Inside SQL Server 2005 Tools

Michael Raheem,
Dima Sonkin,
Thierry D'Hers,
Kami LeMonds

Addison-Wesley

Upper Saddle River, NJ • Boston • Indianapolis
San Francisco • New York • Toronto • Montreal
London • Munich • Paris • Madrid • Capetown
Sydney • Tokyo • Singapore • Mexico City

Many of the designations used by manufacturers and sellers to distinguish their products are claimed as trademarks. Where those designations appear in this book, and the publisher was aware of a trademark claim, the designations have been printed with initial capital letters or in all capitals.

The authors and publisher have taken care in the preparation of this book, but make no expressed or implied warranty of any kind and assume no responsibility for errors or omissions. No liability is assumed for incidental or consequential damages in connection with or arising out of the use of the information or programs contained herein.

The publisher offers excellent discounts on this book when ordered in quantity for bulk purchases or special sales, which may include electronic versions and/or custom covers and content particular to your business, training goals, marketing focus, and branding interests. For more information, please contact:

> U.S. Corporate and Government Sales
> (800) 382-3419
> corpsales@pearsontechgroup.com

For sales outside the United States please contact:

> International Sales
> international@pearsoned.com

Safari BOOKS ONLINE ENABLED — This Book Is Safari Enabled

The Safari® Enabled icon on the cover of your favorite technology book means the book is available through Safari Bookshelf. When you buy this book, you get free access to the online edition for 45 days. Safari Bookshelf is an electronic reference library that lets you easily search thousands of technical books, find code samples, download chapters, and access technical information whenever and wherever you need it.

To gain 45-day Safari Enabled access to this book:

> Go to http://www.awprofessional.com/safarienabled
>
> Complete the brief registration form
>
> Enter the coupon code GWKS-JKHJ-7S7U-BEJS-LIGJ

If you have difficulty registering on Safari Bookshelf or accessing the online edition, please e-mail customer-service@safaribooksonline.com

Visit us on the Web: www.awprofessional.com

Library of Congress Cataloging-in-Publication Data

Inside SQL server 2005 tools / Michael Raheem ... [et al.].
   p. cm.
   Includes indexes.
   ISBN 0-321-39796-7 (pbk. : alk. paper) 1. SQL server. 2. Database management. 3. Client/server computing.
I. Raheem, Michael.
   QA76.9.D3I54584 2006
   005.75'85—dc22

                                                            2006025109

ISBN 0-321-39796-7
Text printed in the United States on recycled paper at R.R. Donnelley & Sons in Crawfordsville, IN.
First printing, October 2006

Inside SQL Server 2005 Tools

Contents

Chapter 7   Inside Tuning and Optimization Tools 237

Chapter 8   Inside Scheduling Tools 273

Foreword

SQL Server has always distinguished itself by, among other things, its management tools. One of the earliest design principles for the team was "It just works." We accomplished this by replacing the usual database knobs and levers with intelligent defaults and adaptive behavior. We never felt that we could or should remove all administrator control. Instead we delivered Enterprise Manager in SQL Server 7.0 and SQL Server 2000. Enterprise Manager grew a huge fan base over the years. So it was with some trepidation that we undertook a massive rewrite, yielding SQL Server Management Studio (SSMS) in SQL Server 2005.

The most nerve-wracking experience for software developers is receiving the user initial feedback on a new product or feature. We released an early version of SSMS in SQL Server 2005 Beta 1. You might recall this as Yukon Beta 1. When we received the summary of an early user survey, we were delighted to find SSMS as the most liked new feature in the beta release. At the same time, we were mortified to also find it as the most disliked feature!

Getting past our bewilderment, we realized that we were getting incredible feedback from our users. In fact, we found out that we had two distinct user populations. We had taken our management tools in the direction of supporting DBAs as developers in addition to administrators. The feedback told us we were on the right track, but that we had serious work to do. The users that felt like developers—that is, those that wrote and maintained scripts, schemas, stored procedures and other objects—loved the new paradigms in the product. This affirmed our assumptions and research. The users that felt like administrators—that is, they worried about users and user access, backup and restore and other operations—hated the new paradigms. We had assumed that most DBAs were both developers and administrators. With the amazing growth of SQL Server, it is not surprising that DBAs have specialized.

Armed with user feedback, we made substantial changes to SQL Server Management Studio. Your authors were in the thick of the action. They shaped the feature set and the user interface you use when you manage your SQL Server. They know the tool set inside and out. I had the privilege of working with them for five years. I'm delighted to see them write this book and deliver their insights, their advice, and a behind the scenes perspective.

Several chapters stand out. Chapter 4 covers administration, vital to keeping your server running optimally and securely. DBAs receive constant requests to move data for users. SQL Server 2005 features Integration Services, the successor to Data Transformation Services. Chapter 16 covers this new and improved tool. And as the guy who drove Business Intelligence in SQL Server, I of course recommend the coverage of this topic in Chapter 13. BI is growing rapidly in our industry. Even if you are not engaged in BI, this chapter is worth your time. You will be getting requests for Business Intelligence in the future.

Enjoy this book, and enjoy SQL Server 2005!

Bill Baker
General Manager, SQL Server Business Intelligence
Redmond, WA
June 2006

Preface

This book reveals the power of the SQL Server 2005 tools to database management system professionals, enabling you to maximize productivity. The authors of the book have been working on the SQL Server 2005 team since its inception, they share the philosophy behind the design of the tools, and they are familiar with insider tips and tricks.

The SQL Server 2005 family of products consists of Database Engine, Analysis Services, Reporting Services, Integration Services, Notification Services, and SQL Server Mobile Edition (SQL Server Everywhere Edition). This book describes the core functionality of all the SQL Server 2005 tools, and closely examines the Database Engine tools. The book provides solutions for installation, upgrade, configuration, schema design, management, authoring, development, optimization, deployment, operation, and troubleshooting. It covers the Installation Wizard, Upgrade Advisor, SQL Server Configuration Manager, SQL Server Management Studio, Database Tuning Advisor, SQLCMD, Database Mail, SQL Server Agent, and SQL Server Profiler. It also touches on technologies that these tools are built upon, such as SQL Server Management Objects (SMO), the Windows Management Instrumentation (WMI) Provider, and ADO.NET.

The book describes individual features and how they work together to create end-to-end scenarios. For the beginning user, we have screenshots and code samples. We provide examples with code snippets where applicable. When we introduce particular aspects of tool behavior or scenarios, we start first by describing them and relating them to other previously described tasks. Screen shots show how these things look inside the tools. For the more experienced users, we provide tips and insight. In addition, we provide code snippets to illustrate how particularly interesting functionalities can be implemented with underlying APIs.

In summary, the book will provide:

- Hundreds of time-saving solutions
- Tips, tricks, and workarounds
- Solutions for working smarter
- A vehicle through which you can expand your existing knowledge of SQL Server tools

Who Should Read This Book?

The book is targeted at both new and experienced database professionals. New professionals who have never used the SQL Server tools will learn how to efficiently use each tool to perform specific tasks. More experienced database professionals can update their existing knowledge of the tools, learn about new features, and learn tips and tricks of the SQL Server 2005 toolset.

The purpose of this book is not to introduce you to the basic concepts of databases. We assume that you have been working with databases for at least one year. This book will show you how the tools can be used to maximize productivity while performing common SQL Server 2005 tasks. After reading this book you will be very comfortable using the tools for day-to-day tasks.

How to Use This Book

The book is organized by SQL Server tools and scenarios. Each chapter presents a tool or set of tools and also includes a number of relevant scenarios that illustrate the use of the tools. If you are interested in specific tools or scenarios, you can move straight to those chapters, or you can read through the book in a linear fashion for a more complete understanding of all the tools and features.

What This Book Covers

Here's a brief overview of each chapter and appendix.

Chapter 1: Inside the Fundamentals

This chapter covers the history of SQL Server, as well as background on the SQL Server tools. The rest of the chapter provides an overview of the new toolset in SQL Server 2005, as well as a mapping between tools from previous releases and the current version. In addition, there is a brief summary of each tool.

Chapter 2: Inside the Installation and Upgrade Tools

The features included with each edition of SQL Server 2005 are highlighted in this chapter. It also provides brief descriptions of the target audience for each edition. You can find step-by-step instructions on installations, upgrade, gotchas to avoid during the install process, and information on backward compatibility issues. The new Upgrade Advisor is also covered in detail.

Chapter 3: Inside the Configuration Tools

Confused by the variety of configuration tools available in SQL Server 2005? This chapter will help you understand which tool to use for which task. You can also find descriptions and the architecture of each configuration tool. SQL Server Configuration Manager, SQL Server Surface Area Configuration, and Usage and Error Reporting tools are all covered in this chapter, as well as common configuration tasks. Because security is such a hot button issue, this chapter also covers surface area reduction.

Chapter 4: Inside Management and Administration Tools

This chapter is a must-read for all SQL Server users. You will find information on everything from how the new toolset is laid out, how to register servers, using the management dialogs, and understanding Object Explorer. There is also a discussion of management and administration scenarios that describes how to leverage Management Studio to accomplish common tasks.

Chapter 5: Inside Data Authoring Tools

Running and editing queries are two of the most common tasks you are likely to perform in SQL Server. This chapter describes the new querying tool (Query Editor) available in SQL Server Management Studio. This chapter is a must-read for anyone interested in modifying their editing environment or learning inside tricks for using Query Editor. Bulk Copy Utility can also be used when moving external data to SQL Server, and a full review of Bulk Copy Utility architecture and scenarios is covered.

Chapter 6: Inside SQLCMD Query Tools

Wondering what happened to your old friend OSQL? SQLCMD is the replacement tool, where you will find backward compatibility for much of OSQL as well as many enhancements. This chapter gets you up to speed on working with the new tool. You can also find descriptions of all the command line options and insider tips and tricks.

Chapter 7: Inside Tuning and Optimization Tools

As soon as you understand the new query editing environment, you may want to enhance query performance. This chapter reviews the SQL Server Management Studio query optimizations and takes a comprehensive look at SQL Server Profiler. The SQL Server Profiler user interface has undergone a makeover since the last release, so this chapter may be helpful for even experienced users. You can also find information on the trace API, which enables users to automate creation of the trace and perform trace data reading and manipulations programmatically. Finally, this chapter covers the Database Tuning Advisor that replaces the Index Tuning Wizard in this release of SQL Server. We cover detailed architecture of the tool and its advanced options.

Chapter 8: Inside Scheduling Tools

Task scheduling through SQL Server Agent is covered in detail in this chapter. You can read about everything from creating job steps to job scheduling and execution. Essential information on SQL Server Agent security is included, to ensure that you understand the changes from previous releases as well as how to refine permissions as much as possible. If your environment requires running jobs on multiple machines at the same time, the information on multi-server administration will be very helpful.

Chapter 9: Inside Monitoring Tools

One of the most essential administration tasks is monitoring the server for potential or immediate problems. This chapter describes the monitoring tools, such as Activity Monitor, SQL Server Agent, and SQL Server Profiler, as well as reviews some of the core monitoring scenarios.

Chapter 10: Inside Email Tools

If you are considering using a mailing solution with SQL Server, you will want to fully understand the new email tools. In this chapter you will learn tips and tricks for working with the legacy tool (SQL Mail), as well as in-depth configuration information on Database Mail, new for SQL Server 2005. A brief overview of SQL Agent mail is also included.

Chapter 11: Inside Programming Object Models

You will accomplish many core administration tasks by using a programming model rather than the user interface. Given the importance of understanding the programming models and how they work, this chapter is a must-read. SQL Server 2005 introduces an entirely new programming model (SMO), and this chapter covers basic SMO concepts, usage scenarios, and internal SMO architecture with advanced performance and optimization topics.

SQL Server Management Objects (SMO) is a brand-new API. SMO is implemented as a .NET library and replaces SQL-DMO (COM server with multiple automation interfaces) that shipped as part of earlier releases and is deprecated with SQL Server 2005.

Chapter 12: Inside Replication Tools

Today's data increasingly needs to be in multiple locations at the same time and the data must be kept synchronized. Database developers must consider scale-out requirements for performance and growth and roll-up requirements for reporting and data warehousing when planning and building applications. Disconnected users, such as sales or service personnel, need to take data with them when they enter the field. Keeping this disparate data synchronized on an ongoing basis is a difficult task.

Fortunately, SQL Server offers powerful technology for replicating and synchronizing data. Database replication was introduced in SQL Server version 6.5, but SQL Server 2005 brings a new level of power, performance, and ease of use to this complex functionality. This chapter provides an insightful look at the tools, as well as tips and tricks for accomplishing common tasks.

Chapter 13: Inside Analysis Services OLAP Tools

This chapter covers all aspects of designing, deploying, and managing OLAP databases. In addition, this chapter describes over 20 business scenario solutions and techniques that take full advantage of the Business Intelligence development studio. Also included on the CD are three full samples for some of these scenarios (that is, a full SQL Server Integration Services and SQL Server Analysis Services self documentation tool and two KPI samples). These samples are not only great examples of design best practices, but are also immediately useful in your day-to-day activities.

Chapter 14: Inside Analysis Services Data Mining Tools

This section covers all the Data Mining tools from designing to training a model, to defining prediction, to actually embedding data mining techniques in your ETL job or your reporting environment.

This is not an exhaustive list of scenarios, and you may find many other tips, techniques, and best practices through your own experience. These tools are extremely rich and will surely provide great satisfaction to any data analyst aspiring to gain knowledge from and insight into large data sets.

Chapter 15: Inside Notification Services Tools

Are you new to Notification Services? Or did you use Notification Services 2.0, but want to understand the improvements made in SQL Server 2005? This chapter briefly describes Notification Services, and then introduces the Notification Services tools, including the command prompt utility that has been carried forward from Notification Services 2.0, the new SQL Server Management Studio interface, the built-in stored procedures and views, and the new management API. This chapter then walks you through the use of Management Studio and the command prompt utility to deploy and administer instances of Notification Services.

Chapter 16: Inside Integration Services Tools

Even if you were familiar with DTS (Data Transformation Services) in SQL Server 2000, you will want to review this chapter to learn about its replacement in SQL Server 2005 (Integration Services). The extract, transform, load (ETL) component of SQL Server was redesigned from the ground up in SQL Server 2005.

Integration Services introduces a rich set of tools to support the development, deployment, and administration of ETL solutions. The tools support the simplest solutions in which you just want to perform tasks such as copying data from one location to another to enterprise-level solutions in which you develop a large number of complex packages in a team environment. This chapter describes the Integration Services tools and service in the context of the life cycle of the ETL solution: development and testing, deployment to the test or production environment, and administration in the production environment.

Chapter 17: Inside the Reporting Services Tools

This section describes and illustrates with many business scenarios the various aspects of the reporting cycle. From upgrading, to designing, to managing a report infrastructure, to scheduling, to integrating reporting with other BI components such as SQL Server Integration Services and SQL Server Analysis Services, this section helps you make the most of the Reporting Services capability.

Appendix A: Sample KPI Client Code—Retrieving and Exposing Your First KPI

This sample shows the basics of how to query and retrieve KPI information such as value, goal, trend, and status with ADOMD.

Appendix B: KPI Utilities—Code for Parsing Display Folders and Getting Image Indexes

This sample is a little bit more sophisticated than Appendix A. It navigates through the list of KPIs, retrieves the Display folder, and categorizes the KPIs using their display folders.

Appendix C: KPI Viewer

This sample contains the entire code for building an ASP application that connects to a cube, retrieves and categorizes KPIs using their display folders, and lets the user select a dimension to drill through on selected KPIs.

Appendix D: Complete List of Data Mining Stored Procedures

The full list of available data mining stored procedures, as well as their definitions, can be found in this appendix.

Preparing to Use This Book

Before starting to use this book you should have access to SQL Server 2005. For further information on how to get a copy of SQL Server 2005 and the supported Windows operating system, see www.microsoft.com/sql. You don't need to purchase the full-blown version of SQL Server 2005 if you just want to check it out. The evaluation version of SQL Server 2005 and SQL Server Express are free. It would be good to have SQL Server 2005 installed so you can follow along with the steps. Both SQL Server Express and the evaluation version are currently available for download on the www.microsoft.com/sql site, under "Download Trial Software."

What's on the CD-ROM

The enclosed CD-ROM can be used to view sample code from the book as well as any corresponding Visual Studio project files.

Acknowledgments

Kami LeMonds, Michael Raheem, Dima Sonkin

SQL Server 2005 was such an enormous project that no one person can provide a comprehensive description of the tools as well as insider tips and scenarios. As a result, we were privileged that the subject matter experts on each team were able to help us with their areas of expertise. With the SQL Server team of over 1,000 people, it is difficult to acknowledge everyone who has helped us. Publishing a book is more than just writing technical content. Euan Garden and Andrew Nechayev added a great deal of value to the book through their technical reviews. The team at Addison-Wesley kept us on track (or, tried to!), and provided extensive editing feedback that enhanced the clarity of the text. Special thanks to Elizabeth Peterson, Karen Gettman, and Chris Zahn. This book was truly a joint effort with some of the tools experts on our team. An incredible thank you to the other contributing authors: Sunil Agarwal, Phillip Garding, Diane Larsen, Brian Welcker, and Marianne Willumsen.

Thierry D'Hers

Special thanks to all the members of the Picasso team who helped me assemble the scenarios. Particularly, I would like to thank the Data Mining dev team: Raman Iyer, Bodgan Crivat, Wayne Guan, Scott Oveson, and Jamie McLennan. I also want to extend a special thank you for those who have contributed to this book by sharing some of their work and providing the great samples such as the KPI viewer and the Documenter. Olivier Pieri, Microsoft Consultant in France, provided the KPI viewer. Mohit Chand, Puneet Taneja, Sushil Darekar, and Naveen Babu out of our Microsoft India development center have provided the Documenter for SQL Server, Analysis Services, and Integration Services.

About the Authors

Sunil Agarwal is a Program Manager in the SQL Server Storage Engine Group. Prior to joining Microsoft, Sunil had worked in companies like DEC, Sybase, BMC Software, and DigitalThink, with a primary focus on core database engine technology and related applications. Sunil holds a BS in Electrical Engineering from IIT, Kanpur, India, and has done graduate work in Computer Science at the University of Rhode Island and at Brown University

Thierry D'Hers is a Lead Program Manager in the SQL BI Analysis Services team. Thierry has over 12 years experience in the BI industry. For the last five years, Thierry has been responsible for designing and specifying many of the functionalities of the Analysis Services tools. Beyond participating in the product design, Thierry is also a technical evangelist for the SQL BI product line. In this role, Thierry spends a large amount of time educating customers and partners on the various benefits of the SQL BI components.

Before joining Microsoft, Thierry spent seven years at Hyperion where he occupied various positions. He began as a consultant, and then moved into technical Sales for Hyperion France. Next he was asked to join Hyperion Corp as a Product Manager, and then he became the Group Product Manager on Hyperion OLAP (renamed Hyperion MBA), Hyperion Business Rules, and a few other Hyperion products
initiatives.

Phillip Garding is a Senior Program Manager in the SQL Server Database Replication team. Phillip has driven the design for the administration and monitoring tools for database replication in SQL Server versions 7.0, 2000, and 2005 and helped define the overall user interface experience in SQL Server 2005. In addition, he has contributed more broadly to developing the wizard and error messaging designs at Microsoft. Phillip is a 17-year veteran at Microsoft, and he worked on Microsoft Access and Microsoft Word prior to joining the SQL Server team in 1995.

Diane Larsen is a technical writing lead on the SQL Server User Education team. She has written documentation and articles about several SQL Server 2000 and SQL Server 2005 features, including Notification Services, DTS, Upgrade Advisor, and SQL Server Surface Area Configuration. She worked with the incredible Notification Services development team for over four years, and enjoyed (almost) every minute of it. The times she didn't enjoy it were due to lack of sleep.

Kami LeMonds is a Documentation Manager for the SQL Server User Education team at Microsoft and manages a team of technical writers. In the past eight years at Microsoft, she has been a technical writer and lead, primarily on SQL Server Management Tools. In addition, she has contributed to the Answers from Microsoft column in *SQL Server Magazine*, as well as the SQL Server 2000 Resource Kit. Kami recently completed a Technology Management MBA from the University of Washington.

Michael Raheem is a Senior Product Manager in the SQL Server Marketing team at Microsoft. Michael currently leads the SQL Server enterprise marketing efforts, including High Availability, Scalability, Performance, and SQL Server Always On Technologies. Prior to joining the marketing team, he led the design and implementation of several SQL Server 2005 tools such as Management Studio, Upgrade Advisor, Database Mail, and Surface Area Configuration. Michael has spoken at several conferences, including TechEd, TechReady, PASS, and SQL Connections. Additionally, he has contributed to the Answers from Microsoft column in *SQL Server Magazine* and has over 13 years of experience in designing and developing solutions with Microsoft SQL Server.

Dima Sonkin is a Software Design Engineer Lead at Microsoft Corporation working in SQL Server Management Tools product group. He has been with Microsoft for over seven years. His development team owns such components as SQL Server Agent, SMO/DMO, SQL Profiler, Database Tuning Advisor, Database Mail/SQLMail, SqlCmd/OSQL, and many others. Dima has been through entire shipping cycles of SQL Server 2000 and SQL Server 2005. He has filed over a dozen patents in database management tools space. He holds multiple Microsoft certifications, including MCSD and MCDBA. He has spoken at several professional conferences. Prior to Microsoft, Dima held the position of Staff Software Engineer with IBM Corporation. His formal education includes a master's degree in Engineering from St. Petersburg Technical University and an MSEE from the University of South Florida.

Brian Welcker is Group Program Manager for SQL Server Reporting Services, part of the SQL Server product group. His team is focused on delivering the premier managed and ad-hoc enterprise reporting platform as part of SQL Server 2005, as well as delivering developer reporting components for Visual Studio 2005. A 10-year Microsoft veteran, Brian is one of the founding members of the Reporting Services team; he previously worked as the lead program manager for SQL Server Meta Data Services, as well as a technical evangelist in Microsoft's

Developer Relations Group. He joined Microsoft after working for a company in his home town of Raleigh, North Carolina building software for hospitals and doctors' offices. Brian resides in Seattle, Washington with his wife and two children.

Marianne Willumsen is a documentation manager on the SQL Server user education team. Before she joined the management team, she was the lead writer for the Integration Services user education team. In that role, she developed the table of contents and wrote reams of Integration Services documentation for SQL Server Books Online, as well as many samples. Writing is what she does, and prior to joining the SQL Server user education team she was a writer on the Exchange SDK team.

CHAPTER 1

Inside the Fundamentals

Microsoft SQL Server provides a powerful and comprehensive platform for data management and business intelligence. SQL Server includes a number of products, as well as sophisticated management and development tools that automate standard daily activities. SQL Server graphical tools and designers simplify tasks related to setup, upgrade, database design, management, development, performance tuning, and operations. This gives database professionals time to focus on more strategic business tasks and meet the rising demand of supporting business applications.

History of SQL Server Tools

Part of SQL Server's success story is due to its powerful and versatile tools. Microsoft was one of the first pioneers to introduce graphical tools in its standard database platform. For me, it all started with SQL Server 4.21 while I was employed as a junior database administrator in a small start-up company. Our company built software that was supported on two database system platforms: Sybase System 10 and Microsoft SQL Server 4.21. My job was to create and maintain a number of database scripts to perform daily management tasks, such as create databases, back up and restore databases, create tables, manage indexes, and develop stored procedures. At that time, the Microsoft and Sybase database systems were very similar. For my daily activities, I used the ISQL command line tool to execute my scripts on both database platforms. A year later, Microsoft released SQL Server 6.0 with a number of graphical tools such as ISQL/w and Enterprise Manager. These tools were very exciting to me. I never forget the first time that I launched Enterprise Manager. My jaw dropped! Wow! With one click, I could look up objects on a database server and with a couple more clicks, I could create a backup device.

I no longer needed my scripts. Although I was a little worried about my job security, I was amazed by the power of the tool and the potential for additional productivity. Six months later, my productivity with SQL Server had gone up so much that I convinced the upper management to minimize support for Sybase altogether and fully focus on development against SQL Server. Ten years later, working in the Microsoft SQL Server team, I can see that the evolution of the tools continues. With every release of SQL Server, Microsoft builds innovative tools to keep up with the rising demands of managing complex environments.

Today, the SQL Server 2005 tools are smarter and more powerful than ever before. The tenet behind delivering the tools remains the same: The tools take advantage of hardware and software innovations to make ordinary tasks easier and complex tasks possible.

Why Database Tools Are Important

In the old days, the responsibility of database administrators (DBAs) was to make sure every byte of data was stored safely, and data was always available for quick delivery to business applications. Today, database system professionals have a much more complex job. Not only are they the gatekeepers of the system, but they are also responsible for a variety of complex tasks, such as

- Installation and upgrade
- Configuration
- Administration
- Querying and reporting data
- Business intelligence
- Management
- Development
- Deployment
- Monitoring
- Tuning and optimization
- Maintenance

Database professionals must be efficient with the tools to support these complex tasks. When they are faced with a business requirement, they need to identify database tasks quickly and choose the right tool to perform these tasks. These database tasks are no longer limited to just the relational database. SQL Server now has a family of products that database professionals must support and maintain to meet business requirements.

Introducing the SQL Server 2005 Family of Products

Today's applications demand more than just the database relational engine. They require analytical, intelligence, reporting, and delivery features beyond those available in the database engine. Microsoft has included a number of products in SQL Server 2005, which collectively provide a complete data processing platform. These products are

- Database Engine
- Analysis Services
- Reporting Services
- Integration Services
- Notification Services
- SQL Server Everywhere Edition (also known as SQL Server Mobile Edition)

Database Engine

SQL Server 2005 Database Engine is the core component for storing and processing data. Database Engine enforces data integrity and transaction processing to ensure consistency and recoverability of data. Database Engine provides concurrency so that data can be simultaneously viewed by multiple users and applications. Database Engine also provides a security model so that stored data can be viewed and manipulated by privileged users.

Analysis Services

SQL Server 2005 Analysis Services uses the data stored in Database Engine or other data sources to provide a platform for online analytical processing (OLAP) and data mining. Through its new development and management environments, it delivers a platform for designing, creating, deploying, and managing business intelligence applications. The Data Mining component of Analysis Services gives you access to the information needed to make intelligent decisions about business problems.

Reporting Services

SQL Server 2005 Reporting Services provides a set of tools and services to create, publish, and manage reports based on data stored in Database Engine, Analysis Services, or other data sources. Reporting Services provides tools for creating, developing, and managing subscription and delivery of reports, as well as viewing reports through a URL in a Web browser.

Notification Services

SQL Server 2005 Notification Services provides a programming platform for creating applications that generate and deliver notifications. Notifications could be based on the occurrence of an event or based on a schedule defined by you or the subscriber. Notifications are based on the "push" model. The application enables your enterprise, customers, and partners to specify what information is of interest to them, and then automatically notifies them when something of interest occurs. In addition, the application can deliver notifications to other services or applications to automate business processes.

Integration Services

SQL Server 2005 Integration Services is a platform for building integration solutions to extract, transfer, and load data between data sources. Integration Services provides a rich set of built-in tasks, containers, transformations, and data adapters that support

- Merging data from heterogeneous data sources
- Populating data warehouses and data marts
- Cleansing and standardizing data
- Building business intelligence into a data transformation process
- Automating administrative functions and data loading

For those of you who are familiar with earlier versions SQL Server, Integration Services is a replacement for Data Transformation Services (DTS).

SQL Server Everywhere Edition

SQL Server Everywhere Edition is a compact relational database with a small footprint that can be embedded in mobile and desktop applications. SQL Server Everywhere Edition is supported on desktop and mobile devices, which makes it a strong platform for building occasionally connected applications. SQL Server Everywhere Edition provides replication and synchronization functionality with SQL Server Database Engine to support scenarios where you need to take bits and pieces of enterprise data and integrate them into a mobile application.

SQL Server 2005 Tools

SQL Server 2005 has a number of graphical and command line tools that enable administrators and developers to perform a variety of tasks. The tasks and the supporting tools are described in the following sections.

Installation and Upgrade Tools

This class of tools provides the functionality to install SQL Server 2005 components or to upgrade an existing installation of SQL Server 7.0 or SQL Server 2000. The two major tools are the Upgrade Advisor and the SQL Server Installation Wizard.

Upgrade Advisor

SQL Server 2005 Upgrade Advisor is an analysis and reporting tool to prepare installations of SQL Server 7.0 or 2000 to upgrade to SQL Server 2005. The tool has two main components: an analysis wizard and a report viewer. The wizard scans the old installation and verifies its components against a predefined set of rules embedded in the tool. The result of the analysis is stored in a file, which you can view in the Upgrade Advisor report viewer. The report displays the upgrade and backward compatibility issues that need to be addressed before or after upgrade to ensure a smooth upgrade.

TIP
Run the Upgrade Advisor before upgrading or migrating to SQL Server 2005 to address upgrade issues before proceeding to the Setup Wizard.

SQL Server Installation Wizard and Command Line Tool

The SQL Server 2005 Setup tool provides the functionality to install SQL Server products. The Setup tool can be launched in two ways: through the Setup Wizard and through the Command line. The Installation Wizard provides a graphical user interface, which assists the user through the installation process. The wizard guides the user through installation steps such as system requirements, product key registration, product selection, instance naming, service account configuration, and collation settings, and shows installation progress.

The Setup command line tool can be executed from a Windows command shell and provides advanced installation options such as remote installation, and can be more suitable for large enterprise installations.

Both the Setup Wizard and command line tool provide functionality to upgrade the existing installations of SQL Server.

Configuration Tools

SQL Server 2005 provides a number of tools for the configuration and setup of individual products. Using these tools, you can perform a variety of tasks such as controlling the state of services, configuring client and server protocols, and enabling or disabling features.

SQL Server Configuration Manager

The SQL Server Configuration Manager tool provides functionality to control the configuration options associated with all SQL Server 2005 services. In addition, the tool allows configuration of protocols for both the client and server. The SQL Configuration Manager is a graphical user interface tool built as a Microsoft Management Console (MMC) snap-in. The tool can also be accessed from Windows Computer Management to configure a remote computer. SQL Server Configuration Manager does not make a SQL connection; instead, it makes a Distributed Component Object Model (DCOM) connection to use Windows Management Instrumentation (WMI) on the target server to manipulate its services and Registry key.

Surface Area Configuration

To create a secure initial installation, some functionalities of SQL Server 2005 are disabled by default. This reduces the surface area of your installation for potential security attacks and decreases the number of features and components that you need to manage. The surface area functionality includes service states associated with SQL Server 2005 components, some features of the components, and the remote connectivity option for some of the components.

You can use the Surface Area Configuration tool to switch on features after you have installed an instance of SQL Server. The Surface Area Configuration tool provides a graphical user interface to start and stop or enable and disable services and features for both local and remote computers. In addition, the tool provides an advisory help interface to better understand the implications of enabling or disabling a feature. There is also a command line version of the tool, which provides functionality to export and import the surface area settings between computers.

Reporting Services Configuration

The Reporting Services Configuration tool provides a vehicle to configure and control the Reporting Services settings on an installation of SQL Server 2005. This tool can also be used for the deployment of Reporting Services if the user has chosen the option to copy the files during the initial installation (from the SQL Server Installation Wizard). Like SQL Server Configuration Manager, this graphical user interface tool takes advantage of WMI to manipulate the configuration files and Registry keys. The tool can be used to connect to both local and remote installations of SQL Server 2005 Reporting Services.

Usage and Error Reporting

SQL Server 2005 offers you the option to send information about product usage and report errors to Microsoft. The user can use the Usage and Error Reporting tool to opt in or out of this option. The tool provides a matrix where the user has the option to send feature usage information or error reports or both for each of the installed products. The Microsoft SQL Server team uses the error reports to improve the functionality and quality of SQL Server in future releases and service packs.

Management and Administration Tools

SQL Server 2005 provides comprehensive management and administration tools for all products of SQL Server 2005. These tools enable you to use a graphical interface for tasks or give you the option to run queries to manipulate data or perform administration tasks.

Management Studio

SQL Server Management Studio is an integrated and comprehensive environment for management, administration, authoring, and monitoring for all SQL Server 2005 products. The tool has several integrated components that support various classes of tasks. The Object Explorer (the tree view in the left pane) and the new management dialogs provide a rich graphical user interface for management and administration of the server objects on both local and remote installations of SQL Server. Management Studio supports management of all SQL Server 2005 components, as well as Database Engine in SQL Server 2000.

Report Manager

Report Manager is a web-based tool for managing Reporting Services reports via an HTTP connection. The tool can be accessed via Microsoft Internet Explorer and it provides the functionality to manage security and subscriptions of reports and models. In addition, the tool allows managing of schedules for execution and delivery of reports.

OSQL

OSQL is a command line script execution tool, which provides the functionality to execute Transact-SQL (T-SQL) scripts on a Database Engine. The T-SQL scripts can contain statements in both Data Manipulation (DML) and Data Definition Language (DDL).

NOTE
OSQL is one of the SQL Server legacy tools and it is officially deprecated in SQL Server 2005. If you are planning to use OSQL, you should consider using SQLCMD instead.

SQLCMD

SQLCMD is the next generation of the T-SQL script execution tool. SQLCMD is a replacement for OSQL and ISQL and it enables you to execute T-SQL scripts against a Database Engine. SQLCMD supports all features of OSQL, as well as powerful new features such as support for scripting variables, startup scripts, and better error handling.

Query Editors in Management Studio

SQL Server Management Studio has query editors for editing and execution of scripts against SQL Server components. These include a query editor for Transact-SQL (T-SQL) language against a Database Engine or a SQL Server Everywhere database, a query editor for editing and execution of Multidimensional Expression (MDX) and XML for Analysis (XMLA) against an Analysis Services database, and a query editor for editing and execution of DMX queries against a mining model in Analysis Services. In addition, there is a code editor for editing of XML files and viewing of the XML query results. Management Studio has a Dynamic Help feature, which displays relevant help links in the context of the query being typed.

Management Studio provides a project system for building solutions with Database Engine, Analysis Services, and SQL Server Everywhere scripts. Management Studio can be added to its integrated source control provider so that you can maintain copies of scripts as they change over a development cycle.

BCP

The bulk copy command line tool is perhaps one of the oldest tools in Microsoft SQL Server and it is one of a DBA's best friends. The tool provides the capability to import and export data between SQL Server Database Engine and an operating system file in a specified format. The high performance of the BCP makes it an ideal tool to copy large number of rows in and out of tables. BCP can be used in a variety of scenarios, such as copying or transferring all or a subset of rows between two tables on two separate computers, or extracting data to be viewed in an external application such as Microsoft Office Excel. The tool is versatile and requires little knowledge of T-SQL, as long as the user understands the structure of files and tables.

Monitoring and Operations Tools

SQL Server 2005 provides you with several tools for monitoring activities in the Database Engine, for mirroring, and for replication, as well as the capability to schedule and automate tasks.

Activity Monitor in Management Studio

Activity Monitor in SQL Server Management provides information for monitoring activities in SQL Server Database Engine. The activities can be grouped and viewed by current user connections, process numbers, status, locks, commands that applications are running, locked database objects, and types of locks that currently exist in the system. In addition, activities can be filtered based on user-defined criteria and refreshed at specific intervals.

Database Mirroring Monitor in Management Studio

Database Mirroring is a new high availability feature in SQL Server 2005 Database Engine. Database Mirroring maintains two copies of a database on different installations (instances) of SQL Server Database Engine. One server instance acts as the principal server, whereas the other server instance acts as a mirror server. As the data changes on the principal server, Database Mirroring automatically applies the changes to the mirror server. In case of a failure on the principal server, the system fails over to the mirror server, ensuring database availability for the client applications.

The Database Mirroring Monitor in Management Studio provides the functionality to verify the flow of data between the principal and mirror servers. Database Mirroring Monitor is also helpful in troubleshooting causes of data flow interruption between principal and mirror servers.

SQL Server Agent

SQL Server Agent is a SQL Server 2005 Database Engine subsystem that executes scheduled maintenance and operational tasks specified by the system administrator. The tasks are grouped by jobs and each job can have one or more job steps corresponding to each task. SQL Server Agent jobs run manually or automatically based on scheduled intervals. In addition, SQL Server Agent provides a monitoring and alerting mechanism for system events. After an alert is triggered, it can fire a job or notify an operator via email, pager, or network alerts.

New in SQL Server 2005, SQL Server Agent supports execution of job steps. A job contains one or more steps and each job step can be a Database Engine, Analysis Services, or Integration Services task. Also, SQL Server Agent supports alerts based on WMI events. These new features open up a new world of monitoring and alerting opportunities, which you'll find discussed later in this book.

SQL Server Replication Monitor

SQL Server Replication provides technologies for copying and synchronizing data between databases located locally or on a remote server. SQL Server Replication Monitor is a graphical user interface tool for monitoring the overall status and performance of replication between sites. Replication Monitor also provides the functionality to set up warnings, thresholds, and alerts, so the system administrator can be informed about status and performance in a timely manner.

Microsoft Operations Manager

Microsoft Operations Manager (MOM) is a platform for monitoring the operations of server products in a large IT organization. Each product is monitored via a Management Pack, which is a set of configuration settings and alerts designed specifically for the product. SQL Server 2005 has a Management Pack for Microsoft Operations Manager (MOM). The SQL Server Management Pack monitors the performance and availability of all SQL Server 2005 products, including the SQL Server Agent and Replication. In addition, MOM monitors database health, free space, clustering, and the security settings of Database Engine.

Database, Schema, and Report Design Tools

There are a number of database, schema, and report designer tools in SQL Server 2005. The database and schema design tools are hosted in SQL Server Management Studio and Business Intelligence Development Studio. The Reporting Service report design tool is also hosted in Business Intelligence Development Studio. In addition, Reporting Services provides an easy-to-use tool for building reports called Report Builder. Report Builder, with its simple interface, is targeted for information workers.

Management Studio Designers

SQL Server Management Studio has a number of graphical database tool designers that provide functionality to design databases, tables, views, and queries. These designers are also available in Visual Studio 2005.

Database Diagram Designer (see Figure 1-1) is a graphical tool that can be used to design entities and relationships in a database. The tool allows creation, modification, or deletion of database objects such as tables, columns, keys, constraints, indexes, and relationships. The tool also enables you to construct a database diagram by adding or removing the illustrated entities such as tables, columns, keys, and relationships.

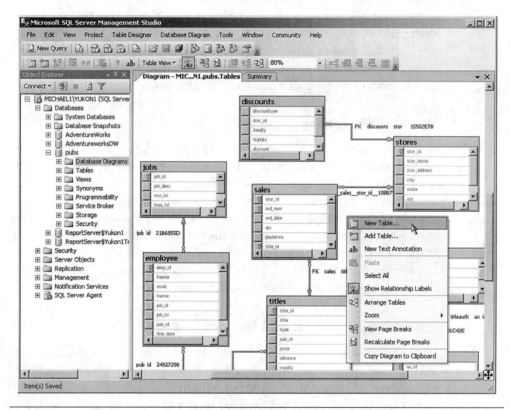

Figure 1-1   Database Diagram Designer in SQL Server Management Studio.

Table Designer is another graphical tool that allows creation or modification of tables in a Database Engine. Table designer also makes it possible to design table columns, relationships, primary and unique keys, constraints, indexes, and change scripts. In addition, table designer provides the functionality to view and edit data stored in a table.

The Query and View Designer tool allows graphical creation of Transact-SQL queries and views. The tool supports various types of queries such as SELECT, UPDATE, DELETE, MAKE TABLE, INSERT VALUES, and INSERT RESULT queries. Also, Query and View Designer provide the functionality to modify data in the resultset of executed queries.

Development Tools

SQL Server 2005 provides a rich development tool as well as tight integration with Visual Studio. This integration enables you to utilize both SQL Server 2005 features as well as Visual Studio functionality for developing solutions.

Business Intelligence Development Studio

Business Intelligence Development Studio in an integrated development environment (IDE) for SQL Server 2005 business intelligence components. Business Intelligence Development Studio provides the functionality to build and deploy solutions for Analysis Services, Integration Services, and Reporting Services projects. Under the surface, Business Intelligence Development Studio is Microsoft Visual Studio 2005 IDE with special business intelligence project types. The project types have a rich set of graphical design tools and wizards to develop objects.

Visual Studio 2005

Visual Studio 2005 provides a comprehensive development environment for SQL Server 2005. Visual Studio 2005 provides a number of visual database tools, some of which are shared with SQL Server Management Studio. However, Visual Studio 2005 is the only tool that allows debugging of Database Engine stored procedures, user-defined functions, and triggers. New in Visual Studio 2005 is the functionality to debug managed Common Language Runtime (CLR) assemblies running inside the SQL Server 2005 process.

Deployment Tools

SQL Server 2005 supports several options for deploying data and metadata to a server. These options include deploying an application from a project file, a source server, or a previous version of Database Engine or Analysis Services.

Management Studio

SQL Server Management Studio has a number of components to deploy data objects on a target server.

Generate Script Wizard enables you to generate Transact-SQL script for all databases, one database, or a subset of objects in one database. After the script from the source SQL Server Database Engine is generated, it can be executed on the target server.

Import and Export Data Wizard provides the functionality to copy data from one SQL Server Database Engine to another. In addition, the tool enables you to import data from any Object Linking and Embedding Database (OLE DB) provider, which makes it a powerful tool for creating objects from any data source, such as a Microsoft Office Excel spreadsheet.

Copy Database Wizard

Copy Database Wizard is a component of SQL Server Management Studio, designed for copying the databases and their objects from one SQL Server Database Engine and deploying them on another Database Engine. With the wizard, you can copy all or a subset of database objects, server logins, and SQL Server Agent jobs to the destination server. The Copy Database Wizard is built on top of the SQL Server 2005 Integration Services (SSIS) technologies. The result of the copy or move options in the wizard is saved as an SSIS package that is wrapped in a SQL Server Agent job. The job can run immediately, or it can be scheduled to run at a later time or on a recurring basis. This provides the functionality to copy objects when the source and destination servers are not busy.

TIP

Copy Database Wizard provides an excellent tool for migration of SQL Server 7.0 or 2000 to SQL Server 2005.

Analysis Services Deployment Wizard

The Analysis Services project contains definitions of objects in a database such as cubes, dimensions, measure groups, and so on. You can deploy an Analysis Services project on a target server by using the Analysis Services Deployment Wizard. Aside from specifying the source database file in the project and the destination server, the wizard provides additional options for controlling the configuration settings and connection strings.

The Deployment Wizard can also run from a command prompt. The user can specify the same deployment switches as the wizard with the option to deploy immediately or generate an XMLA script to be executed later.

Query Tuning and Optimization Tools

SQL Server 2005 includes modifications to some familiar tools that enable you to tune and optimize a broader set of SQL Server products.

SQL Server Profiler

SQL Server Profiler is a graphical user interface that captures events for SQL Server Database Engine or Analysis Services, which can then be used to monitor server events and save trace data to a file or table. The events in the trace can later be analyzed to investigate system performance, troubleshoot a server problem, or audit actions performed on a server.

Profiler also makes it possible to replay the captured trace data from files or tables. This is extremely useful for troubleshooting scenarios where there is a problem on one server instance and you would like to reproduce the problem on another instance and verify a fix.

TIP

SQL Server Profiler and Replay provide an excellent tool for verifying two side-by-side systems, such as after an upgrade.

Database Engine Tuning Advisor

The Database Tuning Advisor tool enables you to analyze data and make recommendations to improve the performance of a Database Engine. The tool works in two stages: analysis and recommendation. In analysis stage, the tool measures the effects of performance while a set of Transact-SQL statements are executed on the Database Engine. When analysis is complete, the tool provides recommendations to add, remove, or modify physical design structures such as clustered indexes, nonclustered indexes, indexed views, and partitioning.

The Database Tuning Advisor is great for tuning the performance of a database without requiring an expert understanding of the structure of the database, the workload, or the internals of SQL Server Database Engine.

Maintenance Tools

You can create Database Engine Maintenance Plans by using the Maintenance Plan Designer or Maintenance Plan Wizard. These tools enable you to automate common maintenance tasks and to time these tasks so they make the least impact on your system.

Maintenance Plan Designer and Wizard in Management Studio

The Maintenance Plan designer in SQL Server Management studio provides the functionality to create a workflow required to maintain your system. The maintenance tasks can back up your databases regularly, check for data inconsistencies, or update indexes and table statistics to make sure your system retains its performance. Management Studio also offers a wizard for the creation of maintenance plans. Although the Maintenance Plan Wizard can be used only for creating basic maintenance plans, the designer provides more flexibility in task selection and control flow. Maintenance Plan designer is built on top of Integration Services, and each plan creates a SQL Server Agent job that runs automatically at a scheduled time.

Email Delivery Tools

SQL Server 2005 contains both the previous email solution, as well as a new and more reliable option. These email delivery tools enable you to send emails from the database engine.

SQL Mail

The SQL Mail feature of SQL Server 2005 enables you to send or read email messages from the database engine. These email messages could include the result of a query execution as well as file attachments. SQL Mail requires installation of an Extended Messaging Application Programming Interface (Extended MAPI) such as Microsoft Outlook. Extended MAPI is a collection of COM objects that provide an interface between client applications such as SQL Mail and email servers. Although SQL Mail is a powerful and popular feature amongst database administrators and developers, there are limitations in configuration, troubleshooting, and support on 64-bit and clustered systems.

NOTE
It is worth noting that Microsoft has deprecated SQL Mail in SQL Server 2005 and you should consider using Database Mail for sending email messages from Database Engine.

Database Mail

Similar to SQL Mail, the Database Mail feature of SQL Server 2005 provides the functionality to send email messages from the Database Engine. However, Database Mail does not require installation of Microsoft Outlook or any other Extended MAPI clients. Instead, it uses a Simple Mail Transfer Protocol (SMTP) server for sending email messages, which can be installed on the same computer or a remote computer. In SQL Server 2005, Database Mail is designed from the ground up as a high-performance and highly available enterprise mail solution. Unlike SQL Mail, Database Mail is easy to configure and troubleshoot, and it supports 64-bit and clustered systems.

Programming Object Models

Several programming object models are available in SQL Server 2005. The object models enable you to manage SQL Server products programmatically.

SQL Server Management Objects (SMO)

SQL Server 2005 Database Engine has a new object model called SQL Server Management Objects (SMO). SMO provides a complete set of Microsoft.NET Framework objects for use in managed applications, such as those developed in Microsoft Visual Basic .NET or Microsoft C#. SMO replaces the legacy SQL Distributed Management Objects (SQL-DMO) and has a number of performance and functionality improvements over DMO. The goal in the design of SMO has been to support all features of SQL Server 2005 and SQL Server 2000 Database Engine.

The Analysis Management Objects (AMO)

SQL Server 2005 Analysis Service has a new object model, Analysis Management Objects (AMO). AMO provides the functionality to manage SQL Server 2005 Analysis Services objects and perform administrative tasks such as processing cubes and backing up databases. AMO can be used only against SQL Server 2005 Analysis Services.

Replication Management Objects (RMO)

Similar to SMO, Replication Management Objects (RMO) enables you to programmatically configure and manage a replication topology in SQL Server 2005. The goal in the design of RMO has been to support the programming of all aspects of SQL Server 2005 replication. In addition to SQL Server 2005, RMO supports SQL Server 7.0 and SQL Server 2000 replication topologies.

SQL Distributed Management Objects (SQL-DMO)

The SQL Distributed Management Objects (SQL-DMO) is the legacy object model for programming against SQL Server 2000 and SQL Server 2005. SQL-DMO has been replaced by SMO and it is available only for backward compatibility with legacy applications. SQL-DMO supports only features that were available in SQL Server 2000; it does not support the new features of the database engine in SQL Server 2005. To reduce the surface area of SQL Server 2005, SQL-DMO is not installed by default.

TIP
SQL Distributed Management Objects (SQL-DMO) is deprecated in SQL Server 2005. You should consider using SQL Server Management Objects (SMO) instead.

Comparing SQL Server 2005 with SQL Server 2000 Tools

As already noted, SQL Server 2005 has improved some of the old tools and introduced a number of new tools. However, for those of you who have worked with the earlier versions of SQL Server, you may see that some of the tools no longer exist. Of course, this does not mean that the tasks and scenarios that the old tool supported have been removed from the product. To the contrary, improvements have been made to the tool or it has been integrated with another tool to increase productivity.

The goal in SQL Server 2005 has been to increase productivity. One of the points of improvements has been to integrate the same experience across all SQL Server products to provide ultimate productivity. For example, Query Analyzer in SQL Server 2000 provided a good authoring experience for SQL Server 2000 Engine. However, the tool for execution of MDX queries against Analysis Services 2000 was a tool named MDX Sample Application. In SQL Server 2005, both these tools have been integrated into SQL Server Management Studio.

For those of you who were familiar with the old tool set and would like to be able to find your way through the new tool set, see Table 1.1.

Analysis Manager, MDX Sample Application, Enterprise Manager, and Query Analyzer are consolidated into SQL Server Management Studio. In fact, Management Studio is an integrated and comprehensive environment for management, administration, authoring, monitoring, and development for all SQL Server 2005 products (see Figure 1-2).

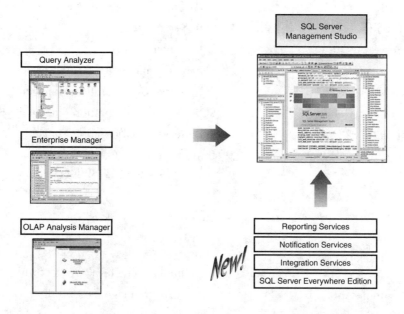

Figure 1-2   Integration of legacy tools in SQL Server Management Studio.

SQL Profiler has had a small name change: In SQL Server 2005 it is called SQL Server Profiler.

The Index Tuning Wizard launch point was only from Enterprise Manager in SQL Server 2000. In SQL Server 2005, it has a number of impressive features that make it a first-class tool. The new name is Database Engine Tuning Advisor, and it can be launched from the Windows Start menu.

ISQL is not included in the SQL Server 2005 tool set. Microsoft officially deprecated ISQL in SQL Server 2000 and it is not shipped in SQL Server 2005. As its replacement, you should consider using SQLCMD.

Table 1-1 describes the relationship between functionality of SQL Server 2000 and SQL Server 2005 Tools.

Table 1-1   Relationship Between SQL Server 2000 and 2005 Tools

SQL Server 2000 Tool	SQL Server 2005 Tool
Query Analyzer	SQL Server Management Studio
Enterprise Manager	SQL Server Management Studio
SQL Profiler	SQL Server Profiler
SQL Server Agent	SQL Server Agent
Index Tuning Wizard	Database Engine Tuning Advisor
Service Manager	SQL Server Configuration Manager
Client Network Utility	SQL Server Configuration Manager
Server Network Utility	SQL Server Configuration Manager
Import and Export Data	Import and Export Data Wizard in SQL Server Management Studio
BCP	BCP
ISQL	SQLCMD
OSQL	OSQL
Analysis Manager	SQL Server Management Studio and Business Intelligence Development Studio
MDX Sample Application	SQL Server Management Studio
Reporting Services Report Manager	Reporting Services Report Manager
None	Business Intelligence Studio
None	Upgrade Advisor
None	Surface Area Configuration

SQL Server 2000 Tool	SQL Server 2005 Tool
None	Analysis Services Deployment Wizard
None	Report Builder
None	Reporting Services Configuration
None	Error and Usage Reporting

Summary

This chapter provided you with an overview of the tools in SQL Server 2005. It began with a bit of the historical development of SQL Server and then provided a rundown of the tools in SQL Server 2005. The rundown included some comparisons of the tools and their locations between SQL Server 2000 and SQL Server 2005.

CHAPTER 2

Inside the Installation and Upgrade Tools

Microsoft SQL Server 2005 is no longer just the relational database engine. It is packaged with a number of components and tools to provide the ultimate data management and business intelligence platform. Designing the installation and ensuring a smooth upgrade to SQL Server 2005 was not an easy task. The SQL Server development team had to provide a consistent experience for the installation and upgrade of all SQL Server 2005 components. With the installation and upgrade being the first out-of-the-box experience, the team wanted to create a positive first impression. The installation interface had to have a friendly and easy-to-use interface to guide the novice user through the installation steps; yet it had to be robust and versatile to meet the advanced specifications of large IT organizations. Using technologies such as Windows Installer, MSI, WMI, and Wizard UI, the team was successful in creating a setup application for the installation experience. However, upgrade was a different story. The early adopter customers who were part of the beta and CTP (Community Technology Preview) program were reporting numerous backward compatibility issues. SQL Server 2005 was a long release and during its five-year cycle, some legacy features had gone through many changes, some of which were no longer backward compatible with earlier releases of SQL Server. This meant customer applications that used these features in SQL Server 7.0 or SQL Server 2000 did not work after the server was upgraded to SQL Server 2005. This was unacceptable. Two teams were formed just to focus on and tackle the upgrade and backward compatibility issues. These teams collected all the reported issues and they classified the issues into four categories:

- Features that broke the setup and upgrade process (also known as upgrade blockers).

- Features that were discontinued in SQL Server 2005.
- Features that exhibited a different behavior in SQL Server 2005.
- Features that were switched off by default after installation.

The first class of issues was simply awful. They were problems that simply prohibited customers from upgrading their systems to SQL Server 2005. What it made it worse was the "point of no return scenario," where the upgrade blockers terminated the setup program at a point where it had partially updated the system to SQL Server 2005. This meant the upgrade could not be rolled forward or backward and the system was left in an unusable state. To solve this class of issues, the team set a high-quality bar and triaged each of the upgrade blockers with the development team. Soon, the number of upgrade blockers diminished: At first there were 23, then the number dropped to 14, and it finally stopped at 9. These 9 issues were true edge cases that rarely happen in real life scenarios. You can find these issues under the topic "Issues that Prevent Upgrading" in Upgrade Advisor help. In addition, the setup program added the logic to check for the upgrade blockers prior to updating the system. This prevented the "point of no return" scenario.

The effort behind tackling the second and third classes of upgrade issues was huge. Although the team worked hard to minimize the number of features with different behavior, it ran into two major issues. For some features, it was too late to revert or redesign the feature to achieve backward compatibility. The development team proved that redesigning some features would impact the stability of these features, weakening their quality. Another issue was related to discontinuation of undocumented and unsupported features. For example, for years authors of SQL Server books and articles had written about undocumented system stored procedures (like xp_regread) and customers had implemented these undocumented features in their applications even though they were not officially supported by Microsoft. The SQL Server development team needed to extend, enhance, or replace some of these undocumented features with the new and more powerful features, but with lack of documentation, it was impossible to understand all customer scenarios. The question became how to inform and educate customers on the upgrade and compatibility issues that are relevant to their environments. The answer was a new tool name, Upgrade Advisor. The goal behind the design of Upgrade Advisor was to improve the SQL Server 2005 upgrade experience. The tool had to run before any upgrade to inform the user of the compatibility issues, thereby eliminating any surprises during or after the upgrade. In addition to detecting issues, Upgrade Advisor had to provide guidance and documentation for fixing or implementing workarounds. The upgrade checks (rules) in Upgrade Advisor also had to be easily updatable, so as the team came across additional issues they could easily be added to the tool.

For the fourth class of upgrade issues, the team decided to build a new tool named Surface Area Configuration (described in Chapter 3). The idea behind the tool is simple: Provide an integrated and easy-to-use tool to enable and disable elements that were switched off by default. In addition, the Surface Area Configuration had to provide advisory documentation to describe each of the surface area elements in detail to help administrators understand the side effects of enabling or disabling an element.

Both the Upgrade Advisor and the Surface Area configuration tools were introduced in the July 2005 CTP release of SQL Server 2005 and they were an immediate success. The number of upgrade-related issues reduced significantly. By the next CTP release, the upgrade issues were almost non-existent.

Once again, this proves the significance of SQL Server's tools in its success story. The Setup and Installation tools, Upgrade Advisor, and Surface Area Configuration have been crucial in the success of SQL Server 2005.

This chapter is in three main parts. The first part describes pre-installation considerations and the installation tools. The second part walks you through the installation process step-by-step. The third part focuses on upgrades and scenarios that are enabled by the upgrade tools. We also share some of the tips and tricks for ensuring a smooth and trouble-free installation and upgrade to SQL Server 2005.

SQL Server 2005 Installation Issues

Whether you are installing SQL Server Express Edition on your personal notebook or SQL Server Enterprise Edition on a 32-processor 50-node cluster environment, a smooth installation of SQL Server requires an installation plan. The scope and number of tasks in your installation plan size depends on the size and complexity of your hardware and application, but at a minimum, you need to plan for three types of installation tasks:

■ Tasks to perform before the installation (pre-installation)

- Tasks to perform for the installation (installation)
- Tasks to perform after installation (post-installation)

Although installation planning for the large IT organization is beyond the scope of this book, we briefly state the pre-installation tasks and go through the steps for installation.

Pre-installation Tasks

Prior to the installation of SQL Server on a computer, we suggest you make a checklist of items to ensure a successful installation.

- Verify that the computer specifications meet the minimum hardware and software requirements (especially the Windows service pack) as described in SQL Server Books Online.
- You cannot install SQL Server on a compressed disk or folder. Verify that the disk or folder where you will be installing SQL Server is not compressed.
- The computer may already have an installation of SQL Server. Check the installed components in Add/Remove Programs in Control Panel before you install SQL Server.
- If SQL Server is already installed, investigate the installed components, the purpose of the previous installation, and whether there are enough system resources to handle the previous installations and your installation. You should also back up the existing installation of SQL Server.
- The installation process may require a product key; look up the product key prior to the installation.
- Prepare a domain account to assign to SQL Server services.
- If you are planning to install SQL Server 2005 Express Edition, the installation program will not install .NET Framework 2.0. You must install .NET Framework 2.0 before installing SQL Server 2005 Express Edition. .NET Framework 2.0 can be downloaded from the Microsoft website.
- The SQL Server setup program has a dependency on Windows Installer 3.1 (or later) and Microsoft Data Access Components (MDAC) 2.8 SP1 or later. You should download both these components from the Microsoft website.

Choosing the Right SQL Server Edition

As we mentioned before, SQL Server is a collection of components, and each component has a number of features to support various aspects of a database application. Microsoft has bundled these components and features into various editions to better accommodate system capacity, performance, and the price requirements of its customers. Prior to acquiring and installing SQL Server, you should study all editions of SQL Server to find the best match for your application and business needs.

As stated in Table 2.1, SQL Server has several different editions, each packaged with different components and functionality. One of your main decisions before any installation of SQL Server should be selecting the edition that suits your personal or business needs. In a large organization, the selection process should include both the database and business stakeholders such as database administrators, database developers, and business unit owners. Everyone should carefully review the functionality of each of edition of SQL Server 2005 to determine which functionality matches the business's current and future needs. This review process should also include an audit of the existing functionality, determination of immediate future functionality, and consultation with business units on functionality needed to support their goals in the next 2–3 years. After compiling a listing of required functionality, the database administrator should match the required functionality with the SQL Server functionality provided in each edition.

Understanding SQL Server Instances

Prior to the installation of SQL Server, it is important that you understand the significance of SQL Server instances because the installation is instance-based. A computer can run multiple instances of SQL Server simultaneously, and each instance runs independently of other instances. A server can have only one default instance of SQL Server, but multiple named instances up to the resources available on the computer. SQL Server 2005 supports multiple instances on a single server. However, not all SQL Server components are instance-aware. Table 2-2 describes components that are instance aware.

The maximum number of instances supported in SQL Server 2005 is based on the editions and cluster configuration of your system, as described in Table 2-3.

Table 2-1   SQL Server 2005 Editions

SQL Server 2005 Edition	Main Components	32-bit & 64-bit Support	Description
SQL Server Express Edition	SQL Server Databases Engine[1] Reporting Services[1]	32-bit [2]	SQL Server Express Edition is a free, easy-to-use and lightweight version of SQL Server 2005. SQL Server Express has limited performance and capacity and it is targeted for low-end users, hobbyists, developers, and students.
SQL Server Workgroup Edition	SQL Server Databases Engine[1] Reporting Services[1]	32-bit [2]	SQL Server Workgroup provides data storage and reporting features that are targeted for small businesses or Web servers.
SQL Server Developer Edition	SQL Server DatabasesEngine Analysis Services Reporting Services Integration Services Notification Services	32-bit and 64-bit	SQL Server Developer Edition has the same components and feature set as the Enterprise Edition, but is licensed to only one developer for development, test, and demonstration use.
SQL Server Standard Edition	SQL Server DatabasesEngine[1] Analysis Services[1] Reporting Services[1] Integration Services[1] Notification Services	32-bit and 64-bit	SQL Server Standard Edition is the data management and analysis platform for small and medium-sized organizations. It includes the essential functionality needed for OLTP, data warehousing, and line-of-business solutions. Standard Edition's integrated business intelligence and high-availability features provide organizations with the essential capabilities needed to support their operations.

SQL Server 2005 Edition	Main Components	32-bit & 64-bit Support	Description
SQL Server Enterprise Edition	SQL Server DatabasesEngine Analysis Services Reporting Services Notification Services	32-bit and 64-bit	SQL Server 2005 Enterprise Edition is the high-end edition of SQL Server 2005 and it is targeted for the mission-critical enterprise systems that demand a high-performance, high-capacity, and high-availability data management system. The Enterprise Edition also includes comprehensive business intelligence, reporting, and robust analytic capabilities.
SQL Server Enterprise Evaluation Edition	SQL Server DatabasesEngine Analysis Services Reporting Services Integration Services Notification Services	32-bit and 64-bit	SQL Server Evaluation Edition is a 180-day trial version of SQL Server that has the same functionality as the Enterprise Edition. The Evaluation Edition is targeted for customers who want to explore and examine the features and functionality of SQL Server 2005 before they choose one of the other editions.

[1] Available with limited functionality or capacity.
[2] 64-bit is supported in Windows on Windows (WoW) mode only on the x64 platform, not the Itanium IA64 platform.

Table 2-2   SQL Server Instance-Aware Components

SQL Server Component	Instance-aware?
SQL Server Database Services (includes SQL Server Agent, Full-Text Search, and Replication)	Yes
SQL Server Analysis Services	Yes
SQL Server Reporting Services	Yes
SQL Server Integration Services	No
Notification Services	Yes—instances are created after installation; not during setup.
Workstation components and tools	No

Table 2-3   Maximum Number of Instances by Edition in a Clustered and Nonclustered Configuration

SOL Server Editions	Maximum Instances Allowed
Enterprise, Developer, and Evaluation Editions	50
Enterprise , Developer, Evaluation Editions in a clustered configuration	25
Standard, Workgroup, and Express Editions	16
Standard, Workgroup, and Express Editions in a clustered configuration	16

Each instance of SQL Server is made up of a distinct set of services with separate settings for collations and other options. The directory structure, Registry structure, and service names all reflect the specific instance name that you specify during the installation of an instance. A SQL Server instance can be either the default instance or a named instance. Although you can technically configure up to 50 instances of SQL Server on a computer, in reality the maximum number of instances you can deploy depends upon the hardware resources available.

A named instance can be installed either as the first or only instance, or in a subsequent installation of SQL Server. The first time you install SQL Server on a computer with no existing installations of SQL Server, the installation program assumes installation of the default instance, although you can choose to install SQL Server as a named instance without installing the default instance first.

SQL Server Installation Tool

SQL Server 2005 has a new installation tool called SQL Server 2005 Setup. The Setup tool can be launched in two ways: through a wizard and in the command line. The Setup Wizard provides a graphical user interface, which guides the user through the installation process. The Setup command line tool is executed from a Windows command prompt and it has several advanced installation options such as remote installation. The Setup command line is more suitable for large enterprise installations. Both the Setup wizard and the command tool provide an integrated solution for installing and upgrading all components of SQL Server.

SQL Server Setup Wizard

The Setup Wizard is an integrated graphical tool for installation and upgrade of all SQL Server 2005 components, namely,

- Database Engine
- Analysis Services
- Reporting Services
- Notification Services
- Integration Services
- Replication
- Management Tools
- Connectivity Components
- Sample databases, samples, and SQL Server 2005 documentation

Installing SQL Server 2005

Microsoft SQL Server 2005 Setup is the tool for installation of all SQL Server components. The setup tool provides the functionality to install a new instance of SQL Server, upgrade an existing instance, or add a component to an existing instance.

The installation steps are consistent for all SQL Server components. We start by describing the installation steps for SQL Server Database Engine, and for other components we refer to the common steps described for the Database Engine.

Installing SQL Server Database Engine

Here are the steps for installing the Database Engine component:

1. Log on to the computer that will be hosting the SQL Server instance with a user account that has local administration privileges.
2. If you have a SQL Server DVD, insert the DVD in the DVD drive and let Autoplay launch the splash screen. If Autoplay does not run, you can manually launch it by running **splash.hta** on the DVD. On the splash screen (see Figure 2-1), click the **Run the SQL Server Installation Wizard**.

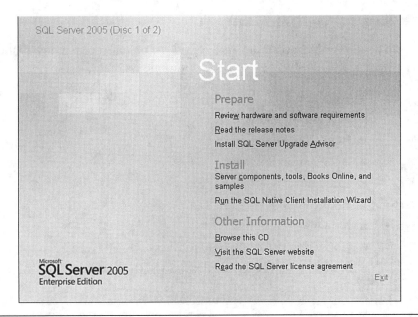

Figure 2-1 The main screen of SQL Server 2005 DVD provides a set of installation and preparation options.

If you have downloaded or copied the SQL Server installation files, navigate to the **Servers** folder and run **Setup.exe**. This launches the **Microsoft SQL Server Setup Wizard**, as illustrated in Figure 2-2.

3. Read the end user license agreement. If you agree with these terms and conditions, select **I accept the licensing terms and conditions** and click on **Next**.

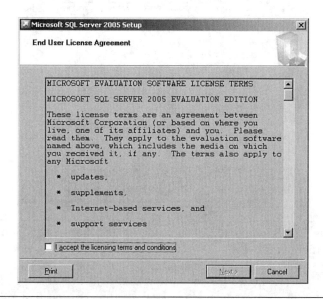

Figure 2-2 The SQL Server 2005 Setup Wizard guides the user through the pre-installation options, such as the licensing terms and conditions.

4. The SQL Server 2005 Setup program itself requires installation of three components, as illustrated in Figure 2-3. These components are

- Microsoft .NET Framework Version 2.0
- Microsoft SQL Server Native Client
- Microsoft SQL Server 2005 Setup Support Files

To proceed with the installation of these components, click on **Install.**

NOTE
SQL Server 2005 has a dependency on .NET Framework 2.0, which takes a while to install on most computers. Although the SQL Server Setup wizard installs .NET Framework 2.0 before the installation process, you can preinstall this prerequisite before installing SQL Server 2005 to speed up the installation process.

Figure 2-3   The SQL Server 2005 Setup program requires installation of three components.

You should be aware that if any of the prerequisite components have already been installed, that component does not appear in the list. In addition, the setup program does not remove these components if the installation fails or it is cancelled. If you want to remove these components after a failure, use **Add or Remove Programs** in **Control Panel**.

5. After the setup prerequisites are installed, the setup program launches the SQL Server Installation Wizard, as illustrated in Figure 2-4. Click on **Next** to proceed with the installation.

6. On the next screen (see Figure 2-5), System Configuration Check (SCC) examines the computer against a predefined set of conditions that would prevent the installation wizard from doing a successful installation. SCC retrieves the status of each condition and compares it to the required status. If a condition is not met, it provides an advisory message next to the item. For a complete list of check items, conditions, and remedies, see the "Check Parameters for the System Configuration Checker" topic in Books Online. Click on **Next** to proceed with the installation.

7. On the **Registration Information** screen (see Figure 2-6), enter your username and optionally your company. Depending

Figure 2-4   The SQL Server 2005 Installation Wizard guides the user through the installation options.

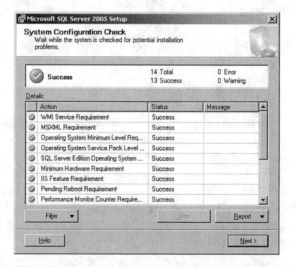

Figure 2-5   SQL Server Installation Wizard examines the system settings and existence of dependent components to ensure a successful installation.

on the edition of SQL Server that you are installing, you may have to enter the product key. You can look up the product key from the sticker on the SQL Server 2005 DVD packaging. The product key needs to be entered only for the first installation.

During the subsequent installations, the product key appears automatically on this screen and it cannot be changed.

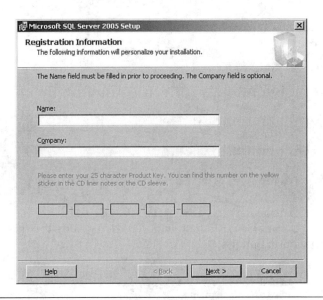

Figure 2-6   SQL Server Registration Information screen.

8. To install an instance of SQL Server Database Engine, follow the instructions for installing the installation Wizard. Click on **Next.** On the **Component to Install** screen, select **SQL Server Database Services** (see Figure 2-7).

9. On the **Instance Name** screen (see Figure 2-8), select **Default instance**. If you are installing a named instance, enter the name of the named instance. Click on **Next** to proceed.

    The installation wizard examines the specified default or named instance and performs different tasks depending on the following conditions:

    - If the specified instance does not exist, it creates the instance and installs the selected components in that instance. In this scenario, where SQL Server Database Services was just selected, the installation wizard installs just the Database Engine component. But if we had selected additional components such as Analysis Services, it would have installed both Database Engine and Analysis Services in the specified instance.

Figure 2-7   SQL Server Installation Wizard provides the option to install Database
Engine along with other components.

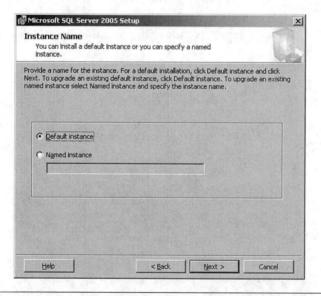

Figure 2-8   You can install the default instance or a named instance of SQL Server
2005.

- If the instance already exists and it is a SQL Server 7.0 or SQL Server 2000 instance, the installation wizard upgrades the selected components to SQL Server 2005 components. We discuss this further in the upgrade section in this chapter.

- If the specified instance is a SQL Server 2005 instance and the selected components do not exist in the specified instance, the installation wizard installs and adds the selected components to the instance.

- If the specified instance is a SQL Server 2005 instance and the selected components already exist in the specified instance, the installation wizard tries to upgrade the editions of selected components. For example, if the selected instance already has a Database Engine Workgroup Edition and you are running the installation wizard from a SQL Server Enterprise Edition, the installation wizard upgrades the Database Engine component to Enterprise Edition.

10. The next screen of the wizard, titled **Service Account** (see Figure 2-9) provides the functionality to specify credentials for SQL Server services and their startup behaviors. SQL Server services typically run with the same security credentials, but if

Figure 2-9   SQL Server Installation Wizard provides the option to assign service accounts.

you want to specify a different credential for each of the services, use the option **Customize for each service account**.

SQL Server services can also run by using one of the security credentials of the local computer accounts. As depicted in Figure 2-10, you can choose the option **Use the built-in System account** to specify **Local System**, **Network Service** or **Local Service.** To run the services with a specific domain credentials, select the option **Use a domain user account** and enter its username, password, and domain on this screen.

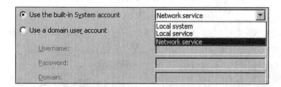

Figure 2-10   SQL Server service accounts can be one of the built-in system accounts.

We recommend that you do not use any of the built-in accounts for the SQL Server services because they may be too powerful and prone to security threats. Instead, use a local user or a domain user account with the lowest possible privileges. For more information and best practices, see "Security Considerations for a SQL Server Installation" in Books Online.

NOTE
After installation, you can change the service accounts by using SQL Server Configuration Manager as described in Chapter 3.

You can specify the startup behavior of SQL Server services after the installation and when Windows is started by using the **Start services at the end of setup** options on the bottom of the screen (refer to Figure 2-9). You should know that SQL Server Agent Service has a dependency on SQL Server Database Engine service; therefore, SQL Server Agent cannot be started unless SQL Server Database Engine is already started.

NOTE
Although the installation wizard displays only three services for each instance of Database Engine, it creates two additional services named SQL Server Full-Text Search and SQL Server VSS Writer, which are not displayed on the installation wizard. During installation, the wizard assigns the same credential as the SQL Server service to the SQL Server Full-Text Search service, and the built-in local System credential to the SQL Server VSS Writer service.

SQL Server Database Engine can use SQL Server Authentication or Windows Authentication to authenticate client connections to the server. In Windows Authentication mode, SQL Server applies users' Windows credentials without requiring users to provide a username or password. In SQL Server Authentication mode, users must provide a login and password, which are stored in the database engine. The option for Database Engine to use **Windows Authentication Mode** or **Mixed Mode** (Windows Authentication plus SQL Server Authentication) can be specified during the installation of the engine. We recommend that you use **Windows Authentication Mode** because it is more secure than **Mixed Mode**. New in SQL Server 2005, you can enable enforcement of strong passwords and password expiration, and more importantly configure your server with Kerberos protocol encryption, which is essential for implementing a secure system. These topics are thoroughly described in SQL Server Books Online.

11. On the **Authentication Mode** page of the installation wizard (see Figure 2-11), you have the option to specify **Windows Authentication Mode** or **Mixed Mode**. If you choose **Mixed Mode**, you must also provide a password for the sa (system administrator) account. Once again, we want to reemphasize that you choose **Windows Authentication Mode**, but if you must use mixed mode, you should specify a strong sa password for the sa account. For additional information, see "Strong Password Guidelines" in SQL Server Books Online.

NOTE
After installation, you can change the authentication mode by using the Server Properties dialog in SQL Server Management Studio.

Figure 2-11   SQL Server Database Engine security options during installation process.

12. The next page of the installation wizard (see Figure 2-12), titled **Collation Settings**, provides the functionality to specify the default Database Engine collation settings. Generally, you do not need to modify the default value for the collation. The installation wizard suggests the most appropriate collation based on the system locale for your computer. You need to change the **Collation designator and sort order** only if the collation setting for this instance of SQL Server must match the collation of another instance of SQL Server. You can also change the **SQL Collation** to use a collation that is compatible with previous versions of SQL Server (perhaps as part of an upgrade scenario).

13. SQL Server 2005 provides the functionality to send information about feature usage and serious system errors to Microsoft. This information helps the SQL Server team to improve the product by fixing the most common bugs, and it gives them a better understanding of product usage scenarios. The **Error and Usage Report Settings** page of the installation wizard (see Figure 2-13) gives the option to opt in or out of each of these error and usage reporting options.

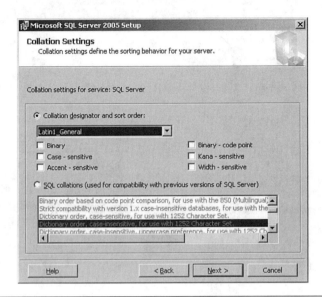

Figure 2-12   Setting SQL Server collation during the installation process.

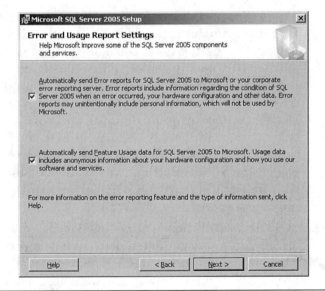

Figure 2-13   SQL Server Installation Wizard provides the option to opt in or out of error and usage reporting for all its components.

The usage reporting option is applicable to the following components and tools:

- SQL Server Database Engine
- Replication
- Analysis Services
- Reporting Services
- Integration Services
- Notification Services
- Business Intelligence Development Studio

NOTE

After installation, you can change or fine-tune the error and usage reporting settings by using the Error and Usage Report Settings tool, as described in Chapter 3.

14. Up until this point, the installation wizard has been gathering configuration information about the installation options, and aside from the setup prerequisites, it has not installed any files or Registry keys. The **Ready to Install** (see Figure 2-14) page displays the components that it is about to install. Click on **Back** if you want to go to the previous pages of the wizard to review or change your selections. Click on **Install** to proceed with the actual installation.

15. While the wizard is busy with the installation process, the **Setup Progress** screen (see Figure 2-15) displays the progress and status of the installation. You can click on the status link for each component to view its installation log. Clicking on **Cancel** is not a good idea because it cancels the installation of only those components that are incomplete; not the ones that have already been installed.

16. When the installation is completed, the wizard displays the completion page, as illustrated in Figure 2-16. The page provides a link to the installation summary log, where you can view information about errors that may have occurred during the installation. It is good practice to always view the log after installation. To learn about reading logs, search for the topic "How to Read a SQL Server 2005 Setup Log File" in SQL Server Books Online.

Figure 2-14   After you specify the installation option, the installation wizard provides a report of the components that will be installed.

Figure 2-15   Progress and status reporting during the installation process.

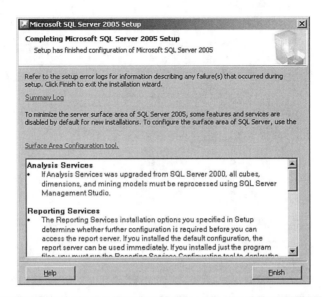

Figure 2-16 Final screen of SQL Server Installation Wizard provides a link to the installation log.

Installing Analysis Services

Installation of Analysis Services is similar to the installation of Database Engine, except on the **Components to Install** screen of the installation wizard, you choose the **Analysis Services** option, as illustrated in Figure 2-17. Analysis Services can be installed as a standalone component or in conjunction with other components.

Analysis Services can be installed in the same instance as other components, such as Database Engine, or in a separate instance; the instance can be the default or a named instance. New in SQL Server 2005, you can install multiple instances of Analysis Services on the same computer.

Installing Reporting Services

Installation of Reporting Services is similar to the installation of Database Engine, except that on the **Components to Install** page of the installation wizard you choose the **Reporting Services** option, as illustrated in Figure 2-18. Reporting Services can be installed as a standalone component or in conjunction with other components in the same instance.

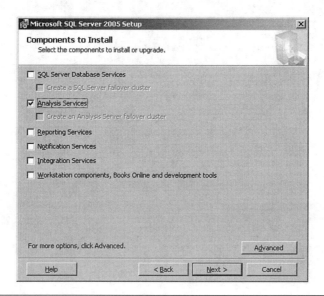

Figure 2-17 SQL Server Installation Wizard provides the option to install an instance of Analysis Services.

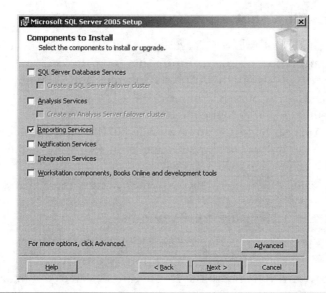

Figure 2-18 SQL Server Installation Wizard provides the option to install an instance of Reporting Services.

On the **Components to Install** page, you may find the **Reporting Services** option disabled. This is because the installation wizard could not find Internet Information Services (IIS) on your computer. To install IIS, cancel the SQL Server Installation Wizard, launch **Control Panel**, open **Add/Remove Program**, open **Add/Remove Windows Component**, select **Internet Information System** and click **Next** (see Figure 2-19).

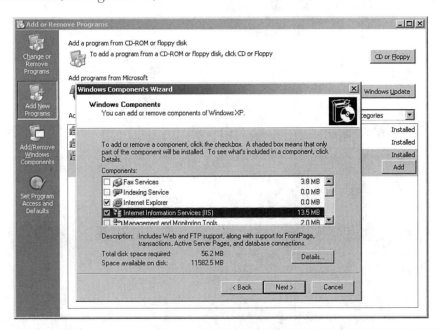

Figure 2-19   Reporting Services requires installation of Internet Information Services (IIS).

Installing Integration Services

Installation of Integration Services is similar to the installation of Database Engine, except that on the **Components to Install** screen of the installation wizard you choose the **Integration Services** option, as illustrated in Figure 2-20. The installation Wizard does not prompt you to specify an instance because Integration Services is not an instance-aware component. Integration Services can be installed as a standalone component or in conjunction with other components in the same instance. There is no user interface in the installation wizard to assign a service account to the Integration Services service. The installation wizard automatically assigns the built-in Network Service account to the service. You can change the Integration Services service account in SQL Server Configuration Manager after the installation, as described in Chapter 3.

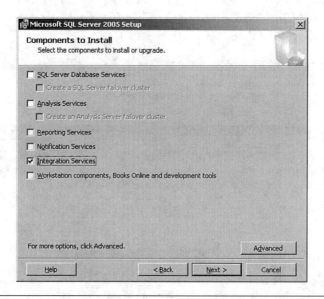

Figure 2-20   SQL Server Installation Wizard provides the option to install Integration Services.

NOTE
The legacy Data Transformation Services (DTS) runtime utilities are installed with the legacy components under Workstation components.

Installing Notification Services

To install Notification Services, select the **Notification Services** option on the **Component to Install** screen of the installation wizard as depicted in Figure 2-21. However, the installation wizard does not really install Notification Services; it copies the necessary files for creation of a Notification Services instance. To create a Notification Services instance, you need to use SQL Server Management Studio, as described in Chapter 15. Therefore, it is a good idea to install the workstation components when you install Notification Services.

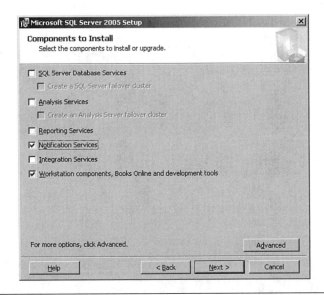

Figure 2-21   SQL Server Installation Wizard provides the option to install the files for Notification Services.

Installing SQL Server Tools and Workstation Components

As illustrated in Figure 2-22, you can select the **Workstation components, Books Online and development tools** option on the **Components to Install** screen of the installation wizard to install SQL Server tools and client components. This includes the following:

- SQL Server Management Studio, SQL Server Configuration Manager, SQL Server Profiler, Database Engine Tuning Advisor, and Replication Monitor
- Business Intelligence Development Studio
- Connectivity Components: Network libraries for DB-Library, OLE-DB for OLAP, ODBC, ADODB, and ADOMD+
- Software development kits
- SQLXML Client Features
- Legacy Components: Data Transformation Services (DTS) run-time utilities, SQL-DMO
- SQL Server Books Online

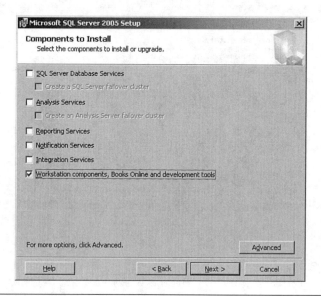

Figure 2-22   SQL Server Installation Wizard provides the option to install workstation components, which include tools and Books Online.

To limit the installed component just to tools or other components, you can click on **Advanced** and use the menu option **Entire feature will be unavailable** to exclude the unwanted components, as depicted in Figure 2-23.

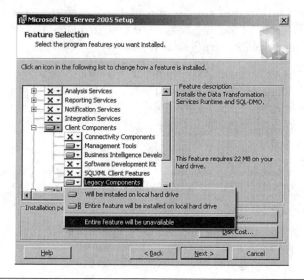

Figure 2-23   You can exclude installation of the unwanted client components.

Installing SQL Server Books Online

SQL Server Books Online is a comprehensive set of product documentation that helps you better understand the SQL Server features and functionality. Books Online is filled with feature explanations, examples, and best practices that makes it a DBA's best friend. We highly recommend that you install Books Online as part of every SQL Server installation.

To install SQL Server Books Online, select the **Workstation components, Books Online and development tools** option on the **Components to Install** screen of the installation wizard. This option installs a number of other components that you may not need. If you need to just install Books Online, on the **Components to Install** page of the installation wizard do not select any components and click on **Advanced**. On the **Feature Selection** dialog, expand **Documentation, Samples, and Sample Databases**, click on **SQL Server Books Online**, and select the **Will be installed on local hard drive** menu option as illustrated in Figure 2-24.

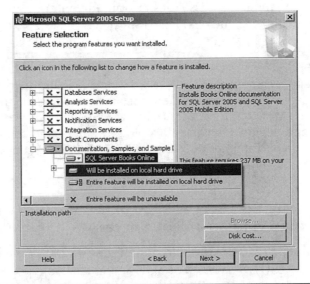

Figure 2-24   SQL Server Installation Wizard provides the option to install Books Online.

Installing Sample Databases, Sample Codes, and Sample Applications

SQL Server 2005 Database Engine has a new set of sample databases:

- AdventureWorks—New Online Transaction Processing (OLTP) sample database for Database Engine.
- AdventureWorksDW—New data warehouse sample database for Database Engine.
- Adventure Works DW—New Analysis Services sample database.

These sample databases are not installed by default. However, you have the option of installing them during the installation of a new instance, or copying the database files to attach them to an existing instance. For both options, you start by clicking on **Advanced** in the **Components to Install** screen of the installation wizard. Next, click on the **Feature Selection** dialog, expand **Documentation, Samples, and Sample Databases**, click on **Sample Databases** and select the **Will be installed on local hard drive** menu option, as illustrated in Figure 2-25. Click **Next**.

On the next page (see Figure 2-26), the installation wizard prompts you for sample database installation options: You can choose to either copy the sample database files to your computer or attach the database to an existing instance of Database Engine.

NOTE

The legacy sample databases, Northwind and Pubs, are not included in the SQL Server 2005 sample databases. You can download these databases from the Microsoft Developer Network (MSDN) Download Center by performing a search or entering this URL: www.microsoft.com/downloads/details.aspx?FamilyId=06616212-0356-46A0-8DA2-EEBC53A68034&displaylang=en.

Installing SQL Server 2005 on a Computer with a Previous Version of SQL Server

As we stated before, installing a SQL Server 2005 in an exiting instance that has a SQL Server 7.0 or SQL Server 2000 component upgrades the components. To install SQL Server 2005 components next to a SQL Server 7.0 or SQL Server 2000 installation, SQL Server 2005 must be installed in a different instance. This is true for all components of SQL Server 2005. If the previous version of SQL Server is installed as a default instance, SQL Server 2005 must be installed as a named instance.

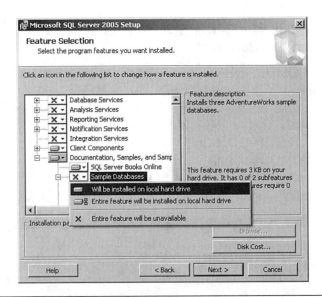

Figure 2-25　SQL Server Installation Wizard provides the option to install the sample databases.

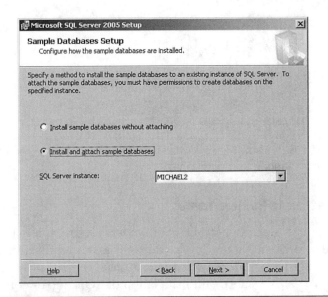

Figure 2-26　Sample databases can be installed and attached to a new or existing SQL Server Database Engine instance.

Adding or Removing SQL Server Components from an Existing Instance

To add a SQL Server component, you can rerun the installation wizard as previously described for SQL Server Database Engine. To remove a component, open **Add/Remove Programs** in **Control Panel**, select **Microsoft SQL Server 2005**, and click **Remove**. This launches the SQL Server 2005 Uninstall Wizard displayed in Figure 2-27. The wizard provides the functionality to remove all or a selection of SQL Server components. To remove all SQL Server components, select instance components and then the **Common Components** option in the wizard.

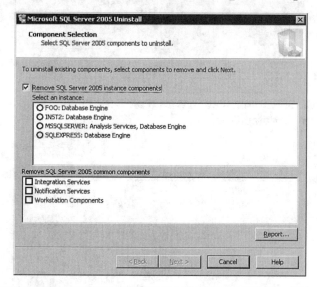

Figure 2-27 SQL Server Uninstall Wizard provides the option to remove a selection of instances and components.

Post-installation Tasks

After an installation of SQL Server, we suggest you make a checklist of items to ensure setup has performed a successful installation and the system is prepared for your application.

To verify a successful installation of SQL Server components, try to start the service by using the SQL Server Configuration Manager tool described in Chapter 3.

You may also need to enable some of the features that are disabled on a new installation of SQL Server. By default, SQL Server disables some features and components (such as remote connections) to minimize the security risk and reduce the exposed surface area of SQL Server. If your application is leveraging any of the disabled features, you need to enable these features by using the Surface Area Configuration tool accessible from the Start menu. For more information about the Surface Area Configuration tool, see Chapter 3.

Upgrading to SQL Server 2005

Every release of SQL Server is filled with data management innovations to meet business demands. SQL Server 2005 is no exception. It provides a highly secure, efficient, and highly available data management platform for relational data as well as data warehousing, analytics, and reporting for business intelligence to meet the needs of today's business applications. If your business is already running on earlier versions of SQL Server, exploiting the new SQL Server 2005 capabilities requires upgrading the existing system to SQL Server 2005. However, you may have concerns about the upgrade. Upgrades can be painful and messy. They can run into problems during the upgrade process and introduce backward compatibility issues. After an upgrade is complete, there is still the risk of existing applications not exhibiting the same behavior, resulting in customer dissatisfaction.

Upgrade issues can be avoided, or at least minimized, with proper education, planning, and testing. A successful upgrade also requires leveraging the right tools to facilitate the process.

In this section, we will briefly discuss upgrade planning, strategies for upgrading, preparing for upgrading by using the Upgrade Advisor tool, and how to actually perform the upgrade.

Upgrade Planning

To ensure a smooth and successful upgrade, you must create an appropriate plan to meet your business requirements. The scope and number of tasks in your upgrade plan depends on the size and complexity of your application, but at a minimum, you need to divide tasks into three stages:

- Pre-upgrade tasks
- Upgrade tasks
- Post-upgrade tasks

Pre-upgrade Tasks

Preparing for a SQL Server 2005 upgrade requires understanding the two general upgrade strategies: **In-place** upgrade and **Side-by-side migration**.

   In-place upgrade is an automated process where an old installation of SQL Server is updated to a SQL Server 2005 while the data, metadata, and configuration settings of the old instance are maintained. Performing an in-place upgrade is simple: You run the SQL Server 2005 setup program (the same program as the one you use for installing a new instance) and point it to the old instance name. The setup program shuts down the old service, updates the service with the new binary files, updates the data and metadata to the SQL Server 2005 format, and restarts the service. Notice the instance name remains the same during an in-place upgrade (see Figure 2-28), but the instance is not available during the upgrade.

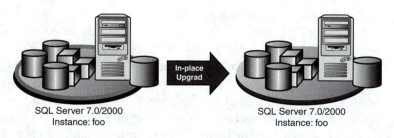

SQL Server 7.0/2000
Instance: foo

In-place
Upgrad

SQL Server 7.0/2000
Instance: foo

Figure 2-28   Instance name remains unchanged during an in-place upgrade. Instance is down during upgrade.

Side-by-side migration is a manual process where you install a new instance of SQL Server 2005, and manually copy the metadata, data, and configuration settings of the old instance. During a side-by-side migration, both the old and new instance remain online until the migration is complete and client applications are pointed to the new instance (see Figure 2-29). At the end of the migration, you can remove the old instance if you choose. Performing a side-by-side migration is not as easy as performing an in-place upgrade, but you have full control over the migration. You can choose to bring all or part of the system and perform a checkpoint, testing to make sure the old and new instance exhibit the same behavior.

   The main difference between an in-place upgrade and a side-by-side migration is how much granular control you need over the upgrade process. With the in-place upgrade, the old instance is replaced by a new instance, whereas in side-by-side migration you can migrate a single database, a table, or even a row from the old instance to the new instance. Another distinction between the two strategies is the amount of down time that your organization can incur during the upgrade. A side-by-side migration results in less down time if you can upgrade the system in phases. As soon as a phase is complete, you can switch the client applications from the old instance to the new instance. Side-by-side migration also provides access to both the new and old instances, allowing verification and comparison of the old and new environments. You should thoroughly study the characteristics of your application before choosing an in-place upgrade or side-by-side migration strategy.

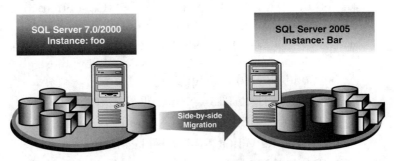

Figure 2-29   Instance or server names cannot be the same during a side-by-side migration. Both instances are available.

Backward Compatibility Issues

One of the main issues in a successful upgrade is your level of prepared-ness for the backward compatibility issues. Although Upgrade Advisor does a great job of examining your server objects, scripts, and trace files for backward compatibility issues, there may be dynamic code in an application or a script that may still be affected by the compatibility issues. One of the best practices is to review the list of compatibility issues with developers and DBAs in your organization as part of your pre-upgrade tasks. Below is a list of general backward compatibility issues that may affect your environment:

- Any object with Unicode character 0xFFFF as part of its name will be invalid after the upgrade if the database compatibility level is set to 90.

- The database ID 32767 is reserved in SQL Server 2005 for the resource database, and any current database with that ID number must be detached before an upgrade can be attempted.

- Data Definition Language (DDL) statements cannot be performed on the inserted and deleted tables inside DML triggers. SQL Server 2005 DML triggers must be modified to remove DDL statements before an upgrade can be attempted.

- SQL Server 2005 does not allow duplicate index names on tables or views. Duplicate indexes must be renamed before an upgrade is attempted.

- SQL Server 2005 cannot create or upgrade databases residing on compressed or READ-ONLY drives.

- Set the AUTO_UPDATE_STATISTICS option to ON before attempting an upgrade to SQL Server 2005.

- The behavior of the following SQL Server statements and commands have changed, and scripts containing these objects should be modified before an upgrade:

  - DBCC PINTABLE—No replacement.

  - DBCC UNPINTABLE—No replacement.

  - DBCC ROWLOCK—No replacement.

  - DISK INIT—No replacement as this is legacy behavior from SQL Server 6.x.

  - DISK RESIZE—No replacement as this is legacy behavior from SQL Server 6.x.

  - The old rebuild master database utility, rebuildm.exe, is not available in SQL Server 2005. You can use the REBUILD-DATABASE option of Setup.exe.

- The Northwind and the pubs database are no longer installed as sample databases. Database administrators can upgrade the databases for use in SQL Server 2005 if they want to, or they can modify scripts to use the new AdventureWorks sample database instead.

- Database administrators should modify any remote setup scripts, including the TARGETCOMPUTER parameter. This parameter is no longer supported.

- The behavior of trace flags has changed in SQL Server 2005. Trace flags are no longer restricted to the session that calls them; they can affect all sessions opened after they are set.

- SQL Server 2005 contains many changes to system stored procedures (parameters, values returned, and columns returned), ANSI views (columns), and system tables (columns). Database administrators need to review the latest SQL Server 2005 Books Online articles to understand changes to system objects before attempting a SQL Server upgrade to modify any scripts that utilize the changed objects.

- Indexed views have been modified in SQL Server 2005 and scripts containing index view creation syntax may need to be modified before an upgrade.

- Current backup scripts should be reviewed to see whether those scripts utilize named pipes. Backups to named pipes are no longer valid in SQL Server 2005.

- Index definitions should also be checked to determine whether current indexes contain references to functions or collations that have undergone changes in SQL Server 2005. These indexes may be disabled during an upgrade to SQL Server 2005 and may require rebuilding after the upgrade completes.

- Presentation of some data fields displayed as query results in Management Studio may look different from those displayed with Query Analyzer. This is because under the hood Management Studio uses a different data provider (ADO.NET) as opposed to ODBC in Query Analyzer.

- The OSQL utility no longer supports the ED or !! commands. To use these commands database administrators must use the SQLCMD utility.

- Itwiz.exe has been replaced with the Database Tuning Advisor utility and references to this tool should be removed or modified.

- The ISQL utility has been replaced with the SQLCMD utility and all references to ISQL should be removed or modified.

- SQL Mail no longer allows mail attachments and now requires either the Outlook XP or Outlook 2003 client. SQL Mail is also deprecated in SQL Server 2005 and replaced with a new component called Database Mail.

- English Query is no longer supported, and there is no replacement in SQL Server 2005.

- Meta Data Services 3.0 is no longer available in SQL Server 2005 and there is no replacement for it.

- The SQL-DMO WMI provider is not available in SQL Server 2005.

Although almost all the security settings from SQL Server 7.0 and SQL Server 2000 upgrade without a problem, you should be aware of the following security changes:

- SQL Server fixed server role names are reserved in SQL Server 2005 and cannot be used for user-defined logins. Any user-defined login using a fixed server role name must be modified before the upgrade process.
- SQL Server 2005 does not allow duplicate security identifiers (SID). You must remove one of the logins and its associated users with a duplicate SID before you begin the upgrade process.
- Password hashes from SQL Server 6.5 are saved in a format that is no longer supported in SQL Server 2005. SQL Server logins with SQL Server 6.5 password hashes must have their passwords reset before you begin the upgrade process.
- The database being upgraded cannot have a user with the name of sys. The sys name is reserved in SQL Server 2005 and any database user with this name must be renamed before you begin the upgrade process.
- Password comparisons that are not case sensitive are no longer supported, and applications attempting these comparisons need to be modified before the upgrade process to ensure continued functionality.
- Scripts using the BCP utility should be reviewed because the permission requirements for the BCP utility have changed. Users need to have the ALTER permission in addition to the INSERT and SELECT permissions to insert data into a table while disabling CHECK constraints on the target table, which is the default behavior of BCP.
- Do not use the ALL permission to grant all object or statement permissions to a user. Scripts assigning permissions to users need to be reviewed and this grant modified.
- Scripts and processes that view system metadata in virtual tables or system objects may need to be modified because access to virtual tables and system metadata is no longer available to guest users or members of the public role.

- Execute permission has been strengthen for the sp_addtype system stored procedure, and users attempting to execute this stored procedure must be members of the db_ddladmin or the db_owner fixed database roles.

- Users executing the sp_changeobjectowner system stored procedure because they have membership in the db_ddladmin or the db_securityadmin fixed database role must also have the CONTROL permission set for target objects.

- SQL Server 2005 no longer supports setting remote logins as trusted. Scripts using the sp_remotelogin system stored procedure to mark remote logins as trusted must be modified.

SQL Server maintenance plans are upgraded during an in-place upgrade. However, you should be aware of several changes to in maintenance plans:

- Maintenance plans no longer support log shipping. Log shipping must be configured outside the maintenance plan.

- Maintenance plans no longer attempt the repair of minor problems currently configured under the Database Integrity Check task of the Maintenance Plan Wizard.

- Maintenance plan metadata is migrated to the new catalog views during the upgrade process. Any code that references the old maintenance plan system tables should be modified to reference the new catalog views.

The following SQL Server Agent upgrade issues may affect your environment:

- The SQL Server Agent is available only for members of the sysadmin, SQLAgentUserRole, or MaintenanceUserRole roles.

- The SQL Server Agent service account no longer allows SQL Server Authentication.

- Upgrade all target servers (TSX) before you upgrade master servers (MSX).

You need to be aware of the following Replication and Log Shipping upgrade issues:

- Log shipping does not upgrade and must be rebuilt after the upgrade process is complete.
- Several discontinued functionalities affect all replication methods:
    - Creating push subscriptions without an active connection
    - Using file transfer protocol (FTP) to initialize subscribers running SQL Server version 7.0
    - Creating subscriptions in Windows Synchronization Manager
    - Subscribing to a publication by locating it in Active Directory
    - Embedding the Snapshot Agent in applications
    - Remote agent activation
    - Subscriptions using Microsoft Access (Jet 4.0)
- The following discontinued functionality affects transactional replication:
    - The Microsoft Message Queuing (MSMQ) option for queued updating subscriptions.

The following discontinued functionality affects merge replication:

- Publishing from SQL Server 2005 Express Edition

You should perform a few additional checks in your pre-upgrade stage:

- Ensure that you have additional disk size for the system databases in SQL Server 2005, which is necessary because of changes in system database schema.
- Ensure that you have additional disk space in the PRIMARY file group of each user database.
- Ensure that you have additional space required by transaction log files of user databases, which is necessary because of changes in how the transaction log handles database recovery.
- If your application has a dependency on DMO, you must install the component as a legacy component.
- If you upgrade from SQL Server 7.0 to SQL Server 2005, you must manually re-create the proxy accounts for job steps that utilize proxies.

Upgrade Tasks

The main upgrade task uses the Upgrade Advisor tool.

Upgrade Advisor

To help you find the upgrade issues prior to upgrading to SQL Server 2005, Microsoft has created the SQL Server 2005 Upgrade Advisor tool. SQL Server 2005 Upgrade Advisor is a tool for database system professionals and developers to analyze their current environments for upgrade blockers, compatibility issues, behavioral changes, deprecated features, and tasks that need to be done before and after an upgrade. The Upgrade Advisor also provides links to additional documentation that describes the recommended changes and the steps required to perform a workaround. We highly recommended that you run Upgrade Advisor against your system before performing an upgrade.

Upgrade Advisor supports analysis of the following components:

- Database Engine
- Analysis Services
- Reporting Services
- Notification Services
- Data Transformation Services
- Transact-SQL scripts
- SQL Trace files

Upgrade Advisor Architecture

The architecture of Upgrade Advisor is simple (see Figure 2-30). Upgrade Advisor parses and extracts the objects in the upgrade target and verifies them against a predefined set of rules. Each upgrade rule has a detection logic and a number of attributes such as title, description, severity, and a link to a topic in the Upgrade Advisor documentation. Objects that match the upgrade rules are stored in an XML file. The report viewer of Upgrade Advisor performs a transformation on the XML file and generates a report.

Installing Upgrade Advisor

You can install Upgrade Advisor in either of two ways. You can install it from the **redist** folder of your SQL Server 2005 media or download it for

free from the Microsoft SQL Server Web site: www.microsoft.com/
downloads/details.aspx?familyid=451FBF81-AB07-4CCB-A18B-
DA38F6BCF484&displaylang=en.

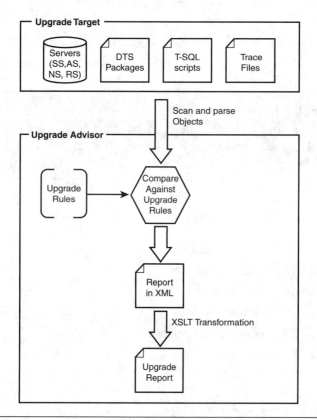

Figure 2-30   Upgrade Advisor architecture.

Upgrade Advisor has a dependency on the Microsoft .NET Framework 2.0,
which is available on the SQL Server DVD, or it can be downloaded
from Microsoft Web site: www.microsoft.com/downloads/details.aspx?
FamilyID=0856eacb-4362-4b0d-8edd-aab15c5e04f5&DisplayLang=en.

Running Upgrade Advisor

Upgrade Advisor (see Figure 2-31) can connect to both local and remote
servers. You can run it on the server you are planning to upgrade, or run
it on a remote computer and point it to the target server. The remote
functionality of Upgrade Advisor works well for situations in which the

target server is not physically accessible or there is a restrict standard for installing software on production servers.

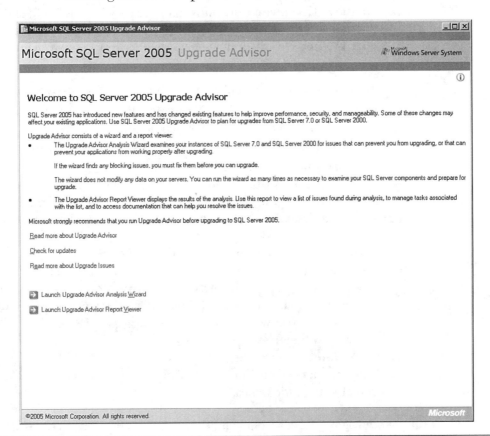

Figure 2-31   Welcome to SQL Server 2005 Upgrade Advisor screen.

NOTE
A direct upgrade from SQL Server 6.5 or older to SQL Server 2005 is not supported and database administrators needing to upgrade their SQL Server 6.5 or earlier environments. They must perform a two-step upgrade and move the older environment to SQL Server 7.0 or 2000 before attempting an upgrade to SQL Server 2005.

Upgrade Advisor Analysis Wizard

To launch the upgrade Advisor Analysis Wizard, follow these steps:

1. On the Upgrade Advisor start page click **Launch Upgrade Advisor Analysis Wizard**.

2. On the **SQL Server Components** page (see Figure 2-32), enter the name of the server to scan in the **Server name** box and then click **Detect**. Use the following guidelines for the server name:

   ■ To scan non-clustered instances, enter the computer name.

   ■ To scan clustered instances, enter the virtual SQL Server name.

   ■ To scan non-clustered components that are installed on a node of a cluster, enter the node name.

3. Review the list of components detected, modify the selections as necessary, and then click **Next**.

4. On the **Connection Parameters** page, select the instance of SQL Server you want to scan, select the authentication method, and, if necessary, enter the username and password information and then click **Next**.

5. The default instance name is MSSQLSERVER.

6. For selected components, enter the requested information. On the **Confirm Upgrade Advisor Setting** page, review the information that you entered. You can select **Send reports to Microsoft** if you want to submit your upgrade report. You can also review the privacy policy.

7. Click **Run** to analyze the instance of SQL Server.

8. When the analysis is finished, click **Launch Report** to view the detected upgrade issues.

Upgrade Advisor Analysis Command Line

You may run into situations in which you need to run the Upgrade Advisor Analysis tool against many servers (perhaps tens or hundreds), and the wizard does not scale because its interface allows analysis of only one server. The solution is the UpgradeAdvisorWizardCmd utility.

UpgradeAdvisorWizardCmd is a command line version of the Upgrade Advisor analysis tool that can run from a Windows command prompt. The command line switches of UpgradeAdvisorWizardCmd provide the same capabilities as the wizard.

```
UpgradeAdvisorWizardCmd [ -? ] |
    [ -ConfigFile filename | <server_info> ]
    [ -SqlUser login_id -SqlPassword password ]
    [ -NsSqlUser login_id -NsSqlPassword password ]
    [ -CSV ]
```

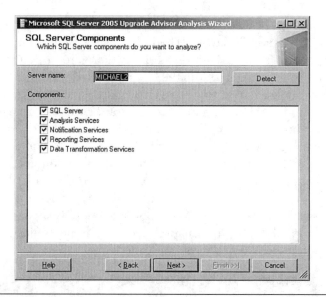

Figure 2-32   Upgrade Advisor Analysis Wizard provides an interface for analyzing all SQL Server 7.0 and 2000 components.

where *<server_info>* is any combination of the following:

- -**Server** server_name
- -**Instance** instance_name
- -**NSInstance** NS_instance_name

For example, to analyze the **Yukon** instance of **server1, server2, server3,** and **server4**, you can include the following commands in a batch file and run it from a command prompt.

```
UpgradeAdvisorWizardCmd -Server server1 -Instance Yukon
UpgradeAdvisorWizardCmd -Server server2 -Instance Yukon
UpgradeAdvisorWizardCmd -Server server3 -Instance Yukon
UpgradeAdvisorWizardCmd -Server server4 -Instance Yukon
```

You can look up the full description of the command line parameters in the Upgrade Advisor documentation in Books Online.

Upgrade Advisor Report Viewer

To view an Upgrade Advisor report, click **Launch Upgrade Advisor Report Viewer** from the Upgrade Advisor start page. When Upgrade

Advisor Report Viewer starts, the reports in the default directory are loaded. Reports are not displayed if Upgrade Advisor Report Viewer does not find any reports in the default directory. If there are no reports in the default directory, you can either run the Upgrade Advisor Analysis Wizard to create a report or load an existing report from another server or a sub-directory.

When XML files from the Upgrade Advisor Analysis Wizard are loaded into the Upgrade Advisor Report Viewer, a report for each component is displayed (see Figure 2-33). The report contains all the known issues, both detectable and undetectable, that you need to address. For each issue there is an icon indicating importance, a label informing you when the issue must be fixed, and a short description. When you expand an issue, you see a longer description, a link to issue details, and a link to the help file. The information for each issue is designed to provide enough information for you to fix the issue.

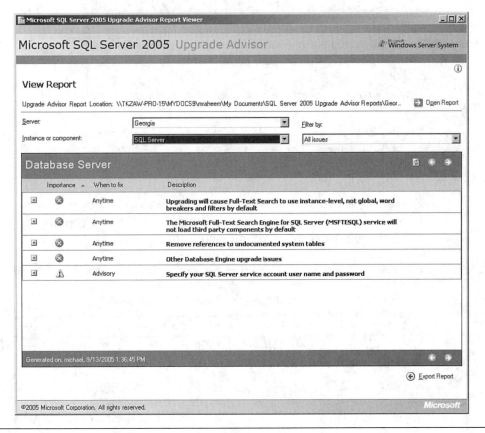

Figure 2-33   Upgrade Advisor report viewer.

Most components have issues that cannot be detected. To view these issues, expand the Other Upgrade Issues item for that component and then click the link to view additional information about the issues in the documentation.

Choosing an Upgrade or Migration Tool

SQL Server 2005 setup is the only tool for performing an in-place upgrade, but there are tools for performing a side-by-side migration. Table 2-4 shows the in-place upgrade and side-by-side migration tools and techniques for each of the SQL Server components.

Table 2-4   In-place Upgrade and Side-by-side Migration Tools for SQL Server 7.0/2000 Components

SQL Server Component	In-place Upgrade Tool	Side-by-side Tools and Technique
Database Engine	SQL Server 2005 Setup	Backup/Restore, Detach/Attach, Copy Database Wizard
Analysis Services	SQL Server 2005 Setup	Analysis Services Migration Wizard
Reporting Services	SQL Server 2005 Setup (for default configuration only)	Manual deployment of reports
Integration Services	None	DTS Migration Wizard
Notification Services	None	Migration steps

Performing an In-place Upgrade

As mentioned earlier, performing an in-place upgrade is similar to installing a new instance of SQL Server. To upgrade an old instance of SQL Server, run the SQL Server 2005 Setup program on the same computer and follow the same installation instructions described in this chapter under the title "Installing SQL Server Database Engine." After you get to the Instance Name screen of the wizard (refer to Figure 2-8), specify the instance of the old installation. The installation wizard verifies the version information and applied service pack of the old instances, and examines the feasibility of upgrading the old instance by checking it against the upgrade blockers. If these conditions are verified, the wizard proceeds with the upgrade.

Post-upgrade Tasks

After the upgrade is completed, you should build a checklist of tasks to address. These tasks need to address changes to the maintenance, security, disaster recovery, and configuration options of SQL Server Database Engine. The following list provides you with issues and information that you will want to consider, check, or otherwise investigate in building your task checklist:

- The model database is set to a database compatibility mode of 90 after an in-place upgrade. This may affect the behavior of scripts in or against this database.
- The PAGE_VERIFY database option of the model database will be set to CHECKSUM.
- After an upgrade, all SQL Server Agent user-defined proxy accounts are changed to a temporary global proxy account named UpgradedProxyAccount. The UpgradedProxyAccount is granted access to only those subsystems that were explicitly used, and does not have access to all subsystems after upgrading.
- Log into SQL Server using Windows Authentication and verify the maintenance plan tasks.
- The value of **max server memory** is a hard limit for the buffer pool size in SQL Server 2005. SQL Server 2005 no longer allows the buffer pool to exceed this setting, even if additional memory is available. Queries fail with an insufficient system memory error if the value of **max server memory** is reached.
- Changes in the query cost modeling may affect the successful execution of queries in SQL Server 2005 if the **query governor cost limit** option has been set in the upgraded installation. Review the value of this option and reset to a higher value or set to 0 to specify no time limit.

  ```
  sp_configure [ [ @configname = ] 'option_name'
  [ , [ @configvalue = ] 'value' ] ]
  ```

- Direct system catalog updates are no not supported in SQL Server 2005. Review the **allow updates** option of sp_configure to determine whether direct updates are allowed before upgrading to SQL Server 2005. Scripts updating system tables must be modified to use documented commands instead of direct updates.

- The **open objects** option of sp_configure has been deactivated in SQL Server 2005. This option is present but it does not function. Review scripts and modify scripts, using this option.

- The '**set working set size**' option of sp_configure has been deactivated in SQL Server 2005. This option is present but it does not function. Modify scripts containing this option.

- You must register each extended stored procedure using the full path for the DLL name. Extended stored procedures registered without the full path do not function after an upgrade to SQL Server 2005.

- The behavior of the following SQL Server statements and commands have changed and scripts containing these objects should be modified:

  - FOR LOAD option of CREATE DATABASE—Should be modified to take advantage of the fact that RESTORE operations can create a database.

  - DBCC DBREPAIR—Use the DROP DATABASE command.

  - DBCC NEWALLOC—Use the DBCC CHECKALLOC command.

  - DBCC TEXTALL—Use the DBCC CHECKDB command.

  - DBCC CHECKDB—DBCC CHECKDB now includes DBCC CHECKCATALOG, making a second call to this DBCC command unnecessary in SQL Server 2005 maintenance scripts.

  - DBCC TEXTALLOC—Use the DBCC CHECKTABLE command.

- You should review the use of trace flags in administration scripts to determine whether the trace flag still exists or whether the functionality of the trace flag has not changed in SQL Server 2005.

- If upgrading target servers from SQL Server 7.0, you must manually reenlist them with the upgraded master server.

- The syntax for calling tokens in the SQL Server Agent job steps has been changed and must be modified after an upgrade to SQL Server 2005.

- SQL Server Agent 2005 uses a new format for error messages written to the job step log files, you must modify any custom or third-party applications that parse the new format.

- Scripts using the xp_sqlagent_proxy_account extended stored procedure must be modified to remove references to this extended stored procedure after an upgrade to SQL Server 2005.

Summary

This chapter covered pre-installation issues, installation, and upgrade tasks. To understand more about the sweeping changes made to SQL Server 2005 that will be faced by database administrators, you are strongly encouraged to not only execute the SQL Server 2005 Upgrade Advisor but also to review the Books Online coverage of Upgrade Advisor as well. A thorough review of the SQL Server 2005 Books Online articles that cover upgrading will help database administrators and developers to understand many of the changes they will face during their upgrade to SQL Server 2005.

CHAPTER 3

Inside the Configuration Tools

SQL Server 2005 provides a number of tools for configuration of its components. The configuration tasks are tasks you perform after installing an instance of SQL Server. The configuration tasks cover a wide variety of things in SQL Server 2005. Some configuration tasks change attributes of the Windows services associated with SQL Server components. Others change the Registry and file settings that affect networking and connectivity behavior. Although there is no crisp distinction between configuration, management, and administration tasks, it is important for you to understand the tasks that SQL Server treats as configuration tasks so you can start with the right tools. Here are the types of tasks that are classified as configuration tasks:

- Tasks that are usually performed after a system installation. Typically, they are not everyday maintenance tasks.
- Tasks that can be performed only by system administrators and not by low-privileged users.
- Tasks that for the most part do not require a connection to SQL Server components.
- Tasks that change Windows services and Registry keys.
- Tasks that require viewing or manipulating of SQL Server installation options.

We've broken this chapter into two main parts to give you a broad perspective on configuration. The first part briefly describes the configuration tools and their architecture. The second part focuses on the tasks and scenarios that are enabled by these tools. As database system professionals, you can apply these tasks to the everyday scenarios you encounter on the job.

SQL Server Configuration Tools

SQL Server 2005 has a new set of configuration tools. The tools provide an integrated solution for configuration of all SQL Server 2005 products; however, some of the tools are richer and deeper than others. We will spend more time covering these tools (Configuration Manager, Surface Area Configuration Tool) and will provide introductory information about the other tools such as the Usage and Error Reporting tool. The following sections provide descriptions for each tool and its architecture.

SQL Server Configuration Manager

SQL Server Configuration Manager provides the functionality to configure and control Windows services associated with each SQL Server component. As you can see in Figure 3-1, it also allows configuration of client and server network protocols for SQL Server Database Engine. For those of you who are familiar with SQL Server 2000 tools, SQL Configuration Manager is a replacement for legacy tools such as Service Manager, Server Network Utility, and Client Network Utility.

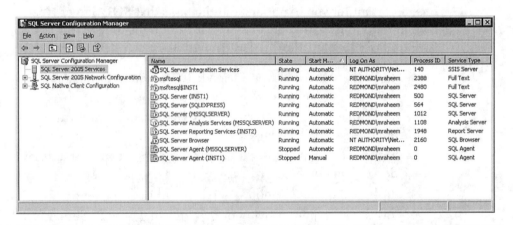

Figure 3-1   SQL Server Configuration Manager tool.

SQL Server Configuration Manager is built on top of Microsoft Management Console (MMC) technology. The tool is an MMC snap-in named SQLServerManager.msc, which is installed in the Windows directory. The tool can be launched several different ways: from its shortcut in the Windows Start menu, from the Services node in Windows Computer

Management, or from manual addition of the snap-in to an MMC console. The most common way of launching the tool is from its shortcut from the Windows Start menu. To launch it from Windows Start menu, point to **All Programs**, **Microsoft SQL Server 2005**, **Configuration Tools**, and select **SQL Server Configuration Manager**. If you want to configure a remote computer, launch SQL Server Configuration Manager from Computer Management—we will cover this scenario later in this chapter.

NOTE

SQL Server Configuration does not support configuration of SQL Server 7.0 or SQL Server 2000 installations. To configure older versions of SQL Server, you must use the SQL Server 7.0 or SQL Server 2000 tools. If you need to configure both old and new versions of SQL Server from the same computer, you can install both tools on the same computer.

As depicted in Figure 3-2, most functionality of SQL Server Configuration Manager is accomplished by manipulating Windows services and Registry keys. SQL Server Configuration Manager uses Windows Management Instrumentation (WMI) as a unified way of interacting with the API calls that manage Registry and service operations. Because it uses WMI, SQL Server Configuration Manager does not need to make a connection to any SQL Server components. This means (unlike some of the other tools such as SQL Server Management Studio) SQL Server services do not need to be running for Configuration Manager to configure these services or Registry key values. However, WMI itself has a Windows service, and the dependency of SQL Server Configuration Manager on WMI requires that the WMI service be running. Also, WMI has a dependency on the Distributed Component Object Model (DCOM) and firewall settings for communicating with a remote computer. For further information about opening a DCOM port and adding client applications to the Windows Firewall Exception list, see Microsoft Knowledge Base article found at http://support.microsoft.com/default.aspx?scid=kb;en-us;875605.

TIP

If you are planning to use SQL Server Configuration Manager against a remote computer, you need to make sure DCOM is enabled on both the client and remote computers.

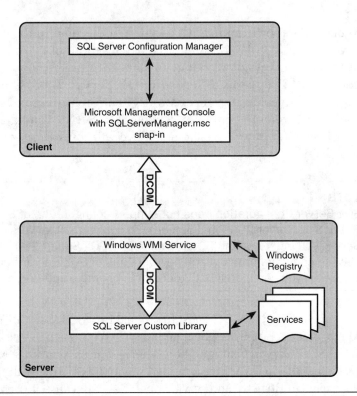

Figure 3-2   The high-level architecture of SQL Server Configuration Manager illustrates its dependency on WMI.

SQL Server Surface Area Configuration

SQL Server 2005 provides a tool named Surface Area Configuration to handle all aspects of surface area configuration for all components. The tool is installed with all editions of SQL Server 2005 and works locally or remotely against a computer.

The architecture of Surface Area Configuration tools looks very similar to that of SQL Server Configuration Manager, except it leverages the object model libraries of the components to configure its surface area (see Figure 3-3). These objects models are SQL Management Objects (SMO) for Database Engine, Analysis Management Objects (AMO) for Analysis Services, and Reporting Services WMI Provider. Both SMO and AMO are installed during installation of Surface Area Configuration on the client. On the server side, Surface Area Configuration has a dependency on Windows WMI service and DCOM.

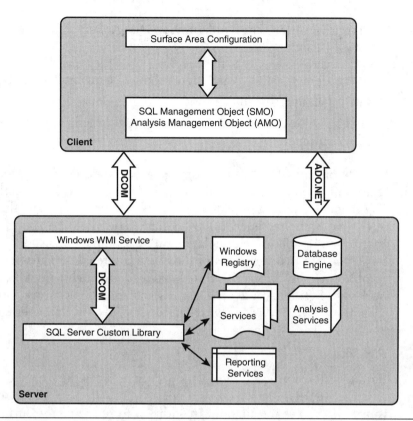

Figure 3-3   SQL Server Surface Area Configuration has a dependency on WMI, DCOM, SMO, and AMO.

It is a good security practice to disable unused services and features to reduce the surface area of SQL Server. This greatly reduces the risk of security attacks. A good analogy is the threat of a thief breaking into your house. A house with fewer doors and windows has less risk of a break and entry than a house with several doors and windows. Another advantage of reducing surface area is lowering the cost of managing and maintaining your server. The fewer components and features you use, the less cost you incur in management and maintenance of your server. Using the house analogy, the fewer doors and windows, the less time and money needed to maintain locks and door handles.

During the development of SQL Server 2005, the Microsoft SQL Server team made an extensive effort in reviewing security threats to all features and components and decided on providing configuration options for only those features that were subject to security threats.

The scope of surface area configuration in SQL Server 2005 was defined in three categories:

- By default, which components should be enabled or disabled
- Capability to enable or disable remote connections
- Capability to disable or enable higher-risk features in each component

In addition, the SQL Server team's goal was to design a product that is secure by default, yet it is usable and does not break legacy applications. The team also had to provide a tool for customers to enable those features that were switched off by default, and describe the effects of enabling or disabling a particular feature or component.

There are two variations of the Surface Area Configuration tool: a graphical user interface (GUI) tool and a command line tool. Both tools work with SQL Server 2005 instances, but they do not work with older versions of SQL Server, such as SQL Server 7.0 or SQL Server 2000.

GUI Tool

Reducing the surface area of your server reduces the exposed surface area for security attacks, but it is not a sufficient measure for securing your SQL Server installation. In addition to reducing the surface area of your SQL Server, you must implement the general security practices to prevent unauthorized access to your server. SQL Server Books Online has a number of security topics that you may find useful is securing your server.

To launch the surface area configuration GUI tool from Windows Start menu, point to **All Programs, Microsoft SQL Server 2005, Configuration Tools**, and select **SQL Server Surface Area Configuration**. The main dialog of Surface Area Configuration tool (see Figure 3-4) provides links to launch additional dialogs for enabling or disabling services, remote connections, and features. In addition, there is a link for the tool to connect to a remote computer.

Command Line Tool

The command line tool is called SAC.EXE and it is installed in the Shared folder of your SQL Server installation (for example, if SQL Server is installed on the C drive, you can find it at C:\Program Files\

Microsoft SQL Server\90\Shared\SAC.EXE). The functionality of the GUI and command line tool is very similar except the command line tool provides the additional functionality to export and import surface area settings to and from a file. This functionality enables deployment scenarios, especially for large enterprise customers with hundreds or thousands of servers. We cover this scenario in detail later in this chapter.

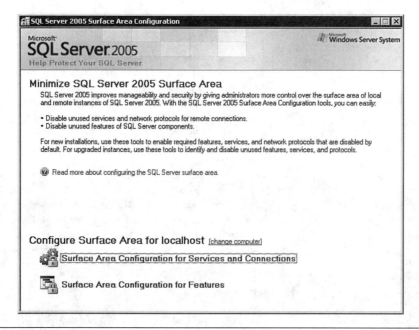

Figure 3-4   The main panel of Surface Area Configuration tool.

The SAC command line utility has a number of switches that control the surface area settings that are exported or imported from a file. To get a listing of SAC commands, run **SAC/?** in a command window:

```
C:\Program Files\Microsoft SQL Server\90\Shared>sac /?
Imports and exports SQL Server 2005 surface area settings.
  sac {in | out} filename [-S computer_name]
      [-U SQL_login [-P SQL_password]]
      [-i instance_name ]
      [-DE] [-AS] [-RS] [-IS] [-NS] [-AG] [-BS] [-FT]
      [-F] [-N] [-T] [-O]
      [-H | -?]
  in              Import the surface area settings from a file.
```

out	Export the surface area configuration settings from an instance to a file.
filename	Full path of the import or export file.
-S computer_name	Name of a remote computer. Default is local computer.
-U SQL_login	SQL Server Authentication login for the Database Engine connection. Default is Windows Authentication.
-P SQL_password	Password for SQL_login.
-i instance_name	SQL Server instance to run sac against. Default is all instances on the specified computer.
-DE	Import or export Database Engine settings.
-AS	Import or export Analysis Services settings.
-RS	Import or export Reporting Services settings.
-IS	Import or export Integration Services settings.
-NS	Import or export Notification Services settings.
-AG	Import or export SQL Server Agent settings.
-BS	Import or export the SQL Browse service settings.
-FT	Import or export the Full-Text Search service settings.
-F	Import or export the state of features.
-N	Import or export the state of network protocols.
-T	Import or export the state of Windows services.
-O	Name of the file that receives command-line output.
-H | -?	Display command syntax. Other arguments are ignored.

Secure by Default and Upgrade

The goal behind SQL Server 2005 "secure by default" is to provide a secure environment for new installations, but not to break customer applications after an upgrade. For example, **xp_cmdshell** is a legacy Database Engine extended stored procedure that was initially introduced in SQL Server 6.5. xp_cmdshell is a powerful utility for executing operating system commands from a database engine and is used in some client applications and administration scripts. In new installations of SQL Server 2005 Database Engine, xp_cmdshell is disabled by default. However, to avoid breaking legacy applications, xp_cmdshell remains enabled after a previous installation of SQL Server is upgraded. On the other hand, this upgrade behavior is applicable only to older features of SQL Server. The new features of SQL Server remain disabled after an upgrade. For example, integration of Common Language Runtime (CLR) in Database Engine is a new feature of SQL Server 2005 that allows development of stored procedures, user-defined functions, triggers, and user-defined types with any Microsoft .NET Framework language. This new feature is disabled on both new and upgraded installations of Database Engine.

Reporting Services Configuration

The Reporting Services Configuration tool (see Figure 3-5) provides a vehicle to configure and control Reporting Services settings on a SQL Server 2005 installation. This tool can also be used for the deployment of Reporting Services, if the user has chosen the option to just copy the files during the initial installation (from the SQL Server Installation Wizard). Similar to SQL Configuration Manager, this graphical user interface tool takes advantage of WMI to manipulate the configuration files and Registry keys. The tool can be used to connect to both local and remote installations of SQL Server 2005 Reporting Services.

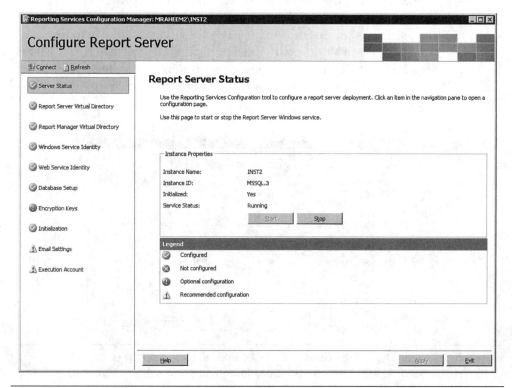

Figure 3-5   SQL Server Reporting Services has a dedicated tool for all aspects of its configuration.

Usage and Error Reporting Configuration

SQL Server 2005 provides the functionality to send information about product usage and serious system errors to Microsoft. You can use the

Usage and Error Reporting tool to opt in or out of this option (see Figure 3-6). To launch the tool, go to Windows **Start** menu, point to **Microsoft SQL Server 2005,Configuration Tools,** and select **SQL Server Error and Usage Reporting.** The tool provides two views: simple and advanced for the error and usage reporting.

In the simple view, you can choose to opt in or out for all components and all instances on the computer. In the advanced view, a grid view represents all SQL Server instances and components where you can opt in or out of sending information for a particular component. Sending this information enables the SQL Server team to identify and fix the most commonly encountered bugs and improve the product in future releases of SQL Server. Another advantage of enabling this feature is that when a fatal error occurs, you may see a response from Microsoft in the Windows Event Log that points to a Microsoft Knowledge Base article. These articles are written based on highest hits from users, so errors and events hit most often will have regularly updated articles.

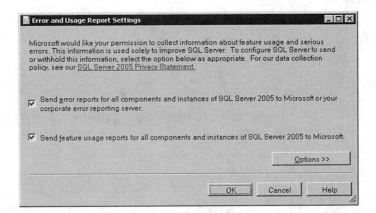

Figure 3-6   Error and Usage Report Settings enable you to opt in or out of sending information about product usage and system errors to Microsoft.

Error and Usage Report Settings cannot configure a remote computer. If you need to configure a remote computer, you must log on to the computer or use the Remote Desktop tool to run Error and Usage Report Settings on the remote computer.

Common Configuration Scenarios

SQL Server configuration tools enable a number of scenarios that you may encounter in your daily activities. The following sections describe a number of the common configuration scenarios and how to use the configuration tools to perform these tasks.

Identifying SQL Server Instances and Components on a Computer

Whether it is your initial configuration or part of your daily administration of SQL Server, you will encounter situations where you need to identify instances of SQL Server that are installed on a given computer. You may also need to find out the physical association of components and instances, and the state of services for each of the installed components. But before we describe how you can perform this sort of tasks, you need to understand the relationship between SQL Server instances, components and services.

As described in Chapter 2, SQL Server allows multiple instances of SQL Server to run simultaneously on the same computer. Each instance of SQL Server consists of a number of components, and each component has a separate set of services. For example, on a given computer that has two SQL Server instances named Accounting and Sales, the Accounting instance may have a Database Engine and a Reporting Services component, and the Sales instance may have a Database Engine and an Analysis Services component. End-user applications can connect to any of these components in the Accounting or Sales instances the same way they would connect to these components if they were installed on two separate computers. You should also know that not all SQL Server components can be installed in multiple instances on the same computer. For example, Integration Services is not associated with any instances of SQL Server and it can only be installed once on a computer. There are also services that are shared between all instances on a computer. For example, SQL Server Browser service, which provides instance name resolution for all instances, is not associated with a particular instance. In addition, there are auxiliary services that are not exposed to client applications but support other services such as SQL Server Active Directory Helper and SQL Server VSS Writer. These services are typically installed along with the main services and you do not need to install them explicitly.

Table 3-1 Describes SQL Server components and their corresponding services.

To identify SQL Server instances and components on a computer, you can use SQL Server Configuration Manager or Surface Area Configuration tools.

To launch SQL Server Configuration Manager, point to Windows **Start** menu, **All Programs, Microsoft SQL Server 2005, Configuration Tools**, and select **SQL Server Configuration Manager**. SQL Server Configuration Manager has two panes. Selecting an entry in the left pane displays members of the entry in the right pane. To view services, select **SQL Server 2005 Services** in the left pane and the right pane (see Figure 3-7) displays all services that are installed on the computer.

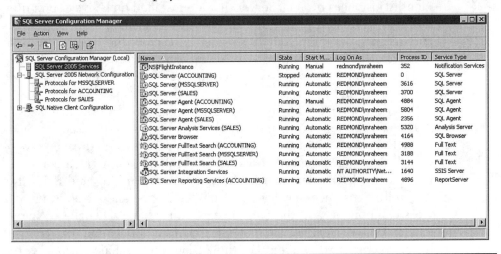

Figure 3-7   The right pane of Configuration Manager displays information about SQL Server services.

The service names in the right pane of SQL Server Configuration manager appear in the format, *component name (instance name)*. For example, SQL Server Analysis Services (Sales) refers to the service for the Analysis Services component in the Sales instance of SQL Server. The instance name MSSQLSERVER refers to the default instance. SQL Server Reporting Services (MSSQLSERVER) refers to the service for the Reporting Services component in the default instance of SQL Server. You may have noticed that the association of instances with services is not very distinguishable in SQL Server Configuration Manager. In fact, if you have multiple instances and several components in each of the instances, the list of services and instances becomes too long and it becomes difficult to understand the relationship between instances and components. In such scenarios, you can use the Surface Area Configuration tool to discover the instances.

In addition to discovery of SQL Server instances and components on a computer, you can use the Surface Area Configuration tool to easily identify the relationship between instances and components.

To launch Surface Area Configuration from Windows Start menu, point to **All Programs, Microsoft SQL Server 2005, Configuration Tools**, and select **SQL Server Surface Area Configuration**. To view or change SQL Server service states, and to enable or disable remote connections, select **Surface Area Configuration for Services and Connections** from the main panel. The Surface Area Configuration for Services and Connections dialog has two panes. The left pane (see Figure 3-8) provides a hierarchal view of the installed instances and components, and the right pane displays service information for the selected component in the left pane.

Figure 3-8   The left pane of SQL Server Surface Area Configuration provides a hierarchal view of installed instances.

The information in the left pane of Surface Area Configuration can be used to quickly answer questions like:

- How many instances of SQL Server are installed on this computer?
- What components are in a particular instance of SQL Server?

Let's go through an example and discover how you can use the tool to answer these questions. In Figure 3-8, the View by Instance tab in the left pane shows four instances of SQL Server, namely MSSQLSERVER (or default instance), ACCOUNTING, SALES, and FlightInstance. In addition, you see Integration Services and SQL Server Browser components that are not associated with any instances of SQL Server. Figure 3-8 also shows that the ACCOUNTING instance has four components: Database Engine, Reporting Services, SQL Server Agent, and Full-Text Search.

If you switch to View by Component (see Figure 3-9), you can view the instances by components. The information now can be used to answer questions such as

- Which components of SQL Server are installed on this computer?
- What instances of SQL Server contain a particular component?

Figure 3-9   The left pane of SQL Server Surface Area Configuration provides a hierarchal view of installed components.

Following the previous example, Figure 3-9 now displays the same information by component. The left pane displays that there are eight installed components on this computer. Furthermore, the Database Engine is installed in three instances, namely MSSQLSERVER (or default instance), ACCOUNTING, and SALES.

You should be aware that not all SQL Server services described in Table 3-1 are displayed in SQL Server Configuration Manager or the Surface Area Configuration tool. Auxiliary services such as SQL Server Active Directory Helper and SQL Server VSS Writer are not exposed in these tools. You do not need to configure these services, and their initial configuration during setup is sufficient to run these services. However, in emergency situations, you may want to configure or manage these services. In that case, you can view and configure these services from the Windows Service Manager. You can launch the Windows Service Manager from the Start menu by pointing to **All Programs, Administrative Tools**, and selecting **Services**.

Table 3-1 SQL Server Components and Service Descriptions

Display Name	Service Name	Instance-based	Description
SQL Server Database Services	MSSQLSERVER	Yes	Provides storage, processing, and controlled access of relational data and rapid transaction processing.
SQL Server Analysis Services	MSSQLServer OLAPService	Yes	Supplies online analytical processing (OLAP) and data mining functionality for business intelligence.
SQL Server Reporting Services	ReportServer	Yes	Manages, executes, renders, schedules, and delivers reports.
SQL Server FullText Search	SQL Server Full-Text Search	Yes	Quickly creates full-text indexes on content and properties of structured and semi-structured data to allow fast linguistic searches on this data.
SQL Server Agent	SQL Server Agent	Yes	Executes jobs, monitors SQL Server, fires alerts and allows automation of administrative tasks.
SQL Server Integration Services	MsDtsServer	No	Provides support for Integration Services package storage and execution.
Notification Services	NS$instance_name	Yes	A registered instance of a programming frame-work for generating and sending notifications.
SQLBrowser	SQL Server Browser	No	Provides instance name resolution service to clients that are connecting to any instances of SQL Server. This service is shared across multiple instances of SQL Server.
SQL Server Active DirectoryHelper	MSSQLServerADHelper	No	Enables integration with Active Directories.
SQL Server VSS Writer	SQLWriter	No	Provides the interface to back up/restore Microsoft SQL server through the Windows VSS infrastructure.

Starting, Stopping, and Viewing State of Services

As described earlier, there is a Windows service associated with each component of SQL Server. SQL Server components use Windows services to connect and respond to requests from client applications. Stopping a service results in refusal of new connections and termination of the existing connections. There are a number of scenarios where you need to stop, pause, or start a service. For example, you may have to terminate all connections to investigate a problem or to perform a system update. Similarly, a DBA may need to pause the Database Engine service to deploy a new build of an application. There are circumstances where you need to change a setting, but the new setting will not take effect until the service is stopped and restarted. You can also change the behavior of service startup. You may need to change the startup behavior of a service so it does not automatically start when the operating system is started. You can also view the state of a service. An application may suddenly stop connecting to the server and you need to view the state of the service to isolate the problem to either service or network issues.

SQL Server Configuration Manager is the primary tool for starting, stopping, and viewing SQL Server service states. But you can also use Surface Area Configuration to perform these tasks. The right pane of SQL Configuration Manager provides a summary view for the state of all services on a given computer (see Figure 3-10). SQL Server Configuration does a better job of grouping components by instances.

Name ▽	State	Start Mode	Log On As	Pr...	Service Type
SQL Server Integration Services	Stopped	Automatic	NT AUTHORITY\N...	0	SSIS Server
SQL Server Browser	Running	Automatic	REDMOND\mraheem	632	SQL Browser
SQL Server Agent (MSSQLSERVER)	Running	Automatic	REDMOND\mraheem	3580	SQL Agent
SQL Server (MSSQLSERVER)	Paused	Automatic	REDMOND\mraheem	1432	SQL Server
SQL Server FullText Search (MSSQLSERVER)	Running	Automatic	REDMOND\mraheem	3844	Full Text
SQL Server Analysis Services (MSSQLSERVER)	Running	Automatic	REDMOND\mraheem	3448	Analysis Server
SQL Server Reporting Services (MSSQLSERVER)	Running	Manual	REDMOND\mraheem	3248	ReportServer
NS$FlightInstance	Stopped	Other (Boot, System, Disabled or Unknown)	redmond\mraheem	0	Notification Services

Figure 3-10   The right pane of SQL Server Configuration Manager provides a summary view for the state of all services.

A service could have one of these three states: Stopped, Started, or Paused. In the right pane of SQL Server Configuration Manager, the state of the service is displayed in the State column and in a small traffic light icon next to its name. In Figure 3-10, you can see that Integration Services and Notification Services are stopped and SQL Server (MSSQLSERVER), which is the default instance of SQL Server Database Engine, is paused. The right pane also has a column named Start Mode, which describes when and how a service is started. A service can have one of the three start modes: Automatic, Manual, and Disabled. In Figure 3-10, SQL Server Reporting Services has start mode of Manual, and the Notification Services instance named NS$FlightInstance is disabled.

To start, stop, or resume a service, right-click on the service and select the appropriate action. You can select the **Properties** option to view additional information about the service, as shown in Figure 3-11.

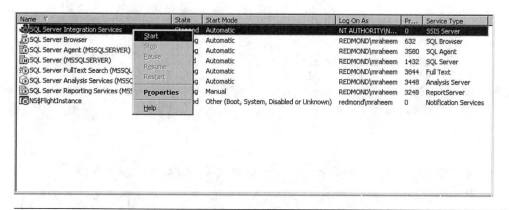

Figure 3-11   SQL Server services can be started, stopped, paused, resumed, and restarted from the right pane of SQL Server Configuration Manager.

Alternatively, you can start, stop, pause, and resume a service from the Surface Area Configuration tool (see Figure 3-12). To launch Surface Area Configuration for Services and Connections, select a component in the left pane and click on one of the buttons to Start, Stop, Pause, or Resume the service.

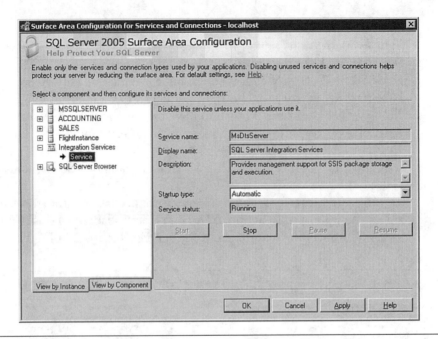

Figure 3-12   SQL Server Surface Area Configuration tool can be used to stop, start, pause, and resume services.

Configuring SQL Server Services in Windows Service Manager

By now you may ask, can we use Windows Service Manager to configure SQL Server services? The answer is maybe—it depends on the nature of your task. If you are trying just to stop, start, or change the startup behavior of a service, you can use Windows Service Manager. If your goal in stopping a service is to reduce the surface area of SQL Server, we highly recommend that you use Surface Area Configuration. Using Surface Area Configuration to stop some services, such as Reporting Services, not only stops its service but it also disables its Web services and URLs. In general, it is good practice to use SQL Server tools rather than Windows tools when you are working with SQL Server components. SQL Server configuration tools are specifically designed to configure SQL Server services and they do more than Windows Service Manager.

Configuring Service Account and Password

SQL Server services need to access system resources such as files, folders, and protected Registry keys. This requires that the service account logs on to an account to access these resources. The account to which a service logs on can be a built-in system account or a user account. To specify a service account, launch **SQL Server Configuration Manager** (see Figure 3-13), select the service, and choose **Properties**. In the service properties dialog, you can use either one of the built-in accounts or a user account.

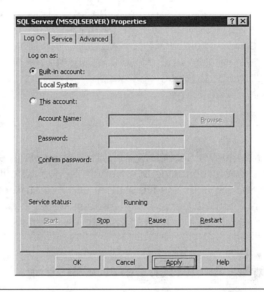

Figure 3-13   SQL Server Configuration Manager provides the functionality to view or change a service account.

Changing a service logon account requires restarting the service. However, new in SQL Server 2005, changes to the account password do not require restarting the service.

Whether you decide to log on as one of the built-in accounts or a user account, it is highly recommended that you run SQL Server services with the lowest possible privileges. This minimizes the escalation of privileges in the event that your service is compromised.

Choosing the Right Account for a Service

SQL Server services can be configured to be logged on to through a user account or any of the three available built-in accounts: Local System, Local Service, and Network Service. Some system administrators choose to log on to the service through the Local System account, which may not be the best practice. You should think of the System Account as the same account as that on which the operating system runs. Local System is an authoritative account that has full access to all objects in the system. For example, if a service is logged on through the Local System account and the system happens to be a domain controller, that service has access to the entire domain. It may be more suitable for the service to be logged on to through the Local Service or Network Service accounts, which are similar to authenticated user accounts. Local Service or Network Service accounts have the same level of access to system resources and objects as members of the Users group. This limited access helps protect your system if the service is compromised.

NOTE
Do not use Windows Service Manager to change SQL Server service accounts. Properly changing SQL Server service accounts requires setting special permissions on the file system and Registry keys that can be performed only with SQL Server Configuration Manager. Always use SQL Server Configuration Manager to change service account information.

Configuring Advanced Service Settings

In addition to the status and startup mode, additional configuration properties of a service can be viewed or manipulated in the Advanced tab of the Service Properties dialog (see Figure 3-14). Although some of this information is available if you make a connection to the server and execute system queries, SQL Configuration Manager also makes this information available without a connection. This is useful for situations in which the service is not running and you need to look up a particular property quickly, especially on a remote computer.

Advanced properties can be used to answer questions such as

- What version of SQL Server is running on this instance?
- Which service pack is applied to this instance?
- What edition of SQL Server is installed on this instance?

- Is this instance cluster aware? If so, in which virtual server is it installed?
- Is this a 32-bit instance running on a 64-bit operating system?
- What is the Instance ID of this instance?

Figure 3-14　SQL Configuration Manager enables you to view and change advanced properties of a service without a connection.

Following is a description of the advanced properties and how you can use these properties to answer these questions.

Clustered and Virtual Server Name

As mentioned in Chapter 2, a service can be installed as a resource of a clustered server or as a regular standalone service. You can use the values of the Clustered property to quickly identify whether a service is clustered. You can look up the Virtual Server Name that hosts the instance of SQL Server. These two properties are particularly useful for identifying SQL Server clustered services on remote computers.

Customer Feedback Reporting

SQL Server 2005 provides the option for its users to send information about their product usage to Microsoft. You can use the Customer

Feedback Reporting property to opt in or out of sending usage information for a service. Notice Customer Feedback Reporting performs the same functionality as the Error and Usage Reporting tool, but at a more granular level. Customer Feedback Reporting property controls a service, whereas the Error and Usage Reporting tool controls one or more components of an instance, or all components of all instances of SQL Server. The functionality of the Error and Usage Reporting tool is described earlier in this chapter.

Dump Directory and Error Reporting

When a service has a fatal error, SQL Server creates a memory dump and optionally sends it to the SQL Server team. The Microsoft SQL Server team uses the error reports to improve the functionality and quality of SQL Server products. You can use the Dump Directory property to specify the location of the memory dump, and Error Reporting to specify whether you want to send the memory dump to Microsoft. Error Reporting performs the same functionality as the Error and Usage Reporting tool but at a more granular level. The Error Reporting property controls a service, whereas the Error Reporting tool controls one or more components of an instance, or all components of all instances of SQL Server.

Instance ID

Instance ID displays the internal identifier of this instance of SQL Server assigned by the system during an installation of the instance. Instance ID is used by the system for installing instance files in a folder named as the Instance ID. Instance ID is a read-only field in the format, SQL.1, SQL.2, SQL.3,... and is different from Instance Name, which is specified by the user during installation of an instance. For example, on a computer with multiple instances of SQL Server, an instance could be named Sales with an Instance ID of MSSQL.6. This means all the files relevant to the Sales instance are installed under the folder C:\Program Files\Microsoft SQL Server\MSSQL.6. Without knowing the Instance ID, it would be difficult for the user to find the database or backup files of the Sales instance.

Language

Language is a read-only property that displays the identifier of the default language for SQL Server messages. The mapping between the language identifier and language name is listed in Table 3-2.

Table 3-2 Language ID and Language Name Correlation

Language ID	Language Name
1028	Traditional Chinese
1031	German
1033	English
1036	French
1040	Italian
1041	Japanese
1042	Korean
1043	Dutch
1046	Portuguese Brazilian
1049	Russian
1053	Swedish
2052	Simplified Chinese
3082	Spanish

Registry Root

Registry Root is a read-only property that displays the root of the Registry that holds the keys for the instance of SQL Server.

Service Pack Level

Service Pack Level is a read-only property that displays the service pack level for the instance of SQL Server. Service Pack level of 0 implies that no service packs have been applied to the instance.

HINT

Look up the value of the Service Pack Level property for situations in which you need to determine the version of SQL Server service pack on a local or remote computer, even if the service is not running.

Startup Parameters

Startup Parameters specifies the parameters that are applied when the instance of SQL Server is started. Each of the parameters is separated by a semicolon from the previous parameter. For further information about startup parameters and their supporting scenarios, see "Configuring Database Engine Startup Parameters" in this chapter.

Stock Keeping Unit Name

Stock Keeping Unit Name is a read-only property that displays the instance edition information. The edition value could be Express Edition, Workgroup Edition, Standard Edition, Enterprise Edition, or Evaluation Edition.

Version

Version is a read-only property that displays the version of SQL Server service.

HINT
You can use the value of the Version property for situations in which you need to determine the version of SQL Server service on a local or remote computer, even if the service is not running.

Configuring Database Server Network Protocols

SQL Server Database Engine and client applications communicate via network packets inside a standard communication protocol. This is done using network libraries on both server and client computers. The network packets are formatted in Tabular Data Stream (TDS) format. The network protocol could be one of the SQL Server-specific protocols, namely Shared Memory, TCP/IP, Named Pipes, or Virtual Interface Adapter (VIA). There is no need to install network libraries on the server computer; they are always installed as part of the database engine installation. However, the client network libraries need to be installed as part of the SQL Native Client installation. There is no need for the system administrator to configure the network packet or network libraries on a client or server computer. However, the communication protocols need to be configured on both the client and server computers.

To enable and configure network protocols for an instance of Database Engine server, launch SQL Server Configuration Manager on the server computer, expand **SQL Server 2005 Network Configuration** in the left pane and select the instance. The right pane (see Figure 3-15) displays all available SQL Server 2005 protocols on the server and each protocol's status.

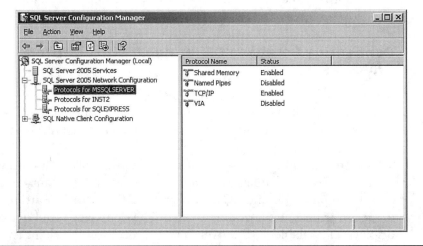

Figure 3-15   The right pane of SQL Server Configuration Manager provides a list of available network protocols for a Database Engine instance.

A Database Engine instance could use one or many network protocols to communicate with client applications. To enable a protocol (see Figure 3-16), select the protocol, right-click, and choose **Enable**.

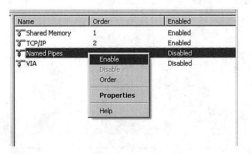

Figure 3-16   SQL Server Database Engine network protocols can be enabled or disabled from the right pane of SQL Server Configuration Manager.

Additionally, you can choose **Properties** to view or change network properties. SQL Server Configuration Manager reads and writes the status of protocols and their properties from the Windows Registry.

These properties are read when the Database Engine service starts. Therefore, making any changes to the protocols while the service is running has no effect.

Changes to the state of server network protocols and their properties require a service restart for the changes to take effect.

Configuring Database Client Application Network Protocols

As described earlier, a Database Engine server can be configured to communicate with clients using one or more network protocols. A client must also be configured to communicate with the server using one of the enabled protocols on the server.

To enable and configure client network protocols for an instance of Database Engine, launch SQL Server Configuration Manager on the server computer, expand **SQL Server 2005 Network Configuration** in the left pane, and select the instance. The right pane (see Figure 3-17) displays all available SQL Server 2005 protocols on the client computer and each protocol's status.

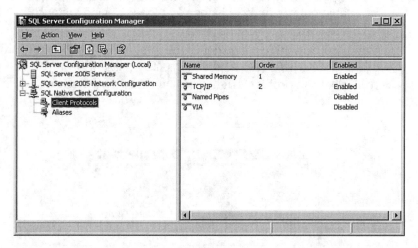

Figure 3-17   SQL Server Configuration Manager provides a list of available client network protocols on a computer.

A client computer could use one or many network protocols to communicate with a database engine instance. To enable a protocol (see Figure 3-18), select the protocol, right-click, and choose **Enable**. Also, a server and client could be configured to use multiple network protocols.

When a client tries to connect to a server, it sequentially tries each of the enabled protocols until there is a match with one of the protocols on the server. The order in which the client tries each protocol is stored in the Registry, and it can be viewed and changed in SQL Server Configuration Manager. After a connection is established, the client and server continue to communicate through the specified protocol until the connection is terminated.

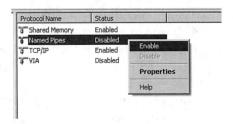

Figure 3-18   SQL Server client network protocols can be enabled/disabled and reordered from the right pane of SQL Server Configuration Manager.

The Shared Memory protocol is not available to client applications on remote computers and is available only for client applications that run on the same computer as the server instance.

NOTE
For troubleshooting scenarios where you suspect client network and server protocols are not configured properly or client applications cannot connect to the server, use the shared memory protocol to connect locally to the server.

The SQL Server client network protocols are installed as part of the SQL Native Client library installation. If the client and server are on the same computer, the SQL Native Client library is installed automatically during the installation of the SQL Server instance. If the client is a remote computer, you must install the SQL Native Client manually by running sqlncli.msi (or sqlncli_x64.msi for Windows 64-bit). The file sqlncli.msi can be found on SQL Server 2005 DVD or media. There are two options for configuring network protocols on a remote client computer. You can either install and run SQL Configuration Manager on the remote computer, or run SQL Server Configuration manager on a remote computer and connect to the client computer. To connect SQL Server Configuration Manager to a remote computer, see the following "Configuring a Remote Computer" section.

Configuring a Remote Computer

Configuring a remote computer is a common administration task. However, connecting SQL Configuration Manager to a remote computer is not intuitive (see Figure 3-19). If you launch **SQL Server Configuration Manager** from the Windows Start menu, it can connect to only the local computer. However, you can launch SQL Server Configuration Manager from **Computer Management** or **SQL Server Management Studio** to connect to a remote computer.

To connect SQL Server Configuration Manager to a remote computer from Computer Management, follow these instructions:

1. On the **Start** menu, point to **All Programs, Administrative Tools** and select **Computer Management**.
2. In the right pane, select **Computer Management (Local)** and from the **Action** menu, select **Connect to another computer**. Alternatively, you can right-click on **Computer Management (Local)** and select **Connect to another computer**.

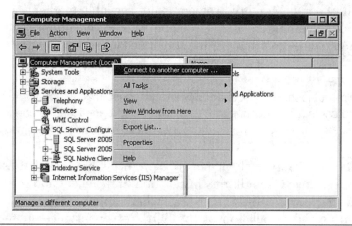

Figure 3-19   Computer Management provides the functionality for SQL Server Configuration to connect to a remote computer.

3. In the **Select Computer** dialog (see Figure 3-20), choose **Another computer**, enter the name of the remote computer, and click **OK**.
4. Back in the **Computer Management** right pane, you can see the name of the remote computer appended to the **Computer Management** label. For example, if the name of the remote

computer is **ComputerXYZ**, you will see **Computer Management (ComputerXYZ)**.

5. In the right pane, expand **Services and Application** and select **SQL Server Configuration Manager** to configure the remote computer.

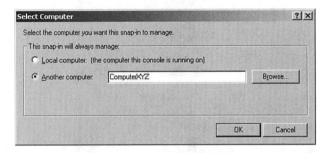

Figure 3-20   Select Computer dialog allows Computer Management to connect a remote computer.

Alternatively, you can connect **SQL Server Configuration Manager** to a remote computer from the Registered Servers window in SQL Server Management Studio (see Figure 3-21).

1. On the Start menu, point to **All Programs, Microsoft SQL Server 2005 and select SQL Server Management Studio**.
2. Click on **Cancel** if the **Connect to Server** dialog pops up.
3. In Management Studio, click on the **View** menu and select **Registered Servers**.
4. In the **Registered Servers** window, right-click on **Database Engine**, select **New** and then **Server Registration**. This will launch the New Server Registration dialog.
5. In the New Server Registration dialog, enter the name of the remote computer in the Server name field, click on **Test** and then **Save**. If the Database Engine on the remote computer requires SQL Server authentication, you have to change Authentication to SQL Server Authentication to enter the username and password.
6. Back in the Registered Servers window in SQL Server Management Studio, right-click on the remote computer and select **SQL Server Configuration Manager** to configure the remote computer.

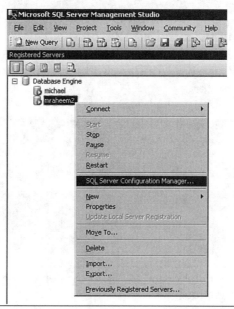

Figure 3-21 SQL Server Management Studio provides the functionality for SQL Server Configuration Manager to connect to a remote computer.

Encrypting Connections to Database Engine

You can enable encrypted connections between clients and an instance of SQL Server Database Engine by configuring a certificate for the Database Engine. Note that the same certification authority must issue a certificate for the clients and Database Engines. To configure a certificate for an instance of Database Engine on a computer, you must first install a certificate on the computer and then configure the Database Engine instance to use the certificate and accept encrypted connections.

To install certificates on a computer follow these steps:

1. Log on to the computer as an Administrator. Make sure the certificate file is accessible to import.
2. On the Windows Start menu, select **Run**, type **mmc**, and click **OK**.
3. On the File menu in MMC console, select **Add/Remove Snap-in...**, and then click **Add**.
4. In Add/Remove Snap-in dialog, click **Add**.

5. In Add Standalone Snap-in dialog, select **Certificates** and click **Add**.

6. In Certificate snap-in dialog, select the **Computer account** option and click **Next**.

7. In the Select Computer dialog, select **Local Computer** and then click **Finish**.

8. Back on Add Standalone Snap-in dialog, click **Close**.

9. In **Add/Remove Snap-in** dialog, click **OK**.

10. Back in the mmc Console Root tree, expand **Certificates**, expand **Personal**, and right-click on **Certificates**. Point to **All Tasks** and select **Import** (see Figure 3-22).

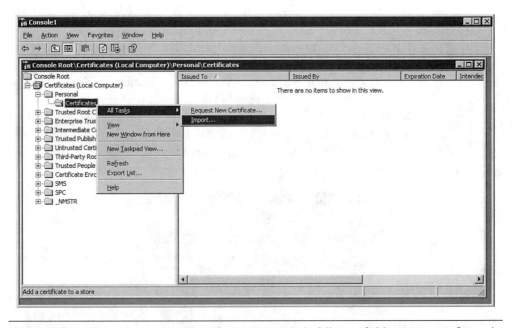

Figure 3-22   You can use the Certificates snap-in in Microsoft Management Console to import a computer account certificate.

11. In Certificate Import Wizard, click on **Next**.

12. In the next page of the wizard, click **Browse**, select the file for your certificate, and click **Next**.

13. Select the option **Place all certificates in the following store** and make sure **Personal** is the selected Certificate Store. Click **Next** and **Finish**.

To configure a Database Engine instance to use the certificate and accept encrypted connections, follow these steps:

1. Launch SQL Server Configuration Manager, and expand the SQL Server 2005 Network Configuration node.
2. Right-click on the node **Protocols for MSSQLSERVER** if you are configuring the default instance of Database Engine. If you are configuring a named instance of Database Engine, right-click on the node **Protocols for named-instance**.
3. In the Protocols for <instance name> Properties dialog (see Figure 3-23), change **ForceEncryption** to **Yes**. Switch to the **Certificate** tab, and in the **Certificate** drop-down select the certificate from the previous section and click **OK**.

Figure 3-23   Protocol Properties in SQL Server Configuration Manager provides the functionality to install a certificate for SQL Server Database Engine.

4. Restart the Database Engine service.

Configuring Database Engine Startup Parameters

As discussed earlier, each instance of SQL Server Database Engine has a service that needs to be started for the instance to service client requests. When a service starts, it reads its startup parameters from the Registry. Some of these startup parameters, such as location of master database and log files, are specified during installation of the service. Other parameters, such as behavior of the engine and enabling or disabling of features, can be specified by the system administrator after the service installation. You can use SQL Server Configuration Manager to view or change the startup parameters.

To view or change the startup parameters of a SQL Server Database Engine instance, launch SQL Server Configuration Manager, right-click on the service, and select the **Properties** option in the menu (see Figure 3-24). On the Properties dialog, choose the **Advanced** tab and select **Startup parameters** in the grid.

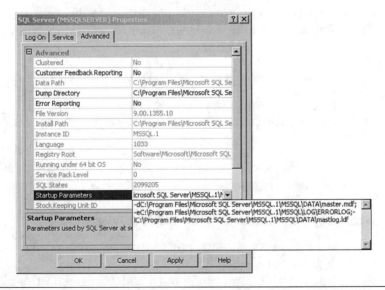

Figure 3-24 Service Properties dialog in SQL Server Configuration Manager provides the functionality to view or change the startup parameters.

Each startup parameter is specified by a dash character followed by a letter and its value. A Database Engine service has multiple startup parameters. Each parameter is separated by a semicolon. For example, in Figure 3-24 there are three startup parameters.

```
-dC:\Program Files\Microsoft SQL Server\MSSQL.1\ MSSQL\DATA\
    master.mdf;
-eC:\Program Files\Microsoft SQL Server\MSSQL.1\MSSQL\LOG\ERRORLOG;
-lC:\Program Files\Microsoft SQL Server\MSSQL.1\MSSQL\DATA\
    mastlog.ldf
```

The first parameter starts with -d, which specifies the location of the master database data file. The second parameter starts with -e which specifies the location the operation log file. The last parameter starts with -l, which specifies the location of the master database log file.

Starting Database Engine in Single User Mode

There are situations in which a DBA needs to change certain Database Engine configuration parameters or recover the master database, which require starting the Database Engine in single-user mode. This can be done by following the same instructions as in the previous scenario to edit the startup parameters and append ;-m to the startup parameters. For example, to start the service in Figure 3-24 in single-user mode, the startup parameters would be

```
-dC:\Program Files\Microsoft SQL Server\MSSQL.1\MSSQL\DATA\
    master.mdf;
-eC:\Program Files\Microsoft SQL Server\MSSQL.1\MSSQL\LOG\ERRORLOG;
-lC:\Program Files\Microsoft SQL Server\MSSQL.1\MSSQL\DATA\
    mastlog.ldf;-m
```

Remember, any change to service startup parameters requires a service restart for the change to take effect.

Starting Database Engine with a Trace Flag

Database Engine trace flags are startup parameters that change the server behavior or enable/disable a particular feature. Starting a server with a trace flag is typically temporary and it is used for troubleshooting server problems, particularly to investigate performance issues. To start a database engine with a particular trace flag, you need to append the trace switch –t followed by the trace flag number. For example, trace flag 1204 registers the resources and types of locks participating in a deadlock and the current command affected in the database engine log

To start the database engine in Figure 3-24 with trace flag 1204, the startup parameters would change to

```
-dC:\Program Files\Microsoft SQL Server\MSSQL.1\MSSQL\DATA\
    master.mdf;
-eC:\Program Files\Microsoft SQL Server\MSSQL.1\MSSQL\LOG\ERRORLOG;
-lC:\Program Files\Microsoft SQL Server\MSSQL.1\MSSQL\DATA\
    mastlog.ldf;-t1204
```

Enabling Database Mirroring

Database Mirroring is a powerful feature for increasing availability of a database. In the first release of SQL Server 2005, this feature is not supported and is available for evaluation purposes only. However, there is a good chance that this feature may be supported in the future service packs or releases of SQL Server 2005. To enable database mirroring for a particular instance of Database Engine, change the service startup parameter to include trace flag 1400 (see Figure 3-25). Follow the same instruction as in the previous section and append `;-t1400` to the startup parameters.

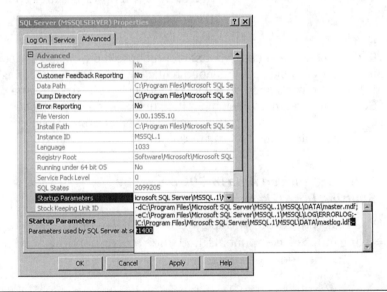

Figure 3-25   Database Mirroring can be enabled by adding trace flag 1400 to startup parameters.

After appending the trace flag 1400 to the startup parameters, you need to restart the service to enable Database Mirroring. To make Database

Mirroring fully functional, you need to further configure it in SQL Server Management Studio.

Configuring Surface Area of SQL Server

As mentioned before, there are three concepts behind surface area configuration in SQL Server 2005:

- Reducing the surface area of SQL Server by shutting down unused components (by default, some components are disabled after installation)
- Reducing the surface area of SQL Server by disabling remote connections
- Reducing the surface area of SQL Server by disabling higher-risk features in SQL Server Database Engine, Analysis Services, and Reporting Services.

The following sections describe each aspect of surface area configuration.

NOTE
Reducing surface area of your server reduces the exposed surface area for security attacks, but it is not a sufficient measure for securing your SQL Server installation. In addition to reducing the surface area of your SQL Server, you must implement the general security practices to prevent unauthorized access to your server. SQL Server Books Online has a number of security topics that you may find useful in securing your server.

Reducing Surface Area of SQL Server by Shutting Down Unused Components

You can reduce the surface are of SQL Server by stopping and disabling unused components and their corresponding services. These services include

- SQL Server Database Engine (including SQL Server Agent and Full-text Search)
- Analysis Services
- Reporting Services
- Integration Services

- Notification Services
- SQL Server Browser

Each SQL Server service has a Startup attribute that specifies when the service is started. A service could have one of the startup modes: Automatic, Manual, and Disabled. A service with Automatic startup is automatically started when the operating system starts. A service with Manual startup remains stopped until the system administrator manually starts the service or a dependent service starts the service. A service with Disabled startup cannot be started until its Startup attribute is changed to Manual or Automatic.

You can use the Surface Area Configuration tool to stop and disable SQL Server services. Launch Surface Area Configuration for Services and Connections, select the unused component in the left pane, and click on **Stop** in the right pane to stop its service (see Figure 3-26). If you want to further disable the service, you can set its Startup type to **Disabled**. Conversely, the tool allows starting, pausing, and resuming of a service.

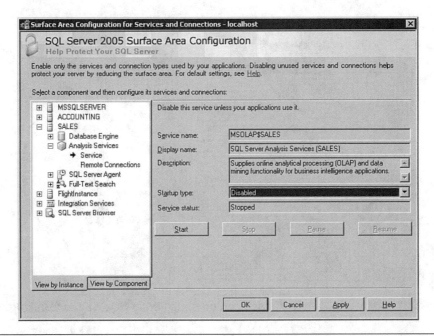

Figure 3-26   You can start, stop, pause, and resume SQL Server services with the Surface Area Configuration tool.

NOTE
Although at a glance you may think stopping and starting a component in the Surface Area Configuration tool merely stops and starts its corresponding service, the tool actually performs more than service manipulation for some of the services. For example, stopping and starting Reporting Services also enables and disables the Reporting Services web services and URLs.

For this reason, it is recommended that you use the **Surface Area Configuration** tool for disabling or enabling all SQL Server 2005 components.

Alternatively, you can use SQL Server Configuration Manager to start and stop a SQL Server service and change its startup mode. You already saw how to start and stop a service earlier in this chapter. To disable a service, launch **SQL Server Configuration Manager,** select a service on the right pane, right-click, and choose **Properties**. This launches the Service Properties dialog (see Figure 3-27). In the Service Properties dialog click on the **Service** tab and set the Start Mode to **Disabled**.

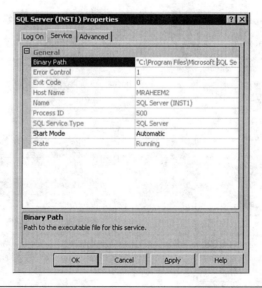

Figure 3-27   Start mode of a service can be specified in SQL Server Configuration Manager.

Reducing Surface Area of SQL Server by Disabling Remote Connections

A SQL Server client application can reside either locally on the same computer as the SQL Server installation or remotely on a separate computer. One of the effective ways to reduce security attacks is to disable the capability for remote client applications to connect to SQL Server.

SQL Server 2005 provides the functionality to disable remote connections for Database Engine and Analysis Services components. For Database Engine, you do so by disabling network protocols that are used for remote connections. A remote client application uses one of the protocols TCP/IP, Named Pipes, or VIA to connect to a SQL Server Database Engine. So, by disabling TCP/IP, Named Pipes, and VIA protocols, you can disallow remote connections to your server. A local client application can use Shared Memory protocol to connect to the server. You can further disable Shared Memory protocol, but then no local client applications including SQL Server tools can connect to manage the server. In most cases you want to enable Shared Memory protocol, so tools such as SQLCMD and Management Studio can connect to the server.

To enable or disable remote connections for Database Engine and Analysis Services, launch **Surface Area Configuration for Services and Connections,** select the instance, the component, and **Remote Connection** in the left pane (see Figure 3-28). The right pane displays the current remote connection state of the selected component. To disable remote connections, select **Local connections only**. To enable remote connections, select **Local and remote connections** and choose one or both of the TCP/IP and Named Pipes protocols. It is good security practice to only enable the protocol that is needed by your application but not both protocols. Enabling or disabling remote connections for a component requires restarting the service associated with the component.

NOTE
By default, remote connections are disabled in certain editions of SQL Server 2005 such as Express, Evaluation, and Developer editions, and are enabled in all other editions. After installing SQL Server, you can use the Surface Area Configuration tool to enable or disable remote connections.

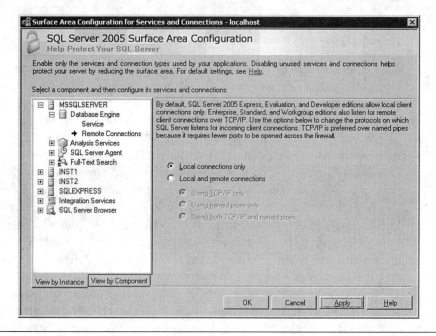

Figure 3-28   Use the Surface Area Configuration tool to enable remote connections to Database Engine and Analysis Services.

Reducing Surface Area of SQL Server by Disabling Features in Database Engine, Analysis Services, and Reporting Services

The third aspect of surface areas configuration that can reduce the surface areas of SQL Server, as mentioned previously, is concerned with the features in Database Engine, Analysis Services, and Reporting Services.

Enabling and Disabling Database Engine Features

SQL Server 2005 Database Engine provides the functionality to configure surface area by disabling or enabling its features. The option to enable or disable is not available for all features of Database Engine. The Microsoft SQL Server team made an extensive effort in reviewing all product features and decided on providing configuration options only for those features that were subject to a security threat. The goal of the team has also been to design a product that is secure by default. Most of these features are disabled by default. Accessing any of the disabled features returns an error indicating that the feature is disabled for the purposes of surface area reduction. For example, executing the stored procedure xp_cmdshell when it is disabled generates the following error:

```
Msg 15281, Level 16, State 1, Procedure xp_cmdshell, Line 1
SQL Server blocked access to procedure 'sys.xp_cmdshell' of
component 'xp_cmdshell' because this component is turned off as
part of the security configuration for this server. A system
administrator can enable the use of 'xp_cmdshell' by using
sp_configure. For more information about enabling 'xp_cmdshell',
see "Surface Area Configuration" in SQL Server Books Online.
```

To enable or disable a feature of Database Engine, launch **Surface Area Configuration** from the Windows **Start** menu, select **Surface Area Configuration for Features**, select the Database Engine instance and the feature in the left pane, and enable or disable the feature on the right pane (see Figure 3-29). The right pane also provides a provisionary description of the feature, with additional details available if you click on **Help** or from Books Online.

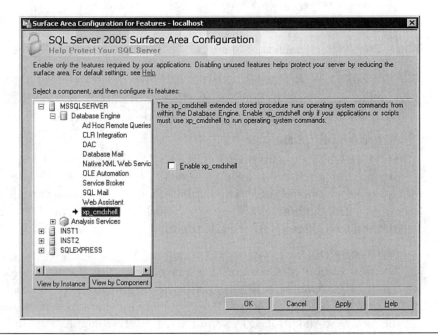

Figure 3-29   Use the Surface Area Configuration tool to enable or disable Database Engine features.

Enabling or disabling SQL Server Database Engine features for a particular instance requires the Database Engine service for that instance to be running. In fact, the left pane of the **Surface Area Configuration** for Features dialog displays only components that are currently running. For example, in the scenario illustrated in Figure 3-29, the default instance (MSSQLSERVER) has two components: Database Engine and Analysis Services. If Database Engine is stopped, the left pane shows only Analysis Services under MSSQLSERVER instance. If Analysis Services is also stopped, the left pane does not display the MSSQLSERVER instance at all. In the event that all components are stopped, launching of **Surface Area Configuration for Features** dialog displays the error message show in Figure 3-30.

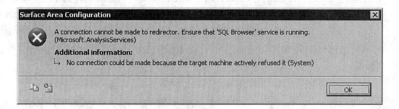

Figure 3-30   Enabling or disabling of features of a SQL Server component requires its service to be running.

The following sections describe the Database Engine features that could be enabled or disabled, along with a brief description of each feature.

Ad-hoc Remote Queries

The two T-SQL functions OPENROWSET and OPENDATASOURCE provide the functionality to run ad-hoc remote queries without necessarily defining a linked server. By default, these two functions are disabled on new installations of SQL Server 2005 Database Engine but enabled in instances upgraded from SQL Server 2000 or SQL Server 7.0.

CLR Integration

The integration of Common Language Run-time (CLR) inside SQL Server 2005 Database Engine provides the functionality to create and execute CLR-based objects. These objects include types, user-defined functions, stored procedures, and triggers. By default, running CLR objects is disabled, which means you can create, alter, or drop CLR-based objects but you cannot access these objects and run the CLR code.

Remote DAC

The dedicated administrator connection (DAC) is a high-priority connection to the server for troubleshooting when the server is "hung" and does not accept new connections. This feature is always available for tools and applications that run locally on the same computer as Database Engine. By default, DAC is disabled from a remote computer.

Database Mail

Database Mail is a new subsystem for sending e-mail messages from Database Engine. Database Mail relies on Service Broker and a few extended stored procedures that are disabled by default. Disabling Database Mail while it is busy processing emails in its queues does not stop Database Mail from sending the emails. If you need to stop Database Mail immediately, execute the stored procedure msdb.dbo.sysmail_stop_sp. For more information about Database Mail see Chapter 10.

SQL Mail

SQL Mail is the legacy subsystem for sending and receiving email messages from Database Engine. SQL Mail relies on a few extended stored procedures that are disabled by default in a new installation of SQL Server Database Engine but enabled in installations upgraded from SQL Server 2000 or SQL Server 7.0.

NOTE

The dependency of SQL Mail on Microsoft Outlook has been problematic for many customers. In SQL Server 2005, Microsoft has introduced a new subsystem called Database Mail, which uses SMTP for sending email messages. SQL Mail will be removed in future versions of SQL Server. If you are planning to use SQL Mail, consider using Database Mail instead.

Native XML Web Service

Native XML Web Service is a new feature in SQL Server 2005 that provides access to Database Engine through use of Simple Object Access Protocol (SOAP) messages over user-defined HTTP endpoints. HTTP endpoints can be stopped and disabled to reduce risk of malicious access to Database Engine.

OLE Automation

OLE Automation provides functionality to create and access OLE Automation objects from Database Engine. The OLE Automation functionality is exposed through a number of extended stored procedures, namely, sp_OAGetProperty, sp_OASetProperty, sp_OAMethod, and sp_OAGetErrorInfo. These stored procedures are disabled in new installations of SQL Server Database Engine, but enabled in installations upgraded from SQL Server 2000 or SQL Server 7.0.

Service Broker

Service Broker is a new feature in SQL Server 2005 that provides queuing and reliable messaging for Database Engine. Service Broker uses Simple Object Access Protocol (SOAP) messages over an endpoint to communicate with remote applications. Service Broker endpoints can be stopped and disabled to reduce the surface area of SQL Server.

Web Assistant

Web Assistant consists of a few stored procedures that generate HTML files from tables of a Database Engine. These stored procedures are sp_makewebtask, sp_dropwebtask, sp_runwebtask, and sp_enumcodepages. The Web Assistant stored procedures are disabled in new installations of SQL Server Database Engine, but enabled in instances upgraded from SQL Server 2000 or SQL Server 7.0.

NOTE

Web Assistant will be removed in future releases of SQL Server. If you are planning to use this feature, consider using Reporting Services instead.

---

xp_cmdshell

xp_cmdshell is a system extended stored procedure that runs a given operating system shell command. By default, xp_cmdshell is disabled in new installations of SQL Server Database Engine but enabled in instances upgraded from SQL Server 2000 or SQL Server 7.0.

SQL Server Agent Stored Procedures

SQL Server Agent is a component of SQL Sever that executes scheduled jobs. SQL Server Agent consists of a service and a number of stored procedures that provide the interface to manage features of the agent. SQL Server Agent stored procedures are enabled and disabled when the service is enabled or disabled.

Enabling and Disabling Analysis Services Features

SQL Server 2005 Analysis Services has a number of features that can be disabled to reduce surface area. By default, these features are disabled on a new installation of Analysis Services, and you should enable these features only if they are needed for your application. To enable or disable these features for an instance of Analysis Services, you can use SQL Server Surface Area Configuration tool (see Figure 3-31).

   1. Verify the instance of Analysis Services that the server is running.

2. From Windows **Start** menu, point to **All Programs/SQL Server 2005, Configuration Tools** and select **SQL Server Surface Area Configuration**.

3. On the main dialog of Surface Area Configuration, click on **Surface Area Configuration for Features**.

4. On the left pane of Surface Area Configuration for Features dialog, select the instance of Analysis Services and its features. The right pane displays the current state of the feature. Using the controls in the right pane, you can enable or disable each of the Analysis Services features.

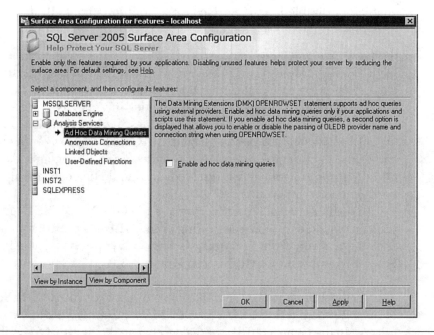

Figure 3-31   Use the Surface Area Configuration tool to enable or disable Analysis Services features.

Enabling or disabling of Analysis Services features requires the Analysis Services service to be running. In addition, configuring named instances (instances other than the default instance) requires SQL Server Browser service to be running. Viewing features of a named instance of Analysis Services while the SQL Server Browser Service is not running generates the error message shown in Figure 3-32.

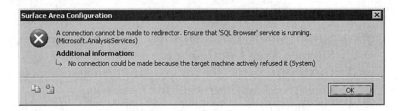

Figure 3-32   Connections to named instances of Analysis Services require the SQL
Server Browser service to be running.

The following sections detail the Analysis Services features that can be
enabled or disabled in the Surface Area Configuration tool, along with a
brief description of each feature:

Ad Hoc Data Mining Queries

Data Mining Extensions (DMX) is a language that allows execution of
Data Manipulation Language (DML) and Data Definition Language
(DDL) statements against a mining model in Analysis Services. The
OPENROWSET function in DMX provides the functionality to use an
Object Linking and Embedding Database (OLEDB) provider to execute
an ad-hoc data mining query on a remote server. By default, **Ad Hoc
Data Mining** functionality is disabled and should be enabled only if it is
needed in your application.

To further control the surface area of the OPENROWSET function,
you can enable or disable the passing of the OLEDB provider name and
connection string from the **Analysis Server Properties** dialog in **SQL
Server Management Studio** (see Figure 3-33).

1. On Windows Start menu, point to **All Programs/SQL Server
   2005**, and select **SQL Server Management Studio**.
2. In the Connect to Server dialog, change the **Server type** option to
   Analysis Services and enter the Analysis Services server name.
3. In Management Studio, locate the Object Explorer window,
   right-click on the server node (top-level node in the tree) and
   select **Properties** from the exposed menu.
4. In the Analysis Server Properties dialog, select the **Show
   Advanced (All) Properties** option, located on the bottom of
   the dialog.
5. Locate the server property named **DataMining\Allow-
   ProvidersInOpenrowset** and set its **Value** to **true** or **false** to
   enable or disable it.

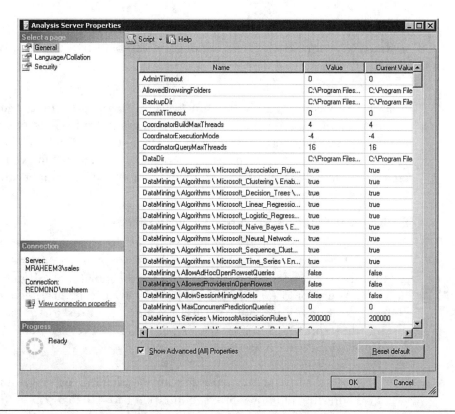

Figure 3-33   Although most of the Analysis Services surface area settings are exposed in the Surface Area Configuration tool, some of the advanced settings can be controlled only from the Server Properties dialog in SQL Server Management Studio.

Anonymous Connections

The Anonymous Connections feature of Analysis Services enables users to connect to Analysis Services with no authentication. The Anonymous Connections feature is disabled by default and it is highly recommended that you keep this feature disabled unless it is absolutely needed by your application.

Linked Objects

Analysis Services provides the functionality to link objects such as measure groups and dimensions between two instances of Analysis Services. To enable this functionality, you need to enable one option on each of the instances. On the instance where the linked object is created, you need to enable the **Enable links to other instances** option, and on the referenced instance you need to enable the **Enable links from other instances** option. Both these options are disabled by default on new installations of Analysis Services.

User-Defined Functions

Analysis Services provides the functionality to create and run user-defined functions based on Common Language Runtime (CLR) or Component Object Model (COM) objects. By default, execution of CLR and COM-based user-defined functions is disabled, which means you can create or delete this type of user-defined function, but you cannot run the CLR code by accessing these functions.

Enabling and Disabling Reporting Services Features

SQL Server 2005 Reporting Services provides the functionality to configure surface area by disabling or enabling some of its features. By default, these features are disabled on a new installation of Reporting Services. You should enable these features only if they are needed in your applications. To enable or disable these features for a specific instance of Reporting Services, you can use **SQL Server Surface Area Configuration** (see Figure 3-34):

1. Verify the instance of Reporting Services that the server is running.
2. From the Windows **Start** menu, point to **All Programs, SQL Server 2005, Configuration Tools** and select the **SQL Server Surface Area Configuration** tool.
3. On the main dialog of **Surface Area Configuration**, click on **Surface Area Configuration for Features**.
4. On the left pane, select the instance of Reporting Services and one of its features. In the right pane, you can view, enable, or disable the feature.

Enabling or disabling of Reporting Services features for a particular instance requires the Reporting Services service for that instance to be running. The right pane of the **Surface Area Configuration for Features** dialog does not display Reporting Services instances that are disabled.

The following sections describe the Reporting Services features that can be enabled or disabled in the Surface Area Configuration tool.

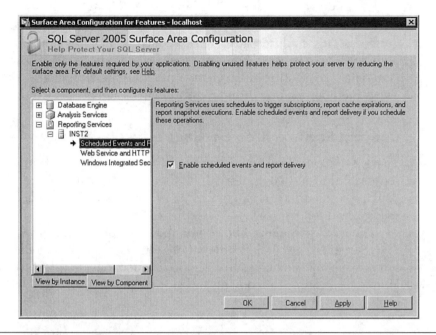

Figure 3-34 Use the Surface Area Configuration tool to enable or disable Reporting Services features.

Scheduled Events and Report Delivery

You can reduce the surface area of SQL Server 2005 Reporting Services by disabling its Scheduled Events and Report Delivery feature. Scheduled Events and Report Delivery provides the functionality to schedule operations such as taking report snapshots, delivering reports, and sending cache expiration notifications. You should enable this feature if your implementation of Reporting Services requires report subscription or scheduling report snapshots.

Web Service and HTTP Access

Tools and client applications can use SOAP and URL requests to access a Reporting Server. You can reduce the surface area of Reporting Services by disabling the Web Service and HTTP Access feature. However, disabling this feature also prevents some of the SQL Server tools such as Report Manager, Report Builder, and Management Studio from connecting to the Reporting Services instance.

Windows Integrated Security

A report in Reporting Services accesses and aggregates data from a variety of data sources. With the Windows Integrated Security feature enabled, the credentials of the user running the report are used to access the data. This could create security concerns if user's credentials are used without the user's consent. You can disable the Windows Integrated Security feature and use other methods for accessing report data. These methods include Prompted Credentials and Stored Credentials.

Copying Surface Area Settings between Two Computers

There are situations in which you need to copy all or part of surface area settings from one computer to another. The You may even need to deploy these surface area configuration settings to hundreds or thousands of computers.

The **SAC** command line utility allows exporting and importing of SQL Server surface area configuration settings to and from a file. These settings include service states, remote connections, and feature states. Here are the steps for copying surface area settings for all SQL Server components from Computer_A to Computer_B:

1. Using the Surface Area Configuration tool, verify the surface area settings on Computer_A. This includes the states of all services, remote connection and state of features.
2. On Computer_A, open a command prompt window and change the current directory to the same directory as SAC.EXE. For example, if SQL Server tools are installed on the C: drive, change the current directory to **C:\Program Files\Microsoft SQL Server\90\Shared**.
3. At the command prompt, run **SAC.EXE** to export the surface area settings of Computer_A to a file name sac_settings.xml, as follows:

```
sac out sac_settings.xml -S Computer_A
```

4. At the same command prompt, run **SAC.EXE** on to import the surface area settings from file sac_settings.xml to Computer_B:

```
sac in sac_settings.xml -S Computer_B
```

There are a couple of tips worth noting: SAC exports the feature settings only for components that are running. After exporting and importing the surface area settings, if you notice that certain features are not deployed on your target computer it is most likely because the corresponding components are not running on the source computer. To verify the export operation, you can open the export file in Notepad or Internet Explorer and search for an XML tag named <Features>. If you cannot find the tag, start the component and rerun the command in step 3. Second, execution of the command in step 4 requires remote connections to be enabled on Computer_B. There are two ways to work around this issue. You can run Surface Area Configuration on Computer_A, connect it remotely to Computer_B, enable remote connections on Computer_B, restart the service, and run the command in step 4. Another option is to copy the exported file to Computer_B and run the command in step 4 in a command prompt window on Computer_B.

If you want to deploy the surface area settings to several computers (e.g., Computer_B, Computer_C, Computer_D, …), you can create a batch file with the command in step 4 for each of the computers. Once again, this assumes remote connections are enabled on the target computers:

```
sac out sac_settings.xml -S Computer_A
sac in sac_settings.xml -S Computer_B
sac in sac_settings.xml -S Computer_C
sac in sac_settings.xml -S Computer_D
sac in sac_settings.xml -S Computer_E
```

The commands in steps 3 and 4 copy the surface area settings for all components of SQL Server on the source computer. If you need to deploy a subset of the settings, you can use the SAC command line switches. The SAC command line switches enable you to fine-tune the settings deployed between two computers. For example, if Computer_A has several instances of SQL Server and you want to deploy just the Database Engine features of one instance to Computer_B, you can use the -I , -DE, and -F switches to accomplish this.

```
sac out sac_DE_mssqlserver_settings.xml -S Computer_A -I
MSSQLSERVER -DE -F
```

Remember, the default instance of SQL Server is named MSSQLSERVER.

Stopping SQL Server Services Across Multiple Instances

Consider the situation in which you urgently need to stop all SQL Server services on all computers in your network. One option is to log on to every computer and stop the services manually, but the manual operation will not scale if you have to stop tens or hundreds of instances of SQL Server.

You can use the SAC command line utility to stop all SQL Server services on a computer. Here are the steps:

1. Choose a computer that has the same instances and components as your production computers. Using the **Surface Area Configuration** tool or **SQL Server Configuration Manager**, stop all SQL Server services on this source computer.

2. Using the SAC command line utility, export the service settings of the source computer to a file:

```
sac out sac_stop_all_services.xml -T
```

3. Use SAC to import the file to any computer in your network to stop its services. You can create a batch file with multiple SAC commands to stop services on several computers (e.g., Computer_B, Computer_C, Computer_D, ...)

```
sac in sac_stop_all_services.xml -S Computer_B
sac in sac_stop_all_services.xml -S Computer_C
sac in sac_stop_all_services.xml -S Computer_D
sac in sac_stop_all_services.xml -S Computer_E
```

Notice that the export file also includes the services startup mode, which is applied to the target computers upon import of the file. As part of step 1, you need to make sure the service startup modes are set the same as those on the target computers.

Configuring Surface Area of a Remote Computer

Both the Surface Area Configuration tool and SAC command line utility provide the functionality to configure the surface area of a SQL Server on a remote computer. To connect SAC to a remote computer, you can use its command line -s switch. To connect Surface Area Configuration to a remote computer, click on the link **change computer** on its main dialog (see Figure 3-35).

Clicking on **change computer** launches the Select Computer dialog, where you can enter the name of a remote computer or select the option to connect to the local computer (see Figure 3-36).

The name of the remote computer is displayed back on the main Surface Area Configuration dialog (see Figure 3-37). This is useful for situations in which you need to quickly figure out the name of the computer to which Surface Area Configuration is connected.

Now, if you launch the Surface Area Configuration for Services and Connections or Surface Area Configuration for Features dialogs, they

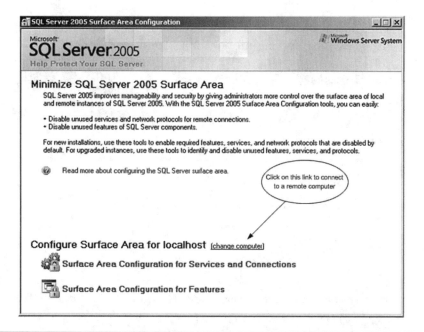

Figure 3-35   Surface Area Configuration can connect to a remote computer.

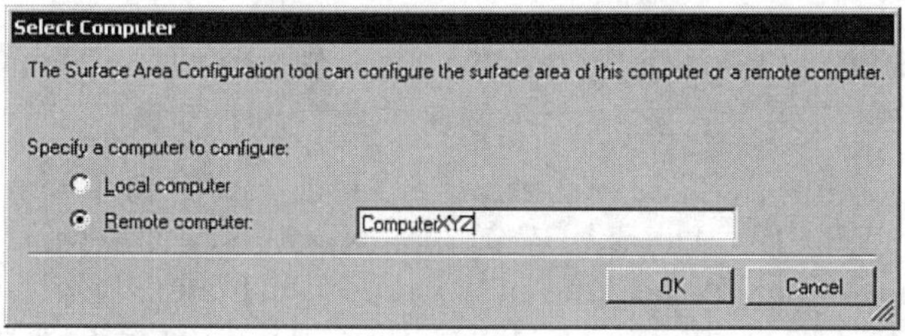

Figure 3-36   The Select Computer dialog.

will be launched in the context of the remote computer. The name of the remote computer is also displayed in the title bar of these dialogs.

Sending Information About Feature Usage and Serious Errors to Microsoft

SQL Server 2005 provides functionality to send information about feature usage and serious system errors to Microsoft. This information helps the SQL Server team to improve the product by fixing the most common bugs and gives them a better understanding of product usage scenarios. You can choose to opt in or out of each of these options for all instances on your computer or for a specific component.

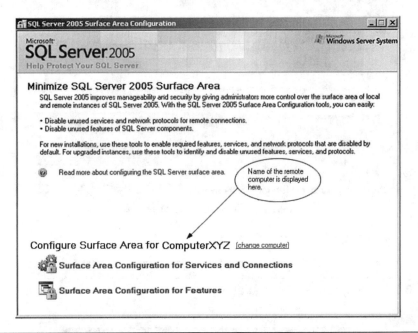

Figure 3-37   Surface Area Configuration can connect to a remote computer.

By default, SQL Server error and usage information is collected once per day at 12:00 a.m. If 12:00 a.m. is not a suitable time for your server, you can change the time of collection by manually editing the Registry key that controls the collection time. There is a Registry key for each SQL Server instance identified by its instance ID. For example, the following is the Registry key with instance ID of MSSQL.1.

```
HKLM\Software\Microsoft\Microsoft SQL Server\MSSQL.1\CPE\
TimeofReporting
```

The value of the Registry key is the number of minutes from 12:00 a.m. when the information will be sent to Microsoft. For example, a value of 30 would set the collection at 12:30 a.m., and value of 600 would run the collection at 10:00 a.m.

The information that is sent to Microsoft is classified in two categories: Error Reporting and Feature Usage. These two options can be found in the Error and Usage Report Settings dialog. As you can see in

Figure 3-38, the labels for these two options are somewhat wordier than what we have been calling them. This happened after the labels were reviewed by the Microsoft legal team.

The **Error and Usage Report Settings** dialog (see Figure 3-38) has two modes: Simple and Advanced. In the simple mode, you can choose to opt in or out of error and usage reporting for all components in all instances of SQL Server.

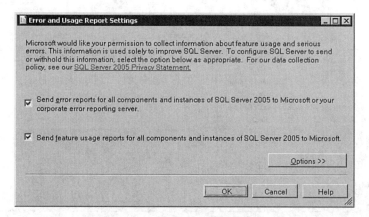

Figure 3-38   The simple view of Error and Usage Report Settings provides the functionality to opt in or out of sending information for all components.

The advanced mode of the Error and Usage Report Settings dialog (see Figure 3-39) provides a more granular control of components that can send error and usage reports to Microsoft. On the Error and Usage Report Settings dialog, click on **Options** to view the error and usage settings for every component in every instance.

At first glance, you may find the information in the grid rather confusing. However, as soon as you understand the rules applied to classify the information, you will likely find it intuitive. There is a row for each of the instance-aware components such as Database Engine, Analysis Services, and Reporting Services. Other components are presented as **Others** in **All Instances**. Also, unlike other tools, the default instance is displayed as **<Default>**.

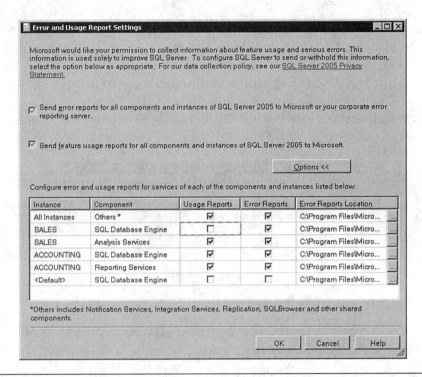

Figure 3-39   The advanced view of Error and Usage Report Settings provides the functionality to opt in or out of sending information for a specific component.

Summary

The first part of the chapter briefly described the configuration tools and their architecture, including SQL Server Configuration Manager, SQL Server Surface Area Configuration tools, Reporting Services configuration, and Usage and Error Reporting configuration. The second part of the chapter covered specific tasks and scenarios that are addressed by these tools.

CHAPTER 4

Inside Management and Administration Tools

The Microsoft SQL Server Team had two main goals for the design of the new SQL Server 2005 management tools. The first goal was to provide a consistent management experience for all components of SQL Server. The second goal was to provide an innovative tool to make database professionals more productive at querying, managing, and administrating SQL Server. To achieve these goals, the team had to choose an environment that was easily extensible, user-friendly, and familiar to the database professionals. While we were studying different hosting environments, or as we called them "shells," we soon concluded that the Microsoft Management Console (MMC) shell was not suitable to host the new tools. The MMC model was old, monolithic, and it did not provide the extensibility needed. For example, the MMC model stipulated that the management dialogs had to be modal with a fixed size optimized for a desktop size of 640 × 480 pixels. However, as the high-resolution computer monitors became more popular and the average size of the desktop increased to 1024 × 768, the legacy Enterprise Manager users hated this restriction. They consistently asked us why they could not resize the management dialogs to take advantage of the full size of their screens. However, deviating from the MMC model was not that easy. A new shell would definitely solve some of the issues, but it would also break a long-term trend. For two generations of SQL Server, database professionals had used the Enterprise Manager or Analysis Manager, both of which were MMC snap-ins. The innovative new shell had to eliminate some of the legacy restrictions but also had to be familiar to users.

One of the environments that looked very attractive was the Integrated Development Environment (IDE) upon which Visual Studio was built. The IDE had provided extensibility and a proven, user-friendly environment for developers for several years. It also offered several engineering advantages, such as a ready-to-use editor, a debugger, and a powerful help model, and it could host some of the components that were built by the Visual Studio team. After studying several prototypes, the team decided to use the IDE for the new shell. The tool was called SQL Server Workbench and it was distributed to a number of early adopter customers and SQL Server Most Valued Professionals (MVPs). By the Beta 1 release, SQL Server Workbench created a lot of controversy in the community. The feedback was very bipolar; customers either loved or hated it. While the developers found the environment extremely friendly, the DBAs found the user interface confusing. Some DBAs thought the shift to a development-like environment unnecessary, and it required a steep learning curve. The engineering team faced a tough task addressing these issues. The decision was to cut down some of the features and use the resources to address these important usability issues. The team carefully collected all the feedback and redesigned the environment to bridge the gap between the legacy tools and the new innovative tool. We also made the environment simpler and friendlier for the DBAs. By the Beta 2 release, the tool was called SQL Server Management Studio, and it received positive feedback from both developers and DBAs. The results were successful, but it came at the price of cutting some features such as the T-SQL debugger and Object Search functionality.

With almost six months since the release of SQL Server 2005 at the time of this writing, I (Michael) can see that the team made the right decision to achieve its goals. SQL Server Management Studio provides the ultimate integrated management and authoring experience for all components of SQL Server and it is a productive and user-friendly environment. You may not find all the functionality of Enterprise Manager or Query Analyzer in the new tool, but it certainly increases your productivity. As for the missing features, you can find them in other tools—as with the T-SQL debugger now found in Visual Studio—or look for them in the future releases of SQL Server. Remember, the SQL Server team is always looking forward to your feedback: http://connect.microsoft.com.

SQL Server Management Studio

Management Studio is a comprehensive integrated environment to manage, administer, and author queries for all components of SQL Server, namely Database Engine (including Replication, SQL Server Agent, and Full-Text Search), Analysis Services, Reporting Services,

Integration Services, Notification Services, and SQL Server Mobile. Management Studio is a collection of rich tools in the form of dialogs, wizards, tool windows, designers, and editors (see Figure 4-1).

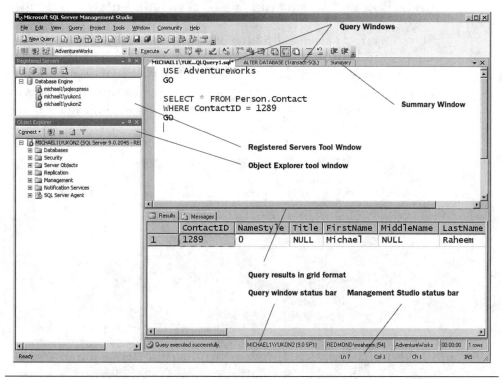

Figure 4-1 SQL Server Management Studio and some of its main components.

The Management Studio environment or "shell" leverages the same technologies as the Visual Studio Integrated Development Environment (IDE). However, Management Studio and Visual Studio are two completely different products. Management Studio is specifically designed for management and authoring of SQL Server products, whereas Visual Studio is an integrated development environment for all types of development such as Windows, Office, web, and mobile applications.

One of the main productivity gains in Management Studio is the integration of authoring and management in a single environment. For those of you who are familiar with SQL Server 2000/7.0 tools, Management Studio combines the functionality of Enterprise Manager, Query Analyzer, MDX Sample Application, and Analysis Manager in a single environment. In addition to SQL Server 2005, SQL Server Management Studio can manage SQL Server 2000 Database Engine.

Installing and Launching SQL Server Management Studio

SQL Server Management Studio can connect locally or remotely to a server. To install Management Studio, run the SQL Server Setup program and proceed with the setup screens until you see the **Components to Install** screen. On this screen, select **Workstation components, Books Online and development tools** (see Figure 4-2), and continue with the rest of the setup screens.

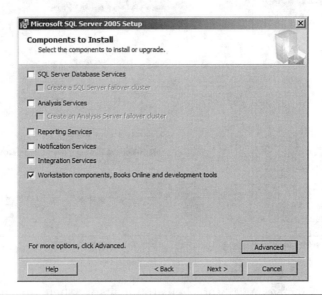

Figure 4-2   Management Studio can be installed as part of the workstation components from the SQL Server setup program.

NOTE
The option, Workstation components, Books Online and development tools in the setup program installs more than just Management Studio. If you want to install only the management tools, click on Advanced and exclude all other components but Management Tools in the subsequent screen.

To launch Management Studio from Windows Start menu, point to **All Programs/Microsoft SQL Server 2005**, and select **SQL Server Management Studio**.

Management Studio Components

Management Studio hosts a number of components for the authoring, administration, and management of SQL Server products. The following sections present a description of the main components in Management Studio along with their functionality.

Connection Dialog

Connection dialog provides the functionality to specify the necessary parameters to connect to a server (see Figure 4-3).

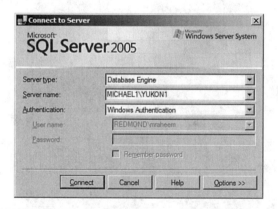

Figure 4-3   Connection dialog in SQL Server Management Studio.

Using the fields **Server type** and **Server name,** you can connect Management Studio to any of the SQL Server products on a given server. These products could be Database Engine, Analysis Services, Reporting Services, Integration Services, or SQL Server Mobile. As described in Chapter 2, you can install named instances of Database Engine, Analysis Services, and Reporting Services. To connect to a default instance of any server type, you can enter the name of the server in **Server name**. To connect to a named instance, enter the name of the server followed by the \ character and then the name of the instance. For example, in Figure 4-3 the user has entered MICHAEL1\YUKON1 in the **Server name** field to connect to a database engine instance named YUKON1 on server MICHAEL1.

NOTE
You can substitute the full server name with (local) or . (dot character) to connect to a local server. For example, in Figure 4-3 if Management Studio were running on the same computer as MICHAEL1, you could enter (local)\YUKON1 or .\YUKON1 in the Server name field of the connection dialog.

On the connection dialog, you can optionally click on the **Options** button to access the advanced connection options (see Figure 4-4). You can find a description of these options in SQL Server Books Online. For most scenarios, you do not need to change any default values.

Figure 4-4   Advanced connection options for SQL Server Database Engine.

Upon clicking on **Connect**, the Connection dialog tries to establish a connection with the specified server. While the connection is being established, the narrow orange band on top of the dialog moves from left to right and you can click on **Cancel** to cancel the connection. During the connection cancellation, the narrow orange band changes its movement to the opposite direction, moving from right to left.

Registered Servers

Registered Servers (see Figure 4-5) is a Management Studio tool window that provides the functionality to keep links to your frequently used servers. You can use these links to quickly view the status of the server, connect to the server to manage its objects, or to execute a query. Each user has a separate list of Registered Servers stored in a file on the local computer (the same computer that is running Management Studio).

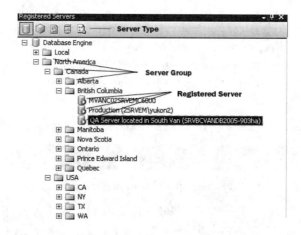

Figure 4-5 Registered Servers provides a list of the frequently used servers.

You can organize the Registered Servers in server groups (similar to the files and folders) to match the logical or physical grouping of the servers in your organization. For example, in Figure 4-5 the registered servers are grouped by physical location of the servers—in other words, by continent, country, region, state, and so on. You can create registered servers for all server types. The toolbar on top of the Registered Servers window allows quick switching between different server types: Database Engine, Analysis Server, Reporting Services, SQL Server Mobile, and Integration Services. Alternatively, you can use **View, Registered Server Types** from the main menu in SQL Server Management Studio to switch between server types.

TIP

You can create Registered Servers for SQL Server 2000 and SQL Server 2005 instances. However, there are no iconic or graphical representational differences between a SQL Server 2000 and SQL Server 2005 registered server. If you are planning to create registered servers for both your SQL Server 2000 and SQL Server 2005 servers, it is a good idea to create your SQL Server 2000 registered servers in a separate server group named something like "SQL2000." This will help you to distinguish the SQL Server 2000 registered servers quickly.

By default, the Registered Server window appears on the top-left corner of Management Studio. You can easily move, hide, or autohide the window to allocate more space to other components. To quickly view the window, choose **Ctrl+Alt+G** or **View, Registered Servers** from the main menu.

The Registered Servers window enables you to view and change the state of a server from the registered server. To view the status of a server, look at the icon to the left of to the registered server and match it to Table 4-1.

Table 4-1   Status of Servers in the Registered Servers Window

Icon	Status	Description
	Started	Service is up and running.
	Stopped	Service is stopped.
	Paused	Service is paused.
	Unknown	The state of the service is unknown. Registered Server cannot access the service possibly because of network or WMI security issues—see "Troubleshooting Registered Servers to Show Server Status" in this chapter.

The context menu on a registered server (see Figure 4-6) provides the capability to change the state of a service, along with a variety of management options that are covered later in this chapter.

Object Explorer

Object Explorer (see Figure 4-7) is one of the main components of SQL Server Management Studio. It provides a hierarchical tree view of the objects on a server. The tree displays nodes in folders representing the server's logical structure. Object Explorer is the manifest for performing management operations on the server objects for Database Engine

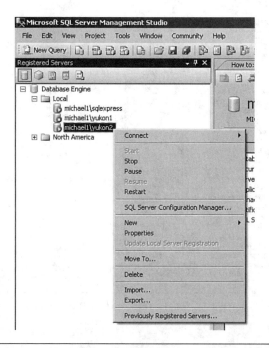

Figure 4-6 The Registered Servers menu provides a variety of management options.

(including SQL Server Agent, Replication, and Full-Text Search), Analysis Services and Data Mining, Reporting Services, Integration Services, and Notification Services. Each folder or a node in Object Explorer has a context menu with a variety of options to perform an action on the server. For those of you who are familiar with SQL Server 2000 tools, Object Explorer is the replacement for the left tree in Enterprise Manager and Analysis Services, and Object Browser in Query Analyzer.

By default, the Object Explorer window appears on the left side of Management Studio, docked under the Registered Server window. You can move, hide, or autohide the window to allocate more space to other components. There are several ways to quickly show the Object Explorer window. You can press **F8** on the keyboard, select **View, Object Explorer** from the main menu, or click on the Object Explorer button on the main toolbar in Management Studio.

NOTE
Closing the Object Explorer window (clicking on the [x]) does not disconnect it from the server; it only hides it.

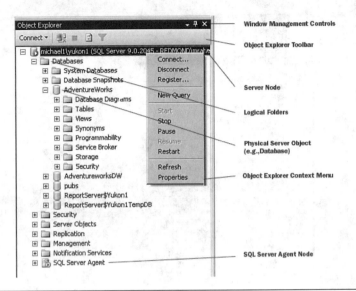

Figure 4-7   Object Explorer and its various sub-components.

To connect Object Explorer to a server, you can right-click on a registered server and choose the option **Connect, Object Explorer**. You can also click on **Connect** in the toolbar of Object Explorer and select one of the server types. Alternatively, you can choose **File, Connect Object Explorer** from the Management Studio main menu. All these connection options, with the exception of the registered server, pop up the connection dialog, where you can enter the server name and other connection options. After you are connected, you can expand and collapse the nodes to navigate through the objects and use the context-menu to perform operations on the objects. To disconnect, click on **Disconnect** in the toolbar or right-click on the server node and choose the option **Disconnect**. The context menu of the server node has an option to register the server. This is particularly useful for situations in which you have connected to a server and you want to quickly add it to your registered servers for subsequent connections.

You can use Object Explorer to connect to multiple servers in the same window. The servers could be of the same type or different types, installed locally or remotely. This is a great productivity feature because you can manage all servers in your organization without launching a separate management tool or opening multiple instances of the same tool for each of the servers. In addition, Object Explorer supports connections to the SQL Server 2000 database engine. This is a useful option during upgrade and migration processes, where you can use Object Explorer to manage both SQL Server 2000 and SQL Server 2005 environments and remove the old tools altogether.

In addition to managing objects, Object Explorer can assist you in programming and writing queries. As shown in Figure 4-8, you can right-click on an object (such as a table) and choose the option to create a DML (INSERT, UPDATE, DELETE), or a DDL (CREATE, ALTER, DROP) statement. You can optionally send the generated script to a new query window, a file, or the clipboard to subsequently paste into other editors. In addition, you can drag an object from Object Explorer to a query window rather than typing it. This is extremely useful in a situation in which you have objects with long names or names that are too difficult to spell.

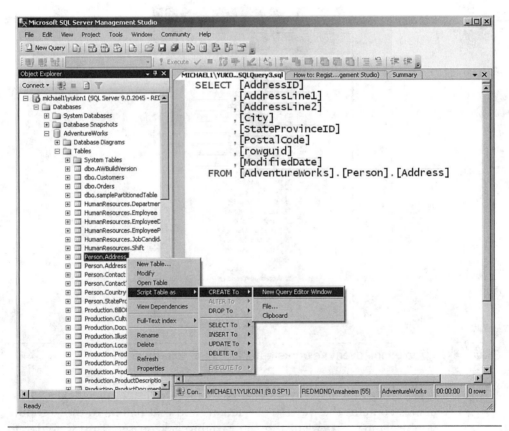

Figure 4-8   Object Explorer provides the functionality to create DML and DLL statements for an object.

NOTE
You cannot select multiple objects in the Object Explorer window; use the Summary Window instead.

Object Explorer has several productivity features such as filtering. If you plan to work with a large number of objects, consider creating a filter. Filters enable you to view and work with only a subset of objects at a time. The filtering is applied just like a WHERE clause; it restricts the object list to only those objects that meet the filtering criteria. Let's go through a filtering example and see how it works:

Figure 4-9 shows a snapshot of tables in the AdventureWorks database prior to filtering.

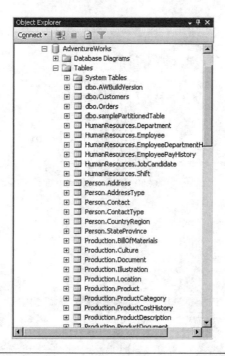

Figure 4-9   Tables in AdventureWorks database prior to filtering.

Imagine that the objective is to create a filter to display only tables whose names contains the word "Transaction" and that belong to the "Production" schema. To create the filter, right-click on the **Tables** folder in Object Explorer and select **Filter, Filter Settings** in the context menu.

In the Object Explorer Filter Settings dialog, enter the filtering criteria to match the objective. For the **Name** property, pick the operator **Contains** and enter **Transaction** for its value. For **Schema**, pick the operator **Equals** and enter **Production** for the value. The finished filter settings are shown in Figure 4-10.

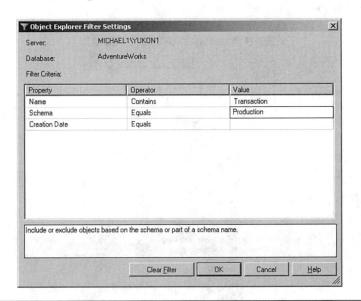

Figure 4-10   Object Explorer filter settings for AdventureWorks tables.

After you click **OK**, the Object Explorer displays only two tables that matched the filtering criteria. Notice the word "filtered" is now appended to **Tables**, in parentheses, indicating that filtering is in effect (see Figure 4-11). To remove the filtering, you can right-click and select the option **Filter, Remove Filter**.

NOTE
The Object Explorer filter settings are removed and not persisted after you disconnect Object Explorer from the server.

Under the hood, Object Explorer uses a component called Enumerator to query the meta-data of objects on a server and displays them in a tree control. As the user clicks on each node of the server, Object Explorer sends a query that looks very much like an XML Path Language (XPath) query to the enumerator. Enumerator interprets the XPath-like query into a metadata query, which is understood by the particular server type. The enumerator fetches the query result from the server and passes it to Object Explorer in XML format. Object Explorer transforms the XML into the graphic format and appends it to the appropriate node in the tree.

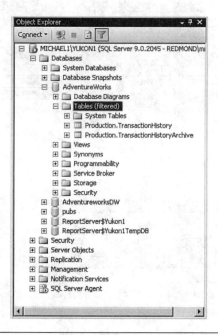

Figure 4-11   Tables in AdventureWorks database after filtering.

Summary Window

The Summary window (see Figure 4-12) works in conjunction with Object Explorer to display additional information about the selected object in Object Explorer. In addition, the Summary window provides an alternative method to Object Explorer for navigating through the objects in a server. You can find the title and relative location of the current object in the area just under the toolbar. The grid displays the down-level objects relative to the current object. You can double-click on the objects in the grid to further navigate their down-level objects. Double-clicking an object with no down-level objects opens a dialog where you can view/change properties of the object. To view the up-level node, click on the **Up** button in the Summary Window toolbar. Navigating through

Object Explorer automatically changes the current node in the Summary window, but not vice versa. To change the current node in Object Explorer to the same node in the Summary window, you need to click on the **Synchronize** button on in the Summary window toolbar. Just as you can with Object Explorer, you can use filtering by clicking on the **Filter** button in the Summary window toolbar.

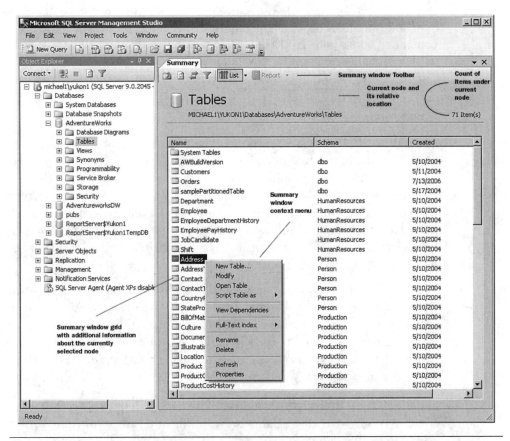

Figure 4-12 The Summary window provides an alternative method for viewing objects on the server with additional metadata.

The Summary window provides two views, **List** and **Details**, that can be selected from the **List** button on the toolbar. In Details mode, the Summary window grid displays additional metadata information for the down-level objects. You can sort the metadata information in the grid in ascending or descending order by clicking on the column headers. This metadata information is useful for the times when you want to find the creation date of an object quickly or you need to find objects with the same name in different schemas.

TIP

The Summary window performs better than Object Explorer for populations of nodes with many objects. The difference becomes more visible when populating nodes with 1,000 or more objects. It is recommended that you use the Summary window for navigation if the population of Object Explorer becomes a bottleneck.

Management Dialogs

Management Dialogs are components of SQL Server Management Studio that provide the functionality to manage objects or perform actions on a server through a graphical user interface. There are over 200 management dialogs in Management Studio, which support all SQL Server 2005 products. Some of these dialogs are very simple and some are complex. However, they all follow a consistent layout and flow to ensure a low learning curve for the user. Figure 4-13 displays a typical management dialog and its various components.

You launch most of the management dialogs by selecting an entry on the Object Explorer context menu. The Object Explorer context menu is carefully designed to provide a link to dialogs and actions that are relevant to the currently selected node. For example, from the **Databases** folder in Object Explorer you can launch the following management dialogs that are relevant to databases:

- **New Database**—Allows creation of a new database.
- **Attach**—Creates a database from files that were previously used to store a database.
- **Restore Database**—Restores a database from a full or transaction log backup.
- **Restore File and Filegroups**—Restores specific files or file groups of a database.

The concept of management dialogs is not new in SQL Server 2005, and they have been around since SQL Server 6.0. However, a few innovations in SQL Server 2005 management dialogs could significantly improve your productivity. These innovations provide a new generation of dialogs that are resizable, non-modal, scriptable, and schedulable.

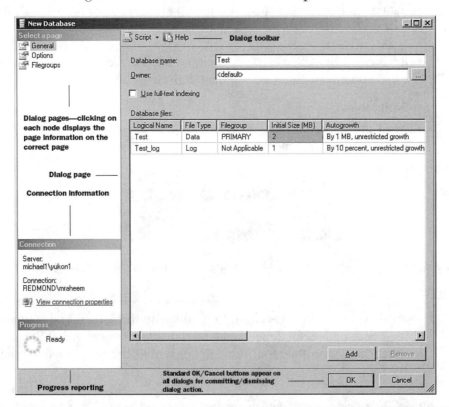

Figure 4-13   A typical management dialog in SQL Server Management Studio.

Resizability

One of the strong bits of feedback from SQL Server 2000 customers was related to the shortcomings of management dialogs in Enterprise Manager. The dialogs were too small and not resizable. New in SQL Server 2005, almost all management dialogs are resizable. You can discover the resizability of a dialog from the size-grip [image] displayed on the bottom-right corner of the dialog.

Non-Modality

Another problem with SQL Server 2000 Enterprise Manager dialogs was their modality: Only one dialog could be opened at any given time. This was extremely frustrating in situations where the user was in the middle of creating an object and wanted to look up properties of another object. To do this, the user had to cancel the first dialog, which meant losing all the data already entered. Next, the user had to open up the second dialog, look up the information, close the second dialog, and open the first dialog again and re-enter the information. This was a big hindrance to productivity. New in SQL Server 2005, multiple instances of management dialogs can be opened without any stipulation to close the previous ones.

Scriptability

Most management dialogs provide several scripting options that can be accessed from the management dialog toolbar (see Figure 4-14).

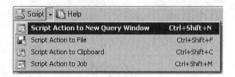

Figure 4-14   The management dialog toolbar provides various scripting options

The scripting options provide a means of generating a script for the action that the dialog is about to perform on the server. The language of the generated script depends on the type of server to which the management dialog is connected. Table 4-2 describes the script type for each of the server types.

Table 4-2   Server Types and Script Languages Generated by the Management Dialogs

Server Type	Script Language and Execution Environment
Database Engine (including SQL Server Agent and Full-Text Search)	Transact-SQL; the generated T-SQL script can be executed in Management Studio or other command line T-SQL execution tools such as SQLCMD, OSQL, etc.
Analysis Services	XMLA; the generated XMLA script can be executed in Management Studio.
Reporting Services	VBScript; the generated script cannot be executed in Management Studio, but you can use any script runtime such as CScript or Visual Studio to run and debug the script.

Server Type	Script Language and Execution Environment
Integration Services	None; Integration Services dialogs are not scriptable.
Notification Services	None; Integration Services dialogs are not scriptable.
SQL Server Mobile	None; SQL Server Mobile dialogs are not scriptable.

The scripting options are useful for situations in which you want to review and perhaps tweak the script that the management dialog is about to execute on the server prior to its execution. Another usage scenario would be to use the scripting option of the dialogs as a template generator for scripts with long and difficult-to-remember syntax, such as the Analysis Services XMLA.

Schedulable

The action of the management dialogs can be scripted as SQL Server Agent jobs to run at a later time or on a recurring schedule. This is particularly useful, for example, in situations in which you want to create a recurring job to back up a database or reorganize an index on the production server at a later time, when the server is not so busy. To create a job for the dialog action, click on the **Script** button on the dialog toolbar and select **Script Action to Job**. On the **New Job** dialog (See Figure 4-15), switch to the **Schedules** page and select or create a new schedule for the job.

Architecturally, all management dialogs are inherited from a base class. This ensures consistency in the layout, formatting, and behavior of the dialogs. In addition, almost all management dialogs use an object model to create/manipulate and perform actions on the server (see Figure 4-16). As a matter of fact, the Microsoft SQL Server team enforced a development policy that all management dialogs must use the object models rather than make a direct connection and embed metadata queries in the dialogs for creation of or performing actions on the server. Enforcing this level of abstraction has been a huge win for SQL Server because it ensured quality in the management tools and reinforced the versatility and flexibility of SQL Server management object models.

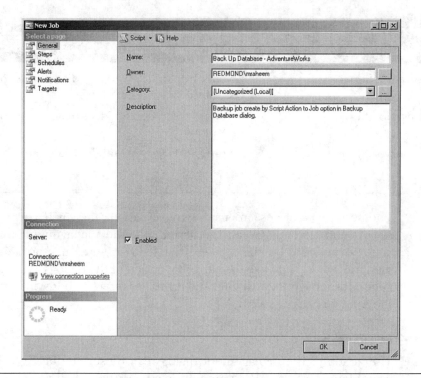

Figure 4-15   The management dialog toolbar provides various scripting options.

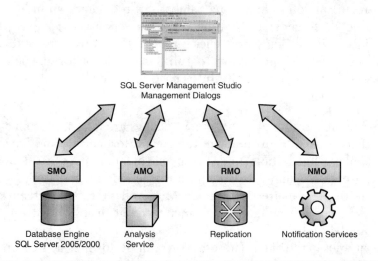

Figure 4-16   Management dialogs leverage SQL Server object models to perform actions on Database Engine, Analysis Services, Replication, SQL Server Agent, and Notification Services.

Wizards

A wizard is a graphical user interface element similar to a management dialog that guides you step by step through a set of complex tasks. Management Studio has a number of wizards to assist the user with management tasks. Similar to the management dialogs, all wizards are inherited from the same class to provide a consistent user experience. Table 4-3 provides a list of the SQL Server Database Engine wizards and a brief explanation of their functionality.

Table 4-3 SQL Server Database Engine Wizards.

Wizard Name	Functionality
Generate SQL Server Scripts Wizard	Creates T-SQL scripts for all or a subset of objects in a database.
Import and Export Data Wizard	Allows copying, transformation, and loading of data between supported data sources and the Database Engine.
Copy Database Wizard	Provides the functionality to move or copy one or more databases from a source to a target instance.
Maintenance Plan Wizard	Creates scheduled jobs to perform routine database tasks such as back up, update statistics, check integrity, and so on.
Database Mail Wizard	Allows management and configuration of Database Mail.
Configure Distribution Wizard	Configures a server to be a replication distributor.
New Publication Wizard	Provides the functionality to choose objects to replicate.
New Subscription Wizard	Create one or more subscriptions to a publication for replication purposes.

Query Editors

SQL Server Management Studio hosts a number of rich code editors that provide the functionality to create, edit, and execute script-language queries against SQL Server Database Engine, Analysis Services (including

Data Mining), and SQL Server Mobile. Table 4-4 shows which editors work with which server type and through which script language. In addition, Management Studio hosts an XML editor for editing XML files and viewing XML data in query resultsets.

Table 4-4   Query Editors in Management Studio by Server Type and Script Language

Server Type	Script Language	Query Editor in Management Studio
Database Engine	Transact-SQL (T-SQL)	T-SQL Query Editor
Analysis Services	Multidimensional Expression (MDX)	MDX Query Editor
	Data Mining Extensions (DMX)	DMX Query Editor
	XML for Analysis (XMLA)	XMLA Query Editor
SQL Server Mobile	Transact-SQL (T-SQL)	.SQL Server Mobile Query Editor

Figure 4-17 illustrates various components of a query window. The query pane is where you type a query. The database drop-down in the toolbar provides the functionality to specify the database where you want to execute the query. To execute the query, you can click on the **Execute** button on the query tool bar, select **Query, Execute** from Management Studio main menu, or press **F5**, **Ctrl+E**, or **Alt+X** on the keyboard. You also have the option to execute part of the query by selecting the script and clicking on the Execute button (or pressing any of the aforementioned keyboard shortcuts). The result of the query execution appears in the Results pane. The Results pane has tabs for displaying various components of a query result: Data appears in the **Results** tab, messages are displayed in **Messages** tab, query execution plan is displayed in **Execution plan** tab, and client statistics appear in the **Client Statistics** tab. The data for query results can be displayed in a grid or as text, or it can be redirected to a file. These options can be selected from **Query, Result to** in the main menu of Management Studio, or you can press **Ctrl+T**, **Ctrl+D**, and **Ctrl+Shift+F** for **Results to Grid**, **Results to Text**, and **Results to File**. You can also access these options from buttons ⊡⊡⊡ on the query tool bar. You can hide and show the Results pane by selecting **Window, Hide Result Pane** from Management Studio main menu or by pressing **Ctrl+R** on the keyboard to give you more screen space for editing the query.

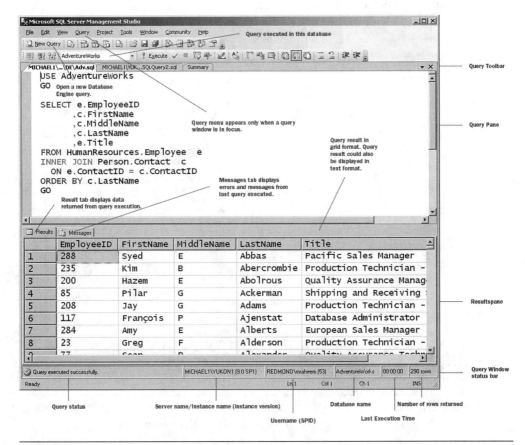

FIGURE 4-17   Management Studio Query Editor and its components.

As shown in Figure 4-17, the query window has a status bar on the bottom of the window that displays useful information about the status of the last executed query.

Help and Dynamic Help Window

The Dynamic Help window in Management Studio displays links to relevant help topics while you are performing a task. This is particularly useful in query editors, where the dynamic help window displays help links as you are typing a query. You can click on a help link to launch Books Online in the context of the help topics as shown in Figure 4-18. This is particularly useful in situations where you want to look up the syntax in Books Online quickly. Alternatively, you can highlight a statement and click F1 to launch help in the context of the statement.

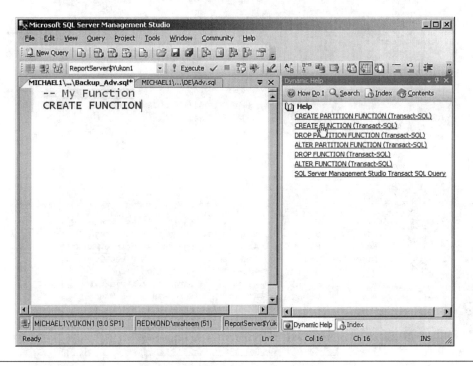

Figure 4-18   The Dynamic Help window automatically displays links to help topics relevant to the statements in the Query Editor window.

To open the Dynamic Help window, select **Help, Dynamic Help** from the main menu in Management Studio.

To launch Help from Management Studio, press F1 at any time. By default, Help opens as an external window to the Management Studio shell. However, the help windows are still associated with Management Studio, so when you close Management Studio, the help windows close as well. You can optionally open Help as a document window inside Management Studio.

You can configure Help and SQL Server Books Online to launch as document windows inside Management Studio window by following these steps:

1. On the **Tools** menu in Management Studio, select **Options**.
2. In the **Options** dialog, expand **Environment**, expand **Help**, and click on **General**.
3. In the left pane, click the **Show Help Using** drop-down arrow, select **Integrated Help Viewer** (see Figure 4-19), and click **OK**.

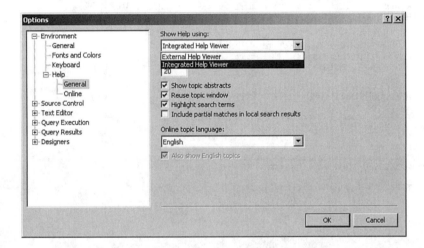

Figure 4-19   The Integrated Help Viewer option will set Help and SQL Server Books Online as document windows inside Management Studio.

You may need to restart Management Studio for the new setting to take effect.

Solution Explorer

Solution Explorer is a component of Microsoft SQL Server Management Studio that enables you to view and manage project items and perform item management tasks in a solution or a project (see Figure 4-20). It also enables you to use the SQL Server Management Studio editors to work on items associated with one of the script projects. Solution Explorer provides an interface with version control software and the functionality to check in and check out scripts.

To view Solution Explorer, you can press **Ctrl+Alt+L** on the keyboard, or select **View, Solution Explorer** from the main menu in Management Studio.

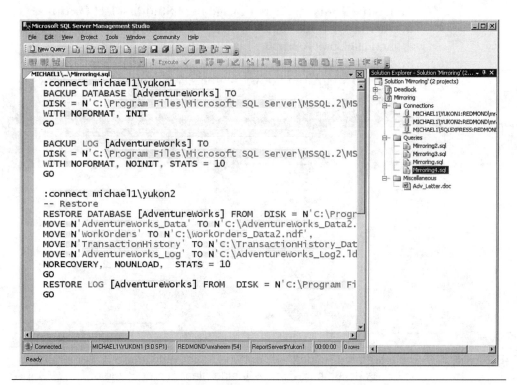

Figure 4-20 Solution Explorer in Management Studio.

Properties Window

The Properties window (see Figure 4-21) provides the functionality to view and change properties of a selected object that are located in editors and designers. By default, the **Properties Window** is located in the bottom-right corner of Management Studio. By default, the Registered Server window appears in the top-left corner of Management Studio. You can easily move, hide, or autohide the window to allocate more space to other components. To quickly view the **Properties** window, click **F4** or choose **View, Properties Window** from the main menu in Management Studio.

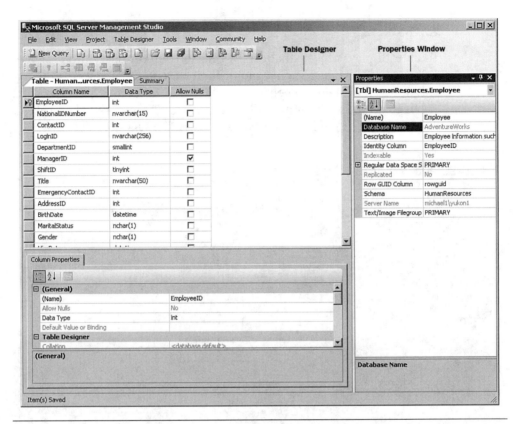

Figure 4-21   The Properties window supports changing properties of objects that are located in editors and designers.

Properties window

Each field in the Properties window displays different types of editing fields, depending on the particular property. Properties shown in grey are read-only.

NOTE
Do not confuse the Properties window with Properties dialogs. Properties dialogs are rich management dialogs that provide the functionality to modify properties of an object on the server. To launch Properties dialogs, select **Properties** from the Object Explorer context menu.

Toolbox

Toolbox displays objects that can be dragged and dropped into designers and editors. In Management Studio, Toolbox is empty, and it is populated only when the Maintenance Plan Designer is in focus. In Figure 4-22, Toolbox displays a number of Maintenance Plan tasks that can be dragged and dropped into the Maintenance Plan Designer.

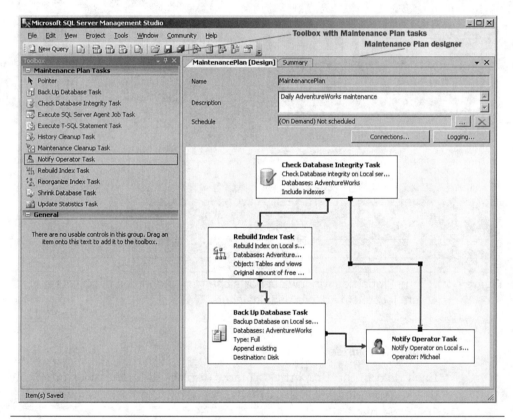

Figure 4-22   Toolbox is populated with Maintenance Plan tasks only when Maintenance Plan designer is in focus.

Web Browser

SQL Server Management Studio has an embedded Internet Explorer, which enables you to browse web pages in a document window (see Figure 4-23). This is particularly useful because you can search external resources such as the Microsoft Developer Network (www.msdn.com)

or other community web pages without leaving SQL Server Management Studio. You can open the Web Browser window from the main menu in Management Studio. In the main menu, point to **View**, **Web Browser** and then select **Home** or **Search**. Alternatively, you can open the browser window by selecting **Community, Developer Center** in the main menu.

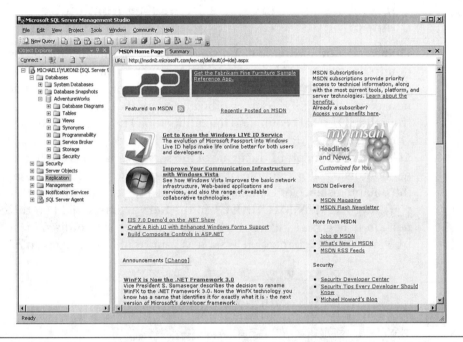

Figure 4-23   The embedded browser in Management Studio provides web browsing functionality without the need to leave the environment.

Management and Administration Scenarios

In this section, we originally started writing about the typical management scenarios such as how to back up and restore a database, how to manage indexes, or how to administer security. However, we soon realized that we were just reiterating the scenarios that are already described in product documentation. Instead, we decided to focus on describing real-life (and some painful) scenarios that customers have usually asked us about in person, via newsgroups, or during our presentations. We will also be describing some interesting scenarios and some features that are not fully supported by Microsoft. Please be cautious in using the undocumented features. We highly recommend that you try to test these results in your development/testing environment before applying them to your production servers.

Connecting to a Server via Dedicated Administrator Connection

Dedicated Administrator Connection (DAC) is a high-priority connection to the server. DAC is a powerful connection, and it should be used only for troubleshooting, when the server is "hung" and does not accept new connections. SQL Server officially supports DAC connections only from the SQLCMD command line utility tool. However, you can also use Query Editor in Management Studio for DAC connections. To make a DAC connection, prefix the name of the server with **ADMIN:** in the connection dialog. For example, if you want to make a DAC connection to the default instance of Database Engine on a server named MICHAEL1, you enter **ADMIN:MICHAEL1** in the **Server name** field on the connection dialog (see Figure 4-24). It is good practice to disconnect and free up the DAC connection as soon as your troubleshooting is complete.

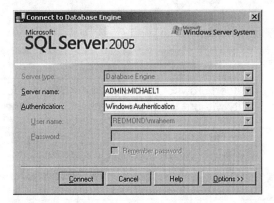

Figure 4-24 Making a DAC connection from Management Studio.

DAC is limited to only one connection. If you use DAC for a query window and try to open other components of Management Studio such as Object Explorer in the context of the same connection, you will get strange errors. This is one of the reasons Microsoft does not support making DAC connections with Management Studio.

NOTE
By default, you cannot make a remote DAC connection. Remote DAC is disabled on new installations of SQL Server. See the topic "Remote DAC" in Chapter 3 for information about enabling this option.

Removing Most Recently Used (MRU) Server Names from the Connection Dialog

The **Server name** drop-down list box in the Connection dialog stores the 10 most recently used (MRU) server names (see Figure 4-25). The Connection dialog stores the server name after it has successfully connected to the server. Although this is a convenient feature, there are situations in which you may want to remove the dormant servers from this list or remove all the entries for security reasons. You may also want to copy the list to another workstation or share it with another user.

The server name MRU list is distinct for each user on a computer. The list is stored in a file named **mru.dat** under the **Application Data** directory for each user:

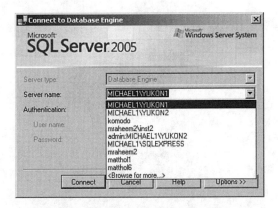

Figure 4-25   Making a DAC connection from Management Studio.

```
C:\Documents and Settings\<user name>\Application Data\
Microsoft\Microsoft SQL Server\90\Tools\Shell\mru.dat
```

To remove all server entries from the list, delete or rename the file to oldmru.dat. To share the MRU list with another user, identify the user's mru.dat file, and replace it with the source mru.dat file. To copy the connection dialog server MRU list to another server, simply copy the source mru.dat file from the source to the target server.

Changing Default Startup Behavior of Management Studio

By default, launching Management Studio displays the connection dialog, prompting you for a connection to a server. After it is connected, it opens Object Explorer in the context of the specified server. You have the option to change this default behavior to opening a new query window, opening Object Explorer and a new query window, or not being prompted for a connection at all.

To change the startup behavior of Management Studio, do the following:

1. Click on the **Tools** menu in Management Studio and select **Options**.
2. In the **Options** dialog, expand **Environment** and select **General**.
3. In the **At Startup** drop-down, select the desired startup behavior (see Figure 4-26). Click **OK**.

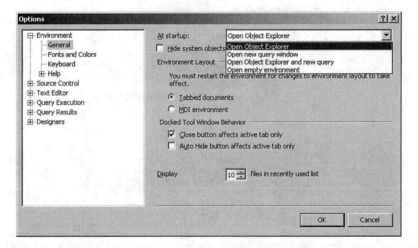

Figure 4-26   You can change the startup behavior of Management Studio to better suit your everyday tasks.

You may need to restart Management Studio for the new setting to take effect.

Updating Registered Servers with Local Instances

When a user launches SQL Server Management Studio for the first time, it discovers the local instances of SQL Server and automatically adds them to the list of registered servers for that user. However, if new instances are added or old instances are removed, the registered servers could get out of synch with the actual instances. Of course, the user could add or delete instances manually (see Figure 4-27), but there is an automated way to register the local instances quickly.

Figure 4-27   Updating Registered Servers list with local instances of SQL Server.

To add or update the list of your registered servers automatically with local instances of SQL Server on a computer, right-click on the root node of a server type (such as Database Engine), and select **Update Local Server Registration**. Be aware that this option works only for the selected server type. To update all server types, you have to select the server type from the Registered Server toolbar and perform an update.

Importing Registered Servers from Enterprise Manager

SQL Server 2005 provides the functionality to keep your SQL Server 2000 registered servers during both upgrade and migration to SQL Server 2005.

If you upgrade an instance of SQL Server 2000 to SQL Server 2005 by using the SQL Server 2005 setup program, the old Registered Servers in Enterprise Manager are automatically upgraded to registered servers in Management Studio. However, if you do a side-by-side installation of SQL Server 2005 on the same computer as SQL Server 2000, Enterprise Manager and Management Studio do not share the same registered servers. In this case, you can optionally import the SQL Server 2000 Enterprise Manager registered servers to Management

Studio. To do this, right-click on the **Database Engine** node in the Registered Servers window in Management Studio and select **Previously Registered Servers** (See Figure 4-28).

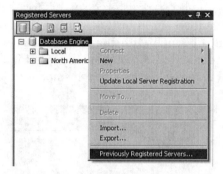

Figure 4-28   Migrating registered servers from Enterprise Manager.

Referencing Registered Servers with a Friendly Name

Server names do not usually correspond to the functionality of or the role of the server. In addition, some server names may be too long or too similar to one another, which makes you more prone to performing the wrong task on the wrong server. Management Studio provides the capability to register a server with a friendly name.

Figure 4-29 displays the **New Server Registration** dialog. The name shown in the field **Server name** is the physical name of the server, but the one shown in the field **Registered server name** could be the same or different from the physical name. By default, **Registered server name** is the same as **Server name**. As you type a name in the **Server name** field, the same name is automatically entered in **Registered server name**. However, after entering **server name** you can override the **Registered server name** with a friendly name. In Figure 4-29, the physical name of the server is **SRVBCVANDB2005-903ha**, but its registered server name is **QA Server located in South Vancouver**.

As shown in Figure 4-30, registered servers are displayed by registered server name, followed by server name in parentheses. In the example, it is displayed as **QA Server located in South Vancouver (SRVBCVANDB2005-903ha)**.

The preceding paragraphs described how to register a new server with a friendly name. You can also assign a friendly name to a previously registered server by editing its properties. To do so, right-click on the

Registered Server window and select **Properties** in the exposed context menu. This launches the **Edit Server Registration Properties** dialog, where you can change the value of the **Registered server name** field.

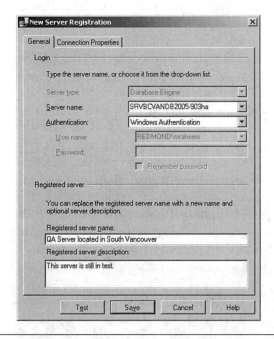

Figure 4-29 You can assign a friendly name to your registered servers.

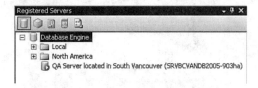

Figure 4-30 Registered Server window displays the friendly names.

Copying Registered Servers Between Users and Computers

Registered servers are stored on the local computer where Management Studio is running. The registered server information is stored for each user and it is not shared between users. To copy the registered server information between two computers or two users, you need to use the import and export functionality of registered servers.

You can follow these steps to export the registered server information for a user on a particular computer:

1. Log in as the user to the computer that contains the registered server information.
2. Launch SQL Server Management Studio.
3. From the main menu, select **View, Registered Servers**.
4. From the **Registered Server** toolbar, select a server type, such as **Database Engine**.
5. In the Registered Server window, right-click and select **Export** from the context menu. This launches the Export Registered Servers dialog, as shown in Figure 4-31.
6. In the Export Registered Servers dialog, you have the option of exporting all or just a subset of the registered servers. To export all registered servers for the selected server type, select the root node (e.g., **Database Engine** in Figure 4-31). To export a subset of the servers, select the server group (e.g., **Canada** in Figure 4-31).
7. Specify the **Export file** by either typing the path and name of the file or choosing the browse option next to it. Click **OK**.

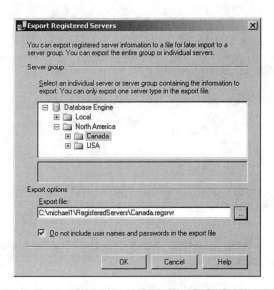

Figure 4-31   Management Studio provides the functionality to export registered servers.

NOTE
The option **Do not include user names and password in the export** file is applicable only to registered servers that used the SQL Server Authentication option and specified a password during registration. For security reasons, we highly recommend you do not include the passwords in the export file and let the user who imports the file specify the passwords after importing the file.

To import the registered server information for a user on the same or a different computer, follow these steps:

1. Follow the same export steps 1–4 as just described.
2. In the Registered Server window, right-click and select **Import** from the context menu. This launches the Import Registered Servers dialog, as shown in Figure 4-31.
3. Specify the **Import file** by either typing the path and name of the file or choosing the browse option next to it.
4. Select the server group to import the file (e.g., **North America** in Figure 4-32). Click **OK**.

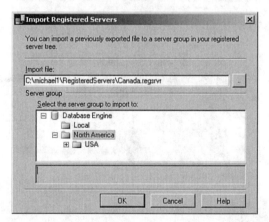

Figure 4-32 Management Studio provides the functionality to import the registered server's information from a previously exported file.

NOTE
It is good security practice to delete the registered servers import file after you have completed the import operation.

Adding Registered Servers to an Export File

As you have seen above, Management Studio provides a user interface to add registered servers. But what if you are in a situation where you have to create tens or hundreds of registered servers? The answer is to leverage the SQL Management Objects (SMO). SMO's `Microsoft.SqlServer.Management.Smo.RegisteredServers` namespace provides a rich library of classes that you can use in your Visual Basic .NET or C# code to create, remove, and manage registered servers. You can look up the library in Books Online.

However, there is an undocumented and perhaps easier way to manipulate the registered servers' information without using SMO. The registered servers export file is in XML format. You can append the new registered servers to the XML file.

To understand the schema of the export file, try creating a registered server named **Server1** and export the registered server to a file named `S.regsrv`. Next, open `S.regsrv` in the XML editor in Management Studio. As shown in Figure 4-33, you can see that the server information is surrounded by <Server> tags.

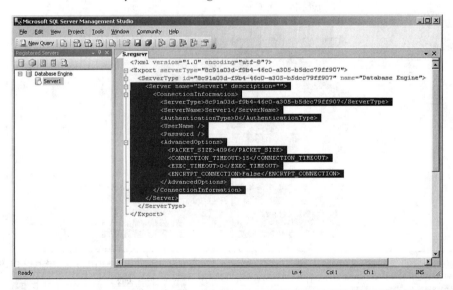

Figure 4-33   Editing a registered server export file in the XML editor in Management Studio.

To add a server named **Server2** to the export file, copy and paste the text between server tags. Next, in the pasted text change **Server1** to **Server2** (indicated in bold characters as follows):

```
<Server name="Server2" description="">
  <ConnectionInformation>
    <ServerType>8c91a03d-f9b4-46c0-a305-b5dcc79ff907</ServerType>
    <ServerName>Server2</ServerName>
    <AuthenticationType>0</AuthenticationType>
    <UserName />
    <Password />
    <AdvancedOptions>
      <PACKET_SIZE>4096</PACKET_SIZE>
      <CONNECTION_TIMEOUT>15</CONNECTION_TIMEOUT>
      <EXEC_TIMEOUT>0</EXEC_TIMEOUT>
      <ENCRYPT_CONNECTION>False</ENCRYPT_CONNECTION>
    </AdvancedOptions>
  </ConnectionInformation>
</Server>
```

Next, save the `s.regsrv` export file and try importing it in Management Studio. You will see Server1 and Server2 in the Registered Servers window, as shown in Figure 4-34.

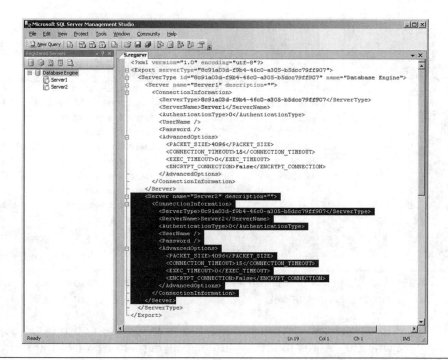

Figure 4-34   Manipulating the registered server export file to add a new registered server.

Copying Query Result to Excel Spreadsheet

You can copy part or all of a query result to a Microsoft Office Excel spreadsheet or any other text editors. To export all the resultset, right-click on the results grid and select **Save Results As** in the context menu. This option saves the results in a Comma-Separated Value (CSV) file, which you can subsequently open in Excel. Alternatively, you can select all or part of the data in the results grid and copy and paste it in an Excel spreadsheet. To select all the cells in the result set grid, you can right-click and choose **Select All**, or click on the top-left corner of the results grid as displayed in Figure 4-35.

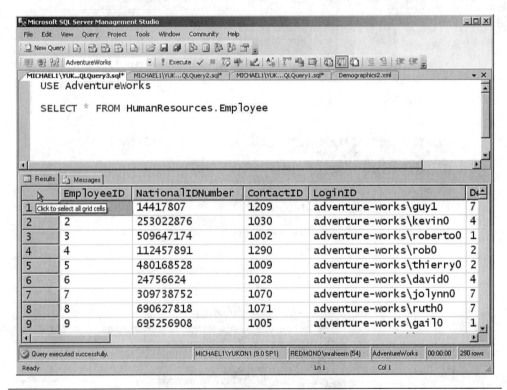

Figure 4-35   You can click on the top-left corner of the result grid to select all data in a query result set.

If you followed these instructions, you may have noticed that neither saving the results to a CSV file or copying all or part of the result set includes the column headers. To include the column headers in the file or copied data, follow these steps:

1. Click on the **Tools** menu in Management Studio and select **Options**.
2. In the Options dialog, expand **Query Results,** and **Results to Grid**. Select **Results to Grid** (see Figure 4-36).
3. Select **Include column headers when copying or saving the results**. Click OK.

You may need to re-execute your query in a new query window for the new setting to take effect.

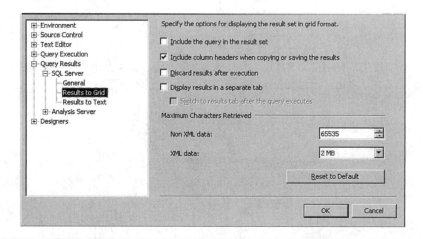

Figure 4-36 You can choose the option to include column headers when copying a resultset to Excel.

Configuring WMI to Show Server Status in Registered Servers

Registered Servers and Object Explorer windows display the state of SQL Server services through a small icon appearing to the left of the server node. Both Registered Servers and Object Explorer use Windows Management Instrumentation (WMI) to query the state of the services. To query the status of the services successfully, two things must happen: 1) The computer that hosts the SQL Server services must have WMI installed, and 2) the user who is running Management Studio must have permissions to access the WMI object remotely on the computer that hosts the SQL Server services.

You can follow these steps to grant WMI permission to a particular user.

1. Log on to the computer that is hosting the SQL Server services.
2. On the Windows Start menu, select **Run**, type **mmc**, and click **OK**.
3. From the **File** menu in the **MMC** console, select **Add/Remove Snap-in**, and then click **Add**.
4. In the **Add Standalone Snap-in** dialog, select **WMI Control**, and click **Add**.
5. On the Change Managed Computer dialog, select **Local computer** and click **Finish**.
6. In the Add Standalone Snap-in dialog, click **Close**.
7. In the Add/Remove Snap-in dialog, click **OK**.
8. In the **MMC** console, right-click on **WMI Control (Local)** and select **Properties**.
9. In the WMI Control (Local) Properties dialog, select the **Security** tab, expand the **Root** node, and select **CIMV2** (see Figure 4-37).

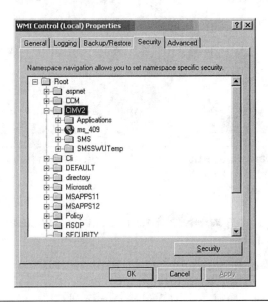

Figure 4-37   To view the state of SQL Server services, the user must have permissions to the WMI CIMV2 namespace.

10. Click on **Security** at the bottom of the dialog.
11. Add the user or a group of which the user is a member to the **Group or user names** box and select it.

12. In the **Permissions for <group or user>** box, select the **Allow** column for the **Remote Enable** permission and click **OK**.
13. Close the MMC console.

Leveraging an Asynchronous Population of Objects in Object Explorer

You can take advantage of the asynchronous operation of Object Explorer, especially when you are dealing with a large number of server objects. This means that while Object Explorer is busy populating nodes, Management Studio remains responsive and you can continue performing other tasks such as editing or executing a query, expanding another node in Object Explorer, connecting Object Explorer to another server, and even canceling the population of the nodes. The capability to cancel is a great feature for situations in which you have accidentally expanded a highly populated node and you want to cancel the population and apply a filter instead.

To better understand the asynchronous operation of Object Explorer, make use of the following script. First, you need to create a highly populated node in Object Explorer. You can execute the following script below to create 25,000 tables in the AdventureWorks database.

```
-- This script creates 25,000 tables in AdventureWorks database
USE AdventureWorks
GO

DECLARE @i          INT
        ,@table_ddl  VARCHAR(4000)

SET @i = 100001

WHILE @i - 100000 <= 25000
BEGIN
  SET @table_ddl = 'CREATE TABLE Table'
                   + SUBSTRING(CONVERT(CHAR, @i), 2, 5)
                   + '(ID INT NULL)'
  EXECUTE(@table_ddl)
  SET @i = @i + 1
END
```

After the script has executed successfully, try connecting Object Explorer to the server and expanding the Tables node. Notice that while Object Explorer is busy populating the Tables node, the phrase (expanding…) is appended to the end of Tables node (see Figure 4-38). Now you can collapse the Tables node and perform other tasks in Management Studio. You can even click on the Stop button in the Object Explorer toolbar to stop populating the nodes.

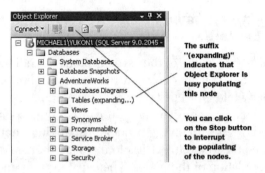

Figure 4-38   Asynchronous operation of Object Explorer provides the functionality to stop the population or perform other tasks during the population of the node.

The asynchronous behavior of Object Explorer is due to its multi-threaded operation. Object Explorer can spawn up to four threads for its population of the nodes. This means you expand up to four highly populated nodes in Object Explorer and continue performing other tasks in Management Studio.

Editing Queries in Disconnected Mode

Unlike Query Analyzer in SQL Server 2000, Management Studio enables you to edit queries without connecting to a server. This is particularly useful in situations in which the server is not available and you still want to take advantage of the rich editor features such as keyword color-coding, dynamic help, or source control. Another potential situation is one in which you want to guard yourself against accidental execution of an incomplete script against the server.

If you want to open a new script in disconnected mode, select **File, New, Database Engine Query** (or any other query type). Next, click on **Cancel** in the Connection dialog. The editor is now ready to type a new query. Notice the title of the query says **not connected** and the query window status bar also says **Disconnected**. As soon as you are ready to execute the query, you click on the connect button 🔌 in the query toolbar or select **Query, Connection, Connect** from the Management Studio main menu.

If you want to open an existing query in disconnected mode, simply click on **Cancel** in the connection dialog.

If you have a query that is already connected and you want to continue editing it in a disconnected mode, click on the disconnect button in the Management Studio query toolbar or select **Query, Connection, Disconnect** from the main menu. 🖳

To disconnect all queries, select **Query, Connection, Disconnect All Queries** from the main menu in Management Studio.

Using Query Designer for Writing Queries

Management Studio provides a graphical query designer for authoring Transact-SQL queries. To design a new query, open a new query window, and press **Ctrl+Shift+Q** on the keyboard or select **Query,** and **Design Query in Editor** from the main menu in Management Studio. In the **Add Table** dialog, you can select tables, views, functions, or synonyms for your query. The Query Designer automatically discovers the relationship between the selected objects. After you have selected the objects, you can define the output columns, sorting, or grouping in the resultset. While you are designing the query graphically, the SQL pane on the bottom of the query designer displays the T-SQL syntax of your query (see Figure 4-39).

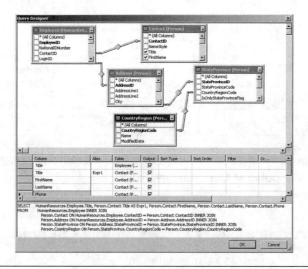

Figure 4-39   Query Designer in Management Studio provides the functionality to graphically author a Transact-SQL query.

You can also get a graphical representation of an existing query in Query Designer by selecting all or part of the T-SQL script in a query window and selecting the option **Design Query in Editor** from the context menu or the main menu in Management Studio (see Figure 4-40). Any changes to the query in Query Designer updates the query in the query window.

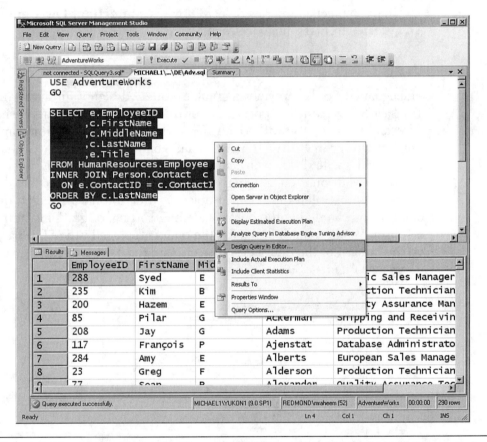

Figure 4-40   Management Studio provides the functionality to design all or part of a T-SQL query in Query Designer.

Executing a Query Across Multiple Servers

One of the common management actions is executing a script across multiple servers. The query editors in Management Studio provide a couple of solutions for executing scripts across multiple servers.

The first option is to use the Change Connection feature of query editors in Management Studio. Let's go through an example and see how you can leverage this feature. Suppose your objective is to execute the following T-SQL script to back up the AdventureWorks database across three servers: SERVER1, SERVER2, and SERVER3.

```
-- To permit log backups, before the full backup, alter the database
-- to use the full recovery model
USE master
GO
ALTER DATABASE AdventureWorks
    SET RECOVERY FULL

-- Back up the full AdventureWorks database
BACKUP DATABASE AdventureWorks
    TO DISK = 'C:\BAK\Adv_Full.bak'

-- Back up the AdventureWorks log
BACKUP LOG AdventureWorks
    TO DISK = 'C:\BAK\Adv_Log.bak'
```

Open up a new database engine query, connect to SERVER1, copy and paste this script, save the query as **backup.sql**, and execute it. To execute the same script on SERVER2, you do not need to close the script and reopen it (as you had to in SQL Server 2000 Query Analyzer). Instead, click on the **Change Connection** button 🔲 on the query toolbar, or right-click in the query window and select **Change Connection** from the context menu (see Figure 4-41). This will launch the connection dialog, where you can connect to **SERVER2** and execute the script. You can change the connection again to execute the script on **SERVER3**.

Another option to execute a T-SQL query across multiple servers is to use the SQLCMD Mode feature of the T-SQL query editor. Let's go through the same example and see how you can execute the script across SERVER1, SERVER2, and SERVER3 by using SQLCMD mode.

In Management Studio, open the **backup.sql** file that you saved earlier. Right-click on the tab of the query window and select **Copy Full Path,** as shown in Figure 4-42. The full path in the example is C:\BAK\Adv_Full.bak.

Next, open a new query window, select SQLCMD mode by either clicking on the SQLCMD button 🔲 on the query toolbar or selecting **Query, SQLCMD Mode** from the Management Studio main menu. Now, the query is ready to accept SQLCMD extensions. You can use **:connect** <*servername*> to connect to SERVER1, SERVER2 and

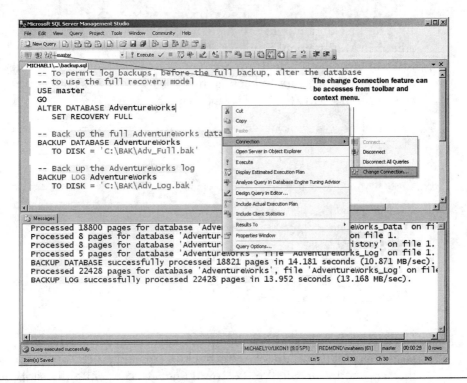

Figure 4-41   The change connection feature of Management Studio enables you to connect a query to another server.

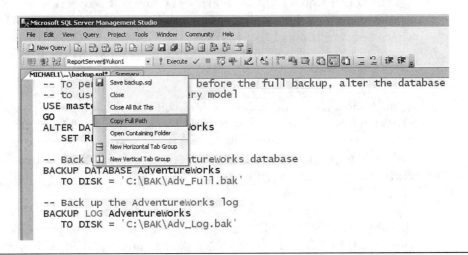

Figure 4-42   Context menu of the query window provides a number of features, such as copying the full path of the query.

SERVER3 and use **:r** *<file path>* to include the backup script. You can paste the copied file path rather typing it. Notice the lines of code that contain SQLCMD extensions appear with a grey background. Your script should look like the script shown in Figure 4-43.

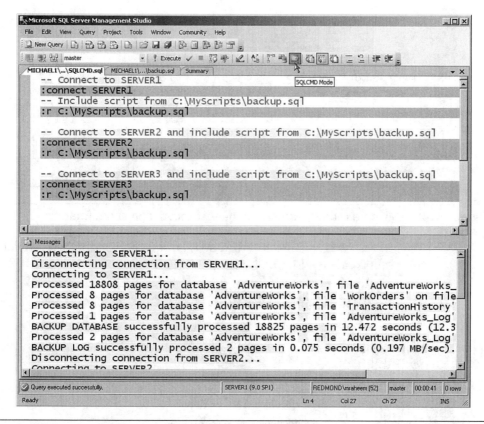

Figure 4-43   Management Studio provides the functionality to execute queries in SQLCMD mode.

Viewing and Editing XML Data

Management Studio hosts a rich XML editor. In addition, the XML editor is integrated with T-SQL query editor for viewing XML data. To open an XML file in Management Studio, select **File, Open, File** in the main menu and select the XML file in the Open File dialog.

With the XML datatype now being a native datatype in SQL Server, the XML query result is displayed as a link in the grid format (see Figure 4-44).

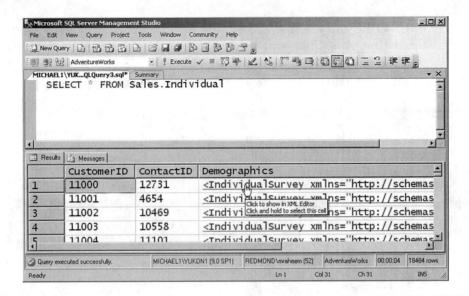

Figure 4-44 XML data returned as part of query execution in grid format.

To view the XML resultset in the XML editor, click on the **XML** link in the results grid (see Figure 4-45).

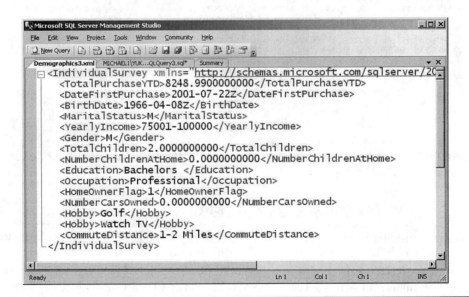

Figure 4-45 XML query results can be viewed in the XML Editor of Management Studio.

Deleting and Scripting Multiple Objects

Using Object Explorer, you can delete or generate a script for one object. So how would you go about deleting multiple objects or quickly generating a DDL script for a selection of objects? The answer is in the Summary window. The Summary window allows deletion of multiple objects and the generating of CREATE and DROP scripts. To select a range of nodes, click on the first node, hold the **Shift** key, and click on the second node. To select an individual node, click on the first node, hold the **Ctrl** key, and click on the subsequent nodes. After the nodes are selected, choose the **Script** or **Delete** options in the Summary window context menu (see Figure 4-46).

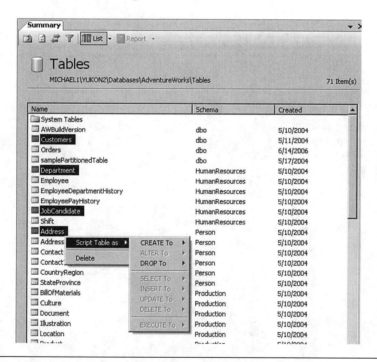

Figure 4-46   The Summary window provides the functionality to delete or script multiple objects.

NOTE
The Summary window provides only simple scripting options. For more advanced scripting options, use the Generate SQL Server Scripts Wizard.

Summary

As you have seen in this chapter, SQL Server Management Studio is a rich and comprehensive tool that enables many management and administration scenarios. We have also given you some tips and tricks for using the tool. However, the scenarios described in this chapter represent just a few of the things you can do with Management Studio. You can find additional usage scenarios in the product documentation and in Books Online.

CHAPTER 5

Inside Data Authoring Tools

This chapter covers Query Editor as the main part of SQL Server Management Studio's data authoring environment and Bulk Copy Utility (BCP), which allows you to move data between different data sources.

Query Editor in SQL Server 2005, in addition to T-SQL, enables you to edit XML, as well as MDX, DMX, and XMLA queries. This integration is made possible via SQL Server Management Studio's integration with Visual Studio's development environment framework. A few improvements, which have been made specifically to retrieval and display of results in Query Editor, are also covered in this chapter.

Bulk Copy Utility has existed since the first release of the product. The entire feature will be covered thoroughly in this chapter, as well as new improvements made to BCP for the SQL Server 2005 release, such as support of new file formats, the XML data type, and security enhancements.

Query Editor in SQL Server Management Studio

Editing and submitting queries to the database engine is probably the most common operation you will perform when working with SQL Server. This functionality is provided by Query Editor, part of SQL Server Management Studio. Thus, Query Editor is the graphical tool of choice when working with SQL Server. As soon as you are connected to the server, you can invoke Query Editor by clicking on the **New Query** button on the standard SQL Server Management Studio toolbar. Alternatively, you can first select the type of query you wish to author from the **File** menu, as shown in Figure 5-1, and you will be prompted with the Connection Parameters dialog.

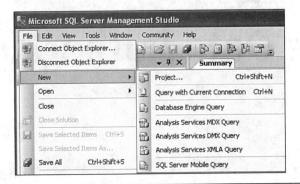

Figure 5-1   Invoking Query Editor.

As you can see, Query Editor supports authoring and executing multiple query types, including Analysis Services and SQL Server Mobile. Analysis Services querying capabilities are covered in great depth in Chapter 14, "Inside Analysis Services Data Mining Tools."

Functionally, a SQL Server Mobile query is a subset of a Database Engine query and differs only in the connection type. Upon connection you need to either provide a valid database connection file or create a new one. Because query syntax is also just a subset of true SQL, the query carries the extension sqlce instead of sql.

Let's concentrate our efforts on Query Editor support for SQL Server Database Engine. After you type a query, you typically want to execute it against the database engine right away to see the results. You can do it directly from the standard tool bar, using the **Execute** button.

TIPS AND TRICKS
Several hotkey combinations in Query Editor perform the same function (F5, Ctrl+E, Alt+X). You can pick the hotkey combination you feel most comfortable with, depending on your background.

By default, results appear in the bottom pane in grid format. You can switch the view to display textual output directly. This option comes in handy if you want to cut and paste text.

If you want to change the font used by Query Editor, you can easily change it by following the Tools > Options menu items. Keep in mind that new settings will be global and not for a particular instance of your authoring session, so after you are finished, you need to go back and restore the defaults by clicking the **Use Defaults** button, as shown in Figure 5-2.

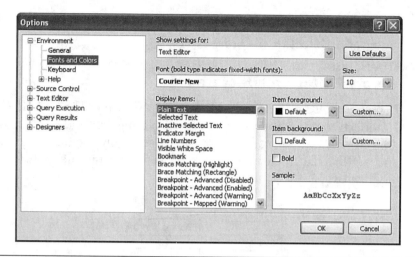

Figure 5-2   Query Editor: Changing fonts and colors.

From the same Options dialog, you can also change many of the configuration options for Query Execution, as shown in Figure 5-3.

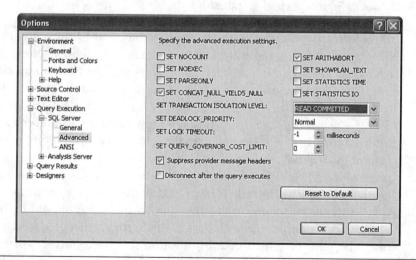

Figure 5-3   Query Editor for SQL Server Database Engine Advanced Execution options.

When you execute a query that brings back a large result set, you may notice that the first rows start showing up immediately and the scroll bar continually reflects new rows constantly coming in. Moreover, even if the result set is huge, overall process memory of SQL Server Management Studio remains steadily low, and scrolling and viewing of the data is not affected. To understand how this is accomplished, let's look at the internal architecture of Query Editor.

Query Editor Architecture

The Query Editor internal architecture is shown in Figure 5-4. The user interface component responsible for displaying data and scrolling is called the Grid Control. It does not contain data; its only responsibility is coordinating what data is currently in a scroll view and which needs to be fetched for display.

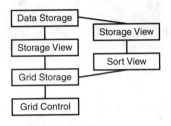

Figure 5-4   Query Editor internal architecture.

Data fetched from the server is immediately placed into physical Data Storage, that is, a temporary file on the disk. These files get created for each outstanding query that has any results and get cleaned up after the query window is closed or a new execution is initiated. Data that needs to be read from the file is retrieved by a series of data readers called Storage View components. A Storage View component understands the internal format of the storage data file and can access the file in random fashion, de-serializing any data column object that is requested by the presentation layer. The Grid Storage component sits between the data layer and the user interface layer and provides "glue" that ties everything together. For example, the Grid Storage component produces application-specific formatting of the data for display. It's worth noting that when a user moves columns around the grid control or sorts data, the actual data on disk remains intact, and only the display changes. Grid Storage keeps track of those changes and translates physical data into data for display. If row sorting is requested, another component called Sort View gets involved. Sort View has its own Storage View component that references Data Storage data, performs all required sorting operations, and builds an index of the relative order of rows in storage required for display. The Grid Storage component constantly references Sort View to find out the absolute row number for the relative row requested for display, and subsequently makes the proper request to its own Storage View to fetch data.

XML Result Support

When query data contains data of the XML data type, Query Editor handles it in a special way. It provides a link inside the grid for each value of such data type, as shown in Figure 5-5.

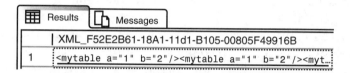

Figure 5-5   XML data type link.

By clicking on the link you can bring up the XML editor with column data conveniently loaded.

Bulk Copy Utility (BCP)

As a DBA or System Administrator, you are often faced with the task of moving data from external sources to the Database Engine efficiently. BCP is one of tools enabling you to accomplish this task.

The external data can come from a variety of sources, ranging from a Database Engine, to a database server from another vendor, to hardware devices (e.g., network controller), to applications such as Excel. Because each data source stores data in its native format, the Database Engine (or any native tool) cannot automatically interpret it for loading. The general strategy used to facilitate such data movement is to export the data into an intermediate format, commonly to a file, and then use the intermediate format to import the data into Database Engine. The Database Engine or tools can then read this file directly, transform its data to a representation that Database Engine understands, and then send the data over using Transfer Data Stream (TDS). Note, you need to send data over TDS when using tools, but not when Database Engine reads the file directly. TDS is an internal protocol used to communicate with Database Engine for sending or receiving both command and data. There are, however, some restrictions on how the data should be represented in the intermediate format before it can be imported into Database Engine. For example, when using Bulk Insert (a TSQL command), by default the data file must either be a TSV (tab-separated values) unless you are using a format file or have data represented in Database Engine's native format. These restrictions do not apply to client programs, but the downside is that you need to write a custom client program that interprets the data in the file before sending it to Database Engine. BCP is one such client application that ships with SQL Server, but it has restrictions similar to those listed previously for Bulk Insert. To be precise, actually it is the other way around. Bulk Insert was implemented much later than the BCP client application and was designed to be compatible with BCP (that is, to be able import the same data as BCP). In addition, there is another option for moving data: SQL Server Integrations Services (SSIS) can be used to import data into Database Engine. SSIS uses BCP or Bulk Insert at lower levels to import data and is geared toward more complex data transformation and workflow scenarios. Later in this chapter you will learn when to use BCP over other options available in SQL Server.

In addition to using BCP to import data, you can use BCP to export data out of Database Engine and to generate a format file. You invoke BCP in a command shell window with parameters that specify the operation type: import/export, location of the data file, target or source table, an optional format file to describe the data, and various others. For example, BCP in represents the import operation, whereas BCP out represents an export operation. We will highlight some of the key parameters later in this chapter.

The BCP client application has been available as part of SQL Server from the very beginning, starting with SQL Server 4.2. There have been some improvements over the releases, but mostly these improvements are to support the Database Engine functionality, such as new data types. However, there have been a few exceptions as follows:

- BCP clients on or before SQL Server 6.5 were based on DBLIB APIs, a legacy from Sybase. Starting with SQL Server 7.0, the BCP clients are built on ODBC APIs. The BCP 6.5 client is still supported on SQL Server 2005.
- SQL Server 7.0 introduced a special BU lock (a server-side change) to enable parallel BCP. Multiple BCP clients could now import data into the same target table concurrently.

BCP Architecture

As mentioned earlier, the BCP client application is used to import/export data into/out of Database Engine. This section provides a high-level description of data flows into and out of Database Engine.

For an import operation, BCP reads from a data file, optionally interprets the data using a format file, converts it into a Database Engine native format, and then calls ODBC (BCP 7.0 or later) or DBLIB (BCP 6.5) to send one or more data rows over TDS. On the server side, the bulk load module processes then generates an OLEDB rowset for the rows to be inserted and sends it to the relational engine to insert into the target table. Two special cases need to be mentioned here. First, the large objects (LOBs) import is optimized (using the API provided by Storage Engine, a lower layer of Database Engine) by directly storing the LOBs instead of copy, getting a pointer to the LOB data, and then inserting this pointer into the OLEDB rowset for the corresponding row/column. These steps are repeated for each LOB column in the target table. Second, if the target column type is XML, an XML validation component is called to validate and convert it into an internal format. After that it is processed the same way as other LOB data.

Figure 5-6 illustrates the data flow from a data file to the target table in Database Engine.

The architecture during export operation (i.e., BCP out) is similar to its import counterpart except the data flow is reversed, as shown in Figure 5-7.

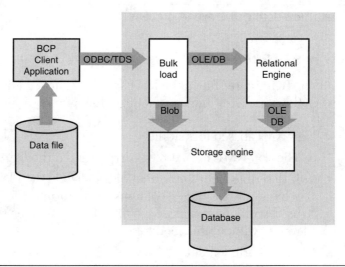

Figure 5-6   Data Flow during BCP import process.

The export operation retrieves data by executing a SELECT command on the target table and then writes the data into a file (in native or character mode, depending on command line options or as specified in the format file). Additionally, you can use BCP to generate a format file that describes output format (for export) of the data in the file or the input format (for import) of the data in the file. To export data out of Database Engine, you must have SELECT permission on the target table.

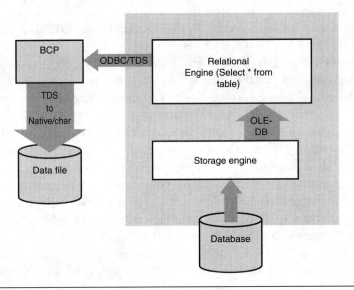

Figure 5-7   Data Flow during BCP export process.

New in SQL2005 BCP

Although BCP core functionality has not changed since previous releases, there are a few improvements as follows:

- New XML-based format file.
  - The non-XML format file is cryptic and difficult to understand.
  - It describes both the format of the data in the file and also the schema of the target columns. This format file can then be used with OPENROWSET by BULK rowset provider to generate a rowset without the need to specify a target table.
- Better security model.
  - BCP now has stricter validation of the data being imported.

- Whenever possible, elevation of privileges has been eliminated. For example, previously you could import data with constraints and triggers disabled, even if you did not have ALTER table permission.
- Support for the XML data type.

BCP Command Syntax

At a high level, three components of a BCP command are of interest. The first component is the table. The table is either the target or the source of data to be transferred. The second component is the data file itself that, like the table, is either the source of or target for the data. The third component is the set of parameters that provide a wide range of choices such as error handling, locking, parallel BCP, handling of constraints/triggers, and how to interpret data in the file. Here is the full range of parameters available with BCP. Not surprising given the lineage of Database Engine (Sybase Adaptive Server was initially developed on the UNIX platform), you will notice the parameters have a UNIX flavor to maintain backward compatibility.

```
bcp {[[database_name.][owner].]{table_name|view_name}|"query"}
    {in | out | queryout | format} data_file
    [-mmax_errors] [-fformat_file] [-x] [-eerr_file]
    [-Ffirst_row] [-Llast_row] [-bbatch_size]
    [-n] [-c] [-w] [-N] [-V (60 | 65 | 70 | 80)] [-6]
    [-q] [-C {ACP|OEM|RAW|code_page}] [-tfield_term]
    [-rrow_term] [-iinput_file] [-ooutput_file] [-apacket_size]
    [-Sserver_name[\instance_name]] [-Ulogin_id] [-Ppassword]
    [-T] [-v] [-R] [-k] [-E] [-h"hint [,...n]"]
```

For full details on all of these parameters please refer to product documentation (SQL Server Books Online), but a few key parameters are highlighted here:

- -b: Used to specify the batch of rows that are imported into Database Engine as one transaction. This is commonly used to group data to be imported into smaller chunks so that in case of failure, you need to start loading from only the last failed batch. In that scenario you would use the -F parameter to specify from which data row to start the reload.

- -h: Used to specify one or more hints to Database Engine for higher performance. These hints can be used to do parallel BCP, to enable constraints/triggers, and to specify the sort order of the input data.

- -n: Specifies that the data is in native Database Engine format. This is the most efficient way to move data from one Database Engine to another because it reduces the size of the data to be transferred and eliminates data conversion. For example, an integer value in native format is represented as a 4-byte value, whereas in character format it can be up to 11 characters. In addition, the data needs to be converted from native to character mode during export and then from character to native mode during import. Data transfer in native mode is not always possible: for example, when transferring data from a Microsoft Excel application to Database Engine. In this case, you can export data from the Microsoft Excel application as comma-separated-values (CSV) and then import it into Database Engine. Similarly, you can use a CSV file to transfer data from DB2 to Database Engine.

- -f: Used to specify the format file. For an import operation, this parameter describes how to interpret the data in the file. For an export operation, it describes how the data needs to be structured and formatted (e.g., comma-separated character values or native representation) in the data file.

BCP Usage Scenarios

The bcp command provides a huge number of command line options that enable many scenarios. This section covers a few representative scenarios. Most of the scenarios are based on the following Employee table. This table has one unique index on EmpID and one constraint that checks that all employees are older than 18.

```
Employee (EmpID varchar(10) unique,
          EmpAge int check (EmpAge > 18),
          EmpDept varchar(100),
          EmpSalary decimal)
```

Simple Export and Import

Suppose this table exists in SQL Server 2000 and you want to transfer this table to SQL Server 2005. There are multiple ways to accomplish this. You can, for example, use backup and restore to move the entire database to a

SQL Server 2005 instance and then extract the Employee table. However, the downside of this is that you are forced to copy the whole database, and it requires a higher level of privileges. This can be particularly painful if the Employee table is a small fraction of the overall database. Alternatively, you can use Linked Server functionality to directly access the Employee table in a SQL Server 2000 instance and move it to a SQL Server 2005 instance. However, in both of these cases the data transfer is not fully optimized (e.g., the insert into the target table is fully logged). On the other hand, the BCP client application provides a much simpler and more efficient way to transfer this data using the following steps:

1. Use BCP to export the data from a SQL Server 2000 instance. The following command exports (note the use of `out`) the data into a data file in native format. You only require `Select` privileges on the source table. You can always use a format file, but the `-n` parameter is convenient when you are transferring all the data from the source table "as is" to the target table.

```
bcp <dbname>..Employee out <datafile> -S<instance-name> -n -T
```

2. Create a target table in the appropriate database in the target instance. Note that the data file does not have any information on the target table and its schema. Ideally, if the table schema could be exported like the data file, then it potentially could be used to create the target table transparently. Although this is desired functionality, it is not currently available.

3. Use BCP to import data into a SQL Server 2005 instance. The command shown here is almost identical to the export command, with two exceptions. First, `in` is used to indicate import. Second, the privilege requirements are more complicated. By default, BCP disables constraints on the target table. `Alter Table` permissions are required to import the data. If you know that data in the file does not violate the constraint, there is no reason not to enforce the constraint. In this case you will only require INSERT permission but not ALTER Table permission.

```
bcp <dbname>..Employee in <datafile> -S<instance-name>
➥-n -T -h "CHECK_CONSTRAINTS"
```

Error Handling

The preceding scenario assumed that everything was correct with no chance of error. However, in real-life situations, the System Administrators and DBAs have a small window in which to import data and limited capacity to recover should anything go wrong. Some common errors that can cause failure during an import operation are

- A subset of input data is incorrectly formatted. For example, in a character-mode data file, an integer is represented as xyz, but the BCP expects digits.
- A subset of input data violates the constraints. For example, a data row with a value 10 for the EmpAge column will cause the import to fail.

BCP provides a few parameters to handle errors like these, as follows:

```
bcp <dbname>..Employee in <datafile> –S<instance-name>
➥-c –T –m 100 –e <error-file>
```

By using the –m parameter, you are instructing BCP to ignore the first 100 format errors in data representation. By default, BCP ignores the first 10 errors. You can move the rows that have format errors into a separate error file for analysis by using the -e option. Similarly, by not specifying the -h option, you are, in fact, disabling the constraints checks. If you enable the constraint checks, and any row violates the constraint, the bcp command is terminated and all newly inserted rows are removed. If this or any other error happens toward the end of a large load, it can result in wasted resources of Database Engine and time. To get around this, you can use the -b parameter that lets you commit a set of rows (i.e., a batch) at a time. This way, if a subsequent batch fails because of some errors, the SysAdmin or DBA needs to reload data from only that batch, eliminating the need to reload the data that was already successfully imported. The following bcp command specifies a batch size of 1000.

```
bcp <dbname>..Employee in <datafile> –S<instance-name>
➥-c –T –m 100-e <error-file> -h "CHECK_CONSTRAINTS" -b 1000
```

Generating and Using Format Files

So far, we have only considered the case where both the source and target tables had identical schema. Another common case involves fields in a data file that do not match with the target table, neither in number of columns nor in ordering. To import this data, you need a way to map data fields in the file to the corresponding columns in the target table. Format files can be used to provide this mapping. Like TSQL Insert, any column that is not mapped must have a default or must allow NULLs for the import operation to succeed. You can generate this format file as part of exporting data, or you can create it explicitly through the BCP program. Let us consider a new target table, NewEmployee, with the following schema (note that it does not have an EmpDept column):

```
NewEmployee (EmpID varchar(10) unique,
             EmpAge int check (EmpAge > 18),
             EmpSalary decimal)
```

Assume that you need to import data that was generated during an export from the Employee table into this new target. To do this, the first step is to generate an XML format file that uses the source table as follows:

```
bcp <dbname>..employee format nul -f employee-fmt-xml.xml -x
➥-c –S<instance-name> –T

<?xml version="1.0"?>
<BCPFORMAT
xmlns="http://schemas.microsoft.com/sqlserver/2004/bulkload/format"
           xmlns:xsi="http://www.w3.org/2001/XMLSchema-instance">
  <RECORD>
      <FIELD ID="1" xsi:type="CharTerm" TERMINATOR="\t"
             MAX_LENGTH="10
             COLLATION="SQL_Latin1_General_CP1_CI_AS"/>
      <FIELD ID="2" xsi:type="CharTerm" TERMINATOR="\t"
             MAX_LENGTH="12"/>
      <FIELD ID="3" xsi:type="CharTerm" TERMINATOR="\t"
             MAX_LENGTH="100"
             COLLATION="SQL_Latin1_General_CP1_CI_AS"/>
      <FIELD ID="4" xsi:type="CharTerm" TERMINATOR="\r\n"
             MAX_LENGTH="41"/>
  </RECORD>
  <ROW>
      <COLUMN SOURCE="1" NAME="EmpID" xsi:type="SQLVARCHAR"/>
      <COLUMN SOURCE="2" NAME="EmpAge" xsi:type="SQLINT"/>
      <COLUMN SOURCE="3" NAME="EmpDept" xsi:type="SQLVARCHAR"/>
      <COLUMN SOURCE="4" NAME="EmpSalary" xsi:type="SQLDECIMAL"
             PRECISION="18" SCALE="0"/>
  </ROW>
</BCPFORMAT>
```

Because the new target table does not have EmpDept, the above format file needs to be modified to match the target table. To do this, the column row associated with EmpDept is removed and the third column is mapped to the fourth field in the data file.

```
<?xml version="1.0"?>
<BCPFORMAT xmlns="http://schemas.microsoft.com/sqlserver/2004/
              bulkload/format"
xmlns:xsi="http://www.w3.org/2001/XMLSchema-instance">
 <RECORD>
      <FIELD ID="1" xsi:type="CharTerm" TERMINATOR="\t"
            MAX_LENGTH="10"
            COLLATION="SQL_Latin1_General_CP1_CI_AS"/>
      <FIELD ID="2" xsi:type="CharTerm" TERMINATOR="\t"
            MAX_LENGTH="12"/>
      <FIELD ID="3" xsi:type="CharTerm" TERMINATOR="\t"
            MAX_LENGTH="100"
            COLLATION="SQL_Latin1_General_CP1_CI_AS"/>
      <FIELD ID="4" xsi:type="CharTerm" TERMINATOR="\r\n"
            MAX_LENGTH="41"/>
 </RECORD>
 <ROW>
      <COLUMN SOURCE="1" NAME="EmpID" xsi:type="SQLVARYCHAR"/>
      <COLUMN SOURCE="2" NAME="EmpAge" xsi:type="SQLINT"/>
      <COLUMN SOURCE="4" NAME="EmpSalary" xsi:type="SQLDECIMAL"
            PRECISION="18" SCALE="0"/>
 </ROW>
</BCPFORMAT>
```

Now you can use the following command to import the data:

```
bcp <dbname>.NewEmployee in <datafile> -f <formatfile>
➥-S<instance-name> -n -T
```

Note we could have done the same using the non-XML format file as follows:

```
9.0
4
1       SQLCHAR         0       10      "\t"        1       EmpID
SQL_Latin1_General_CP1_CI_AS
2       SQLCHAR         0       12      "\t"        2       EmpAge
""
3       SQLCHAR         0       100     "\t"        0       EmpDept
SQL_Latin1_General_CP1_CI_AS
4       SQLCHAR         0       41      "\r\n"      3       EmpSalary
""
```

If you compare both format files, a couple of things stand out. First, the XML-based format file is much easier to understand. Second, it explicitly defines the target column types. Target column types are useful, not as much in the context of BCP, but when used with BULK INSERT and OPENROWSET.

There is, however, one restriction with XML-based format files. Unlike non-XML format files, you cannot use them to skip columns in the target table. You can get around this issue by creating a view on the target table and map the columns as needed and then import the data into the view.

Optimized Bulk Import

So far we have focused only on functional scenarios. One of the main benefits of BCP is that it can be used to efficiently load data into Database Engine. The optimizations available during bulk import are

- Optimized logging. Under this optimization, individual data rows are not logged. Only page/extent allocations are logged. This optimization is available only under special conditions described later in this section.

- Parallel load. Multiple BCP threads can import data into the target table without blocking each other. On a multiple-CPU machine, this can reduce your data import time significantly. Like logging optimizations, this optimization is available only under special conditions.

- Skipping the sort. If the data to be imported is already sorted on the clustered key column, the sort step can be skipped.

- Skipping enforcement of constraints and firing of the trigger. If you already know that the data to be imported does not have any constraint violations, you can skip constraint checking to speed up the import. Alternatively, as discussed before, if the data does have constraint violations, you may still want to ignore constraint checking to eliminate constraint-related errors during the import operation.

In the simplest case, you can import data into a heap (a table with no indexes) or into an empty table if there are indexes using optimizations listed above; however there are a few exceptions. For heaps, because there is no index, the optimization related to sorting is irrelevant. For the empty table with an index, you cannot do parallel load with optimized logging at the same time. In the case of an index, you have to choose whether you want optimized logging or parallel load. Another interesting point is that for an index, the optimized logging is available only when the target index is empty. If you want to import data in multiple batches, then by definition, the target index is not empty after the completion of the first successful batch. And finally, to be able to do optimized logging, your database must be configured for the "Bulk Logged" or "Simple" recovery model. As you can see, identifying cases for bulk optimizations can be tedious. Table 5-1 lists these cases, assuming there is no lock escalation.

Table 5-1 Cases for Bulk Optimizations

Table Schema	Empty	TABLOCK	Locks	Logging
Heap	Yes	Yes	BU-Tab	Bulk-logged
Heap	Yes	No	IX-Tab	Fully logged
Heap	No	Yes	BU-tab	Bulk-logged
Heap	No	No	IX-Tab	Fully logged
Heap + non-clustered index	Yes	Yes	SCH-M	Bulk-logged
Heap + non-clustered index	Yes	No	IX-Tab	Fully logged
Heap + non-clustered index	No	Yes	SCH-M	Data-bulk-logged Index-fully logged
Heap + non-clustered index	No	No	IX-Tab	Fully logged
clust Index	Yes	Yes	SCH-M	Bulk-logged
clust Index	Yes	No	IX-Tab	Fully logged
clust Index	No	Yes	X-TAB	Fully logged
clust Index	No	No	IX-Tab	Fully logged

You should note a few points in this table. First, the parallel Bulk Load is available only when the locking mode is BU lock. BU lock is a special table-level lock that enables multiple BCP threads to load data concurrently, but conflicts with all other locks. Second, you must specify the TABLOCK hint to be able to do optimized bulk logging. It is a necessary but not sufficient condition. The following bcp command imports data into the target table Employee with the preceding optimizations, assuming the table was empty to start with:

```
bcp <dbname>..employee in empoyee-dat-c.dat
➥-SSUNILA2\BLD1313 -c -T -h "TABLOCK"
```

Because the employee table in this example has an implicit index (because of the unique constraint on the column EmpID), you cannot execute multiple BCP threads concurrently. One good strategy under this situation is to drop the index(es) so that the target table becomes a heap, use multiple BCPs to load the data in parallel, and then finally re-create the index. Because the target table was empty to start with, there is no additional cost to drop the index and then re-create it after the data has been imported. This is, however, not as black and white when you want to load incremental data into a target table with multiple indexes with a large number of existing rows. You need to weigh the cost of dropping and re-creating indexes and the availability requirements of the table against the benefits from doing an optimized bulk import with BCP. There is another choice available in SQL Server 2005 that uses table partitioning. If applicable, you can load incremental data into an empty heap by using bulk optimizations, creating required indexes, and then snapping in the table as a new partition into a partitioned table. For details on partitioned tables, please refer to SQL Server Books Online.

Summary

This chapter covered different ways to invoke Query Editor from within SQL Server Management Studio and then touched on the new capabilities of Query Editor in SQL Server 2005. It then described the architectural details of the Query Editor data retrieval mechanism and finished up with the new XML data type support.

Both BCP and Bulk Insert commands provide very similar functionality for an import operation. However, there are some subtle differences you may want to consider. BCP is a client application that typically runs on a computer other than Database Engine. So the work to read and parse the data file and to convert the data into native format is done on the client machine. It sends data over a TDS stream, which can be an issue on a slow network. Bulk Insert, on the other hand, runs as part of the Database Engine process. It thereby uses Database Engine resources to read and parse the data file. Neither of these operations provide any transformation (e.g., aggregate) of the data during import. You can categorize these options under ETL (extract, transform, and load) with a missing T—that is, no transformation of data. If you need to do some data transformation before the import, you may want to consider OPENROWSET with the BULK rowset provider for simple transformations and SSIS for complex transformations.

CHAPTER 6

Inside SQLCMD Query Tools

SQLCMD is a new tool developed for SQL Server 2005. Its main purpose is to let the user connect to a SQL Server Database Engine Instance directly from the command line and run ad hoc T-SQL statements and scripts. One of the original design goals of SQLCMD was backward compatibility with the deprecated OSQL tool, to simplify migration. SQLCMD supports most of the legacy command line options supported by OSQL, plus some new ones. Aside from the command line options, SQLCMD also introduces many other useful features to make implementing some core DBA scenarios extremely efficient.

TIPS AND TRICKS

SQLCMD uses the OLE-DB provider, whereas OSQL used the ODBC provider. Although many of the command line options look the same, the underlying technology of the two tools is radically different, so some differences in behavior (especially in the returned provider error codes) are to be expected.

This chapter covers all the SQLCMD options, special commands supported by the tool, and scripting variables. It also describes typical usage scenarios of SQLCMD for miscellaneous database management operations. To simplify authoring and execution, SQL Server Management Studio Query Editor has support for SQLCMD scripts. Later in this chapter you will find discussion on how to leverage this feature, as well.

Command Line Options

This section begins with an overview of the command line options and a brief introduction to the use of variables in SQLCMD. Specific options are then covered throughout the rest of the section.

Overview of Command Line Options

Any discussion of console applications such as SQLCMD invariably starts with examining command line options, i.e., its entry points. However, before covering the individual command line options of SQLCMD, it's a good idea to look at the help output of SQLCMD and highlight the options that existed in OSQL.

```
C:\>SQLCMD /?
Microsoft (R) SQL Server Command Line Tool
Version 9.00.1187.07 NT INTEL X86
Copyright (C) Microsoft Corporation.  All rights reserved.

usage: SQLCMD          [-U login id]       [-P password]
  [-S server]          [-H hostname]       [-E trusted connection]
  [-d use database name] [-l login timeout]   [-t query timeout]
  [-h headers]         [-s colseparator]      [-w screen width]
  [-a packetsize]      [-e echo input]        [-I Enable Quoted
                                                   Identifiers]
  [-c cmdend]          [-L[c] list servers[clean output]]
  [-q "cmdline query"] [-Q "cmdline query" and exit]
  [-m errorlevel]      [-V severitylevel]   [-W remove trailing
                                                   spaces]
  [-u unicode output]  [-r[0|1] msgs to stderr]
  [-i inputfile]       [-o outputfile]        [-z new password]
  [-f <codepage> | i:<codepage>[,o:<codepage>]] [-Z new password
                                                   and exit]
  [-k[1|2] remove[replace] control characters]
  [-y variable length type display width]
  [-Y fixed length type display width]
  [-p[1] print statistics[colon format]]
  [-R use client regional setting]
  [-b On error batch abort]
  [-v var = "value"...]  [-A dedicated admin connection]
  [-X[1] disable commands, startup script, environment variables
         [and exit]]
  [-x disable variable substitution]
  [-? show syntax summary]
```

As you may notice, SQLCMD's options are case sensitive, so a letter may have a different meaning depending on its case. Also a forward slash (/) may be provided in place of dash (-) in front of the option.

In many cases, in addition to using a command line option, you can induce the same behavior by setting the environment or scripting variable. However, if provided, a command line option always overwrites a variable setting. As each individual option is described, the corresponding variable will also be listed if it exists.

Let's touch briefly on usage of variables in SQLCMD. Any environment variable of the command shell gets inherited by SQLCMD.exe as
its child process and thus becomes available inside its session. At that
point it is referred to as a "scripting variable."

To illustrate the usage of variables in SQLCMD we are going to
manually set an environment variable DBNAME and then later use it
inside a SQLCMD session as follows:

```
C:>SET DBNAME=pubs
C:\>SQLCMD
1> use $(DBNAME)
2> go
Changed database context to 'pubs'.
```

In addition to directly using environment variables for scripting, scripting variables can also be defined explicitly inside a SQLCMD session.
Later, you'll learn exactly how this is done.

Now rather than define scripting variables manually for each session as
you saw in the previous example, you can set their values permanently via
the Advanced System Properties tab in the control panel (see Figure 6-1).

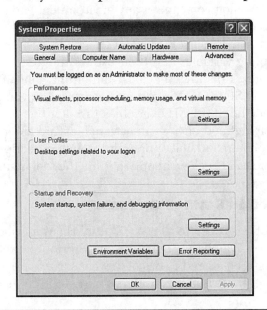

Figure 6-1   Advanced System Properties Windows dialog.

When you click on the Environment Variables button the dialog shown in Figure 6-2 appears.

Figure 6.2 Environment Variables Windows dialog.

From this dialog you can set any environment variable for your specific user session and keep its value private and globally for all sessions, regardless of which user is logged on.

Scripting variables and their use will be discussed in depth later in this chapter. For now, the most important point to remember is that while using SQLCMD in the interactive mode you can always obtain a list of specific SQLCMD variables through the command :listvar. All previously defined environment variables and any new values obtained via either command line options or through the script are displayed. This is how you can check what option value the tool is currently using.

Connection Related Options

These options relate to the way SQLCMD establishes a connection to a SQL Server Database Engine Instance. Prior to establishing connection there might be a need to discover what servers are available on the network. This phase is also considered part of the connection options.

-L[c]

Suppose you want to list all locally configured servers and the ones broadcasting their names across the network. -L is an option that can provide this information:

```
C:\>SQLCMD /L
Servers:
     MYSERVER
     MYSERVER\INST1
```

When -L is followed by lowercase c, you get clean output, without the Servers: string and without leading spaces before each server name, to simplify programmatic parsing of the output.

-S

This option can be used to specify to which SQL Server Database Engine instance SQLCMD should connect. If a server instance name is not specified, SQLCMD checks the value of the SQLCMDSERVER environment variable. If the environment variable is not defined, it tries to connect to the default instance of SQL Server running on the same computer.

-U and -P

To connect using SQL Authentication, you have to provide -U to enter the username and -P to enter the password. If the -U option is not provided, SQLCMD checks for the SQLCMDUSER environment variable. If that variable is missing, SQLCMD checks for the OSQLUSER environment variable kept for backward compatibility purposes with the OSQL tool. Similarly, for the password, SQLCMD checks for SQLCMDPASSWORD and then OSQLPASSWORD if the -P option is not present.

TIPS AND TRICKS

If a username is provided without a password, SQLCMD prompts the user for a password before establishing a connection. You can use this trick to avoid revealing the password in your batch scripts.

-E

This option instructs the tool to connect to SQL Server Database Engine using Windows Integrated Security. If this option is used, it takes precedence over any environment variable definition mentioned in the previous section.

TIPS AND TRICKS
If none of the environment variables specifying username have been set, you can omit this option and SQLCMD assumes you intend to use Windows Integrated Security as the default.

Here's how to connect to the default server instance running on the computer by explicitly instructing SQLCMD to use integrated security:

```
C:\>SQLCMD /E
>
```

The caret symbol (>) indicates that the connection succeeded and you are now ready to execute T-SQL and SQLCMD commands. At this point, you communicate with SQLCMD by typing in the console.

-A

Unlike a regular SQL Server connection, this connection option instructs SQLCMD to log in to the server using the dedicated administrator connection (DAC). The dedicated administrator connection runs on a special thread inside SQL Server and thus does not contend with other clients for resources. If DAC is not available (for example, if it is already being used) or the server does not support it, an error message is printed and SQLCMD immediately exits.

TIPS AND TRICKS
DAC connection is new to SQL Server 2005, and earlier versions of SQL Server do not support it. Just because this option has been added to the tool does not imply earlier versions of SQL Server can be accessed this way.

WARNING
You should use the DAC connection only as a last resort when you must access your server to perform emergency management operations, such as killing a runaway process, and the regular connection is not available.

-l and -t

Another important connection-related option, -l, specifies the login timeout in seconds. This argument must contain a numeric value in the range 0 through 65534, where 0 is used in place of infinite timeout. SQLCMD's default for this option is 8 seconds. Somewhat similar, the option -t defines the statement timeout. The corresponding environment variables for these two options are SQLCMDLOGINTIMEOUT and SQLCMDSTATTIMETOUT.

-H

The -H option enables you to specify a workstation name. You can use this to distinguish different SQLCMD sessions from each other when executing the sp_who stored procedure or during Profiler tracing. This option corresponds to the environment variable SQLCMDWORKSTATION.

-d

The initial database name option -d may be used instead of the USE <dbname> statement. This option is most useful when you need to submit a T-SQL query for batch execution in a specific database context. This option corresponds to an environment variable named SQLCMDDBNAME.

-q and -Q

To submit a specific command for immediate execution, you would use -q or -Q, depending on the intent. Q instructs SQLCMD to exit when the command line terminates, whereas q leaves SQLCMD in interactive mode. An example follows:

```
C:\>SQLCMD /E /q"select * from HumanResources.Department"
➥/dAdventureWorks
```

TIPS AND TRICKS
Keep in mind that you cannot submit multiple batches as part of one command. SQLCMD does not recognize batch separators when processing commands for immediate execution.

-a

Option -a is used to specify a packet size in the range of 512 through 32767. It has no visible effect on the output. Increased packet size can enhance performance of a large script execution by packing more data in the envelope. However, the provider can choose not to grant this request, in which case SQLCMD defaults to the server default packet size.

This option corresponds to an environment variable SQLCMD-PACKETSIZE.

-I

Option –I sets the QUOTED_IDENTIFIER setting for the connection to ON. The default setting for this option is off. When SET QUOTED_IDENTIFIER is ON, identifiers can be delimited by double quotation marks, and literals must be delimited by single quotation marks.

Formatting Options

These options relate to the way SQLCMD processes and formats query results. Multiple control points are available to the user concerning how data is going to be displayed or stored in the output file, and they are covered in this section.

-h

This option controls the number of rows printed between column headings. This results in the entire resultset being split into batches of the size specified in the –h setting, with each one preceded by its own set of headings. A default value of 0 instructs SQLCMD not to split the resultset.

In this example compare the default output

```
C:\>SQLCMD /E
1> select top(3) name from sys.objects
2> go
name
-----------------------------------------
sysrowsetcolumns
sysrowsets
sysallocunits
```

with the following output obtained when the value 1 was supplied for this setting, essentially meaning split the results into batches of one row each.

```
C:\>SQLCMD /E /h1
1> select top(3) name from sys.objects
2> go
name
--------------------------------------------------------
sysrowsetcolumns
name
--------------------------------------------------------
sysrowsets
name
--------------------------------------------------------
sysallocunits
```

This setting corresponds to the environment variable SQLCMDHEADERS.

TIPS AND TRICKS

Use a value of -1 to specify that no headers should be printed. If -1 is supplied, there must be no space between the parameter and the setting, that is, -h-1. Otherwise, SQLCMD interprets it as a separate option and fails.

-s

Option -s provides a different default for the column separator in place of blank space. To use characters that have special meaning to the operating system, enclose the character in double quotation marks. This option corresponds to the environment variable SQLCMDCOLSEP.

TIPS AND TRICKS

If you don't want to have any separation between columns, you can pass in an empty string as follows -s"".

-w

Option -w specifies screen width. The default value is 80. When the printed output reaches the specified value, it wraps to a new line. This option corresponds to the environment variable SQLCMDCOL-WIDTH.

-e

Option -e causes contents of the script file (i.e., queries) to be written to stdout in addition to the regular output.

TIPS AND TRICKS
This option may be useful for troubleshooting when a script is produced from other files being read with the `:r` command or from scripting variables that are expanded inside a SQLCMD session.

-W

This option strips spaces from the ends of the columns, causing all columns of each row to be printed next to each other without regard for column justification.

TIPS AND TRICKS
This technique is especially useful when preparing data for import into another program in combination with option `-s` and `-h`.

Suppose you need to create a comma-separated file of query results for subsequent import into a spreadsheet application. Assuming the query is stored in the in.sql script file, you can produce the desired output as follows.

```
C:\>SQLCMD -i in.sql -s, -W -h-1 -o out.csv
```

WARNING
You cannot combine this option with options `-y` or `-Y`; they are mutually exclusive.

-y <column width >

This option limits the number of characters that are printed for large variable-length types. These types are varchar(max), nvarchar(max), varbinary(max), XML, user-defined types, ntext, text, and image. If the returned column data is shorter than the specified display width, the output is padded up to that limit. If 0 is specified, the column output is returned without any truncation. This option corresponds to environment variable SQLCMDMAXVARTYPEWIDTH.

TIPS AND TRICKS
In reality, SQLCMD allows a fine level of control for this option only in the range of 1 through 8000. After that, any value is treated as if 0 was provided.

WARNING
Keep in mind that even if 0 is supplied, the SQLCMD output is limited to a sufficiently large but finite number of characters for performance reasons, so some data truncation is still possible.

-Y <column width>

This option controls truncation of fixed-width character data types. These types include char(1…8000), nchar(1…4000), varchar(1…8000), nvarchar(1…4000), and variant. This option corresponds to environment variable SQLCMDMAXFIXEDTYPEWIDTH. The default value for this option is 0, which means there will be no truncation or unlimited column width.

-k [1\2]

This option causes any control characters, such as tab (\t), newline (\n), and others, to be removed from the output. This allows column formatting to be preserved when requested column data contains special characters. Possible values for this option include 1 and 2. A value of 1 instructs SQLCMD to replace control characters with a single space. A value of 2 instructs SQLCMD tool to apply a single space to any sequence of special characters. For example, when supplying –k2, the following sequence

```
\t\t\t\r\n
```

is automatically replaced with a single blank space ( ) if it is encountered in the script.

Command Execution Options

Command execution options relate to the way SQLCMD executes queries and treats errors if they occur. Sometimes users also might want to record query execution statistics.

-c

By default, commands are terminated and sent to SQL Server Database Engine if GO is entered on a line by itself. The default batch separator can be changed with the –c option.

TIPS AND TRICKS

When you reset the batch terminator, do not use Transact-SQL reserved words or characters that have special meaning to the operating system, whether preceded by a backslash or not, even though this was allowed by legacy.

-m error_level

The error level –m option customizes display of the error messages. Any error higher than the specified number gets reported, along with its message number, state, and error level. A value of -1 specifies that all headers are returned with messages, even informational messages. This option corresponds to environment variable SQLCMDERRORLEVEL.

–p [1]

This option enables you to print performance statistics. An example follows:

```
Network packet size (bytes): 4096
2 xact[s]:
Clock Time (ms.): total 321  avg 321.00 (3.12 xacts per sec.)
```

As you can see, there was one total transaction processed by SQL Server Database Engine. It took 321 milliseconds to execute, with the same average time per transaction, enabling the server to run 3.12 transactions of this type per second.

Note that performance statistics are printed for every resultset. If optional argument 1 is provided, statistics output is printed in a colon-separated format that can be easily imported into a spreadsheet, or processed by a script.

For the previous example the results would look like this:

```
4096:1:321:321.00:3.12
```

TIPS AND TRICKS

Performance statistics information comes directly from SQLCMD and does not add any additional burden on SQL Server Database Engine Query Processor, so it is safe to use even under heavy server load, which is when it becomes most useful. SQLCMD uses OLE-DB technology under the covers to get the statistics, but it does not do any calculations internally.

File Stream and Redirection Options

Unless you want to simply connect to the server and execute ad-hoc T-SQL queries, you are going to start developing scripts and run them together. SQLCMD enables you to specify input and output files during execution specifically for this purpose.

-i input_file[,file2...]

This option enables you to supply one or several script files for immediate execution. When multiple files are specified, they are processed in the same order as they are specified on the command line. File names should not be separated by spaces. If the file name contains embedded spaces, the file name needs to be enclosed within double quotes.

For example:

```
C:\sqlscripts>SQLCMD -i"file 1.sql","file 2.sql"
```

SQLCMD first checks whether any of the files are missing before attempting to execute them.

-o output_file

This option enables you to specify an output file for SQLCMD session execution.

TIPS AND TRICKS
If you combine the output file option with the –u switch, the output file is saved in Unicode format.

-r [0| 1]

This option redirects message output, also referred to as stderr, to the screen. If you specify 0, only error messages with a severity level of 17 or higher are redirected. This is also the default option. If you specify 1, all message output is redirected.

Error Handling and Reporting Options

Error handling and reporting is an important part of any program. SQL-CMD enables you to control how errors affect script execution based on their severity.

-V <severity level>

This option specifies the minimal severity level that will be reported by SQLCMD. If a T-SQL script reports a lower severity error than the severity level provided with –v option, 0 is reported; otherwise, the severity level is returned.

-b

This option makes SQLCMD exit upon error. At the same time SQLCMD sets the value of environment variable ERRORLEVEL.

When SQL Server Database Engine reports an error of severity greater than 10, SQLCMD sets the ERRORLEVEL value to 1; otherwise, it sets it to 0. If a SQLCMD script contains a bad instruction, the ERRORLEVEL value is set to 1 as well.

Most operating system batch files can test the value of this environment variable and handle the error appropriately.

Let's first create a script file c:\sqlscripts\myscript.sql containing the following code:

```
select 1
go
-- we expect for this batch to fail
select * from nonexistent_table
go

select 2
go
```

At this point we are going to create an operating system batch script run_script.cmd that will invoke the SQLCMD tool by passing script file in as an argument and examine the ERRORLEVEL value after the tool returns.

```
sqlcmd /i"c:\sqlscripts\myscript.sql"

echo %ERRORLEVEL%
```

Running batch script produces the following output:

```
C:\sqlscripts>run_script.cmd

C:\sqlscripts>sqlcmd /i"c:\sqlscripts\myscript.sql"
```

```
--------------------
                   1

(1 rows affected)
Msg 208, Level 16, State 1, Server KOMODO_Q5, Line 2
Invalid object name 'nonexistent_table'.

--------------------
                   2

(1 rows affected)

C:\sqlscripts>echo 0
0
```

If we now modify the batch script to use option -b, the result is different.

```
C:\sqlscripts>run_script.cmd

C:\sqlscripts>sqlcmd /i"c:\sqlscripts\myscript.sql" /b

--------------------
                   1

(1 rows affected)
Msg 208, Level 16, State 1, Server KOMODO_Q5, Line 2
Invalid object name 'nonexistent_table'.

C:\sqlscripts>echo 1
1
```

Two things in this example are worth highlighting. First, the T-SQL script gets aborted after the second batch that contains an invalid statement. Second, the ERRORLEVEL environment variable indicates there was a problem running SQLCMD session and the batch script can examine its value to make subsequent logical decisions.

TIPS AND TRICKS

If the -v option is used along with the -b option, errors are not reported when the severity level raised is lower than the severity level specified with -v.

Language-Specific Conversion Options

These options direct SQLCMD how to treat input and how to format output so it is interpreted correctly in non-English speaking countries.

-R

This option directs SQLCMD to use client regional settings when converting currency, date, and time data to character data. By default server side settings are used.

-u

This option instructs the tool to store the output file in Unicode format, regardless of the format of the input script file.

-f <codepage> [i:<codepage>][,o:<codepage>]

The main option, -f, drives codepage specification. Before you dive into how to specify a codepage, it's important to understand what it is. A codepage defines a character set, which can include numbers, punctuation marks, and other glyphs specific to each language. Naturally, codepages are not the same for each language. Some languages, such as Japanese and Hindi, have multi-byte characters, whereas others, such as English and German, need only one byte to represent each character. Therefore, you would only use option -f and define a codepage by its specific numeric value, if you were dealing with multiple codepages within your environment and needed to either resolve the ambiguity or simply force the output in a certain way.

When used by itself, option -f is applied to both the input and output codepage. Optionally, the user can supply separate parameters to drive input codepage (i:) or output codepage (o:). If an input codepage is not provided, SQLCMD tries to use the current codepage to interpret the input file. If the input file is already in Unicode format, no conversion is needed. Similarly, if an output codepage is not provided, SQLCMD uses the console codepage for printing data to display.

WARNING
Do not supply output codepage specifications when using the -u option. Codepage specifications conflict with the Unicode format.

You can understand conversion specification better if you look at a few examples.

This example prescribes the use of Ansi Latin 1 as the codepage for an output file:

```
SQLCMD -i in.sql -o out.txt -f o:1252
```

This example instructs SQLCMD to use Ansi Latin 1 as the codepage for an input file and to provide output in Unicode format:

```
SQLCMD -i in.sql -o out.txt -f 1252 -u
```

This command tells SQLCMD to use Ansi Latin 1 as the input file codepage and to produce an output file using an ISO-8859-1 codepage:

```
SQLCMD -i in.sql -o out.txt -f i:1252,o:28591
```

Security and Scripting Options

Two new command line options in SQLCMD provide a certain degree of protection when you are running untrusted scripts: -x and -X. This section also looks at the –v option.

-X

This option causes SQLCMD to ignore scripting variables completely. Keep in mind while using the -x flag that all variable-related commands or command line options are still allowed, for example, :setvar or -v, except that the variable substitution will not take place.

Take a look at the following example:

```
INSERT INTO mytable VALUES
➡('Hourly rate will be calculated as $(price)/number of hours')
```

-X [1]

This option disables commands that may potentially compromise system security when SQLCMD is executed from a batch file. They include ED and !! <command> and are described in detail later in this chapter. These commands are still recognized by the tool, and SQLCMD issues a warning message and continues on unless option argument 1 is provided. In such case, SQLCMD issues an error message and exits.

Additionally, environment variables are not passed on to SQLCMD, and, subsequently, the startup script specified with SQLCMDINI environment variable is not executed.

Please note that the -x option provides a different aspect of protection than -x listed, so both options may be combined if desired.

-v <variable name>="<variable value>"

This option enables you to define one or more variables right on the command line before running a script. The variable value needs to be enclosed in double quotes only if it contains blank spaces. This option is discussed later in this chapter when it covers different scripting usage scenarios. Multiple variables can be supplied this way, separated by a blank space.

Scripting Variables

It's a good idea to discuss scripting variables at this point before discussing different SQLCMD commands, primarily because certain commands reveal their true power only via leveraging scripting variables.

SQLCMD variables are different from T-SQL variables in many aspects. The easiest way of thinking about SQLCMD variables is that they are similar to macros that you can define in many text editors and development environments. Wherever such a variable is referenced, the query editor substitutes it with the text associated with the variable, which makes using them much more convenient then using just T-SQL variables.

Another major benefit of such variables is that they are carried forward between multiple batches. If you define a SQLCMD variable on the first batch, you can use it in all subsequent batches (unless it was undefined). Moreover, as you'll see in the next sections, these commands can be used to parameterize queries stored in different files.

Scripting variables have the following format: $(<variable name>). The variable name is not case sensitive. Scripting variables can be defined in one of the following ways:

- via command line option –v;
- through the :SETVAR command described later in this chapter;
- by defining an environment variable prior to running SQLCMD.

If an environment variable name conflicts with a –v or :setvar definition or command line option, the command line option takes precedence. If a variable is referenced in a script whose value is not defined, an error message is returned and the SQLCMD session terminates. Let's consider a very simple but illustrative example of scripting variable usage.

Suppose you want to create a generic script that backs up a database to a specific location on the disk. The following line is going to be placed in the backup.sql script file:

```
BACKUP DATABASE $(db) TO DISK = "$(path)\$(db).bak"
```

Now to use it effectively you can pass in values of two variables on the SQLCMD command line as follows:

```
C:>SQLCMD -ic:\backup.sql -vdb="pubs" path="c:\data"
```

You can see that to back up a different database or back up to a different location, you can execute this script again and again by modifying scripting variables and not touching the script itself.

SQLCMD Commands

SQLCMD commands give the script developer substantially more flexibility beyond what would normally be supported by T-SQL language. They are part of the SQLCMD tool, and as such get executed on the client computer before the query is submitted to the server. You need to keep this in mind while using them. All the commands supported by the tool are described in this section.

Overview of SQLCMD Commands

As mentioned earlier, in addition to command line options, SQLCMD also supports many powerful commands. A SQLCMD command always starts with a new line and is preceded by a colon. A colon is required to make a clear distinction between a SQLCMD command and a T-SQL script command. However, for backward compatibility with OSQL, some legacy commands are recognized without the colon prefix.

How do you find out what commands SQLCMD supports? There is a "help" command for this, and here is the output:

```
1>:help
:!! [<command>]
  - Executes a command in the Windows command shell.
:connect server[\instance] [-l timeout] [-U user [-P password]]
  - Connects to a SQL Server instance.
:ed
  - Edits the current or last executed statement cache.
:error <dest>
  - Redirects error output to a file, stderr, or stdout.
:exit
  - Quits SQLCMD immediately.
:exit()
  - Execute statement cache; quit with no return value.
:exit(<query>)
  - Execute the specified query; returns numeric result.
go [<n>]
  - Executes the statement cache (n times).
:help
  - Shows this list of commands.
:list
  - Prints the content of the statement cache.
:listvar
  - Lists the set SQLCMD scripting variables.
:on error [exit|ignore]
  - Action for batch or SQLCMD command errors.
:out <filename>|stderr|stdout
  - Redirects query output to a file, stderr, or stdout.
:perftrace <filename>|stderr|stdout
  - Redirects timing output to a file, stderr, or stdout.
:quit
  - Quits SQLCMD immediately.
:r <filename>
  - Append file contents to the statement cache.
:reset
  - Discards the statement cache.
```

```
:serverlist
  - Lists local and SQL Servers on the network.
:setvar {variable}
  - Removes a SQLCMD scripting variable.
:setvar <variable> <value>
  - Sets a SQLCMD scripting variable.
1>
```

It's worth noting that SQLCMD commands (unlike command line options) are not case sensitive.

TIPS AND TRICKS

It is safe to mix SQLCMD command with T-SQL statements in the same batch because they all get pre-processed before T-SQL is submitted to the server. However, you should be aware that for any given batch, all SQLCMD commands are pre-processed and only after that is T-SQL sent to the server. It means that sometimes you can get unexpected results if you try doing too many things in the same batch. Consider, for example, the SET-VAR command mentioned earlier that defines a scripting variable.

```
use AdventureWorks

:setvar tablename Person.Address
select * from $(tablename)
:setvar tablename HumanResources.Department
select * from $(tablename)
go
```

One could expect that the first select would be from Person.Address and the second one from HumanResources.Department. However, that's not the case. As already mentioned, all SQLCMD commands in a given batch are pre-processed first, and only after that is the resulting T-SQL sent to the server. In this example, both selects are from HumanResources.Department. To fix that, put the batch separator (go in the default case) between the two SETVAR commands:

```
:setvar tablename Person.Address
select * from $(tablename)
go
:setvar tablename HumanResources.Department
select * from $(tablename)
```

Explanations and Examples of SQLCMD Commands

This section provides more information on each of the SQLCMD commands.

GO [count]

Although it does not get prefixed by colon, a batch terminator can also be considered a special command. Not only that, a batch terminator can accept a numeric value as a parameter. If supplied, the current batch executes the specified number of times, as shown in the following example:

```
C:\>SQLCMD
1> select 1
2> go 3
-----------------
          1
(1 rows affected)
-----------------
          1
(1 rows affected)
-----------------
          1
(1 rows affected)
1>
```

[:]RESET

All T-SQL statements are held in the statement cache until a batch terminator is encountered. The RESET command clears the statement cache.

TIPS AND TRICKS

The statement cache can also be cleared by typing the ^C escape sequence at the console. However, if this sequence is used when the cache is empty, the entire SQLCMD execution session is terminated.

[:]ED

This command enables the user to call an editor on the current query buffer. The editor of choice is defined by the SQLCMDEDITOR environment variable. The default editor is "edit," provided by the operating system. After the editor exits, the entire batch is entered directly into the statement cache.

TIPS AND TRICKS
The ED command also enables you to edit the last executed batch if the current statement cache is empty. This is especially useful when you realized you made a mistake and the previous batch returned syntax errors. Quick editing and submitting can save time.

[:]!! <command>

Typing !! allows the user to pass essentially any operating system command straight to the command line interpreter for direct execution and passes the output back to your display.

WARNING
This is a very powerful option that can allow a malicious script writer to break through your security. If you are not sure of the contents of the script, you should consider using the -x command line option while executing it.

Support of the !! command and its implementation makes interesting scenarios possible while inside Query Editor that have never been possible before. For example, you can see a list of all files in your Program Files folder on your local machine inside the Messages tab if you do the following while in SQLCMD mode:

```
!!dir "%programfiles%"
```

Note that there is no dir.exe command, but it is available while inside the cmd.exe command interpretor, so the command works successfully; it gets expanded to something like this (depending on location of your Windows directory).

```
"C:\WINDOWS\system32\cmd.exe /C dir"
```

In general, any command is passed as a parameter to the Windows cmd.exe shell.

TIPS AND TRICKS
As with other SQLCMD commands, !! supports specifying a SQLCMD variable as its parameter.

Consider an example of backing up the Pubs database to a share. Remember that the database is on the server to which your query window is connected, but the command specified to the !! command is executed on your local computer on which you run SQL Server Management Studio. For the purpose of this example, imagine that your file server name is "myserver" and the share name that you (and the account under which SQL Server service runs) can access is called "backups."

```
:setvar backupDir "\\myserver\backups\pubs"
!!if not exist $(backupDir) md $(backupDir)
GO
   BACKUP DATABASE [pubs] TO
   DISK = N'$(backupDir)\pubs.bak' WITH NOFORMAT, NOINIT,
   NAME = N'pubs-Full Database Backup', SKIP, NOREWIND,
   NOUNLOAD,  STATS = 10
GO
```

In this query, SQLCMD variables are used to share context between the !! command and the SQL Query. The first line introduces a new SQLCMD variable called backDir and initializes it with the file share. The second line uses the command interpretor's language to ensure that the directory exists. After that, the directory name is passed in to the T-SQL backup database statement to back up the database to the specified share.

TIPS AND TRICKS

If you try executing this example and you receive an Access Denied message output to your Messages tab, it probably means that either you or the user under which SQL Server runs do not have write permission for the share.

This example uses command shell language directly inside a query window. Usually it is preferable to encapsulate it into a batch file and then call the file from the !! command. Let's rework this query to use the batch file to create a directory for the BAK file.

Open your favorite text editor and create a c:\batches\prepare.bat that contains the following statement:

```
if not exist "%1" md "%1"
```

This means that it checks to see whether the directory specified as the first parameter to the batch file exists, and if it does not, then it creates it.

After that, adjust the query like this:

```
:setvar batchFile c:\batches\prepare.bat
:setvar backupDir "\\myserver\backups\pubs"
!!$(batchFile) $(backupDir)
GO
   BACKUP DATABASE [pubs] TO
   DISK = N'$(backupDir)\pubs.bak' WITH NOFORMAT, NOINIT,
   NAME = N'pubs-Full Database Backup', SKIP,
   NOREWIND, NOUNLOAD,  STATS = 10
GO
```

It does exactly the same thing as the previous query, only this time it calls the batch file and specifies the `backupDir` SQLCMD variable as the parameter.

[:]QUIT

This command immediately ends the current SQLCMD session without running any statements in the statement cache.

[:]EXIT[(statement)]

This function has three distinctly different formats.

- `:EXIT` supplied without parenthesis has the same affect as `QUIT`.
- `:EXIT()` first executes previously accumulated statements and only then exits the session.
- `:EXIT(query)` first executes previously accumulated statements, then the supplied query. Finally it quits after returning results of the query as a return value from the SQLCMD tool. If the query is a `SELECT` statement returning multiple result sets, the first column of the first row of the last result set is converted to a four-byte integer value and is used as the return code from the program.

TIPS AND TRICKS

In general, SQLCMD propagates an error message number as the return code to the calling program.

Suppose a script causes the following RAISERROR statement to be executed: RAISERROR(30301, 16, 130). The error causes SQLCMD to end and the message ID 30301 to be returned to the client.

In case SQLCMD is not able to process the supplied query and return a value to the client, it can return one of the following reserved error codes for which a calling program can test:

- -100 means an error occurred prior to selecting the return value
- -101 means no rows were returned by the query
- -102 means a conversion error occurred when selecting the return value

:SETVAR <variable name> ["<variable value>"]

The SETVAR option, already mentioned earlier during the discussion on scripting variables, enables you to set their values programmatically inside the script.

One interesting aspect of the SETVAR command is that it is possible to assign a value that consists of multiple words. In this case, the variable value should be enclosed into the double quotes characters.

```
:setvar querytext "select * from pubs..authors"
$(querytext)
```

The query above results in "select * from pubs..authors" being submitted to the server.

It is possible to define a variable that spans multiple lines, as long as it is enclosed in quotes and can be executed as one batch.

Try executing

```
:setvar querytext "select au_lname from pubs..authors
where au_id = '172-32-1176'
"
$(querytext)
```

You'll see the following result:

```
au_lname
-----------------------------------
White
(1 row(s) affected)
```

In order to undefine a previously defined variable, use the SETVAR syntax without specifying the variable value:

```
:setvar <variable name>
```

It undefines the previously defined variable. For example,

```
:setvar ProcName sp_who
exec $(ProcName)
go
:setvar ProcName
exec $(ProcName)
go
```

results in the following error during execution of the second exec statement: "A fatal scripting error occurred. Variable ProcName is not defined."

:r <filename>

This option enables the script writer or interactive user to read the contents of a specified script file and include it in the current execution session. The included file is processed in-place; in other words, every command encountered is processed the same way, as if it was just typed in or was part of the original file.

The read command enables you to create complex compound scripts to potentially leverage simpler generic scripts and drive their execution through different scripting variable settings.

Let's use a previously created backup.sql script containing the following entry

```
BACKUP DATABASE $(db) TO DISK = '$(path)\$(db).bak'
```

Only this time it is included inside the compound script and backs up two databases at once, as follows.

```
:setvar db pubs
:setvar path C:\data
:r "c:\sqlscripts\backup.sql"
GO
:setvar db northwind
:setvar path C:\data:r "c:\sqlscripts\backup.sql"
GO
```

TIPS AND TRICKS
The extension of the file specified to the `:r` command does not matter.
You could have TXT or any other extension; SQLCMD simply treats the file
as a text file containing T-SQL statements.

A very helpful feature of the `:r` command is that you can specify a SQL-CMD variable as the parameter. That enables you, among other things, to quickly try different queries depending on a variable value or to logically include setting a file name into the variable definition part of your queries. Consider the following example:

```
:setvar filename "c:\sqlscripts\sp_who.sql"
:r $(filename)
go
:setvar filename "c:\sqlscripts\sp_lock.sql"
:r $(filename)


This is equivalent to the following:

:r c:\sqlscripts\sp_who.sql
go
:r c:\sqlscripts\sp_lock.sql
```

By itself, this doesn't look like a useful feature, but consider what happens when you have multiple `:r` commands that read different files. In this case, you can have SQLCMD variables with filenames defined at the top of your query file and use them as needed later:

```
:setvar firstQuery "c:\sqlscripts\sp_who.sql"
:setvar secondQuery "c:\sqlscripts\sp_lock.sql"
:setvar thirdQuery "<some file>"

:setvar finalQuery "<some file>"

<100 lines of SQL statements>
:r $(secondQuery)
GO
<200 lines of SQL statements>
:r $(firstQuery)
GO
<more SQL statements>
... .
etc
```

SQLCMD enables you to include nested :r statements, causing one file to include another one and so on. Be careful, however, with the level of nested files that you load with the :r command. If you end up with too many levels on indirection (you load a file that loads a file that loads a file, etc.), it might be difficult to debug the resulting script and to maintain it. After all :r commands have been processed, the query editor doesn't have information about which file contained which executed batch, so if there are errors during execution, it might be a challenge to correlate them with the correct query file. In such situations it's a good idea to use print statements to trace the execution order. For example, you might want to adjust your stored_proc.sql statement like this:

```
:setvar filename "c:\sqlscripts\sp_who.sql"
print '$(filename)'
:r $(filename)
go
:setvar filename "c:\sqlscripts\sp_lock.sql"
print '$(filename)'
:r $(filename)
```

To summarize, the :r command enables the user to easily group and parameterize your SQL queries so you can have a set of SQL files doing different logical operations that can later be combined into a single query. With this command, you don't have to maintain one huge SQL query that does hundreds of different things. You can keep different operations in their own files and combine and parameterize them as needed by using the :r command and SQLCMD variables, as demonstrated by the preceding short examples.

:SERVERLIST

This command corresponds to the command line option -L, listing all locally configured servers and the names of the servers broadcasting on the network. How does it help you to know the names of all servers when you are already connected? SQLCMD enables a user to reconnect to a different server within a session. Here is how:

```
:CONNECT <SQL Server Database Engine instance name>
➥[-l timeout] [-U user [-P password]]
```

As soon as SQLCMD connects to a new server, the current connection is closed. At the same time the SQLCMDSERVER variable is updated accordingly.

An optional login timeout switch allows infinite timeout (0), or some finite number of seconds. If not specified, the default comes from the SQLCMDLOGINTIMEOUT variable.

The default authentication mode is Windows integrated security. However, if the environment variable SQLCMDUSER is set or option -U specified, SQLCMD attempts to use it to establish a connection instead. In lieu of a password value provided via SQLCMDPASSWORD or the -P flag, SQLCMD interactively asks the user to enter a password on the command line.

:LISTVAR and :LIST

The LISTVAR command was mentioned earlier during the introduction of scripting variables. It lists currently defined variables and, as such, is handy in troubleshooting SQLCMD.

There is a different command, LIST, which enables you to list contents of the current statement cache.

:ERROR <filename>/ STDERR/ STDOUT

This command enables the user to redirect error output, either to a specified file or to standard error/standard output console streams. You may want to refer back to command line option -r, discussed earlier in this chapter.

TIPS AND TRICKS
Error redirection instructions can appear multiple times in the same session or script, each time changing where errors are going to be reported.

Similar redirection options exist for output and performance trace data.

:OUT <filename>/STDERR/STDOUT

This command redirects all query results output that by default gets sent to standard output.

:PERFTRACE <filename>/STDERR/STDOUT

The :PERFTRACE command redirects all performance information (see the discussion of the -p option) that by default goes to standard output.

:ON ERROR [exit/ignore]

This command instructs SQLCMD on how to handle errors during script execution. The following options are available:

- `exit`—Exits the program with the appropriate error value
- `ignore`—Ignores the error and continues execution. An error message is printed.

:XML [ON/OFF]

When you expect XML data to be coming back from the server, for example because of a FOR XML clause in your query, you should set XML mode to ON via this command, to properly format the output. By default it is set to OFF and thus displays unformatted data in a continuous stream.

One side effect of setting the XML mode to ON is that error messages also appear in XML format. This option does not affect formatting of any other non-XML columns present in the returned data set.

TIPS AND TRICKS

Setting XML mode ON and OFF needs to be done only upon the start of a new batch; otherwise, results are indeterminate. Consequently, XML and regular data results cannot be mixed in the same batch or data of one of these two types becomes unreadable.

SQLCMD Startup Script

SQLCMD can run a startup script defined by the environment variable SQLCMDINI.

Suppose you want to always execute the following query when you are connected to the server:

```
SELECT @@SERVERNAME, @@VERSION
```

Place this command inside the init.sql file and define the following environment variable:

```
C:\SET SQLCMDINI=c:\sqlscripts\init.sql
```

Then whenever you start a SQLCMD session, the script automatically executes and displays query output listing the server name and full version string.

Authoring of SQLCMD Queries Using SQL Server Management Studio Query Editor

The SQL Server Management Studio Query Editor has support for SQLCMD scripts authoring and execution. The following section demonstrates how to enable this feature and how to use it.

Turning the SQLCMD Feature On and Off

While you are inside SQL Server Management Studio, SQLCMD mode can be turned on and off for SQL Queries on both a per-window and global basis. To toggle the mode for a particular query window, use the Query>SQLCMD Mode menu item or the corresponding button on the query window toolbar (see Figure 6-3).

Figure 6-3 SQL Server Management Studio toolbar.

TIPS AND TRICKS

If you find this mode useful, you can make it the default for all SQL Query windows. To do that, go to the Tools>Options dialog (see Figure 6-4) and select Query Execution>SQL Server>General category on the left side of the dialog. After that, check the check box at the bottom of the page on the right side of the dialog that says **By default, open new queries in SQLCMD mode.**

While adding support for SQLCMD syntax to Query Editor, the development team envisioned two primary scenarios. One scenario is to make Query Editor more powerful by supporting new commands in addition to GO. The other one is to enable writing and debugging SQLCMD scripts in Query Editor so that they can be executed later from batch files with the SQLCMD.EXE command line tool.

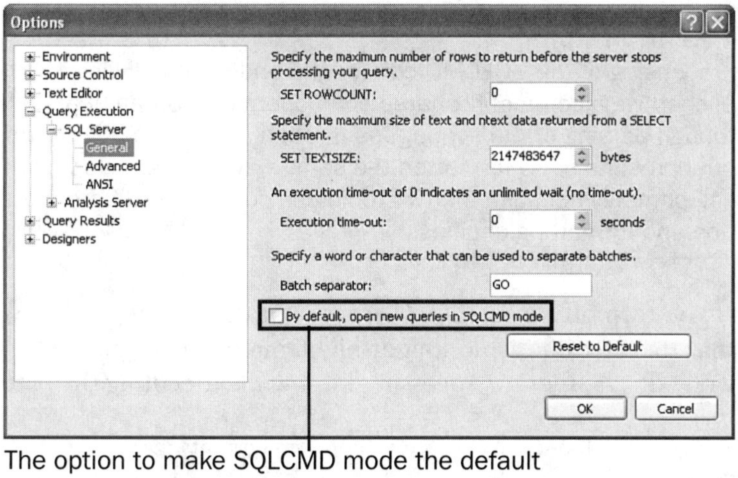

The option to make SQLCMD mode the default

Figure 6-4   SQL Server Management Studio Options dialog.

Colorizing of SQLCMD Commands and Variables

Now you can try using this mode to author and execute in Query Editor a simple query that selects all columns from a table whose name is specified by a SQLCMD variable.

Create a new query window and connect to AdventureWorks. Turn on the SQLCMD mode. After that, type the following in the text editor area of the query window:

```
:setvar tablename HumanResources.Department
go
select * from $(tablename)
go
```

Please note the same rules apply as if we were working in console mode, that is, the command should be the first statement on the line.

Notice that the line containing the `:setvar` SQLCMD command is highlighted. All recognized SQLCMD commands are highlighted this way so that it is clear that the command is not part of T-SQL syntax.

SQLCMD Mode Script Execution in Query Editor

Any highlighted commands are going to be recognized by the execution engine. If you run a query in the Query Editor, the results appear the same way as if you were to execute it from within the console application.

TIPS AND TRICKS
Processing of the SQLCMD commands and scripting variables is accomplished via a commonly shared component called BatchParser. Even though parsing of the script goes through a common engine, do not expect query results to be formatted the same way. They are close, but not identical, primarily because the two tools use completely different query execution and formatting engines.

If you turn off the SQLCMD mode for this query window you'll notice that the first line is no longer highlighted—it means that query editor won't do any special processing for it while executing the batch:

```
:setvar tablename HumanResources.Department
go
select * from $(tablename)
go
```

If you run the query in this mode, execution fails because the SETVAR command is submitted directly to SQL Server Database Engine, and the engine doesn't recognize its syntax.

TIPS AND TRICKS
Batch terminator, which is also considered a special command in SQL-CMD, as mentioned earlier in this chapter, is still recognized by Query Editor even when SQLCMD mode is off. This applies to its supplied argument, as well specifying the number of times the batch is to be executed.

It is important to know that any definitions and settings introduced by a SQLCMD command during previous query execution are not carried over and remembered for the next execution. This is a significant difference from the command line tool. Query Editor remembers only settings that are specified with UI elements of SSMS. For example, suppose you execute the following:

```
:setvar tablename HumanResources.Department
go
```

If after that you execute the following query separately from the preceding execution, you get an error that the tablename variable is not defined:

```
select * from $(tablename)
go
A fatal scripting error occurred.
Variable tablename is not defined.
```

To correct this problem you need to execute both batches in one shot:

```
:setvar tablename Person.Address
select * from $(tablename)
go
```

It is important to note that all major Query Editor features are usable while queries execute in SQLCMD mode. For example, you can still parse the text and view the graphical execution plan. However, some particular aspects of the Query Editor behavior are slightly different when you are working in this mode. Some of the SQLCMD commands are not supported at all and some have limitations.

SQLCMD Commands Not Supported by Query Editor

The list of SQLCMD commands that are not supported by Query Editor demonstrates the main difference between SQLCMD.exe and SSMS. The former is an interactive command line tool where the interaction with the user happens via Windows console window. The latter has graphical user interfaces and interacts with the user via menu commands and graphical elements. Therefore, not all interactive SQLCMD commands are supported inside Query Editor. What follows is the list of nonsupported commands—Query Editor issues a warning in the Message tab if it encounters these commands while in SQLCMD mode:

- :serverlist—Lists local and SQL Servers on the network.
- :reset—Discards the statement cache.
- :perftrace—Redirects timing output to a file, stderr, or stdout. This is not supported because Query Editor doesn't have this concept.
- :listvar—Lists the set SQLCMD scripting variables.
- :ed—Edits the current or last executed statement cache.
- :help—Shows the list of supported commands.

When one of these commands is used in a SQLCMD query, Query Editor issues a non-fatal warning into the Messages tab during execution and continues on.

```
:help
select 1


Scripting warning.
Command Help is not supported. String was not processed.


------------------
1

(1 row(s) affected)
```

One other important difference between Query Editor and SQL-CMD.EXE is that Query Editor doesn't support built in SQLCMD and OSQL variables. If you try specifying them in the query that you execute inside SSMS you'll see an error about an undefined variable:

```
print '$(SQLCMDSERVER)'
go

A fatal scripting error occurred.
Variable SQLCMDSERVER is not defined.
```

Redirecting Results and Errors in Query Editor

Query Editor still supports the following SQLCMD commands: `:out <destination>` and `:error <destination>`. As explained earlier, their purpose is to redirect the output and error messages respectively into a file, stderr, or stdout location.

Suppose you're working on a query and you want to always have results in a file separate from error messages that should be in a different file. Assuming you have a c:\output folder, you can do the following:

```
:out c:\output\queryresults.txt
:error c:\output\queryerror.txt
GO
exec sp_who
go
exec sp_who 'foo'
```

If you execute it, you'll notice that the results of the first sp_who execution will be in the first TXT file, and unless you have a login 'foo,' the error message from the second sp_who execution will be in the second TXT file.

TIPS AND TRICKS
One important aspect of the Query Editor behavior is that it silently over-writes the files if they exist. So, be sure to back them up as needed.

Because SQL Server Management Studio is a UI application and not a command line tool, it can't really support strerr and stdout parameters to these commands. However, it does accept them and redirects subsequent output to the Messages window. For example, executing the following puts the results of exec sp_who 'sa' into the text file and the results of exec sp_who into the Messages window.

```
:out c:\output\queryresults.txt
GO
exec sp_who 'sa'
GO
:out stdout
GO
exec sp_who
```

You may notice that it is similar to the Results to File and Results to Text query execution modes that Query Editor has. The major difference is that by utilizing these commands, you can change the result mode dynamically for different parts of the query. This might be useful for large scripts that do multiple logical operations, for which you want to track results independently.

TIPS AND TRICKS
The :out command results in both tabular results and the non-error messages being redirected to the specified destination.

Summary

This chapter has covered SQLCMD, a brand-new command execution tool shipped with SQL Server 2005. It went over SQLCMD options, grouping them into different functional categories, special commands supported by the tool, and scripting variables. Finally, it covered support that was added to SQL Server Management Studio Query Editor for authoring and executing SQLCMD scripts.

CHAPTER 7

Inside Tuning and Optimization Tools

This chapter will cover various SQL Server tools that can be used for tuning and optimization of database queries. It should give you a detailed overview of what is available and help provide you with some guidance on what tool to use in your particular situation.

The chapter starts with discussion of execution plan capture and analysis features of SQL Server Management Studio. Then it looks at the internals of SQL Server Profiler and highlights many new features related to advanced tracing and data analysis that were added to the tool in the SQL Server 2005 release of the product. Following a discussion of tracing, you get a brief look at the new tracing application programming interface and see several related scenarios along with corresponding code samples. A somewhat underutilized feature of SQL Profiler is covered separately: Replay. This chapter also covers the Replay application programming interface exposed by the tool. Finally, it takes an in-depth look at Database Tuning Advisor, including its internal architecture and multiple usage scenarios.

Using SQL Server Management Studio for Query Optimization

The simplest way to tune performance of a single query is by using Query Editor (part of SQL Server Management Studio) and turning on one of the two execution plan options available under the **Query** menu item.

Display Estimated Execution Plan for a query does not actually execute any T-SQL statements in your batch; it captures a query execution plan in XML format associated with each of your statements and produces a graphical representation in the bottom pane of the window (shown in Figure 7-1).

NOTE
SQL Server releases prior to 2005 do not use XML format for describing execution plans.

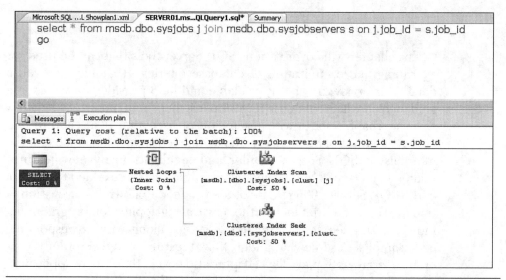

Figure 7-1 Display Estimated Execution Plan query results.

Display Estimated Execution Plan is accomplished when you use the SET SHOWPLAN_XML ON command. The SQL Server Database Engine parses any T-SQL submitted following the aforementioned command. The server produces well formed XML describing the estimated execution plan as if the statement actually ran and sends it to the client as a regular resultset.

Include Actual Execution Plan waits for you to actually run the queries on the server, then displays the results and also includes the execution plans. Query Editor achieves this by executing SET STATISTICS XML ON before running the batch.

TIPS AND TRICKS
It is also possible to extract execution plan information and automatically save it to a file by using SQL Server Profiler. This technique will be described further later in this chapter.

Another interesting option exposed by Query Editor is **Include Client Statistics**. This option utilizes SQL Server Managed Data Provider and does not impose any additional processing workload on Database Engine. Results of selecting this option are shown in Figure 7-2.

	Trial 4		Trial 3		Trial 2		Trial 1		Average
Client Execution Time	20:45:56		20:45:52		20:43:44		20:43:17		
Query Profile Statistics									
Number of INSERT, DELETE and UPDATE statements	0	→	0	→	0	→	0	→	0.0000
Rows affected by INSERT, DELETE, or UPDATE statem...	0	→	0	→	0	→	0	→	0.0000
Number of SELECT statements	2	→	2	→	2	→	2	→	2.0000
Rows returned by SELECT statements	1	→	1	→	1	→	1	→	1.0000
Number of transactions	0	→	0	→	0	→	0	→	0.0000
Network Statistics									
Number of server roundtrips	3	→	3	→	3	→	3	→	3.0000
TDS packets sent from client	3	→	3	→	3	→	3	→	3.0000
TDS packets received from server	5	→	5	→	5	→	5	→	5.0000
Bytes sent from client	236	→	236	→	236	→	236	→	236.0000
Bytes received from server	11711	→	11711	→	11711	→	11711	→	11711.0000
Time Statistics									
Client processing time	10	↑	0	→	0	→	0	→	2.5000
Total execution time	40	↓	120	↓	130	↑	120	→	102.5000
Wait time on server replies	30	↓	120	↓	130	↑	120	→	100.0000

Figure 7-2   Include Client Statistics output.

Note how with each query run the statistics results get updated with new processing times, including change of direction for each value.

TIPS AND TRICKS
Note how the client statistics in Figure 7-2 indicate that there were two select statements in the batch when in reality there was only one. They do so because the previously selected **Include Actual Execution Plan** option was not turned off. You have to be careful to look at only pure values when comparing different runs and filter out other activity generated by the graphical tool.

Two separate tuning and optimization tools are located in the **Performance** folder: SQL Server Profiler and Database Engine Tuning Advisor. The following section takes a detailed look at each of them.

SQL Server Profiler

Virtually all serious SQL Server Database administrators have used the SQL Server Profiler more than once. It is a graphical tool used to monitor the internal state of the server being traced. Sometimes people confuse SQL Server Profiler with the internal server component that actually produces trace data. In the case of SQL Server Database Engine this component is called SQL Trace.

NOTE

Keep in mind that running a trace always puts some additional load on the server. The SQL Server development team worked very hard to minimize this impact of tracing, and in the SQL Server 2005 release it is smaller than ever before. However, it can never be eliminated completely.

SQL Profiler has a fairly simple user interface: You establish a connection to the server you want to trace, select events and columns, and run the actual trace. The subject of monitoring SQL Server and Analysis Server via SQL Profiler is covered in greater depth in Chapter 9, "Inside Monitoring Tools." If you are unfamiliar with the internals, it might be worthwhile now to take a look at how tracing is actually accomplished behind the scenes.

We are going to investigate what SQL Profiler is doing behind the scenes by using Profiler itself. First, connect to a running instance of SQL Server Database Engine. The **Trace Properties** dialog depicted in Figure 7-3 has several advanced options that are discussed later in this chapter. For now, **Looking at events generated by Profiler** is typed in the **Trace name** box to define the trace.

TIPS AND TRICKS

Keep in mind that the literal trace name is not being persisted anywhere and exists only for the benefit of the user while looking at the trace window. When trace data is saved to a file or a table, this information is permanently lost.

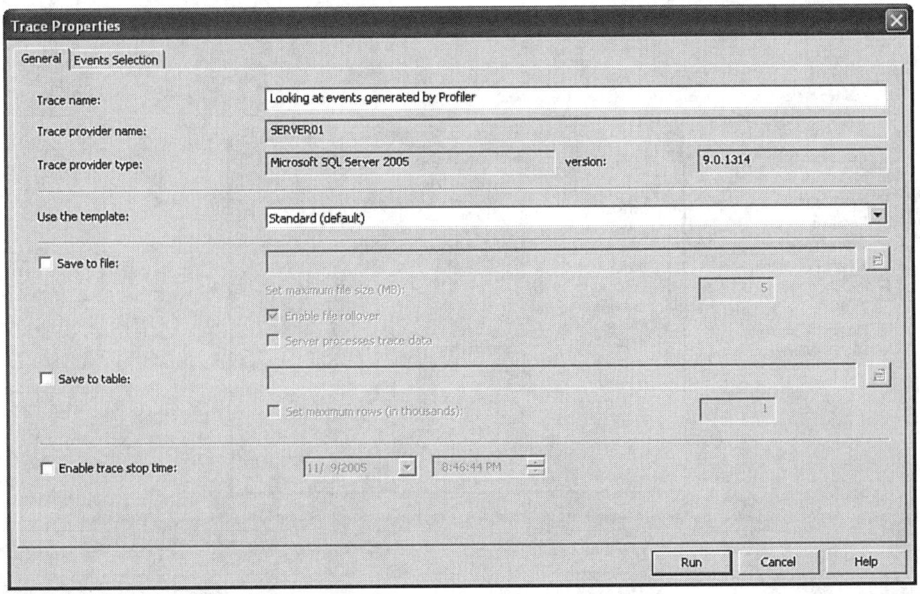

Figure 7-3   Trace Properties dialog.

Before starting the trace, let's switch over to the **Events Selection** tab and click the **Application Name** column header. The **Edit Filter** dialog is displayed as shown in Figure 7-4.

You may notice that the application name associated with a given SQL Server Profiler session is filtered out via a "Not Like" clause. The purpose of this pre-set filter created by the SQL Profiler infrastructure is not to trace actions generated by SQL Profiler itself. We are going to change it so that the application name filter is set to "Like=SQL Server Profiler%." This causes Profiler-generated events to be displayed, regardless of the session from which they came.

TIPS AND TRICKS
You can edit a SQL Profiler filter by clicking directly on the text you want to modify. This initiates in-place activation of the text control.

Make sure you delete the GUID-like value displayed after the Profiler name in the original filter if you are using cut-and-paste, and replace it with a percent sign. In this case, it serves as a wild card. The actual session to be traced is not this session but the session that will start next and that will have a different, unknown GUID.

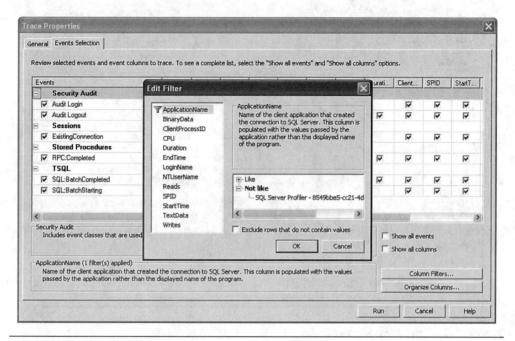

Figure 7-4   Edit Filter dialog.

When the filter setting is finished, click the **Run** button to start collecting trace data.

At this point we are going to start another trace session. Establish a new connection to the same Database Server Instance and start a new trace.

Now it's time to switch back to the window where the original trace is being captured and examine the collected data. It's easy to see all the activity generated by Profiler when starting a second trace. To create a trace, SQL Profiler uses the sp_trace_create stored procedure. After the trace object is created on the server and a handle is passed back to the client, SQL Profiler makes a series of sp_trace_setevent calls, listing each event and column ID combination that the user is interested in receiving. Finally, the sp_trace_setfilter stored procedure is called and sets the filter on the **Application Name** column. Then the sp_set_tracestatus call is made to actually turn tracing on. After that, SQL Profiler executes the sp_trace_getdata stored procedure, which starts feeding it with a never-ending resultset until the trace status is changed to "pause" or "stop" on a separate thread.

Trace Definition

To make proper sp_trace_setevent calls, SQL Profiler obtained information on each event column intersection straight from the events selection matrix shown in Figure 7-5.

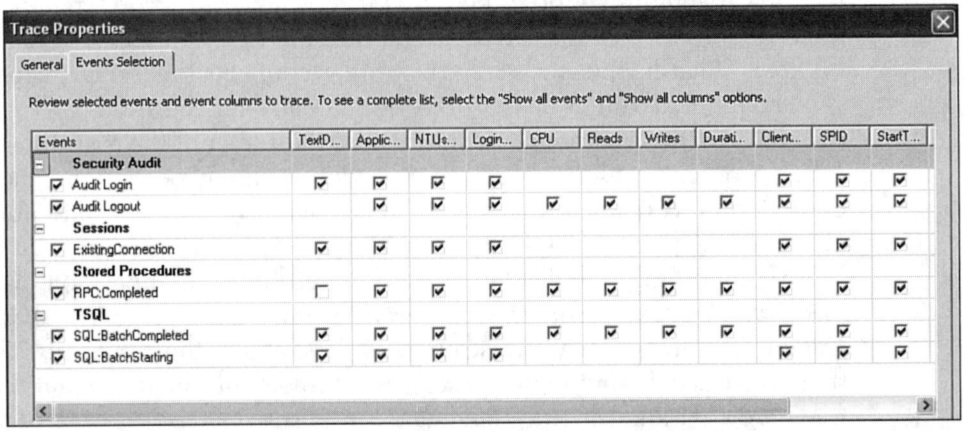

Figure 7-5   SQL Server Profiler events selection matrix.

How does SQL Server Profiler know what possible event-column combinations to display for a specific server, and how does it later perform name-to-ID translation when generating DDL statements? All this information is stored in an XML file located inside the %Program Files%\Microsoft SQL Server\90\Tools\Profiler\TraceDefinitions folder. If you open a file named Microsoft SQL Server TraceDefinition 9.0.0, after general information you will see the following pattern:

```
<EVENTLIST>
<EVENT>
   <ID>139</ID>
   <NAME>Broker:Forwarded Message Sent</NAME>
      <EVENTCOLUMNLIST>
         <EVENTCOLUMN>
            <ID>7</ID>
         </EVENTCOLUMN>
         <EVENTCOLUMN>
            <ID>23</ID>
         </EVENTCOLUMN>
```

This information is used by SQL Server Profiler to present the user with an event selection matrix and to translate the user selections back into valid event and column ID values. This folder also contains files corresponding to other server types supported by SQL Profiler. In fact, the SQL Profiler user interface code is agnostic to server capabilities; those unique capabilities get described to SQL Profiler by the corresponding trace definition file. Each trace definition file also contains a version number. What happens when SQL Profiler connects to a server with a version number different than the one already on the disk? In such cases, SQL Profiler attempts to interrogate the server of the trace metadata it exposes via a series of stored procedure calls and persists the trace definition on disk for future reference. To figure out the version information in the protocol, you can use tracing as you saw before.

It's important to understand that although the communication protocol with Analysis Server is different from SQL Server Database Engine, the underlying infrastructure is essentially the same, that is, there is a trace definition that describes complete information about the trace provider and the trace metadata it exposes. The user is presented with an event selection matrix based on the information found in the corresponding trace definition file. User selections are turned into appropriate DDL calls to set up a trace and start consuming data.

TIPS AND TRICKS
SQL Profiler enables you to extract the required sequence of DDL calls when starting a trace without having to capture T-SQL statements as you saw in the exercise. With a currently active trace window you would like to script out, go to the menu **File, Export, Script Trace Definition** and select one of the available options. Notice that scripting for SQL Server 2000 is presented as a separate option from scripting for SQL Server 2005. Even though underlying stored procedures have not changed considerably, many new events were added for SQL Server 2005 that did not exist in SQL Server 2000. Thus, if your trace contains these new events, they are skipped when you script a trace definition for a down-level (earlier than SQL Server 2005) server.

Advanced Tracing Options

If you refer back to Figure 7-3 you can see several advanced tracing options. SQL Profiler enables you to specify possible ways to save trace information while tracing the server. You can save it to either a file or a table. When saving to a file you can have SQL Server perform the actual I/O. However, even under this option you will be getting data back to the grid. Does SQL Profiler read the data as it has been written to the server file system? In reality it cannot, because Database Engine can be running on a different machine under different security credentials than the graphical tool. How is this accomplished? SQL Profiler creates two different traces. One trace tells SQL Server Database Engine to write to a file on disk and another trace feeds data back to the client. When you run SQL Profiler, you may notice that the number of concurrent server connections indicated in the right corner of the status bar is one more than you would expect. This is not a very efficient use of SQL Server resources, so it is a good practice to write to a file from SQL Server only when you are not using SQL Profiler at all but are instead starting/stopping traces from the console or in a batch mode.

NOTE
When SQL Server writes trace data to the file system, it has a guaranteed assurance of never losing the data. However, when data is sent to Profiler over the network and the server load is too heavy, some events may actually get dropped. When this happens, you will see a special event displayed in the SQL Profiler grid indicating that some of the original trace events have been dropped because of resource constraints.

In general, you can have trace data written to either a file or database table as shown in the diagram in Figure 7-6,

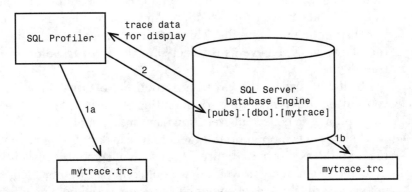

Figure 7-6   Saving trace data to the file system or into a database table.

Either SQL Profiler or Database Engine can write to a file (1a, 1b) but only SQL Profiler can write to a trace table (2), including the one located on a different physical server than you are tracing. When writing trace data to a file, you have to specify a maximum file size in megabytes. After the maximum specified size is reached, the file is closed and all new data is redirected into a new one with the same base name but with a numeric suffix. This feature is called "file rollover." File rollover enables you to move the old file to a new location and free up disk space. When replaying trace data, (the replay feature is described later in this chapter) SQL Profiler treats multiple rollover files as one and loads them sequentially into one execution scheduler. If you uncheck the **Enable file rollover** check box that was shown in Figure 7-3, trace recording stops as soon as maximum file size is reached. Even though the check box shown in the figure is grayed out, it gets enabled when the **File**, **Save** option is selected.

TIPS AND TRICKS

If you did not select an option of saving trace data to a file or table before the trace starts, you can always do it later directly from the **File** menu. One issue with this is that if the trace is still running while you are saving data, only data currently displayed in the grid will be recorded and new data coming in after that point will not be—as opposed to recording everything from start to finish.

Another advanced tracing option is the capability to stop a trace at some point in time. This is done to prevent unnecessary consumption of server resources beyond a reasonable time interval of interest.

Some of the advanced tracing options are hidden from immediate view and get enabled only when certain user selections are made. For example, you can capture execution plans described at the beginning of the chapter to a separate file. This option gets enabled only when one of the Showplan XML events is selected in the **Events Selection** matrix (see Figure 7-7).

Switching over to the **Events Extraction Settings** tab in Figure 7-8, you will see different options for persisting execution plans to file system. One option is to collect all execution plans into a single XML file.

Later you can open up the execution plans in SQL Server Management Studio as shown in Figure 7-9. If you collected each execution plan in its individual file you would have only one picture per plan, but it is not necessarily more convenient because you would not know which one of multiple files you needed to open before trying each individual one.

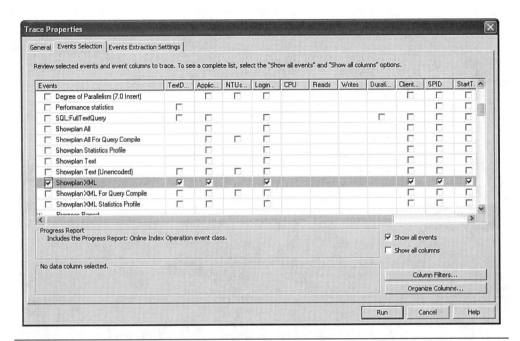

Figure 7-7   Selecting Showplan XML events in SQL Profiler.

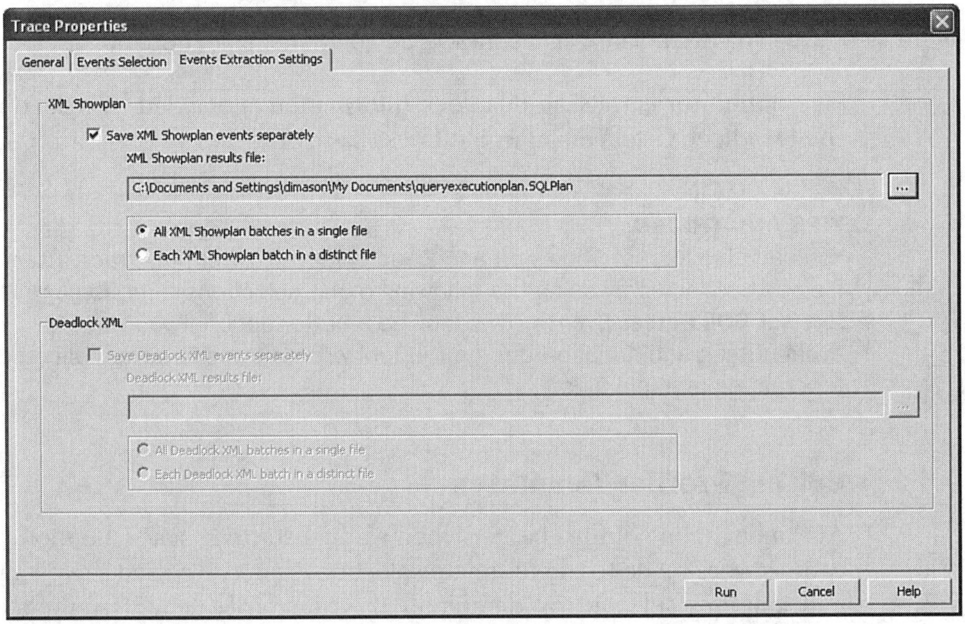

Figure 7-8   Showplan and Deadlock XML Extraction while tracing.

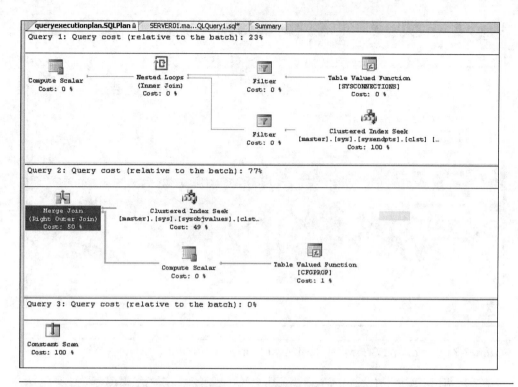

Figure 7-9 Opening Showplan XML file in SQL Server Management Studio.

The option for extracting deadlock information is enabled by selecting the Deadlock Graph event in the Locks category.

TIPS AND TRICKS

You can also extract Showplan and Deadlock events from the trace after it's been collected by using the following menu selections: **File, Export, Extract SQL Server Events**. This may be a better option if you want to avoid putting additional burden on the tool while a trace is being collected for creating multiple files.

Editing Profiler Templates

At the beginning of the chapter when we first started a trace, no modifications were made to the template selection; that is, we used the events and columns selected by default in the Standard (default) template. Many pre-defined templates are supplied with SQL Server Profiler. You can refer to Chapter 9 "Inside Monitoring Tools," to get an overview of each one. Here we discuss an option of creating a custom template that satisfies your needs. This is easy to do in SQL Profiler. From the **File** menu, select the **New Template** in the **Templates** submenu, as shown in Figure 7-10.

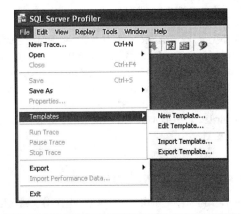

Figure 7-10   Templates submenu.

This will launch the template editor (see Figure 7-11).

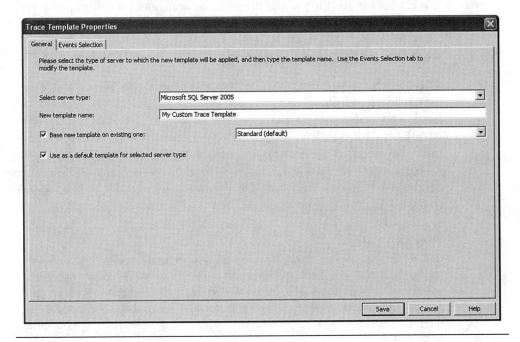

Figure 7-11   Template Editor.

Here you can create a new template based on an existing template and customize the event/columns selection, or you can select events and columns from scratch. You can also make this new template your default template for starting SQL Profiler traces.

TIPS AND TRICKS

You may need to experiment with the trace before you determine the optimal event and column information to collect. If you already have a trace, it is much easier to create a template by directly exporting it from the trace itself. With the trace window open, select **File**, **Save As Trace Template** and give it a name. This is by far the quickest and most effective way to create a template. Later you can edit the template in the template editor and make it the default.

Saving a Trace in XML Format

Trace data is being saved following a well-defined XML schema and can be accessed programmatically by other tools. The biggest advantage of saving trace data in XML format is to allow easy editing of the data before using Replay (described later in this chapter). There is an option to save as **Trace XML File for Replay**, which strips all the non-relevant columns from the original trace except for those used by the Replay execution engine.

Performance Counter Correlation

The correlation of trace data and the performance monitor log is a cool new feature of SQL Profiler. This correlation enables the person troubleshooting SQL Server performance problems to see how trace data correlates with Windows performance counter data. To use this correlation, you need to use Performance Monitor logging while tracing the server to collect performance counter data separately. Performance Monitor data needs to be stored in a comma-delimited log file, as shown in Figure 7-12, and trace data can be stored in a regular trace file.

TIPS AND TRICKS

SQL Profiler can read binary log files as well; however, because the binary format has changed between different versions of the Windows operating system, it is possible that a file captured on one computer (server) might not be successfully read on the computer where Profiler is installed (client). Thus, saving to a comma-delimited file is safer, although performance may be impacted.

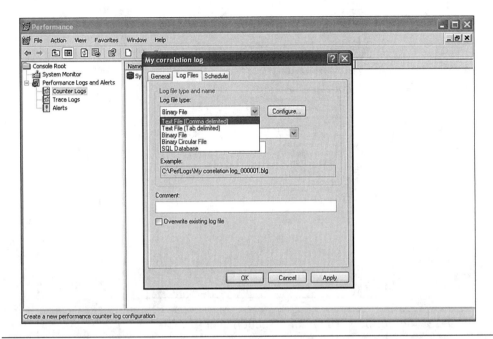

Figure 7-12   Saving performance counter data into comma-delimited log file.

After the data collection stage, you can start correlation by first loading the trace file and then choosing the **File**, **Import Performance Data** menu option. This launches the counter selection dialog shown in Figure 7-13.

This dialog is used to keep SQL Profiler from reading all the counters captured in the log file. Reading too many counters can be quite costly and should be avoided unnecessarily. After all counters have been selected, the user is presented with the correlation graph shown in Figure 7-14.

The graph itself reflects value changes for each counter. The vertical red bar can be positioned anywhere on the graph. The trace window scrolls in correlation with the selected timestamp. You can also scroll through the trace data and change positioning of the vertical bar at the same time.

TIPS AND TRICKS
Only the timestamp is used in correlating of two different sources of data. Therefore it is imperative that the trace file contains StartTime and End-Time columns collected for each trace event.

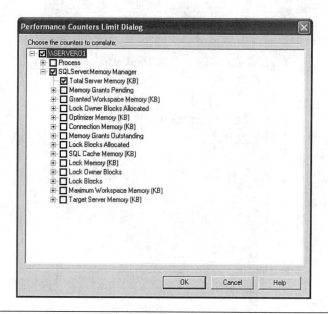

Figure 7-13 Performance counter selection dialog.

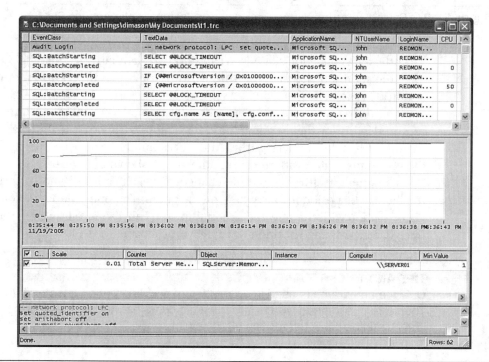

Figure 7-14 Trace-Performance counter correlation graph.

Trace Objects API

One of the hard-to-discover features of SQL Profiler is exposed through a completely different mechanism. There is an application programming interface (API) layer around SQL Profiler called Trace Objects. With this API, the SQL Profiler development team wanted to enable users to automate creation of the trace and perform trace data reading and manipulations programmatically. It is a managed API; that is, it can be accessed by any .NET language.

Trace Objects

Trace objects enable the user to start a new trace, read and write trace log files, and trace tables. There are three main classes:

1. TraceServer—Starts and reads a new trace.
2. TraceFile—Reads and writes to a trace file.
3. TraceTable—Reads and writes to a trace table.

All these classes are part of the Microsoft.SqlServer.Management.Trace namespace contained in managed assembly %Program Files%\Microsoft SQL Server\90\SDK\Assemblies\Microsoft.SqlServer.ConnectionInfo.dll.

TraceServer is a read-only abstraction, whereas TraceFile and Trace-Table can be used for both reading and writing of trace data.

Scenario 1— Starting a New Trace

To start a new trace, you first need to create the TraceServer object:

```
TraceServer reader = new TraceServer();
```

Next you need to create an object responsible for storing connection information and indicate that you want to use Windows Integrated Security for connecting the server:

```
ConnectionInfoBase ci = new SqlConnectionInfo("localhost");
((SqlConnectionInfo)ci).UseIntegratedSecurity = true;
```

Now you can pass connection information to the TraceServer object as part of its initialization routine. The second argument is the name of the trace template file (creation and editing of SQL Profiler templates were described earlier in this chapter).:

```
reader.InitializeAsReader(ci, @"Standard.tdf");
```

At this point you can start consuming trace data by repeatedly calling the `Read()` method in a loop. Contents of each data record can be examined in a way standard to any data provider via the `IDataRecord` interface members (for more information, see the .NET Framework documentation):

```
while (reader.Read())
{
        // do something with data when it comes back
        Console.Write( reader.GetValue(0).ToString() );
}
```

TIPS AND TRICKS

The `reader.Read()` call is synchronous, meaning that it will not return until the event is read or the trace is stopped. To stop a trace, you need to call `TraceServer.Stop()` from a separate thread.

After getting out of the reader loop, close the reader:

```
reader.Close();
```

The same code is applicable to starting a trace against Analysis Services, except a different connection object (OlapConnectionInfo) and tracing template need to be used in this case.

Scenario 2— Saving Trace File Data to a Table

Often users perform tracing through stored procedures and have SQL Server write directly to the file system. As soon as tracing is complete, however, they need to analyze data with the SQL Server query mechanism, so data needs to be loaded into the table. One way to solve this is by using an insert statement and reading the trace data via the `fn_trace_gettable` built-in function that projects trace results directly from the file. However, this function does not work if the trace data file is in legacy format—for example, Microsoft SQL Server 7.0 or SQL Server 2000 files. Another advantage of using trace objects is the capability to process data as it has been read and optionally modify the data being written (very valuable for Replay) or discard unnecessary events.

Just as in the code example described above, the following assembly needs to be referenced for the project to compile: %Program Files% \Microsoft SQL Server\90\SDK\Assemblies\Microsoft.SqlServer.ConnectionInfo.dll.

Here is a code segment that demonstrates how to perform this operation:

```
public void FileToTable()
{
    SqlConnectionInfo connInfo = new SqlConnectionInfo("localhost");
    connInfo.DatabaseName = "pubs";

    TraceFile  reader = new TraceFile();
    reader.InitializeAsReader("TraceInputFile.trc");

    TraceTable writer = new TraceTable();
    writer.InitializeAsWriter(reader, connInfo, "OutputTraceTable");

    writer.WriteNotify += new WriteNotifyEventHandler(OnWriteNotify);

    while( writer.Write() ){};
    writer.Close();
}
```

One interesting detail of this code sample is a callback mechanism that uses WriteNotifyDelegate. This mechanism is used to examine each individual record being written. You can optionally suppress this event from being written out by setting the SkipRecord boolean flag to true. You can also modify the contents of each individual column. The following demonstrates a sample implementation of this method:

```
protected void OnWriteNotify(object sender, TraceEventArgs args)
  {
    IDataRecordChanger recordChanger = args.CurrentRecord

    if( recordChanger["ApplicationName"].ToString() != "myprogram" )
    {
       args.SkipRecord = true;
    }
    else
    {
       recordChanger.SetValue(1, "Changed by user");
       recordChanger.SetValue(2, 10);
    }
  }
```

Scenario 3—Saving Trace File Data to a Table

With moderate modifications, you can change the preceding utility to save the contents of a trace table to a file, that is, go in the opposite direction.

First, you need to initialize this routine by creating the `SqlConnectionInfo` object:

```
SqlConnectionInfo connInfo = new SqlConnectionInfo("localhost");
connInfo.DatabaseName = "pubs";
```

Then you need to create and initialize the `TraceReader` class:

```
TraceFile  reader = new TraceFile();
reader.InitializeAsReader("InputTraceFile.trc");
```

Create and initialize the table writer object:

```
TraceTable writer = new TraceTable();
writer.InitializeAsWriter(reader, connInfo, "OutputTraceTable");
```

Set up the `OnWriteNotify` event handler as before if you want to perform optional writing:

```
writer.WriteNotify += new WriteNotifyEventHandler(OnWriteNotify);
```

Sit in the loop and write:

```
while( writer.Write() ){};
```

As writing is done, close the writer (which closes the reader as well):

```
writer.Close();
```

SQL Profiler Replay

SQL Profiler Replay is an integral part of SQL Profiler. The purpose of replay is to reproduce the original load on the server based on original trace data. For example, the original trace captured three different clients executing three distinct queries in a specific order. When the trace is replayed, identical queries will be executed on different connections following the same order. Moreover, all client connection options

affecting execution, such as ANSI_PADDING, QUOTED_IDENTI-
FIERS, and so on, will be properly set for each connection as well.

Some of the events captured by the trace require special interpreta-
tion during replay. For example, a client tool or database provider itself
is using the API server cursor by calling sp_cursorprepare, then sp_cur-
sorfetch multiple times, and finally sp_cursorclose. SQL Profiler Replay
needs to understand that sp_cursorprepare creates a server-side cursor,
and then accepts and stores cursor handle returned from the server.
Subsequently, this new handle must be used in place of an old one when
executing sp_cursorprepare and sp_cursorclose statements. In cases
where multiple statements get fetched at the same time on the same
connection, Replay must remember all original handles and make
proper substitutions based on that information.

Understanding that the Replay feature of SQL Profiler requires special information to properly reproduce complex customer scenarios will
help you justify the existence and enforcement of the TSQL_Replay
trace template. Only when the trace is captured with this template does
SQL Profiler have a chance to replay it properly. In fact, this information
is so critical that SQL Profiler now enforces minimum required information in a trace file when trying to start Replay against a SQL Server 2005
Database Engine instance.

TIPS AND TRICKS

In reality, trace replay may encounter errors even when using the right template. There are multiple reasons for these errors. For one, client actions
may have started prior to the trace capture, making cursor creation information unavailable in the trace. Or client connection options reported via
an "ExistingConnection" event might not have been set when the statement was replayed. Or perhaps the database is not in the same state as it
was when trace was captured, or the database user is no longer valid.

Let's use the correct template to capture trace data, storing it in the file
at the same time. After the trace is stopped, open the file and wait until
it's fully loaded. There are three ways to start replay from the shell. First,
select the **Replay**, **Start** menu option. Second, you can click on the toolbar. Third, press the F5 function key. In each case you must first connect
to the replay server. Then you are presented with the basic Replay Configuration options dialog shown on Figure 7-15.

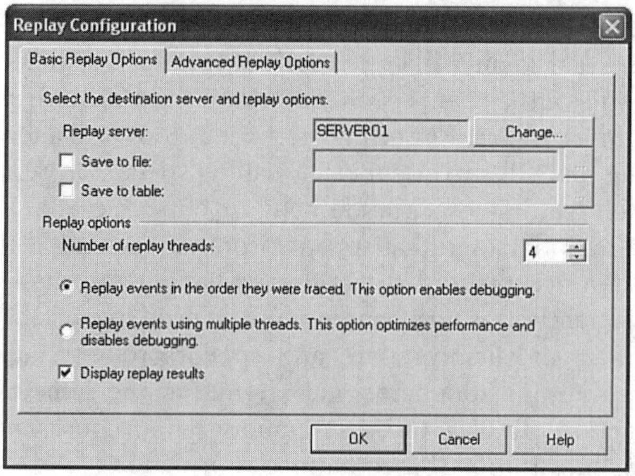

Figure 7-15 Basic replay configuration options.

Replay Execution Modes

There are two main mutually exclusive replay execution modes, indicated by radio buttons: **Replay events in the order they were traced** and **Replay events using multiple threads**. These names/descriptions can be quite confusing. Wouldn't you expect replay to preserve the order of the events? At the same time wouldn't it make sense to always use multiple threads while replaying? The fact of the matter is both of these statements are true. Let's try to introduce a better naming scheme. Call the first mode "Full Synchronization" and second mode "Connection-Level Synchronization." When replay occurs in Full Synchronization mode, all events collected in the original trace are replayed sequentially. Events that were originated from different connections are still replayed on different threads, but overall order of execution is preserved unconditionally. When replay occurs in Connection Level Synchronization mode, the order of events within each connection remains the same, but different connections are not assumed to be dependent on each other. Figure 7-16 shows the relative sequence of execution of events replayed in Full Synchronization mode.

As you can see from the picture, two events each are collected on connections A, B, and C. The order of replay follows exactly the relative order along the timeline.

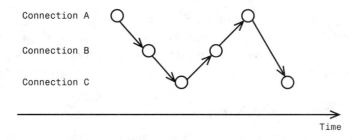

Figure 7-16   Full Synchronization replay mode.

TIPS AND TRICKS

Even during Full Synchronization Replay mode, the replay engine uses multiple threads. This makes it possible to properly replay simple blocking scenarios where the order of submission for each event is different than the actual order of execution. In reality, only a few replay threads are active at the same time because of frequent synchronizations, so setting the thread pool number too high will not help replay, and in fact it will run slower because of the unnecessary overhead of context switching.

Figure 7-17 shows the relative sequence of execution of events replayed in Connection Synchronization mode.

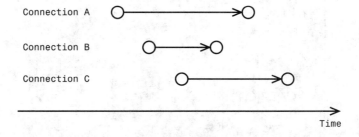

Figure 7-17   Connection-level synchronization replay mode.

As you can see from the picture, only relative order of events within each individual connection is preserved. Connections are assumed to be independent of each other. This mode of operation provides the highest replay throughput and server stressing. However, the exact results of replay are going to be non-deterministic if there is any correlation between clients, because absolute order of events is not guaranteed and can vary between different replay sessions. It should be obvious from the diagram why Connection Level Synchronization replay does not allow setting replay breakpoints for debugging. Because global serialization is not used, it's impossible to halt all replay threads at any point in time deterministically because they run independently of each other.

Additional Basic Replay Options

During replay, the original trace window is going to be split into two. The bottom half represents the replay output. It is possible to save replay output data to either a file or a table for further analysis.

Another useful basic replay option is the capability to hide replay results. When verifying correctness of replay, it's not necessary to look at individual resultsets for each individual query. Any actual replay error is going to be reflected in the "Replay Statistics" event generated at the end of the replay session.

Advanced Replay Options

Switching to the **Advanced Replay Options** tab before beginning a replay will launch the dialog shown in Figure 7-18.

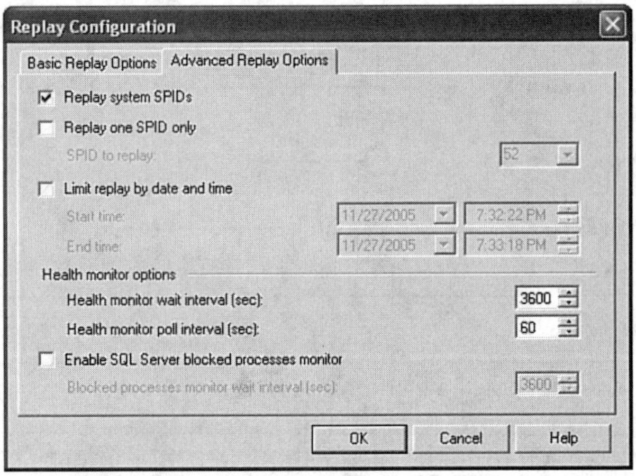

Figure 7-18   Advanced Replay Options.

This option enables you to replay SPIDs (unique client connections) that are considered internal system processes or filter them out. The option also enables you to replay a single SPID within a certain time range. The most useful advanced replay options are related to health monitoring.

The replay engine has an internal health monitor thread that periodically checks for the status of each outstanding request. If the request has been outstanding longer than the predefined maximum allowed interval, the statement is cancelled and the thread moves on to the next event. The health monitor also allows the replay engine to periodically check and terminate requests that are blocked by other requests.

Replay Objects API

Similar to the Trace Objects API, you can completely control Replay programmatically via managed code.

Replay objects contain two classes: the TraceReplay class, which implements all replay functionality, and the TraceReplayOptions helper class, which helps configure the TraceReplay object.

TraceReplay class exposes the following methods, properties, and events.

- **Methods**
  - `Start()`—Starts replay.
  - `Pause()`—Pauses replay.
  - `Stop()`—Stops replay.
- **Properties**
  - `Source`—A mandatory TraceReader object that contains the trace to be replayed.
  - `OutputFile`—An optional file to which the output will be streamed.
  - `OutputTable`—An optional table to which the output will be streamed.
  - `Connection`—Mandatory Connection information objects. TraceReplay replays the trace against the server that is specified in this connection object.
  - `Options`—Configuration options.
- **Events**
  - `OnReplayStart`—A handler is invoked on Replay Start.
  - `OnReplayPause`—A handler is invoked on Replay Pause.

- `OnReplayStop`—A handler is invoked on Replay Stop.
- `OnReplayEvent`—A handler is invoked before replaying an event.
- `OnReplayResultEvent`—A handler is invoked on every result of replayable event.

`TraceReplayOptions` provides the following configuration options:

- `NumberOfReplayThreads`—The number of threads Replay uses.
- `HealthMonitorPollInterval`—How often the health monitor wakes up and examines stale threads.
- `HealthMonitorWaitInterval`—The stale thread maximum time to live.
- `Mode`—The mode of replay (either Full Synchronization or Connection Level Synchronization).
- `KeepResults`—Specifies whether to keep the replay results.

Let's look at sample usage of the Replay Objects API.

Scenario – Replay Trace File

The first thing to do is instantiate a new `TraceReplay` object and initialize a replay source file:

```
TraceReplay replay = new TraceReplay();
TraceFile source = new TraceFile();
source.InitializeAsReader("InputTraceFile.trc");
replay.Source = source;
```

Next, create a replay connection:

```
SqlConnectionInfo connection = new SqlConnectionInfo();
connection.ServerName = "localhost";
connection.UseIntegratedSecurity = true;
replay.Connection = connection;
```

Then sign up for event notification when an event is about to be submitted for replay:

```
replay.OnReplayEvent += new
➥TraceReplay.OnReplayEventHandler(OnReplayEvent);
```

As part of the callback mechanism, you can examine and change the details of any event before it gets replayed or skip the event all together.

```
public static void OnReplayEvent( int recordNumber,
➡ITraceObjectsTraceEvent currentEvent, out bool skipRecord )
{
   skipRecord = false;

   currentEvent.SetValue(1, "new text data to be replayed", true);
}
```

Finally, it's time to start the replay.

```
replay.Start();
```

TIPS AND TRICKS
The Start method does not return until Replay is finished. To stop the replay you need to call the `Stop` method on a separate thread.

Database Tuning Advisor

Database Engine Tuning Advisor (DTA) is a brand new tool that replaced the previously shipped Index Tuning Wizard (ITW). However, this is not just a name change. DTA is a full-blown application that has many powerful features never available in the old tool.

Let's try to start a simple tuning session to better understand DTA's capabilities. You can launch the tool from the **Start** menu. DTA is located under the **Microsoft SQL Server 2005\Performance Tools** folder.

TIPS AND TRICKS
Using the **Start** menu is not the only way to launch DTA. The tool can be launched from within SQL Server Management Studio Query Editor window by following the **Analyze Query in Database Engine Tuning Advisor** menu selection. In this case DTA will be launched with pre-populated workload information, connection, and database context. If a portion of the text was selected in Query Editor window, it will become the default query to be analyzed instead of the entire script.

TIPS AND TRICKS

Upon initial installation of SQL Server 2005, you need to run the tool first by connecting to Database Engine as a member of the sysadmin fixed server role. During the initial connection, DTA goes through an initialization process by creating special objects on the SQL Server Database Engine instance. After the first run, the application repository database is fully initialized, and from that point forward any user who is a member of the db_owner fixed database role can use DTA to tune tables on databases on his or her own.

Immediately after launching the tool you are presented with a connection dialog. After you establish a Database Engine connection you come to a new session creation screen, shown in Figure 7-19.

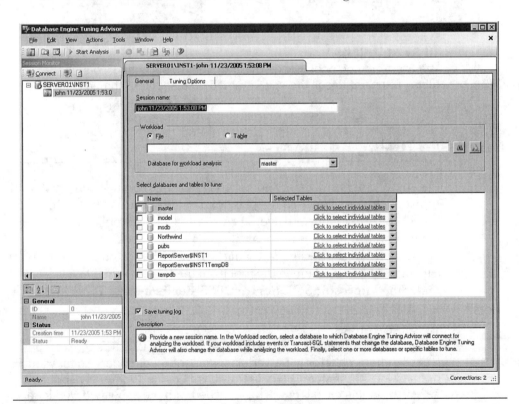

Figure 7-19 Database Tuning Advisor—new session creation.

The first thing to note is the **Session Monitor** window in the left pane. Every session configuration, including tuning results, is stored inside the MSDB database of the SQL Server Database Engine Instance; therefore, it can be retrieved later at any point. In fact, along with performing tuning in real time—that is, while the user is watching the screen—DTA supports disconnected tuning mode, where the graphical tool is fully closed but tuning continues behind the scene until finished. The user can always connect back to the server to monitor tuning progress. Thus, the purpose of Session Monitor is to present a list of all tuning sessions currently stored on the server. The default session name is fairly descriptive and comprises the current SQL Server Login name and timestamp when the session was first created.

The next thing to note is the database and table selection grid. DTA makes it possible to do narrow tuning to a specific set of databases and even tables within those databases. There is also a concept of a default database ("Database for workload analysis") to be used for workload analysis when the query itself does not specify the "use database" clause and does not contain fully-qualified object names.

Before you go any further, it is critical to supply either a workload file or a workload table to the tuning engine. DTA accepts three types of workload files: trace files that can be opened by SQL Profiler, T-SQL query scripts, and XML files. Using XML files as a workload input is discussed later in this chapter, during the description of the DTA internal architecture.

TIPS AND TRICKS

When DTA consumes a trace table or file that contains the "LoginName" column as a workload, it impersonates the user specified by that column during tuning. If this user does not have sufficient permissions to execute and produce Showplans for the statements contained in the trace, DTA cannot tune to those statements. To resolve this you can either grant Showplan permission to each affected user or remove the "LoginName" column from those events that are not tuned.

DTA Tuning Options

Switch to the **Tuning Options** tab to examine the DTA tuning options shown in Figure 7-20.

The first thing to note is a time limit on how long tuning should proceed. DTA runs for a predetermined amount of time and gives the best set of recommendations it's able to come up with under the constraints. This enables you to schedule tuning in the time window allocated for database maintenance without affecting other clients.

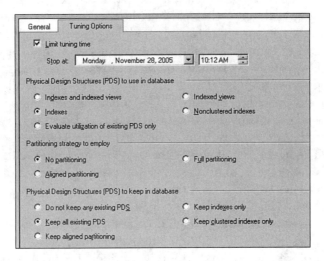

Figure 7-20   Database Tuning Advisor session tuning options.

A list of different tuning options and their meanings is presented in the Table 7-1.

Table 7-1   Tuning Options

Option	Meaning
Indexes and indexed views	Include recommendations for adding clustered/nonclustered indexes and indexed views.
Indexed views	Include only recommendations for adding indexed views.
Indexes	Include only recommendations for adding clustered and nonclustered indexes.
Nonclustered indexes	Include only recommendations for nonclustered indexes.
Evaluate utilization of existing PDS only	Evaluate the effectiveness of the current indexes, but do not recommend additional indexes or indexed views.

Table 7-1   Tuning Options

Option	Meaning
No partitioning	Do not recommend partitioning.
Full partitioning	Include recommendations for partitioning.
Aligned partitioning	New recommended partitions will be aligned to make partitions easy to maintain.
Do not keep any existing PDS	Recommend dropping unnecessary existing indexes, views, and partitioning for a given workload.
Keep indexes only	Keep all existing indexes but recommend dropping unnecessary indexed views, and partitioning.
Keep all existing PDS	Keep all existing indexes, indexed views, and partitioning.
Keep clustered indexes only	Keep all existing clustered indexes but recommend dropping unnecessary indexed views, partitions, and nonclustered indexes.
Keep aligned partitioning	Keep partitioning structures that are currently aligned, but recommend dropping unnecessary indexed views, indexes, and non-aligned partitioning. Any additional partitioning recommended will align with the current partitioning scheme.

Advanced tuning options are shown in Figure 7-21.

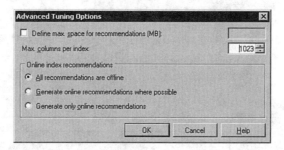

Figure 7-21   DTA advanced tuning options.

Here you have an opportunity to limit the maximum space consumed by recommended physical data structures and the maximum number of columns per index, covering included columns as well.

This enables users to impose online recommendation constraints on the tuning engine.

Assuming you are happy with all selected tuning options, you can start analysis from the toolbar or by selecting the **Actions**, **Start Analysis** menu item.

The first phase of the tuning process as indicated by the progress report is called "Submitting Configuration Information." During this phase, all tuning options become part of the newly generated configuration XML that gets entered into the MSDB database through a special configuration stored procedure. After the tuning session is fully configured, the tuning engine gets invoked. While running, the tuning engine starts consuming a workload file or table data, at the same time performing incremental tuning analysis. Finally, reports and recommendations are generated and ready for examination.

At this point, the user can selectively apply recommendations right away, schedule applying recommendations later, or save the recommendations script for future use. All these options are available from the **Actions** menu. Before applying recommendations you can selectively choose which ones you would like to apply by using check boxes, as shown in Figure 7-22.

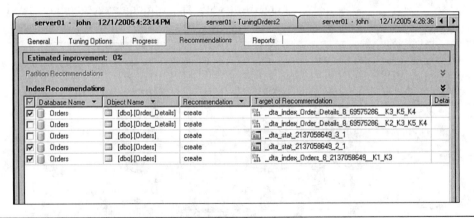

Figure 7-22 DTA recommendations.

You can even evaluate the impact of applying a partial set of recommendations via a feature called "Evaluative Tuning" described later in this chapter.

DTA Architecture

The DTA Architecture is described in Figure 7-23.

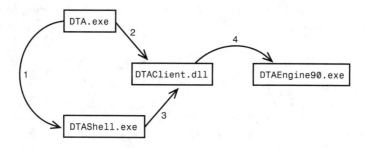

Figure 7-23   DTA architectural diagram.

There is a command line interface to DTA called DTA.exe. It supports most of the options exposed through the user interface.

TIPS AND TRICKS

You can always get a full list of options supported by the tool by using the -?
switch as follows:

```
C:\>DTA.exe -?
```

When invoked with the –u flag, DTA.exe launches a graphical interface to DTA called DTAShell.exe (1) and passes all supplied options to it as well. If a user intends to perform tuning via the console, DTA.exe makes direct calls to the DTAClient.dll (2) shared component. DTAShell.exe also uses shared components for tuning (3). The DTAClient.dll component contains the necessary infrastructure to create a proper XML configuration file and store it in the MSDB database. When the tuning session is created, it calls the DTAEngine90.exe component that actually performs the tuning. Because the DTAEngine90.exe is running as a separate process, it is possible to close the graphical tool and continue tuning in the background.

DTA interactions between DTAClient.dll and DTAEngine90.exe always happen via reading and writing to the MSDB database, as shown in Figure 7-24.

Before first launching the DTAEngine90.exe process, the DTA-Client.dll writes session information into the database (1). After it is running, DTAEngine90.exe consumes the information straight from

MSDB (2). As tuning progresses it continues to update progress information in MSDB, eventually producing tuning recommendations (3). Tuning recommendations and reports are consumed by console or graphical tool from MSDB (4). This closes the interaction loop between DTA components.

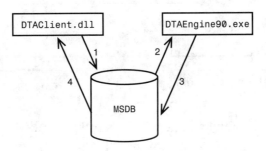

Figure 7-24   DTA component interactions via MSDB database.

TIPS AND TRICKS
All information exchanged between different DTA components is in XML. The XML input file uses the published Database Engine Tuning Advisor XML schema, which can be found at the following location in your Microsoft SQL Server 2005 installation directory:
C:\Program Files\Microsoft SQL Server\90\Tools\Binn\schemas\sqlserver\2003\03\dta\dtaschema.xsd

Evaluative Tuning

One very important action available after tuning is done is "Evaluate Recommendations." You can use this to pick and choose from a set of recommendations provided by the tool to evaluate the impact of applying a subset of those recommendations. When this menu item is selected, a new tuning session is created with essentially the same options as the old one, but a modified configuration XML section now contains the subset of selected recommendations.

TIPS AND TRICKS

You don't have to stop with working only with a subset of given recommendations. You can actually learn the format of the XML configuration file and supply your own custom recommendations to the tool for evaluation.
To see the configuration section, use the link provided at the bottom of the session screen (see Figure 7-25).

Figure 7-25 shows the session configuration XML preview dialog.

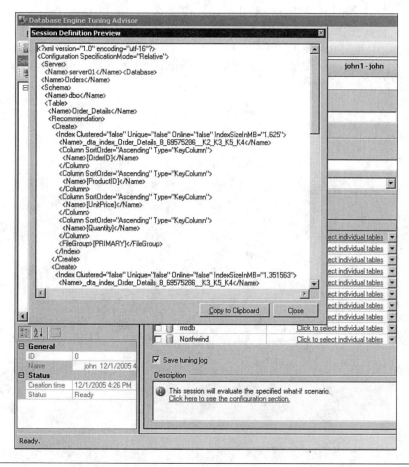

Figure 7-25   DTA configuration section of XML document.

Even though the graphical tool does not support direct editing of the configuration section of the XML, a configuration XML file can be provided as an input to the console program DTA.exe described earlier via the "-ix" option.

Summary

This chapter covered the tuning and optimization features of SQL Server Management Studio, SQL Server Profiler, and SQL Profiler Replay. It also covered tracing and replay application programming interfaces. At the end there was a detailed examination of the Database Tuning Advisor.

CHAPTER 8

Inside Scheduling Tools

In this chapter we look at SQL Server Agent as the main task scheduling tool for SQL Server. In the SQL Server 2005 release of the product, SQL Server Agent has undergone substantial changes in terms of functionality, performance, monitoring, and security. All the changes are covered in this chapter, along with a detailed description of the architecture of SQL Server Agent and advanced service configuration options.

SQL Server Task Scheduling Via SQL Server Agent

The primary SQL Server task scheduling tool is SQL Server Agent. Although SQL Server Agent runs as a separate Windows service process, users can access the SQL Server Agent service through the SQL Server Database Engine by executing T-SQL commands. The SQL Server Agent process runs on the same computer as SQL Server Database Engine, and there is a strict one-to-one correspondence between SQL Server Database Engine and SQL Server Agent. For example, if you have two instances of SQL Server Database engine running on the same computer, you have two distinct instances of SQL Server Agent running as well. This is a known limitation of the current architecture.

Supported Task Types

What kind of tasks can SQL Server Agent run? The most popular type of task is TSQL scripts. In addition to TSQL, there are several other built-in task execution environments called subsystems. These subsystems include the following functionality:

- Executing operating system commands (CmdExec)
- Running Visual Basic, Java, and Perl scripts (ActiveScripting)
- Executing SQL Server Integration Services packages (SSIS)

- Running XMLA Queries and commands against the Analysis Services engine (ANALYSISQUERY, ANALYSISCOMMAND)
- Executing specialized tasks for Replication (Snapshot, LogReader, Distribution, Merge, QueueReader).

Later in this chapter, during the coverage of proxy accounts, you will find a discussion on the security aspects of running different tasks and their run-time execution credentials. Another important aspect of these task execution environments, the per-subsystem thread pool limit, will be covered as part of the general SQL Server Agent architecture.

TIPS AND TRICKS

In previous releases of SQL Server, all subsystem information was stored in the Registry. In SQL Server 2005, you can get general information about SQL Server Agent subsystems by looking directly at the contents of the msdb.dbo.syssubsystems table, using any SQL Server Database Engine query tool, such as Query Editor or SqlCmd.

All subsystems are loaded upon SQL Server Agent service startup. However, the SSIS subsystem may be deployed or removed later (after SQL Server Agent is already running), as part of a separate installation. SQL Server Agent can handle reconfiguration of this particular subsystem dynamically and does not require a restart.

WARNING

Do not attempt to modify the contents of the msdb.dbo.syssubsystems table directly or certain tasks may not function properly. If a particular subsystem fails to load, jobs that have job steps belonging to that subsystem get marked internally as "suspended" and cannot be reset back to normal programmatically. There are two ways to fix the situation if it happens. First, jobs can be deleted and then re-created. Another option is to restart the SQL Server Agent service.

Jobs and Job Steps

SQL Server Agent tasks are called job steps. They are executed as part of a larger entity called a job. A single job can contain multiple job steps of any supported type already described. Most jobs are scheduled to run regularly via the SQL Server Agent scheduling mechanism.

TIPS AND TRICKS
In previous releases of SQL Server, the job schedule was tied directly to a specific job and could never be reused. In SQL Server 2005, a user can create a schedule and then link multiple jobs to it. However, other users cannot link to a shared job schedule for security reasons.

In addition to running on a schedule, jobs can started by direct TSQL commands through use of the sp_start_job stored procedure, they can be triggered by an alert, instructed to run during CPU idle cycles, or they can be directed to run by a master server in a MSX/TSX (master server/target server) distributed execution environment.

Conceptually, jobs, job steps, and job schedules are connected together, as shown in Figure 8-1.

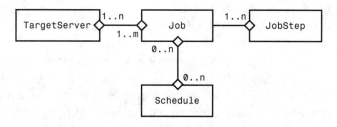

Figure 8-1   SQL Server Agent job conceptual diagram.

As you can see from the diagram, a single job can consist of multiple job steps, can execute on multiple target servers, and can be linked to multiple schedules.

Creating Jobs

The Jobs folder appears under the SQL Server Agent node in the tree view of SQL Server Management Studio (the Object Explorer). By expanding the Jobs folder, you can see a list of all jobs currently configured on your server as shown in Figure 8-2.

Suppose you want to create a job that automatically rebuilds an index on one of your tables every night. We will walk through this scenario step by step to demonstrate the process of creating a simple job through the graphical user interface. Later we examine the stored procedure calls that the graphical tool calls behind the scenes to run SQL Server Agent.

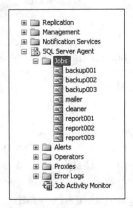

Figure 8-2   Object Explorer view of the Jobs folder.

Right-click the Jobs folder to bring up the **New Job** option. Select **New Job**, and you will see the dialog for creating new jobs. On the General page (see Figure 8-3) fill in the job name and a brief description of the job functionality. Although providing the job description is optional, a good set of comments will help others understand your intentions later on and cut down on other users contacting you unnecessarily. By default, the **Owner** field will show all currently logged on users. As the system administrator, you can access more options by clicking the Browse button (...) on the right. Leave the default value for job category since it is used only to group different jobs for display purposes, but does not effect how a job is executed. After filling in job information, click on **Steps** in the **Select a page** tree view on the left to create at least one job step for the job.

Creating Job Steps

After selecting Steps you will see the **New Job Step** dialog (see Figure 8-4). Start creating job steps by giving the first step a name. The job step name should be descriptive to help you distinguish between other steps defined as part of the job. Next, choose Transact-SQL script (T-SQL) as the job step subsystem type. This determines how your job step command is executed by SQL Server Agent. Leave the **Run as** field blank for now. This field is discussed later as part of the proxy accounts topic. Make sure you select the correct database in which your step is to execute, or the step will fail unless all objects used in your script contain the full name resolution path. Notice how GO is used as a batch separator to split different parts of the script. SQL Server Agent respects this batch separator and issues a separate query against SQL Server Database Engine for each batch. Keep in mind that the job step creation dialog does not perform any token colorization the way Query Editor does. It is a known limitation of the tool, so if you are developing any advanced scripts you may want to use Query Editor first and then cut and paste your query into this dialog after you are finished.

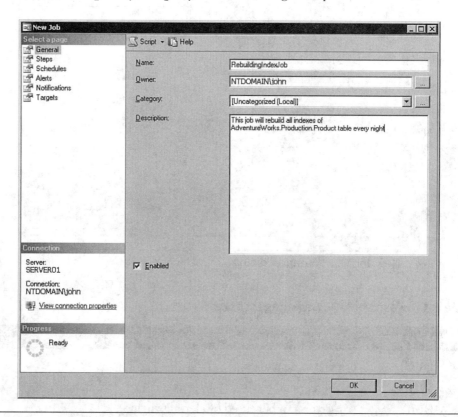

Figure 8-3   New Job creation dialog—general page.

Another thing worth mentioning is the use of a well-known job step token: $(DATE). At runtime, SQL Server Agent dynamically evaluates and substitutes a real value for the token. For a list of recognized SQL Server Agent tokens see Table 8-1.

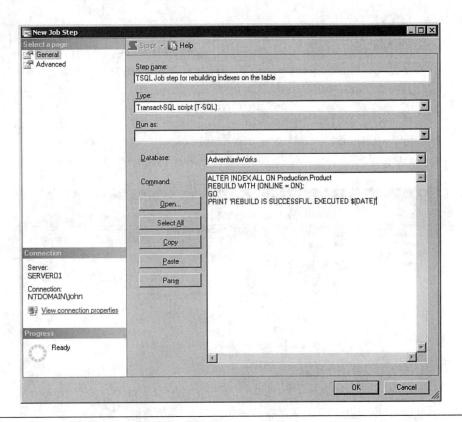

Figure 8-4   New Job Step creation dialog.

Table 8-1   Reserved SQL Server Agent Tokens

Token	Description
$(A-DBN)	Database name.
$(A-SVR)	Server name.
$(A-ERR)	Error number (used by alerting engine).
$(A-SEV)	Error severity (used by alerting engine).
$(A-MSG)	Message text (used by alerting engine).
$(DATE)	Current date (in YYYYMMDD format).
$(INST)	Instance name. For a default instance, this token is empty.
$(JOBID)	Job ID.
$(MACH)	Computer name.

Token	Description
$(MSSA)	Master SQLServerAgent service name.
$(OSCMD)	Prefix for the program used to run CmdExec job steps.
$(SQLDIR)	The directory in which SQL Server is installed. By default, this value is C:\Program Files\Microsoft SQL Server\MSSQL.
$(STEPCT)	A count of the number of times this step has executed (excluding retries). Can be used by the step command to force termination of a multistep loop.
$(STEPID)	Step ID.
$(SRVR)	Name of the computer running SQL Server. If the SQL Server instance is a named instance, this includes the instance name.
$(TIME)	Current time (in HHMMSS format).
$(STRTTM)	The time (in HHMMSS format) at which the job began executing.
$(STRTDT)	The date (in YYYYMMDD format) on which the job began executing.
$(WMI(property))	Value of specified WMI property retrieved by alerting engine.

TIPS AND TRICKS

The token pattern syntax changed in SQL Server 2005. Previously, tokens had square brackets rather than dollar signs and parentheses. This change is handled dynamically as part of a SQL Server Database Engine upgrade through the MSDB schema update. You should be careful, however, to always use new syntax for new job step definitions.

There were several reasons for this change. First, because it is valid T-SQL to use square brackets to delimit identifier name, SQL Server Agent would have an internal conflict trying to resolve a token that had the same name as the real object name in the script. Second, SQL Server Agent started using the unified Batch Parser component widely adopted across the entire tools suite (SqlCmd, QueryEditor, SMO). This meant syntax needed to be consistent as well.

At this point the necessary job step details have been defined for this scenario. It's time to add a schedule for running this job. You do so by clicking Schedule in the tree view on the left.

Creating Job Schedules

Although it would have been possible to use another shared schedule already defined on the system, assume there is not an appropriate schedule, so that it's necessary to create a new schedule. Follow the user interface as shown in Figure 8-5 to create this schedule.

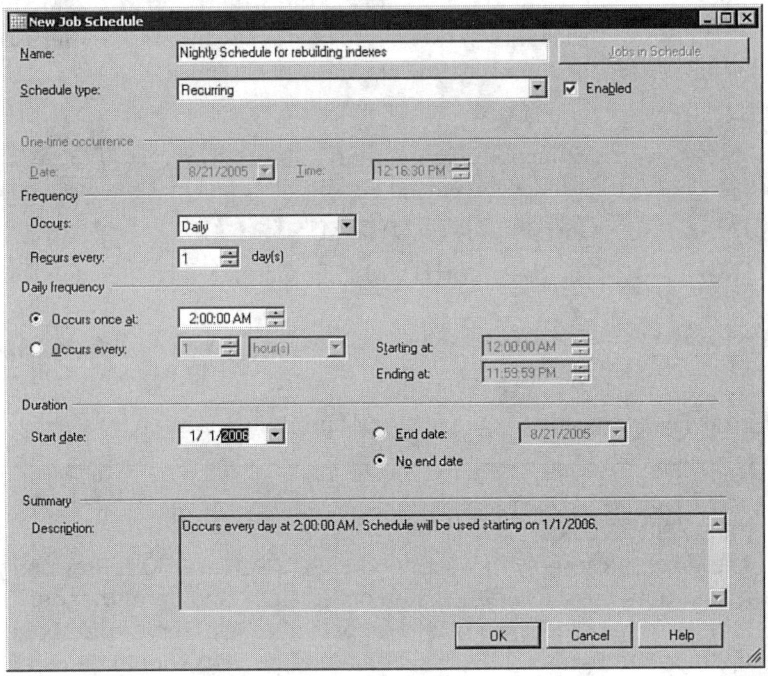

Figure 8-5 New Job Schedule creation dialog.

This schedule should be recurring, executing daily at 2:00 AM. Now it's necessary to decide whether it will execute forever or have some finite end date.

With schedule creation over, it's time to finish the job creation process. Before that, you might want to ask SQL Server Management Studio to script the entire job creation process to a new Query Editor window by selecting the Script menu option. The following is the approximate script that gets created and split into logical pieces.

The first stored procedure call creates a SQL Server Agent job object and obtains a job identifier to report to the caller.

```
DECLARE @jobId BINARY(16)
EXEC  msdb.dbo.sp_add_job @job_name=N'RebuildingIndexJob',
            @enabled=1,
            @notify_level_eventlog=0,
            @notify_level_email=2,
            @notify_level_netsend=2,
            @notify_level_page=2,
            @delete_level=0,
            @description=N'This job will rebuild all
➥indexes of AdventureWorks.Production.Product table',
            @category_name=N'[Uncategorized (Local)]',
            @owner_login_name=N'REDMOND\dimason',
            @job_id = @jobId OUTPUT
select @jobId
```

Then the job gets associated with the job server that is going to run it.

```
EXEC msdb.dbo.sp_add_jobserver @job_name=
➥N'RebuildingIndexJob', @server_name = N'KOMODO_P6'
```

The next thing is to add a job step to the job providing all necessary execution details.

```
EXEC msdb.dbo.sp_add_jobstep @job_name=
➥N'RebuildingIndexJob',
            @step_name=N'TSQL Job step for rebuilding
➥indexes on the table',
            @step_id=1,
            @cmdexec_success_code=0,
            @on_success_action=1,
            @on_fail_action=2,
            @retry_attempts=0,
            @retry_interval=0,
            @os_run_priority=0, @subsystem=N'TSQL',
            @command=N'ALTER INDEX ALL ON Production.Product
➥REBUILD WITH (ONLINE = ON);
GO
PRINT ''REBUILD IS SUCCESSFUL. EXECUTED $(DATE)''',
            @database_name=N'AdventureWorks',
            @flags=0
```

The next stored procedure call is somewhat redundant and only serves the purpose of identifying the step number from which to start execution.

```
EXEC msdb.dbo.sp_update_job @job_name=
➥N'RebuildingIndexJob',
            @enabled=1,
            @start_step_id=1,
            @notify_level_eventlog=0,
            @notify_level_email=2,
            @notify_level_netsend=2,
            @notify_level_page=2,
            @delete_level=0,
            @description=N'This job will rebuild all indexes
➥of AdventureWorks.Production.Product table every night',
            @category_name=N'[Uncategorized (Local)]',
            @owner_login_name=N'REDMOND\dimason',
            @notify_email_operator_name=N'',
            @notify_netsend_operator_name=N'',
            @notify_page_operator_name=N''
```

Finally, the job schedule gets created. Even though we called a legacy-style stored procedure, sp_add_jobschedule, rather than explicitly created a schedule through sp_add_schedule, the schedule still gets created behind the scenes and can be reused later.

```
DECLARE @schedule_id int
EXEC msdb.dbo.sp_add_jobschedule @job_name=
➥N'RebuildingIndexJob',
            @name=N'Nightly Schedule for
➥rebuilding indexes',
            @enabled=1,
            @freq_type=4,
            @freq_interval=1,
            @freq_subday_type=1,
            @freq_subday_interval=0,
            @freq_relative_interval=0,
            @freq_recurrence_factor=1,
            @active_start_date=20060101,
            @active_end_date=99991231,
            @active_start_time=20000,
            @active_end_time=235959,
            @schedule_id = @schedule_id OUTPUT
select @schedule_id
```

Almost any operation with SQL Server Agent metadata can be translated the same way into a series of simple stored procedure calls.

The scenario job just created is not very resource consuming, so it is safe to run it at least once in real time to make sure it executes successfully. You can run the job from the Object Explorer tree by right-clicking the newly created job and selecting Start job.

Monitoring Job Execution

Frequently you might want to know what's going on with your job at any given time. This section is going to concentrate on monitoring individual SQL Server Agent jobs and global performance counters for the entire service.

Looking at the Job History

After the Job Status dialog shows successful completion of the job, you can drill further into the job's history from the Object Explorer through selecting **View History** and bringing up the job step details (see Figure 8-6).

Notice how the step execution statistics appear in the bottom pane of the dialog, followed by the printed messages.

Job Activity Monitor

The Job Activity Monitor is a powerful feature of SQL Server Management Studio that enables you to monitor the status of jobs defined on this system. You can view the Job Activity Monitor by double-clicking the last item in the Jobs folder of Object Explorer (see Figure 8-7).

Using the Job Activity Monitor, you can filter out jobs in your view by applying a dynamic filter. You can also set a refresh rate for your view so job information can be updated at a regular interval.

TIPS AND TRICKS

Job Activity Monitor uses the extended stored procedure xp_sqlagent_enum_jobs to bring job information into view. This retrieval mechanism has an inherent delay because the request must first reach SQL Server Agent and then fetch data from its internal memory structures and send this data back to SQL Server Database Engine as a resultset. If multiple requests are issued at the same time, they will be queued through synchronization mechanisms inside SQL Server Agent. A second issue with this approach is the volatility of this information; it is available only while

SQL Server Agent is running. An immediate and more robust way to get job activity is to use the msdb.dbo.sysjobactivity table. SQL Server Agent uses this table to log success or failure of each job step immediately on execution. Moreover, when the SQL Server Agent service is restarted, a new session is created in the table, preserving old data. This can be especially useful if you are trying to recover after an unexpected failure or on a cluster failover. Because this table contains specific information about which job steps were in progress before a failure occurred, the administrator can decide which steps need to be re-run to assure full recovery of the system. SQL Server Agent itself cannot make this determination, but it can provide sufficient information for the user to take appropriate actions.

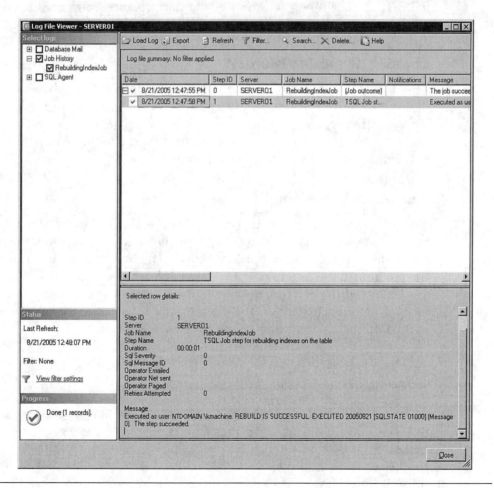

Figure 8-6 Job history dialog.

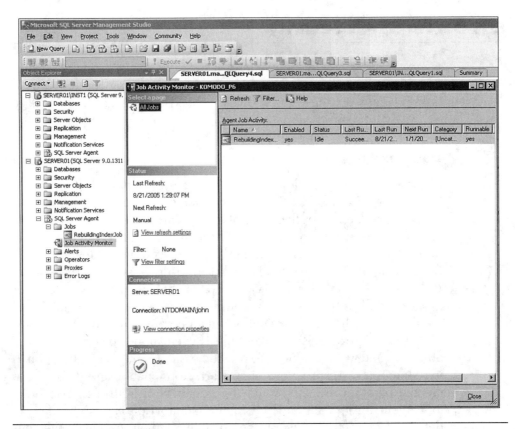

Figure 8-7   SQL Server Agent Job Activity Monitor.

SQL Server Agent Performance Monitor Counters

Another great way to look at the overall health of SQL Server Agent and monitor potential problems is through the Windows Performance Monitor. In SQL Server 2005, SQL Server Agent has several performance objects: SQLAgent:Alerts, SQLAgent:Jobs, SQLAgent:JobSteps, and SQLAgent:Statistics. Some of the most useful performance counters include Active jobs, Failed jobs, Queued jobs, and Activated alerts. You should look at the first three to make sure the job execution engine is functioning properly and the last counter to spot trouble areas.

SQL Server Agent Security

How can a user create and run tasks using SQL Server Agent? How can I let him or her use a set of credentials for performing certain types of tasks? To answer these questions you need to look at the new SQL Server Agent security model.

Database Roles

SQL Server Agent is no longer accessible to every authenticated user, as in previous releases of SQL Server. User access and rights for SQL Server Agent are controlled through one of three major security-related database roles in MSDB. The most basic role is **SQLAgentUserRole**. Members of this role can create SQL Server Agent jobs. Most users will be associated with this role. The next level up is **SQLAgentReader-Role**. Members of this role can read job details and job history for jobs created by other users. Therefore, these users can perform simple monitoring of the Agent execution environment. The next level up is **SQLAgentOperatorRole**. This role is even more powerful than the other two and was introduced to provide basic administrative functionality. Members of this role can view, start, stop, enable, and disable jobs created by other users. None of the members of SQLAgentUserRole, SQLAgentReaderRole, and SQLAgentOperatorRole can modify any job details. If they could, it would be possible for them to inject malicious contents into a job step and therefore cause elevation of privileges during job execution. That is why this is not allowed by the system.

WARNING
In an ideal world, members of SQLAgentReaderRole and SQLAgentOperator-Role would be restricted to viewing and acting upon only those jobs that run in the databases to **which** they have access. Unfortunately, the SQL Server Agent security model does not allow this finer-granularity filtering. Therefore, when you make a user a member of these roles you must realize the implied security consequences to avoid unintentional information disclosure.

Proxy Accounts

Why does SQL Server Agent need proxy accounts? Every job step executes under a specific set of credentials that defines its execution context. It would be wrong for SQL Server Agent to let an average user run his job under the credentials of the SQL Server Agent service account. If this happened, the user could execute dangerous operating system commands, and see and modify SQL Server data not normally accessible. SQL Server Agent has no access to the job owner's password, so it cannot impersonate a job owner directly. Therefore SQL Server Agent needs to rely on a known set of credentials and a mapping that instructs SQL Server Agent to use these credentials on behalf of the user for a given subsystem task. This logical mapping is provided through a proxy account, that is, an account to be used as a proxy for the user. Most subsystems, except T-SQL, use proxy accounts.

The T-SQL subsystem does not need a proxy account because it uses a different impersonation mechanism provided directly by SQL Server Database Engine. Upon each connection and before executing a T-SQL subsystem task, SQL Server Agent runs the `EXECUTE AS LOGIN = N '<login_name>' WITH NO REVERT` command, providing the job owner's login as a parameter. SQL Server Database Engine switches execution context of the current session to this login and does not allow reverting back to the account that initiated the connection.

Figure 8-8 shows a logical diagram that should help you understand the mapping that the proxy account provides.

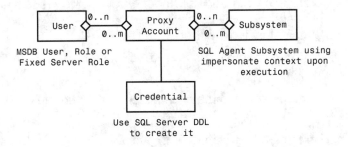

Figure 8-8   Proxy account logical diagram.

By itself, the proxy account object does not store usernames and passwords. The account needs to be mapped to a specific credential object that contains the username and password. The proxy account also needs to be associated with a subsystem that is going to use impersonated context for task execution. Finally, a proxy account needs to be tied to a user, allowing the user to create tasks belonging to a subsystem to be run under the aforementioned set of credentials. The term "user" can be viewed in a rather broad sense. Access to the proxy account can be granted to a valid MSDB user, MSDB role, or a fixed SQL Server role. Please note that to use SQL Server Agent in SQL Server 2005, a the non-administrative login has to have a valid user in the MSDB database and be part of one of the special SQL Server Agent roles (SQLAgentUserRole, SQLAgentReaderRole, or SQLAgentOperatorRole) anyway.

Using Proxy Accounts to Restrict Access

In comparison to earlier releases of SQL Server, SQL Server 2005 allows for much finer granularity when it comes to proxy accounts. There used to be a single proxy sccount shared by all SQL Server Agent subsystems and bythe xp_cmdshell extended stored procedure. In SQL Server 2005, xp_cmdshell runs under its own unique credential, which is no longer tied to SQL Server Agent, and the SQL Server Agent administrator can define multiple proxy accounts and tie them to multiple subsystems. Thus, the SysAdminOnly Registry flag and corresponding @sysadmin_only configuration parameter no longer work against SQL Server 2005 and are kept only for backward compatibility reasons.

In practical applications, sometimes, it makes sense to define multiple SQL Server Agent proxy accounts and link them to the same credential object to restrict different users to specific subsystems.

Some examples might include the following:

- User A needs to be able to create ActiveScripting tasks and run them under Account X.

- User B needs to be able to create CmdExec tasks and run them under Account X.

- User C needs to be able to create both ActiveScripting and CmdExec tasks and run them under account X.

- User D needs to be able to create both ActiveScripting and CmdExec tasks and run them under account Y.

An administrator can satisfy these requirements by performing the following actions:

1. Create proxy account "X Active Scripting" and associate it with User A and User C.

2. Create proxy account "X CmdExec" and associate it with User B and User C.

3. Create proxy account "Y Active Scripting and CmdExec" and associate it with User D.

Setting up the multiple SQL Server Agent proxy accounts in this fashion creates the fine-grained control required.

When a proxy account is first created, SQL Server Agent verifies that it is linked to a valid set of credentials. Upon each job step execution, SQL Server Agent makes sure the user is still granted access to the proxy account and fails the job if the user does not have access. Underlying credential objects can be manipulated while jobs are running, (such as when updating passwords and changing the security context of the object). One thing to keep in mind is that all jobs linked to the proxy account associated with this credential object will be affected.

Setting Up a Proxy Account

Now that you understand the theory behind proxy accounts, let's go through the process of creating one. Suppose you need to have a special account for running a CmdExec task whose purpose is to run queries against Analysis Server and generate textual reports.

Under the Proxies folder in Object Explorer, there are multiple subfolders that contain proxies associated with different SQL Server Agent subsystems. There is also a special folder at the end that contains unassigned proxies. Right-clicking on the Proxies folder and selecting **New Proxy** opens the New Proxy Account dialog.

TIPS AND TRICKS

Make sure you created an appropriate Credential object before attempting to create a proxy account. The Credentials folder is located under the Security folder in Object Explorer. The main requirement for a Credentials object to be used later for proxy account association is to have a valid Windows account identity and password. For most tasks that do not establish connections to other computers across the network, it may be sufficient to create a local computer account instead of a domain account. In this scenario, job steps using such an account run faster because account authentication can occur locally without contacting a domain controller.

For a new proxy account you need to fill in the proxy account name, a valid previously created credential object name, and subsystem associations (see Figure 8-9).

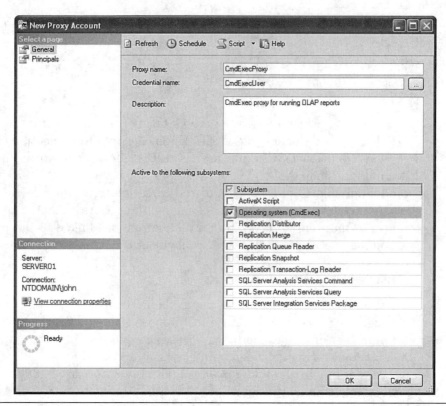

Figure 8-9   Creating a new proxy account.

If you already know which users will be using this proxy account, you can add them at this stage as well by clicking on Principals in the left tree view (See Figure 8-10).

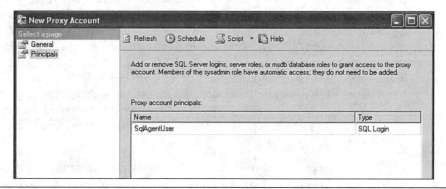

Figure 8-10   Proxy account principal associations.

Now that the proxy account is ready, you can create the job running the CmdExec task (see Figure 8-11). One additional caveat here is the need to preserve full job step output because this is how a report actually gets generated. By default, only the first 1024 characters of any job step output are persisted in the database, and even then most of this space is consumed by statistical information about runtime, execution credentials, and so on.

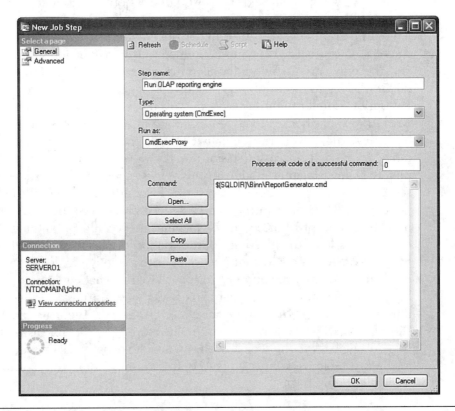

Figure 8-11 CmdExec task creation.

Following normal job creation procedure, we will concentrate more on CmdExec job step creation. One thing to notice here is the proxy account selection under the **Run as** option. The drop-down list will be populated with all available proxies associated with the current subsystem to which the user has access.

Click on the Advanced item in the left tree view to get to the job step logging options.

Job Step Logging

The SQL Server Agent reporting engine prints output to the console. Therefore it needs to be persisted. First let's cover available options for output persistence.

SQL Server Agent enables the user to optionally log job step output beyond what gets recorded into msdb.dbo.sysjobhistory table. If users are members of the sysadmin fixed server role, they can choose to log to a file. File logging is performed under the credentials of the SQL Server Agent service account. The most common way of logging job step output and the only way for non-administrator users (starting in SQL Server 2005) is to log to the msdb.dbo.sysjobstepslogs table. Logging to a table has options similar to those of logging to a file, such as append and overwrite. If a user chooses to append the output, a new row is created for each new run. Overwrite actually replaces the previous entry to the table. It was not an easy decision for the development team to completely change logging models in this release, potentially breaking the setups of existing customers. However, logging to a file could not be done securely without introducing a special proxy account. If all users used the same proxy account for logging, they could potentially read each other's logs, thus leading to information disclosure. Alternatively, SQL Server Agent could continue to log with a highly privileged service account but restrict the output to a special folder. That could potentially have the same affect. The final choice was made in favor of a correct long-term strategy. Indeed, because all SQL Server Agent metadata is stored in MSDB tables it seems natural to store logs to a table as well.

Getting back to the scenario, all you need to do is check the option of logging to table as well as the sub-option of appending the output, as shown in Figure 8-12.

SQL Server Agent Multi-Server Administration

In many enterprise installations there is a need to run jobs on multiple machines at the same time while controlling all executions from one central location. SQL Server Agent supports this scenario by allowing multi-server administration.

Master Server–Target Server Distributed Job Execution Environment is also referred to as MSX/TSX. Here's how it works in principal. First, the administrator of the Target Server (TSX) needs to enlist in the

Master Server (MSX). Enlistment has to be initiated from the TSX side because of security implications. Basically, TSX implicitly vouches to download and execute any job assigned to it by MSX. This means that the MSX server has full control over which jobs get executed on the TSX side. In the process of enlistment, a special account called the MSX Account gets created on the MSX server side and added to a special MSDB role called TargetServersRole.

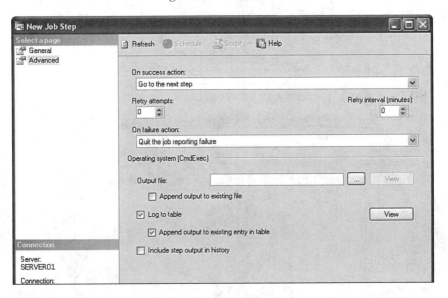

Figure 8-12   Job step advanced options.

SQL Server Management Studio makes the creation of a distributed environment very easy by wrapping it inside the Master Server Wizard.

Right-clicking on the SQL Server Agent node inside Object Explorer launches the menu shown in Figure 8-13. Choosing **Make this a Master** brings up the Master Server Wizard. The first step in the wizard is creation of a master server operator that will receive notifications for all distributed jobs associated with the current master server. The next step is to select target servers to be controlled by this master server, as shown in Figure 8-14. Keep in mind that even though the Wizard is run on the client side, it has to be able to connect to both servers as a member of the sysadmin fixed server role to execute this operation successfully.

After the administrator selects which target servers should be enlisted into the master, the Wizard provides the option of creating an MSX login account (see Figure 8-15).

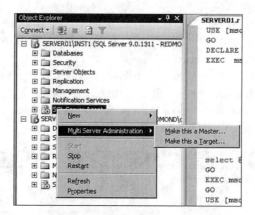

Figure 8-13   Multi-Server Administration option.

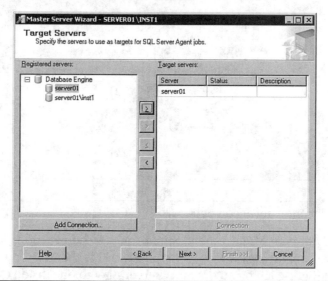

Figure 8-14   Master Server Wizard—Create enlistments.

After you have created a master server you can later dynamically add or remove target servers to and from it. If you navigate from the TSX server side, the process is made even simpler if you use the Target Server Wizard, and involves a single step of picking a master server.

After enlistment, SQL Server Agent of the target server makes periodic connections to the master server, using MSX account credentials, and looks at the contents of the msdb.dbo.sysdownloadlist table. If there is a new or changed job posted for download, it is transferred over and entered into the system on the TSX side.

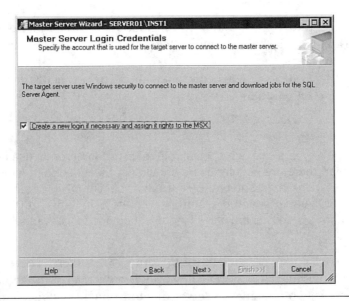

Figure 8-15   Master Server Wizard—Create an MSX account.

How do you assign a job to the target server? You can do so as part of the job creation process by following the "Targets" item in the tree view on the left, as shown in Figure 8-16.

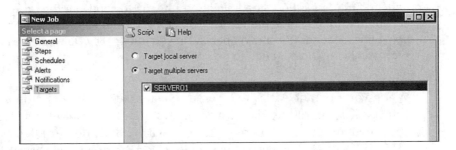

Figure 8-16   Assigning a job to the target server.

Now, under the Jobs folder in Object Explorer, two subfolders have been created: Local Jobs and Multi-Server Jobs. Keep in mind that downloaded jobs cannot be modified on the TSX side; otherwise, master and target server configurations would get out of synch with each other.

Jobs get executed as scheduled, and their execution history gets transferred back to the master server and entered into msdb.dbo.sysjobservers table. Note this is different from all local jobs whose entries are stored in msdb.dbo.sysjobhistory table. The history contains only basic job status information.

The entire process continues until TSX explicitly defects from the MSX configuration.

WARNING

TargetServersRole is a special role reserved for internal use by SQL Server Agent; therefore, regular users should not be added to it. Although members of the TargetServersRole have very similar privileges to members of the SQLAgentReaderRole, starting with the SQL Server 2005 release they cannot see local jobs, only the jobs scheduled for distributed execution.

One MSX server can control multiple TSX servers. There is no explicit limit defined in the system; however, for practical purposes and to reduce extra load on the master server due to frequent polling connections, it is recommended to keep the number of TSX servers under 100.

TIPS AND TRICKS

If the MSX job being downloaded contains job steps that require proxy accounts, propagation does not happen automatically. Several things must happen first. First, the TSX administrator needs to configure the proxy accounts with the same names as the ones corresponding to the jobs being downloaded. Second, a special Registry flag, AllowDownloadedJobsToMatchProxyName, needs to be set to 1 (true).

When you upgrade MSX/TSX server clusters, it is recommended that you start by upgrading the target servers first. SQL Server 2005 level TSX recognizes and can communicate with a SQL Server 2000 post-SP3 MSX server. However, if a previous version of a SQL Server TSX server is enlisted and tries to download information from a higher-level MSX, the download will fail because of multiple metadata changes introduced in the new release of SQL Server 2005.

SQL Server Agent Architectural Overview

As mentioned earlier, the SQL Server Agent service does not have its own authentication mechanism; therefore, it relies on SQL Server to validate the user. A SQL Server Agent user connects to SQL Server via any TSQL client and executes stored procedure commands. Even if the user uses the SQL Server Management Studio user interface or writes managed programs using SQL Server Management Objects, eventually the user actions will still get translated into a series of stored procedure calls. User actions typically result in metadata changes inside the SQL Server store. If such a change requires an immediate update of SQL Server Agent's internal data cache or a direct response from SQL Server Agent, the extended stored procedure xp_sqlagent_notify is called to place a formatted message in a shared memory object from SQL Server. SQL Server Agent continuously looks at this communication channel and processes all information placed into the shared memory object sequentially. The overall architecture of SQL Server Agent is shown in Figure 8-17.

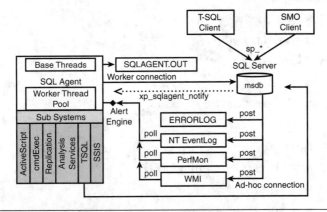

Figure 8-17   SQL Server Agent architectural diagram.

WARNING
The shared memory object has a finite capacity, although a very large one, so it can hold only a certain limited number of messages. As each message gets processed by SQL Server Agent, it is removed from the temporary storage, enabling the system to reclaim this piece of memory.

Thus, it is theoretically possible to reach shared memory saturation by executing too many metadata operations in parallel. In this case, a user message will be returned from the stored procedure call that lets the user know to hold off making a request until new memory becomes available.

SQL Server Agent stores all its metadata exclusively in the MSDBdatabase. Most SQL Server Agent stored procedures are also contained within this database. Here is a list of some of the most significant metadata tables SQL Server Agent uses, divided by area:

- **Jobs**
  - sysjobs
  - sysjobsteps
  - sysjobhistory
  - sysjobstepslogs
  - sysjobactivity
  - syscategories
- **Schedules**
  - sysschedules
  - sysjobschedules
- **Alerts**
  - sysalerts
  - sysoperators
  - sysnotifications
- **Security**
  - syscachedcredentials
  - sysproxies
  - sysproxysubsystem
  - sysproxylogin
- **MSX/TSX**
  - sysjobservers
  - systargetservers
  - systargetservergroups
  - sysdownloadlist

WARNING
Do not attempt to modify any of these tables directly. They are meant to be updated via management stored procedures.

The preferred way of viewing and interpreting table data is through "help" procedures. Take a look at sp_help_job, sp_help_jobstep, sp_help_schedule, sp_help_operator, sp_help_alert, sp_help_proxy, and others. Merging data from related metadata tables using these procedures performs all the necessary security checks, so they may be the only option for a user who is not an administrator on the system and therefore does not have access to all underlying tables.

To pull metadata from a SQL Server Database Engine MSDB database, SQL Server Agent establishes regular SQL Server connections from one of its worker threads. SQL Server Agent has an internal thread pool servicing the job execution engine; it no longer creates a thread for each new job as it did in previous releases. The total number of threads in a thread pool is limited by the Registry value MaxWorkerThreads. Thus at any given time only a certain number of jobs can run concurrently. What happens to the job if a thread is not available when it needs to execute? The job remains in the internal job queue until it has a chance to run. This internal balancing assures the system never starves for resources while attempting to maximize throughput.

In addition, every subsystem in SQL Server Agent has its own limit on the number of threads it is allowed to use concurrently. This limit is stored in the msdb.dbo.syssubsystems table and by default is proportional to the number of processors the computer has. For example, the TSQL subsystem is defined as the number of processors multiplied by 20. This limitation is different for every subsystem and also serves as a limiting factor in determining how many jobs are going to run in parallel. Consider a situation in which 100 jobs are scheduled to run at the same time, each consisting of at least one T-SQL step. Because the system allows at most only 20 concurrently executing T-SQL steps, 80 jobs will be sitting in the queue waiting for the first 20 to complete, even though each job has its own thread available.

As you saw in Figure 8-17, SQL Server Agent establishes separate ad-hoc connections to SQL Server for running T-SQL subsystem job steps. That is actually one of the reasons the number of concurrently running T-SQL job steps is limited.

SQL Server Agent has its own error log file called SQLAGENT.OUT. By default it is stored in the same location as SQL Server logs, but can be redirected through the Registry entry ErrorLogFile and also exposed by the stored procedure sp_set_sqlagent_properties through the @error_log_file parameter. SQL Server Agent logging can also be controlled through the ErrorLoggingLevel Registry entry. This flag is a bit mask that enables you to combine the following basic set of values: log error messages (0x01), log warning messages (0x02), and log informational messages (0x04). Thus if you would like to log all messages, you need to supply a value of 0x07.

NOTE

0x07 is the only value that can be set through the SQL Server Agent Properties dialog part of SQL Server Management Studio. It corresponds to the **Include execution trace messages** check box.

Similar to SQL Server Database Engine, SQL Server Agent cycles error logs on each service restart.

TIPS AND TRICKS

You can cycle the internal SQL Server Agent error log without restarting the service by calling the sp_cycle_agent_errorlog stored procedure.

The monitoring and alerting capabilities of SQL Server Agent are covered as part of Chapter 9. As for the principal architecture of the SQL Server Agent monitoring mechanism, there is a dedicated thread that polls three different alert sources (Windows Event Log, SQL Server Performance Monitor Counters, and Windows Messaging Instrumentation Provider) in a round-robin fashion. This thread is responsible for firing alerts in response to some particular value that satisfies a pre-configured condition.

SQL Server Agent Advanced Service Configuration

SQL Server Agent service has a run-time dependency on the corresponding SQL Server Database Engine instance process. There are several reasons for this. SQL Server Agent uses Database Engine for its metadata store and leverages the SQL Server security mechanism for user authentication.

NOTE

From this point on, any SQL Server Agent-related Registry flag mentioned will be located under the implicit common Registry hive \HKEY_LOCAL_MACHINE\SOFTWARE\Microsoft\Microsoft SQL Server\<instance_name>\SQL Server Agent\.

TIPS AND TRICKS

SQL Server Database Engine and SQL Server Agent are closely related and can be configured to monitor each other's state and to restart each other if needed, such as upon abnormal termination. Both configuration settings are exposed on the General Page of the SQL Server Agent Properties dialog and are stored in the Registry as RestartSQLServer and MonitorAutoStart. If upon startup the SQL Server Agent service is instructed to monitor Database Engine service, it creates a special monitoring thread that continuously polls Database Engine status through a common shared memory object. The process of Database Engine monitoring SQL Server Agent is more convoluted. SQL Server Database Engine does not know it is supposed to monitor SQL Server Agent until the xp_sqlagent_monitor extended stored procedure is invoked on SQL Server Database Engine by SQL Server Agent, essentially telling it to monitor itself.

Upon initial installation, the SQL Server Agent service is in a disabled state. Therefore, to start SQL Server Agent, the Windows server administrator must manually enable the service, using the Service Control Manager or SQL Server Configuration Manager. As soon as SQL Server Agent is started, it loads metadata from the SQL Server store and subsequently starts running tasks, monitoring, and responding to alerts.

The SQL Server Agent component is Off-By-Default (OBD). This means all the extended stored procedures and some stored procedures are not accessible while the service is not running. Upon startup, the SQL Server Agent service enables its own OBD component, called Agent XPs, via the sys.sp_configure system configuration procedure when it first connects to SQL Server and turns the extended stored procedures back on. SQL Server Agent turns itself off upon shutdown by calling the same procedure.

TIPS AND TRICKS

While the SQL Server Agent OBD component is off, any of the metadata configuration procedures, such as sp_add_job, sp_add_schedule, sp_add_alert, and so on, can still be invoked. In other words, it is possible to fully configure SQL Server Agent in a shutdown state so when it comes back up, it starts functioning right away. The only stored procedures truly blocked from being invoked are the ones that require communication to the running Agent service, such as sp_msx_set_account.

In a MSX/TSX distributed execution environment, the target server determines whether it needs to download jobs from the master and to which master server it needs to connect via the MSXServerName Registry flag. The RegularMsxConnections registry flag tells SQL Server Agent to use either integrated security or obtain credential information for SQL Authentication from the SQL Server Database Engine Credentials Store. These two settings are typically not set by the user directly; they are created during the enlistment process. Several other related Registry flags may need some tweaking. The MSXDownload-BatchSize Registry setting determines the number of download instructions to the cache at one time, and MSXPollInterval defines how frequently the target server needs to connect to the master server to check for pending updates.

SQL Server Agent can be configured to send out email notifications for certain types of alerts (there is more on alerting in the next chapter). For this reason, SQL Server Agent has its own MAPI-based mailing component. Unlike SQLMail, which can use only Extended MAPI, SQL Server Agent can use Simple MAPI if Extended MAPI is not available. In SQL Server 2005, SQL Server Agent can optionally use the new SQL Server mailing solution (based on the SMTP protocol) called Database Mail. If SQL Server Agent is configured this way through UseDatabaseMail and DatabaseMailProfile, Registry flags will call the msdb.dbo.sp_send_dbmail stored procedure for mail delivery. However, when SQL Server is down and the stored procedure unavailable, SQL Server Agent uses cached profile and account information and sends mail via a low-level API layer, using the same basic infrastructure (including a failover mechanism) as the DatabaseMail90.exe process when it is running. Mail in this case is still sent without logging in the msdb.dbo.sysmail_mailitems table.

SQL Server Agent service account needs to be a member of the sysadmin fixed server role on its corresponding instance of SQL Server.

WARNING
Starting with SQL Server 2005, SQL Server Agent can no longer use SQL Authentication when connecting to SQL Server. Therefore, if before the upgrade SQL Server Agent was configured to use @host_login_name and @host_login_password configuration parameters, it will no longer be able to connect to SQL Server and will fail to start. The parameters are left on the interface for backward compatibility reasons but no longer serve any useful purpose. The same is true for the @regular_connections parameter.

On the positive side, the SQL Server Agent service account no longer needs to be a member of the local Administrators group on the box. The SQL Server development team did a lot of work to remove this requirement and lower the potential security vulnerability of the system as a whole by lowering the minimum account privileges. To accomplish this goal, storage of the proxy and master server account credentials had to be removed from LSA. Starting with the SQL Server 2005 release, SQL Server Agent completely relies on the SQL Server Database Engine credential store to handle storage of this confidential information.

Summary

This chapter covered the functionality of SQL Server Agent, the primary task scheduling tool of SQL Server. It looked under the hood at SQL Server Agent's architecture as well as advanced configuration settings of the service.

CHAPTER 9

Inside Monitoring Tools

This chapter describes four principal tools used to monitor SQL Server: Activity Monitor, which is a component of SQL Server Management Studio, SQL Server Agent, SQL Server Profiler, and Microsoft Operations Manager (MOM) using the SQL Server Management Pack. Chapter 9 also contains numerous monitoring scenarios that should guide readers in tool selection and usage decisions.

Monitoring Server Activity

This section concentrates on SQL Server Management Studio Activity Monitor and provides examples of some typical problems that can be solved using the tool.

Activity Monitor

Activity Monitor is a SQL Server Management Studio component that displays information about client applications and processes that are currently running on an instance of Database Engine. In addition, Activity Monitor provides the functionality to view the T-SQL statements each process last executed and any locks the statement is holding. Activity Monitor also allows a system administrator to view blocked processes and optionally terminate or "kill" the blocking process (or any problematic process).

To start Activity Monitor for an instance of Database Engine, launch SQL Server Management Studio, connect Object Explorer to the instance of Database Engine, expand the **Management** node, right-click on **Activity Monitor** and select **View Processes** (see Figure 9-1). You can select **View Locks by Process** and **View Locks by Object** if you want to launch Activity Monitor for the purposes of monitoring locks, but all three menu options launch Activity Monitor in the context of one of its three pages.

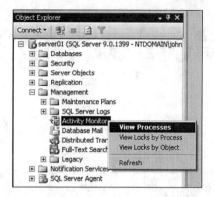

Figure 9-1 Activity Monitor is launched from Object Explorer in SQL Server Management Studio.

Activity Monitor has three pages for displaying processes and lock information on the server. The first page is called **Process Info** (see Figure 9-2), and it displays information about processes such as process ID or SPID, status of the process, the blocking process, username, application name, host name, network protocol, login time, last batch executed time, CPU, and memory usages. The **Locks by Process** page displays locks grouped by connection. The **Locks by Object** page displays locks by the object name.

New in SQL Server 2005, Activity Monitor provides auto-refresh functionality, which allows the user to specify an interval of time after which to automatically fetch and display server activity information. To specify the refresh settings, click on **View refresh settings** on the left side of the Activity Monitor dialog. This will launch the Refresh Settings dialog (see Figure 9-3) where you can enable or disable the auto-refresh option. Enabling the auto-refresh option allows you to specify the amount of time for the auto-refresh interval. Be aware that specifying a low auto-refresh interval may not be a good idea. Activity Monitor runs specific queries on the server, which could hinder system performance, depending on the load and size of your system.

The additional new functionality in the Refresh Settings Dialog is the capability to specify filtering criteria for information displayed in Activity Monitor (see Figure 9-4). The filtering is particularly useful when there are tens or hundreds of connections on the server and the system administrator must monitor activity for a particular database, application, username, blocked processes, or other system phenomenon.

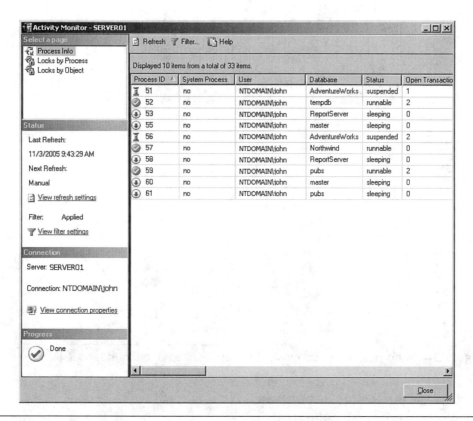

Figure 9-2 Activity Monitor provides information about user connections on a server.

Figure 9-3 The Refresh Settings Dialog box.

SQL Server Management Studio also provides the capability to run multiple Activity Monitor dialogs simultaneously. This allows the system administrator to designate a specific monitoring task in each Activity Monitor dialog. For example, a DBA may decide to launch three Activity Monitor dialogs and set the filtering settings such that the first dialog monitors activity on a specific database, the second dialog monitors blocked processes, and the third dialog monitors activity from a specific application or user.

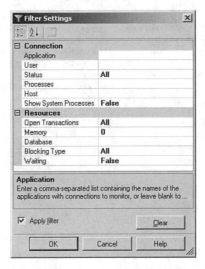

Figure 9-4 Information in Activity Monitor can be filtered to target a specific scenario.

Monitoring Scenarios

Although system stored procedures such as **sp_who** or **sp_who2** have traditionally provided server activity information, these stored procedures do not provide the same versatility as a graphical tool such as Activity Monitor. Activity Monitor provides monitoring of blocking and lock information in the same interface, with options such as filtering and auto-refresh. It also enables you to view the T-SQL statements for each of the processes and the option of killing a process, which makes it a handy tool for monitoring processes on a server.

Identifying Blocked Processes on a Server

Using Activity Monitor, you can quickly view the status of processes and identify blocked processes on a server. To identify a process and determine whether or not it is blocked, launch Activity Monitor. Click on the **Process Info** page to view all processes currently running on the server. To identify blocked processes in the Activity Monitor grid, look for processes with a status of **suspended**, scroll to the left and look for a non-zero value in the **Blocked By** field.

Figure 9-5 depicts an example where process 57 is blocked by process 56.

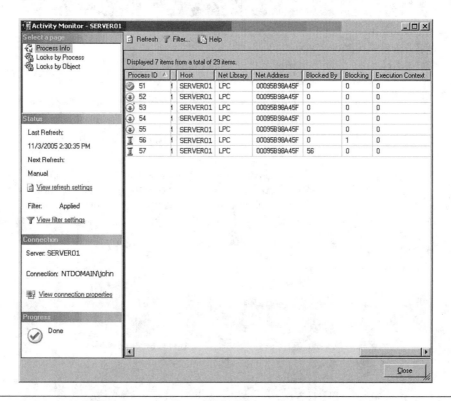

Figure 9-5   Activity Monitor can be used to identify blocked processes.

Alternatively, you can use the suspended icon next to the **ProcessID** field to identify the suspended processes. The icons for process status are described in Table 9-1.

Filtering Blocked Processes in Activity Monitor

In the previous scenario, **Status** and **Blocked By** fields were used to visually identify blocked processes, but what if there are hundreds or thousands of connections to the server? The answer is to use the filtering functionality of Activity Monitor. In the **Filter Settings** dialog, change the **Blocking Type** to **Blocked** (see Figure 9-6) to view only those processes that are blocked by other processes. You can use other values in **Blocking Type** to view just blocking and/or blocked processes in Activity Monitor.

Table 9-1   Process Status Icons

Icon	Status	Description
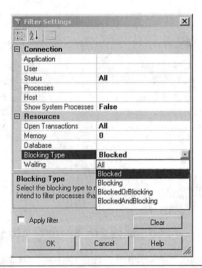	Running	Process is currently performing work.
	Runnable	Process has performed work in the past and it currently has no work to perform.
	Sleeping	Process has work to perform but it is waiting for a lock or some other system resource.
	Background	Process wakes periodically to execute work.
	Suspended	Process has work to perform but it has been stopped. The **Wait Type** field may contain information about why the process is suspended. A non-zero value in the **Blocked By** field indicates the blocking process.
	Other	Any status other than the ones already described.

Figure 9-6   Activity Monitor Filter Settings.

As mentioned before, filtering in Activity Monitor enables additional scenarios where you can set filtering criteria to view activities in a particular database, application, user, and so on.

Identify Last Executed Command from a Connection

In addition to describing processes and locking information, Activity Monitor provides the functionally to view the last executed command for each process on the server. To view the last Transact-SQL batch executed by a connection, identify the process related to the connection in the Activity Monitor, right-click, and select **Details**, (see Figure 9-7).

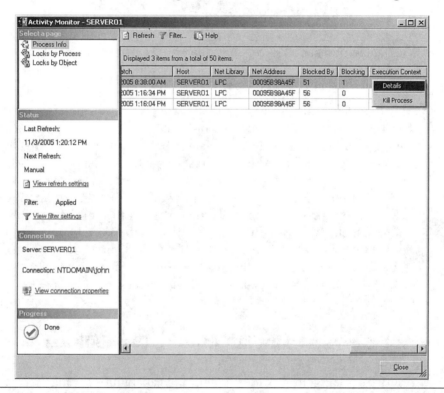

Figure 9-7 Activity Monitor provides the functionality to view the last executed command by each process.

In the Process Details dialog, you can view or select and copy the last executed T-SQL batch as shown in Figure 9-8. Although the dialog launches in a small window, you can easily resize or maximize it to view long T-SQL batches. There is refresh functionality on this dialog to view subsequent T-SQL batches that were issued by the same process. Also, you can use Kill Process directly from this dialog.

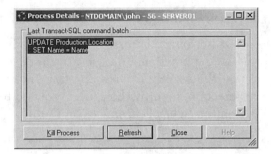

Figure 9-8   The last Transact-SQL command batch executed by process 56.

Terminating or Killing a User Connection

In some scenarios the system administrator must terminate a user connection from the server. A common scenario is when one process blocks another process, which in turn blocks another process, and the chain of blocking continues. Although resolving the locking and blocking requires a thorough investigation, the best temporary solution for the DBA is to ask end-users to cancel operations from their applications. However, in some cases cancellation is not possible, or the end-users are not available. In these situations, the best solution would be to terminate or kill the process at the head of the blocking chain.

To kill a process from Activity Monitor, identify the process in the Activity Monitor grid, right-click, and select **Kill Process** (see Figure 9-9).

Using SQL Server Agent Monitoring Capabilities

SQL Server Agent provides monitoring capabilities through its internal alerting engine. It supports the following three types of alerts.

- SQL Server Event alerts
- SQL Server Performance alerts
- Windows Management Instrumentation alerts

In response to any alert, SQL Agent can start a job or send a notification via email or pager, or through use of a net send command. The following sections define each type of alert and consider its best application. However, prior to defining the first alert it's best to create an operator to be notified when an alert gets triggered.

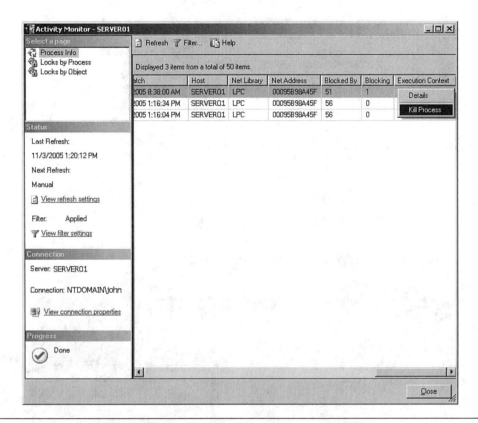

Figure 9-9   Activity Monitor provides the functionality to kill a process.

SQL Server Agent Operator

To define an operator, expand **SQL Server Agent** in SQL Server Management Studio Object Explorer and right-click on **Operators** (see Figure 9-10).

Selecting **New Operator** brings up a New Operator dialog (see Figure 9-11). Assume the operator has a valid email address and carries a pager during normal business hours. Later, when selecting the notification method for an alert, you can indicate the preferred way to contact the person.

Notice how the pager information shows up in regular email format. SQL Agent uses the same mailing capabilities (either internal MAPI-based component or Database Mail solution), based on the configuration, for both kinds of delivery.

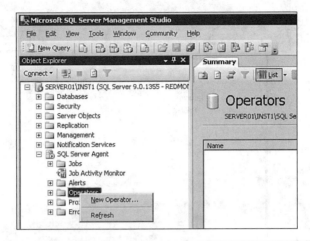

Figure 9-10   Operators Node inside Object Explorer.

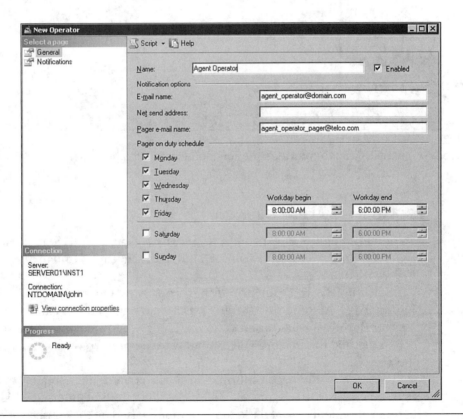

Figure 9-11   New Operator dialog.

SQL Server Event Alerts

Now you are ready to define a SQL Server Event Alert. You can launch the New Alert dialog (see Figure 9-12) by right-clicking the **Alerts** node in object Explorer.

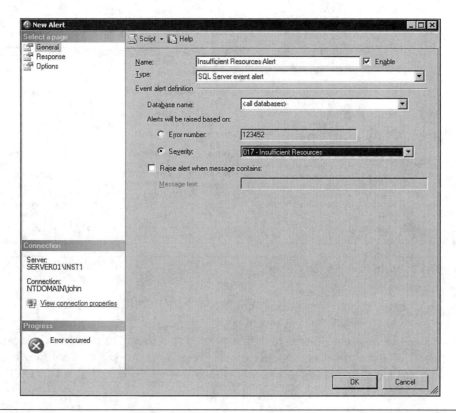

Figure 9-12   New Alert dialog.

TIPS AND TRICKS

SQL Agent is constantly polling the Windows Event Log for SQL Server Database Engine-generated events and tries to match event instances with criteria specified for each alert. Therefore, any alert SQL Agent needs to respond to can be viewed directly if you use the Windows Event Viewer tool. You can find this tool inside the Windows Administrative Tools folder (see Figure 9-13).

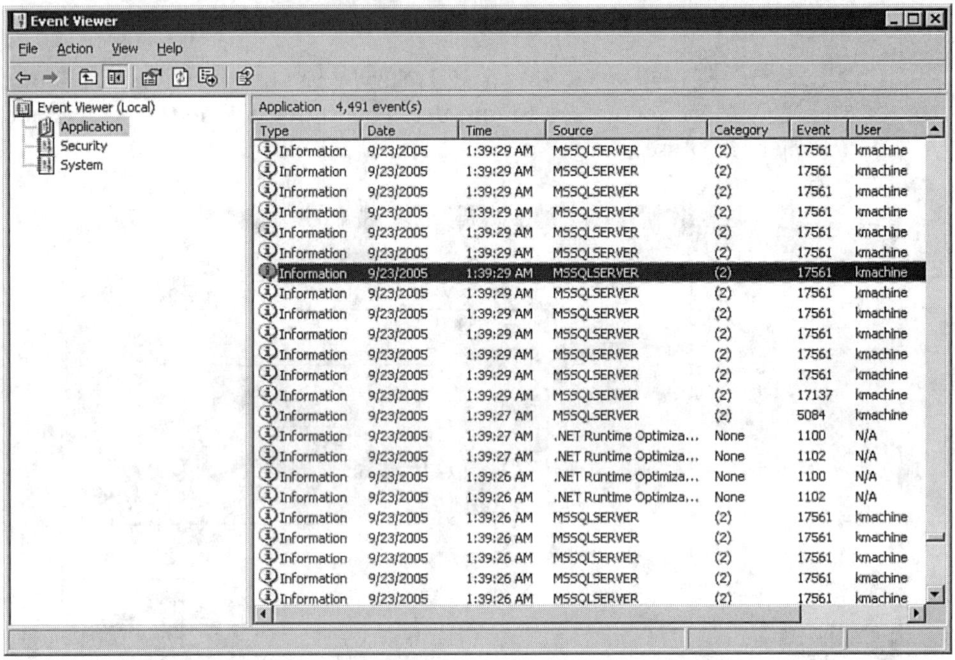

Figure 9-13   Windows Event Viewer.

Virtually any event that has MSSQLSERVER specified as an event source can be intercepted by SQL Agent.

You can define an alert based on a specific error number or severity. The error number actually corresponds to a message_id column in the sys.messages system view and the Event column as displayed by Windows Event Viewer.

TIPS AND TRICKS

In SQL Server 2000, predefined alerts shipped with SQL Agent. These alerts were removed from SQL Server 2005 for various reasons having nothing to do with functionality. One of the alerts that existed in SQL Server 2000 and that is still considered good practice to use today was one that monitored events with error number 9002 for your database, indicating that the transaction log is full and needs to be backed up.

If you want to raise a more generic alert based on the severity of the message, you can also do that by selecting the appropriate radio button.

There is a pre-defined list of error severity levels supported by the system. Table 9-2 lists general ranges for different severity levels and what they mean.

Table 9-2   Error Severity Level Ranges

Severity Level	Description
0-10	Indicate informational messages and non-severe errors
11-16	Indicate errors that can be corrected by the user
17-19	Indicate software errors that cannot be corrected by the user
20-25	Indicate system problems and fatal errors

Another important option when defining an alert is the capability to specify an exact string that must be found inside event message text for an alert to be raised. You enable this option by clicking the check box in the lower part of the dialog, and it should help you further filter out unwanted events.

On the Response tab of the New Alert dialog you can select previously defined operators and a desired notification method (see Figure 9-14).

In addition, you can also select a job to run, possibly to compensate for the event action or to provide other notification not directly supported by SQL Agent infrastructure. Response tab options are common for all types of SQL Agent alerts, but specifics of an alert definition vary with its type.

SQL Server Performance Alerts

SQL Agent will monitor SQL Server Database Engine-related performance counters and compare them to pre-defined alerting thresholds.

TIPS AND TRICKS
To see the current performance counter value you can select data from the sys.sysperfinfo system view. This is the same mechanism used by the SQL Agent alerting engine when performing periodic polling of the counters to determine when an alert needs to be raised.

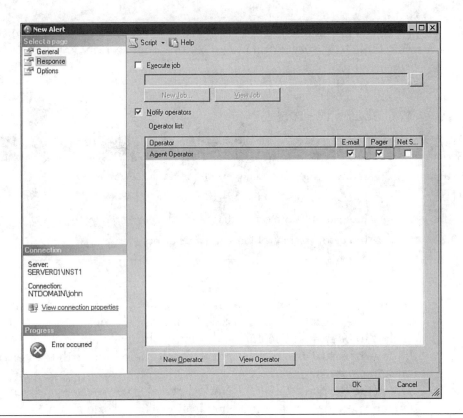

Figure 9-14   New Alert dialog Response tab.

Figure 9-15 defines an alert on the total number of lock timeouts in the SQL Server system. The alert is to fire when a selected performance counter value exceeds 100 lock timeouts per second. Other possible conditional clauses in addition to "rises above" include "falls below" and "becomes equal to," which together essentially cover all possible scenarios.

Windows Management Instrumentation Alerts

Windows Management Instrumentation (WMI) alerts are possible only starting with SQL Server 2005. To define a WMI alert you need to know how to write WQL queries. Let's define an alert that will monitor SQL Server Database Engine for creation of a new database. This alert needs to fire automatically, creating a backup job for new databases in addition to sending a notification message to the previously defined operator.

Go to the already familiar dialog for alert creation (see Figure 9-16) to create an alert.

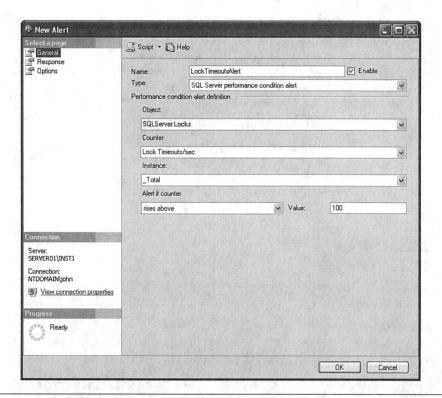

Figure 9-15   Creating a new performance alert dialog.

Notice when the dialog first shows up that the WMI namespace name is automatically filled in by the tool based on the specific Database Engine instance name. The query only looks like T-SQL; in reality it is in WQL.

Now it's time to write and execute the next few required steps directly in the Object Editor window. You could do everything with management dialogs, but job creation was already covered in the previous chapter, so this demonstration uses T-SQL directly.

The first task is to add a backup device for this instance of SQL Server.

```
USE [master]
GO
exec master.dbo.sp_addumpdevice  @devtype = N'disk',
        @logicalname = N'MyBackups',
        @physicalname = N'C:\Backups\MyBackups2.bak'
GO
```

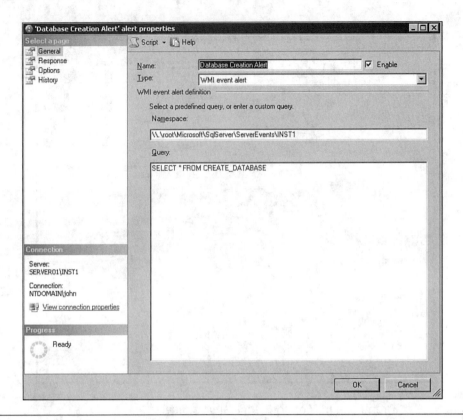

Figure 9-16   Windows Management Instrumentation Alert properties.

Next you need to create a job that is going to execute required T-SQL to create another job. Notice how it obtains the WMI property value DatabaseName dynamically during execution.

```
use msdb
exec sp_add_job @job_name=N'Automatically create a backup job'
GO
exec sp_add_jobstep @job_name=
➥N'Automatically create a backup job',
        @subsystem=N'TSQL',
        @database_name=N'msdb',
        @on_success_action=3,
        @step_name=N'Create Backup Job',
        @command=N'sp_add_job @job_name=N''Backup
➥$(WMI(DatabaseName))'''
GO
```

```
exec sp_add_jobstep @job_name=
➥N'Automatically create a backup job',
            @subsystem=N'TSQL',
            @database_name=N'msdb',
            @on_success_action=3,
            @step_name=N'Add Backup Step',
            @command=N'sp_add_jobstep @job_name=
➥N''Backup $(WMI(DatabaseName))'',
            @step_name=N''Issue BackupCommand'',
            @database_name=N''msdb'',
            @command=N''BACKUP DATABASE
➥$(WMI(DatabaseName)) TO MyBackups'''
GO
exec sp_add_jobstep @job_name=
➥N'Automatically create a backup job',
            @subsystem=N'TSQL',
            @step_name=N'Give job a jobserver',
            @database_name=N'msdb',
            @command=N'sp_add_jobserver
➥@job_name=N''Backup $(WMI(DatabaseName))'''
GO
exec sp_add_jobserver @job_name=
➥N'Automatically create a backup job'
GO
```

Now we are ready to associate our previously created alert with the job as follows.

```
EXEC msdb.dbo.sp_update_alert @name=N'Database Creation Alert',
            @job_name=N'Automatically create a backup job'
GO
```

If you create a new database on the server, you will immediately notice creation of the job.

Using SQL Server Profiler for Monitoring Server Activity

SQL Server Profiler is a graphical tool that allows the user to get a continuous list of events reflecting server activity. (Note the word *server* instead of SQL Server Database Engine: Starting with SQL Server 2005,

SQL Profiler also enables users to look at current activity happening inside Analysis Server.)

Detailed examination of SQL Profiler capabilities was performed earlier in Chapter 7. Here you'll skim through the monitoring capabilities of Profiler traces. Let's begin by examining a SQL Server Database Engine trace first.

After a server connection is established, the Trace Properties dialog appears (see Figure 9-17). On the General tab, the user can select one of the pre-defined templates to be used for tracing.

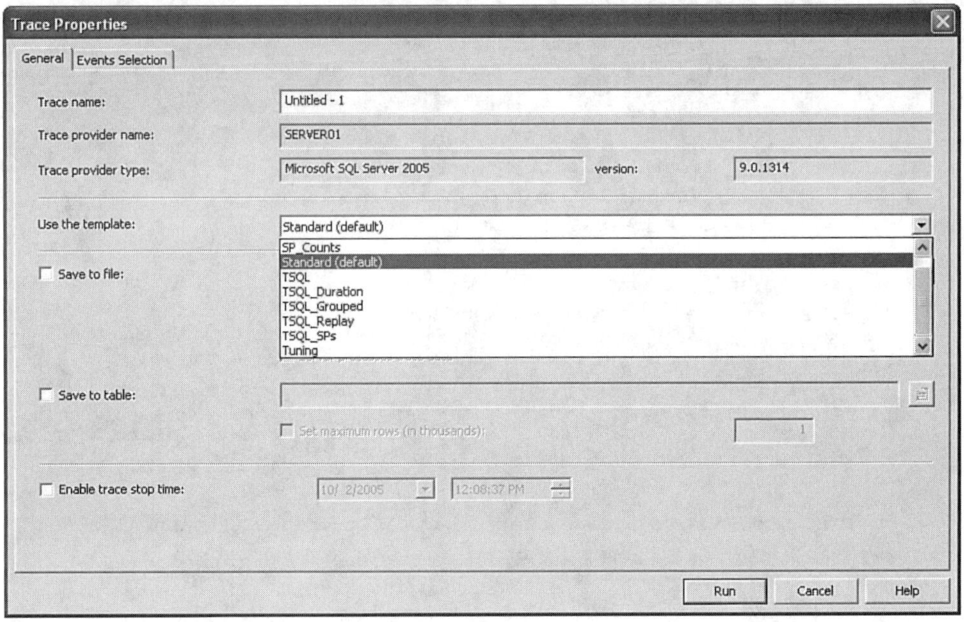

Figure 9-17   SQL Server Profiler Trace Properties dialog.

The Standard template is a good starting point if you want to monitor general server activity. By flipping to the Events Selection tab you can see that the Standard template automatically selects connection events, T-SQL batch events, and RPC events. Thus when starting a trace by clicking the **Run** button, you should be able to immediately see all SQL Server Database Engine Instance users. Those users who are already connected to Database Engine are going to be reflected via the Existing-Connection event, new connections via the Audit Login event, and disconnects via the Audit Logout event. You will also see all T-SQL batches that users are submitting for execution, as well as all RPC calls made via the programming API by database applications. All data appears directly in the trace window that will constantly scroll as new data comes in.

TIPS AND TRICKS
If you don't like auto-scrolling of the trace window data, you can uncheck the Auto Scroll option under the Windows menu or click the appropriate button on the Profiler toolbar ▣.

Please note another useful feature of Profiler that enables you to see event details more closely. Hover over the specific event in the trace and it will display corresponding textual data in the bottom pane of the split window. This is how you can investigate T-SQL data in more depth.

If you are not satisfied with general monitoring using the Default template, you can select one of the specialized templates meant to assist in troubleshooting a specific issue with SQL Server Database Engine Instance. You can also use any of the templates as a base and select additional events that you would like to see monitored on the Database Engine.

In addition to the Standard template, you can pick one of the other pre-defined templates listed in Table 9-3.

Monitoring of Analysis Server is very similar to SQL Server Database Engine, but it comes with its own set of templates. Two templates that ship with SQL Profiler for Analysis Server are "Standard," used for regular monitoring of Analysis Server activity, and "Replay," used to capture trace information sufficient to replay data against Analysis Server.

Monitoring Using Microsoft Operations Manager and SQL Server Management Pack

Microsoft Operations Manager (MOM) provides a way to manage multiple solutions in your enterprise environment, not just SQL Server (see Figure 9-18). Management Pack is a plug-in to the Microsoft Operations Manager whose purpose is to monitor SQL Server specifically. MOM monitoring is architected so there is a central MOM server and multiple MOM Agents reporting to it. Actual monitoring is performed by a MOM agent. One agent per computer is sufficient, and the agent can monitor multiple instances of SQL Server Database Engine at the same time.

Table 9-3 Predefined Profiler Templates

Template Name	Template Purpose	Event Classes
SP_Counts	Captures stored procedure executions.	**SP:Starting**
TSQL	Captures all T-SQL statements that are submitted to SQL Serverby clients and the time issued. Used to debug client applications.	**Audit Login** **Audit Logout** **ExistingConnection** **RPC:Starting** **SQL:BatchStarting**
TSQL_Duration	Captures all T-SQL statements submitted to SQL Server by clients and execution time (in milliseconds), and groups them by duration. Used to identify slow executing queries.	**RPC:Completed** **SQL:BatchCompleted**
TSQL_Grouped	Captures all T-SQL statements submitted to SQL Server and the time they were issued, and groups information by user or client that submitted the statement. Used to investigate queries from a particular client or user.	**Audit Login** **Audit Logout** **ExistingConnection** **RPC:Starting** **SQL:BatchStarting**
TSQL_Replay	Captures detailed information about T-SQL statements that is required if the trace will be replayed.Used by Profiler Replay for purposes of verification and performance benchmarking. Also used by Database Tuning Advisor for iterative tuning.	**CursorClose** **CursorExecute** **CursorOpen** **CursorPrepare** **CursorUnprepare** **Audit Login** **Audit Logout** **Existing Connection** **RPC Output Parameter** **RPC:Completed** **RPC:Starting** **Exec Prepared SQL** **Prepare SQL** **SQL:BatchCompleted** **SQL:BatchStarting**

Template Name	Template Purpose	Event Classes
TSQL_Sps	Captures detailed information about all executing stored procedures. Used to analyze component steps of stored procedures.	**Audit Login** **Audit Logout** **Existing Connection** **RPC:Starting** **SP:Completed** **SP:Starting** **SP:StmtStarting** **SQL:BatchStarting**
Tuning	Captures information about stored procedures and T-SQL batch execution. Used to produce trace output that Database Engine Tuning Advisor can use as a workload to tune databases.	**RPC:Completed** **SP:StmtCompleted** **SQL:BatchCompleted**

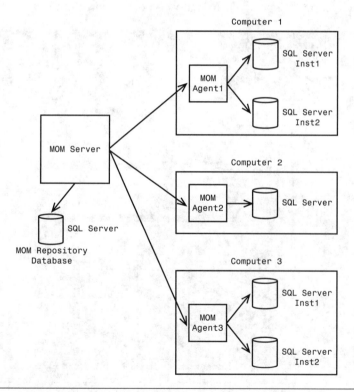

Figure 9-18   MOM architectural diagram.

The MOM Agent does not depend on the state of the components it is monitoring, so it detects failure of SQL Server and reports its state back to the central console. If for some reason the MOM Agent itself or the computer on which it's running is down, the Central MOM Server generates an alert because it fails to receive a successful heartbeat from its agent.

The MOM user interface consists of two main applications. The Administrator Console is used to perform MOM configuration when you need to customize the management pack. The Operator Console is used to actually do the monitoring.

Administrator Console

To start monitoring, you have to install MOM on a central machine, import SQL Server Management Pack, and then assign SQL Servers to it. Let's examine these steps. First you need to launch the MOM 2005 Administrator Console and import SQL Server Management pack by clicking on the Import/Export Management Packs link and following the Management Pack Import/Export Wizard steps as depicted in Figure 9-19.

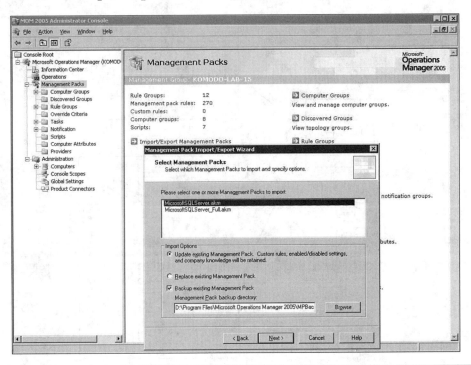

Figure 9-19   Microsoft Management Console—Administrator Console.

Note that installing SQL Server Management Pack requires a separate download from Microsoft because it is not shipped in the same box as SQL Server 2005 itself.

MOM uses multiple rules to determine what data to collect, how frequently to collect it, and how to analyze it. SQL Server Management Pack comes pre-configured with default rules and configuration settings, so immediately after installation it can be used for direct monitoring of assigned SQL Server instances. It does not require extra configuration effort right away and can wait until you feel the need to modify some of the existing rules or add new ones. Another important point is that SQL Server Management Pack, shipped with SQL Server 2005, also includes monitoring capabilities for SQL Server 2000, so you don't need to look for it separately.

How do you actually begin monitoring a SQL Server instance? After importing SQL Server Management Pack, you need to deploy the MOM Agent on the computer you want to monitor. You can do it directly from the MOM Administrator Console by first checking all monitored computers and then following the pop-up menu as shown in Figure 9-20.

This launches the Install/Uninstall Agents Wizard (see Figure 9-21). Follow the wizard steps until you get to the final screen (Completing the Install/Uninstall Agents Wizards), describing the series of actions about to occur.

After you select **Finish**, the MOM Agent is going to be deployed on the target machine and start monitoring as prescribed by the configuration rules.

Rule Groups

What are some of the most important rule groups of SQL Server 2005? The Client Side Monitoring group (see Figure 9-22) is used to monitor connectivity to the monitored SQL Server Database Engine instance. It also catches possible network latency problems.

Client Side Monitoring rules have default values, but to actually start monitoring you will have to do a little configuration work. First, you need to decide what remote computer will be performing connectivity checks. That computer needs to be added to the appropriate computer group, as shown in Figure 9-23.

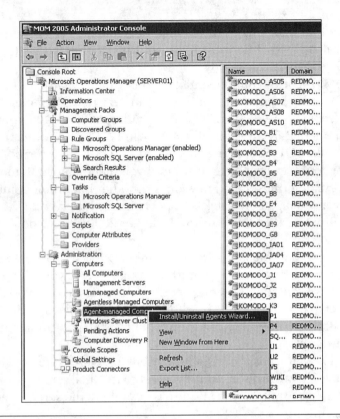

Figure 9-20 Installing the MOM Agent.

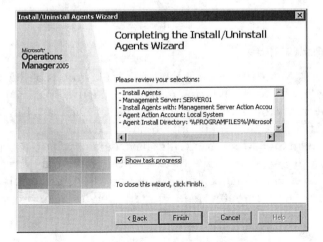

Figure 9-21 Install/Uninstall Agents Wizard.

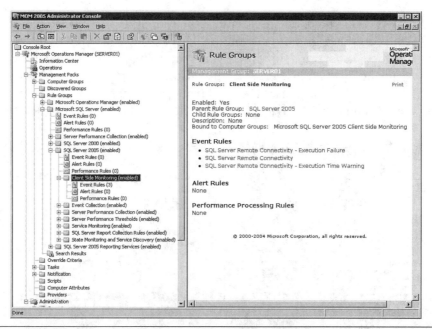

Figure 9-22   Microsoft Management Pack—Client-Side Monitoring.

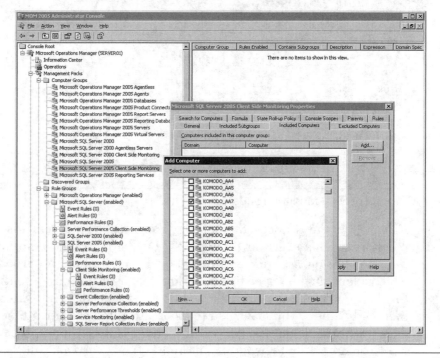

Figure 9-23   Client-Side Monitoring computer group.

Next you need to decide what instances of SQL Server Database Engine the computer is going to monitor. That setting is located under the rules group. Let's bring up the Event Rule Properties dialog by double-clicking on the SQL Server Remote Connectivity event. Inside the dialog, switch to the Responses tab. Highlight the pre-configured script and click **Edit**. The resulting Launch a Script dialog is shown in Figure 9-24.

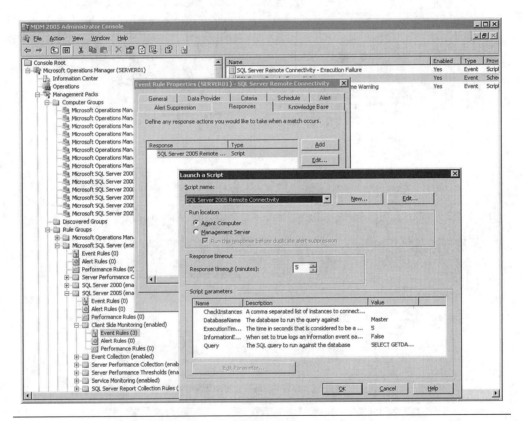

Figure 9-24   Client-Side Monitoring customizations.

From within the Launch a Script dialog you can change several essential monitoring characteristics. Suppose you have strict performance requirements on a specific query used by the application. You may want to consider using this specific query directly for monitoring. You can do this by double-clicking the Query property inside the grid. After you modify the query, you may need to adjust expected execution time and database through the ExecutionTime and DatabaseName properties. Now you are ready to assign monitored SQL Server Database Engine instances to this MOM Agent by modifying the CheckInstances property and providing a comma-separated list of instance names. Only after the instance name list is populated will the MOM Agent start client-side monitoring.

The Event Collection group combines more that 200 various SQL Server-specific events that can be collected by the MOM Agent.

TIPS AND TRICKS

SQL Server Database Engine event collections are based on readings of the Windows Application Event Log. This event collection process is conducted in a fashion similar to how SQL Server Agent collects them. This means the same technique described earlier (in the section SQL Server Event Alerts) for selecting the correct event still applies.

Creating a new event collection rule is very simple. Right-click the event rule tree node under the desired group or subgroup folder (see Figure 9-25), and step through a simple wizard, describing the required event criteria.

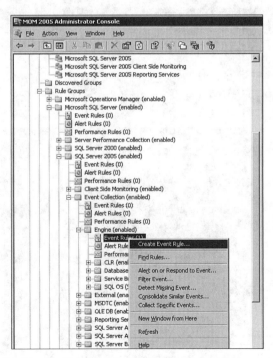

Figure 9-25   MOM Create Event Rule.

The Performance Monitoring group covers a collection of performance counters affecting SQL Server Database Engine internal performance characteristics, such as lock timeouts/sec and average wait times in milliseconds. It also includes resource monitoring, such as CPU performance and disk and memory usages. This grouping makes sense because computer resources directly affect application performance.

The Service Monitoring group checks on the state of different services. In addition to SQL Server Database Engine itself, MOM Management Pack monitors SQL Service Broker, SQL Browser Service, Notification Services, and other services.

The State Monitoring and Service Discovery group monitors the overall health of the SQL Server Database Engine. One of the most important aspects of this group is space monitoring. Let's bring up the pre-configured settings for monitoring database space usage and see whether modifications are necessary. You can do this by double-clicking the SQL Server Database Space Analysis event, as shown in Figure 9-26.

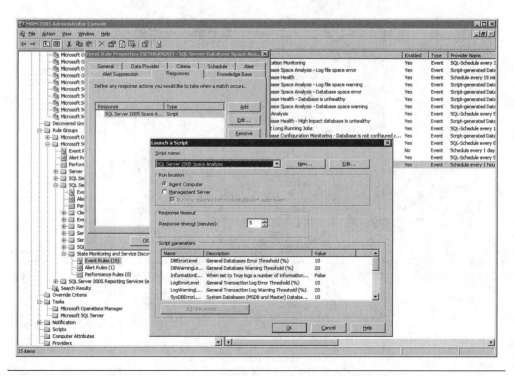

Figure 9-26   MOM State Monitoring—space analysis configuration.

Now bring up the Responses tab and edit the pre-configured response. As you can see from Figure 9-26, in the current configuration a warning will be generated if available database space drops below 20%. If available space is below 10%, an error is generated. You may want to modify these configuration values to fit your particular space usage patterns and requirements.

TIPS AND TRICKS

If you want any configuration changes made to the MOM Management Pack to take effect immediately, you need to follow a special procedure shown in Figure 9-27. Choose **Commit Configuration Change**. This causes the MOM Server to broadcast all changes to the entire network of MOM Agents right away.

Figure 9-27   MOM committing configuration changes.

NOTE

If you don't force the configuration to be committed, changes will be picked up, but after a built-in delay of several hours.

Operator Console

Operator Console is split into different views (see Figure 9-28). The Alerts view is the most important one, and covers all current alerts on all the systems aggregated together. You can also see specific alert details in the bottom pane of the screen.

Figure 9-28 MOM Operator Console—Alerts view.

The State view (see Figure 9-29) shows the state of your monitored computer and different components, including the MOM Agent, MOM Server, and SQL Server.

As you may notice in Figure 9-30, placing the cursor on a specific row in the grid enables you to see the details of this alert and drill down by double-clicking on the alert.

Now you can see a full history of the specific alert with an explanation of what could be causing it.

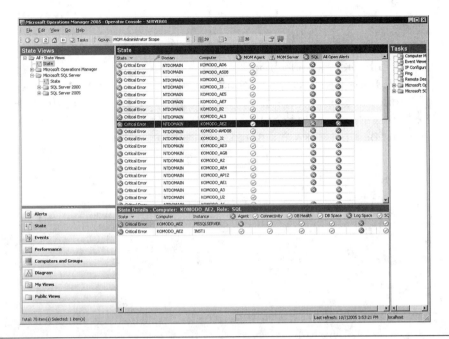

Figure 9-29   MOM Operator Console—State view.

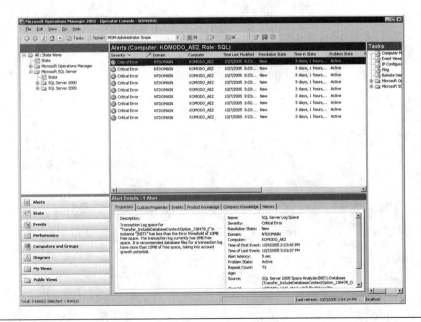

Figure 9-30   MOM Operator Console—Alert drill-down.

Summary

This chapter talked about several tools used to monitor SQL Server: SQL Server Management Studio Activity Monitor, SQL Server Agent Monitoring and Alerting, SQL Server Profiler, and Microsoft Operations Manager (MOM) via SQL Server Management Pack. It also described some best practices and usage scenarios for each tool.

CHAPTER 10

Inside Email Tools

Two principal email solutions ship with SQL Server 2005: the legacy component previously shipped with SQL Server 2000 (SQL Mail) and a newly developed mailing solution (Database Mail). The two solutions are completely different, have different architectures, and utilize different underlying mail delivery protocols. SQL Mail uses Extended MAPI, whereas Database Mail utilizes SMTP. This chapter talks first about SQL Mail and then Database mail, describing each solution separately and highlighting critical differences along the way.

SQL Agent also has its own mailing capabilities, but these are used only for sending out notifications and cannot be used directly by external clients. However, for completeness we cover SQL Agent Mail as well as the other two email solutions in this chapter. We begin with SQL Mail, move on to Database Mail, and finish with SQL Agent Mail.

SQL Mail

SQL Mail has been around for several releases of SQL Server and has not undergone significant changes since SQL Server 2000. It is asynchronous in nature: that is, each call to the underlying mailing infrastructure is blocked until the requested operation is completed. SQL Mail uses Extended MAPI for mail delivery, so it needs to be installed and configured outside of SQL Server Database Engine before SQL Mail actually can be used.

Overview

SQL Mail is a collection of extended stored procedures for sending, reading, and deleting mail items that share the same MAPI profile. There is also a regular T-SQL stored procedure (sp_process_mail) that calls several extended stored procedures to perform work. Table 10-1 lists all the procedures and describes their purposes.

Table 10-1 SQL Mail Stored Procedures

Stored Procedure Name	Main Function
xp_startmail	Initializes an extended MAPI mail session and logs on to the mail server.
xp_stopmail	Closes the MAPI mail session and performs mail server log off.
xp_sendmail	Sends mail, optionally executing T-SQL queries and formatting results to be sent as attachments or body text.
xp_readmail	Reads mail messages from the mail box.
xp_findnextmsg	Navigates mail messages by finding the next message after given one.
xp_deletemail	Deletes mail messages from the mail box.
sp_process_mail	Reads and deletes all the messages in the inbox, converting mail items into resultsets and returning them to the caller.
xp_get_mapi_default_profile	Retrieves the default MAPI profile.
xp_get_mapi_profiles	Enumerates MAPI profiles accessible to the SQL Server Database Engine service account.
xp_test_mapi_profile	Performs MAPI profile validation by logging on and off the mail server.
xp_issqlmailstarted	Checks whether a mail session has been initialized.

By default, only members of the sysadmin fixed server role have execute permissions for any of the SQL Mail procedures, but these permissions can be granted to other users.

TIPS AND TRICKS
Most users need to have permission to only send mail, so it is sufficient to grant them the xp_sendmail procedure with the execute privilege.

The SQL Mail component is OFF by default on a brand new installation of SQL Server 2005 and needs to be explicitly enabled before the first use. If, however, SQL Server Database Engine has been upgraded from a SQL Server 2000 instance, the component remains enabled to provide full backward compatibility.

Before we consider different mailing scenarios that use SQL Mail, it is worthwhile to spend some time talking about SQL Mail configuration.

SQL Mail requires extended MAPI to be deployed on the machine from which mail is going to be sent, that is, where the SQL Server Database Engine instance is installed. It's worth noting that because of its reliance on extended MAPI, SQL Mail does not work on any 64-bit platform. The simplest supported way to install extended MAPI is through a Microsoft Outlook installation.

TIPS AND TRICKS

Microsoft has released multiple versions of extended MAPI. It is very important to know exactly which version is used by SQL Mail. Although Outlook's MAPI will work, many enterprise customers prefer using versions of MAPI shipped with Exchange server because it may be more robust and scalable. However, these versions are not supported by PSS.

After extended MAPI is deployed, you need to configure the email profile to be used by SQL Mail. Because SQL Mail will be running inside a SQL Server Database Engine process, SQL Mail accesses email facilities using service account credentials. Thus, if you intend to use Outlook configuration facilities, you need to configure the email profile while logging in to the Windows server under this account. You can configure Outlook 2003 mail account settings by using the Custom Installation Wizard at installation time, and then change them later using the Custom Maintenance Wizard.

When configuring email accounts you can set up multiple ones and then select which one to use via the xp_startmail extended procedure, passing its profile name as a parameter. If the parameter is missing, SQL Mail uses the default profile configured for the user.

Setting up and testing the default profile for SQL Mail can also be done through SQL Server Management Studio, as shown in Figure 10-1. To bring up the SQL Mail Configuration dialog, you need to right-click on the **SQL Mail** folder and select **Properties**.

TIPS AND TRICKS

If you want SQL Mail to use the default account, the xp_startmail call can be omitted all together. Mail session initialization will be done as part of the first xp_sendmail call.

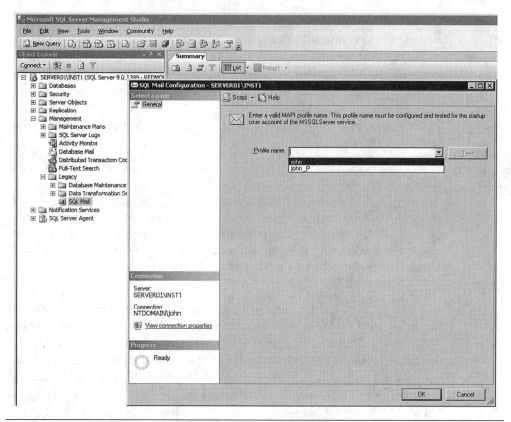

Figure 10-1   SQL Mail configuration.

Calling the xp_stopmail extended procedure has the reverse effect of xp_startmail; it closes the MAPI session and allows the user to change the mail profile on the next xp_startmail call.

TIPS AND TRICKS

Frequent calling of xp_startmail/xp_stopmail is not recommended because of architectural design limitations of SQL Mail and can cause memory and handle leaks inside the SQL Server Database Engine process.

Sending Mail

After the mail session is initialized, you are ready to send mail. Let's examine different options of the xp_sendmail extended stored procedure. Here is the accepted syntax.

```
xp_sendmail { [ @recipients= ] 'recipients [ ;...n ]' }
    [ ,[ @message= ] 'message' ]
    [ ,[ @query= ] 'query' ]
    [ ,[ @attachments= ] 'attachments [ ;...n ]' ]
    [ ,[ @copy_recipients= ] 'copy_recipients [ ;...n ]'
    [ ,[ @blind_copy_recipients= ] 'blind_copy_recipients [ ;...n ]'
    [ ,[ @subject= ] 'subject' ]
    [ ,[ @type= ] 'type' ]
    [ ,[ @attach_results= ] 'attach_value' ]
    [ ,[ @no_output= ] 'output_value' ]
    [ ,[ @no_header= ] 'header_value' ]
    [ ,[ @width= ] width ]
    [ ,[ @separator= ] 'separator' ]
    [ ,[ @echo_error= ] 'echo_value' ]
    [ ,[ @set_user= ] 'user' ]
    [ ,[ @dbuse= ] 'database' ]
```

One of the most important options is specifying the query to be executed against Database Engine. When this parameter is supplied, the mail procedure establishes an internal connection to SQL Server Database Engine under service account credentials, changes the security context to the caller, and then runs the query. Results of the query get formatted and included in the message body. Here is an example:

```
EXEC master.dbo.xp_sendmail
    @recipients = N' john_smith@mydomain.com;
tracy_miller@mydomain.com',
    @subject = N' contents of the authors table',
    @query = N' select * from pubs..authors'
GO
```

Notice how email addresses for multiple users are separated with a semicolon. If the table name was not fully qualified, you could have specified the @dbuse parameter instead.

Query results can also be attached as an output file, as in the following example:

```
EXEC master.dbo.xp_sendmail
    @recipients = N'john_smith@mydomain.com;
tracy_miller@mydomain.com',
    @query = N'select * from pubs..authors',
    @subject = N'contents of the authors table',
    @attach_results = 'TRUE',
    @attachments = N'query_results.log'
GO
```

If the `@attachments` parameter was not supplied, the output file name would be automatically generated and have a `.txt` extension. The `@attachments` parameter specification also allows SQL Mail to attach existing files to the email message. If users attempting to attach files are not members of the sysadmin fixed server role, SQL Server Database Engine impersonates the user before accessing the file system. If the user is connected to SQL Server through SQL Authentication, he is not able to attach files at all.

NOTE
This behavior is different from SQL Server 2000, where a global proxy account was used to validate permission access to the file for non-sysadmin users.

Another parameter that deserves special consideration is `@set_user`. If this parameter is supplied, SQL Mail issues a SETUSER request to SQL Server Database Engine before query execution takes place. However, for the SETUSER statement to succeed, the caller needs to have sufficient privileges for impersonation, or the SETUSER statement will fail.

Most other options of xp_sendmail have to do with query results formatting and need be experimented with only when you are trying to conform the desired output to a template or make it easily parsable by automated tools.

In general, it's worth noting that SQL Mail processes query execution, formatting, and sending the mail message synchronously with the user request. Thus, the xp_sendmail procedure does not return until the message is either successfully sent or has failed in formatting or delivery. Sometimes, the back-end server can experience a temporary outage or network connectivity issue that will interfere with mail delivery, and this might cause the SQL Mail thread to appear hung. This has been a source of numerous customer complaints and could not be fully rectified without re-designing the SQL Mail solution. This problem was the driving force behind creation of a different type of asynchronous solution in SQL Server 2005, based on the SMTP mail delivery protocol, called Database Mail. Database Mail design and architecture are examined later in this chapter.

Reading Mail

Before you can call xp_readmail, you need to obtain a valid message ID. This is done via the xp_findnextmsg extended stored procedure. Here is the accepted syntax:

```
xp_findnextmsg [ [ @type= ] type ]
     [ , [ @unread_only= ] 'unread_value' ]
     [ , [ @msg_id= ] 'message_id' [ OUTPUT ] ]
```

@msg_id is actually an input as well as an output parameter into the procedure. On the very first call its value is going to be NULL and from that point on it will be populated with the ID of the next message in the inbox waiting to be read.

After receiving a valid (non-NULL) message ID, you can call xp_readmail with the following syntax:

```
xp_readmail [ [ @msg_id= ] 'message_id' ]
     [ , [ @type= ] 'type' [ OUTPUT ] ]
     [ , [ @peek= ] 'peek' ]
     [ , [ @suppress_attach= ] 'suppress_attach' ]
     [ , [ @originator= ] 'sender' OUTPUT ]
     [ , [ @subject= ] 'subject' OUTPUT ]
     [ , [ @message= ] 'message' OUTPUT ]
     [ , [ @recipients= ] 'recipients [ ;...n ]' OUTPUT ]
     [ , [ @cc_list= ] 'copy_recipients [ ;...n ]' OUTPUT ]
     [ , [ @bcc_list= ] 'blind_copy_recipients [ ;...n ]' OUTPUT ]
     [ , [ @date_received= ] 'date' OUTPUT ]
     [ , [ @unread= ] 'unread_value' OUTPUT ]
     [ , [ @attachments= ] 'attachments [ ;...n ]' OUTPUT ])
     [ , [ @skip_bytes= ] bytes_to_skip OUTPUT ]
     [ , [ @msg_length= ] length_in_bytes OUTPUT ]
     [ , [ @originator_address= ] 'sender_address' OUTPUT ] ]
```

As you can see, there are only a handful of input parameters for this procedure other than @msg_id. @peek is used to flag the message as read if the value is FALSE, or leave it unread if set to TRUE. @suppress_attach avoids creation of temporary attachment files on the server when the mail message is read if set to TRUE.

Finally, after reading the email message, you can delete it by calling xp_deletemail with the following syntax:

```
xp_deletemail { 'message_id' }
```

For a good example of how to use these three procedures (xp_ findextmsg, xp_readmail, and xp_deletemail) you can look at the contents of stored procedure sp_processmail for putting them all together.

TIPS AND TRICKS
To see the contents of sp_processmail, execute the following command from the Query Editor tool:

```
sp_helptext 'sp_processmail'
```

Database Mail

Database Mail is an SMTP-based asynchronous mailing solution shipped in SQL Server 2005. It relies on SQL Server Service Broker queuing technology for asynchronous guaranteed mail delivery support. Unlike SQL Mail, Database Mail does not allow the user to read mailbox items. In fact, there is no mailbox to speak of; it can only send mail.

Mail Accounts and Mail Profiles

Depending on the configuration, a user can have access to multiple mail profiles for sending mail. Each profile can have multiple mail accounts associated with it.

When a profile is fully configured, it starts delivering mail using the account with the lowest sequence number. If the mail server specified by the account is not available for any reason, the DatabaseMail90.exe process tries it a specified number of times after a pre-configured delay interval and moves on to the next account in sequence. This process when one account fails and another one is used in its place is called *account failover* and is shown in Figure 10-2. All accounts under Profile1 are going to be exercised according to their sequence numbers: 1, 2, and 3.

In general, a profile can be **public**, that is, accessible to any user, or **private**, that is, accessible only to members of the sysadmin fixed server role or to any user that has been granted explicit access to this role.

Configuring Database Mail

Similar to SQL Mail, Database Mail is OFF by default on a new installation of SQL Server Database Engine and needs to be explicitly enabled by the administrator before it can be used.

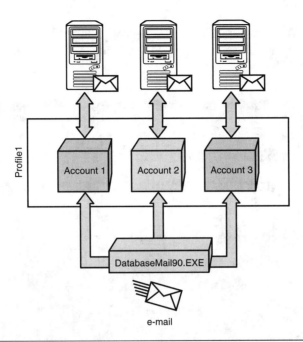

e-mail

Figure 10-2   Mail account failover.

You can configure a Database Mail solution by using the **Database Mail Configuration Wizard** in SQL Server Management Studio, shown in Figure 10-3. You invoke the wizard by clicking on the Database Mail folder inside the Object Explorer. You can run this wizard multiple times, performing different configuration tasks after email is already in operation. For now, it makes sense to select the first option that takes us through the basic setup stages, so let's click the **Next** button.

First, you need to configure the email profile and account. Account configuration can be tricky because you need to specify several important server characteristics. Please reference Figure 10-4 for details. You need to know the name and port number of the outgoing SMTP server. You also need to consider whether the SMTP server supports SSL. Finally, you need to decide on the server authentication mechanism. Database Mail supports the following authentication mechanisms:

- Anonymous authentication—The least secure option.
- Basic authentication—By providing user name and password in clear text.

■ Windows authentication—By using Database Engine service credentials. This is by far the most secure option and it leverages network security.

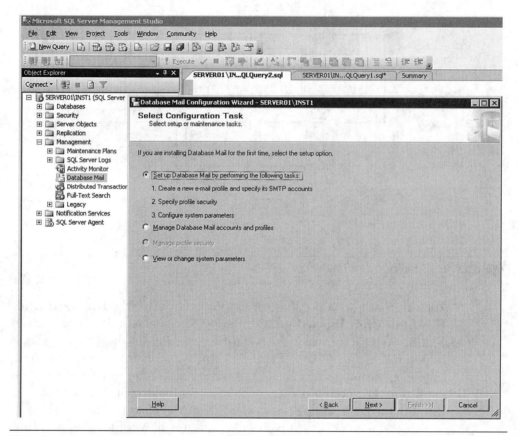

Figure 10-3 Database Mail Configuration Wizard.

Which one you choose depends on your environment and, more specifically, how much control you have over the back-end server configuration.

Database Mail Security

After the profile is fully configured, you need to decide which user(s) will have access to it. Assuming you don't want to make the profile public, you need to switch to the **Private Profiles** tab and select the user who will have access to the profile (see Figure 10-4). You also need to decide whether any given profile should be considered the **default** profile for this user. The default profile is used for sending mail by this particular user, calling sp_send_dbmail if the profile name is not specified as part of the stored procedure call.

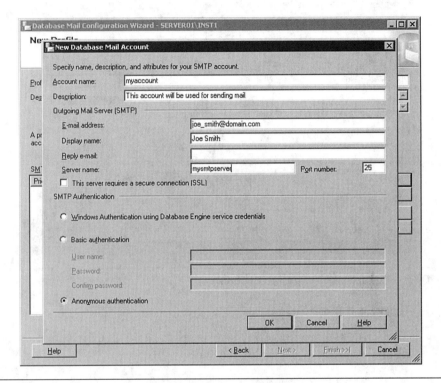

Figure 10-4   Configuring New Database Mail Account.

TIPS AND TRICKS
If the profile name is not specified for sending mail, Database Mail first checks for a private default profile and then checks the public default profile.

The drop-down list will be populated with all users that are defined in the MSDB database; however, only users that are members of the DatabaseMailUser database role can call sp_send_dbmail and use any profiles for sending mails.

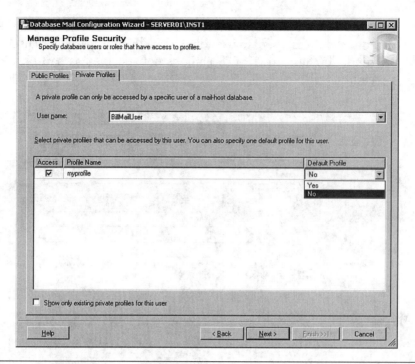

Figure 10-5   Database Mail profile access.

Sending Mail

The principal stored procedure used to send mail is called sp_send_ dbmail, which has the following syntax:

```
sp_send_dbmail [ [ @profile_name = ] 'profile_name' ]
     [ , [ @recipients = ] 'recipients [ ; ...n ]' ]
     [ , [ @copy_recipients = ] 'copy_recipient [ ; ...n ]' ]
     [ , [ @blind_copy_recipients = ] 'blind_copy_recipient [ ; ...n ]']
     [ , [ @subject = ] 'subject' ]
     [ , [ @body = ] 'body' ]
     [ , [ @body_format = ] 'body_format' ]
     [ , [ @importance = ] 'importance' ]
     [ , [ @sensitivity = ] 'sensitivity' ]
     [ , [ @file_attachments = ] 'attachment [ ; ...n ]' ]
     [ , [ @query = ] 'query' ]
     [ , [ @execute_query_database = ] 'execute_query_database' ]
     [ , [ @attach_query_result_as_file = ]
  ➥attach_query_result_as_file]
     [ , [ @query_attachment_filename = ]
  ➥query_attachment_filename ]
     [ , [ @query_result_header = ] query_result_header ]
```

```
[ , [ @query_result_width = ] query_result_width ]
[ , [ @query_result_separator = ] 'query_result_separator' ]
[ , [ @exclude_query_output = ] exclude_query_output ]
[ , [ @append_query_error = ] append_query_error ]
[ , [ @query_no_truncate = ] query_no_truncate ]
[ , [ @mailitem_id = ] mailitem_id ] [ OUTPUT ]
```

As you might have noticed, the parameters are very similar to those supplied for xp_sendmail (part of SQL Mail discussed earlier in this chapter), especially those related to formatting.

TIPS AND TRICKS

Do not expect the formatting of the query results to be the same between SQL Mail and Database Mail. In early pre-released versions of SQL Server 2005, both solutions shared the same formatting engine, but that has changed. The main reason for this change is deficiencies of the old SQL Mail-based formatting engine with respect to the new data types introduced in SQL Server 2005, such as nvarchar(max), varchar(max), xml, and so on.

This similarity is intentional because Microsoft wanted to simplify customer migration to Database Mail by providing full backward compatibility. Still, a few extra parameters exist that need to be considered as definite improvements. First, the @body parameter can indicate the HTML body type of a sent message that instructs the SMTP delivery mechanism about special character escaping for HTML element tags or lack thereof that is required to handle the message. Second, there is a capability to specify the importance of the mail message via the @importance parameter that can accept the following values: Low, Normal, and High. There is also the @sensitivity parameter, which accepts Normal, Personal, Private, Confidential flags.

You may also notice that the capability to run the query as a user is no longer there. It is believed that users that are not members of the sysadmin fixed server role won't have necessary privileges to impersonate others, whereas server administrators can simply supply the EXECUTE AS clause as part of the query itself, thus eliminating the need for the extra logic.

Finally, you need to consider the last parameter, @mailitem_id, which gets the actual value of the mail message ID assigned to it automatically for delivery by Database Mail engine. What do you do with this value? You can look later at one of the management views showing mail delivery status and see whether your message has been delivered to the mail server.

Now consider the entire process of calling **sp_send_dbmail** and look at all the moving parts. Please refer to Figure 10-6 for a sequence diagram representing the mail delivery process: The steps involved are these:

1. Sender connects to SQL Server Database Engine and calls sp_send_dbmail in the context of MSDB database.
2. The entire body of the message (including necessary attachments) gets loaded into one of the internal MSDB tables supporting the Database Mail solution.
3. A special message ID is inserted into the External Service Broker queue.
4. Service Broker, in response to the newly inserted queue item, calls a special activator stored procedure.
5. The activator procedure checks whether a DatabaseMail90.exe process is already running and launches it if necessary.
6. The DatabaseMail90.exe process connects back to the SQL Server Database Engine instance and reads the Service Broker Queue Message.
7. After the message is read, the mailer process selects the message details from the internal mail table by its message ID.
8. Message details include a profile name that gets resolved into the appropriate mail accounts to be used for delivery.
9. The DatabaseMail90.exe process attempts to contact all mail servers, following the normal mail account failover routine as described earlier.
10. When the message is successfully delivered to the mail server, DatabaseMail90.exe posts a response message onto a special Service Broker Internal Queue.
11. The Service Broker Internal Queue activation stored procedure gets launched.
12. The activation procedure reads the response message and updates the internal status table for a given message ID, indicating successful delivery.

It is worth noting that after the DatabaseMail90.exe process is launched, it continues running for a pre-defined period of time, even after the External Queue is depleted, that is, there are no more messages to be delivered. This inactivity timeout period and other similar global settings are part of the Database Mail global configuration parameters.

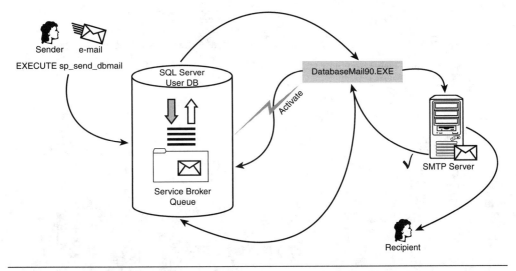

Figure 10-6   Delivering mail.

System Configuration Parameters

Let's examine the Database Mail system configuration parameters via the Database Mail Configuration Wizard, shown in Figure 10-7.

Each parameter value can be changed right inside the grid. To quickly look up what purpose a particular parameter serves, it is sufficient to simply switch focus to the desired grid line and look at the help text at the bottom of the dialog. Table 10-2 contains a brief summary of system configuration parameters and their possible values.

Monitoring and Troubleshooting Database Mail

Database Mail has a log that can contain different types of events, based on a specified preconfigured Logging Level. You can view the Database Mail Log easily by right-clicking on the **Database Mail** node in the Object Explorer and selecting the **View Database Mail Log** pop-up menu item. The Database Mail Log File Viewer is shown in Figure 10-8.

A number of monitoring views and stored procedures have also been added to Database Mail to simplify monitoring and potential troubleshooting of email issues. Although they do not have direct graphical

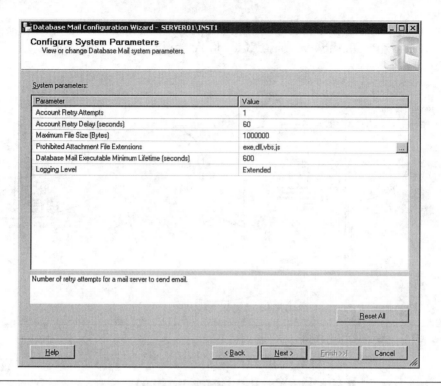

Figure 10-7   Database Mail System configuration parameters.

support in SQL Server Management Studio, you can access them by executing simple queries via Query Editor.

For example, the msdb.dbo.sysmail_allitems view enables the user to see all email items processed by the system. There are specialized snapshots of this view for viewing only successfully sent items (msdb.dbo.sysmail_sentitems), unsent items (msdb.dbo.sysmail_unsentitems), and failed items (msdb.dbo.sysmail_faileditems). Any member of the DatabaseMailUserRole MSDB has access to these views, but regular users can see only specific items they personally tried to send.

Stored procedure sysmail_help_status_sp is used to view the status of Database Mail queues. Possible values returned are STARTED and STOPPED.

TIPS AND TRICKS
Under normal operation, you would not have a need to start or stop mail queues yourself, but if you ever want to do this you can use the sysmail_start_sp and sysmail_stop_sp procedures to do this.

Table 10-2 System Configuration Parameters

Parameter Name	Recommended Value(s)	Possible Values	Purpose
Account Retry Attempts	1–3	Any positive number	Number of times the DatabaseMail90.exe process should try to connect to a given mail server before giving up. If more than one mail account is associated with the mail profiler, the failover sequence is started.
Account Retry Delay	10–60	Any positive number	Number of seconds to wait before trying to connect to the same mail server again.
Maximum File Size	100,000–1,000,000	Any positive number	Maximum size of the attachment file that can be sent via email.
Prohibited Attachment File Extensions	exe, dll, vbs, js	Comma-separated string of the file extensions	If the attachment has one of the specified potentially dangerous not be sent extensions, it will not be sent out.
Database Mail Executable Minimum Lifetime	60–180	Any positive number	Number of seconds the DatabaseMail90.exe process will wait before shutting down after all mail is sent.
Logging Level	2-Extended, Normal, Extended, Verbose		Normal—Log errors only. Extended—Log all errors and warnings. Verbose—Log all errors, warnings, and informational messages.

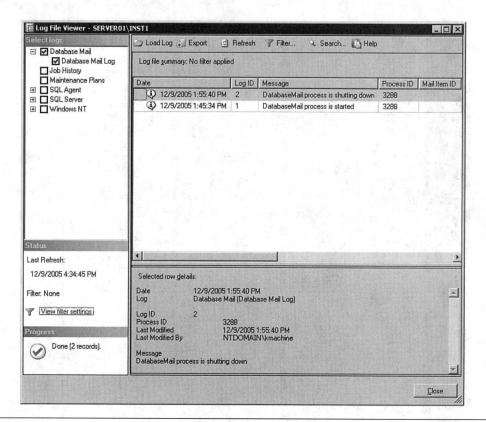

Figure 10-8 Database Mail Log File Viewer.

There is also a procedure that allows you to view the status of Database Mail queues explicitly. It is called sysmail_help_queue_sp, and it returns a resultset with the status of each mail queue.

Managing Database Mail Storage

Because Database Mail uses the MSDB database as its repository, it is important to be able to clean up old messages. A special management stored procedure exists specifically for this purpose: sysmail_delete_mailitems_sp, which allows the administrator to delete all mail items sent earlier than a specified date, and optionally allows you to restrict deletion by specific mail item status (sent, unsent, failed, retrying).

SQL Agent Mail

SQL Agent can be configured to use either its own internal mailing facilities based on MAPI or the Database Mail solution described earlier. Keep in mind that SQL Agent never uses legacy SQL Mail components, so when you look at the SQL Server Agent Properties dialog shown in Figure 10-9 the component name is slightly confusing. We will refer to SQL Agent MAPI mailer as SQL Agent Mail.

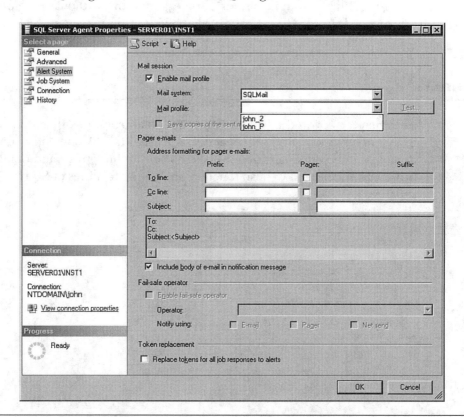

Figure 10-9   SQL Server Agent Properties dialog—Mail Session Configuration.

SQL Agent Mail, by default, targets extended MAPI for mail delivery, but when extended MAPI is not present, SQL Agent Mail starts using simple MAPI instead. Unlike SQL Mail, which runs in the context of the SQL Server Database Engine service account, SQL Agent Mail uses the SQL Agent service account because it is completely embedded within the SQL Agent internal process space.

When configuring SQL Agent to use Database Mail, you need to first pre-configure the Database Mail profile because SQL Agent expects explicit profile name specification at the configuration stage. SQL Agent uses Database Mail just as any other SQL Server client does: by executing the sp_send_dbmail stored procedure. However, if its corresponding SQL Server Database Engine instance is down and mail cannot be sent through this route, SQL Agent instead uses a low-level Database Mail API, using cached profile and account information. This way, mail still goes out in case of an emergency, but without being properly logged into MSDB repository along with other messages.

Summary

This chapter covered in depth two main email solutions that ship with SQL Server 2005: SQL Mail and Database Mail. Along the way we demonstrated significant differences in their architectures and delivery protocols. At the end we also touched on mailing facilities of SQL Agent service.

CHAPTER 11

Inside Programming Object Models

SQL Server 2005 ships with two programming object models that allow programmatic management of SQL Server objects. SQL Server Management Objects (SMO) is a brand-new API. SMO is implemented as a .NET library and replaces SQL-DMO (COM server with multiple automation interfaces), which shipped as part of earlier releases and is deprecated with SQL Server 2005. SMO has an object tree hierarchy similar to SQL-DMO and provides most of the functionality of SQL-DMO, plus added support for all new objects added to SQL Server Database Engine in SQL Server 2005. SQL-DMO has also been upgraded to manage SQL Server 2005 Database Engine Instance, but no new functionality has been added to it. Therefore, customers using new SQL Server 2005-specific Database Engine features, such as, SQL Server Service Broker, Http Endpoints, and so on, will have to migrate to SMO.

TIP

Old applications written based on SQL-DMO will continue to function after an upgrade to SQL Server 2005 as long as the client computer using SQL-DMO has an upgraded version of the SQL-DMO library as well. Consider upgrading client computers before upgrading your server to ensure a smooth transition to the new platform.

SMO can manage SQL Server 2000 and SQL Server 2005 Database Engine instances. It cannot, however, manage earlier versions of Database Engine.

SMO, similar to DMO, is freely redistributable with your application, provided you comply with certain licensing restrictions. A special redistribution module contains SMO assemblies and registration code that you can download and that ship as part of your product. It is called XMO installer package and includes a few other assemblies in addition to SMO. You can download the RTM version from http://download. microsoft.com/download/f/7/4/f74cbdb1-87e2-4794-9186-e3ad6bd54b41/ SQLServer2005_XMO.msi.

Please keep in mind that you don't need to download it separately if you are planning to install SQL Server 2005 on your computer anyway. In this case SMO components are installed automatically when you select the Client Tools option.

This chapter covers SMO through multiple usage scenarios, then covers internal SMO architecture, and finally dives into performance and optimization topics.

The SMO Object Model

A high-level fragment of the SMO Object Model diagram is shown in Figure 11-1.

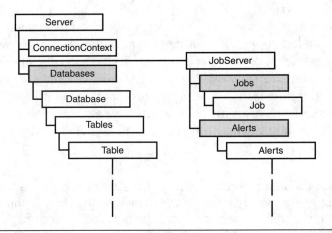

Figure 11-1   SMO Object Model diagram fragment.

As you notice in the picture, some of the names are plural. These plural names represent collections of objects. For example, the top level Server object has a collection of Databases holding actual Database instance objects present in the given Database Engine instance. Subsequently each database has a collection of Table objects and so on. If you can imagine this diagram extended to cover nearly every object inside SQL Server 2005, you will have an idea how large this object model is. Just to give you some idea, SMO has over 150 instance classes.

Some Uses of SMO Objects

Let's perform a few simple operations on SMO objects to demonstrate their multiple uses. Most objects support Create, Alter, and Drop operations, so in this section you will see an example of each operation.

TIP

To treat objects polymorphically and check at runtime whether a given object supports Create, Alter, or Drop operations, you can check whether the object implements the ICreatable, IAlterable, or IDroppable interface and act on it correspondingly.

To use SMO in projects, the user needs to include a few namespace references:

- Visual Basic .NET
  - Imports Microsoft.SqlServer.Management.SMO
  - Imports Microsoft.SqlServer.Management.Common
- C# .NET
  - using Microsoft.SqlServer.Management.Smo
  - using Microsoft.SqlServer.Management.Common

The user also needs to reference the following few assemblies in his project:

- Microsoft.SqlServer.Smo.dll
- Microsoft.SqlServer.SmoEnum.dll
- Microsoft.SqlServer.SqlEnum.dll
- Microsoft.SqlServer.ConnectionInfo.dll

In general you can find these assemblies in two places on your computer. First they are located in C:\Program Files\Microsoft SQL Server\ 90\SDK\Assemblies. That is the source from which you need to reference them. The second place you can find them is the Global Assembly Cache (GAC) under some cryptic directory similar to this one:

```
C:\Windows\Assembly\GAC_MSIL\Microsoft.SqlServer.SMO\9.0.242.0__898
45dcd8080cc91.
```

The SDK directory should be used at design time and GAC is used at run time. The SMO redistribution module mentioned earlier handles registration of deployed SMO assemblies with GAC automatically so your programs will be able to locate them when they are running.

Let's dive directly into SMO code through different usage scenarios. Throughout this chapter most of the code samples are provided in two mainstream .NET languages: Visual Basic and C#. Only when syntax is identical or nearly identical will one of the languages be omitted for the sake of brevity.

Create a Simple Login Using SQL Authentication

The first part of the following code snippets is used to a create server object and establish a connection common to all samples, and therefore is omitted from here on. Please make sure to supply the correct `serverName` value, that is, the name of the server operation you want to be performed.

Visual Basic .NET

```
Dim serverInstance As Server
serverInstance = New Server(serverName)
serverInstance.ConnectionContext.NonPooledConnection = True
serverInstance.ConnectionContext.LoginSecure = True
```

C# .NET

```
Server serverInstance = new Server(serverName);
serverInstance.ConnectionContext.NonPooledConnection = true;
serverInstance.ConnectionContext.LoginSecure = true;
```

With the server object created, now you can create a login object on the server. Make sure `loginPassword` satisfies security requirements of SQL Server Database Engine in terms of complexity.

Visual Basic .NET

```
Dim l As Login
l = New Login(serverInstance, loginName)
l.LoginType = LoginType.SqlLogin
l.DefaultDatabase = "AdventureWorks"
l.Create(loginPassword)
```

C# .NET

```
Login l = new Login(serverInstance, loginName);
l.LoginType = LoginType.SqlLogin ;
l.DefaultDatabase = "AdventureWorks";
l.Create(loginPassword);
```

Alter an Existing Table by Changing the Data Type of One of Its Columns to Small Integer

It would have been possible to perform navigation to the column object in one line, but it is split here for the sake of simplicity.

Visual Basic .NET

```
Dim db As Database
Dim t As Table
Dim c As Column
db = serverInstance.Databases(databaseName)
t = db.Tables(tableName, tableSchema)
c = t.Columns(columnName)
c.DataType = DataType.SmallInt
c.Alter()
```

C# .NET

```
Database db = serverInstance.Databases[databaseName];
Table t = db.Tables[tableName, tableSchema];
Column c = t.Columns[columnName];
c.DataType = DataType.SmallInt;
c.Alter();
```

Drop Full Text Index on View

Suppose a view has a full text index defined and you want to remove it.

Visual Basic .NET

```
Dim fti As FullTextIndex
fti = serverInstance.Databases(databaseName).
➥Views(viewName).FullTextIndex;
fti.Drop();
```

C# .NET

```
Full Text Index fti = serverInstance.Databases
➥[databaseName].Views[viewName].FullTextIndex;
fti.Drop();
```

What happened behind the scenes as the code ran? SMO generated proper DDL statements to perform the desired operations on the Database Engine instance and submitted them to the server for immediate execution. Should an error occur during any of these operations, SMO throws an exception containing a specific SQL Server message with an error number and a brief description of why it failed. However, you do not always want to execute DDL immediately against the server. Sometimes it is desirable to obtain a T-SQL script for examination and later execute it in a different environment. SMO provides the functionality to accomplish this in **Capture Mode**. SQL Server Management Studio leverages this feature from all management dialogs when you choose to generate a script.

Capture Mode

To control how generated statements are going to be executed, you need to set the `SqlExecutionMode` explicitly on the ConnectionContext object as follows:

```
serverInstance.ConnectionContext.SqlExecutionModes =
➥SqlExecutionModes.CaptureSql;
```

This enumeration property has several possible values: `ExecuteSql`, `CaptureSql`, and `ExecuteAndCaptureSql`. The first value is set by default to execute all generated T-SQL statements immediately. The second value enables you to capture generated T-SQL in a special buffer where it can later be accessed, like this:

Visual Basic .NET

```
Dim scriptBatches As StringCollection
scriptBatches = serverInstance.ConnectionContext.

➥CapturedSql.Text;
```

C# .NET

```
StringCollection scriptBatches =
➥serverInstance.ConnectionContext.CapturedSql.Text;
```

TIP
The reason captured T-SQL is retrieved as a `StringCollection` is to avoid the need for parsing different batches, as each batch is represented by its own string entry in the collection. Actually, the SMO `ServerConnection` object enables you to execute a collection of batches directly as follows:

```
serverInstance.ConnectionContext.ExecuteNonQuery
➥(scriptBatches);
```

To use `StringCollection` do not forget to add a reference to the System.`Collections`.`Specialized` namespace.

Finally, the `ExecuteAndCaptureSql` option enables the user to run the DDL and capture it at the same time for examination and running later against a different server or via other means.

Scripting

In many cases you need to get a DDL script to re-create an object, possibly against a different server. For this purpose you will use a feature called **scripting**. Any object that implements the `IScriptable` interface uses two overloaded `Script` methods. The first method takes no parameters and the second method accepts different scripting options via a special class called `ScriptingOptions`. Both methods return `StringCollection`, which contains the DDL for this particular object. Using one of these two scripting methods of the object is by far the simplest way to obtain its script. However, this is not the only way to obtain a script and does not satisfy a complex scenario of scripting several objects at once while respecting their dependencies. For example, when you have a view V1 that relies on another view V2 and that view in turn relies on table T1, you likely want to generate the script in the right order, that is, T1, V2, V1. To accomplish this, you need to use a standalone `Scripter` object. In a simple case, you instantiate the `Scripter` object, supply it with a list of objects to script and some scripting options, and get back a complete DDL for creation of all the objects you specified plus any dependent objects `Scripter` discovers. However, this happens only if you set the `WithDependencies` flag to true on the `ScriptingOptions` object.

TIP

Scripter also enables you to generate drop statements for the objects in the proper sequence. To accomplish this you should set the aforementioned `WithDependenices` option as well as the `ScriptDrops` flag.

A single-phase scripting is shown in Figure 11-2. Notice how the Scripter is treated as a "black box" by the user. In other words, after scripting is invoked, you expect to get the full script back in one section without interruption.

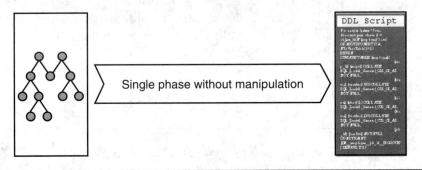

Figure 11-2 SMO scripting in a single phase.

Let's look at a code sample for this scenario.

Single Phase Scripting

Create a `Scripter` object by passing a reference to previously instantiated server object (see earlier examples):

Visual Basic .NET

```
Dim scripterInstance As Scripter
scripterInstance = new Scripter(serverInstance)
```

C# .NET

```
Scripter scripterInstance = new Scripter(serverInstance);
```

Set different scripting options:

```
scripterInstance.Options.WithDependencies = true;
scripterInstance.Options.ClusteredIndexes = true;
```

```
scripterInstance.Options.NonClusteredIndexes = true;
scripterInstance.Options.DriPrimaryKey = true;
scripterInstance.Options.DriUniqueKeys = true;
```

Generate a list of objects to script:

Visual Basic .NET

```
Dim db As Database
Dim scriptList(2) As SqlSmoObject
db = serverInstance.Databases("pubs");
scriptList(1) = db.Tables("authors")
scriptList(2) = db.Tables("publishers")
```

C# .NET

```
Database db = serverInstance.Databases["pubs"];
SqlSmoObject[] scriptList = new SqlSmoObject[]

➥{db.Tables["authors"], db.Tables["publishers"]};
```

Now invoke scripting:

Visual Basic .NET

```
Dim scriptStrings As StringCollection
scriptStrings = scripterInstance.Script(scriptList);
```

C# .NET

```
scriptStrings = scripterInstance.Script(scriptList);
```

Behind the Scenes

Let's examine what happens behind the scenes and consider some of the advanced scripting features exposed by the `Scripter` object. Figure 11-3 shows multiple scripting phases.

The first scripting phase is called **Dependency Discovery** or **Discovery** for short. This is when SMO figures out object interdependencies and builds an internal tree of objects. To accomplish this in code you write the following:

```
DependencyTree depTree = scripter.DiscoverDependencies
➥ (smoObjectsList, true);
```

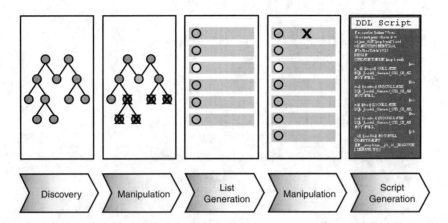

Figure 11-3   SMO scripting in multiple phases.

After Discovery is finished, the user has a chance to manipulate the dependency tree and remove unnecessary branches for objects that do not need to be scripted. The user can navigate the dependency tree in a simple manner. Each node in a tree is represented by the DependencyTreeNode object, which can have any number of dependent child nodes. You can walk through each level of dependent child objects as follows:

```
If (depParent.HasChildNodes)
{
depChild = depParent.FirstChild;
    while ( null != depChild )
{
            // do something with the node

    depChild = depChild.NextSibling;
    }
}
```

While navigating the tree, you can remove any of its branches by calling the Remove method on any node. This causes the particular node and any of its dependent nodes to not be scripted.

The second scripting phase is called **List Generation**. During this phase, the scripter walks the dependency tree and comes up with a flat list of objects for scripting. This is how you can perform the navigation through the `Scripter` object:

```
DependencyCollection depCollection =
 ➥scripter.WalkDependencies(dependencyTree);
```

After a list of objects is generated, it may be desirable for a user to manipulate it further by adding or removing nodes.

The final phase of the scripting process is called **Script Generation** and actually involves scripting each object on the list individually. Here is how you accomplish it:

```
StringCollection scriptBatches =
 ➥scr.ScriptWithList(dependencyCollection);
```

Previously, you saw how scripting can be performed in a single step. Here is how you can invoke each phase individually and accomplish the same goal but with more granular control of the process, as was shown in Figure 11-3.

Advanced Scripting

Rather than call the `Script` method, as the previous example did, let's call each scripting phase individually:

Visual Basic .NET

```
Dim depTree As DependencyTree
Dim depCollection As DependencyCollection
Dim scriptBatches As StringCollection

depTree = scripterInstance.DiscoverDependencies
 ➥ (scriptList, true);

'do something with a tree
' ...

depCollection = scripterInstance.WalkDependencies(depTree);

'do something with a list
' ...

scriptBatches = scripterInstance.ScriptWithList(depCollection);
```

C# .NET

```
DependencyTree dependencyTree =
scripterInstance.DiscoverDependencies

➥(scriptList, true);

// do something with a tree
// ...

DependencyCollection dependencyCollection =
➥scripterInstance.WalkDependencies(dependencyTree);

// do something with a list
// ...

StringCollection scriptBatches =

➥scripterInstance.ScriptWithList(dependencyCollection);
```

This discussion of scripting would not be complete without mention of the advanced scripting callback mechanism. Users can sign up to be notified via a callback function during the dependency walk before each tree node is added to the flat list of objects for scripting. Another notification point is during the scripting phase, when the script for the object is about to be generated. Here is how you can declare a filter function and sign up for the event:

Visual Basic .NET

```
Public Function CustomScriptingFilter(objectUrn As Urn)

➥As Boolean
'logic to determine whether object needs to be skipped.
'If so, return True

Return False
End Function ' CustomScriptingFilter
```

C# .NET

```
bool CustomScriptingFilter(Urn urn)
{
      // logic to determine whether object needs to
      // be skipped. If so, return true.

      return false;
}
```

Sign up for the event before the desired stage of the scripting process as follows:

Visual Basic .NET

```
scripter.FilterCallbackFunction = New ScriptingFilter

➥ (AddressOf CustomScriptingFilter);
```

C# .NET

```
scripter.FilterCallbackFunction = new ScriptingFilter

➥ (CustomScriptingFilter);
```

TIP

If you want to script objects for the entire database, you should consider using the `Transfer` object instead of `Scripter`. In addition to transferring metadata between two databases via script, the `Transfer` object can also move actual data by utilizing a specialized SQL Server Integration Services task. Here is an example of how you can generate a script for all tables and views inside the database for creation on a SQL Server 2005 server:

```
Transfer transfer = new Transfer(database);
transfer.CopyAllObjects = false;
transfer.CopyAllTables = true;
transfer.CopyAllViews = true;
transfer.Options.TargetServerVersion =
➥SqlServerVersion.Version90;
StringCollection scriptBatches =
➥transfer.ScriptTransfer();
```

Backup and Restore

SMO also provides utility classes to simplify some of the essential database operations. Some of the most widely used classes are `Backup` and `Restore`. The following sections demonstrate how to use these classes with a few examples.

Back Up the AdventureWorks Sample Database to a Disk with Mirroring

To back up the database, begin by creating a backup object and initializing it with options:

```
Backup backupInstance = new Backup();
backupInstance.Database = "AdventureWorks";
backupInstance.Action = BackupActionType.Database;
backupInstance.Checksum = true;
backupInstance.FormatMedia = true;
backupInstance.Initialize = true;
backupInstance.SkipTapeHeader = true;
```

Create backup devices:

```
backupInstance.Devices.AddDevice(@"c:\back1a.bak",

➥DeviceType.File);
backupInstance.Devices.AddDevice(@"c:\back1b.bak",

➥DeviceType.File);
```

Create a backup device list for mirroring:

```
BackupDeviceList l1 = new BackupDeviceList();
l1.AddDevice(@"c:\Backups\back2a.bak", DeviceType.File);
l1.AddDevice(@"c:\Backups\back2b.bak", DeviceType.File);

BackupDeviceList l2 = new BackupDeviceList();
l2.AddDevice(@"c:\Backups\back3a.bak", DeviceType.File);
l2.AddDevice(@"c:\Backups\back3b.bak", DeviceType.File);

BackupDeviceList[] la = new BackupDeviceList[2];
la[0] = l1;
la[1] = l2;
backupInstance.Mirrors = la;
```

Create a script backup operation:

```
StringCollection scriptBacthes =

➥backupInstance.Script(serverInstance);
```

Perform Asynchronous Database Backup

To perform asynchronous database backup, begin by declaring a progress event notification handler function that prints the completion percentage to the disk:

Visual Basic .NET

```
Sub OnPercentComplete (ByVal sender As Object, ByVal a As
PercentCompleteEventArgs)
     Console.WriteLine(a.Percent.ToString +
➥"% backed-up")
End Sub
```

C# .NET

```
void OnPercentComplete (object sender,

➥            PercentCompleteEventArgs a)
{
    Console.WriteLine("Progress = {0}%", a.Percent);
}
```

Declare an operation completion notification function that checks for errors during backup and reports a final status:

Visual Basic .NET

```
Sub OnComplete (ByVal sender As Object, ByVal a As
ServerMessageEventArgs)
If backup.AsyncStatus.ExecutionStatus <>
➥ExecutionStatus.Succeeded
        Console.WriteLine("Backup had an error: " +
➥ backup.AsyncStatus.LastException.Message);
    Else
        Console.WriteLine("Backup completed successfully");
End If
End Sub
```

C# .NET

```
void OnComplete(object sender, ServerMessageEventArgs e)
{
if( backup.AsyncStatus.ExecutionStatus !=
➥    ExecutionStatus.Succeeded )
{
        Console.WriteLine("Backup had an error: " +
➥backup.AsyncStatus.LastException.Message);
}
```

```
        else
        {
                Console.WriteLine("Backup completed successfully");
        }
}
```

Create a `Backup` object and initialize it:

Visual Basic .NET

```
Dim backupInstance As Backup
backupInstance = new Backup()
backupInstance.Database = "AdventureWorks"
backupInstance.BackupSetName = "AdventureWorks Backup"
backupInstance.BackupSetDescription =
➡"Weekly Backup of AdventureWorks"
backupInstance.MediaName = "Set 1"
backupInstance.MediaDescription = "Backup Media Set # 1"
backupInstance.Devices.AddDevice(@"c:\north.bak",
➡DeviceType.File)
backupInstance.Initialize = true
backupInstance.UnloadTapeAfter = true
backupInstance.PercentCompleteNotification = 10
backupInstance.RetainDays = 14
backupInstance.Action = BackupActionType.Database
```

C# .NET

```
Backup backupInstance = new Backup();
backupInstance.Database = "AdventureWorks";
backupInstance.BackupSetName = "AdventureWorks Backup";
backupInstance.BackupSetDescription =
➡"Weekly Backup of AdventureWorks";
backupInstance.MediaName = "Set 1";
backupInstance.MediaDescription = "Backup Media Set # 1";
backupInstance.Devices.AddDevice(@"c:\north.bak",
➡DeviceType.File);
backupInstance.Initialize = true;
backupInstance.UnloadTapeAfter = true;
backupInstance.PercentCompleteNotification = 10;
backupInstance.RetainDays = 14;
backupInstance.Action = BackupActionType.Database;
```

Add event handlers to the backup object:

Visual Basic .NET

```
AddHandler backupInstance.PercentComplete,

➥AddressOf OnPercentComplete
AddHandler backupInstance.Complete, AddressOf OntComplete
```

C# .NET

```
backupInstance.PercentComplete += new
PercentCompleteEventHandler(OnPercentComplete);
backupInstance.Complete +=

➥new ServerMessageEventHandler(OnComplete);
```

Start the asynchronous backup operation. You could also have used the `SqlBackup` function call to perform the operation synchronously:

```
backupInstance.SqlBackupAsync(serverInstance);
```

Restore a Complete Database by Replacing the Existing One

Another backup and restore operation that can be scripted is restoring a database by replacing the existing one. Start by creating a `Restore` object and initialize it:

Visual Basic .NET

```
Dim restoreInstance As Restore
restoreInstance = new Restore()
restoreInstance.Database = databaseName;
restoreInstance.Devices.AddDevice(BackupFileName,
➥DeviceType.File)
restoreInstance.ReplaceDatabase = true
restoreInstance.PercentCompleteNotification = 25
```

C# .NET

```
Restore restoreInstance = new Restore();
restoreInstance.Database = databaseName;
restoreInstance.Devices.AddDevice(BackupFileName,
➥DeviceType.File);
restoreInstance.ReplaceDatabase = true;
restoreInstance.PercentCompleteNotification = 25;
```

Add an event handler to show periodic progress, as in the previous example.

Visual Basic .NET

```
AddHandler restoreInstance.PercentComplete,

➥AddressOf OnPercentComplete
```

C# .NET

```
restoreInstance.PercentComplete +=

➥new PercentCompleteEventHandler(OnPercentComplete);
```

Finally, start the synchronous restore process:

```
restoreInstance.SqlRestore(serverInstance);
```

Architecture

Now that you have looked at some important functional components of SMO and their uses, it's time to look at the big picture and understand how the object model is structured from an architectural perspective. SMO consists of the following major components exposed to the user and shown in Figure 11-4.

- **Instance classes** include concrete objects representing objects that exist inside Database Engine, e.g., Table, View, Index, Trigger, StoredProcedure, SqlAssembly, PartitionScheme, etc.

- **Scripter Classes** include Scripter itself and all its helper classes, such as ScriptingOptions, DependencyWalker, DependencyTree, etc.

- **Utility Classes** provide special complementary functionality, e.g., Backup/Restore, WMI Provider, Server Configuration, Full-Text indexing, Transfer, Tracing/Replay (described in depth in Chapter 9, "Inside Monitoring Tools"), etc.

To obtain object properties, all SMO instance classes have to go through an internal component called Enumerator. Enumerator accepts generic metadata requests from its clients asking for a specific set of object properties. It turns these requests into valid T-SQL metadata queries and executes the queries against back-end Database Engine via a connection object. The Enumerator converts data coming back from the server into a usable format and returns it back to the caller. Although the major portion of Enumerator's functionality is dedicated to working with SQL Server Database Engine, it also has branches dealing with other types of data that need to be retrieved. For example, there are Enumerator branches that talk to Analysis Server, Notification Server, and WMI Provider.

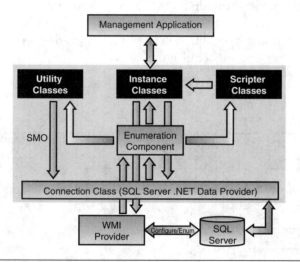

Figure 11-4   SMO architectural diagram.

To uniquely identify any SMO object, Enumerator uses the notion of Urn. It is a common property for all instance classes. Here is a sample Urn for the pubs.dbo.authors table:

```
Server/Database[@Name='pubs']/Table[@Name='authors'
➥ and @Schema='dbo']
```

TIP
Urn can also be used to instantiate an object directly through a class factory as follows:

```
Table table = serverInstance.GetSmoObject(tableUrn)
➥as Table;
```

Local Trees

SMO, unlike SQL-DMO, does not have a global object tree with an Application object as its root. Instead, SMO enables users to create multiple object trees called **Local Trees** using the Server object as root. After each tree is populated, it represents a snapshot of the Database Engine metadata at the time the tree population took place. Local trees are not synchronized with each other. In other words, changes made to any Database Engine object represented in the tree, including the changes made through another tree of the object model itself, are not propagated to other instances of the same object in other trees. At any point in time any local tree can be released and objects in collections can be emptied, as shown in Figure 11-5.

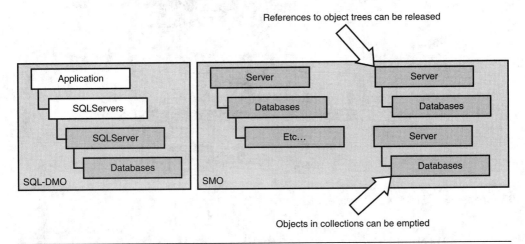

Figure 11-5   SMO local trees with releasable state vs. SQL-DMO global tree.

TIP
If you believe the object to which you are holding a reference is stale and want to refresh its internal properties before making further modifications or discarding previous ones, you can accomplish this by directly calling the `Refresh` method on the object.

Monitoring Server Events

SQL Server Database Engine exposes certain internal events via its WMI provider. Clients using SMO can optionally subscribe to these events and have them routed to a particular object of interest to monitor any changes made externally to an object, such as monitoring for table structure changes, audit logins, and so on. The Internal SMO event routing mechanism is shown in Figure 11-6. Notice how events can be aggregated at the higher-level object. For example, any table object event such as creation of an index can be propagated to the database object or even to the server object, depending upon the level at which you sign up for it.

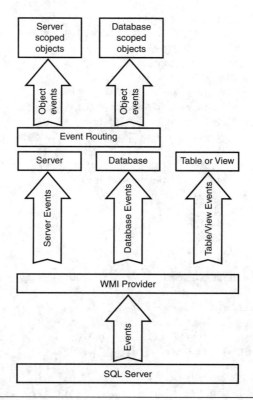

Figure 11-6   Server events.

To help refine your understanding of this sort of monitoring, let's examine some server monitoring scenarios.

Monitor Table Create/Drop Events at the Server Instance Level

To set up monitoring of table create/drop events at the server instance level, begin by declaring an event callback function that prints the contents of each event to the console.

Visual Basic .NET

```
Private Sub OnDdlEvent(ByVal sender As Object,
➥ByVal args As ServerEventArgs)
    SyncLock Me
        Console.WriteLine("------ {0} ------",
➥args.EventType.ToString())
        Console.WriteLine("SPID    : {0}", args.Spid)
        Console.WriteLine("Time    : {0}", args.PostTime)
        Console.WriteLine("Instance: {0}", args.SqlInstance)
        Console.WriteLine()
        For Each EventProperty entry in args.Properties
            Dim valueType As String
            If entry.Value Is Nothing Then
                valueType = String.Empty
            Else
                valueType = Entry.Value.GetType().ToString()
            End If
            Console.WriteLine("{0,25}: {1} ({2})",
➥entry.Name, entry.Value, valueType)
        Next
    End SyncLock
End Sub
```

C# .NET

```
public void OnServerEvent (object sender, ServerEventArgs args)
{
    lock (this)
    {
        Console.WriteLine("------ {0} ------",
➥args.EventType.ToString());
        Console.WriteLine("SPID    : {0}", args.Spid);
        Console.WriteLine("Time    : {0}", args.PostTime);
        Console.WriteLine("Instance: {0}", args.SqlInstance);
        Console.WriteLine();

        foreach(EventProperty entry in args.Properties)
        {
            Console.WriteLine("{0,25}: {1} ({2})",
```

```
➡    entry.Name, entry.Value,
➡    (entry.Value != null)?
➡     entry.Value.GetType().ToString() : string.Empty);
       }
    }
}
```

Next, simply subscribe to events and start monitoring:

Visual Basic .NET

```
Dim serverEventSetInstance As New ServerEventSet
serverEventSetInstance.CreateTable = True
serverEventSetInstance.DropTable = True
Dim serverEventHandlerInstance As ServerEventHandler
serverEventHandlerInstance = New ServerEventHandler(AddressOf
OnServerEvent)
serverInstance.Events.SubscribeToEvents(serverEventSetInstance,
serverEventHandlerInstance)
serverInstance.Events.StartEvents();
```

C# .NET

```
serverInstance.Events.ServerEvent += new ServerEventHandler(this.
OnServerEvent);
serverInstance.Events.SubscribeToEvents(ServerEvent.CreateTable);
serverInstance.Events.SubscribeToEvents(ServerEvent.DropTable);
serverInstance.Events.StartEvents();
```

Upon program exit make sure you unsubscribe to all events:

```
serverInstance.Events.UnsubscribeAllEvents();
```

Monitor an Index Creation Event on a Table Object Level

Using a previously declared event handler function, you can subscribe to an index creation event as follows:

Visual Basic .NET

```
Dim tableInstance As Table
tableInstance = serverInstance.Databases("pubs").
➡Tables("authors")
Dim tableEventSetInstance As New TableEventSet
tableEventSetInstance.CreateIndex = True
Dim serverEventHandlerInstance As ServerEventHandler
```

```
serverCreateEventHandler = New ServerEventHandler(AddressOf
OnServerEvent)
serverInstance.Events.SubscribeToEvents(tableEventSetInstance,
serverEventHandlerInstance)
tableInstance.Events.StartEvents();
```

C# .NET

```
Table table = serverInstance.Databases["pubs"].Tables["authors"];
table.Events.SubscribeToEvents(TableEvent.CreateIndex);
table.Events.ServerEvent +=
➥new ServerEventHandler(OnServerEvent);
table.Events.StartEvents();
```

Monitoring a Trigger Alter or Drop at the Object Level

SMO enables you to monitor for any external modifications to a database object, provided your application that is calling into the SMO function is running while modification is taking place.

Visual Basic .NET

```
Dim db As Database
Dim trig As Trigger
db = serverInstance.Databases("AdventureWorks")
trig = db.Tables("Address", "Person").Triggers("TRIG_ADDRESS")
Dim triggerEventSet As New ObjectEventSet
triggerEventSet.Alter = True
triggerEventSet.Drop = True
Dim serverEventHandlerInstance As ServerEventHandler
serverCreateEventHandler =
➥New ServerEventHandler(AddressOf OnServerEvent)
serverInstance.Events.SubscribeToEvents(triggerEventSet,
➥serverEventHandlerInstance)
trig.Events.StartEvents();
```

C# .NET

```
Database db = serverInstance.Databases["AdventureWorks"];
Trigger trigger = db.Tables["Address",
"Person"].Triggers["TRIG_ADDRESS"];
trigger.Events.ServerEvent +=
➥new ServerEventHandler(this.OnServerEvent);
trigger.Events.SubscribeToEvents(ObjectEvent.Alter +
➥ObjectEvent.Drop);
trigger.Events.StartEvents();
```

Optimized Instantiation

Optimized Instantiation, also called **Lazy Instantiation**, is one of the performance features of SMO. When an object is first created, by default all its properties are not immediately retrieved from the server; only the essential properties needed for scripting are retrieved. This is done to improve the performance of the object model by saving extra CPU cycles and internal process memory needed for retrieval of properties that are infrequently used. The state of the object when only partial properties are available is called the **partially instantiated** state. You can also request for an object to be fully populated with properties upon creation. The state of an object when all its properties, including more and less frequently used ones, are retrieved from the server is called the **fully instantiated** state. Requesting a fully instantiated object on creation will reduce load on the network and query engine because if all properties are going to be needed, it makes sense to retrieve them once and thus submit fewer queries to the Database Engine. Some objects may also have **expensive** properties that are retrieved only when requested, even after an object is already in a fully instantiated state. Figure 11-7 demonstrates the tradeoffs of delayed instantiation versus full instantiation.

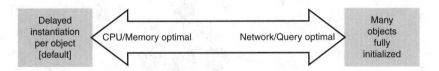

Figure 11-7   Optimized instantiation design trade-offs.

For the advanced programmer, there is an even finer-grained control over what properties are retrieved when an object is first created. You can actually request and specify what properties are retrieved for any object type by calling the `GetDefaultInitFields` and `SetDefaultInitFields` methods on a `Server` object. This way, you can even request any of the expensive properties be retrieved up front. For example, the following sets default fields for any Database object to be its Name and Collation:

```
serverInstance.SetDefaultInitFields(typeof(Database),

➥new string[] { "Name", "Collation" });
```

If you want any Database object to be fully instantiated from the start, you make the following call:

```
serverInstance.SetDefaultInitFields(typeof(Database), true);
```

Suppose the object is already created and you want to make sure it is fully initialized. You can achieve this goal by calling the object's `Initialize` method and passing the Boolean value "true" as an argument.

Pre-fetch Capability

Pre-fetch is another important performance-related feature of SMO. Sometimes the user knows he needs to walk through an entire collection of objects of some type. For this purpose, it makes sense to retrieve the entire collection of properties from the server in one trip, using the aforementioned `SetDefaultInitFields` setting. This concept can be better demonstrated with Figures 11-8 and 11-9. Figure 11-8 shows how the entire tree is populated by default. The legacy SQL-DMO model followed this pattern as well.

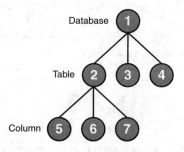

Figure 11-8   Sequential object instantiation (SQL-DMO Model).

Figure 11-9 shows how you can efficiently cut down on the number of queries submitted to the Database Engine by using pre-fetch. The entire Table objects collection is retrieved in one query, and all table columns are retrieved in the next query.

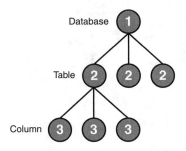

Figure 11-9   Per-Level Object Instantiation (SMO Pre-fetch Model).

TIP
Pre-fetch is used extensively by SMO itself to simplify scripting operations. However, sometimes SMO can make the wrong choice on whether to use pre-fetch or not based on how many objects actually need to be scripted. In this case, you may need to tune the application by calling pre-fetch yourself or by setting the `PrefetchObjects` flag on the `Scripter` object to false.

Let's demonstrate forcing pre-fetch by example. Suppose you want to pre-fetch all Table objects of a particular database before accessing the collection. This is how it is done:

```
database.PrefetchObjects(typeof(Table));
```

Pre-fetching all tables of the database significantly speeds up subsequent access to the tables collection.

Summary

This chapter covered basic SMO concepts and went over multiple usage scenarios. It also talked about internal SMO architecture, and at the end covered very advanced performance and optimization topics.

CHAPTER 12

Inside Replication Tools

One of the biggest challenges in designing tools for database replication is to make administration and monitoring simple when the technology is complex. As with any distributed database technology, you have to think not only about database interactions, but also about connectivity, cross-server security, network performance and reliability, conflicting data changes, and many other factors that can affect the success of your deployment. Our quest has always been to make understanding and configuring replication easy so you can focus on your database and application design and let us handle the rest.

During the development of SQL Server 2005, we had countless discussions about how we could simplify the tools by asking better questions, having better defaults, automatically handling more unexpected circumstances, and crafting the paradigms and terminology to make the technology easy to understand. The tools in SQL Server 2005 represent tens of thousands of hours of effort to simplify the management of database replication.

In this chapter, we discuss the major components for administering and monitoring database replication in SQL Server 2005. After examining how replication objects and tasks are represented in Management Studio, we look at the New Publication Wizard and the New Subscription Wizard. Finally, you can see inside the new Replication Monitor.

Database Replication Basics

This chapter assumes you have at least a basic understanding of replication functionality. However, if you do not, I offer a very brief overview to get you started.

A Brief Overview of Replication

Today's data increasingly needs to be in multiple locations at the same time and the data must be kept synchronized. Database developers must consider scale-out requirements for performance and growth and roll-up requirements for reporting and data warehousing when planning and building applications. Disconnected users, such as sales or service personnel, need to take data with them when they enter the field. Keeping this disparate data synchronized on an ongoing basis is a difficult task.

Fortunately, SQL Server offers powerful technology for replicating and synchronizing data. Database replication was introduced in SQL Server version 6.5, but SQL Server 2005 brings a new level of power, performance, and ease of use to this complex functionality.

Replication in SQL Server uses a "publish and subscribe" metaphor in its configuration. The Publisher is the server instance that originally has the data and objects to replicate; a publication is a logical grouping of objects in a database that you want to replicate—tables, stored procedures, views, indexed views, and user-defined functions. Properties of the publication control how the objects are replicated. Depending on your needs, you can choose between three types of publications: snapshot, transactional, or merge. After the publication is created, you can create subscriptions in the locations where you want a copy of the published objects. Replication relies on SQL Server Agent jobs to create the objects at the Subscribers and keep them synchronized.

You can configure replication by using wizards and property sheets in SQL Server Management Studio, by programming to the Replication Management Objects (RMO) managed code assembly, or by calling system stored procedures from T-SQL scripts. Many customers use Management Studio for initial configuration and then generate a script for recovery and future automation. After the publications and subscriptions are configured, you can use the Replication Monitor to monitor ongoing replication activity and troubleshoot problems.

For a complete description of replication functionality and how to prepare your data and application to be replicated, see the topic "SQL Server Replication" in Books Online.

Initializing and Synchronizing Subscriptions

Although the replication wizards make it easy to create publications and subscriptions, the real work of replication (copying the database objects to the Subscribers and keeping the subscriptions synchronized on an ongoing basis) is performed by replication agents, which are usually called from SQL Server Agent job steps.

- **Snapshot Agents** are used for all publication types and run infrequently. They generate scripts that can create the published objects at a Subscriber, and they also take snapshots of the published data. The scripts and snapshots are typically used to initially synchronize or reinitialize subscriptions, although you can initialize the objects and data manually.

- **Log Reader Agents** are used for transactional publications and run continuously. They monitor the transaction log for changes to published objects.

- **Distribution Agents** are used for snapshot and transactional publications and typically run continuously. There is usually one agent per subscription. For snapshot publications, the agent keeps its subscription synchronized by applying snapshots intermittently. For transactional publications, the agent keeps its subscription synchronized by applying snapshots for initialization and by replicating commands processed by the Log Reader Agent.

- **Merge Agents** are used for merge publications only and typically run on a schedule or on demand. There is one agent per subscription, and the agent keeps its subscription synchronized by applying snapshots and merging any data that has been changed since the last synchronization.

After creating publications and subscriptions in the wizards, ensure that the agents are running and working together. Transactional publication agents generally work without intervention because they run continuously. Making sure that new merge subscriptions get their initial synchronization can be challenging because the Snapshot Agent must generate the snapshot files before the Merge Agent can apply the snapshot. If the Merge Agent runs before the Snapshot Agent finishes, the Merge Agent reports that the snapshot is not available and stops. You have to run the Merge Agent again after the Snapshot Agent finishes. If the Merge Agent is scheduled to run once per day, that will not happen until the following day, unless you start it manually. In the meantime, you may wonder why the subscription database has no data.

Management Studio provides tools for configuring replication, but provides minimal help for monitoring the activity of the agents. To track the agent activity, you need to use Replication Monitor. Replication Monitor is a separate application from Management Studio, but you can launch it from Management Studio by using the **Launch Replication Monitor** command on the context menus of nodes under the **Replication** folder in Object Explorer.

TIP

Management Studio includes a report that gives the current state of the Snapshot Agent and, for transactional publications, the current state of the Log Reader Agent. To see the report, select the publication in Object Explorer. In the Summary document window, click **Reports** and select **General**.

To see the status of the Snapshot Agent and start and stop it inside Management Studio, right-click on a publication in Object Explorer and click **View Snapshot Agent Status**. Management Studio displays a dialog box that shows whether the agent is running, the last message from the agent, and buttons to start or stop the agent.

To see the status of a Merge or Distribution Agent and to start and stop it inside Management Studio, right-click on a subscription in Object Explorer and click **View Synchronization Status**. Management Studio displays a similar dialog box to that for the Snapshot Agent.

Wizards in Management Studio

Management Studio relies on wizards to configure replication, and wizards in Management Studio have new features. Before discussing replication, let's take a moment to look at the new things you can do with wizards in SQL Server 2005.

Wizard windows are traditionally a fixed size, but in Management Studio all wizard windows are resizable. Notice that the bottom-right corner of the window has a pattern of dots (see Figure 12-1). This is a visual clue that you can click on that corner to drag the window border to a new size. You will also notice that your mouse cursor changes to a "resize cursor" when you move over that corner. You can also make the wizard fill the screen by clicking the Maximize button in the title bar.

Figure 12-1 Wizard window and starting page.

If you have ever wished you could skip the starting page of wizards, you will like the **Do not show this starting page again** check box at the bottom of the first page of every wizard. If you check the box and open the same wizard in the future, it will start on the second page, saving you one click. Setting the check box in one wizard does not affect other wizards, so you have to check the box in each wizard that you use.

Management Studio wizards have an Information Panel at the bottom of the page that appears when there is additional information to help you understand what the wizard is asking or doing (see Figure 12-2). Any time the Next button is disabled, for example, the Information Panel is displayed with an explanation of what you need to do to continue the wizard. Wizards can use the Information Panel to give a warning of limitations that may not be obvious or the consequences of making a certain choice. The Information Panel is a flexible way for wizards to provide extra information when you need it without requiring any extra clicks to dismiss a message box. The Information Panel is not always displayed, so watch for it when it appears.

Expert users often complain that wizards force them to click through every page regardless of their expertise with the wizard. This is especially troublesome for server administrators who use the same wizards frequently and are very familiar with the questions and default values of the wizard. Management Studio wizards now enable the Finish button as early as possible, allowing you to "fast forward" to the **Complete The Wizard** page, the last page of the wizard. By fast forwarding to the end, you skip over the pages between your current position and the end of the wizard, implicitly accepting the default values for questions on those pages. The button text includes the symbols >>| to indicate this behavior. For example, the New Subscription Wizard asks you to choose the publication to which you want to subscribe, the destination database in which the subscription should be created, and then a series of questions about subscription behavior. If you know that you want the default subscription behavior, you can click **Finish >>|** after choosing the publication and subscription database. In this way, you don't have to click through the pages that require no input. Clicking **Finish>>|** always takes you to the last page, which presents a summary of actions the wizard will take, so you can review the settings from the pages you skipped and back up if you want to change anything.

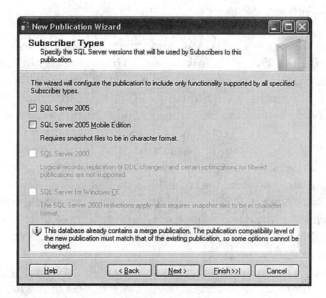

Figure 12-2   Information panel and early finish button in wizards.

On the last page of the wizard, the button text changes from **Finish >>|** to **Finish.** When you click **Finish** on the last page, the wizard performs its actions as always.

Administering Replication in Management Studio

The administration of replication in Management Studio can be accessed from the **Replication** folder, which is under the server folder in Object Explorer (see Figure 12-3).

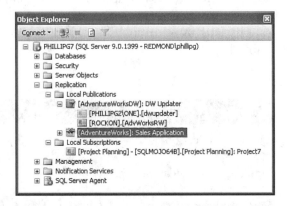

Figure 12-3   Replication folder in Object Explorer.

One server instance can be both a Publisher (publish data to others) and a Subscriber (subscribe to data published by others) at the same time. The **Replication** folder provides a consolidated view of both publication and subscription activity on the server instance. The **Replication** folder is structured as shown in Figure 12-4.

```
Replication
    Local Publications
        <publication 1>
            <subscription 1 to publication 1>
            <subscription 2 to publication 1>
            ...
        <publication 2>
            <subscription 1 to publication 2>
            <subscription 2 to publication 2>
            ...
    Local Subscriptions
            <subscription on <this server> to publication from Publisher <Server 2>>
            <subscription on <this server> to publication from Publisher <Server 3>>
            ...
```

Figure 12-4   Replication folder structure.

All objects in **Local Publications** relate to the "local" server instance (the one to which you are connected) in its role as a Publisher. Thus, publications in **Local Publications** are of objects on this server instance, and the subscriptions below the publications represent the instances receiving copies of those objects. The objects in **Local Subscriptions** relate to the server instance in its role as a Subscriber. These subscriptions indicate objects that are being copied from other Publishers.

Publications and subscriptions in Object Explorer have the icons shown in Table 12-1.

Table 12-1   Replication Icons in Object Explorer

Icon	Meaning
	Snapshot publication
	Transactional publication
	Merge publication
	Subscription—The Distribution or Merge Agent can be administered locally
	Subscription—The Distribution or Merge Agent must be administered at another server instance

Publication icons show the type of the publication. Subscription icons tell whether the agent that synchronizes the subscription can be administered from the local server instance.

TIP
When you see the darker-colored icon for a subscription, you can right-click on the subscription and select **View Synchronization Status**. Management Studio displays a dialog box that shows whether the agent is running and displays the last message from the agent. It also provides buttons to start or stop the agent. When you see the lighter-colored icon for a subscription, you have to connect to another server instance to administer the synchronization agent.

Like table names, publication names are unique within a database, but the same publication name can be used in different databases. Because the **Replication** folder is at the server instance level, the database context for a publication must be explicitly stated. Publications in Object Explorer are identified as

[<publication database>]: <publication>

Note that a colon is used to separate the database and publication names because publications cannot be referenced if they use the standard period separator for database object names.

Identifying a subscription is more difficult than identifying a publication because a subscription doesn't have a name of its own. To uniquely identify a subscription, you need to identify the publication and the subscription database, which requires five pieces of information:

- Publisher
- Publication database
- Publication
- Subscriber
- Subscription database

Subscriptions in **Local Subscriptions** specify all of these except the Subscriber name (the Subscriber is always the instance to which you are connected). Subscriptions in **Local Subscriptions** are identified as

<subscription database> - [<Publisher>].[<publication DB>]: <publication>

Subscriptions under a publication node have a simpler format because the publication context is provided by the parent. These subscriptions are identified as

[<Subscriber>].[<subscription database>]

TIP

Management Studio displays a detailed tooltip such as the one shown in Figure 12-5 that explains the parts of the name when you point to a publication or subscription. For a publication, the tooltip shows the Publisher, publication database, and publication type. For a subscription, the tooltip shows the Publisher, publication database and type, Subscriber, subscription database, and where the synchronization agent runs. The tooltip remains visible for five seconds. If you need more time to read everything, point to the node again to see the tooltip for another five seconds.

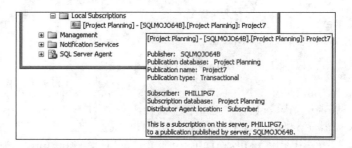

Figure 12-5 Tooltip detailing a local subscription.

All replication commands are available from the context menus on the objects under **Replication**. The commands you see when you right-click on **Local Publications** and its children let you configure the server as a Publisher, such as for creating and editing publications. The commands you see when you right-click **Local Subscriptions** and its children let you configure the server as a Subscriber, such as for creating subscriptions to publications from other servers and synchronizing the subscriptions.

Using the New Publication Wizard to Create Publications

The first step to configuring replication is to create a publication. To start the New Publication Wizard, expand **Replication**, right-click **Local Publications,** and select **New Publication**.

This wizard has about ten pages, although the number of pages varies depending on whether this is your first publication and what type of publication you create. Most pages are straightforward, with good explanations of the task for the page. If you need additional information, click **Help**. This chapter focuses on the most complex pages of the wizard.

The wizard asks you which database (or part of the database) you want to publish. It also asks you to choose the type of publication to create: snapshot, transactional, or merge. If you are not familiar with the publication types and how they fit your needs, SQL Server Books Online discusses this information in detail. Because the publication types have different requirements and properties, the pages you see in the wizard and the options on a given page vary depending on the type of publication you create.

Articles Page of the New Publication Wizard

You choose the database objects to replicate in the publication on the Articles page, shown in Figure 12-6. (To extend the publication metaphor, the objects that are published are referred to as "articles.")

Figure 12-6   New Publication Wizard, Articles page

The Articles page is the core of the wizard. On this page, you select which database objects to replicate and the properties and behavior of the objects as they are replicated. SQL Server allows you to publish tables, stored procedures, views, indexed views, and user-defined functions. The wizard presents these objects in a tree so you can easily navigate the list of objects. You choose an object for publication by checking the box next to the object, and you can easily publish all objects of a certain type by checking the box next to the type name. For example, checking the box next to Tables publishes all table objects that are eligible to be published.

TIP

If you have many objects of one type, such as hundreds of stored procedures, working with the list can be a challenge. To see more of the list at one time, make the window bigger by dragging the bottom-right corner of the window or clicking the Maximize button in the title bar.

To publish only a few objects of one type, expand the type and check the boxes of the objects you want to publish. To publish most, but not all, objects of a specific type, it is faster to first check the box next to the type name to publish all eligible objects of that type, and then uncheck the boxes for objects you don't want to publish.

After you select the objects you want to publish, you can hide the objects you don't want by clicking the **Show only checked objects in the list** box. To see the objects in the list again, uncheck the box.

SQL Server enables you to filter the data in published tables so that only certain columns or rows in the table are replicated. You may filter a table to control access to sensitive information, such as a salary column, or to reduce the size of the data being replicated. You can specify which columns to publish in the Articles page. You can specify which rows to publish on the Filter Table Rows page later in the wizard.

To see the columns of a table, expand the individual table node. The column names are displayed under the table, with check boxes next to each name. When you publish a table, the wizard automatically publishes all eligible columns in the table and checks the boxes next to the columns. If you do not want to publish a column, uncheck the box next to the column.

TIP
To publish only a few columns of a table, expand the table but do not check the box for the table. Instead, check the boxes next to the columns you want to publish. To publish most, but not all, columns in a table, it is faster to first check the box next to the table, and then uncheck the boxes for columns you don't want to publish.

In some cases, SQL Server may not allow you to publish a table if that table does not meet the requirements for an article in the publication you are creating. For example, if a table does not have a primary key, you cannot publish it in a transactional publication. Tables that are not eligible to be published are included in the list, but the icon for that table is marked with a special symbol and you cannot check the box for that table. Similarly, SQL Server may not allow you to publish certain columns of a table. Conversely, SQL Server may require that a certain column, such as the primary key column, be published if the table is published. The icons presented in Table 12-2 are used in **Objects to publish** to help communicate these restrictions.

Table 12-2   Table and Column Icons in the Articles Page

Icon	Meaning
	A table with no restrictions.
	A table that cannot be published.

Icon	Meaning
	A table with possible data type conversion problems. Look at the Article Properties dialog box for more information.
	A table for which synchronization is download-only to the Subscriber.
	A table column with no restriction.
	A table column that must be published if the table is published.
	A table column that is a primary key that must be published if the table is published.
	A table column that cannot be published.

TIP

If a table or column has a special icon to indicate that it cannot be published or it must be published, select the object and the New Publication Wizard explains the reason. When a restricted object is selected, an Information Panel is automatically displayed at the bottom of the page (see Figure 12-7). When you select an object without a restriction, the Information Panel is hidden.

Each article that is published has properties that govern how the object is created at the Subscribers, how the replicated object behaves, and other settings. Although you usually do not have to change the default article properties, it is good to understand what the defaults are so that you know how to adjust them if the need arises.

To view or change the properties of an individual object, select it in **Objects to publish** and click **Article Properties**. When you click the button, a menu is displayed with the following commands: **Set Properties of Highlighted <type> Article** and **Set Properties of All <type> Articles**, where <type> is a Table, Stored Procedure, View, and so on.

If you click **Set Properties of Highlighted <type> Article**, Management Studio displays the **Article Properties** dialog box for the selected article (see Figure 12-8).

Figure 12-7   New Publication Wizard, Articles page, showing filtered columns and table and column restrictions.

Figure 12-8   Article Properties dialog box.

TIP

If you right-click on an object in **Objects to publish**, you get a menu of commands for that object, including the two for article properties. In some cases, you may be able to set common properties directly from the context menu without going through the Properties dialog box.

Like most windows in Management Studio, you can resize the **Article Properties** dialog box to see more properties at one time. The dialog box uses a property grid to display most of the properties. Note that when you click on a property in the grid, a short description of the property is displayed in the Description box below the grid.

TIP

If you cannot read the entire description displayed below a property grid, you can increase the size of the Description box by pointing the mouse at the area between the grid and the Description box. When you see a resize cursor, click and drag up.

You can also change the properties of all articles of a single type at one time. Let's use Tables as an example. After you have checked the boxes for the tables you want to publish, highlight the Tables item or one of the tables in **Objects to publish**. Click **Article Properties** and select **Set Properties of All Table Articles**. Management Studio displays the **Properties For All Tables** dialog box. This dialog box displays the default values for the properties of table articles. If you change a property value and click OK, the value of that property is changed for all the currently published tables and it becomes the new default value for any other tables that you publish in this run of the wizard. Note that the new default value is not remembered the next time you run the New Publication Wizard or if you open the **Publication Properties** dialog box for this publication.

For example, the default value for the table article property **Convert data types** is False. You publish two tables, highlight the Tables item, click **Article Properties**, and select **Set Properties of All Table Articles**. Management Studio displays the **Properties For All Table Articles** dialog box. You change the **Convert data types** value to True and click OK. The value of this property for each published table is changed to True. The default value for this property is also changed to True. You then publish a third table, and **Convert data types** for the new article defaults to True. The next time you run the New Publication Wizard, the default value for **Convert data types** has returned to False.

Filter Table Rows Page of the New Publication Wizard

In some publications, you may need to filter the rows in one or more published tables so that only certain data is replicated to the Subscribers. For snapshot and transactional publications, all subscriptions receive the same data, but for merge publications, you can customize the filters so that different subscriptions receive different data. This can be helpful in circumstances such as a sales application where salespeople need only their own customer and order information. The **Filter Table Rows** page of the New Publication Wizard allows you to define these filters. If you do not need to filter table rows, click **Next** on this page and continue through the wizard. Because filtering in a merge publication offers additional functionality, how this page operates with each publication type is discussed separately.

The **Filter Table Rows** page for a snapshot or transactional publication is shown in Figure 12-9. The **Filtered Tables** list shows each table in the publication for which you have defined a row filter. A row filter is the WHERE clause in the following query:

SELECT <published_columns> FROM <published table> **WHERE <filter criteria>**

When you select a table in the list, the row filter statement is displayed in the **Filter** box. You can add a row filter on another table by clicking **Add**, choosing the table, and specifying the filter statement. Note that a row filter affects only the data replicated from the filtered table. If other tables are dependent on data in that table, such as an order table with a foreign key constraint on a customer table, you must make sure that dependent tables are also filtered as needed.

As shown in Figure 12-10, in the merge publication the Filter Table Rows page looks a little different.

You will notice immediately that merge publications allow filtering across a hierarchy of tables, in addition to filtering each table individually. Unlike other publications, you can configure a merge publication so that when you apply a row filter to one table, dependent tables are automatically filtered so that foreign key and other constraints are not violated in the data that the Subscriber receives. You extend filtering from a filtered table by specifying join filters to define the relationship between the filtered table and the joined tables. SQL Server can then cascade the effects of the filter statement to the joined tables.

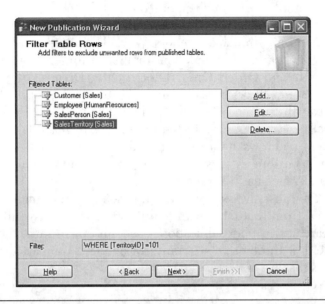

Figure 12-9   New Publication Wizard, Filter Table Rows (snapshot or transactional publication).

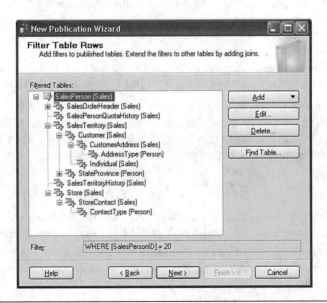

Figure 12-10   New Publication Wizard, Filter Table Rows (merge publication).

For example, your publication contains the tables Customers, Orders, and OrderDetails. You define a row filter on the Customers table that includes only French customers: WHERE Country = 'France'. You then add join filters that link Customers.CustomerID with Orders.CustomerID and Orders.OrderID with OrderDetails.OrderID. When the entire set of filters is evaluated to create a subscription, the Subscriber tables will contain only rows in the Customers table where Country is equal to 'France,' rows in the Orders table that relate to French customers, and rows in the OrderDetails table that relate to the orders from French customers. Customer, order, and order detail data for customers not in France has been filtered out.

You must always begin with a row filter on a single table, and then extend from that table with join filters. You can have filters on several hierarchies in one publication, each starting from a different filtered table, but the hierarchies must not overlap. You can also have filtered tables that are not extended by joins.

TIP

If you have defined primary and foreign key relationships in your database, Management Studio can generate join filters automatically based on those relationships. To do this, click **Add** and select **Automatically Generate Filters** from the menu. In the Generate Filters dialog box, choose the table for the row filter, enter the filter statement, specify how many subscriptions will receive each published row, and click **OK**. SQL Server analyzes the relationships between the tables and creates the join filters that will extend the row filter on your starting table.

If **Filtered tables** contains a large number of tables, it can be difficult to locate a particular table if you want to change its row or join filter or see how it fits in the hierarchy. To quickly find a table, click **Find Table**, select the table, and click **OK**. Management Studio then locates the table, selects it, and expands and scrolls the tree so it is visible.

To add a join manually, select the table in **Filtered tables** from which you want to join and click **Add**. Select **Add Join to Extend Filtered Table**.

The table from which you are joining is automatically specified as the **Filtered table** in the dialog box. In **Joined table**, select the table to which you want to join (see Figure 12-11). When you select the joined table, Management Studio looks to see whether there is a defined relationship between the two tables. If so, it automatically enters the column names in the join builder grid in step 2 of the dialog box. You can remove those columns, add other pairs of columns, or change the operator that defines the relationship between the columns. As you make changes in the builder, you can see in the Preview box how the join statement will look.

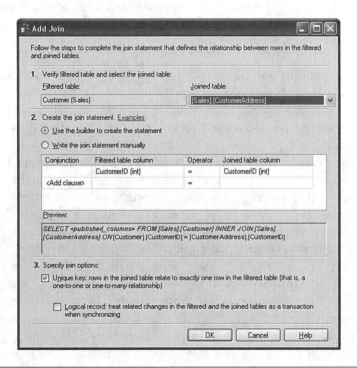

Figure 12-11   Add Join dialog box.

Optionally, you can write the join statement yourself and not use the builder. If you select **Write the join statement manually**, the middle section of the dialog box changes to look like Figure 12-12.

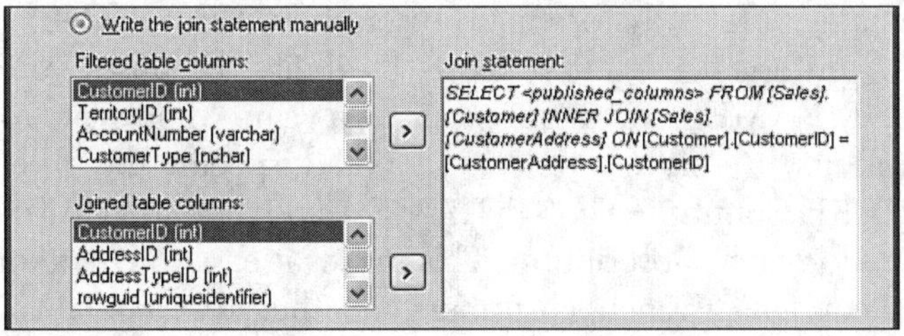

Figure 12-12   Write the join statement manually in the Add Join dialog box.

You can now select columns from the lists and type in the **Join statement** text box.

TIP

Double-clicking a column name in the **Filtered table columns** or **Joined table columns** lists inserts the column name into the **Join statement** text box at the cursor location.

When adding join filters, you can optionally specify that rows in the two tables should be treated as one "logical record." By default, merge replication synchronizes data changes between the Publisher and a Subscriber on a row-by-row basis. If you enable a logical record, related changes are processed as a unit during synchronization. This ensures that during synchronization, related changes always go together. For example, if the Orders and OrderDetails tables are enabled as a logical record, and a change is made to an order and to the details of that order, both changes must be replicated or neither is replicated. If an error occurs when synchronizing the row in Orders, you know that the change to the row in OrderDetails will not be synchronized either.

When you enter the **Add Join** or **Edit Join** dialog box you may find that the **Logical record** option button is disabled or not visible. This happens when the publication and article requirements for logical records are not met. For more information on the requirements, see "Considerations for Using Logical Records" in SQL Server Books Online.

Merge publications also enable you to partition published data so that different subscriptions receive different partitions. You do this by specifying a parameterized row filter instead of a static row filter on a table. In the preceding example, the filter statement WHERE Country = 'France' is a static filter because it compares constant values that evaluate identically for all subscriptions, sending the same rows to everyone. A parameterized filter uses a function, such as SUSER_SNAME() or HOST_NAME(), that evaluates differently for each subscription. Using HOST_NAME() in the filter criteria gives the most flexibility because you can override HOST_NAME() and supply your own value when synchronizing the subscription. In this example, you could specify the filter statement as WHERE Country = HOST_NAME(), and then specify a different country name for each subscription. This makes it easy to create one subscription that contains French customers, another that contains Canadian customers, and so on. For a complete discussion, see the topic "Parameterized Row Filters" in SQL Server Books Online.

TIP
By default, the HOST_NAME() function returns the name of the computer that connects to a SQL Server instance, but you can override this when creating a subscription. In the **New Subscription Wizard**, specify the new value on the **HOST_NAME() Value** page. Note that this changes the value returned by all calls to the function, not just from replication. Be careful that other applications are not dependent on the value of the HOST_NAME() function.

When adding a row filter on a table in a merge publication, the **Add Filter** dialog box has an additional option that is not available for snapshot and transactional publications.

When adding a parameterized filter with the SUSER_SNAME() or HOST_NAME() functions, you can specify how many subscriptions will receive each published row in the table. If the published data is well partitioned by your filters so that a given row will be replicated to exactly one subscription, SQL Server can optimize the performance of the synchronization. For example, you could define a row filter to compare SalesPersonID to HOST_NAME(). Because the ID of each salesperson is unique, each subscription will contain only the rows for that person and no others. Therefore, you can choose **A row from this table will go to only one subscription** (see Figure 12-13). As you extend filtering from this table by adding join filters, the performance improvement extends to all the joined tables as well.

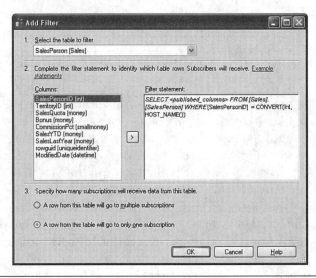

Figure 12-13   Add Filter dialog box for a merge publication.

Snapshot Agent Page of New Publication Wizard

The **Snapshot Agent** page (see Figure 12-14) enables you to schedule when the agent runs and, for transactional publications, whether the snapshot files are persisted. Controlling when the agent runs is important because generating a snapshot can adversely affect the performance of your server, especially if the size of the published data is large. You may want to run the Snapshot Agent during off-peak hours rather than when you are running the wizard.

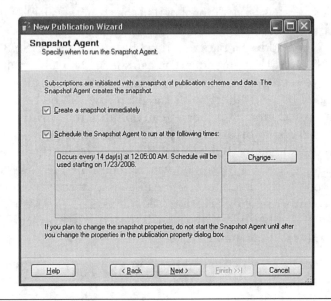

Figure 12-14   New Publication Wizard, Snapshot Agent page (merge publication).

For merge publications, the Snapshot Agent always generates a new snapshot and cleans up previous snapshots. The new snapshot files remain until the Snapshot Agent runs again, and Merge Agents always have a snapshot to use to initially synchronize subscriptions. In this mode, it does not matter whether you run the Snapshot Agent before or after you create a subscription to initialize it.

For transactional publications, however, you can choose whether you want this behavior. If you check the **Create a snapshot immediately and keep the snapshot available to initialize subscriptions** box, the behavior is exactly like that described for merge publications, except it is a Distribution Agent, not a Merge Agent, that applies the snapshot. If you do not check this box, however, the behavior of the Snapshot Agent is different. When the agent runs, it generates a snapshot only if there is a subscription waiting to be initialized or reinitialized, and when all subscriptions have been initialized, the Snapshot Agent deletes the snapshot files. If the Snapshot Agent runs and there are no subscriptions needing initialization and no snapshot files to delete, the agent stops without doing anything. In this mode, you must run the Snapshot Agent after you create a subscription to initialize it.

For a transactional publication, the first check box is different (see Figure 12-15).

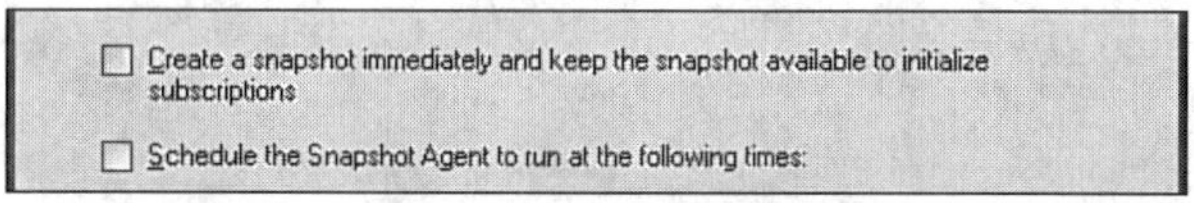

☐ C̲reate a snapshot immediately and keep the snapshot available to initialize subscriptions

☐ S̲chedule the Snapshot Agent to run at the following times:

Figure 12-15   The check box portion of the New Publication Wizard, Snapshot Agent page (transactional publication).

Be aware that keeping the snapshot files may require a large amount of disk space because the snapshot files include a copy of all of the published data. Keeping the snapshot files available can cause SQL Server to keep replicated transactions in the distribution database longer. For more information, see the topic "Subscription Expiration and Deactivation" in Books Online.

TIP

If you do not expect to create subscriptions frequently, do not create a schedule for the Snapshot Agent. If you create all subscriptions as part of an initial configuration, the snapshot is needed for only the time of your configuration. After that, you can generate a new snapshot when circumstances arise, such as when you create a new subscription or need to reinitialize a subscription.

Wizard Actions Page of New Publication Wizard

New Publication Wizard creates your publication when you click **Finish**, but the wizard can also generate a script of the steps needed to create the publication. Having a script is an important part of a recovery plan for the database so you can easily re-create the publication in the future without having to go through the wizard again. The script is also helpful if you plan to make a similar publication. It may be faster to modify and execute the script than to use the wizard again.

Just before the final page of the wizard, you will see the Wizard Actions page. To have the wizard generate a script, check the **Generate a script file** box. With this box checked, when you click **Next**, you will be asked for the file location and other options for creating the script. When you click **Finish** on the last page of the wizard, the wizard creates the publication, generates the script, or both, according to which boxes are checked on the **Wizard Actions** page (see Figure 12-16).

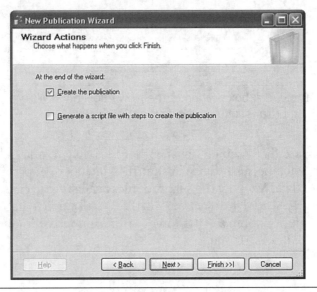

Figure 12-16   New Publication Wizard, Wizard Actions page.

TIP
You can generate a script any time after the publication is created by right-clicking on the publication in Object Explorer and clicking **Generate Scripts**.

Using the New Subscription Wizard to Create Subscriptions

Creating a publication just defines the set of database objects that you want to replicate. To actually get a copy of those objects to other server instances, you must create subscriptions to the publication. You can create a subscription in Management Studio in two ways. You can start from the publication object at the Publisher, or you can start from the **Local Sub-scriptions** folder on the Subscriber. To start from the Publisher, expand the **Replication** folder, expand **Local Publications**, and right-click on the publication. From the context menu, select **New Subscription.** To start from the Subscriber, expand the **Replication** folder and right-click on **Local Subscriptions**. From the context menu, select **New Subscrip-tion.** If you are an administrator or database owner on both server instances, it doesn't matter which method you choose; the wizard is the same, although some of the defaults are different.

In the New Subscription Wizard, begin by identifying the publica-tion to which you want to subscribe (see Figure 12-17).

Figure 12-17 New Subscription Wizard, Publication page.

Select the Publisher from the list or select **<Find SQL Server Pub-lisher>** to see the Connect to Server dialog box. In the Connect to Server dialog box, specify the Publisher and how the wizard should connect to it. The wizard then displays a list of publication databases on the Publisher. Expand the appropriate database and select the publication.

TIP
Databases and publications contains only publications that the account
used to connect to the Publisher has permission to see. If you cannot see
a publication that you think you should be able to see, make sure you have
connected to the Publisher using the appropriate credentials, or have the
administrator of the Publisher add your login to the publication access list
in the **Publication Properties** dialog box.

After selecting the Publisher and publication, you must select one or
more Subscribers and subscription databases (see Figure 12-18).

Figure 12-18   New Subscription Wizard, Subscribers page.

The New Subscription Wizard enables you to create subscriptions in
Oracle or IBM DB2 databases as well as at SQL Server instances. If the
server instance that you want as a Subscriber is not in the list, click **Add
Subscriber** and select **Add SQL Server Subscriber** or **Add Non-
SQL Server Subscriber** from the menu.

   If the subscription database doesn't exist as a SQL Server Subscriber,
you can create one from this wizard page as long as you have the necessary
permissions on the Subscriber. In the **Subscription Database** column,
click the drop arrow and select **<New Database>** from the list. Management Studio displays the **New Database** dialog box.

The remaining pages in the New Subscription Wizard ask for values for the properties of the subscription and the Merge or Distribution Agent. The number of pages varies depending on the type and properties of the publication to which you are subscribing. The pages are straightforward, with good explanations on the page of the question being asked. If you need additional information, click **Help**.

Monitoring Replication Activity in Replication Monitor

Although you might spend hours or even days configuring your replication topology, you are likely to spend months or years monitoring the replication activity of your system. Fortunately, SQL Server 2005 provides Replication Monitor, an excellent tool for watching the performance and activity of your replication agents.

Because monitoring personnel are sometimes separate from the database administrators, Replication Monitor is an independent application from Management Studio (see Figure 12-19). You can launch it directly from Management Studio by using the **Launch Replication Monitor** command on the context menus of all nodes under the **Replication** folder in Object Explorer.

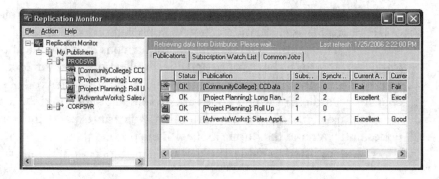

Figure 12-19   Replication Monitor.

Replication Monitor is organized around the hierarchy of Publishers, publications, and subscriptions. The starting point is a Publisher, and you can add as many Publishers as you want. Replication Monitor enables you to organize your Publishers into groups, with the default group being **My Publishers**. After a Publisher is added, Replication Monitor retrieves the list of its publications and subscriptions and their status. This information is automatically refreshed at a frequency that you can set.

The left pane, known as the Navigation Pane, displays a tree with the following levels: Replication Monitor, Publisher group, Publisher, and publication. The right pane, known as the Detail Pane, is a tabbed interface that shows details about the object selected in the Navigation Pane. The Detail Pane often displays a grid that contains a list of subscriptions or replication agents.

TIP

You can see detailed information about a subscription or agent in the Detail Pane by double-clicking its grid row or by right-clicking the row and selecting **View Details**.

By default, Replication Monitor automatically refreshes the data it is displaying on a regular basis. You can set the frequency of the automatic refresh separately for each Publisher in the Publisher Settings dialog box, which is accessible from the context menu of the Publisher. You can see how long ago the data in the Detail Pane was retrieved by looking at the gray ribbon above the tabs where the time of the last refresh for the selected tab is shown. You will also occasionally see the message "Retrieving data from Distributor. Please wait[...]" when Replication Monitor is querying to get fresh data.

The icons in the panes indicate the type and status of the selected object or its children. If a publication or subscription has a status of Error, Warning, or Retry, the status is marked in the icons of the publication, its Publisher, the Publisher group, and the Replication Monitor root node (see Figure 12-20). In this way, Replication Monitor notifies you of status changes regardless of which nodes are expanded or collapsed. When you see a status that requires your attention, you can expand the marked nodes until you find the publication with the problem.

The icons listed in Table 12-3 are used in Replication Monitor.

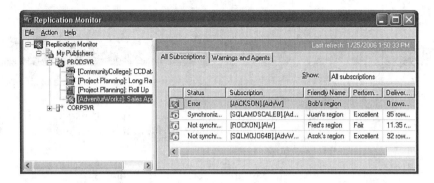

Figure 12-20 Replication Monitor showing an error.

Table 12-3 Icons in Replication Monitor

Icon	Meaning
	Replication Monitor root node
	Publisher group
	Publisher
	Snapshot publication
	Transactional publication
	Merge publication
	Subscription

The status overlays listed in Table 12-4 can appear on the lower-right corner of the icons.

Information about errors, warnings, and retries is always found in the Detail Pane; the status markers in the Navigation Pane are used only to lead you to the object that needs attention. Because almost all replication activity occurs at the publication level, you will usually select a publication in the Navigation Pane and look at the specifics in the Details Pane.

Table 12-4   Status Overlays in Replication Monitor

Icon	Meaning
	Error: An agent has encountered an error. Replication has stopped.
	Warning: There are various warnings: low performance, expiring subscription, etc. Replication is still operating, but a potential problem has begun.
	Retry: An agent has encountered an error, and is retrying the operation. Replication is still operating, but may stop if the retries are unsuccessful.
	Running/Synchronizing: A Distribution Agent is running, or a Merge Agent is synchronizing. (Subscription only)
	Not Running/Not Synchronizing: A Distribution Agent is not running, or a Merge Agent is not synchronizing. The agent shut down normally, without an error. (Subscription only)

Adding Publishers to Replication Monitor

To begin monitoring replication, you must add one or more Publishers to Replication Monitor. If you launch Replication Monitor from a publication node in Management Studio, the Publisher is automatically added to Replication Monitor with default settings. To add a Publisher manually, right-click on the root node, a Publisher group, or a Publisher, and click **Add Publisher**. In the **Add Publisher** dialog box, click the **Add** button and select one of the following from the menu: **Add SQL Server Publisher**, **Add Oracle Publisher**, or **Specify a Distributor and Add Its Publishers**. With SQL Server 2005, you can configure an Oracle server to publish through a SQL Server Distributor. You can also configure a server instance to act as the Distributor for one or more Publishers. The **Add Publisher** dialog box lets you add Publishers from all these configurations.

When you specify the connection to the Publisher or to the Distributor for an Oracle Publisher or when using a remote Distributor, you must also specify how Replication Monitor connects to the server instance. Replication Monitor will remember the connection credentials so that you don't have to enter them when you use Replication Monitor in the future. To monitor replication, the login that you specify must be an administrator on the server instance or a member of the **replmonitor** fixed database role in the distribution database.

TIP

The only way to create a Publisher group is with the **New Group** button in the **Add Publisher** or **Publisher Settings** dialog box. To change the group to which a Publisher belongs after the Publisher is added, right-click on the Publisher and click **Publisher Settings**.

Publisher Detail Pane

When you select a Publisher in the Navigation Pane, the Detail Pane contains three tabs: **Publications**, **Subscription Watch List**, and **Common Jobs** (see Figure 12-21). **Publications** contains a list of publications at the Publisher. The list is displayed in a grid with columns that summarize current activity and status for that publication. **Common Jobs** contains a list of SQL Server Agent jobs that perform background maintenance for all replication components at the server instance. It is rare that you would ever need to work with them, but they are listed here just in case.

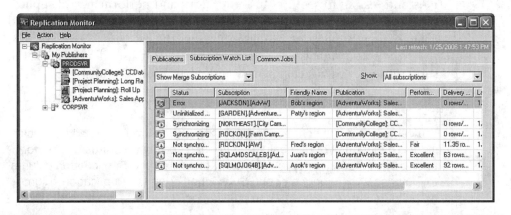

Figure 12-21   Subscription Watch List Tab.

The really interesting tab when a Publisher is selected is **Subscription Watch List**. On **Subscription Watch List**, you can see lists of subscriptions from all publications of one type at this Publisher. (Replication Monitor does not let you see subscriptions of multiple types at one time because the columns and statuses are different for different publication types.)

By default, Replication Monitor sorts the list by status and then by worst to best performance, so that the most worrisome subscriptions are at the top. For transactional subscriptions, the status order is Error, Warning, Retry, Uninitialized Subscription, Not Running, and Running. Subscriptions whose status is Not Running and Running are then sorted by increasing performance ratings. For merge subscriptions, the status order is Error, Warning, Uninitialized Subscription, Retry, Synchronizing, and Not Synchronizing. Subscriptions whose status is Synchronizing and Not Synchronizing are then sorted by increasing performance.

This sort order lets Replication Monitor put the subscriptions that are of greatest concern at the top of the list. Error status comes first because an error means replication has stopped. Warning and Retry statuses indicates that there is a potential problem that could eventually lead to an error. Uninitialized Subscription status notifies you that you have not finished setting up a subscription. For transactional subscriptions, Not Running status is next because these agents typically run continuously, so an agent that is not running may be a problem. For merge subscriptions the opposite is true: Synchronizing status is next because these agents run intermittently, and those that are currently running are the most interesting to see. Because the status and performance of replication agents change frequently, the order of the subscriptions is likely to change when Replication Monitor refreshes the list.

To see the details of a subscription in the list, double-click the subscription or right-click the row and select **View Details**.

TIP

You can sort the subscription watch list by any column in the grid by clicking the header cell of that column. Although sorting on status and performance meets most needs, you may want to sort on the Subscription column to focus on subscriptions at one Subscriber, or on the Publication column to focus on subscriptions to one publication.

You can also filter the watch list by selecting a criterion from the **Show** list. You can filter the list so that it includes only subscriptions with Errors, subscriptions with Warning or Retry status, subscriptions that are Running/Synchronizing or Not Running/Not Synchronizing, or the 25 or 50 worst performing subscriptions.

Transactional Publication Detail Pane

When you select a transactional publication in the Navigation Pane, the Detail Pane looks like Figure 12-22.

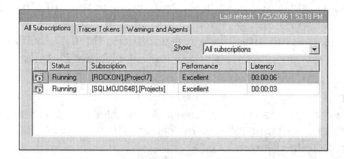

Figure 12-22   Transactional Publication detail pane, All Subscriptions tab.

The default content for the Detail Pane is to see all subscriptions to the publication. The list includes the following information:

- **Status**—The combined status of the Log Reader Agent for the publication and the Distribution Agent that synchronizes this subscription. The status reported is the "worst" status of the two agents. For example, if one agent's status is stopped by an error but the other is running normally, the status for the subscription is Error.

- **Subscription**—The Subscriber and database that contain the subscription.

- **Performance**—A rating of the synchronization performance, as measured by the latency. Performance can be Excellent, Good, Fair, Poor, or Critical. If performance drops to Critical, the status of the agent is changed to Warning: Critical Performance. Ratings are given only if you have defined a warning threshold for the publication on the **Warnings and Agents** tab.

- **Latency**—The time between when a command is committed at the Publisher and when it is committed at the Subscriber. This value measures the performance of both the Log Reader Agent and the Distribution Agent. This measurement is the time it took to move user data through the replication pipeline.

By default, Replication Monitor sorts the list by status and then worst to best performance, so that the most worrisome subscriptions are at the top, as on the **Subscription Watch List** tab when a Publisher is selected in the Navigation Pane. Because the status and performance of replication agents changes frequently, the order of the subscriptions is likely to change when Replication Monitor refreshes the list.

To see the details of a subscription in the list, double-click the subscription or right-click the row and select **View Details**.

TIP

You can sort the subscription list by any column in the grid by clicking the header cell of that column. You can also filter the list by selecting a criterion from the **Show** list.

If you right-click on a subscription row, you get a menu of commands for that subscription, including commands to see the subscription properties and to start or stop the Distribution Agent.

Although the **All Subscriptions** tab shows the performance of ongoing replication activity, the **Tracer Tokens** tab enables you to check connections and measure performance in real time by inserting a tracer token. On the **Tracer Token** tab (see Figure 12-23), click **Insert Tracer** to insert a small amount of data into the transaction log on the Publisher. SQL Server then monitors this data as the Log Reader Agent moves it from the Publisher to the distribution database on the Distributor and the Distribution Agents move it from the Distributor to the Subscribers. While the token is in transit, Replication Monitor shows "Pending" for any unmeasured times. When the token is delivered to the Subscriber, the Total Latency column reports the end-to-end latency for that subscription.

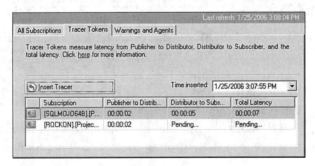

Figure 12-23 Transactional Publication detail pane, Tracer Tokens tab.

TIP
You can review the times of a past token by selecting the time the token was inserted from **Time inserted**.

The **Warnings and Agents** tab (see Figure 12-24) has two purposes: It enables you to define performance warning thresholds so that you can be alerted when a problem is building, and it shows agents for this publication that are common to all subscriptions. For a transactional publication, the common agents are the Log Reader Agent and the Snapshot Agent.

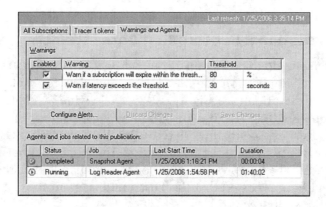

Figure 12-24   Transactional Publication detail pane, Warnings and Agents tab.

If you enable a warning and specify a threshold, SQL Server logs an event to the Windows Event Log if a subscription crosses the threshold. You can define an alert that responds to the event by using SQL Server Agent or any application that watches the event log, such as Microsoft Operations Manager.

TIP
If you make changes to the warnings on this page, you must click **Save Changes**. If you leave the tab without clicking the button, your changes are not saved.

If you want to use SQL Server Agent to define alerts, click **Configure Alerts**, specify the warning on which you want to be alerted, and Replication Monitor opens the **Alert Properties** dialog box. To define alerts in Microsoft Operations Manager or another application, configure alerts in that application.

In **Agents and jobs related to this publication**, you can see the status of the Snapshot Agent and Log Reader Agent. To see the details of a current or past agent session, double-click the agent or right-click its row and select **View Details**. You can also start or stop the agent from the context menu.

TIP

If the Snapshot Agent or Log Reader Agent has an error, Replication Monitor shows an error icon in the **Warnings and Agents** tab so that you know to click on this tab to get information about the error.

Transactional Subscription Detail Window

When you double-click on a transactional subscription in any subscription list, Replication Monitor opens a window to display details about the subscription (see Figure 12-25). The window contains three tabs: **Publisher To Distributor History**, which shows the activity of the Log Reader Agent; the **Distributor To Subscriber History**, which shows the activity of the Distribution Agent; and **Undistributed Commands**, which shows the number of commands that the Log Reader Agent has processed that the Distribution Agent has not yet applied to the Subscriber.

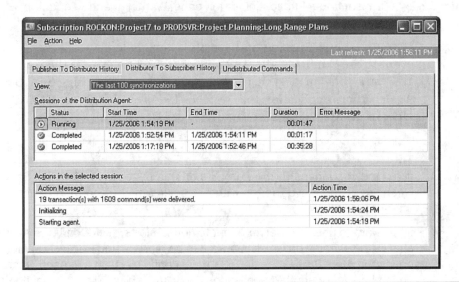

Figure 12-25   Transactional Subscription detail window.

When an agent has stopped because of an error, the bottom of the tab displays the error message and other information. Log Reader Agent errors are displayed on **Publisher To Distributor History**, and Distribution Agent errors are displayed on **Distributor To Subscriber History**. There is often a series of error messages that come from different components involved in the operation that failed. If the error occurred when the agent was trying to execute a command, such as an INSERT statement, the command also is listed in **Last message of the selected session** (see Figure 12-26).

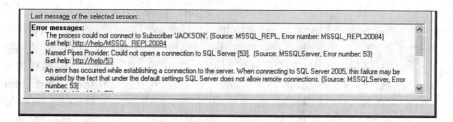

Figure 12-26   Error information in Transactional Subscription detail window.

Merge Publication Detail Pane

When you select a merge publication in the Navigation Pane, the detail pane looks like Figure 12-27.

The default content for the detail pane is to see all subscriptions to the publication. The list includes the following information:

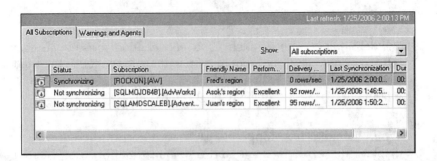

Figure 12-27   Merge Publication detail pane, All Subscriptions tab.

- **Status**—The status of the Merge Agent that synchronizes this subscription.

- **Subscription**—The Subscriber and database that contains the subscription.

- **Friendly Name**—The name that helps identify the subscription. This name is especially helpful when the server and database names are not meaningful, such as "SVR54101." The friendly name is the **Description** property of the merge subscription, which you can set in the Subscription Properties dialog box.

- **Performance**—A rating of the synchronization performance, based on the delivery rate and merge duration. Performance can be Excellent, Good, Fair, Poor, or Critical. If performance drops to Critical, the status of the agent is changed to Warning: Critical Performance. Critical ratings are given only if you have defined a warning threshold for the publication on the **Warnings and Agents** tab.

- **Delivery Rate**—The number of rows per second that were processed during the last merge.

- **Last Synchronization**—The last time that the Merge Agent ran.

- **Duration**—The length of time taken for the last merge.

- **Connection**—The connection type used for the last merge, either Dialup or LAN

By default, Replication Monitor sorts the list by status and then by worst to best performance, so that the most worrisome subscriptions are at the top, as on the **Subscription Watch List** tab when a Publisher is selected in the Navigation Pane. Because the status and performance of replication agents changes frequently, the order of the subscriptions is likely to change when Replication Monitor refreshes the list.

To see the details of a subscription in the list, double-click the subscription or right-click the row and select **View Details**.

TIP

You can sort the subscription list by any column in the grid by clicking the header cell of that column. You can also filter the list by selecting a criterion from the **Show** list.

If you right-click on a subscription row, you get a menu of commands for that subscription, including commands to see the subscription properties, and to start or stop synchronizing.

The **Warnings and Agents** tab (see Figure 12-28) has two purposes: It enables you to define performance warning thresholds so that you can be alerted when a problem is building, and it shows the Snapshot Agent, the only agent for a merge publication that is common to all subscriptions.

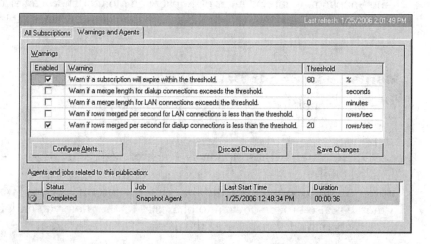

		Last refresh: 1/25/2006 2:01:49 PM		

All Subscriptions | Warnings and Agents

Warnings

Enabled	Warning	Threshold	
☑	Warn if a subscription will expire within the threshold.	80	%
☐	Warn if a merge length for dialup connections exceeds the threshold.	0	seconds
☐	Warn if a merge length for LAN connections exceeds the threshold.	0	minutes
☐	Warn if rows merged per second for LAN connections is less than the threshold.	0	rows/sec
☑	Warn if rows merged per second for dialup connections is less than the threshold.	20	rows/sec

Configure Alerts...   Discard Changes   Save Changes

Agents and jobs related to this publication:

	Status	Job	Last Start Time	Duration
⊘	Completed	Snapshot Agent	1/25/2006 12:48:34 PM	00:00:36

Figure 12-28 Merge Publication detail pane, Warnings and Agents tab.

If you enable a warning and specify a threshold, SQL Server logs an event to the Windows Event Log if a subscription crosses the threshold. You can define an alert that responds to the event by using SQL Server Agent or any application that watches the event log, such as Microsoft Operations Manager.

TIP

If you make changes to the warnings on this page, you must click **Save Changes**. If you leave the tab without clicking the button, your changes are not saved.

If you want to use SQL Server Agent to define alerts, click **Configure Alerts**, specify the warning on which you want to be alerted, and Replication Monitor opens the **Alert Properties** dialog box. To define alerts in Microsoft Operations Manager or another application, configure alerts in that application.

In **Agents and jobs related to this publication**, you can see the status of the Snapshot Agent. To see the details of a current or past session of the agent, double-click the agent or right-click its row and select **View Details**. You can also start or stop the agent from the context menu.

TIP

If the Snapshot Agent has an error, Replication Monitor shows an error icon in the **Warnings and Agents** tab so that you know to click on this tab to get information about the error.

Merge Subscription Detail Window

When you double-click on a merge subscription in any subscription list, Replication Monitor opens a window to display details about the subscription.

When a merge subscription is synchronized, SQL Server records detailed information about the data changes that are processed for each article. All this information is displayed in the subscription detail window. A merge is also broken down into phases to further help you understand the activity that occurred during the merge. The phases are

- **Initialization**—The period in which the Merge Agent starts up and establishes connections to the Publisher and Subscriber.
- **Schema changes and bulk inserts**—The period in which the Merge Agent applies any changes to the schema of the published objects, such as adding a new column to a published table, and performs bulk insert actions such as applying a snapshot to initialize a new subscription.

- **Upload changes to Publisher**—The period in which changes made to published data at the Subscriber are applied to the data at the Publisher.

- **Download changes to Subscriber**—The period in which changes made to published data at the Publisher are applied to the data at the Subscriber.

The amount of time spent in each phase is detailed in **Articles processed in the selected session** (see Figure 12-29). This list further breaks down the upload and download phases to show how much time was spent processing the changes in each article and the types of changes that were made. This information can help you determine whether there are bottlenecks in your publication, such as inefficient row or join filters, that slow down the merge process.

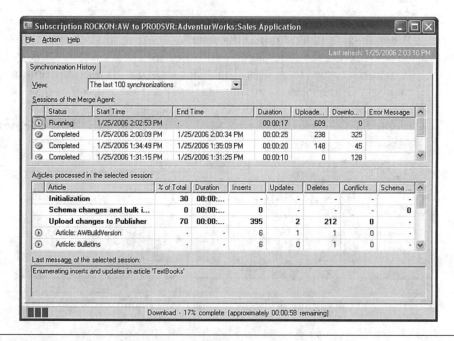

Figure 12-29 Merge Subscription detail window.

When you open the detail window for a subscription that is currently being merged, you can watch these performance values change as they are being recorded. Note that the Merge Agent works on several threads at the same time, so the sum of the times spent per article may appear to be greater than the duration of the merge. When the merge completes, the time spent per article is apportioned according to the final duration of the merge. Replication Monitor also provides a progress bar at the bottom of the window and an estimate of much time it will take for the merge to complete.

TIP

The detail window for a merge subscription sometimes, but not always, automatically refreshes. If the subscription is being synchronized, the window automatically refreshes because the performance details are actively changing. If the subscription is not synchronizing, the window does not automatically refresh. To manually refresh the window, click **Refresh** on the **Action** menu. To toggle automatic refreshes for this window, click **Auto Refresh** on the **Action** menu.

When an agent has stopped because of an error, the bottom of the window displays error messages and other information. There is often a series of error messages that come from different components involved in the operation that failed. If the error occurred when the agent was trying to execute a command, such as an INSERT statement, the command also is listed in **Last message of the selected session** (see Figure 12-30).

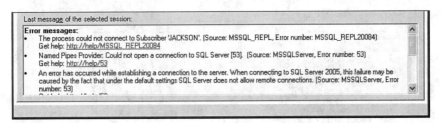

Figure 12-30   Error information in Transactional Subscription detail window.

TIP

Many error messages displayed in Replication Monitor have a help link with a URL of http://help/<error ID>. Although this isn't a URL that you can paste into your browser, when you click on it, Replication Monitor translates it into a complex URL that links to an online error database maintained by Microsoft.

Summary

This chapter gives you a look at the most important parts of the replication tools, but there is much more to them. If the tools seem complex, remember that database replication is complex technology. We recognized that you may need assistance in various places, so we made sure to have a Help button in most wizard pages and dialog boxes.

Significant effort went into making the tools for configuring and monitoring replication in SQL Server 2005 as intuitive and easy to use as possible. We were successful in many ways: Compared to the wizard in SQL Server 2000, the New Publication Wizard has about 50% fewer pages. SQL Server 2000 had two subscription wizards: separate ones for creating push and pull subscriptions. The New Subscription Wizard in SQL Server 2005 combines both into one common experience. Replication Monitor was completely redesigned and focuses more on your replicated data and less on the moving parts of the implementation. Your can debate whether the replication tools qualify as easy, but there is no doubt that completing replication tasks is easier now than in previous versions of SQL Server.

CHAPTER 13

Inside Analysis Services OLAP Tools

Microsoft SQL Server 2000 provided two main tools for developing and managing OLAP cube and Mining Models. Analysis Manager was the main tool. Built on the Microsoft Management Console (MMC) infrastructure, it enabled the Database professional to develop and manage OLAP servers and mining models against a live server. In this tool, Design and Management tasks were combined in one unique environment. The other tool that was available was the MDX Sample. Although it was shipped on the CD as sample code, it turned out to be one of the most useful tools to issue MDX queries against the Analysis Services servers. It was particularly important for testing data and the performance of specific queries.

With SQL Server 2005, Microsoft has redesigned its tool approach to better fit different roles played by different individuals or teams in a company. Most aspects of functionality are now split between the BI Development studio for design tasks and SQL Management Studio for management and other operational tasks. When we started early designs and prototypes in 2000, the decision had not yet been made to integrate the BI development environment with Visual Studio, but very early it was clear that we wanted to provide an experience to the "BI developer." Now the BI developer is often an odd role; it doesn't necessarily map with any existing title in the IT organization. Traditionally, the person in charge of designing the Cubes or Mining model fits one of the two possible molds:

- He or she is in IT yet has a good knowledge and understanding of user requirements or situations.

- He or she is not in IT, belonging instead to the user community, but has good technical ability. This person is fairly comfortable with some DB concepts and writing some business-oriented logic (MDX)

So we rapidly had to make a decision about the level of technical ability that our tool should require as well as what the best Integrated Development Environment (IDE) was for such an environment. Although we decided that we should leverage the Microsoft IDE, which is Visual Studio, we also decided that we would focus on designing tools that would be appropriate for not only developers (coders) but non-developers as well. This is why every single task can be achieved through graphical wizards and designers as well as through scripting and coding using our APIs. We do realize, though, that even though we have made tons of investment in providing a very business-oriented wizard, the IDE environment can still be somewhat overwhelming for the non-developer. Look at the development tools in SQL 2005 as our first step in this direction. I'm sure that as we learn more from customers' experiences and hear more feedback from users and developers, we will refine and provide tools in the future that are even better suited to individual roles, levels of expertise, and tasks.

This chapter tries to walk the reader through many scenarios that cover most of the key functionality of the tools while also providing insights, tips, and techniques. The reader will find a lot of valuable "How to" techniques throughout this chapter.

Analysis Services OLAP Tools Overview

Analysis Services tools in 2005 introduce a whole new way to work with the data and the OLAP and Data Mining objects. In Analysis Services 2000, the very first step a user had to take to design or manage a server was to physically connect to an Analysis Services server. In 2005, you have the choice of two tools to use, depending on the task to be accomplished: BI Development Studio or SQL Server Management Studio. Also, with BI development Studio, you have two choices: work live against a physical server (also called immediate mode) or work in project mode. With SQL Server Management Studio you always work against a live server. Both modes are presented and discussed in the next section.

BI Development Studio

The BI Development Studio is the environment to use for the following type of tasks:

- Designing cubes (see Figure 13-1)
- Designing dimensions

- Designing the mining structure and model
- Changing an existing design before redeployment to a production server
- Enriching the cube with additional analytics (using the BI Wizard, for example)
- Adding business logic, KPI, translations values
- Adding dimension or cell security

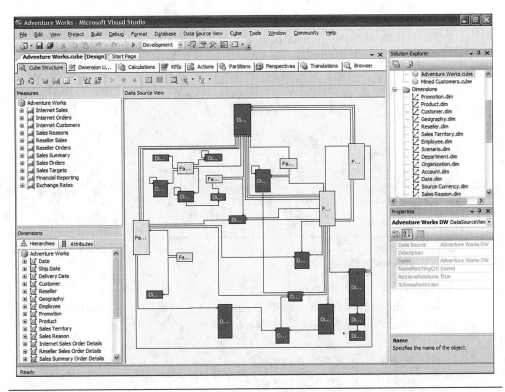

Figure 13-1 Cube designer hosted in the BI Development Studio.

The BI Development Studio is a fundamental revolution for BI development activity. The first major change is that the first operation is to choose either to connect live to a database or work with a project.

A **project** is a collection of XML files that are saved a disk, either local or remote. Additionally, these files can also be saved in a source control system. When a project is loaded or created, graphical designers read from each XML file, parse the information, and display the same data graphically (see Figure 13-1).

To create a new project, you start as if creating any other project in Visual Studio. The main difference is that new project types are made available to you (see Figure 13-2).

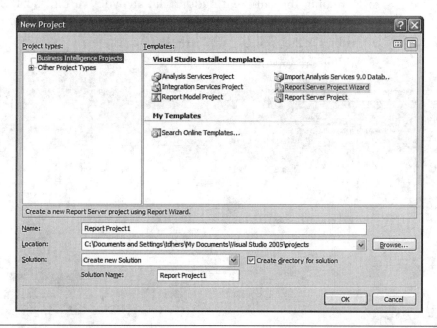

Figure 13-2 New Project dialog.

Thus the database professional can elect to create a solution using any of the available BI project types:

- Analysis Services project
- Integrations Services project
- Report Server project
- Report Model project

The other two projects are just shortcuts for specific tasks:

- Import Analysis Services 9.0 Database project launches a converter that will reverse-engineer a project from a live database.
- Report Server Project Wizard creates a new report project and launches the Report Wizard automatically

Additionally, after the solution has been initially created with one project, other projects can be added later to this solution, whether they are BI projects or any other projects available with Visual Studio (ASP.NET, VB.Net, C+, and so on).

The counterpart to Project mode is Immediate mode or Live mode. In this mode, using the File/Open menu, you can select a physical server and database to connect to, as shown in Figure 13-3. Thus any change made through the BI development studio happens immediately and directly in the live production environment.

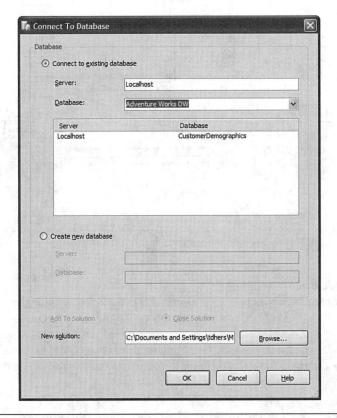

Figure 13-3 Connect To Database dialog.

So one of the first questions you will ask yourself is "Which mode should I use?" This is indeed one of the most important decisions you will make when starting a new project. Project mode is recommended when working with a professional development team made up of several developers or designers. Immediate mode is usually fine when a single person designs and manages the OLAP database and Mining model. Figure 13-4 illustrates the interaction between BI development Studio and the file or live database, as well as interaction between SQL Server Management Studio and the live server.

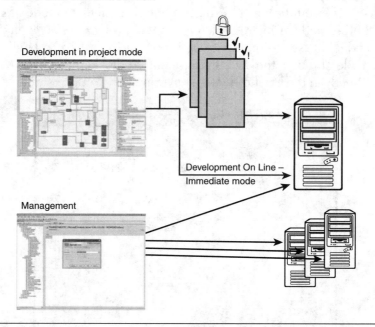

Figure 13-4   SQL Server development and management tools.

WARNING
Avoid as much as possible mixing the two modes. Working against the same database using both modes can be very dangerous because one of your teams or developers may be changing the structure of the Cube in Project mode while another may be changing the same object in Immediate mode. The changes made in Immediate mode will be overwritten next time the project is deployed.

Inside a BI development Studio Analysis Services Project

After you have created an Analysis Services project or are connected live to an Analysis Services database, you find yourself presented with various designers.

Unlike Analysis Manager in SQL 2000, every designer here has been built natively as modeless. That means that you can open as many as you want at the same time.

TIP

Using two screens in a side-by-side mode greatly improves productivity by allowing you to work with and update multiple objects at once.

Let me briefly describe the various designers available in such a project because I will be referencing them further in this chapter:

- Data Source Editor dialog
- Data Source View designer
- Cube designer
- Dimension designer
- Data Mining Structure designer
- Role Security designer
- Cube, Dimension, Mining Model, BI wizard.

The Data Source Editor dialog enables the database professional to set up a connection to various data sources. In Analysis Services 2000, ODBC as well as OLE-DB providers could be used. In Analysis Services 2005, OLE-DB as well as native connectors can be used. In addition, the Data Source editor also provides the environment to customize connection properties such as time-out and impersonation credentials.

The Data Source View Designer is a designer of a new object: the Data Source View (DSV). The DSV lets you model your relational data. One may ask, "Why can't I model it directly in my relational database?" Well, for starters, your source may not be relational. Also, if you are trying to build a reporting and analytical application directly against an OLTP or production database, the database may be read-only to the database professional, thus making it impossible to create additional relationships or views for the purpose of this BI application. Finally, you may need to access multiple heterogeneous data sources. The Data Source View, beyond allowing you to reduce the scope and number of tables you work with, also enables you to access tables coming from multiple data sources (i.e., Oracle and SQL Server, or Teradata and DB2) in a single relational modeling environment and create logical relationships between them or views on top of them.

The DSV Designer is a great environment for doing such modeling. Adding relationships, creating named queries (Views), and creating calculated columns are all common tasks that can be accomplished in this designer.

TIP

When the schema contains a large number of objects (tables, views, and so on), do not hesitate to create multiple Diagram views for portions of the schema. This will make it easier to read and navigate relationships.

TIP

Use the CTRL + Mouse wheel up and down to rapidly zoom in and out in the diagram. This technique works in all other designer diagram views as well.

TIP

If the schema contains a lot of tables that cannot be seen on the screen all at once, use the Diagram Navigator, which you can access by clicking on the double arrow in the bottom right of the diagram (see Figure 13-5) to get an overview (see Figure 13-6) and navigate through the diagram.

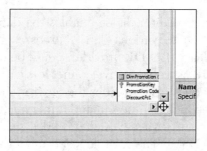

Figure 13-5   Diagram Navigator Anchor.

You can access the Database Designer by right-clicking on the Project name (in this case, AdventureWorksDW) in Solution Explorer. Because the database is the container of the cube, Dimension Object, it doesn't really find its place in the Solution Explorer. This is why we found that the most logical place for the menu to invoke it was a context menu on the project name itself. Experience and time have shown that although it is very logical, it makes it hard to discover for the novice user. The Cube Designer has been much enhanced since Analysis Manager 2000. Because a cube is now a much more powerful and complete object, the Cube Designer now is made up of nine tabs. Because it has so many tabs, we thought originally of using the Microsoft Outlook Metaphor and displaying the tab along the left vertical side of the designer. Usability studies showed that it was consuming too much screen real estate,

which as you have probably noticed already, is one of the most important things to preserve in the VS shell. Each tab enables the database
professional to update the components of the cube definition, which
are usually referred to as second-class objects. (First-class objects are
things such as cubes, dimensions, and Mining Models. Second-class
objects are things such as Measures, Actions, KPIs, Attributes, and
hierarchies.) Because it is sometimes necessary to display the same
information in two different tabs, the Cube Designer ensures that when
some information is updated through one tab, the rest of the designer is
refreshed with the same updates as well. This way, the Cube Designer
ensures that a consistent and coherent view of the second-class object is
displayed at all time.

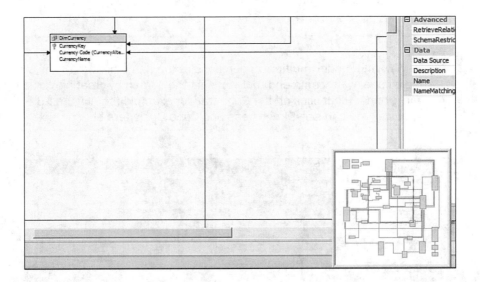

Figure 13-6   Diagram Navigator Overview.

The Dimension Designer, like the Cube Designer, has been enhanced as
well. It now includes three tabs: Dimension Structure, Translation, and
Browser. You will notice that the pane organization inside the Dimension Structure tab is reorganized if you select between the Tree, List,
and Grid views (see Figure 13-7). This is again to optimize screen real
estate usage to a specific view. It is recommended that you play around
with the view, and then find the one that best suits your need. For example, I know I like the Tree view to set the Attribute member properties

relationship (which is important for aggregation design), but I like the Grid view to review attribute key properties all at once.

Figure 13-7   Dimension Structure tab view selection drop- down.

TIP
To view and modify multiple dimensions at the same time that you're editing a cube, we recommend that you split the screen by creating Vertical Tab groups. Right-click on the Cube tab, for example (see Figure 13-8). That way you can see Dimensions and Cube Designers side by side.

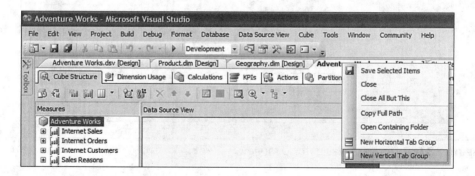

Figure 13-8   Create New Vertical Tab Group.

The Data Mining Model Designer is probably one of the richest of all the designers. It hosts over 25 data browsers. Rich visualization is critical to being able to analyze the findings of the mining model algorithm. Although the designer only has five main tabs (Mining Structure, Mining Models, Mining Model Viewer, Mining Accuracy Chart, Mining Model

Prediction), you will rapidly notice that the Mining Model Viewer tab contains its own set of sub-tabs. The list of sub-tabs is dependent on the mining model algorithm selected.

TIP
Each of the Data viewers available in the mining Model Designer is a component that can be reused as-is in an application.

The Role Designer is a unique designer because it is the only Designer that was designed from day one to be hosted by both the BI Development Studio and the SQL Management Studio. Because setting security is an activity that may be done during the development phase or deployment phase, it is indeed needed in both environments. Thus you will notice that the Role Designer in BI development Studio and the Role Dialog in SQL Management Studio have the same structure. They actually share the same framework and code. Only the hosting frame is different.

NOTE
Unlike in Analysis Manager 2000, the Testing Role is not accessed from the Role Designer. This functionality has been moved to the Cube and Dimension Designers' browser tabs. An icon is available in the toolbar that lets the database professional impersonate a different user or set of roles. The browser can then display the data with the security context of the user or role(s) (see Figure 13-9).

Finally, many wizards are available throughout the BI Development Studio. There are wizards like those in SQL 2000 for creating each first-class object: Cube, Dimension, Mining Model. Some new wizards are also introduced in this release, such as the Deployment Wizard or the BI Wizard. The Deployment Wizard assists the database professional to deploy a specific database to another server. The BI Wizard was designed to assist with enhancing the cube or dimension design with more complex tasks such as adding time intelligence, semi-additive aggregation, or currency conversion. The list of available tasks is different, depending upon the object for which the BI wizard was invoked. More and different tasks are available if the wizard is invoked from a cube rather than a dimension object. Also, this wizard was designed with a specific framework that will enable us to easily enhance the list of available tasks in a future release. We didn't have the time to make this framework fully extensible by external parties in the SQL 2005 release. We hope it will be made possible in the future. This wizard doesn't build anything that cannot be done by hand through the designers directly. The goal of this wizard is to help you complete more complex business tasks in less time, thus improving productivity.

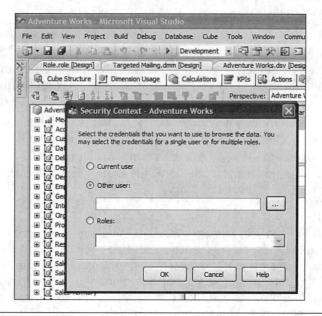

Figure 13-9   Testing roles and users using the Security Context dialog.

SQL Management Studio

The SQL Management Studio is the environment to use for the following types of tasks:

- Migrating a database
- Backing up or restoring a database
- Processing a cube, a partition, a dimension, or a mining structure
- Browsing a cube, a dimension, or a mining model
- Scripting any management task
- Running an MDX, DMX, or XML/A query against the live database
- Changing a server property

Unlike BI development Studio, in SQL Management Studio your first task will always be to select and connect to a specific server, whether local or remote (see Figure 13-10). After you are connected to this server, then all management tasks related to this server become enabled. The server content is displayed in the object browser that comes up on the left side of the window. In some ways connecting to an Analysis Services server with SQL Server Management Studio is equivalent to connecting to an Analysis Services server with Analysis Manager in SQL Server 2000, less all the development tasks.

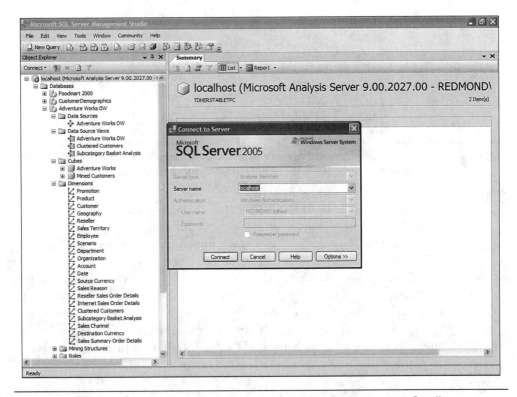

Figure 13-10   Managing Analysis Services using SQL Management Studio.

NOTE
In SQL 2005, the database professional can actually customize some connection properties when connecting to a server with the Advanced option button on the bottom right of the connection string. Clicking the Advanced button yields the properties page shown in Figure 13-11.

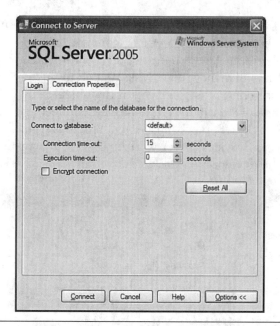

Figure 13-11   Advanced Connection Properties can be set when connecting to Analysis Services with SQL Server Management Studio.

The SQL Management Studio interface is mainly divided into two areas: Object Explorer on the left side and query editors or a summary pane on the right side. In addition, you can achieve most management tasks by invoking a dialog or a wizard to complete these tasks.

Through the Object Explorer, you can access every Analysis Services Database object and trigger task for individual objects. The available task list is different for each Analysis Services object. So, for example, migrating a database or editing Server Properties are available only from the server node. The Running Usage-Based Optimization Wizard is available only from a specific partition or set of partitions.

TIP

One of the best features of the Object Explorer is the capability to script every single object. Scripting an object creates the portion of the XML/A command, which is now the native protocol for Analysis Services 2005 server, that can either be scheduled or run directly from within this environment or copied into an Integration Services package or application code.

As explained in previous chapters, the Summary pane displays statistical and detailed information about the object selected in the Object Explorer.

TIP

Although the object browser itself doesn't allow multi-selection of nodes, it is possible to select multiple objects by using the Summary page on the right pane. For example, if the Cubes node is selected in the Solution Explorer, all cubes can be selected together in the summary pane and the Process command can be invoked on all of them at once.

The MDX sample utility that was so useful with Analysis Services 2000 has been integrated and enhanced in the SQL Management Studio. Now you can directly send MDX, DMX, or XMLA commands, using MDX, DMX, or XML/A query editors. As they do for SQL, these editors support enhanced color coding, tooltips, and region collapsing. As many of these editors as needed can be opened at the same time.

To complete tasks, a set of dialogs and wizards are also available in this environment. The dialogs have been designed to run independently from the SQL Management Studio shell. That means they continue to run even if the shell is closed. That also means they each run as separate executables. This is especially useful for the database professional who can now, for example, run a usage-based optimization wizard while at the same time running a backup on a different database (see Figure 13-12) These dialogs are very powerful because they are themselves entirely scriptable as well as schedulable.

So pretty much everything that can be done graphically through the SQL Management Studio environment can be scripted and scheduled at a specific time. This really brings the level of manageability of Analysis Services objects on par with the SQL relational database objects.

Using Analysis Services Tools to Address Business Scenarios

The following section discusses various scenarios and technical situations in which you may find yourself. The goal of presenting these scenarios is to go beyond the basic step-by-step of how to use the designers or wizards, but to actually provide tips on and insights into some non-obvious capabilities of the designers and wizards.

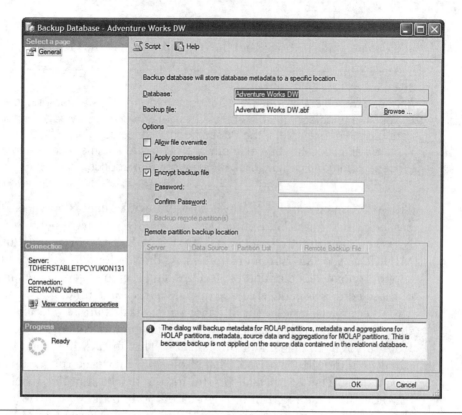

Figure 13-12   Backup Database dialog.

To facilitate your search through these 30+ scenarios, I have categorized them each by the designers and wizards where they take place. Beyond this grouping they are not ordered in any particular way.

- **General**
  - How should I upgrade my existing application? Should I rebuild it, migrate it, or upgrade it?
  - What exactly is the UDM: Is it a DSV diagram, a cache, a very detailed cube? How come I can't find the UDM object anywhere through the tools?
- **BI development Studio**
  - How do I decide whether I should work live on the server or in project mode? How do I switch between modes?
  - How do I deploy a DB across servers? Do I use the Deployment Wizard, Filecopy only?

- How do I take an AS2K cube and enhance it with new AS2K5 features?
- How do I create new templates for cubes and dimensions?
- Why should I be typing my dimensions and attributes with dimension types (Time, Currency, Account, and so on) or attribute types?
- How do I make Visual Development Studio look like Analysis Manager 2000?
- How can I produce documentation for every object contained in my solution?
- When would auto-scrolling during drag-and-drop operations help?

- **DSV Designer**
  - How do I use SQL in cube, dimension, and partition definitions?

- **Cube Wizard**
  - How can I prototype a cube rapidly without pre-requiring any existing data sources?
  - How can I easily use test data to speed development of cubes and dimensions?
  - How do I view sample measures data in the cube wizard?

- **Cube Designer—Dimension Usage Tab**
  - How do I compare two measured groups' dimensionality? Do I use filtering by dimension or by measure group or some other option?
  - How can I have a measure group with a level of granularity above the key?

- **Cube Designer—Calculation, Actions, KPI Tab**
  - How do I change calculation, Action, or KPI MDX templates?
  - Should I use a KPI Display folder or KPI parent property? How do I build a company health index KPI?
  - How can I rebuild my own KPI browser to be similar to the one available in BI Development Studio and embed it in my application?
  - How do I use the cube debugger as a calculation builder? How do I use the MDX debugger to debug complex calculations?

- **Cube Designer—Translation tab**
  - How do I automate loading translation strings into my project?
- **Cube Designer—Partition tab**
  - How do I automatically create a partition for a new data set? How do I set automatic partitioning on a partitioned table?
- **Cube Designer—Cube browser**
  - What is the difference between the cube slicer and OWC filter in the cube browser page? When do I use one versus the other?
  - How do I test my roles and security?
- **BI Wizard**
  - How do I change time intelligence templates?
  - How do I document changes generated by the BI wizard?
- **Dimension Editor**
  - How do I bring pictures into my UDM?
  - Which tree views in the user interface that support multiple selections might help in my case?
  - How do I set up a dimension with Multiple Parents Rollup with Weights?
- **Dimension Wizard**
  - How should I build the time dimension? Should it be server-based or table-based?
- **SQL Management Studio**
  - How do I execute multiple MDX queries from SQL Server Management Studio (SSMS)?
  - How do I find a specific server property?
  - How do I set a process option for more than one object at once in the Process Object(s) dialog?

In the following sections we address each of these questions.

How Should I Upgrade My Existing Application?

This is one of the very first questions you may face. The answer is not that obvious because it depends on your business requirements, resources, and infrastructure. You have four main options:

- Upgrade
- Migrate
- Migrate and enhance
- Rebuild

Let's look at each of these options in detail and evaluate their pros and cons. But before that, let's look at what your cube's situation would look like before and after you have installed Analysis Services 2005 and applied each of these techniques. Figure 13-13 illustrates what version of the software would be running on your server before and after an Upgrade, migration, or building a brand new cube. Each option is discussed in detail in the following sections.

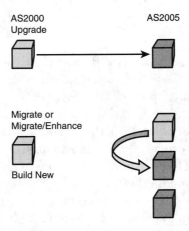

Figure 13-13   Upgrade and migration options.

Upgrade

Upgrade means the database and cube are upgraded from an AS200 to an AS2005 server in the same machine. After the upgrade the AS2000 server and cubes are no longer available, so there is no going back!

Personally I would rarely recommend using the upgrade scenario. The main reason for this is that during an upgrade the cube is moved from an AS2000 to an AS2005 server on the same machine. Because the AS2000 cubes and DB are not available any longer, it is impossible to test after the upgrade and verify that the upgraded cubes return the same results as the cubes in AS2000.

If you decide to upgrade we strongly, no, we STRONGLY recommend that you use the Upgrade Advisor utility before running the upgrade. The Upgrade Advisor can either be downloaded from Microsoft.com or installed from the SQL 2005 setup disk. The Upgrade Advisor provides you with a warning about potential areas affected during the upgrade and information about how to fix some of these issues.

Also, you need to realize that after an upgrade, the AS database and cubes in AS2005 are an exact (as much as possible) image of the AS2000 database and cube, and thus they don't take advantage of any of the new architecture and features available in AS2005.

Also be aware than an upgrade upgrades only the metadata, which means the cube and database need to be processed after the upgrade step.

Migrate

The migration scenario is different than the upgrade scenario in the sense that SQL 2005 is installed side by side with SQL 2000. Although this requires more space on the server, it also provides you with a major benefit over upgrading. This benefit is the fact that after you migrate your AS database to AS2005, the AS2000 Database is still available. Thus both databases can be compared, and, if necessary, the AS2000 database can serve as a reference in case some modification needs to be applied to the newly migrated AS2005 database.

During the migration, the migration wizard provides warnings and information similar to that delivered through the upgrade advisor.

As in the upgrade scenario, the migration migrates only the metadata, so this means that the cubes and dimensions need to be reprocessed.

As in the upgrade scenario, after a migration, the cube and database are an image of the AS2000 cube and database. Thus they don't take advantage of any of the new AS2005 functionality.

Migrate and Enhance

Migrating and enhancing is a slight variation on the migration scenario. Indeed, after a migration the cubes and database are an image of the AS2000 cubes and database. But it is possible to enhance this design to start taking more advantage of the new functionality offered by AS 2005.

The first thing that you want to take advantage of is the new project mode. Working in live mode against the server to modify and develop functionality can work only in situations or companies that do not have a lot of resources and specifically do not have different teams and people in charge of developing and managing the server.

Moving off live mode to the project mode is important because it gives you a lot of possibilities. For one, you can now track versions of the cubes designs by using a source control system. Additionally multiple developers can now work on the project at the same time. And finally, your developers can update the design of the cubes and dimensions without impacting the users using the cubes and database.

You can reverse-engineer the live database to an Analysis Services project by using the Import Analysis Services 9.0 database. Choose **File> New Project** (see Figure 13-14).

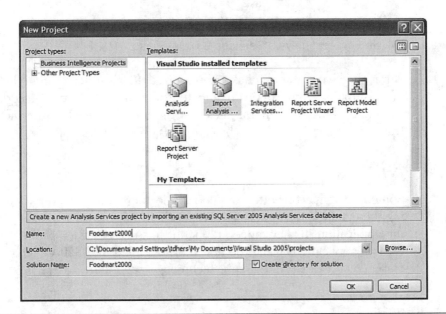

Figure 13-14   Using the Import Analysis Services 9.0 database project.

After you create the project, the Import Analysis Services 9.0 database wizard is launched (see Figure 13-15). You will notice that as an object gets read from the server and imported, the corresponding object is created on the fly in the Solution Explorer.

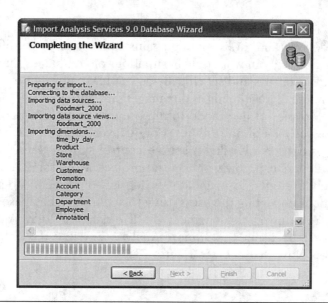

Figure 13-15   Import an Analysis Services 9.0 Database Wizard.

After the live database has been moved to a project, then the rest of the cube's design can be enhanced. For example, KPI can be added to the cube, additional hierarchies can be added to each dimension, or translations can be added to both dimension and cube objects.

Rebuild

Sometime, it may be better to spend a little more time early on when moving the database to Analysis Services 2005, if this provides a longer life to the application. It may indeed be better in some cases for you to rebuild existing applications using the new tools provided by AS2005, such as the Cube Wizard and its intelli-cube technology (see Figure 13-16).

NOTE
Intellicube is not the official name of this functionality. It is now called Autobuild. Interestingly, when Cristian Petculescu, our architect, first started working on this functionality, we called it the One Click cube. That was the result of the challenge that Amir Netz, our Product Unit manager, gave to Cristian. Wouldn't it be cool if we could build the entire cube and dimension automatically in one click. We still used this name internally when we referred to this feature, but we knew it wouldn't be the final one. When it came time to name this feature, the product group recommended Intellicube, because we

are indeed trying to do our best and be as smart as possible in creating the best cube possible. The marketing and branding group came back with this new name which is now the official one: Auto Build. But for us, it is still the Intellicube feature powered by the One Click Cube algorithm.

Figure 13-16   Using the Cube Wizard to automatically build a cube based on a data source.

Anyway, building the cube from scratch may be a slightly lengthier process and a bigger investment in time and resources than upgrading or migrating an existing cube, but it has many advantages.

First, your cube will be fully optimized for the new architecture that AS2005 offers. It will take full advantage of the new attribute-based architecture.

The new cube will provide greater analytic capability: more and finer-grain data, more hierarchies, more measures coming from multiple measure groups, and more calculations.

In conclusion, for this scenario, we offer you options. Don't jump into upgrading everything right away. Take a little time to assess your situation and decide whether it is worth investing some time rebuilding everything or whether things are just fine the way they are. If your cube provides you what you need (as we like to put it, "if it ain't broken, don't fix it"), then migration may be just fine.

What Exactly Is the UDM?

When I do Executive Briefing Center sessions (EBCS) or events like Teched, this is actually one of the most frequently asked questions: What exactly is a Unified Dimensional Model (UDM)? The UDM is the 2005 version of an Analysis Services cube. It is a cube!

One could also wonder, then why did we call that a UDM? It is a cube indeed, but not a cube like the one you may be used to seeing with AS2000 or with other vendor technology. It goes much beyond what people think of traditionally as a cube.

A UDM is a technology that enables you to model all the data contained in your data source(s), not just simple hierarchies. It also contains all the attributes (mapping to columns in the tables) available. Beyond potentially providing the same level of detail as contained in the relational data source(s), it also provides access to this data in real time, thanks to the proactive caching technology.

Furthermore, a UDM or cube can now be modeled directly against a third normal form schema, thus allowing the BI application to be built directly on top of OLTP or an operational system. The Data Source View or DSV is here to enable you to apply relational modeling beneath the UDM in those cases when the underlying data source(s) is read-only and thus cannot be modified for the purpose of the reporting and analytical application (that is, can't add relationship, can't create views).

Finally the UDM is a metadata catalog that can also be enhanced with advanced analytics: KPI, translations, perspectives, MDX script, and actions.

So in summary, a UDM is not the DSV schema, or just a cache, KPI, and business rule catalog or a detailed cube; it is all of it together.

To the OLAP experienced user, the UDM is breaking the barrier of OLAP analytic and relational reporting and can address both of them at the same time. In that sense it goes way beyond a traditional OLAP cube.

To the relational database professional, a UDM is the metadata catalog that provides a business modeling view on top of the relational source, while also enhancing the performance thanks to a disk-based cache.

For all these reasons we didn't want to position this as just a cube, as it would have reduced the impact and perception of this new technology in the marketplace. So we called it a Unified Dimensional Model because it can unify all your data sources in a single metadata catalog while allowing a variety of user experiences (for example, Slice and Dice, highly formatted banded report, KPI Dashboard) and still preserving the single version of the truth.

So why did we not call it a UDM in the tools and object models? The answer is two words: backward compatibility. The cube is one of the first-class objects in an Analysis Services database. Changing its name to UDM would have broken every single existing application that attempted to migrate or upgrade. For this reason alone, we will continue forever to call this a cube, but we sure hope that by now you have realized how much we have broadened the definition of what a cube is.

How Do I Decide Whether I Should Work Live on the Server or in Project Mode?

As noted previously in this chapter, this is one of the first questions you should ask yourself. The answer depends on your context.

My rule of thumb is if only one person will be both developing and administrating the application, then working live against the server is just fine. Connecting to a database to edit it in live mode is fairly straightforward: Just launch the BI development studio and select the following menu sequence: **File > Open > Analysis Services Databases** (see Figure 13-17).

In the Connect To Database dialog, just enter the server name (and eventually instance name) and select the database to which you want to connect. Even though the object appears in the Solution Explorer, you are in live mode, not project mode. What does it mean to your experience? The designers and wizards will look the same, but saving means something extremely different. When working live against a database, saving means save changes and deploy changes immediately on the server. Some structurally breaking changes may result in forcing a reprocessing of the object. By contrast, in project mode, save just means save the changes in the XML file of this object; the live database is not impacted by this change until the project is redeployed.

So when should you use project mode? In any other cases (different teams are developing and managing, or there are multiple developers), I recommend working in project mode. Working in project mode decouples the development cycle from the operational side. One can develop a new version of an application while users still continue querying the current version.

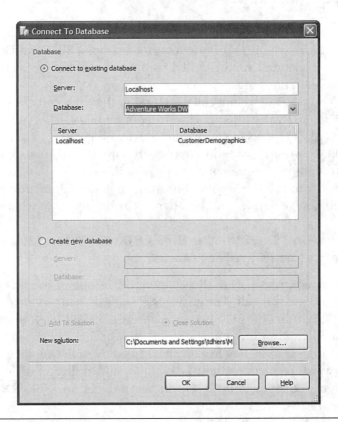

Figure 13-17   Connect to an existing database in live mode.

Project mode also enables you to leverage a source control system to check in files, check out files, create multiple versions, and allow multiple developers to work on the same project simultaneously. Project mode also enables you to fully support the full life cycle of an application:

1. Develop
2. Unit test
3. Integrate and test
4. Deploy to the production environment

By default, projects are saved under the My Documents\Visual Studio 2005\Projects folder, but they can also be stored and retrieved from any file share as well (see Figure 13-18).

   Because in project mode the object definition is saved in XML files in the project folder, do not forget to regularly back up this project folder if you are not using a source control system.

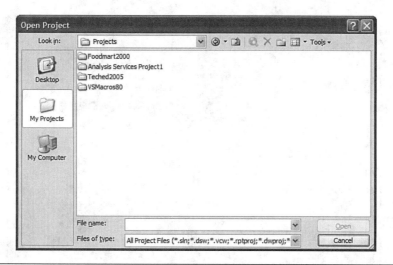

Figure 13-18 Open Project dialog.

How Do I Deploy a DB Across Servers?

Well, in Analysis Services 2000, this was one of the top most-asked questions. Back then, the only answer was to use backup and restore to move the database over to a different server. It was a limited solution because Backup had a 2GB file size limitation and very often cubes were larger than this.

With Analysis Services 2005, we do not provide one solution to this problem; we provide at least four: Deploy the project to a different server, copy the project file on a different machine, use the much revamped Backup/restore, or use the synchronization wizard. Let's review each of them.

The first option is to simply deploy the current project to a different target server. This can easily be achieved by setting a different server name on the Project Properties dialog (see Figure 13-19).

This is a very natural solution for moving from a development machine to a test environment or from a test environment to a production environment. Obviously this option is available to you only if you work in project mode as opposed to live mode against a server.

The second option is to simply copy the project over to a different server and reopen it on that other server with the local BI development studio. Again, this project needs to be deployed on this new server to create the objects on the Analysis Server. Since the project is self contained, it is a very convenient option when you need to move a project between two servers that are on two different domains or that have no network connectivity between them.

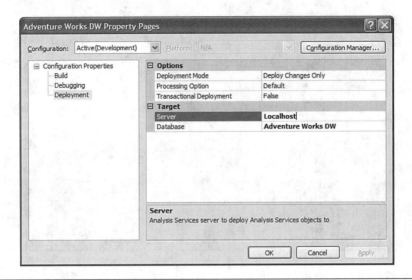

Figure 13-19   Project deployment options.

The third option is to use the much revamped backup and restore utility (see Figure 13-20). The Analysis Services backup and restore has become very similar to the SQL Server relational backup and restore feature. It no longer suffers from a 2GB file limitation. Unlike the two first options, this option enables you to not only move the database object's definition from one server to another but also to move the data as well. This is the preferred choice for moving data and metadata between two production servers. It is obviously the option to use to recover a database in case it becomes damaged.

This solution provides greater flexibility in terms of moving data with or without security definitions. Indeed, you can select to overwrite role definition when restoring the backup file. You also have the capability to rename the database while restoring it.

Finally, the fourth option is to use the synchronization wizard or command (see Figure 13-21). This functionality is very much similar to the replication capability of the relational database. It enables you to define a synchronization rule on a target server. That rule will automatically replicate the database from a source server to the server on which the rule is defined.

This functionality is particularly useful in a scale-out scenario. Indeed it might be very wise in such a situation, where a large number of concurrent users will be querying a fairly large cube, to decouple the server on which a database is processed from the server being queried by users. To do this, you may define an architecture with two servers: One server for processing the data, one for reporting against the data. In such an architecture you need to ensure at all times that both datasets are identical. You can use the synchronization wizard or command to periodically synchronize the data between the two servers.

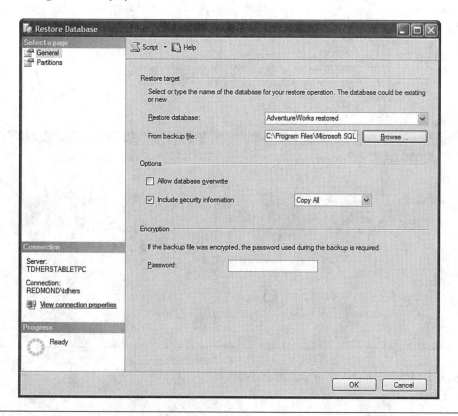

Figure 13-20   Restore Database dialog.

As with every command available through the SQL Management studio, a synchronization script can be generated. This option is actually offered during the last step of the wizard. A script example follows:

```
<Synchronize xmlns:xsi="http://www.w3.org/2001/XMLSchema-instance"
xmlns:xsd="http://www.w3.org/2001/XMLSchema"
xmlns="http://schemas.microsoft.com/analysisservices/2003/engine">
  <Source>
```

```
        <ConnectionString>Provider=MSOLAP.3;
                           Data Source=Localhost;
                           ConnectTo=9.0;
                           Integrated Security=SSPI;
                           Initial Catalog=Adventure Works DW
        </ConnectionString>
        <Object>
          <DatabaseID>Adventure Works DW</DatabaseID>
        </Object>
      </Source>
      <Locations />
      <SynchronizeSecurity>SkipMembership</SynchronizeSecurity>
      <ApplyCompression>true</ApplyCompression>
    </Synchronize>
```

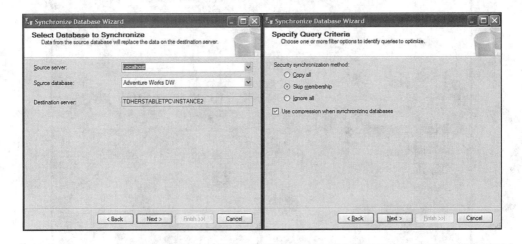

Figure 13-21   Synchronize Database Wizard.

It is then fairly easy to schedule this synchronization to happen at regular intervals by using either SQL Agent jobs (see Figure 13-22) or Integration Services.

SQL Agent has been enhanced to now natively support two new types of steps: the SQL Server Analysis Services Command and the SQL Server Analysis Services query.

In conclusion, you can see that Analysis Services has largely been enhanced in this area to provide you multiple ways to answer this question. Each option is better suited for specific business requirements and situations.

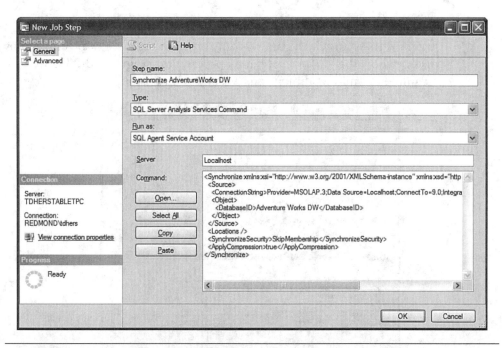

Figure 13-22   Synchronization script automation through a SQL agent job.

How Do I Take an AS2K Cube and Enhance It with New AS2K5 Features?

This scenario is very similar to the Migrate and Enhance option discussed earlier in this chapter. After an Analysis Services 2000 database has been migrated to Analysis Services 2005, you can enhance it by either importing it first into a project, or by connecting to the live database and starting to modify it to add translation, KPIs, or whatever else you need. The detailed procedure is described in the migration scenario earlier in this chapter.

Just remember that migration migrates only metadata, and thus the database needs to be reprocessed before the data and metadata can be queried.

How Do I Create New Templates for Cubes and Dimensions?

One of the new ways to create a cube or dimension in Analysis Services 2005 is without using a preexisting data source. This is not necessarily one of the most advertised features, yet it is very useful for prototyping cube design before the underlying data becomes available. It is also an important feature when designing budgeting or forward-looking forecasting cubes for which data will only become available or be entered by users when the cube is put into production. Figure 13-23 shows an example of building dimensions with the Dimension Wizard.

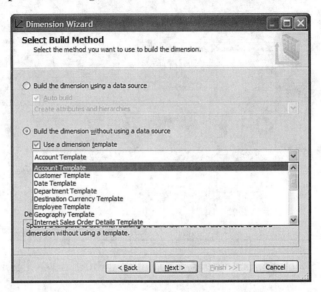

Figure 13-23   Building a dimension using a dimension template.

When creating a cube or dimension without a data source, the database professional can decide to create the object from scratch or use a pre-existing template. Out of the box, one cube template and nineteen dimension templates are provided. The templates are used to pre-fill measures, dimension hierarchies, and attributes while going through the wizard. These templates can be replaced and enhanced.

Cube and dimension templates can contain a lot of pre-defined business content. As a result, it may be interesting to create many company templates so that when database administrators throughout the company create UDMs they do so using company-standard definitions.

To replace or add a new template, simply use the XML file definition of the cube or dimension objects, as found in a project folder, and place it under the dimension or cube template folder under C:\Program Files\ Microsoft SQL Server\90\Tools\Templates\olap\1033 (see Figure 13-24). The path of the folder may be slightly different (that is, other than 1033) if the template needs to be made available in different locales. Here 1033 corresponds to the English U.S. locale.

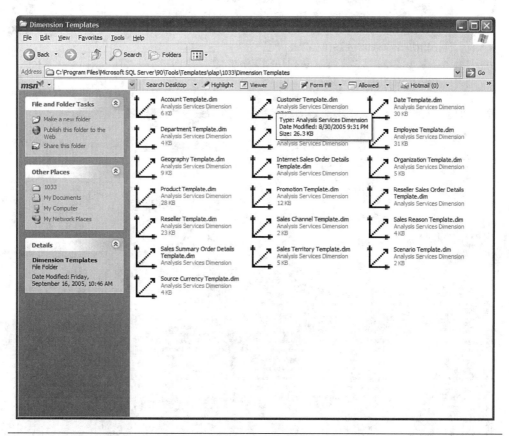

Figure 13-24   Selecting among the built-in dimension template XML files.

Why Should I Be Typing My Dimensions and Attributes with Dimension Types (Time, Currency, Account and so on) or Attribute Types?

In Analysis Services 2000, dimension types (Regular, Product, Time, and so on) or level types (Year, Quarter, Month, and so on) already existed. Typing these objects was important mainly for the time intelligence of the cube. Indeed, for example, YTD and QTD MDX functions needed this information to behave properly and return results.

Attribute types were also used by third-party vendors to add business intelligence and behavior based on the knowledge of the semantic meaning of the dimension or the level. For example, the Microsoft Mappoint OLAP Addin uses this information to determine which dimension and level contains the geographical data. Using this information, the

Mappoint wizard pre-selects the correct dimension and level to use to map the data geographically.

Figure 13-25 shows the Dimension Structure tab grid view used to view attribute types.

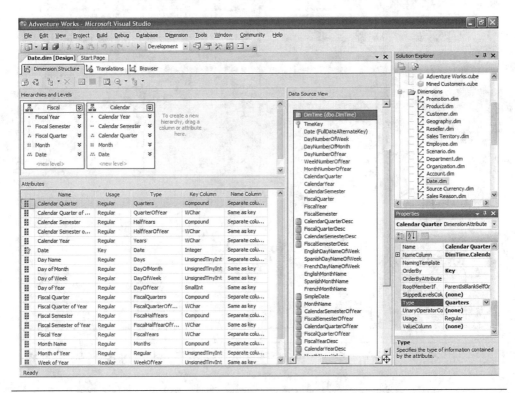

Figure 13-25 Using the Dimension Structure tab grid view to view attribute types.

In Analysis Services 2005, dimension types and attribute types become even more important. The Analysis Services engine has been enhanced with more advanced logics and computations that depend on some semantic knowledge of the data. For example, the system is now aware of accounting logic based on knowledge of account type. (The ByAccount semi-additive aggregation computes aggregation based on the "Account type" type attribute.) The BI wizard can provide more or fewer options based on its detecting of a specific type of dimension (see Figure 13-26). For example, the currency conversion option needs to detect a currency type of dimension in the system to detect which measure groups are potentially the exchange rate measure groups.

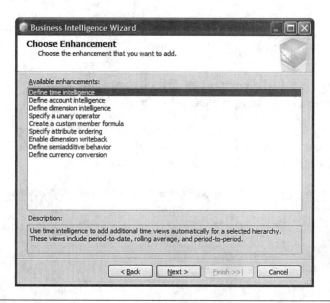

Figure 13-26 Business Intelligence Wizard available enhancements.

How can you set dimension type or attribute type?

Dimension type or attribute type can be set in many ways: through the Dimension wizard, cube wizard, BI Wizard, Cube Editor, Property pane, or the Dimension Structure Attribute pane of the Dimension editor (refer to Figure 13-25).

Which attribute type does Analysis Services take advantage of?

All the time-related attribute types or dimension types are still as important as in Analysis Services 2000. Currency types are now used by the BI wizard to detect exchange rate or source currency dimension. Account types are very important now for the ByAccount semi additive aggregation and currency conversion (for example, some account types are not to be converted.)

Generally, my recommendation is that the more information you can give to the system and eventually a client application, the better. Even if some dimension types and attribute types are not used today by Analysis Services 2005 or a partner application, it doesn't mean that they won't be used in the future, either by a future version or service pack of Analysis Services or by third-party applications. If a type is not used it is simply ignored, so it cannot hurt to set them.

Also, if you are building a custom application, you can query this information and thus take advantage of it to embed business logic and intelligence in your custom application, based on your knowledge of the semantic meaning of these objects.

How Do I Make Visual Development Studio Look Like Analysis Manager 2000?

It is actually fairly easy to customize the Visual Studio environment designers. Each pane can be moved individually. Figure 13-27 shows the standard BI Development Studio interface.

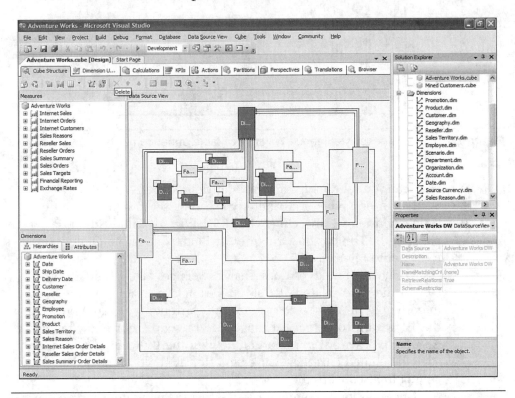

Figure 13-27 BI Development studio before shell customization.

Simply move the Solution Explorer from the right side to the left side of the design environment (see Figure 13-28).

Similarly, just move the Property pane below the Solution Explorer in the left area.

These changes are persisted across sessions.

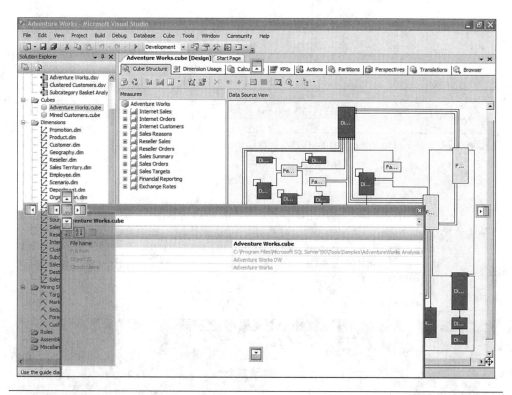

Figure 13-28   Customizing the shell, using drag-and-drop operations on windows.

Now remember that even if you make the BI development studio look like Analysis Manager 2000, it doesn't necessarily mean that it behaves the same. Unless you are in live mode, the BI development studio is still working with only files, not live objects, as the Analysis Manager 2000 does.

The other difference is that unlike Analysis Manager 2000, designers open as tab panes, whereas in Analysis Manager 2000, they open individually, one at a time, as modal dialogs.

The benefit of non-modal dialogs is obvious, yet it requires more screen real estate.

TIP

Right-click on the tab area to split the designer screen in two to see two different designers side by side or one on top of the other (see Figure 13-29).

Figure 13-29   BI development studio tab Context menu.

TIP

In Analysis Manager the property pane could be collapsed. In BI Development Studio, each pane can be pinned or unpinned. If unpinned, they collapse automatically when they lose focus. This is very convenient for maintaining as much usable screen real estate as possible (see Figure 13-30).

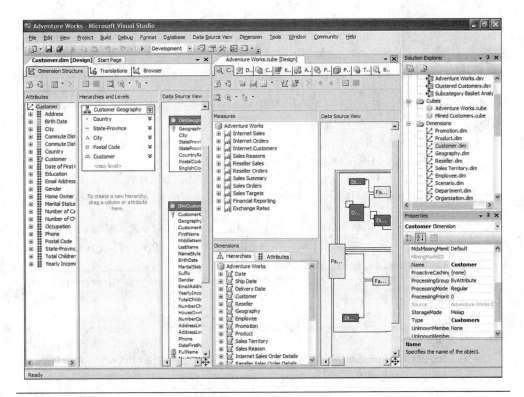

Figure 13-30   BI Development Studio after customization.

How Can I Produce Documentation for Every Object Contained in My Solution?

Although AS2005 tools do not provide such built-in functionality, it is relatively easy to build a utility that can extract metadata and lay it out nicely on either an HTML page or a Word document.

The key is to work in project mode, not live mode. If you work in project mode, then all the metadata is readily available in XML. Indeed, all objects are saved in Solution Explorer as XML files. A program that would be parsing these XML files and organizing the data in an HTML or Word document can be written in a few days or weeks by an intern.

We are including a sample on the CD included in this book of such a documenter utility. This documenter utility works with relational databases, IS packages, and AS cubes and mining models (see Figure 13-31). As soon as the Documenter has been run and completes successfully against either server, it automatically generates an HTML-based document with the format shown in Figure 13-32.

When Would Auto-scrolling During Drag-and-Drop Operations Help?

Some databases are huge. Designing an OLAP solution on top of those databases can be a challenge. Taking into account that the most popular way of designing things in a UI is drag-and-drop operation, we added some auto-scrolling capabilities into UI elements.

If your dimension has many attributes and those attributes are not always related to the key attribute of the dimension, then most probably you need to define attribute relationships (member properties) in the Hierarchies and Levels window or in the tree view of the Attributes window. If you drag an object understandable by the designer (columns from Data Source View or attributes or member properties) and hover the mouse cursor over the upper or lower borders of the windows for approximately one second, then the window scrolls its contents.

If you hover the mouse cursor over a tree node in the tree view for about one second, then the node flips into its expanded state. The expanded node becomes collapsed while the collapsed node becomes expanded. The same thing happens with the Hierarchies and Levels window, but you need to place the mouse cursor at specific areas that you normally use to expand and collapse hierarchical objects with mouse clicks.

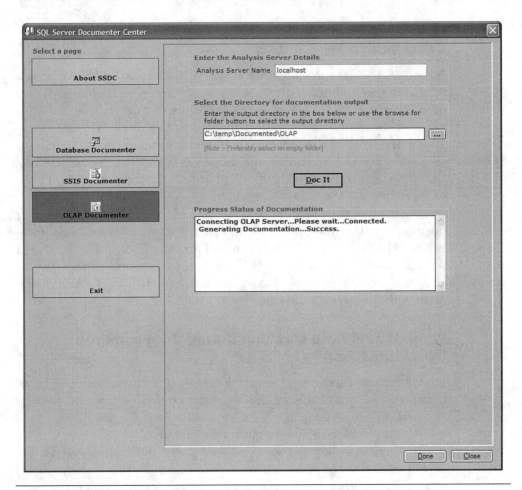

Figure 13-31   SQL Server 2005 Documenter.

Figure 13-33 shows the horizontal areas at the top and bottom that trigger auto-scrolling and, with the small square around the chevrons icon, the areas that trigger the change of the expanded state of the object associated with it.

The same thing happens in Data Source View. Some tables have many columns, and the shapes of the tables are sized smaller. The number of tables in the view can be high. When defining a relationship between two tables with a drag-and-drop operation, one can also benefit from auto-scrolling capabilities. The areas that trigger scrolling of the entire view and the areas that trigger auto-scrolling of the list views of the shapes representing tables are shown in Figure 13-34.

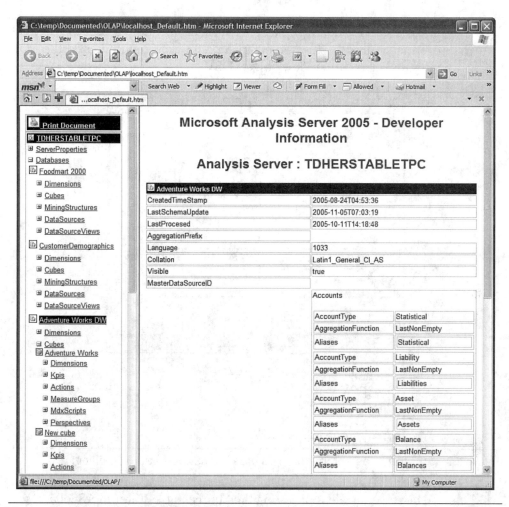

Figure 13-32   Documenter Summary document.

How Do I Use SQL in Cube, Dimension, and Partition Definitions?

AS2000 had pieces of SQL spread around in the definition of cubes and dimensions. For example, the Source Table Filter might contain a WHERE clause and the Member Key Column properties might contain parts of the SELECT clause. Although this provided nice flexibility in defining the cube and dimensions, it had two drawbacks: 1) Cube and dimension definitions became dependent on the SQL dialect of the relational data source, and 2) SQL was spread out in separate pieces that were difficult to locate and validate because each piece was only a part of the SQL eventually used by the server. In AS2005 we've consolidated the SQL into the Data Source View object (DSV).

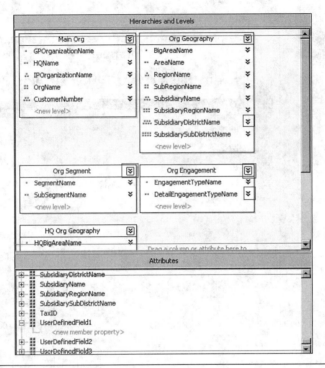

Figure 13-33   Attributes and hierarchies areas sensitive to auto-scrolling.

To do the equivalent of setting the Source Table Filter in AS2005, right-click on the top of the table in the DSV that you want to filter and choose the Replace Table > With New Named Query context menu. Then simply add your own WHERE clause to the query to be used in place of the direct reference to the table. (Use Ctr-Enter to add new lines to the query.) When you are finished, the named query has replaced the table (it has the same ID) and your cubes and dimensions that previously referred to the table in the DSV now refer to the named query.

To do the equivalent of setting the filter on a partition in AS2005, you can use this same technique of replacing the DSV table with a named query. Note that partitions can be defined to point to a table in a DSV or directly to a table in the data source, and only those partitions that point to the table in the DSV will be affected by replacement of the DSV table. When you have multiple partitions, you will want each partition to have a different filter. To do this, you can change the source of the partition to be a query containing the appropriate WHERE clause. You can also change the source to be a different table, named query, or view with the same structure.

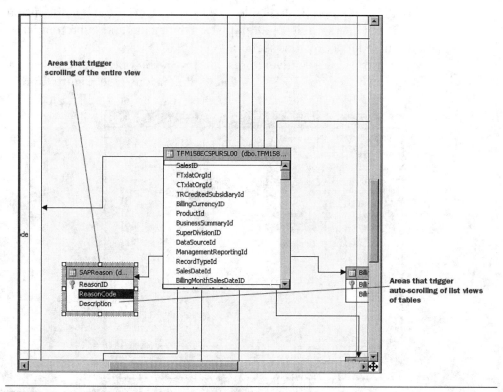

Figure 13-34   DSV areas sensitive to auto-scrolling.

To do the equivalent of putting SQL in the Member Key Column or Member Name Column, you can replace the table in the DSV with a named query as already described or you can create a new named calculation, also available by right-clicking on the top of the table in the DSV. Named calculations provide a way to define additional columns on a table based on SQL expressions. Named calculations are available only on tables, but if you want to add a column to a named query, simply edit that named query.

How Can I Prototype a Cube Rapidly Without Prerequiring Any Existing Data Sources?

This is one of the very powerful yet most unknown features of the new release. Unlike in the previous release, a cube or a dimension can now be built without requiring a previously built underlying data source.

Let's look at the Cube Wizard, for example: The second option in the Select Build Method page enables the user to custom-build a dimension with or without the help of a template. Dimension and cube templates are discussed in a previous section.

The user is consecutively presented with the option to create new measures (see Figure 13-35) and new dimensions (see Figure 13-36).

Figure 13-35   Define New Measures.

Then he can associate the dimension with measures and give a name to the cube (see Figure 13-37).

After this wizard is completed, you can continue editing dimensions and cube objects in each designer by adding or removing measures, attributes, or hierarchies (see Figure 13-38).

You will eventually need to use the Schema generation wizard to generate the underlying tables to store this information (see Figure 13-39).

Figure 13-36   Define New Dimensions.

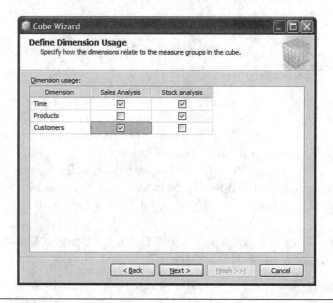

Figure 13-37   Define Dimension Usage.

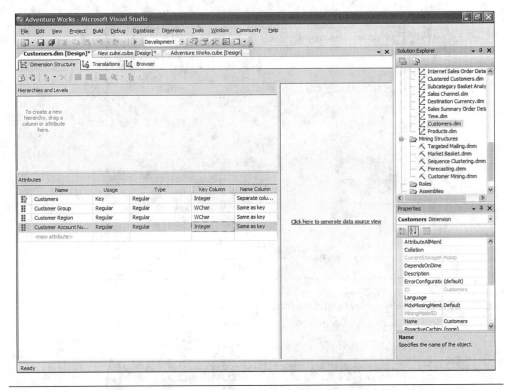

Figure 13-38   Using the link in the Dimension Structure tab DSV pane to generate the Data Source View.

After you have completed this simple step, then it becomes just a matter of using the dimension Writeback capability (assuming the Writeback property was set to True; it is False by default) to start entering dimension members and populating each dimension (see Figure 13-40).

In a few minutes, a cube is created with dimensions populated with members (see Figure 13-41). Now using any Excel add-in or partner or customer application, data can be rapidly entered to populate the cube itself.

How Can I Easily Use Test Data to Speed Development of Cubes and Dimensions?

Often when designing a cube or dimension, you'd like to design and test the structure and calculations on a smaller set of data than what you will deploy on. This is particularly useful in designing calculations, in that it allows you to deploy more quickly and test calculations on known data with which you can more easily verify your results.

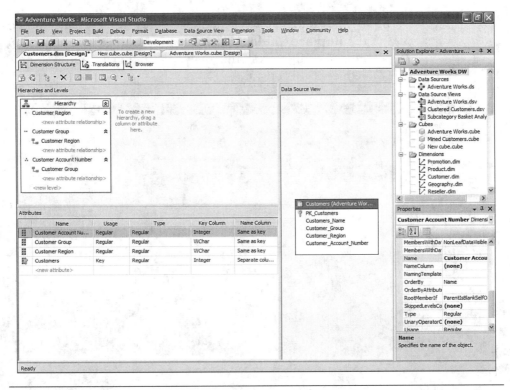

Figure 13-39 Dimension structure pane after the Data Source View has been generated.

This section was written as a tips and trick section by our AS Tools Development lead, Matt Carroll.

Using Replace Table

A simple way to do this when just a few tables are involved is to use the Replace Table feature of the DSV:

1. Edit the DSV behind the cube or dimension on which you are working.
2. Right-click on the header of the table for which you would like to use reduced or simplified data.
3. Choose the **Replace Table** menu item:
   a. If you already have another table with the test data, choose the **Replace Table > With Other Table** sub-menu item and select the appropriate table.

b. If you would like to use a query to restrict test data, choose the **Replace Table > With New Named Query** sub-menu item and then edit the query definition to appropriately reduce the test data.

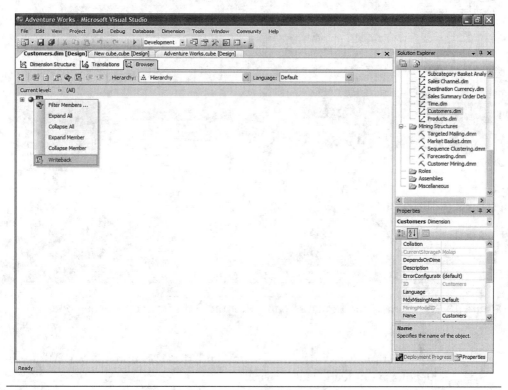

Figure 13-40 Populating dimension members, using Dimension Writeback.

For newly created cubes, the default partition of a measure group whose table has been replaced automatically references the new table or named query. For old cubes or a cube on which you have modified the partitions, be sure to check each partition. Partitions that reference DSV table objects automatically refer to the new table or named query, whereas those that reference DS table objects or queries will not be updated. (It is generally recommended that you design partitions after you've completed the design of cube and dimension structure and calculations.)

When you are finished testing and wish to return to using your production data, simply repeat the preceding steps and replace the table with the original table containing your full data set.

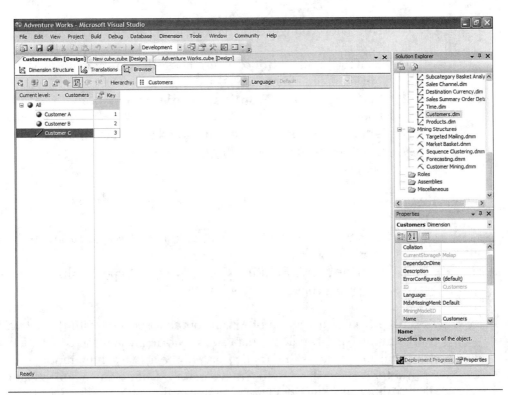

Figure 13-41   Newly created dimension members, using Dimension Writeback.

Modifying the Data Source

Sometimes when many related tables are involved, it's easier to have a separate test relational database. If you have a separate test relational database, then you can very easily use this database by editing the connection string in the Data Source object used by your cubes and dimensions. When you want to return to the production data, just edit the connection string of the Data Source object again.

If the project is shared with other people, has multiple data sources, has other configurable properties such as a target server or database that you'd like to control, or if you just can't seem to remember your connection strings, you may want to follow the more formal process of defining multiple project configurations. The connection string property of the Data Source object is a configurable property, and its value is stored in the active configuration. This enables you to easily switch connection strings by simply switching active configurations.

To create a new configuration, follow these steps:

1. From the top-level **Build** menu, choose the **Configuration Manager** menu item.
2. From the **Active Solution Configuration** drop-down list, choose **<new…>**.
3. In the **New Solution Configuration** dialog, name your new configuration and copy the settings from the existing configuration of your choice.

To switch active configurations, follow these steps:

1. From the top-level **Build** menu, choose the **Configuration Manager** menu item.
2. From the **Active Solution Configuration** drop-down list, choose the existing configuration of your choice.

To set the connection string of a data source associated with the active configuration, simply edit the data source normally and the connection string will automatically be saved as part of the active configuration.

Another alternative is to create a new Data Source object and change the Data Source View to temporarily point to this new Data Source object. This tends to be more complicated because it involves more steps, partitions which directly refer to the Data Source will not be updated, and it cannot be maintained through configurations.

How Do I View Sample Measures Data in the Cube Wizard?

When using the Cube Wizard, measures and measure groups can be generated automatically. The problem is that without seeing the actual data, it is sometimes very hard to make a decision concerning which measures should be used. The solution is simple: Just right-click on any measure and a new window with sample data appears.

How Do I Compare Two Measure Groups' Dimensionality?

One of the major enhancements of the UDM is the capability to model data from different data sources, at different levels of granularity, and in different dimensionality within the same cube. Potentially an entire data warehouse or even multiple OLTP databases and LOB applications can be modeled within the same cube. As a result it is very likely that you can find yourself building a cube with well over a dozen measure groups and dimensions.

In this case, it can become hard to compare the dimensionality of two measure groups or to do an analysis that would yield the measure group in which a specific dimension would participate.

The Cube Designer offers a specific dimension usage tab for this reason (see Figure 13-42).

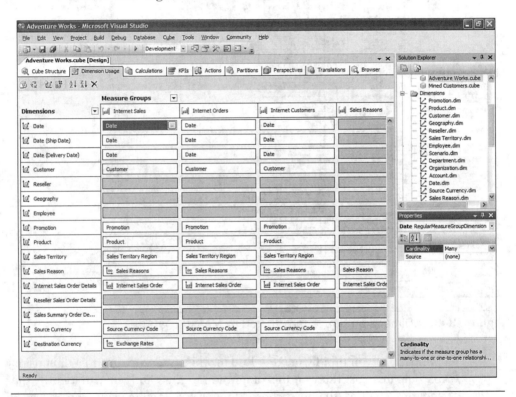

Figure 13-42   Dimension Usage tab, unfiltered.

This tab is great because it offers a grid view of the dimensions and measure group relationships. Yet the span of this grid can sometimes greatly exceed the size of the users' screens.

For this reason, this designer offers the possibility to filter one or multiple measure groups in columns and/or one of multiple dimensions in rows.

This is particularly useful if you need to compare two specific measure groups' dimensionality. By just selecting these two measure groups you have now reduced the view to only the dimensionality of these two objects (see Figure 13-43).

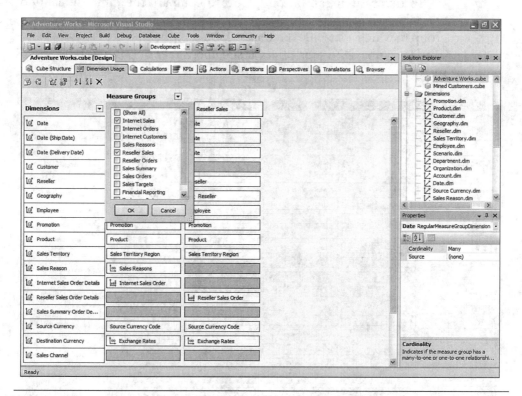

Figure 13-43   Dimension Usage tab, filtered by Measure groups.

Similarly, if you rapidly need to find in which measure group a dimension participates, just filter on this dimension in rows and you can identify the measure groups that use those dimensions. Again using the measure group filter, you can now reduce your view to only these measure groups where this dimension comes into play (see Figure 13-44).

TIP

The value shown in the cell of each intersection in this grid represents the granularity, which means the level of the dimension, at which the measure group intersects.

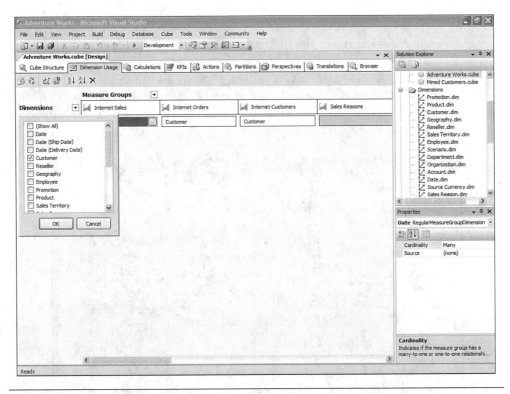

Figure 13-44   Dimension Usage tab filtered by dimensions.

How Can I Have a Measure Group with a Level of Granularity Above the Key?

The Dimension Usage tab of the Cube Designer enables you to view and edit the relationships between a specific measure group and dimensions.

At the intersection of rows and columns, the cell represents the granularity at which a measure group in column is dimensioned by the dimension in row. The granularity represents the attribute that is the lowest level of granularity of the data for this dimension found in the measure group.

Often the granularity of the dimension is also the granularity of the measure groups. But sometime the measure group data is not as granular as the dimension. For example, if a cube contains a Product dimension whose lowest granularity is the SKU level, it is very likely that the actual sales are reported at the SKU level, yet when it comes to Budget or forecast data, this is another story. Budget data is most often entered during the planning cycle at a higher level, such as Product group or Product category.

As a result, Analysis Services enables setting the granularity of a specific measure group at a higher level than the dimension key level.

This can be achieved by simply clicking on the cell that represents the intersection between a measure group and dimension. This brings up the Define Relationship dialog (see Figure 13-45). Through this dialog the bindings between the dimension and a measure group can be set to a different level of granularity.

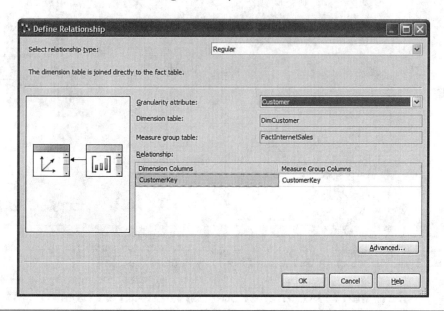

Figure 13-45   Define Relationship dialog.

At first look this seems pretty easy, but the new attribute-based architecture makes some of the mechanics of handling this in the engine slightly more complex. The following sections written by Matt Carroll explain the importance of key uniqueness and attribute relationship when setting a measure group granularity above the dimension key.

As in AS2000, AS2005 enables you to have a measure group joined to a dimension above the lowest level of detail in that dimension. This is common with the time dimension if, for example, your sales are recorded daily but your inventory levels are recorded monthly. For this to work, the server must know what levels of detail are above the selected granularity and thus are still available for slicing the measure group. In AS2000 this was easy because a dimension contained only a single hierarchy and there was no notion of attributes, but only levels within this single hierarchy. In AS2005, dimensions are more flexible and contain many attributes. Each attribute may be contained in zero, one, or many user-defined hierarchies. This flexibility means hierarchies alone do not usually provide sufficient information to the server to know which attributes still apply to the measure group.

Relationships Between Attributes

AS2005 introduces the idea of relationships between attributes to solve this problem (as well as to define member properties). By definition, all attributes are related to the key attribute, so if you know the value of the key, you know the value of any attribute. However, if you use a non-key attribute for the granularity of a measure group, the server must know what attributes are related to the granularity attribute and thus can be used to slice the measure group. To make this work you may need to define additional relationships between attributes. In the dimension, these relationships are defined by AttributeRelationships (called MemberProperties in earlier beta 1 and 2) and can be seen by switching to the tree view layout (now the default) of the attribute list. Let's look at an example.

Given a time dimension with the following attributes

- Date (1/1/2000-12/1/2005) (Key attribute)
- Day of Year (1, 2, 3…366)
- Day of Week (Sun, Mon, Tue…Sat)
- Holiday (True, False)
- Month (Jan 2000, Feb 2000, Mar 2000…Dec 2005)
- Month of Year (Jan, Feb, Mar…Dec)
- Quarter (Q1 2000, Q2 2000, Q3 2000…Q4 2005)
- Quarter of Year (Q1, Q2, Q3, Q4)
- Year (2000, 2001, 2002, 2003, 2004, 2005)

The relationships between these attributes can be described as follows (read ➤ as implies):

Date
   ➤ Day of Week
   ➤ Holiday

➤ Month
  ➤ Quarter
    ➤ Year
➤ Day of Year
  ➤ Month of Year
    ➤ Quarter of Year

Given all this, if you select the key attribute (*Date*) as the granularity attribute, all attributes in the dimension apply to the measure group because the key attribute directly or indirectly implies the values of all attributes in the dimension. If you select *Day of Week* as the granularity attribute, then only *Day of Week* applies to the measure group because it implies no other attributes. If you select *Month*, then the attributes *Month*, *Quarter*, and *Year* apply to the measure group.

Notice that if you select *Month of Year* as the granularity attribute, *Quarter of Year* applies to the measure group, but *Year* does not because the *Quarter of Year* (e.g., Q1) does not imply any year. Making the distinction between *Month* and *Month of Year* is important in AS2005 and is easily overlooked.

Importance of Key Uniqueness

In AS2000, a month lived in a hierarchy, so its meaning was determined by the hierarchy. So if the hierarchy contained Year-Month, then there was no confusion that it was *Month* (Q1 2000 - year specific) and not *Month of Year* (Q1 - year neutral). In AS2000 if the column of month contained just Q1, but it was used in a hierarchy with a year, then you would set UniqueKeys=False to tell the system to combine the key column of that level with the key of the level above to get unique key values. In AS2005, each attribute lives independent of hierarchies, so you must define its key as using both the month and year columns in the attributes key columns collection.

How Do I Change Calculation, Action, or KPI MDX Templates?

One possibly not very well-known enhancement in Analysis Services 2005 is the open extensible template architecture. Calculation templates are very useful to jump-start defining new business logics. The Calculation template, KPI template and Action Templates tab contain well over

100 definitions of the most popular business logics, from how to calculate growth, YTD, and moving average, to more financial ones such as EVA (economic value added), DSO (days of sales outstanding), or return on asset formulas.

But often a consulting company or even an IT department may look at customizing this list to a specific business domain or to the specific taxonomy of a company. All these templates are defined in a clear XML document. This XML template document can be found under C:\Program Files\Microsoft SQL Server\90\Tools\Templates\olap\1033.

The 1033 represents the locale identifier (U.S. English here) under which these templates are stored. This also means that this template can be localized and found in different sub folders.

The template filename is MDXTemplates.XML.

The structure of a template is pretty straightforward. For example, a typical Year to Date MDX calculation will be described as follows:

```
- <Template>
  <Category>Time Series</Category>
  <Name>Periods to Date</Name>
  <Description>Returns the aggregate of a numeric expression from the
  ➡ start of a specified period to the current period.</Description>
- <CalcMemberContent>
  <Expression>Aggregate ( PeriodsToDate ( [<<Target
  ➡Dimension>>].[<<Target Hierarchy>>].[<<Target Level>>],
  ➡ [<<Target Dimension>>].[<<Target Hierarchy>>].CurrentMember ),
  ➡ [Measures].[<<Target Measure>>] ) // This expression will
  ➡ return the aggregated value of the target // measure over the
  ➡ specified time periods, beginning with the // first member of
  ➡ the target level, and ending with the current member.</Expression>
  <FormatString>Standard</FormatString>
  </CalcMemberContent>
  <Type>CalculatedMember</Type>
  </Template>
```

An action template will look like this:

```
- <Template>
  <Category>Reporting</Category>
  <Name>View Report</Name>
  <Description>Launches a SQL Server 2005 Reporting Services report
  ➡ for a selected cube object.</Description>
- <ReportActionContent>
  <Expression />
  <Condition />
```

```
<Target />
<TargetType>AttributeMembers</TargetType>
<Description />
<Type>Report</Type>
<ReportServerName><<Target Server>></ReportServerName>
<ReportServerPath><<Report Server Virtual Directory>>?/<<Path to
➥ Report>></ReportServerPath>
<Invocation>Interactive</Invocation>
<ReportFormat>HTML5</ReportFormat>
</ReportActionContent>
<Type>ReportingAction</Type>
</Template>
```

And a KPI template is defined as follows:

```
- <Template>
<Category>Financial</Category>
<Name>Economic Value Added (EVA)</Name>
<Description>Calculates a financial performance measure
➥ that tries to capture the true economic profit of an
➥ enterprise.</Description>
- <KPIContent>
<ValueExpression><<Net Operating Profit After Tax>> -
➥ ( <<Capital>> * <<Cost of Capital>> )</ValueExpression>
<GoalExpression>/*This can be a fixed value if you know your
➥ Economic Value Added (EVA) goal.*/ <<EVA Goal>></GoalExpression>
<StatusExpression>/*Economic Value Added (EVA) refers to the name of
➥ this KPI. If you change the name, change the reference in these
➥ functions as well. */ IIf ( KPIValue( "Economic Value Added
➥ (EVA)" ) - KPIGoal( "Economic Value Added (EVA)" ) >=0, 1, -1
➥ )</StatusExpression>
<TrendExpression>/*The periodicity of this trend comparison is
➥ defined by the level at which the ParallelPeriod is evaluated.*/
➥ IIf ( KPIValue( "Economic Value Added (EVA)" ) > ( KPIValue(
➥ "Economic Value Added (EVA)" ), ParallelPeriod ( [<<Time
➥ Dimension Name>>].[<<Time Hierarchy Name>>].[<<Time Year Level
➥ Name>>], 1, [<<Time Dimension Name>>].[<<Time Hierarchy
➥ Name>>].CurrentMember ) ), 1, -1 )</TrendExpression>
<Description>This key performance indicator (KPI) is a financial
➥ performance measure that tries to capture the true economic
➥ profit of an enterprise. The Status and Trend expressions
➥ assume that a higher value is better. If this is not the case,
➥ you may need to change the greater than sign (>) to the less
➥ than sign (<) in these expressions.</Description>
</KPIContent>
<Type>KPI</Type>
</Template>
```

Obviously, different types of templates have different tags, but these tags map to the properties of each object generated (calculated member, action, KPI, named set).

Each MDX expression used in these templates is tokenized, using the following convention: <<Token name>>. This convention is not required and is just here for practical purposes.

As many templates can be added or removed as needed. After the file is edited, it just needs to be placed in the same folder with the same name, and the change will be picked up by Development Studio next time it is started.

Should I Use the KPI Display Folder or KPI Parent Property?

Beyond Goal, Trend, or Status a, Key Performance Indicator (KPI) has two properties that enable that KPI to be categorized. The first one is the KPI display Folder. This property is very useful for categorizing a KPI under one or more strategic goals. These strategic goals can themselves be categorized under one or more business perspective. The KPI can belong to one of multiple display folders. Display folders can be nested with no limit of nesting. As a result, a KPI display folder can be defined as

KPI Display Folder = Folder1\SubFolder1\...; Folder2\SubFolder2\...;...

Display folders are simple categorization mechanisms. Display folders do not have Goal, Trend, or Status values.

In contrast, it is sometimes important to show KPIs in a hierarchical manner. In this case, the parent KPI property shall be used. This property makes it possible to define a hierarchy of KPIs. When a KPI is set as a parent of another KPI, the other KPI is automatically displayed beneath the parent KPI. The display folder of the children KPIs is then ignored. Figure 13-46 shows a parent KPI being defined in the KPIs tab.

So the question arises, when should one be used versus the other? Well, if the categorization is needed to model a business or scorecard type of organization, then the display folder is the one to use. But if the KPIs themselves need to be displayed in a hierarchical manner, then the parent KPI property should be used. Figure 13-47 shows an example of using both the display folder and parent KPI properties approaches.

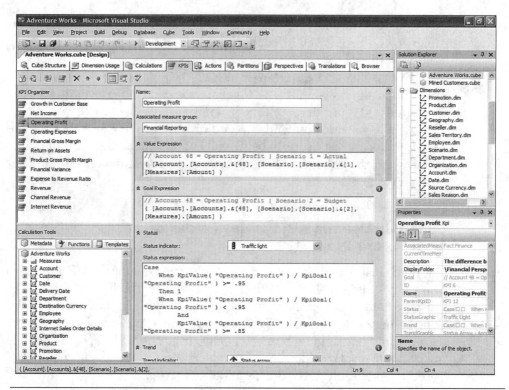

Figure 13-46   Defining the Parent KPI using the KPI tab.

But categorization and hierarchy are often not enough. Most companies that follow a balanced or business scorecard methodology also often like to have some sort of master indicator that would give the overall health index of the entire corporation. Building this Company Health Index is not very difficult.

The Company Health Index is itself a KPI, the values of which depend on other KPIs. But not every KPI is equally important as others for the company. Depending on the overall company strategy, some KPIs may be more critical to the overall Health Index of the company than others. This is where the KPI weight property comes into play. Each KPI must be assigned a weight. This way its importance or criticality can be taken into account when computing the overall Company Health Index.

Let's look at how such a computation would be set up.

Assume 5 KPIs with the following associated weights: KPI1 (1), KPI2 (1), KPI3 (2), KPI4 (2), KPI5 (1).

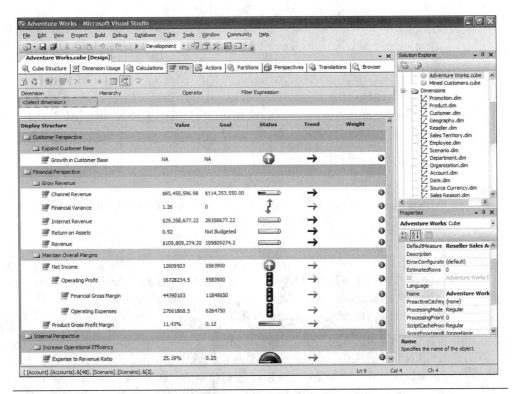

Figure 13-47   Using both Display Folder and Parent KPI properties.

You can now build the Overall Company Health Index (OCHI). Its value should be the aggregation of the status of all the KPIs, weighted by their respective weights:

```
OCHI Value =
  (KPISTATUS(KPI1) * KPIWEIGHT(KPI1)
  + KPISTATUS(KPI2) * KPIWEIGHT(KPI2)
  + KPISTATUS(KPI3) * KPIWEIGHT(KPI3)
  + KPISTATUS(KPI4) * KPIWEIGHT(KPI4)
  + KPISTATUS(KPI5) * KPIWEIGHT(KPI5) )
  / (KPIWEIGHT(KPI1) + KPIWEIGHT(KPI2) + KPIWEIGHT(KPI3)
  + KPIWEIGHT(KPI4) + KPIWEIGHT(KPI5))
```

The OCHI goal is obviously 1.

The OCHI status can be set to any expression that suits your company's objectives.

It is as simple as this, and it provides great value to business users and executive decisionmakers. Because the OCHI KPI is a KPI like any others, it can very easily be queried and retrieved, using any client tool supporting MDX. The KPIVALUE(), KPIGOAL(), KPITREND(), and KPISTATUS() MDX functions can be used against this OCHI KPI. Thus Reporting Services, Microsoft Excel, as well as partner tools such as Proclarity or Panorama can expose this OCHI KPI.

To see more examples of how to query and embed KPIs in your custom application, please look at the three samples provided in the appendices:

- Appendix A: Sample KPI Code: Retrieving and Exposing Your First KPI
- Appendix B: KPI Utilities—Code for Parsing Display Folders and Getting Image Indexes
- Appendix C: KPI Viewer

How Can I Rebuild My Own KPI Browser, Similar to the One Available in BI Development Studio, and Embed It in My Application?

Often, when presenting the product, people ask us whether we are making the KPI debugger/browser available as a control. We currently are not, but on the book's CD you will find a sample that will show you how to build a very simple ASP.NET application that rebuilds a similar control.

This sample was built in a week by a French Microsoft consultant, Olivier Pieri, for one of his customers.

KPIs are accessible through MDX functions (KPIVALUE, KPIGOAL, KPITREND, KPISTATUS, KPIWEIGHT, and so on), so they can be queried like any other measures in the cube. So like any application that would attempt to embed analytical capabilities using MDX, the very same approach can be used with ADOMD.NET to query and display KPIs.

The KPIViewer sample enables the user to connect to a server, select a database, and then be presented with the list of available KPIs (see Figure 13-48).

By default all KPIs are displayed for the default member (most likely *all* members) of every attribute of every dimension (see Figure 13-49).

A control at the bottom enables the user to select a dimension and a hierarchy or attribute on which to drill down when clicking on a specific KPI.

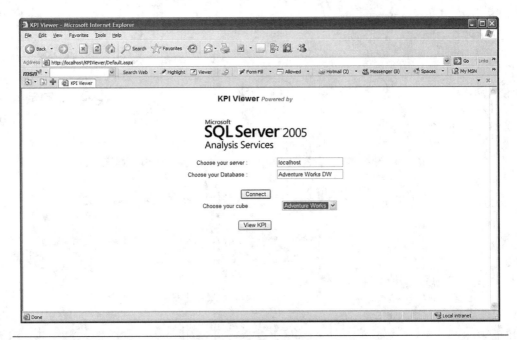

Figure 13-48   KPI Viewer Connection page.

It is possible to select multiple attributes coming from the same or different dimensions successively to drill down in a specific KPI. The path for the dimensions/attributes combination is displayed at the top of the KPI list (see Figure 13-50).

The sample can be found on the CD-ROM. The sample folder contains installation instructions, as well as all the source code and images needed.

How Do I Use the Cube Debugger as a Calculation Builder?

The new SQL Server BI development studio offers a unique capability in the BI Market: a full-blown MDX debugger. This is one of the side benefits of integrating with the Visual Studio development environment. Some of the native Visual Studio debugging services enabled us to build such a capability into our designers.

The following section has been written by one of our most talented developers, Andrew Garbuzov, who actually coded the MDX debugger support in our Cube designer.

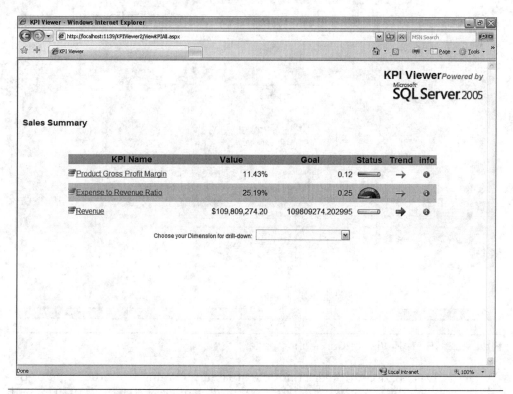

Figure 13-49   Default list of KPIs, unfiltered by any dimensions.

Many users tend to build certain complex calculations and immediately try to verify the correctness of the step they have just completed. This is especially true if the cost of verifying the calculation correctness is not too high. In the Business Intelligence Development Studio, users can build cube calculation scripts on the Calculations page of the cube builder. They have the option to edit the script directly or create calculations one at a time in the user interface windows. Those who prefer creating the script in the text editor rather than in the UI might find the debugger to be a calculations script building tool created just for them.

It is often true that a database designer might want to create the database to be successfully deployed without any calculations, and after that design and apply the calculation script. After you successfully deploy the database you can debug the cube. All you need is to invoke the Debug, Start menu command on the Calculations page of the cube builder. The debugger will run and stop at the first statement. The idea is that you would type your statements, execute them, and explore the cube's state in the pivot table or MDX watch windows. If you do not like the results, you modify your script.

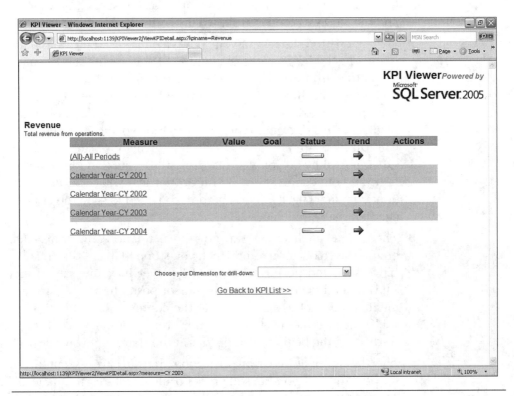

Figure 13-50　　KPI list, filtered on time dimensions.

Tips for Creating Calculations

To help you create good calculations, we have included the following tips:

- On the left side of the debugger you have metadata, functions, and template windows. You can drag contents from there into the calculations script window or MDX windows. Dragging from the Template window allows you to paste the skeleton code for your new calculation. Dragging from the Metadata window gives you unique names of objects. The Functions window reminds you about available functions (see Figure 13-51).

- On the toolbar you have buttons to select font or color, and you can paste them into the current cursor position of the calculation script. This is for the situations in which some font or color needs to be used in the formula. This works for the script text window and the MDX windows, as shown in Figure 13-51.

- Having created the text of your new calculation, you can execute it and check how it works. Execution of statements can be made absolutely arbitrary. Use the context menu commands Set Next Statement and Run to Cursor for arbitrary sequences. Use F5 to run until the next breakpoint or to the end. If you do not like the results and need to get rid of the calculation you have just created, you can type a temporary "Drop your calculation" statement and execute it. Why do you need to drop it? Because you have modified the connection state. If you do not like what you have just done, but liked what you did before, you need to drop the last calculation that you do not like.

- There is a much easier way to return to the connection state before the calculation after which you stopped liking your results. It works if the performance of the server in your case is fine. All you need to do is to move the cursor position to the first statement you do not like and execute the context menu Run to Cursor. If the statement is before your current position, the debugger starts from the beginning and stops at the statement you selected.

- The debugger always runs in a loop. If you have executed the script to the end, you can still press F5 and it restarts automatically. There is no need to use the Debug, Restart menu command. If you set certain breakpoints, you can navigate to the different states of the script very quickly by just hitting F5 and repeating the process all over again to analyze different states of the cube.

- You have four MDX windows (like Watch windows in C++ or C# debuggers in Visual Studio). There you can type MDX statements to show the cell set results you want to monitor (see Figure 13-52). When you step through the script, the MDX you have typed is re-executed. In contrast to the pivot table, which executes many statements, you execute just one MDX statement to see the particular slice you are interested in. If you switch that MDX window to the edit script mode, then the MDX in that window does not execute when you step through your script. This can be useful in cases when the performance is really slow. The results of MDX execution are shown in a grid, similar to the one you can see in SQL Management Studio. Cell and member properties of the currently selected cell in the grid are shown in the Properties window (F4 to activate).

- If you are currently in one "MDX watch" window and want to know which MDX you typed in other windows before switching (because the debugger re-evaluates the MDX to which you are switching and this might be expensive), just hover the mouse over the tabs. The text of the MDX appears in a tooltip.

- After you are finished with the script, just stop the debugging. You are asked whether you want to keep the script or throw it away. Thus you have the capability to try an approach before really accepting it.

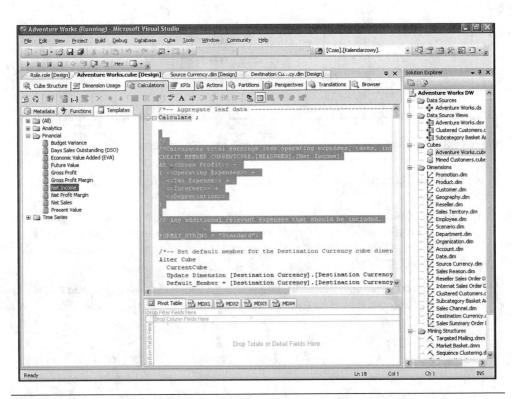

Figure 13-51   Using the MDX Debugger in the Calculations tab.

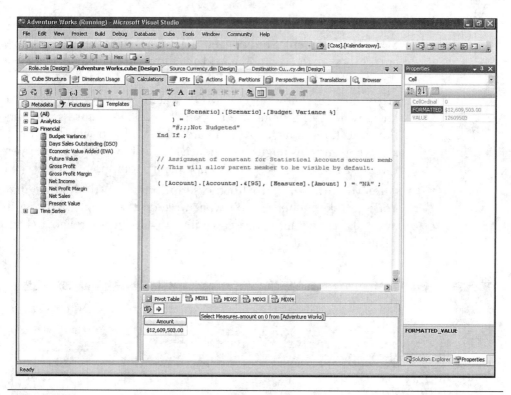

Figure 13-52 Cell Properties in the MDX debugger in the Calculation tab.

TIP

To make it easier to debug a specific calculation, it is often recommended to break down a calculation into as many calculations as possible. For example, imagine that a calculation is made of three sub components: A = (B/C + D/E) / F.

It becomes much easier to debug and find out which portion of the calculation may not be behaving properly if you write the calculation like this instead:

A1 = B/C
A2 = D/E
A = A1 + A2
A = A / F

A1 and A2 enable you to debug each numerator component independently. This saves you a lot of time trying to isolate an issue, if one were to arise. Because the AS engine now handles recursions natively, the last two statements are perfectly valid. The second A= statement reads the value of A on the right side of the equal sign from its previous statement and applies it to the new iteration. After your calculations return the expected result, the four calculations can be merged into one again.

How Do I Automate Loading Translation Strings into My Project?

This is actually a fairly simple process. But first let's review what translations are.

Cubes, dimensions, and mining models all contain metadata. This metadata is made up of descriptions, captions, property names, and values (see Figure 13-53). For dimensions, in addition to metadata, dimension members' names can also be translated. Loading dimension member name translation is just a matter of creating an extra column in the relational table where these members are defined. On the other hand, the metadata is persisted in the XML files describing each of the objects. Obviously this applies only to the case where you work in Project mode and not in Live mode.

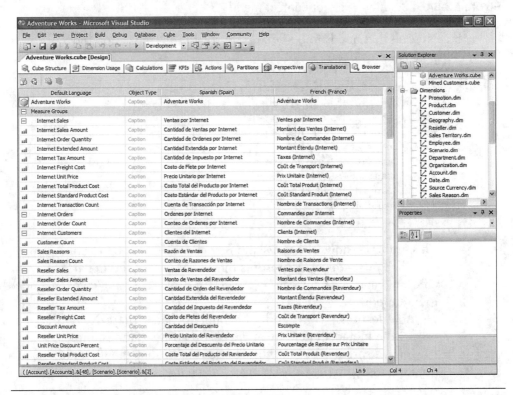

Figure 13-53　　Cube Designer Translations tab.

So the key here is that these translations are persisted in the XML file. This XML file can be edited outside of the designers. You can view the XML file in XML view by simply right-clicking on the cube or dimension name in the Solution Explorer and selecting the View Code menu item (see Figure 13-54).

Figure 13-54   Solution Explorer context menu.

Now all that needs to be done is to isolate the translation block for each piece of metadata:

```
<Translations>
  <Translation dwd:design-time-name="translation1">
    <Language>3082</Language>
    <Caption>Adventure Works</Caption>
  </Translation>
  <Translation dwd:design-time-name="translation36">
    <Language>1036</Language>
    <Caption>Adventure Works</Caption>
  </Translation>
</Translations>
```

This example shows the translation block for the database name.

The `Language` tag represents the LCID (ID of the Locale) of a specific language. As many can be created and added as languages that need to be supported.

A little utility can rapidly be built to parse these XML files and extract the metadata field in an Excel spreadsheet, for example.

Such a spreadsheet can then be sent to various members of the corporation to fill up the translations for each metadata field.

After these translated fields have been completed, a similar utility can read them from the spreadsheet and place them in the appropriate translation block in the XML document.

Saving the XML document and then redeploying it to the server will be sufficient to make these translations become available on the production server.

How Do I Automatically Create Partitions for a New Data Set?

One of the typical data warehouse challenge is refreshing the various parts of the data warehouse after the OLTP or LOB application has received new transactions.

But the data warehouse is often made of several components: the relational data warehouse as well as the dimensional UDM or data marts. One of the issues is then to ensure that the UDM data marts are updated as simultaneously and transparently as the relational data warehouse component itself.

There are several aspects to updating a UDM based on updates in the data warehouse.

Often in a well structured data warehouse, a table partitioning strategy will have been defined to handle and organize new daily, weekly, monthly data.

If such is the case, then one of the first challenges is to create the corresponding OLAP partition for each table partition.

In the AdventureWorksDW set of samples, Dave Wickert from the SQL BI Systems team has created such a sample. It can be found in the following location: C:\Program Files\Microsoft SQL Server\90\Samples\Integration Services\Package Samples\SyncAdvWorksPartitions Sample\SynAdvWorksPartitions.

After the OLAP partitions are automatically created for every new table partition, it is important to ensure that the data remains up to date with the relational data warehouse when it is updated.

For this I recommend setting all the newly created partitions in proactive cache mode. Proactive cache is a great and easy way to let the cube partitions refresh themselves when new data is loaded in the relational partition. The recommended mode is Automatic MOLAP, but advanced settings enable you to customize the latency and refresh the frequency with which the cache is updated (see Figure 13-55).

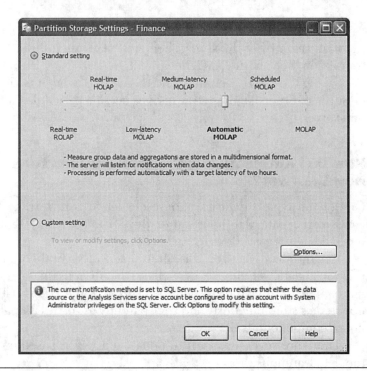

Figure 13-55   Setting partition storage to Automatic MOLAP (proactive caching).

What Is the Difference Between the Cubes Filter Component and the OWC Filter in the Cube Browser Page?

As discussed in the KPI section, the filter control generates a subcube (one for each row in the filter control), whereas OWC filters generate a more traditional WHERE clause.

The main advantage I see of the Filter component is the capability to progressively restrict the cube space as you define successive filters. This is particularly useful when creating reports that use attributes with many members. It also enables much more sophisticated filtering.

For the AS2000 user or the beginning user, using the OWC filter clause is more intuitive and simple. Figure 13-56 shows the Cube Browser filter components and Embedded OWC filter area.

How Do I Test My Roles and Security?

In AS2000, testing role security was done from the Role Manager dialog. Because now an AS database can be either created or edited in Live or Project mode, we had to slightly modify this behavior. Indeed, to test security you have to be able to access the live server, which is not necessarily feasible when working in project mode.

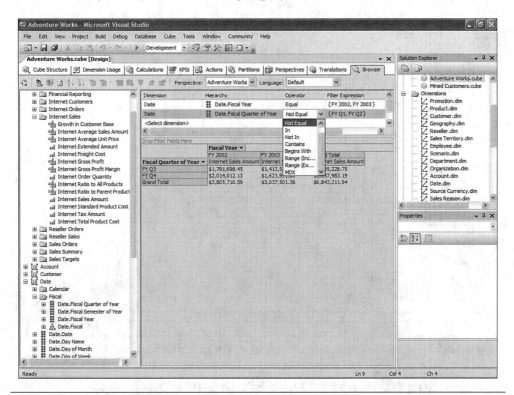

Figure 13-56   Cube Browser filter components and Embeded OWC filter area.

Thus the AS development team decided to change the approach we had in AS2000. So with AS 2005, the testing role can be achieved directly through the cube browser that can be found in SQL Development Studio or BI Development Studio. When starting the Cube browser, the second icon that can be found on the toolbar allows the Database Professional to change the context under which the cube should be browsed (see Figure 13-57).

To change the context, you can choose to switch the current user with a specific selected username or one or multiple roles.

This mechanism enables the database professional to test both cell security as well as dimension security.

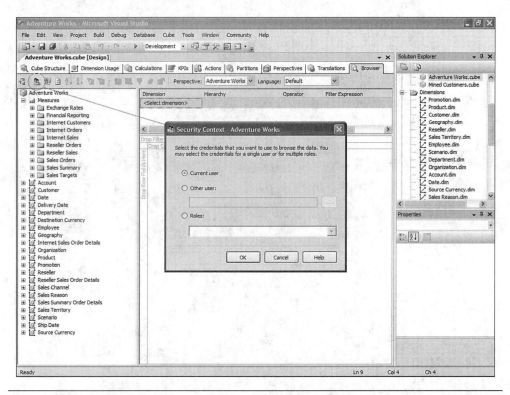

Figure 13-57 Testing Dimension security by changing Role or User context.

How Do I Change Time Intelligence Templates?

The Time Intelligence path of the BI Wizard is a very valuable tool because it offers a very easy way to add most of the more common time-based business logic to your cube. Things like Year-to-Date, Year-over-Year growth, and 12-Month Moving Average can be added in the cube in a matter of literally three clicks (see Figure 13-58).

But often a consulting company or even an IT department may look at customizing this list of predefined time-based business logic to a specific business domain or to the specific taxonomy of a company. All these templates are defined in a clear XML document. This XML template document can be found under C:\Program Files\Microsoft SQL Server\90\Tools\Templates\olap\1033.

1033 represents the locale identifier (U.S. English here) under which these templates are stored. This also means that this template could be localized and found in different sub folders.

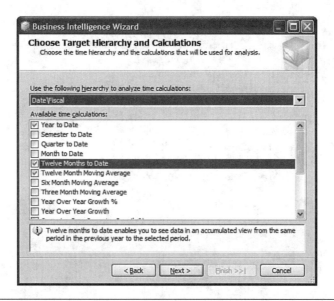

Figure 13-58   Choose Additional Time dimension calculations.

The Template file name is TimeIntelligence.XML.

The structure of a template is pretty straightforward. For example, the 12-Month Moving Average calculation will be described as follows

```
<anyType xsi:type="TimeView">
  <ViewName>Twelve Month Moving Average</ViewName>
  <RequiredLevelGroups>
    <anyType xsi:type="ArrayOfAnyType">
      <anyType xsi:type="xsd:string">Years</anyType>
    </anyType>
    <anyType xsi:type="ArrayOfAnyType">
      <anyType xsi:type="xsd:string">FiscalYears</anyType>
    </anyType>
    <anyType xsi:type="ArrayOfAnyType">
      <anyType xsi:type="xsd:string">ReportingYears</anyType>
    </anyType>
    <anyType xsi:type="ArrayOfAnyType">
      <anyType xsi:type=
      ➥ "xsd:string">ManufacturingYears</anyType>
    </anyType>
    <anyType xsi:type="ArrayOfAnyType">
      <anyType xsi:type="xsd:string">Iso8601Years</anyType>
    </anyType>
  </RequiredLevelGroups>
```

```
        <FormulaComment></FormulaComment>
        <Formula>( [«DestinationDimensionName»].[«NewAttributeName»]
     ➥ .[«CalculatedMemberName»],
     ➥ «CalculatedMeasureListLayout»
[«SelectedCubeDimension»].[«SelectedHierarchySourceAttributeName»]
➥ .[«SelectedHierarchySourceAttributeLevelName»].Members ) =
  Avg(
       {
        ParallelPeriod(
           [«SelectedCubeDimension»].[«SelectedHierarchyName»]
          ➥.[«MonthLevelUniqueName»],
            11,

           [«SelectedCubeDimension»].[«SelectedHierarchyName»]
          ➥ .CurrentMember
          ➥ ) :
          ➥ [«SelectedCubeDimension»].[«SelectedHierarchyName»]
          ➥ .CurrentMember
       },
      «DefaultMember»
  ) ;</Formula>
     <Description>Twelve month moving average enables viewing
     ➥ a rolling average for the previous twelve months from the
     ➥ currently selected period.</Description>
    </anyType>
```

The `RequiredLevelGroups` element is defined when the time-based business logic is presented to the user. Indeed, not every time-based business logic makes sense for every time dimension. For example, if a dimension doesn't contain a Quarter level, then all business logic related to Quarter (for example, Quarter to Date, Quarter over Quarter Growth) is not presented to the users. These level types should map to the Time Attribute Type list. And the business logic is displayed to only the user of the selected hierarchy containing levels, based on which attribute type property has been set to one of these attribute types.

The token used in the formula section cannot be any token (unlike for MDX and KPI templates). The same token must be used in a custom-built formula. Not all of them may be needed, but if the custom logic needs to reference the selected dimension, hierarchy, or level, then these exact token must be used. The BI wizard replaces these tokens at runtime with the matching value from the cube.

As many time templates can be added or removed as needed from this file. After the file is edited, it just needs to be placed in the same folder with the same name, and the change is picked up by the Development Studio next time it is started.

How Do I Document Changes Generated by the BI Wizard?

The BI Wizard can turn just one Boolean property from true of false, or it can change dozens of properties and create huge MDX scripts. If you want to document all those changes, simply, click on the tree view while on the last page of the wizard, and press Ctrl+C. This puts the whole tree view into the clipboard in a format that can be nicely pasted into Excel, Word, or even Notepad.

How Do I Bring Pictures into My UDM?

The UDM supports pictures natively. If installed, you can open the AdventureWorksDW AS Database project that can be found under: C:\Program Files\Microsoft SQL Server\90\Tools\Samples\. Two versions of the samples are installed for the Enterprise SKU, and one is installed for the Standard SKU. Open one of the versions of SQL Server that is installed on your server.

When the project is open, edit the Product dimension, select the Large Photo attribute, and edit its properties as shown in Figure 13-59.

The ValueColumn set of properties determines the Image column to which the attribute is bound.

In addition, it is important to set the DataType to Binary; this is so the UDM knows it is a picture.

Then, and this is not set in the sample project by default, for this image to be rendered in Reporting Services and Report Builder, you need to set the MimeType to the type of the image stored in the relational database. In the case of the Product Large Photo, the type is Jpeg, so the MimeType value must be set to Image/Jpeg.

After this change is done, the project must be redeployed, and if the Report Builder model was already generated, it must be regenerated.

As soon as this is done, you can use Reporting Services Designer or Report builder to build a nice-looking report, entirely built on top of the UDM, that would not just display the entity's attribute, metrics, and KPIs, but pictures as well (see Figure 13-60 and Figure 13-61).

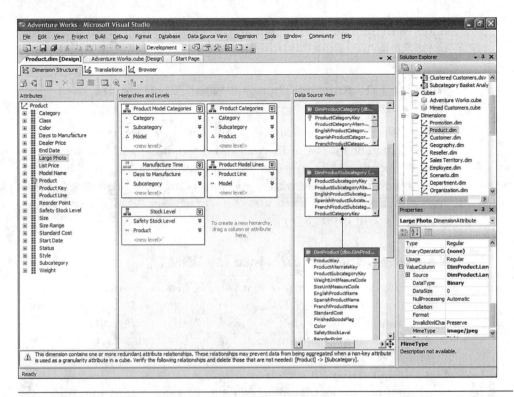

Figure 13-59 Set the MimeType property for the Large Photo attribute in Dimension Designer.

Which Tree Views in the User Interface That Support Multiple Selections Might Help in My Case?

In many areas of the designer, multi-object selection is available. This is often very practical because the Visual Studio shell, for example, enables a common property to be edited for all the selected objects (as long as they all support the same property).

In the Dimension designers, for example, the Tree View supports an alternate grid view, as shown in Figure 13-62.

After the view is switched to grid (see Figure 13-63), then multiple attributes can be selected. All their common properties are displayed in the property pane and can be set for all the attributes at once.

In addition, the context menu makes it possible to create a hierarchy out of these attributes in one click.

In similar ways, many areas of the Cube, Mining Model, or Security designer enable you to select multiple objects in a tree or grid view.

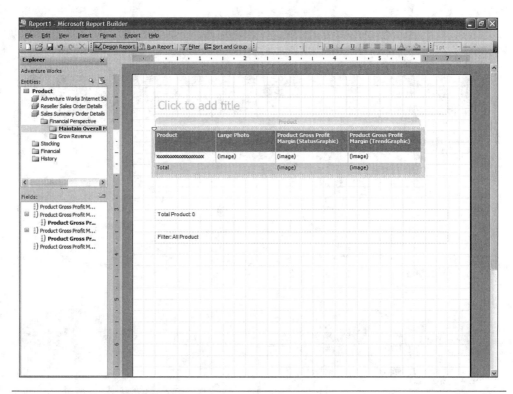

Figure 13-60 Report builder Report design phase.

When in a grid view, you can edit a column for all selected objects by simply using the F2 key.

How Do I Set Up a Dimension with Multiple Parents Rollup with Weights?

Here is a situation where a member needs to be modeled so that it rolls up to multiple parents with different weights. This is perfectly feasible in AS2000 and AS2005 if you use the following steps.

First let's take care of the member-to-multiple-parent issue:

1. Create a duplicate member with the same member name but a different member key: iMember 1 (Key = 1) and Member 1 (Key = 2).
2. The original member is the one linked to your fact data Member 1 (Key = 1).

3. Associate a custom member formula to the shadow member (Key = 2): Member formula = Dimname.hierarchyname.$[1].

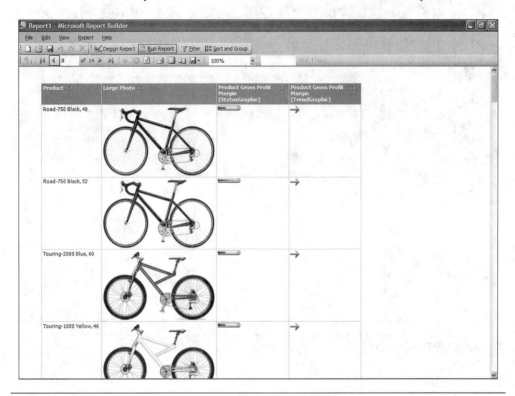

Figure 13-61   Report builder report preview.

Now let's add a weight and/or unary operator to these members to control how they roll up:

1. Add a column in the dimension table with the weight (percentage) that should be associated with each member, including the duplicate ones.
2. For AS2000
   a. Make it a member property of the dimension.
   b. Now let's create a custom rollup formula for the parent level as follows:

```
if(not isleaf([<Yourdimensionname>].currentmember),
SUM([<Yourdimensionname].currentmember.children,
```

```
[<Yourdimensionname].currentmember
➥*VAL([<Yourdimensionname].Currentmember.Properties
➥ ("<Percentage member property name>"))/100),
CalculationPassValue(Measures.currentmember, 0))
```

3. For Analysis Services 2005:
   a. Make the column an attribute of the dimension.
   b. Use this attribute as the unary operator (make sure the percentages are in the 0-to-1 format) and AS2005 does the weighted sum rollup automatically. You can use the BI wizard to define the unary operators.

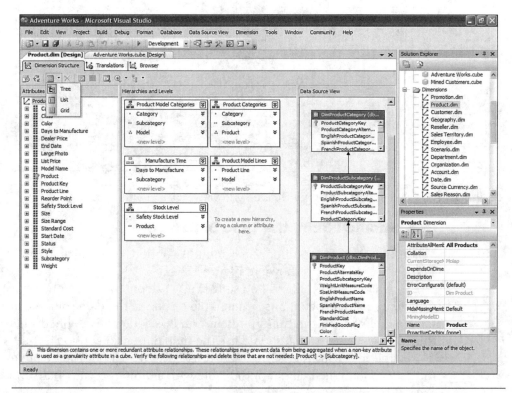

Figure 13-62   Dimension Designer Builder, tree view.

This is pretty straightforward to set up through the tool, but this question has been asked very frequently in the newsgroups, so we felt it would be appropriate to give the answer in this book as well.

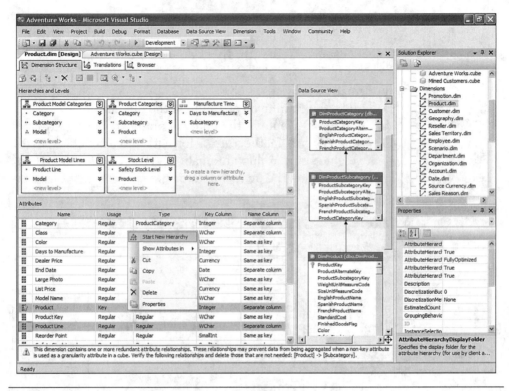

Figure 13-63   Dimension Designer Builder, grid view.

How Should I Build the Time Dimension?

When building a time dimension, multiple options are available in the Dimension Wizard, as shown in Figure 13-64.

So which option should be used? Well, it depends on whether your data source already contains a time table or not. If the data source contains a table where the time frequency and periodicity is defined, then the database professional should use the time dimension option.

In the following steps, the wizard (see Figure 13-65) then enables the user to map the column of the table with a dimension attribute type (Year, Month, Day, etc.).

This step is very important because it makes it possible to assign an Attribute type with each of the dimension attributes. In addition, the wizard generates the appropriate hierarchies automatically.

The second option is the one to use if no time table is available in the data source. In this case, the wizard builds a server-based time dimension. The wizard then lets you create the dimension by hand while providing a lot of advanced business calendar options (see Figures 13-66 through 13-68).

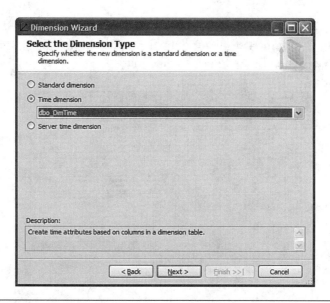

Figure 13-64   Dimension Wizard—Time Dimension.

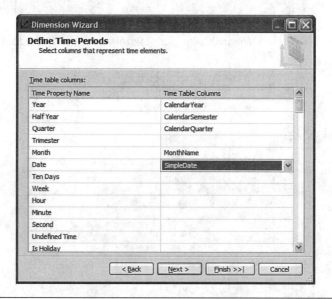

Figure 13-65   Dimension Wizard—time periods definition.

This path of the wizard automatically generates the hierarchies based on the options chosen. As you can see in Figures 13-66–13-68, the five most common business calendars can be set up at once through the wizard.

The hierarchies are generated with the dimension key being a time stamp. As long as the fact data also have a time stamp, this new dimension can then be linked to any fact data.

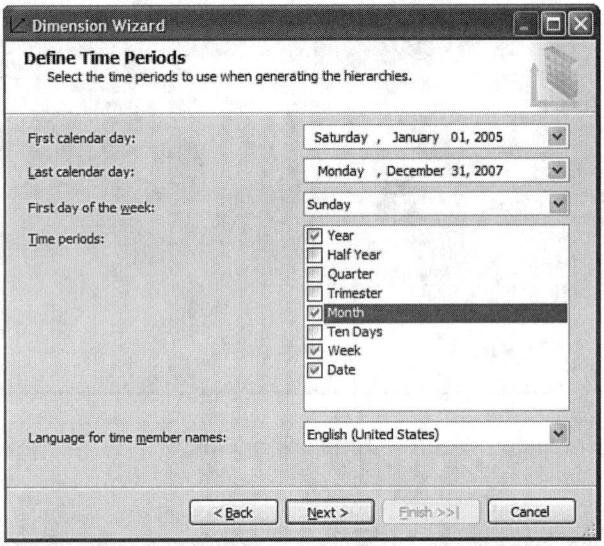

Figure 13-66   Dimension Wizard Calendars Definition: Time Periods.

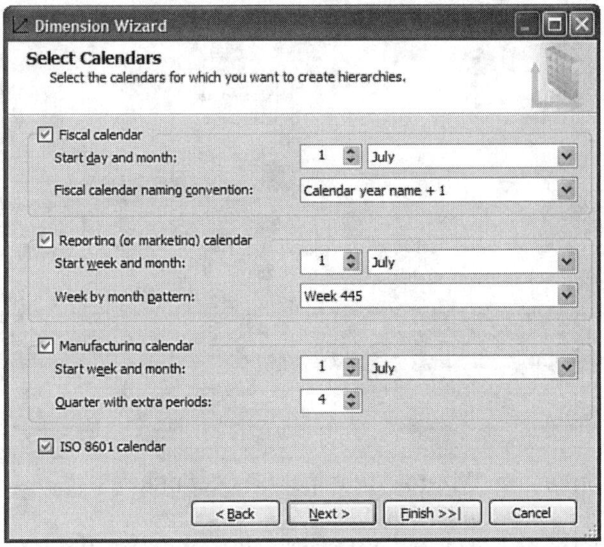

Figure 13-67   Dimension Wizard Calendars Definition: Calendars.

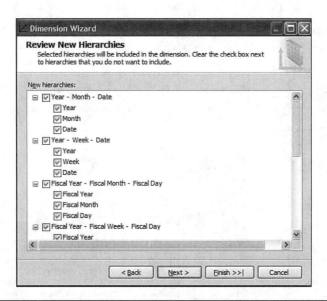

Figure 13-68   Dimension Wizard Calendars Definition: Reviewing Hierarchies.

How Do I Execute Multiple MDX Queries from SQL Server Management Studio?

If you want to execute multiple queries against cubes within the database, then you can do so within SQL Server Management Studio. This section was written as a Tip and Trick by Andrew Garbuzov, who developed all the MDX, DMX, and XML/A query designers for SQL Server Management Studio.

SQL Server 2000 Enterprise manager supported execution of multiple SQL queries and displaying results for various queries in the result pane. SSMS supports the same behavior for SQL queries and MDX queries. All you have to do is separate the MDX queries by GO, as shown in Figure 13-69.

NOTE
Make sure you put a semicolon at the end of the first statement. Also make sure you type GO, not Go because this is case sensitive.

How Do I Find a Specific Server Property?

The server properties in Analysis Services 2005 are much more numerous than in Analysis Services 2000. They can be counted at well over a hundred. In SQL Management Studio, you can use the Server Properties dialog to edit a property value (see Figure 13-70).

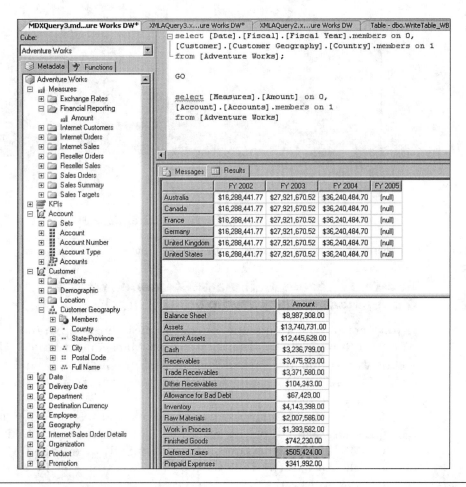

Figure 13-69   Multiple MDX queries in SQL Management Studio.

Because of lack of time at the end of the development cycle, the product team was not able to add any search functionality. We realized later on that it would indeed have been a pretty important feature. The reason for this importance is that the property library is read dynamically from the server. This list can change over the course of service packs. So the list is not hard-coded in the tool at all. Also, the list of properties appears with a full categorization-based path of each property. This makes it very hard to sort the property alphabetically and thus search through the list rapidly. As a result, one of the biggest challenges in this dialog is to actually search for and find a specific property.

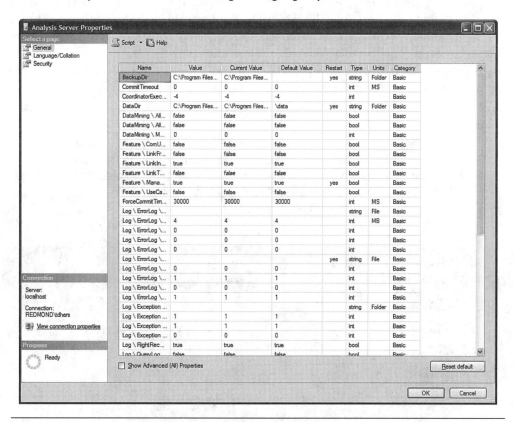

Figure 13-70   Analysis Services Properties dialog.

As the author of this dialog I deeply apologize to our audience for overseeing this during our design process and later for missing the window to address this issue during the life cycle of the product.

To find a property, my recommendation currently is to edit the MSMSDSRV.INI file that can be found in C:\Program Files\Microsoft SQL Server\MSSQL.2\OLAP\Config, and from which these properties are read, and use the Notepad Find feature to find the property.

The server property can be changed directly in the config INI file. If you still want to use the UI, you can just use the INI file to find the path of the property.

How Do I Set a Process Option for More than One Object at Once in the Process Object(s) Dialog?

Often it can be useful to select multiple objects to process them all at once. By default, the Solution Explorer in BI Development studio enables you to select multiple objects. The Partition tab in the Cube Designer also enables you to select multiple objects.

In contrast, in SQL Management Studio the Object Explorer lets you select only one object at a time.

TIP

To select multiple objects in Solution Explorer, just click on the parent Node and all the dependent objects will be displayed in the Summary report page on the right side. In this Summary tab, the object can be multi-selected and an action available in the context menu can be invoked (for example: Process multiple cubes).

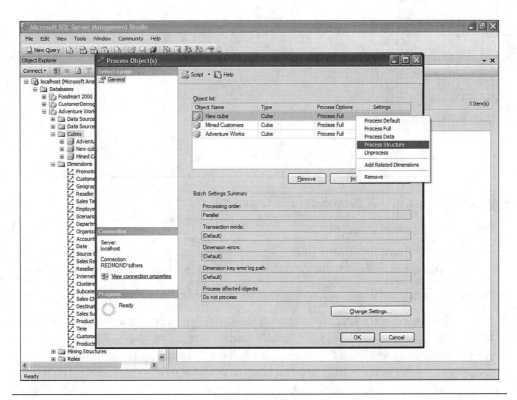

Figure 13-71   Multiple Selection in Process dialog.

After the Process dialog has been invoked for multiple objects, they are each represented in a single row. Multiple rows here again can be selected, but now dropping the option list in the Process option column cancels the multiple selection. To change a selection for a set of objects all at once, the user can simply select all the rows simultaneously and then right-click and select one of the available options displayed in the context menu (see Figure 13-71).

Summary

We hope that through these business scenarios we were able to showcase many Analysis Services development and management tools tips and tricks. These tools should no longer be mysterious to you. Although service packs and the next release (currently code named Katmai) may bring some slight updates and enhancements to these tools, it is unlikely that they will change fundamentally. These tools should be around for a long time.

If you come across specific scenarios that are not properly addressed by this book or by the Books Online, feel free to contact me (Thierry.dhers@microsoft.com) or contact any of the Analysis Services program managers and we will gladly address them in future publications or even build in native solutions in a upcoming release of these tools.

CHAPTER 14

Inside Analysis Services Data Mining Tools

Microsoft SQL Server 2000 provided one main tool for developing and managing mining models. Analysis Manager was the main tool. Built on the Microsoft Management Console (MMC) infrastructure, it enabled the database professional to develop and manage mining models against a live server. In this tool, design and management tasks were combined in one unique environment.

With SQL Server 2005, Microsoft has redesigned its tool approach to better fit different roles played by different individuals or teams in a company. Most functionality is now split between either the Business Intelligence Development Studio for design tasks and SQL Management Studio for management and other operational tasks. When we started early designs and prototypes in 2000, the decision had not yet been made to integrate the BI development environment with VS, but very early it was clear that we wanted to provide an experience to the "BI developer." Unlike the developers using the rest of the BI stack, data mining developers often are analysts, rather than real developers. So the choice to integrate with Visual Studio may sound odd, but it was made so that all the tools are consistent across the stack. Although the analyst needs to work in a Visual Studio shell, he or she will not at any time be required to do any coding.

This is why every single task can either be achieved through graphical wizards and designers, as well as through scripting and coding with the APIs. We do realize that even though we have made tons of investments in providing very business-oriented wizards, the IDE environment can still be somewhat overwhelming for the non-developer. Look at the development tools in SQL 2005 as the first step into this direction. I'm sure that as we learn more from customers' experiences and hear more feedback from users and developers, we will refine and provide tools in the future that are even better suited to individual roles, levels of expertise, and tasks.

This chapter begins with an overview of Analysis Services Tools and then tries to walk the reader through many scenarios that cover most of the key functionality of the tools while also providing insights, tips, and techniques. I hope readers will find a lot of valuable how-to techniques throughout this chapter.

The Inside Scoop on the Data Mining Tools

In SQL Server 2005, all data mining browsers have been designed as stand-alone components. As a result, they can be reused as is in a custom build application. So every scenario described in this chapter can be ported to an embedded application with little coding required.

Also, for data analysts, a great tip is to use the BI development Studio to connect live against the server. This way every analysis and prediction is run live against the data set without requiring any file deployments.

Analysis Services Tools Overview

Analysis Services tools in SQL Server 2005 introduced a new way to work with the data and data mining objects. In Analysis Services in SQL Server 2000, the first step a user had to take to design or manage a server was to physically connect to an Analysis Services server. In SQL Server 2005, the database professional or analyst has two choices: You can either work live against a physical server (also called Immediate mode) or work in Project mode. Also, you have the choice of two tools, depending on the task you must accomplish: BI Development Studio or SQL Server Management Studio.

A detailed description of the BI Development Studio as well as SQL Server Management Studio is available in Chapter 13. In the BI Development Studio the database professional or analyst will be able to work with the Data Mining Model Designer and wizards.

The Data Mining Model Designer is one of the richest designers. It hosts over ten data browsers. Rich visualization is critical to analyzing the findings of the mining model algorithm. Although the Designer only has five main tabs, you will soon notice that the Mining Model Viewer tab contains its own set of sub-tabs. The list of sub-tabs is dependent on the mining model algorithm selected.

TIP

Each of the data viewers available in the Data Mining Model Designer is a component that can be reused as is in an application.

SQL Server Management Studio is the environment to use for the following types of tasks:

- Migrate a database
- Back up or restore a database
- Train a mining structure
- Browse a mining model
- Script any management task
- Run a Data Mining query (DMX) against the live database
- Change a server property

Now that you understand some fundamentals about the toolset, let's look at how it can be used to answer questions and address problems in common business scenarios.

Using Analysis Services Data Mining Tools to Solve Problems in Business Scenarios

The following section discusses various scenarios and technical situations in which you may find yourself. The goal of these scenarios is to go beyond basic step-by-steps of how to use the designers or wizards, and to provide tips and insights about some non-obvious capabilities of our designers and wizards. The scenarios that you are presented within this section are listed here by tool:

- Data Mining Designer
  - Embedding Data Mining controls and sample code in a custom application
  - Interpreting the "Little Diamonds" and how to view them
  - Recoding a column, using the Data Source View
  - Measuring lift over global statistics
  - Creating a Classification Matrix Report
  - Enhancing productivity by multi-selecting in the Data Mining Wizard and Editor in BI Development Studio
  - Using Association rules viewer filtering capability
  - Using the same base column multiple times with different properties in different algorithms (discretized for some, continuous for others)
  - Creating multiple models, using the same algorithm but varying column setting (Input, Predict) or changing properties
  - Copying grid and trees viewers in Microsoft Excel, Microsoft Word, or HTML
  - Using the DMX editor to call the stored procedure to display the data contained in the viewers
  - SQL Server Management Studio:
    - Viewing and customizing DMX templates

How to Embed Data Mining Controls and Sample Code in a Custom Application

In Analysis Services 2000, the data mining offering consisted of two algorithms and three viewers. These viewers couldn't be reused outside of Analysis Manager.

In Analysis Services 2005, the Data Mining offering has been greatly enhanced. The Analysis Services engine now natively supports ten algorithms, and it also contains ten different viewers. The other main difference is that each of these viewers was natively built as components that can be reused and embedded in other applications.

This is particularly important because many of the usage scenarios for data mining are part of an existing application. The value-add of data mining techniques is to make decisions easier for the user by providing extra insight into the data. Thus, data mining is rarely a standalone application, but rather functionality that is embedded in another application.

The following sample illustrates how to embed such functionality in a C# application:

```
// Determine the viewer type based on the model service and
// instantiate the correct viewer
model = conn.MiningModels[modelName];
service = conn.MiningServices[model.Algorithm];
if (service.ViewerType == "Microsoft_Cluster_Viewer")
    viewer = new ClusterViewer();
else if (service.ViewerType == "Microsoft_Tree_Viewer")
    viewer = new TreeViewer();
else if (service.ViewerType == "Microsoft_NaiveBayesian_Viewer")
    viewer = new NaiveBayesViewer();
else if (service.ViewerType ==
            "Microsoft_SequenceCluster_Viewer")
    viewer = new SequenceClusterViewer();
else if (service.ViewerType == "Microsoft_TimeSeries_Viewer")
    viewer = new TimeSeriesViewer();
else if (service.ViewerType ==
            "Microsoft_AssociationRules_Viewer")
    viewer = new AssociationViewer();
else if (service.ViewerType == "Microsoft_NeuralNetwork_Viewer")
    viewer = new NeuralNetViewer();
else throw new System.Exception("Custom Viewers not supported");

// Set up and load the viewer
viewer.ConnectionString = ConnectionString;
viewer.MiningModelName = modelName;
viewer.Dock = DockStyle.Fill;
panel.Controls.Add(viewer);
viewer.LoadViewerData(null);
```

The full sample, as well as many others, can be found on the following data mining website, managed by the Microsoft SQL Server Data Mining development team:

http://www.sqlserverdatamining.com/DMCommunity/Downloads/default.aspx

How to Interpret "Little Diamonds" and How to View Them

The Cluster, Regression Tree, and Time Series viewers use small cyan-colored diamond shapes in their nodes and rowsets.

Figure 14-1 show one such node, for example.

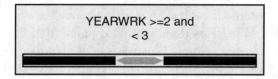

YEARWRK >=2 and
< 3

Figure 14-1 Cluster node illustrating use of little diamond.

We use graphics of this sort for quick visual representation of continuous distributions.

The first thing to note is that the size of the "diamond" symbol is proportional to the standard deviation of the target variable, so the bigger the node diamond, the greater the uncertainty of the predictions based on that node.

Another thing to notice is that in some contexts the diamond is off-center, that is, displaced from the middle of the supporting black bar in either direction, such as in the Cluster viewer snippet shown in Figure 14-2.

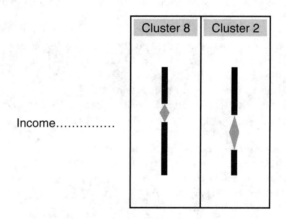

Figure 14-2 Example of cluster viewer snippet.

The supporting black bar represents the range of a continuous variable distribution, and its middle corresponds to the population median (same as marginal mean for normal distribution). The center of a diamond represents a category-specific or node-specific mean and the displacement is proportional to the difference between the two means. Thus in Figure 14.2, the average income of the population in Cluster 8 is above the median, but for Cluster 2 it is below the median. Judging from the displacements, neither of the clusters diverges very far from the population-wide statistical average. However, Cluster 2 shows much greater variation in income than Cluster 8. The range of the black bar is equal to the range of the input data but capped at three standard deviations away from the mean. This is to prevent outliers from skewing the data view and making it meaningless.

The numerical details of the distribution involved are readily accessible from the Mining Legend. The diamond symbols are designed to give just a first-glance impression of the data mining statistics.

Recoding a Column Using the Data Source View

Many times when embarking on a data mining project you need to slightly alter the data source. We're not talking about changing the world; rather we want to look at the data in a subtly but significantly different manner so that it makes more sense to the business problem under examination. In these cases you may need to reduce or change the number of states in a column to those that make sense for your business problem, or change a numeric value into a set of discrete states.

Nominal Recoding

For example, imagine that for your modeling purposes you determine that you need to know the legal marital status of each customer. However, your data has a column called Marital Status with the following values:

- Never Married
- Married
- Separated
- Divorced
- Widowed

Clearly this column does not suit your purposes. What you need is a different column that simply has the values Married and Not Married. Luckily, using the Data Source View editor, you can add such a column without modifying your source data or even touching your source database.

The Data Source View (DSV) enables you to add logical columns to the physical columns in your source tables. To the Analysis Services processing engine, these columns appear the same as any physical column in the table. To create such a column, right-click on a table in the DSV editor and select **New Named Calculation,** which brings up the Create (per Figure) Named Calculation dialog. In this dialog you can enter arbitrary SQL that generates the appropriate values for your column. For recoding, we use the SQL CASE statement to change values from one set to another. The CASE statement looks like the following:

```
CASE <expression>
    WHEN <value>  THEN <value>
    [WHEN <value>  THEN <value>]
    [ELSE <value>]
END
```

For the Marital Status example, the statement would look like this:

```
CASE [Marital Status]
    WHEN 'Married' THEN 'Married'
    WHEN 'Separated' THEN 'Married'
    ELSE 'Not Married'
END
```

To create the Named Calculation, you fill out the Create Named Calculation dialog with the new column name and the SQL fragment, as shown in Figure 14-3.

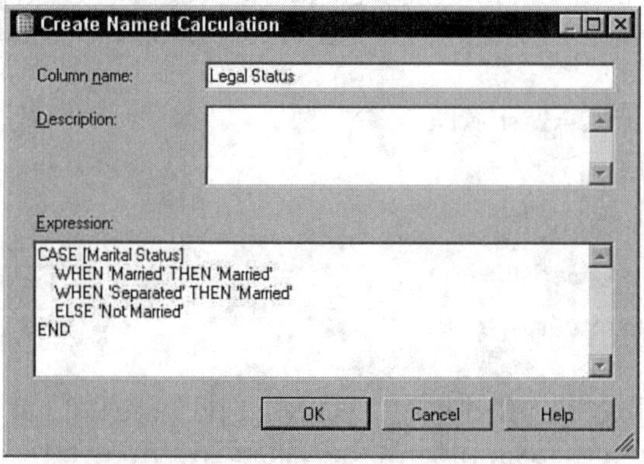

Figure 14-3   Creating a named calculation.

You may also want only to change the column values in some of the cases. For example, if you want to recode the married values into a single value, but preserve all the non-married states, you could use a CASE statement like the following:

```
CASE [Marital Status]
    WHEN 'Married' THEN 'Married'
    WHEN 'Separated' THEN 'Married'
    ELSE [Marital Status]
END
```

Numerical Recoding

The other type of recoding mentioned involves recoding a numerical value into a set of discrete states. For this purpose you use a different form of the CASE statement:

```
CASE
   WHEN <expression> THEN <value>
   [WHEN <expression> THEN <value>]
   [ELSE <value>]
END
```

For example, if you wanted to know whether people were in their twenties or thirties you could use the following SQL expression:

```
CASE
   WHEN [Age] >= 20 AND [Age] < 30 THEN 'Twenties'
   WHEN [Age] >= 30 AND [Age] < 50 THEN 'Thirties'
   ELSE 'Other'
END
```

Verifying Recoding

Verifying your recoding is simple. To see the data that Analysis Services uses to process your model, right-click on the table in the DSV editor and select **Explore Data**. The data viewers use the same mechanism used by the server to pull data from the source, so your data exploration includes the named calculations you added.

Measuring Lift over Global Statistics

One of the typical methods to validate a model is to measure the accuracy of the trained model in terms of correct classification rate. To facilitate this, Analysis Services 2005 supports a lift chart where prediction accuracy of a model is compared with an ideal model and random model. Figure 14-4 presents an example.

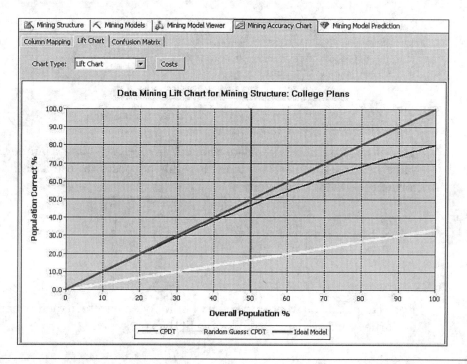

Figure 14-4   Data Mining lift chart.

The chart shows that the model called CPDT significantly outperforms random prediction, which is 0.33 because the target has three states (missing, Yes, No). However, this chart doesn't tell how much better the CPDT model is than marginal prediction (that is, prediction based on just global distribution of the target). What if the global distribution of the target being "Yes" is 85%? As far as the correct classification rate is concerned, the marginal prediction would be better (note that CPDT yields 80% overall). This is why sometimes we also need to know how much the model performs better than marginal. To include a marginal model in the lift chart, you can create a derived model with only the target and key included and all other columns ignored. Figure 14-5 shows the derived model, named CPMG.

Now, try the lift chart with the two models, named CPDT and CPMG, to show lift over the marginal model (see Figure 14-6).

Creating a Classification Matrix Report

Reporting Services makes an excellent delivery vehicle for your data mining results. In addition to exposing query results, you can also use features of

Reporting Services to enhance the functionality of DMX. For example, DMX lacks GROUP BY functionality, so you can take advantage of the Reporting Services grouping capability in data mining reports.

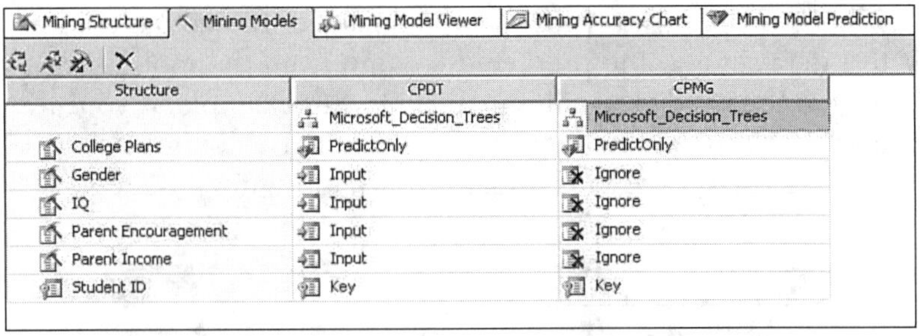

Structure	CPDT	CPMG
	Microsoft_Decision_Trees	Microsoft_Decision_Trees
College Plans	PredictOnly	PredictOnly
Gender	Input	Ignore
IQ	Input	Ignore
Parent Encouragement	Input	Ignore
Parent Income	Input	Ignore
Student ID	Key	Key

Figure 14-5 Example of a derived model.

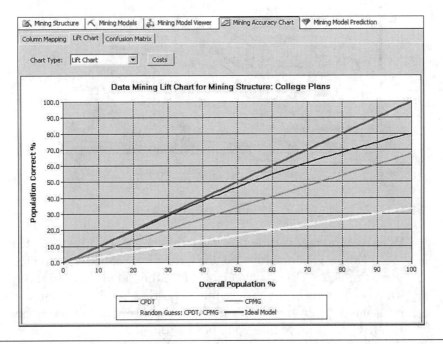

Figure 14-6 Lift chart with two mining models.

Using this capability you can easily emulate the classification matrix functionality of the BI Development Studio in a report that you can deliver to anyone. The first thing you need is a mining model that predicts a discrete attribute and test data. For this example I use a decision tree model built on the movie customer data available on this site to show a classification matrix (also known as a confusion matrix) for the Home Ownership column.

The first thing to do is to create a new Reporting Services project and connect to your Analysis Services database containing your model. When you generate your query, you select the actual column from the test data set and the predicted column from the model. It's a good idea to give the predicted column a name. For example, if your test data column is Home Ownership, then you might call your predicted column Predicted Home Ownership, as shown in Figure 14-7.

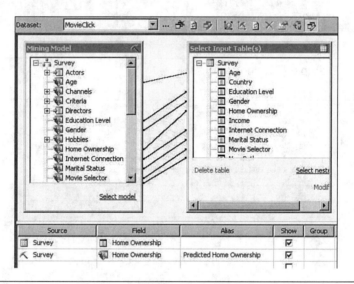

Figure 14-7   Data mining query in Reporting Services.

When you set up the grouping levels for your report, put the actual value (e.g., Home Ownership) into the group box and the predicted value (e.g., Predicted Home Ownership) into the details box. In the end, we want both items in the group, but Reporting Services requires that you put something in the details in the wizard, so you can move Predicted Home Ownership to the group box later.

After you finish the Report Wizard, edit the report layout to move Predicted Home Ownership from the details line to the grouping line, as shown in Figure 14-8. Then you can delete the details row from the report.

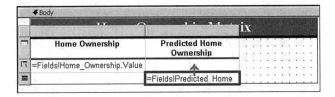

Figure 14-8   Moving Predicted Home Ownership from the details line to the grouping line.

Next, right-click the grouping icon to the left of the row and select Edit Group. Add Predicted Home Ownership to the list of grouping fields and click OK.

Finally, you need to add a new column to the report. For the column header you can type `Count` and for the cell value enter `=CountRows()`. Your final layout should look something like that shown in Figure 14-9 (with some additional formatting):

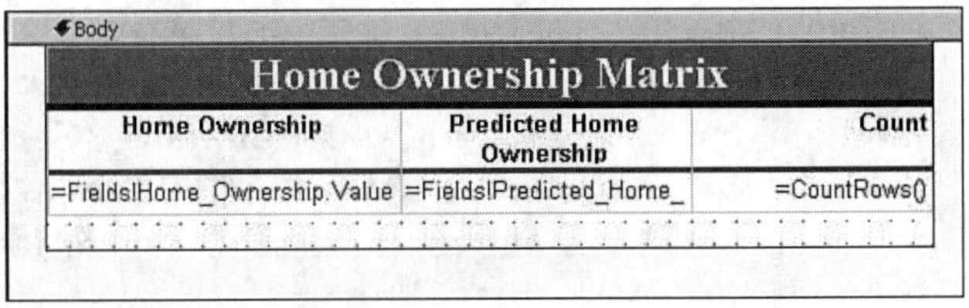

Home Ownership Matrix		
Home Ownership	Predicted Home Ownership	Count
=Fields!Home_Ownership.Value	=Fields!Predicted_Home_	=CountRows()

Figure 14-9   Report preview.

Preview your report and you will receive a thin-client, distributable, portable, classification matrix like the one shown in Figure 14-10.

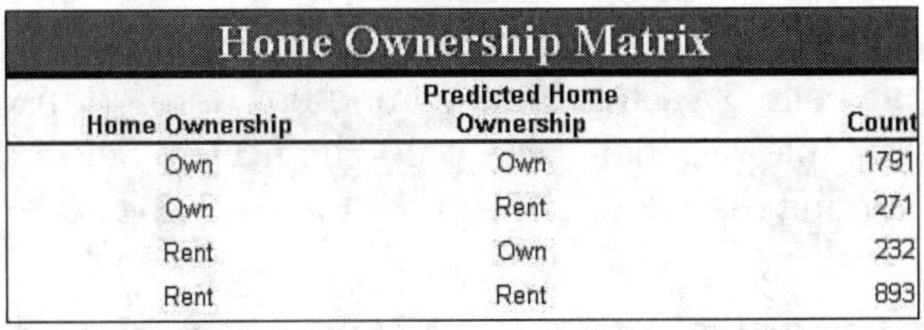

Home Ownership Matrix		
Home Ownership	Predicted Home Ownership	Count
Own	Own	1791
Own	Rent	271
Rent	Own	232
Rent	Rent	893

Figure 14-10   Report Design final layout.

How Multi-Selecting in the Data Mining Wizard and Editor in BI Development Studio Can Enhance Productivity

Several places in SQL Server 2005 Business Intelligence Development Studio support multi-selection of objects, which lets you set the state of many objects at the same time. This can be quite useful in the following scenarios:

- In the Data Mining Wizard, when selecting which columns are input and\or predictable, you can click (use the arrow keys) to position the selection in a cell, then while holding down the Shift key, either scroll and click on another cell to select a range of cells, or use the arrow keys. The cells in the table are all shaded to show that they are all selected. To set the state, press the space bar. Pressing the space bar again toggles the check boxes and un-checks them.

- In the Data Mining Editor's mining structure view, you cannot multi-select columns in the tree to set common properties in the property sheet grid at the same time. However, because the structure columns also appear in the Mining Models view in the leftmost column of the grid, you can multi-select the structure columns there by holding down the Shift key while making the selection and then set properties on several of the structure columns at the same time. Press F4 to show the property sheet if it is not already visible, or choose to show it from the **View** menu. This can be useful when changing several mining structure columns' content type, for example, from discrete to continuous.

- In addition to setting common properties with the property sheet in the Mining Models view, you can also multi-select cells in the mining models grid to set the usage type for several mining model columns and several models all at once. Use the Shift key again to select multiple cells. To activate the combo-box drop-down while retaining the multiple-selection state, press the F2 key. Select the usage type and commit the value. The value is then set across the entire selection.

Using Association Rules Viewer Filtering Capability

The association rule algorithm is useful because it can help with detecting association patterns in the data. For example, the very first rule shown in Figure 14-11 can be read as follows: People who buy ML Road Tire and Sport-100 are likely to buy the Road Tire Tube as well with 100% probability.

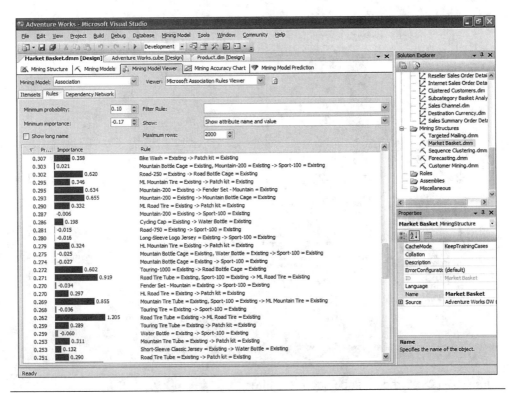

Figure 14-11   Association rule, unfiltered.

Using the AdventureWorks sample cube project, you can browse an association rule mining model called Market Basket. It shows association patterns in the Bicycle Sales data.

An association Mining Model can contain many rules. Because of the high volume, the filter capability is most relevant. A very basic and common filtering is to type a string in the filter dialog.

For example, if you type: "Road Tire" in the Filter combo box, you reduce the number of rules to just 20, which makes it much easier to read and analyze (see Figure 14-12).

But what is not often known is that the Microsoft Association Rules Viewer filtering is based on a .NET regular expression. As a result, the filtering supports more than just wildcards and and/or logic. It also supports all the types of .NET regular expressions, as described at the following page: http://msdn.microsoft.com/library/default.asp?url=/library/en-us/cpgenref/html/cpconregularexpressionslanguageelements.asp.

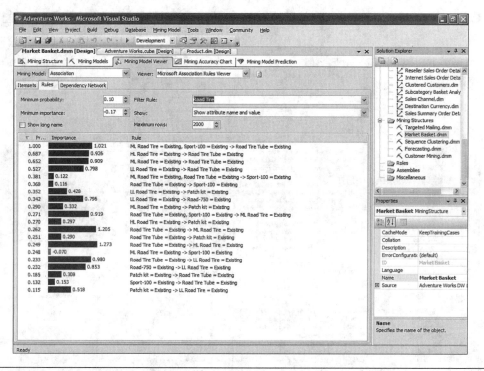

Figure 14-12   Simple association rule filter.

For example, the following filtering expression finds rules having the phrase "Road Tire Tube" on the left side of the rule: `\bRoad\b.\bTire\b.\bTube\b.*->*`, resulting in what is shown in Figure 14-13.

Use the Same Base Column Multiple Times with Different Properties in Different Algorithms

There are many scenarios in which it can be interesting and useful to use the same input list of columns, but with different properties.

For example, some algorithms allow only discrete states (not continuous), such as Naïve Bayes. In other cases, a column may need to be treated as discretized into five buckets for one mining model algorithm (for example: decision tree model), and eight buckets for another model. Creating multiple mining models within the same mining structure allows you to compare how treating this input with a finer granularity of discretization affects the models.

You can create as many model variations as needed.

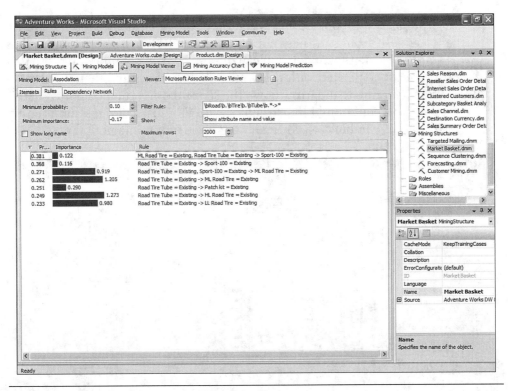

Figure 14-13   Advanced association rule filter.

In Figure 14-14, Yearly Income has been left continuous, whereas Yearly Income 1 has been added from the same base column, but with the Content properties set to discretized in ten buckets.

Creating Multiple Models, Using the Same Algorithm but with Varying Column Settings or Changing Properties

Although most people create a mining structure with multiple models (each one using a different technique), there might be scenarios where it is relevant and useful to use the same Mining Model technique with different combinations of input, predict settings, or properties settings for base columns.

For example, using the same algorithm for two models, if you predict college plans using only Age as input, you get different results than you do if you use Parent Income and Parent Encouragement. A third algorithm that uses all the available columns as input produces different results, as well. Sometimes when there are potentially a lot of columns to choose from, you may not need to use 100 or more columns all as input to train the model. You can discover which columns are those that are most correlated with the predictable attribute and then build additional models that narrow down the scope of important columns. In this case you could build the structure with all those columns and then try different combinations by including some inputs and not others.

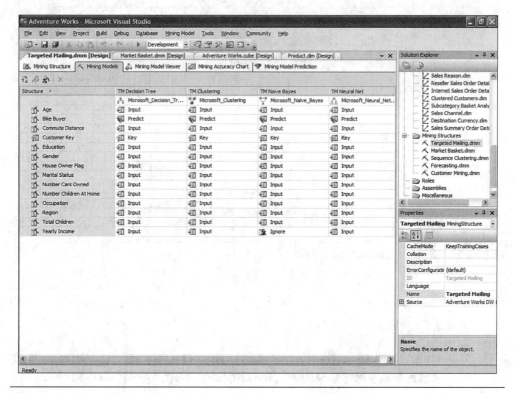

Figure 14-14 DM use of multiple similar base columns.

Copying Grid and Trees Viewers in Microsoft Excel, Microsoft Word, or HTML

Most of the Data Mining viewers are very graphical. Often the graphical shape and overall look of the tree or layout of the cluster distribution can provide as much information as the content itself. This is why each viewer allows you to copy the graphical information to the clipboard and then paste it to Excel, Word, or even a rich format.

The user can use the shortcut key Ctrl+C or right-click on the viewer and use one of the context menu options:

- Copy Graph view, which copies the graph in its current state (see Figure 14-15).
- Copy Entire Graph, which copies the graph entirely, expanded and displayed (see Figure 14-16).

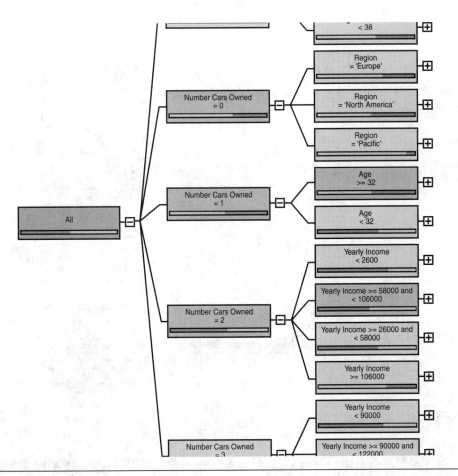

Figure 14-15   Copy Graph view.

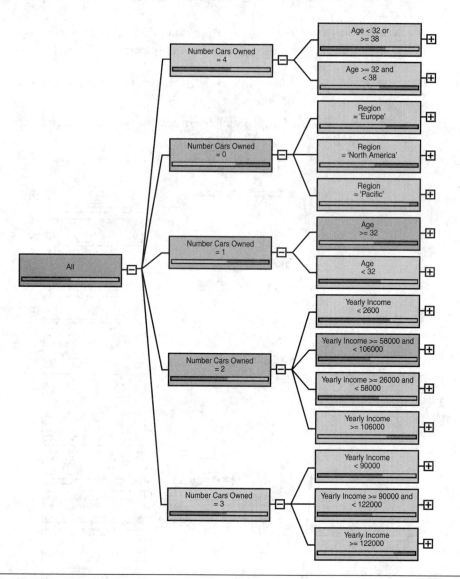

Figure 14-16   Copy entire graph.

DMX Editor Can Call the Stored Proc to Display the Data Contained in the Viewers

This is a slightly more advanced topic. The Data Mining tools make use of many internal stored procedures to query mining model content and display it inside the viewers. These stored procedures can also be used and invoked by the database administrator directly through the DMX query editor in SQL Server Management Studio to query the content of a mining model.

In the following example, the following query queries the first 20 node definitions of the TM Decision Tree Mining Model from the AdventureWorks DW Analysis Services sample:

```
Call
→System.Microsoft.AnalysisServices.System.DataMining.DecisionTree
→sDepNet.
→DTGetNodeGraph('TM Decision Tree', 20)
```

The results of the query can be seen in Figure 14-17.

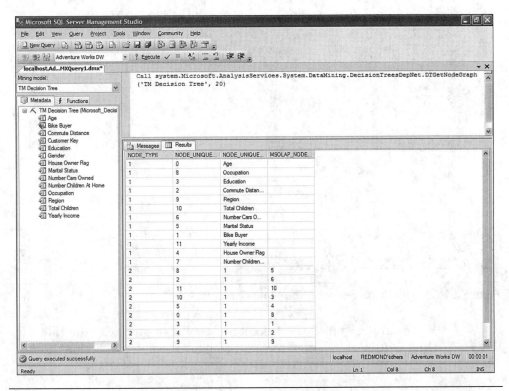

Figure 14-17   Using Stored Procedure to navigate Data Mining Model content.

The full list of available stored procedures, as well as their definitions, can be found in Appendix D.

How to View and Customize DMX Templates

In SQL Server Management Studio, go to View, Template Explorer. The default view shows standard SQL templates. Click the "Cube" icon in the window to get to the Analysis Services templates and open the DMX branch of the tree. There you will find many template DMX syntax examples (see Figure 14-18).

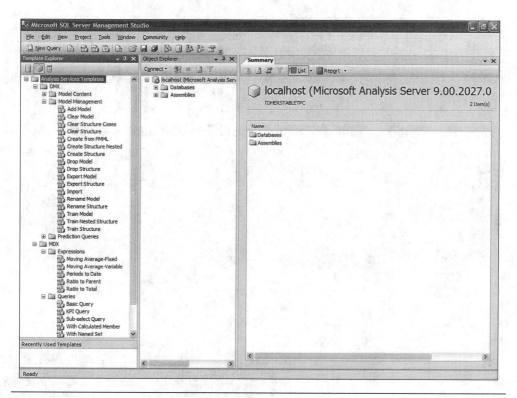

Figure 14-18   Analysis Services Template Explorer.

For example, the "Base Prediction" template gives you the following shell—fill in the parameters and you have a valid prediction query:

```
// =========================
// Base Prediction
// =========================

SELECT <select_list,,> FROM <mining_model,,>
PREDICTION JOIN
```

```
OPENQUERY('<datasource,,>','<query,,>') AS <input_alias,,>
ON <on_clause,,>
WHERE <where_clause,,>
```

This template list is stored on disc in a clear XML file under C:\Program Files\Microsoft SQL Server\90\Tools\Binn\VSShell\Common7\IDE\ sqlworkbenchprojectitems\AnalysisServices.

As with KPI templates and other time intelligence templates, one can easily open any of the XML documents stored in the sub-folders and edit, add, or remove templates. Unlike KPI templates, each query or expression template is stored in a different file; to add a template, create an XML file with the MDX, DXM, or XML/A expression and save it in the appropriate sub-folder.

The MDX, DMX, XML/A folder structure is shown in Figure 14-19.

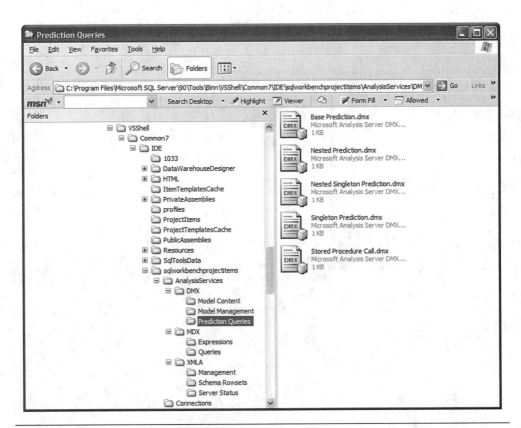

Figure 14-19 DMX template folder structure.

Summary

Through these scenarios we hope to have shown you that much more can be accomplished through these designers and browsers than can be seen at first glance.

These scenarios do not serve as an exhaustive list, and you may find many other tips, techniques, and best practices through your own experience. These tools are extremely rich and will surely provide great satisfaction to any data analyst aspiring to gain knowledge from and insight into large datasets.

Also remember that these browsers can be reused and embedded, as is the case in custom-built applications such as CRM, HR, SCM, and ERP-type applications.

CHAPTER 15

Inside Notification Services Tools

Notification Services first shipped as Notification Services 2.0, an add-on component for SQL Server 2000, in late 2002. Because it was not developed along with the rest of SQL Server 2000, Notification Services tools were not integrated into the SQL Server 2000 toolset. In fact, there were no graphical tools for deployment and management, just a command line utility, stored procedures, views, and performance counters.

With SQL Server 2005 Notification Services, the development team had the opportunity to integrate Notification Services management into the SQL Server 2005 toolset. As a result, Notification Services can be deployed and managed with SQL Server Management Studio and configured with SQL Server Configuration Manager and Surface Area Configuration, in addition to command line utilities.

In addition to the new tools, Notification Services also added the flexibility of a management object model, Notification Services Management Objects (NMO).

Overview of Notification Services

Microsoft SQL Server Notification Services is a set of schemas and APIs for developing applications that generate and send notifications to subscribers, and an engine that runs those applications.

A notification application can be thought of as a "push" application. People (or applications) subscribe to the application, and the application sends information of interest to the subscribers. This enables you build applications that send focused and personalized information to your enterprise, customers, and partners.

Notifications are generated based on the occurrence of an event or based on a schedule defined by you or the subscriber. You can choose to support one or multiple delivery protocols, such as email, Short Message Service (SMS), or raw XML, and format the notifications accordingly.

If your application is for an international audience, you can use the built-in support for multiple formatting options and time zone management. For example, if you are using the built-in Extensible Stylesheet Language Transformations (XSLT) content formatter, you can create one transform per combination of language and device type, such as French cell phone, English cell phone, French email, and English email.

As soon as you learn the basics of the platform and framework, you can quickly define notification applications with Transact-SQL and XML or managed code, and then deploy those applications on SQL Server 2005, a robust and reliable data management platform.

In SQL Server 2005, Notification Services is available in Enterprise Edition, Standard Edition, Developer Edition, and Evaluation Edition.

Notification Services Architecture

To understand the Notification Services tools, it's important to understand the basic architecture of Notification Services. Understanding the architecture will make it easier to understand why the tools work the way they do.

Notification Services uses the concepts of applications and instances. An application is a solution for particular categories of notifications, such as credit card or sports-related notifications. An instance of Notification Services hosts one or more applications.

Applications are separate from each other, which enables you to isolate application data and to tune the performance. However, applications share subscriber and delivery channel information through the hosting instance. Figure 15-1 shows the relationships between applications and instances.

As illustrated in Figure 15-1, applications share subscribers, subscriber devices (such as email addresses and cell phone numbers), and delivery channels (such as email servers or SMS servers) through the hosting instance. However, application data is isolated from other application data. In fact, each application can have its own database (which is why Figure 15-1 does not illustrate the architecture with database diagrams—how you use databases for SQL Server 2005 Notification Services is quite flexible).

If multiple instances and applications share the same database, their objects are isolated from each other through the use of database schemas.

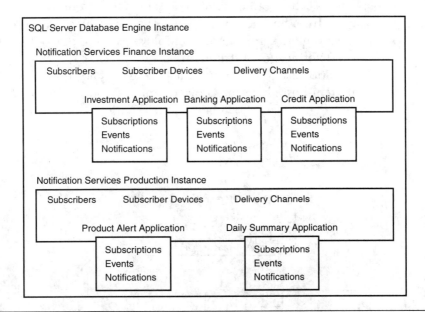

Figure 15-1   Notification Services instances and applications.

Notification Services is also very flexible about how you design applications. Instead of having three finance-based applications (Investments, Banking, and Credit), you could have one application that supports the multiple types of events, subscriptions, and notifications. How you use instances and applications depends on how you want to isolate data versus how you want to share basic application execution settings.

The Notification Services Engine

An instance of Notification Services is controlled by a Notification Services engine. This engine runs event providers, generators, and distributors. For example, if you are using the built-in file-watcher event provider, the engine monitors a folder for XML files and then submits the data to the instance of Notification Services. The generator initiates the processing of events and subscriptions, and the distributor formats notifications and sends them to delivery channels.

In Notification Services 2.0, the engine was always one or more Windows services named NS$*instance_name*. In SQL Server 2005, you can choose to host the Notification Services engine in your own application or process. In either case, the engine can be located on the database server, on a remote server, or on multiple servers to scale out event processing and notification distribution.

In addition to components run by the engine, instances can use external (non-hosted) event providers and subscription management interfaces. Figure 15-2 shows how all these components work together:

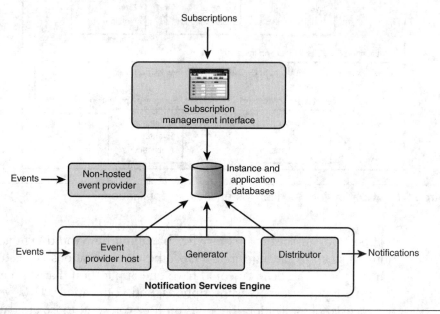

Figure 15-2   How Notification Services components work together.

Building Notification Applications

To build an application, you define schemas and properties for events, subscriptions, and notifications, and then you define operational settings. You can define an application in an XML application definition file (ADF) or using the Notification Services Management Objects (NMO), a managed-code API. ADF and managed code samples are provided in SQL Server Books Online.

There are no specialized tools for developing a Notification Services application. If you are building an application with XML, you can use your favorite XML editor. If you use SQL Server Management Studio, you can use F1 help to get additional information about the XML elements. If you are using NMO, you can use Visual Studio 2005 or other development environments of choice.

In addition to building the core application, you also need to determine how to manage subscriber and subscription data. For many applications, the subscription management interface is a Web or Windows application.

NEW IN SQL SERVER 2005

You can now insert basic subscriber and subscription data into views that Notification Services creates during application deployment. This was added primarily to simplify application development and testing.

You may also choose to develop custom components for gathering event data and distributing notifications. This is optional and depends on the systems into which you are integrating your Notification Services applications.

Defining Instances of Notification Services

To define an instance of Notification Services, you associate applications with the instance and then provide information such as the name of the instance and the name of the SQL Server instance that hosts the Notification Services data. You also define shared components, such as custom delivery protocols and the delivery channels used to deliver notifications from the instance's applications. You can define an instance in an XML instance configuration file (ICF) or using the Notification Services Management Objects (NMO). ICF and managed code samples are provided in SQL Server Books Online.

Again, there are no specialized development tools for Notification Services. Use your favorite XML editor, SQL Server Management Studio, or Visual Studio 2005 to define an instance.

Deploying and Managing Instances of Notification Services

After you have defined an instance and its applications, you deploy the instance, using SQL Server Management Studio, the NSControl command line utility, or, if defining the instance and its applications programmatically, the Notification Services Management Objects (NMO) API. Deploying an instance requires Notification Services to create database objects; for the instance to be registered, enabled, and started; and for all applications that interact with the instance to have the proper permissions. This is all documented in the "Common Deployment and Management Scenarios" section of this chapter.

NEW IN SQL SERVER 2005
You can now deploy Notification Services instances and applications into existing databases. For the instance and each application, you can define the name of an existing database and a schema for the objects.

After deployment, you can use the Notification Services tools to perform management tasks such as updating instances and applications, or temporarily disabling an instance or application for system maintenance.

Overview of the Notification Services Tools

This section looks at the tools available for deploying and administering instances of Notification Services. It starts with the NSControl command line utility because it was used as the underlying framework for the Notification Services tools in SQL Server Management Studio. It then looks at the equivalent commands in SQL Server Management Studio, the NMO API, and then the stored procedures and performance counters you can use to monitor performance.

NSControl Command Line Utility

In the previous release of Notification Services, the NSControl command line utility was the only toolset for deploying and managing instances of Notification Services. This utility still exists in SQL Server 2005 Notification Services, and is the tool of choice for those who like to script deployment and management tasks.

Notification Services Command Prompt

To make it easier to run NSControl commands, SQL Server 2005 installs a Notification Services command prompt. This command prompt opens to the location where the Notification Services binaries are installed. To open this command prompt window, click the **Start** menu, **All Programs,**

Microsoft SQL Server 2005, Configuration Tools, and then click **Notification Services Command Prompt**.

Basic NSControl Syntax

The basic syntax of an **NSControl** command is as follows:

```
nscontrol command command_options
```

Full syntax, permission requirements, and examples for each command are provided in SQL Server 2005 Books Online.

Syntax Example

As an example, let's look at the nscontrol create command, which creates database objects for a new instance of Notification Services. It has the following syntax:

```
nscontrol create
    [-nologo]
    [-help]
     -in instance_config_file
    [-sqlusername name  -sqlpassword password]
    [-argumentkey key]
    [param=value ...]
```

The options are as follows:

- The nologo and help options are standard to all NSControl commands. The nologo option suppresses verbose product information in the command line output. The help option displays the syntax for the command.
- The in option specifies the path and filename of the instance configuration file (ICF) used to compile the instance and its applications. Because many paths and filenames contain special characters, you should enclose the instance_config_file value in quotation marks.
- The sqlusername and sqlpassword options are used only if you are using SQL Server Authentication to connect to the instance of SQL Server. The username and password must be able to create databases or database objects in the existing databases, depending on the database settings defined for the instance and its applications.

- The `argumentkey` option is used to encrypt event provider and delivery channel argument values before storing them in the database. (These parameters sometimes contain sensitive information, such as passwords.)
- And finally, the `param=values` option enables you to provide values for parameters specified in the ICF. You can think of these parameters as a way of doing a search-and-replace before processing the XML.

Usage Example

To learn how the `NSControl` utility works, it helps to see an example. To create database objects for the instance and its applications, you use the `nscontrol create` command. This command validates an XML instance configuration file (ICF), validates referenced application definition files (ADFs), and then creates instance and application database objects.

The following example shows how to create database objects using an ICF named MyICF.xml:

```
nscontrol create -in "C:\NS\MyNSInstance\MyICF.xml"
```

This command gets the MyICF.xml file located in C:\NS\MyNSInstance, processes the file, and then processes referenced application definition files (ADFs). Because the *sqlusername* and *sqlpassword* options are not used, `nscontrol create` uses Windows Authentication to connect to SQL Server and create the database objects. Also, because no *argumentkey* value is provided, event provider and delivery protocol arguments are stored as clear text.

NSControl Commands

In SQL Server 2005, `NSControl` has 13 commands, adding the `nscontrol export` and `nscontrol repair` commands in this release. Table 15-1 lists the commands, the purpose for each command, and the security requirements for running the command.

Table 15-1   NSControl Commands

Command	Purpose	Security Requirements*
`nscontrol create`	Creates databases or database objects for a new instance of Notification Services.	Permission to create databases or add database objects to the specified databases.
`nscontrol delete`	Deletes databases or database objects for an instance of Notification Services (after asking for confirmation).	Permission to drop databases or database objects. (If Notification Services created the databases, `nscontrol delete` drops them; otherwise, `nscontrol delete` drops just the database objects.)
`nscontrol disable`	Disables the specified Notification Services components (instance, application, event provider, generator, or distributor).	Membership in the `NSAdmin` database role (or higher) for updating database tables.
`nscontrol displayargumentkey`	Displays the key used to encrypt delivery channel and event provider arguments	Membership in the Administrators or Power Users groups in Windows (to read the Registry), or must be the same account as used to run the engine.
`nscontrol enable`	Enables the specified Notification Services components (instance, application, event provider, generator, or distributor).	Membership in the `NSAdmin` database role (or higher) for updating database tables.
`nscontrol export`	Exports metadata from the instance and application objects and creates one XML instance configuration file (ICF) and one XML applicationdefinition file (ADF) per application.	Membership in the `NSReader` database role (or higher) for database reading database tables.

Table 15-1 NSControl Commands Continued

Command	Purpose	Security Requirements*
nscontrol listversions	Displays information about the installed versions and registered instances of Notification Services.	No special security requirements.
nscontrol register	Creates or updates local Registry entries and performance counters for an instance of Notification Services, and optionally creates a Windows service.	If creating a Windows service, the account must be a member of the local Administrators group.
nscontrol repair	Updates metadata for the instance of Notification Services. When you upgrade an instance of Notification Services 2.0 to SQL Server 2005, you must run this command to add metadata to the msdb database. If you move an instance of Notification Services or perform any action that removes or alters instance metadata from msdb, run this command to repair the metadata.	Members of the db_owner database role and the sysadmin and dbcreator fixed server roles can run nscontrol repair. If you are not using the server argument, the account that you use to run nscontrol repair must be able to read the Registry.
nscontrol status	Displays the current enabled or disabled status of instances and applications and the current state of associated Windows services.	Membership in of one of the following database roles: NSAnalysis, NSDistributor, NSEvent Provider,NSGenerator, NSReader, NSRunService, NSSubscriberAdmin, or NSVacuum.

Command	Purpose	Security Requirements*
ns control unregister	Removes the Registry information and performance counters for the instance, as well as the local Windows service, if it exists.	Membership in the local Administrators group, which allows nscontrol unregister to access the Notification Services binary files, to update the Registry, and to remove a Windows service.
nscontrol update	Compares the metadata in the ICF and the ADFs to the metadata in the instance and application databases, and then optionally up dates the databases for any differences that it finds.	Membership in the db_owner database role in all instance and application databases affected by the nscontrol update command, or membership in the sysadmin server role.
nscontrol upgrade	Upgrades an instance of Notification Services that was created with an older version of the product to the current version or from a lower edition to a higher edition.	Membership in the db_owner fixed database role or the sysadmin server role.

*All commands require permission to execute the Notification Services binary files; this permission is granted to members of the Administrators and SQLServerNotificationServicesUser Windows groups.

SQL Server Management Studio

In SQL Server 2005, Notification Services added the capability to perform deployment and management tasks in SQL Server Management Studio. For example, rather than provide between one and six options to the nscontrol create command, you can simply right-click Object Explorer's **Notification Services** folder, select **New**, and then complete fields in the resulting dialog box.

NOTE
The Notification Services client components are installed with SQL Server Management Studio, meaning you can do many deployment and management tasks from any installation of SQL Server Management Studio. However, the Notification Services *engine* components are not installed. You must install the Notification Services engine components to locally register and run an instance of Notification Services.

Notification Services Commands

In SQL Server Management Studio, instances of Notification Services appear in the Notification Services folder of Object Explorer. The instances shown have their data in the current instance of SQL Server and have metadata about the instance in the msdb database. If instances do not appear, you may need to run nscontrol repair or you may need to refresh Object Explorer.

Notification Services commands in SQL Server Management Studio are divided into server-level commands and Notification Services instance-level commands. Figure 15-3 shows the server-level commands, which you access by right-clicking the Notification Services folder.

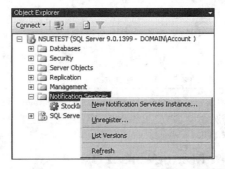

Figure 15-3   Server-level commands.

As mentioned earlier, most SQL Server Management Studio commands for Notification Services are equivalent to NSControl commands. Table 15-2 lists the NSControl equivalents for the server-level commands.

Table 15-2 Notification Services Commands

Management Studio Command	NSControl Command
New Notification Services Instance	`nscontrol create`
Unregister	`nscontrol unregister`
List Versions	`nscontrol listversions`
Refresh	None. However, if deployed instances of Notification Services do not appear, you may need to use `nscontrol repair` to fix instance metadata.

After you create an instance of Notification Services, the instance appears in the **Notification Services** folder. When you right-click an instance of Notification Services, a shortcut menu appears with commands relevant to the instance (see Figure 15-4).

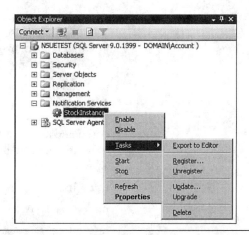

Figure 15-4 Instance-level commands.

Table 15-3 lists the `NSControl` equivalents to these commands.

Table 15-3 Instance Commands

Management Studio Command	NSControl Command
Enable	`nscontrol enable`. For more granular control, use the Properties dialog.

Table 15-3   Instance Commands Continued

Management Studio Command	NSControl Command
Disable	nscontrol disable. For more granular control, use the Properties dialog.
Start	None. If using Windows services to run the instance of Notification Services, this starts all services associated with the instance. For more granular control, use the Properties dialog.
Stop	None. If using Windows services to run the instance of Notification Services, this stops all services associated with the instance. For more granular control, use the Properties dialog.
Properties	nscontrol status. This command also provides more granular control over Enable, Disable, Start, and Stop.
Export to Editor	nscontrol export. The nscontrol export command always exports XML files. The Export to Editor command always exports XML to the SQL Server Management Studio XML Editor.
Register	nscontrol register.
Unregister	nscontrol unregister.
Update	nscontrol update.
Upgrade	nscontrol upgrade.
Delete	nscontrol delete.

What Happens Where?

It is important to note that most Notification Services actions performed within SQL Server Management Studio happen on the instance of SQL Server to which you are connected, but registration commands happen on the local computer.

For example, let's say you have installed Management Studio on Client01, and a default instance of SQL Server on Server01. On Client01, you start SQL Server Management Studio and then connect to Server01. In Object Explorer, right-click **Notification Services** and select **New Notification Services Instance**. The databases or database objects are created on Server01.

However, if you right-click your new instance, point to **Tasks**, and then select **Register**, the instance is registered on Client01, not Server01. In other words, register (and unregister) are local computer operations, and create (along with enable, disable, update, upgrade, and delete) is a database operation.

Start and stop are Windows service operations, but they use instance and application metadata stored in databases to determine where each Windows service is running.

Notification Services Stored Procedures and Views

SQL Server Management Studio provides basic information about instances of Notification Services. But what if you need more information? For example, what if you want to see what event batches were recently processed, and what notification batches were generated as a result? Or what if you want to look at event, subscription, or notification data for troubleshooting purposes?

Notification Services provides stored procedures and views to help you monitor and troubleshoot instances and applications. Although it is debatable whether stored procedures and views are officially "tools," the stored procedures and views are good resources that every Notification Services developer and administrator should know about. Tables 15-4 and 15-5 list the stored procedures and views that are most useful for monitoring and troubleshooting.

Table 15-4   Notification Services Stored Procedures

Stored Procedure	Description
NSAdministrationHistory	Returns information about all applications hosted by the instance, including the events, notifications, and subscriptions processed during a specified time interval.

Table 15-4 Notification Services Stored Procedures Continued

Stored Procedure	Description
NSDiagnosticFailedNotifications	Contains a list of failed notification delivery attempts. Each row in the report includes the notification and subscription classes that produced the notification, the subscriber to which the notification would have been sent, and information about a delivery attempt.
NSEventBatchDetails	Returns detailed information about an event batch in an application. One resultset contains general information about the event batch, such as the event provider name and the time that the event batch was collected. A second resultset displays the events that were submitted in the event batch.
NSEventBatchList	Lists the event batches submitted by an event provider to an event class.
NSNotificationBatchDetails	Contains information about a specified notification batch, such as the rule firing that produced the batch and the notifications contained in the batch. Use this stored procedure to troubleshoot notification generation and to analyze the progression of notifications through the application.
NSNotificationBatchList	Lists the notification batches generated for a notification class.
NSScheduledSubscriptionDetails	Returns information about the subscriptions that are scheduled to be evaluated within a given time period. This stored procedure works only for scheduled subscriptions.
NSScheduledSubscriptionList	Contains information about all scheduled subscriptions for a given subscriber.

Stored Procedure	Description
NSSnapshotApplications	Provides information about all applications hosted by an instance of Notification Services.
NSSnapshotDeliveryChannels	Provides information about the current state of the delivery channels configured for an instance of Notification Services.
NSSnapshotEvents	Produces the events snapshot report. You can use this report to determine how long it has been since an event class has received events from an event provider.
NSSnapshotProviders	Produces the event providers snapshot report, which contains information about each event provider configured for an instance.
NSSnapshotSubscriptions	Produces the subscriptions snapshot report, which contains information about the most recent subscription addition for all subscription classes.
NSSubscriptionCondition Information	Returns the query used to evaluate a user-defined subscription.
NSVacuum	Manually removes older events, notifications, and related data from the application database.

Other stored procedures you might find yourself using to troubleshoot applications include a set of diagnostic stored procedures (NSDiagnostic*) that provide more detail than the snapshot stored procedures, and a set of quantum-related stored procedures (NSQuantum*) that provide detailed information about the generator, which produces notifications.

Table 15-5   Notification Services Views

View Name	Decscription
EventClassNameView	Contains the current set of events to be processed. In SQL Server 2005, this view is always available, and you can insert events into it.
NotificationClassNameView	Contains the current set of raw notification data, which you can use to review the notifications being processed by the application.
NSEventBatchView	Lists the event batches for all event classes in the application.
NSFullTimeZonesView	Lists the Notification Services time zones.
NSNotificationClassName NotificationDistributionView	Lists all delivery attempts for notifications of the associated notification class.
NSSubscriberDeviceView	Lists subscriber and subscriber device information for the instance. You can use this view to manage subscriber devices.
NSSubscriberView	List the subscribers to the instance of Notification Services. You can use this view to manage subscribers.
NSSubscriptionClassNameView	Lists all subscriptions for the associated subscription class. You can use this view to manage subscription data. However, if your application uses the new condition-based subscriptions or scheduled subscriptions, you cannot add subscriptions with this view.

Using SQL Server Management Studio Projects

For each instance of Notification Services, you may find that there is a specific set of queries or stored procedures that you frequently run. To make accessing these queries and stored procedures easier, you may want to create a SQL Server Management Studio solution for Notification Services, and within that solution create a project for each Notification

Services instance. Each project can contain saved queries, XML files, and other files related to that project. For more information about SQL Server Management Studio solutions, see Chapter 4.

API

Finally, you can develop your own tools with the Notification Services APIs. Examples of using the API are not included in this chapter, but SQL Server Books Online contains reference content and sample applications.

The NMO API

The Notification Services Management Objects (NMO) is a managed code API that enables you to define, deploy, and manage Notification Services instances and applications programmatically.

If you develop a Notification Services application with the NMO API, you can deploy that application with the NMO API. Otherwise, use the SQL Server Management Studio or NSControl tools.

However, you can manage an instance of Notification Services programmatically, no matter how you deployed the application. Table 15-6 lists the classes and methods used to manage Notification Services

Table 15-6 NMO Equivalents to Deployment and Management Tools

Class Name	Deployment and Management Methods
Instance Class	Create, Disable, DisableSubscribers, DisableSubscriptions, Drop, Enable, EnableSubscribers, EnableSubscriptions, Export, RegisterLocal, Repair, UnregisterLocal, Update
Application Class	Disable, DisableSubscriptions, Enable, EnableSubscriptions
Distributor, Generator, and Hosted EventProvider Classes	Enable, Disable

For more information about the classes in the NMO API, and the properties and methods that enable you to manage Notification Services, see the Microsoft.SqlServer.Management.Nmo namespace in SQL Server Books Online.

Notification Services Core API

The core Notification Services API is in the Microsoft.SqlServer.NotificationServices namespace. This API is primarily for developing custom event providers, content formatters, delivery protocols, and subscription management interfaces. However, this API also contains the `NSInstance` class, which enables you to start or stop an instance of Notification Services without using the NS$*instance_name* Windows service.

It is important to note that either the Windows service or a custom application can host an instance of Notification Services at any one time. In other words, if you are running an instance of Notification Services using the NS$*instance_name* Windows service, you must use the Windows service, not `NSInstance` class, to stop the instance.

For more information about the `NSInstance` class, see the Microsoft.SqlServer.NotificationServices namespace in SQL Server Books Online.

Other Tools

In addition to `NSControl`, SQL Server Management Studio, and custom tools, SQL Server 2005 and Microsoft Windows provide tools that can be helpful when managing instances of Notification Services, such as the Windows Event Viewer, SQL Server Configuration Manager, SQL Server Surface Area Configuration, and Windows Performance.

Windows Event Viewer

The Windows Event Viewer is one of the most important external tools when using Notification Services. Notification Services writes runtime errors to the Windows Application log, so the Event Viewer is the first place you should look if a Notification Services instance or application is not behaving as expected.

You can use Microsoft Operations Manager to monitor for Notification Services events. The *Management Pack for SQL Server 2005*, available from the Microsoft Download Center, contains rules for monitoring important Notification Services events.

SQL Server Configuration Manager and SQL Server Surface Area Configuration

SQL Server Configuration Manager and SQL Server Surface Area Configuration have different purposes: Configuration Manager is used to configure the services and protocols on the server. Surface Area Configuration helps you ensure that your server is running only those services, protocols, and features used by your applications. However, for Notification Services, you can use either of these tools to stop and start individual Windows services associated with an instance of Notification Services. This is most useful when an instance is located on a single computer, or when you want to stop one service in a scaled-out instance.

If you have a scaled-out instance, and you want to start or stop all Windows services associated with the instance, use the `Start` and `Stop` commands in SQL Server Management Studio.

Windows Performance

System Monitor, part of the Microsoft Windows Performance application, enables you to perform real-time monitoring of instance and application performance, using predefined performance objects that contain performance counters. System Monitor collects counts, rates, and averages about resources and processing, such as notification processing, system CPU activity, and database sizes.

When you register an instance of Notification Services, Notification Services installs performance counters. These performance counters fall into the following categories:

- Delivery channel, distributor, event provider, and generator counters provide information about these components on the local computer.

- Subscribers counters provide information about the subscribers for an instance of Notification Services.

- Subscription counters provide information about the subscriptions for an application.

- Event counters provide information about events for an application.

- Notification counters provide information about notifications created by an application.

- Vacuumer counters provide information about the data removal process.

The name of each performance counter begins with NS$*instance_name* and ends with the name of the object, such as NS$StockInstance: Delivery Channels.

Common Deployment and Management Scenarios

This section contains information about using the Notification Services tools to perform common deployment and management tasks. If the task can be performed with SQL Server Management Studio and NSControl, the instructions for performing the task with SQL Server Management Studio appear first, followed by instructions for performing the task with NSControl.

The primary tasks enabled by the tools are multi-step processes, such as deploying or updating an instance. These tasks also require steps that are not directly performed by the Notification Services tools. For completeness, those external steps are included when necessary.

NOTE
For simplicity and improved security, the following instructions use Windows Authentication. You can modify SQL Server Management Studio instructions to use SQL Server Authentication by providing a SQL Server login and password when registering instances of Notification Services. You can modify `NSControl` instructions to use SQL Server Authentication by adding the `sqlusername` and `sqlpassword` options on `NSControl` commands.

Deploying an Instance of Notification Services

Deploying an instance of Notification Services involves several steps: creating database objects, enabling the instance, registering the instance, and providing Windows and database access to the Notification Services engine (which is usually one or more Windows services), and then starting the engine.

Creating Database Objects and Enabling the Instance

Creating database objects requires you to connect to the instance of the SQL Server database engine where you want to store all instance and application data. For example, if you want to store instance and application data on the default instance on Server01, open SQL Server Management Studio and connect to Server01.

In Object Explorer, you should see a **Notification Services** folder. Right-click this folder and select **New Notification Services Instance**. In the dialog box that appears, click the **Browse** button and select the ICF for the instance you are deploying. Figure 15-5 shows what this dialog box looks like for an ICF named MyICF.xml.

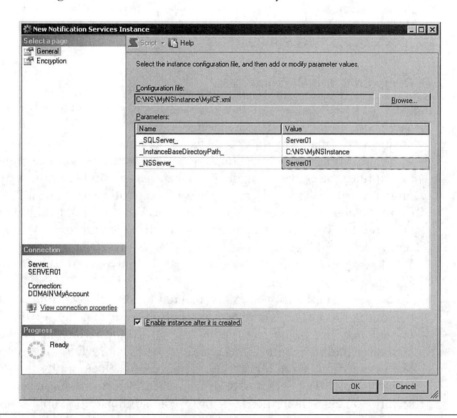

Figure 15-5   New Notification Services Instance dialog.

Notice that this ICF contains three parameters, which are values you define at deployment time. In the ICF, each parameter is surrounded by % characters, such as %_SQLServer_%. In this dialog, you provide the value with which to replace each parameter. Using the values shown, Notification Services replaces each occurrence of %_SQLServer_% (the database server name) with the value Server01, each occurrence of

`%_InstanceBaseDirectoryPath_%` (the base path to instance files) with `C:\NS\MyNSInstance`, and each occurrence of `%_NSServer_%` (the server where the Notification Services engine will run) with the value `Server01`.

Also notice that the **Enable instance after it is created check box** is selected. This is a shortcut. If you select this box, the instance is enabled during creation. However, the instance does not run until it is started.

When you click **OK**, Notification Services replaces parameters, validates the ICF and ADFs, and then creates instance and application database objects. After this process is complete, the instance appears in the Notification Services folder. (If not, right-click the Notification Services folder and select **Refresh**.)

Registering the Instance

Next, you need to register the instance. Registration adds information about the instance and its databases to the local Windows Registry and creates performance counters. Registration can also create a Windows service that runs the Notification Services engine. Unless you are running the Notification Services engine in your own application or process, you must create a Windows service on each computer that runs a hosted event provider, generator, or distributor. This Windows service always has an associated Windows account and password, which it uses for Windows permissions and it can also use for SQL Server access. If you cannot use Windows Authentication to connect to SQL Server, you can specify a SQL Server login and password.

As stated earlier, if you are connected to SQL Server from a client computer, the instance is registered on the client, not the server. This may or may not be correct, depending on the hosted event provider, generator, and distributor `SystemName` values in your ADFs. The bottom line is that you need to register the instance on each computer that runs an event provider, generator, or distributor, and also where you run subscription management interfaces or remote administration applications.

To register an instance of Notification Services on the local computer, right-click the instance, point to **Tasks**, and then select **Register**. The dialog box shown in Figure 15-6 appears.

If you create the Windows service, Notification Services grants most of the necessary Windows permissions to the service logon account, including membership in the `SQLServer2005NotificationServicesUser$Comput-erName` group. You may need to grant additional folder permissions so that the Notification Services engine can pick up events, read content formatter

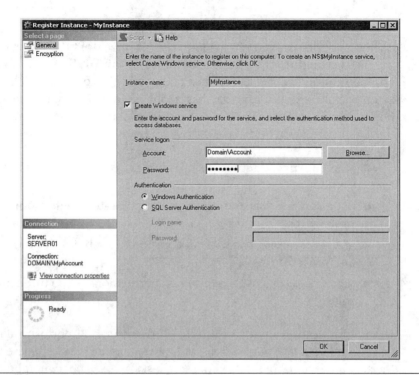

Figure 15-6 Register Instance dialog.

files, and drop notifications. The permissions are documented in the "Granting Windows Permissions" section.

Notification Services does not grant SQL Server permissions to the Windows account or to the optional SQL Server Authentication login. Registration is a process that can happen on several computers, and can be done before or after creating database objects. Also, SQL Server and database permissions should be restricted as much as possible. Therefore, you need to grant database permissions manually.

If you click **OK** with these options selected, Notification Services adds information to the local Registry, creates a Windows service with the specified credentials, and creates local performance counters.

Granting SQL Server Permissions

If using Windows Authentication, the Windows account that the Notification Services engine runs under needs permission to log in to the instance of SQL Server that stores instance and application data. If using

SQL Server Authentication, the SQL Server login associated with the engine needs permission to log in to the instance of SQL Server.

The account used by the engine to log in to SQL Server also needs a user account in each of its instance and application databases. This might be one database or multiple databases, depending on instance and application database settings. These user accounts obtain database permissions through Notification Services database roles:

- `NSEventProvider` has permissions on event-related objects and procedures.
- `NSGenerator` has permissions on generator-related objects and procedures.
- `NSDistributor` has permissions on distributor-related objects and procedures.
- `NSRunService` has the combined permissions of the three previous roles.

If an account used by a Notification Services engine performs all these tasks, grant database permissions with the `NSRunService` database role. If the account is used for a subset of these tasks, use selective membership in the `NSEventProvider`, `NSGenerator`, and `NSDistributor` roles to grant permissions.

For this deployment scenario, the instance is deployed on a single server, and uses Windows Authentication. The instance also uses the default database settings, meaning a new database is created for the instance and each application. Therefore, you need to grant database permissions in one instance database and each application database.

In SQL Server Management Studio, you can create logins and grant database permissions all in one dialog. First, use the Security folder in Object Explorer to make sure the account used by the Notification Services engine has a login account. To create a new login, right-click the **Security** folder, point to **New**, and then select **Login**. To modify an existing login, expand **Security**, expand **Logins**, right-click the login, and then select **Properties**. Both resulting dialog boxes look similar to Figure 15-7.

If creating a new login, enter the name of the login in the **Login name** box. The picture shows how to create a new Windows Authentication login named **DOMAIN\Account**.

To grant database access to DOMAIN\Account, click **User Mapping** in the left pane. For each database associated with the instance,

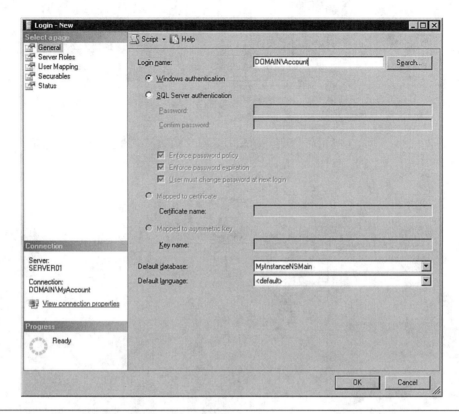

Figure 15-7   The Login dialog's General tab.

select the check box next to the database in the **Users mapped to this login** box, and then select **NSRunService** in the **Database role membership** box, as shown in Figure 15-8.

When you click **OK**, SQL Server creates any new login and user accounts and then grants the specified permissions.

Granting Windows Permissions

When you use Windows services to run instances of Notification Services, most Windows permissions are granted when you register the instance. Other permissions you need to grant depend on your applications. The following list shows the permissions typically required by the Notification Services engine:

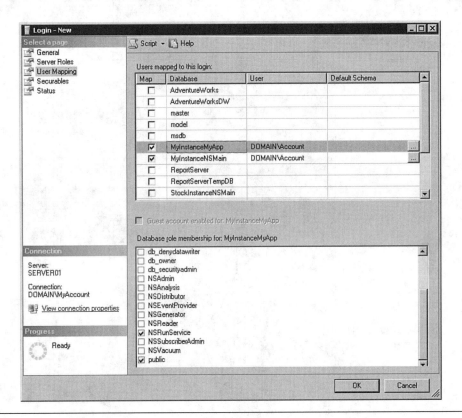

Figure 15-8   The Login dialog's User Mapping tab.

- Read and execute permissions in the Notification Services folder (%ProgramFiles%\Microsoft SQL Server\90\NotificationServices\n.n.nnn) and subfolders. By default, only members of the local Administrators and Power Users groups have access to the files within these folders. Notification Services grants these permissions to the Windows service account when you register the instance by adding the service account to the SQLServer2005NotificationServicesUser$*ComputerName* group.

- Permission to read and write Registry keys at the following Registry locations: HKEY_LOCAL_MACHINE\Software\Microsoft\Microsoft SQL Server\Services\NotificationServices and HKEY_LOCAL_MACHINE\System\CurrentControlSet\Services. This permission is granted to the Windows service account when you register the instance.

- Permission to write to the Windows application log. This permission is granted to the Windows service account when you register the instance.

- For applications using a file system watcher event provider, the event provider must be able to read and rename files in the folder where events are dropped, and must have read access to the event schema file (.xsd).

- For applications using a file delivery protocol to post notifications, the distributor must have write permissions in the folder where the notifications are written.

- For applications using the XSLT content formatter, the distributor must have permission to read the folders that contain the XSLT files. For more information, see XSLT File Locations.

- If an application hosted by the instance uses the local Internet Information Services (IIS) Simple Mail Transfer Protocol (SMTP) service to send notifications, the distributor must send those notifications in the context of an administrator.

Starting the Instance

In this deployment scenario, and in all situations in which the engine is run by one or more Windows services, you start the instance in SQL Server Management Studio by right-clicking the instance and selecting **Start**. This starts all Windows services associated with the instance.

If the instance fails to start, it is typically a problem with the account used to run the service. The account name and password might be mistyped. Or the account might not have the necessary SQL Server and Windows permissions. If the Windows services run on remote computers, make sure SQL Server is configured to accept remote connections. Also make sure the instance was registered with the correct instance of SQL Server and that the SQL Server instance and databases are online and available.

After starting the instance, check the status of all components by right-clicking the instance and selecting **Properties**. All components should be enabled, as shown in Figure 15-9.

If individual components have a current status of Enable Pending, it most likely means that there is a mismatch between the SystemName value specified in the ADF and the name of the system where the Notification

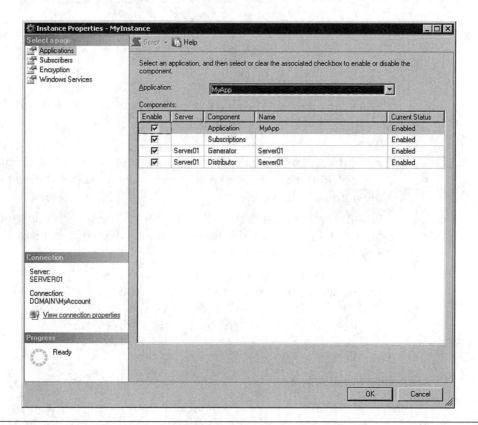

Figure 15-9   Instance Properties dialog.

Services engine is running. However, if you start the instance through SQL Server Management Studio, Notification Services attempts to start the Windows service on each computer specified as a SystemName value, and fails if the Windows service does not exist. Therefore, you are likely to know that something is wrong when a Windows service does not start. If this happens, look closely at the name of each server where Notification Services is attempting to start the instance and make sure it matches the server where you registered the instance.

You can verify that Windows services are running by clicking Windows Services in the left pane of the **Properties** window (see Figure 15-10).

Basic NSControl Deployment Script

Deploying through SQL Server Management Studio is easy, but sometimes you want to script a deployment for more consistent deployment

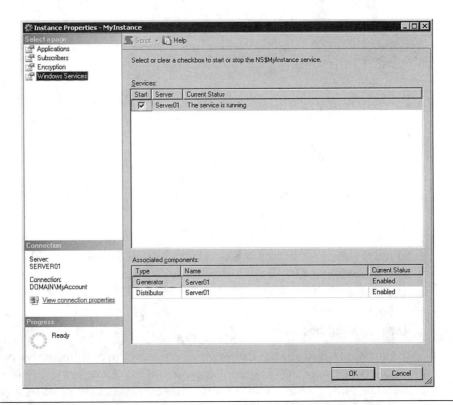

Figure 15-10 Windows Services and associated components.

and recovery experiences. The following script shows how to use the NSControl utility to do the same tasks as shown in the SQL Server Management Studio scenario. Note that you must have the Notification Services engine components installed to create a Windows service when registering an instance.

You should run this script once on the computer where the Notification Services engine will run. Separately register the instance on any additional computers.

```
nscontrol create -in "C:\NS\MyNSInstance\MyICF.xml"
  _SQLServer_=Server01
  _InstanceBaseDirectoryPath_="C:\NS\MyNSInstance"
  _NSServer_=Server01

nscontrol register -name MyInstance -server Server01 -service
➥  -serviceusername "DOMAIN\Account" -servicepassword "password"
nscontrol enable -name MyInstance
```

```
sqlcmd -E -S Server01 -Q "CREATE LOGIN [DOMAIN\Account]
➥   FROM WINDOWS;"

sqlcmd -E -S Server01 -Q "USE MyInstanceNSMain; CREATE USER
➥   [DOMAIN\Account]; EXEC sp_addrolemember
➥N'NSRunService',
➥ N'DOMAIN\Account';"

sqlcmd -E -S databaseServer -Q "USE MyInstanceMyApp;
➥   CREATE USER [DOMAIN\Account]; EXEC sp_addrolemember
➥NSRunService', N'DOMAIN\Account';"

net start NS$MyInstance
```

You may also need to grant Windows permissions for event providers, content formatters, and distributors. Because these permissions are very application-specific, granting them is not shown in the preceding example.

Argument Encryption

You may have noticed the **Encryption** pages in the Notification Services dialog boxes and the `argumentkey` options in `NSControl`. When you define event providers and delivery channels, you may need to specify sensitive information such as server names, logins, and passwords. To keep this information out of your files, you can use parameters, as shown in the deployment scenario. However, unless you use argument encryption, the sensitive information is stored in clear text in the database. If you want to encrypt this information before storing the values, you can set the `EncryptArguments` property to `true` in the ICF and then provide an encryption key when creating and registering the instance. You must also provide this key when updating the instance. The key is a string of up to 2500 characters that will be encrypted and stored in the Windows Registry and in the instance database.

Scale-Out Considerations

If you are running hosted event providers, generators, or distributors on one or more remote servers, you must install the Notification Services client components and then register the instance on those servers to create the Windows service, Registry entries, and performance counters.

If you are running a subscription management interface, non-hosted event providers, or remote administration tools, or are hosting the Notification Services engine on other servers, you must install the Notification Services client components and then register the instance (without creating the Windows service) on those computers.

High-Availability Options

Notification Services supports failover clustering, log shipping, and database mirroring for high availability. Step-by-step instructions for deploying an instance of Notification Services on a failover cluster are provided in SQL Server Books Online. You can use log shipping and database mirroring to maintain a warm standby database server in case the primary database server experiences a failure.

When deploying the Notification Services engine failover cluster, you register the instance on all nodes of the cluster and then create a Generic Service to handle failovers of the Windows service. When defining an application that runs on a failover cluster, the `SystemName` values must be the network name (which is the virtual server name), not the machine name. If the `SystemName` values are not correct, the instance gets stuck in the Enable Pending state.

Using log shipping or database mirroring maintains a warm standby database server. To bring a standby server online, you must re-register the instance to update the name of the database server, and you must update the instance and its applications to update the database server name and the name of the computer where the hosted event providers, generators, and distributors run. You may want to keep standby copies of the ICF and ADFs available with the updated system names so that you can update the instance and its applications quickly. However, be sure that the ICF and ADFs are up to date.

Upgrading an Instance from SQL Server 2000 to SQL Server 2005

Each version of Notification Services is tied to its specific release of SQL Server. Notification Services 2.0 requires SQL Server 2000 databases. SQL Server 2005 Notification Services requires SQL Server 2005 databases.

If you deployed an instance of Notification Services on SQL Server 2000, and you want to upgrade to SQL Server 2005, you must upgrade the instances of Notification Services. Upgrading instances of Notification Services upgrades database objects, adds new views and stored procedures, and removes dependence on extended stored procedures.

Upgrading requires you to prepare the instance, install SQL Server 2005, upgrade the instance, update the instance, recompile any custom components, and then enable and start the instance.

Preparing an Instance for Upgrading

Before you can upgrade an instance of Notification Services, you must disable, stop, and unregister the instance. In Notification Services 2.0, these tasks are done through the Notification Services Command Prompt.

First, open the Notification Services 2.0 command prompt by clicking **Start**, pointing to **All Programs**, pointing to **Microsoft SQL Server Notification Services 2.0**, and then selecting **Notification Services Command Prompt**.

At the command prompt, run the following three commands:

```
nscontrol disable -name MyInstance
net stop ns$MyInstance
nscontrol unregister -name MyInstance
```

If the instance is scaled out across multiple servers, you must run the `net stop` and `nscontrol unregister` commands on the additional servers. After running these commands, you can close the command prompt window.

After unregistering the instance, you should back up all databases used for instance and application data. Having backups enables you to revert back to SQL Server 2000 if necessary.

Installing SQL Server 2005

The next step in the upgrade process is to upgrade the SQL Server 2000 database engine to SQL Server 2005 and install SQL Server 2005 Notification Services. The database engine can be upgraded in place. Notification Services is installed side by side with previous versions, which allows some flexibility in how you upgrade, especially on client computers.

Before upgrading the database engine, you should run SQL Server 2005 Upgrade Advisor, which reports any issues that might prevent you from upgrading or that might cause differences in how applications operate. Fix any issues reported, and then upgrade the database engine and install Notification Services by running SQL Server 2005 Setup. (Notification Services will report that you need to perform the steps in the following sections.)

Also make sure you install SQL Server 2005 Notification Services on any computer that runs components of the Notification Services instance, including event providers, generators, distributors, subscription management interfaces, and remote administration consoles.

After running Setup, make sure you start the database engine so that it is ready for the next upgrade steps.

Upgrading the Instance

After installing SQL Server 2005, you need to run a repair command to add some metadata about the instance to the msdb database. This metadata is added when you use SQL Server 2005 to deploy an instance, but does not exist for instances deployed with SQL Server 2000. One way Notification Services uses this data is to display Notification Services instances within Object Explorer.

Repairing instance metadata is an infrequent task that is typically done only when you upgrade from SQL Server 2000. For this reason, the repair command is available only in the NSControl command-line utility.

To run the repair command, open the SQL Server 2005 Notification Services command prompt by clicking **Start**, pointing to **All Programs**, pointing to **Microsoft SQL Server 2005**, point to **Configuration Tools**, and then selecting **Notification Services Command Prompt**.

At the command prompt, run the following command:

```
nscontrol repair -name MyInstance -database MyInstanceNSMain
➥-schema dbo -server Server01
```

During the upgrade step, Notification Services updates the instances version and edition information with the version and edition of the toolset you are using. (So, to upgrade to SQL Server 2005 Enterprise Edition, you need to use the SQL Server 2005 Enterprise Edition tools.)

We're going to switch back to SQL Server Management Studio, where we can perform most of the remaining upgrade tasks. (You can also perform these tasks from a command prompt window.)

First, open SQL Server 2005 Management Studio and connect to the instance of Notification Services that contains the instance and application data. When connected, you should see a Notification Services folder in Object Explorer. When you expand this folder, you should see your instance of Notification Services. However, the instance will appear with a warning symbol. The warning symbol indicates that the instance's version information is incorrect, which will be fixed when you perform the upgrade step.

To upgrade, right-click the instance of Notification Services and select **Upgrade**. Notification Services compares the version and edition information in the instance database with the version and edition of the current toolset. If the instance is of a lower version or edition than the toolset, Notification Services upgrades the instance.

NOTE
Upgrading changes instance version and edition information, but does not apply any user-defined ICF or ADF changes to an instance. If you want to change any instance or application settings, such as SystemName values, you must do this when you *update* the instance.

Modifying Subscription Rules

In Notification Services 2.0, subscription rules used a Notify function to generate notifications. For example, a rule might use a Notify function as follows:

```
SELECT dbo.FlightNotificationsNotify(S.SubscriberId,
S.DeviceName, S.SubscriberLocale, E.Carrier, E.LeavingFrom,
E.GoingTo, E.Price, E.Conditions)
    FROM FlightEvents E, FlightSubscriptions S
    WHERE E.LeavingFrom = S.LeavingFrom
    AND E.GoingTo = S.GoingTo
    AND ( (E.Carrier = S.Carrier) OR (S.Carrier = '*') )
    AND E.Price &lt; S.Price
```

SQL Server 2005 Notification Services does not use Notify functions. When you upgrade to SQL Server 2005, you will need to modify your subscription rules to insert notifications directly into a view named after the notification class and then update the instance to apply the changes. The following code shows how this rule would be modified as follows to insert notifications into the `FlightNotifications` notifications class:

```
INSERT INTO FlightNotifications(SubscriberId, DeviceName,
SubscriberLocale, Carrier, LeavingFrom, GoingTo, Price,
Conditions)
SELECT S.SubscriberId, S.DeviceName, S.SubscriberLocale,
E.Carrier, E.LeavingFrom, E.GoingTo, E.Price, E.Conditions
    FROM FlightEvents E, FlightSubscriptions S
    WHERE E.LeavingFrom = S.LeavingFrom
    AND E.GoingTo = S.GoingTo
    AND ( (E.Carrier = S.Carrier) OR (S.Carrier = '*') )
    AND E.Price &lt; S.Price
```

At this time, you can also make any other desired changes to your instance and application definitions.

Updating the Instance

After you have modified your subscription rules to replace the Notify function with INSERT statements, you need to apply those changes.

In Object Explorer, right-click the instance of Notification Services, point to **Tasks**, and select **Update** to display the Update Instance dialog. Just as with the **New Instance** dialog, you must click the **Browse** button, select your ICF, provide values for any parameters, and then select the **Enable instance after it is updated** box (see Figure 15-11).

When you click **OK**, Notification Services examines the ICF and its referenced ADFs, compares them to the metadata in the database objects for the instance and its applications, and then presents a screen that summarizes the changes to the instance and its applications (see Figure 15-12).

NOTE

Updating can take a several minutes because of the way underlying APIs compare the data in the XML to data in the database objects.

When you click the **Update** button, Notification Services applies the changes.

Recompiling Custom Components

If your instance uses custom event providers, content formatters, or delivery protocols, recompile those components with the SQL Server 2005 assemblies.

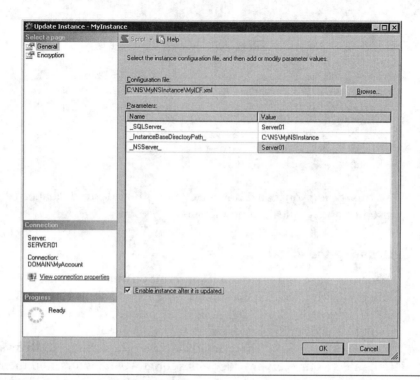

Figure 15-11   Update Instance dialog.

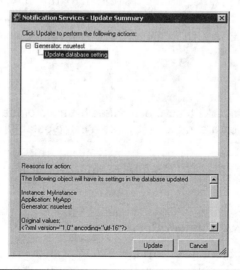

Figure 15-12   Update Summary dialog.

Registering and Starting the Instance

When you re-register the instance, use the same settings and values as you use with SQL Server 2000. Re-registering updates the Registry for SQL Server 2005 binary files.

To register the instance locally, right-click the instance, point to **Tasks**, and select **Register**. To register the instance on other servers, you either need to run SQL Server Management Studio on those servers, or run the `nscontrol register` command, using the SQL Server 2005 version of the Notification Services Command Prompt.

After you register the instance, right-click the instance and select **Start**.

Upgrading Using NSControl

Many of the tasks required to upgrade an instance of Notification Services from version 2.0 to SQL Server 2005 must be done in `NSControl`. The tasks shown as being done in SQL Server Management Studio can be replaced with the corresponding `NSControl` command. Just be sure to perform the initial disable, stop, and unregister commands with the Notification Services 2.0 version of the Notification Services Command Prompt, and to perform the repair, upgrade, update, register, and enable tasks in the SQL Server 2005 version of the Notification Services Command Prompt.

Upgrading to a Different Edition of SQL Server 2005

If you upgrade an instance of SQL Server 2005 to a different edition, such as upgrading an instance from Developer Edition to Enterprise Edition, you must also upgrade instances of Notification Services. The version and edition of the database engine must match the version and edition of Notification Services.

Notification Services supports the following SQL Server 2005 edition upgrades:

- Evaluation Edition to Standard Edition, Developer Edition, or Enterprise Edition.
- Developer Edition to Standard Edition or Enterprise Edition.
- Standard Edition to Evaluation Edition, Developer Edition, or Enterprise Edition.

Upgrading Editions Using Management Studio

To upgrade an instance of Notification Services to a different edition of SQL Server 2005, you must first disable and stop the instance. In SQL Server Management Studio, right-click the instance and select **Disable**, and then right-click the instance and select **Stop**.

Next, install the new edition of SQL Server 2005, making sure to upgrade both the database engine and Notification Services. If you have scaled out instances of Notification Services, make sure to install the new edition on each server.

After the installation is complete, open the upgraded edition of SQL Server Management Studio and connect to the instance of SQL Server that contains instance and application data. In Object Explorer, right-click the instance, point to **Tasks**, and then select **Upgrade**. It is important that you use the new edition to do this, as the upgrade command uses the tool's version and edition information to determine the new version and edition of the instance.

After performing the upgrade, right-click the instance, point to **Tasks**, and select **Update**. In the Update Instance dialog, select the ICF, provide any parameter values, and select **Enable instance after it is updated**. When you click **OK**, Notification Services examines the instance and then displays the Update Summary dialog. Click **Update** to complete the update.

When the update is complete (which can take several minutes), right-click the instance and select **Start**.

Using NSControl to Upgrade Editions

The tasks required to upgrade an instance of Notification Services to a different edition can be done from the command line. Replace the disable, upgrade, update, and enable steps with their NSControl commands. Replace the stop and start steps with net stop and net start.

Viewing the Notification Services Summary Report

For a quick view of the state of the instances on an instance of SQL Server, you can use a simple report that gathers data about your Notification Services instances.

Using Management Studio to View Summary Information

To view the Notification Services summary report, first make sure the Summary window is available. If not, select **Summary** from the **View** menu. In Object Explorer, select **Notification Services**. Then, in the **Summary** window, click Report.

SQL Server Management Studio generates a report similar to that shown in Figure 15-13, which shows the instance names along with some key instance details.

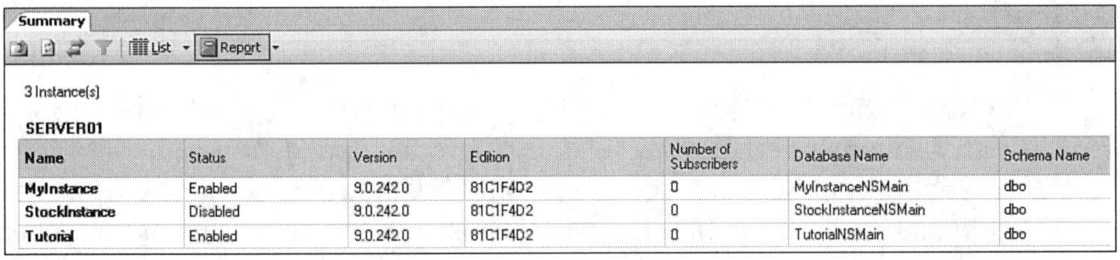

Name	Status	Version	Edition	Number of Subscribers	Database Name	Schema Name
MyInstance	Enabled	9.0.242.0	81C1F4D2	0	MyInstanceNSMain	dbo
StockInstance	Disabled	9.0.242.0	81C1F4D2	0	StockInstanceNSMain	dbo
Tutorial	Enabled	9.0.242.0	81C1F4D2	0	TutorialNSMain	dbo

3 Instance(s)

SERVER01

Figure 15-13 Notification Services summary report.

Using NSControl to View Summary Information

NSControl does not produce a cross-instance summary report. However, you can view the status of individual instances by using the `nscontrol status` command. For example, to view the status of MyInstance, run the following command:

```
nscontrol status -name MyInstance
```

Enabling, Disabling, Starting, and Stopping

After you deploy an instance of Notification Services, you must enable and start the instance. Enabling allows a component to run. Starting the instance runs enabled components. An instance must be both enabled and started for the instance and its applications to process data.

After you deploy an instance, you may need to temporarily halt processing for maintenance or other reasons. Your two options are disabling the instance, application, or components, or stopping the instance:

■ Disabling is like pausing, but with options. The disable command can pause an instance, application, event provider, generator, or distributor, whereas pausing a Windows service pauses the entire instance. When disabled, the component shuts itself down in an orderly manner and resumes when enabled.

- The Notification Services engine can take up to 30 seconds to pick up a change in the enabled/disabled state.
- Stopping happens at the instance level, and you do so by stopping Windows services that run the instance (or any other process that is hosting the Notification Services engine). Stopping halts all processing. SQL Server rolls back any uncompleted transactions.
- Whenever possible, it is best to disable an instance before stopping it.

Notification Services recovers from an instance being disabled or stopped by using its internal clock to start where it stopped. You can control how Notification Services processes older data when restarted by setting "quantum limits," which enables the instance to skip old events and scheduled subscriptions. For more information, see SQL Server Books Online.

If you need to disable an entire application or stop an instance, you can use a process like the following to allow the instance or application to finish processing any current data before it or its components are paused or stopped:

1. Disable all event providers and then wait for the generator to pick up all event batches. The duration depends on the generator's quantum interval setting.
2. Disable the generator and then wait for the distributors to process all notifications. Because of possible delivery failures and retry intervals, this might not be reasonable. But you may want to wait until the distributor has attempted to deliver the notifications.
3. Disable all distributors.
4. If stopping the instance, stop the Windows services or other processes that host the engine.

You can use the NSAdministrationHistory stored procedure to obtain information about event batches pending generation, notification batches pending distribution, and distribution work items in process.

If an instance, application, or component is stopped without following this process, the instance, application, or component recovers and starts processing either where it left off or at the current processing quantum minus the specified quantum limit. The preceding process is simply a recommendation if you want current notifications to move through the "queue" before you perform maintenance activities. Also, to minimize the impact on subscribers, you should attempt to perform maintenance during periods of low activity.

Enabling and Disabling an Instance Using Management Studio

To enable an instance of Notification Services in SQL Server Management Studio, right-click the instance and select **Enable**. To disable an instance, right-click the instance and then select **Disable**.

Enabling and Disabling an Application or Component Using Management Studio

To change the state of an individual application or component in SQL Server Management Studio, use the Instance Properties dialog. To display the Instance Properties dialog, right-click the instance and select **Properties** (see Figure 15-14).

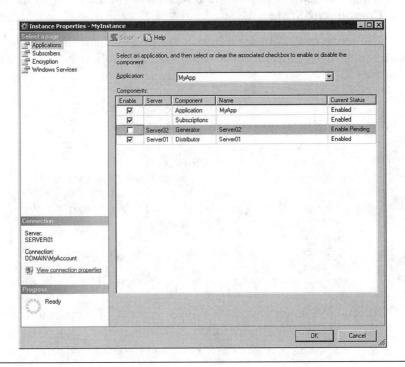

Figure 15-14 Enable and disable, using the Properties dialog.

Select the application to configure in the **Application** box. You can enable the entire application, or you can individually enable its subscriptions, event providers, generator, or distributor by selecting the corresponding **Enable** boxes. You can disable the application or individual components by clearing the **Enable** boxes. Apply changes by clicking the **OK** button.

To enable or disable subscriber management for the instance, select the **Subscribers** page and then select or clear the **Enable** box.

In Figure 15.14, the application, its subscriptions, and its distributor will be enabled and the generator will be disabled when you click **OK**.

Note the Enable Pending state in the picture. If a component is in a "pending" state, the Notification Services engine has not acknowledged the change in state. As stated earlier, it can take up to 30 seconds to pick up the change in state. If the component is stuck in a pending state, there may be a mismatch between where the component is configured to run and the actual name of the computer (or virtual server) where the engine is running.

Using NSControl to Disable and Enable Instance, Application, or Component State

The `NSControl` command line utility provides enable and disable commands. The syntax for these commands is as follows:

```
nscontrol [en|dis]able
    [-nologo] [-help]
    [< component > [...n]]
     -name instanceName
    [-server databaseServer]
    [-application applicationName]
    [-sqlusername sqlUserName -sqlpassword sqlPassword]

where < component > is one or more of the following:
    -events [systemName]
    | -generator
    | -distributor [systemName]
    | -subscriptions
    | -subscribers
```

To disable the generator for the application MyApp in instance MyInstance, you would run the following command:

```
nscontrol disable -name MyInstance -application MyApp -generator
```

When you are ready to enable the generator, you would run the following command:

```
nscontrol enable -name MyInstance -application MyApp -generator
```

Starting and Stopping Windows Services in Management Studio

If you are using Windows services to run your instances of Notification Services, you can stop and start Windows services associated with an instance of Notification Services by using SQL Server Management Studio. To start all services associated with an instance, right-click the instance and select **Start** (see Figure 15-15). To stop all services, right-click the instance and select **Stop**.

Figure 15-15   Starting all Windows services for an instance.

You can also start and stop individual Windows services by using the Instance Properties dialog. To display the Windows Services settings in this dialog, right-click the instance and select Properties, and then in the left pane select Windows Services. Figure 15-16 shows the Windows Services for an instance that is scaled out over two servers, Server02 and Server01:

To start the service on Server02, select the **Start** check box and then click the **OK** button. Or, to stop the service on Server01, clear the **Start** check box and then click the **OK** button.

Starting and Stopping from the Command Prompt

NSControl does not start and stop Windows services. However, you can start and stop individual Windows services by using the net start and net stop Windows commands. The Notification Services engine is named

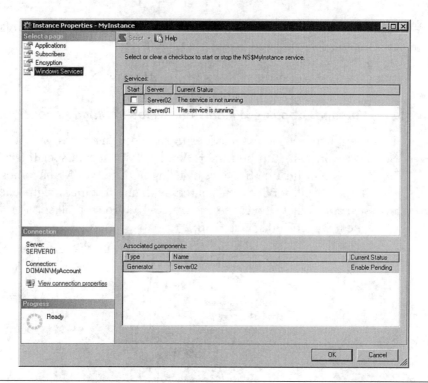

Figure 15-16 Starting individual Windows services, using the Properties dialog.

NS$*instance_name*. The following examples show how to start and stop a Windows service for the MyInstance Notification Services instance.

```
net start ns$MyInstance
```

```
net stop ns$MyInstance
```

Updating an Instance of Notification Services

Whenever you want to modify an instance of Notification Services, such as adding a new application, you must perform a set of steps to update the instance. During the update, Notification Services examines the ICF and ADF files, compares the settings to metadata stored in the instance and application database objects, and then applies the differences to the database objects.

Before you perform the update steps, make your changes to the ICF and ADFs. For example, you might add a delivery channel and application in the ICF, and you might change the application execution settings in the ADF.

Also make sure to back up instance and application databases. Many changes made to event classes, notification classes, or subscription classes cause Notification Services to delete and re-create the underlying database tables. Backing up databases before updating enables you to undo any changes by restoring pre-update data.

Updating Using Management Studio

First, open SQL Server Management Studio and connect to the instance of SQL Server that contains the instance and application data. In Object Explorer, expand **Notification Services** to display all the Notification Services instances on the server.

Next, you need to disable the instance before you can update it. Updating fails on an enabled instance. To disable the instance, right-click the instance and select **Disable**.

After the instance is disabled, you can apply the changes you made to the ICF and ADFs. Right-click the instance of Notification Services, point to **Tasks**, and select **Update**.

In the Update Instance dialog, click the **Browse** button, select your ICF, provide values for any parameters, and then select the **Enable instance after it is updated** box (see Figure 15-17).

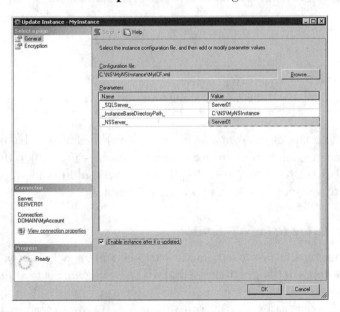

Figure 15-17 Update Instance dialog.

When you click **OK**, Notification Services examines the ICF and its referenced ADFs, compares them to the metadata in the database objects for
the instance and its applications, and then presents a screen that summarizes the changes to the instance and its applications (see Figure 15-18).

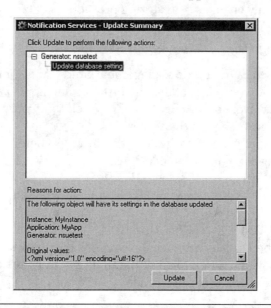

Figure 15-18 Update Summary Dialog.

NOTE
Updating can take a several minutes.

At the Update Summary screen, review the changes. To make the listed
changes, click the **Update** button. Because you enabled the instance via
the Update Instance dialog, there are no additional steps to perform.
The instance has been updated and enabled.

Updating Using NSControl

The steps for using NSControl to update an instance can be derived from
the steps in the previous section. First, run nscontrol disable to disable
the instance. Then run nscontrol update to apply ICF and ADF changes
to the databases. Finally, run nscontrol enable to enable the instance.

Updating Registry Information

When you register an instance of Notification Services, you specify the name of the database server where the instance (and application) data is stored. The Notification Services engine, subscription management interfaces, and other components use this information to access the instance and application data.

If you specify creation of a Windows service during registration, you also supply a Windows account and password for the service, and optionally a SQL Server Authentication login and password. If any of this information changes, you must update the Registry information. The Windows service uses these accounts to connect to the database server.

In SQL Server 2005, updating Registry information requires you to unregister the instance and then register it again.

It is important to note that SQL Server Management Studio registers the instance locally and uses the name of the SQL Server instance to which you are connected as the database server. If these values are not correct, you should use the NSControl command line utility to unregister and register the instance.

Using Management Studio to Update the Registry

First, stop the instance of Notification Services. To stop all Windows services associated with the instance, right-click the instance and select **Stop**. To stop an individual Windows service in a scaled-out instance, right-click the instance, select **Properties**, clear the service's check box on the **Windows Services** page, and then click **OK**.

After stopping the service, right-click the instance, point to **Tasks**, and select **Unregister** (see Figure 15-19).

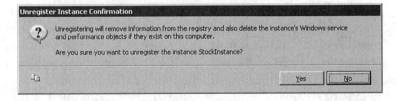

Figure 15-19   Unregistration confirmation.

When you click the **Yes** button, Notification Services removes the instance's information from the Windows Registry.

To re-register the instance, point to **Tasks** and select **Register** (see Figure 15-20).

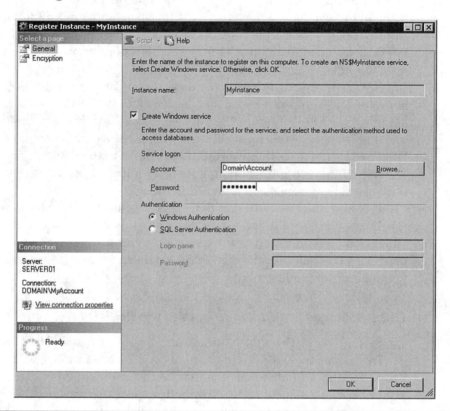

Figure 15-20 Register Instance dialog.

If you use the Windows service to run the Notification Services engine, and the local computer runs a hosted event provider, generator, or distributor, check the **Create Windows service** box and supply a service logon account and password. If you use SQL Server Authentication for connections to SQL Server, select **SQL Server Authentication** and supply a login and password. Remember that the account used to connect to SQL Server must have the permissions outlined in the "Deploying an Instance of Notification Services" section of this chapter.

SQL Server Management Studio registers the instance locally (on the server where you are running SQL Server Management Studio), using the current SQL Server instance as the database server name.

After the instance is registered on all computers where it needs to be registered, you can start all Windows services associated with the instance by right-clicking the instance and selecting **Start**.

Using the NSControl to Update the Registry

When using NSControl, use nscontrol unregister to delete existing registry information and then use nscontrol register to re-register the instance.

Exporting Instance and Application Metadata

In SQL Server 2005, you can export the instance and application metadata from the instance and application databases, creating new copies of the ICF and all ADFs.

The nscontrol export command does not recreate the original ICF and ADFs. It creates files that contain the current instance and application definition, including values that may have been provided through replaceable parameters. If you want to maintain the parameters in your files, you should keep the original ICF and ADFs.

You can export metadata while the instance is running. You do not need to disable or stop the instance.

Using Management Studio to Export Metadata

SQL Server Management Studio uses the current Microsoft Windows locale setting to export the metadata to its XML editor. You can then modify these files and save them.

To export instance and application metadata, right-click the instance of Notification Services, point to **Tasks**, and select **Export to Editor**. Notification Services opens one XML Editor window for the ICF and one window per ADF, as shown in Figure 15-21.

In the SQL Server Management Services XML editor, you can use Dynamic Help to access reference documentation. Put the cursor in an XML element (such as EventClasses, as shown above), and relevant help topics are displayed in the Dynamic Help pane. To display the Dynamic Help pane, click the **Help** menu and then select **Dynamic Help**.

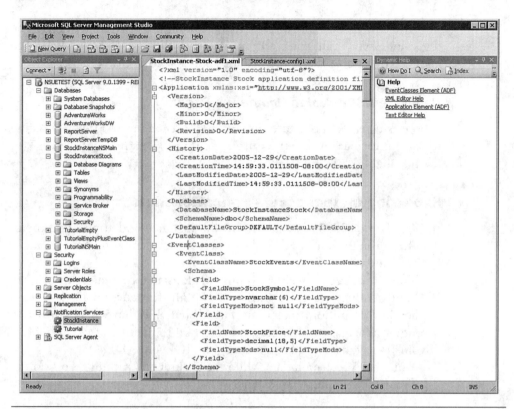

Figure 15-21   SQL Server Management Studio, the XML Editor, and Dynamic Help.

Using the Command Prompt to Export Metadata

You also can export metadata with NSControl. The nscontrol export command writes the files using UTF-8 encoding. To export the configuration and application definition files using other encodings, use SQL Server Management Studio.

Use the following command to export instance and application data with NSControl, overwriting any existing files that have the same names:

```
nscontrol export -name MyInstance -out "C:\NS\MyNSInstance"
-force
```

The resulting ICF is named *instance_name*-config.xml. Each resulting ADF is named *instance_name-application_name*-adf.xml.

Configuring Logging Levels

Notification Services uses configurable logging levels to determine what is written to the Windows Application log. You can control the logging level of an instance of Notification Services by editing the NSservice.exe.config configuration file. The file, which has a default location of C:\Program Files\Microsoft SQL Server\90\NotificationServices\9.0.242\bin, is XML and uses the following format:

```
<?xml version="1.0" encoding="UTF-8"?>
<!--
    The default logging levels for all components is Warning
    Off = 0 < Error = 1 < Warning = 2 < Info = 3 < Verbose = 4

    Change the values of the value attribute to change the
    logging level.

    Setting the logging level enables all log events that are
    less than or equal to the log level setting
-->
<configuration>
    <system.diagnostics>
        <switches>
            <add name="LogAdministrative" value="2"/>
            <add name="LogService" value="2"/>
            <add name="LogEventProvider" value="2"/>
            <add name="LogEventCollector" value="2"/>
            <add name="LogGenerator" value="2"/>
            <add name="LogDistributor" value="2"/>
            <add name="LogVacuumer" value="2"/>
            <add name="LogOther" value="2"/>
            <add name="LogPerformanceMonitor" value="2"/>
        </switches>
    </system.diagnostics>
</configuration>
```

As the file says, you can set the logging level between 0 and 4. The default level is 2 for all switches. Zero turns off all logging, and 4 logs errors, warnings, information, and all status messages.

SQL Server Books Online says that you can set the logging level per instance. This is true, but a bit impractical. When you start an instance of Notification Services, the instance reads the local configuration file and uses those settings until the service is restarted. To control logging at a per-instance level, you would need to separately document the settings and then make sure to update the configuration file prior to each time you start the instance.

It may be better to simply set a reasonable logging level for all instances that run on a particular computer. If you scale out an instance of Notification Services, you can customize the logging level on each computer. However, you also must monitor events on each computer.

Removing Obsolete Data

When a Notification Services application runs, it accumulates event, notification, and operational data in its application database objects. This data can cause tables to grow very large, and can affect application performance.

The best way to remove obsolete application data is to define a vacuuming schedule in each application definition. This schedule determines the retention age for data and how often Notification Services should remove obsolete data, as shown in the following example:

```
<Vacuum>
    <RetentionAge>P3DT00H00M00S</RetentionAge>
    <VacuumSchedule>
        <Schedule>
            <StartTime>23:00:00</StartTime>
            <Duration>P0DT02H00M00S</Duration>
        </Schedule>
        <Schedule>
            <StartTime>03:00:00</StartTime>
            <Duration>P0DT02H00M00S</Duration>
        </Schedule>
    </VacuumSchedule>
</Vacuum>
```

In this example, events are obsolete when they reach the retention age of three days. Notifications are obsolete after the retention age is reached and if the notifications have been delivered or have no future retry attempts. The vacuuming process runs at 23:00 and 3:00 in Coordinated Universal Time (UTC), for two hours each.

You might inherit applications that do not have a vacuuming interval configured. (You can verify this by exporting instance and application metadata and looking for a `Vacuum` element with `RetentionAge` and `VacuumSchedule` child elements.)

If there is no vacuuming schedule, or if you need to remove data between vacuuming intervals, you can manually run the NSVacuum stored procedure in each application database. For example, to run the vacuuming process for a duration of five minutes (300 seconds), you can run the following stored procedure:

```
Use MyAppDatabase;
EXEC MyAppSchema.NSVacuum 300;
```

If you need to save all event and/or notification data, make sure to run your archiving process, such as an Integration Services package, before vacuuming.

Deleting an Instance of Notification Services

Deleting an instance of Notification Services drops all database objects associated with the instance and its applications. If Notification Services created new databases for the instance, those databases are dropped. If Notification Services created database objects within existing databases, only the database objects created by Notification Services are dropped.

Deleting an Instance in Management Studio

In Object Explorer, right-click the instance and select **Disable**, and then right-click the instance and select **Stop**. (If you are hosting the engine in your own application or process, stop the instance through your application or process.)

After the instance is stopped, unregister the instance. If the instance is registered on the computer where you are running SQL Server Management Studio, unregister the instance by right-clicking the instance, pointing to **Tasks**, and then selecting **Unregister**. Otherwise, unregister the instance by using nscontrol unregister.

To drop instance and application database objects, right-click the instance, point to **Tasks**, and then select **Delete**. If Notification Services created the databases, the databases are dropped. Otherwise, only the instance and application objects are dropped.

Using NSControl to Delete an Instance

If you want to use a command-line script to delete an instance, first run nscontrol disable. Then, run net stop and nscontrol unregister on each computer where the instance is registered. Finally, delete the instance by using `nscontrol delete`. You can run the `nscontrol disable` and `nscontrol delete` commands from any computer that has the Notification Services client components.

For More Information

SQL Server Books Online contains conceptual and reference information about Notification Services, as well as a tutorial that builds a basic notification application. Much of the conceptual content was rewritten for this release, and there are now examples in most (if not all) of the XML references.

Books Online is very large, and content tends to be spread across several sections. One good way to find all the Notification Services information is to use filters. To filter the content for Notification Services, first make sure the Contents tab is displayed by selecting **Contents** from the **Help** menu. At the top of the Contents pane is a box named **Filtered By**. In this box, select **SQL Server Notification Services**. When you select this filter, the information in the Contents tab (and also the Index tab) is restricted to information about Notification Services plus information that is applicable across all or most SQL Server components. Figure 15-22 shows Books Online with the filter selected.

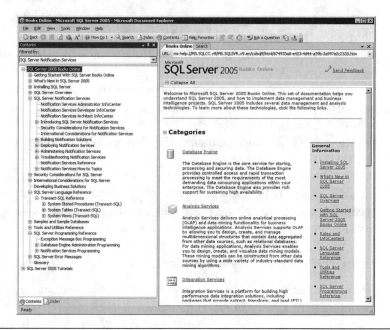

Figure 15-22   Filtered contents in SQL Server Books Online.

I recommend you start with the Notification Services tutorial (but you might want to skip the step of updating the instance on lessons three through seven to save some time) and then use the "SQL Server Notification Services" section to fill in the holes and expand your knowledge. I also recommend using the "Deploying Notification Services" subsection if you need to scale out an instance or use failover clustering. Also, there are several sample applications in the "Samples and Sample Databases" section of Books Online.

In addition to Books Online, the book *Microsoft SQL Server 2005 Notification Services*, by Shyam Pather (Sams Publishing: Indianapolis, 2006), is very good. It focuses on developing Notification Services applications, but it also provides information about deploying and managing instances of Notification Services. It's good information from an insider on the development team.

Summary

Using SQL Server Notification Services, you can quickly create applications that generate and send notifications based on the preferences of subscribers. SQL Server 2005 enhances the NSControl command line toolset available for deploying and managing instances of Notification Services, and also provides a new graphical user interface for most of these commands via SQL Server Management Studio.

This chapter provided information about the NSControl commands and the Notification Services functionality in SQL Server Management Studio, and then showed how to use these tools to perform tasks in common Notification Services scenarios. Using this information, you should be able to easily and effectively deploy and manage your Notification Services applications or the sample applications provided with SQL Server 2005.

CHAPTER 16

Inside Integration Services Tools

SQL Server 2005 introduces a new extract transform load (ETL) component, Integration Services. Integration Services replaces Data Transformation Services (DTS), first introduced in SQL Server 7.0 and enhanced in SQL Server 2000. However, Integration Services is not a new and improved version of DTS; instead, Integration Services is redesigned and rebuilt from the ground up. This means a new and very different object model, an expansive application programming interface (API) for programming the object model, and a plethora of graphical tools and wizards to create the packages that comprise an ETL solution. This includes the SQL Server Import and Export Wizard to quickly build a simple package that extracts and loads data; SSIS Designer to create complex packages with multiple inputs and outputs, in-line business intelligence, and data cleaning capabilities; tools to implement logging, configurations, updatable properties, and variables in packages; and finally, the tools to deploy the ETL solution.

In SQL Server 7.0 and SQL Server 2000, the Microsoft Management Console (MMC) snap-in, Enterprise Manager, hosted the tools for SQL Server components, including DTS. In SQL Server 2005, it's good-bye MMC, and hello to the "studio" environment. SQL Server 2005 introduces two studios: Business Intelligence Development Studio and SQL Server Management Studio. Both environments are similar to Microsoft Visual Studio; they include Solution Explorer and Server Explorer views, a Properties window, and windows for debugging. In addition, many of the tools for Integration Services are tightly integrated with the look and feel of the "studio" environment. For example, the windows germane to Integration Services, such as the ones for working with variables or viewing log entries, behave just like the windows that are an intrinsic part of the "studio" environment.

When you are using Integration Services, you are working in both Business Intelligence Development Studio and SQL Server Management Studio. If you are a developer that uses graphical tools to develop business ETL solutions, you can create, debug, and maintain packages in the Business Intelligence Development Environment. If you are an administrator, you can manage packages in SQL Server Management Studio. Either way, you will find that the tools provided by Integration Services go a long way toward addressing the tasks that were just plain difficult to do in the earlier Microsoft ETL offerings. This chapter tells you about these tools.

Integration Services Overview

Before we begin the discussion of the Integration Services tools, you should be familiar with some Integration Services concepts to help you create Integration Services packages successfully from the very beginning. This is not a comprehensive overview of the Integration Services architecture and object models; we discuss only concepts that are relevant to the use of the Integration Services tools. Those concepts include the following:

- Packages
- Control Flow
- Data Flow
- Connection Managers
- Package Configurations
- Property Expressions
- Data Sources and Data Source Views

A **package** presents a unit of work that addresses a business requirement. The package is the Integration Services object that you save, manage, or run. In SQL Server 2005, Integration Services introduces the concepts of control flow and data flow in packages. A **control flow** consists of the tasks and containers. The tasks perform specific types of work such as executing SQL statements or sending email messages, and the containers define repeating subsets of the control flow or group subsets of the control flow to make the package easier to manage. The tasks and containers are usually connected by precedence constraints that specify the sequence in which tasks and containers are executed and the conditions that must be satisfied to run the next task or container in the control flow. A **data flow** consists of sources that extract data, transformations that modify data, and the destinations that load the data into data stores.

To connect to the data stores, a package uses **connection managers**. The connection managers are defined when you create the package. From the definition, the Integration Services runtime creates a connection at run time.

When you construct a package, you configure properties of the connection managers, control flow and data flow items in the package, as well as the package itself. Frequently, a package must be configured differently for each environment to which you deploy it. For example, the connection string of connection managers may require updating to specify a different server, the location, the location of the data sources it accesses may change, and so forth. Integration Services provides package configurations to support this common scenario. **Package configurations** make it possible to dynamically update properties at run time. A configuration is a name/value pair that maps a property and a value. The configurations are stored outside the package in XML files, Database Engine tables, variables, or Registry entries. When the package is run, the value from the configuration replaces the value of the mapped-to property within the package. The values of the properties are not changed permanently.

You can set property values of packages and package objects in two different ways: directly by setting the value of each property, or indirectly by using property expressions. An expression, mapped to a property, is called a **property expression**. You build property expressions by using the operators and functions that the Integration Services expression language provides and variables. When the package is validated, which occurs when you save the package, the evaluation results of the property expressions replace the original values of properties.

A **data source** is a connection reference that you create and save outside a package, and then use as a source when adding new connection managers to a package. A data source represents a simple connection to a data store and therefore makes all tables and views in the data store available to the package. A **data source view** is built on a data source. It can contain only selected database objects and it can be extended with calculated columns that are populated by custom expressions, new relationships between tables, and queries. You can also apply a filter to a data source view to specify a subset of the data selected. In Integration Services, data sources and data source views are saved within the package definitions of the packages in which they are used.

Integration Services Tools Overview

The extract, transform, load (ETL) component of SQL Server is re-designed from the ground up in SQL Server 2005. The new ETL component, Integration Services, replaces the Data Transformation Services (DTS) included in SQL Server 2000.

Integration Services introduces a rich set of tools to support the development, deployment, and administration of ETL solutions. The tools support the simplest solutions, in which you just want to perform tasks such as copying data from one location to another, to enterprise-level solutions, in which you develop a large number of complex packages in a team environment. This section describes the Integration Services tools and service in the context of the life cycle of the ETL solution: development and testing, deployment to the test or production environment, and finally, administration in the production environment.

This chapter discusses the Integration Services tools for developing and configuring packages, the tools that are available in Business Intelligence Development Studio; as well as the Integration Services management tools that are available in Server Management Studio to import or export packages, assign roles that have read and write permissions on packages, and monitor running packages. The discussion also includes information about the Integration Services command prompt utilities that you use to run or manage packages outside the Studio environments.

Business Intelligence Development Studio

Business Intelligence Development Studio is the SQL Server 2005 studio for developing business intelligence solutions, including Integration Services packages, data sources, and data source views.

In Business Intelligence Development Studio you perform the following tasks:

- Design and create new packages
- Design and create the data source objects that packages use
- Design and create the data source views that packages use
- Modify existing packages
- Debug package functionality
- Create the deployment bundle that you use to deploy packages

In Business Intelligence Developments Studio, you develop your business solutions in the context of a solution and a project. A **solution** is a container that manages multiple projects as one unit. Typically, the projects in a solution are related, and together they support a business solution. A solution can include different types of projects such as Integration Services, Analysis Services, or Reporting Services projects. A **project** contains the items of a specific project type and provides the templates to build those items. The items are saved to disk, locally or remotely, as XML files.

Business Intelligence Developments Studio provides the following project types:

- Analysis Services Project
- Integration Services Project
- Report Server Project
- Reporting Model Project

In addition to starting a new project from scratch and manually constructing project items or adding existing items, you can launch the following tools with Business Intelligence Development Studio:

- Import Analysis Services 9.0 Database to create a new Analysis Services project by importing an existing SQL Server 2005 Analysis Services database
- Report Server Wizard to create a project and launch the Report Server Wizard automatically

The options for project types and tools are presented to you in the New Project window, as shown in Figure 16-1.

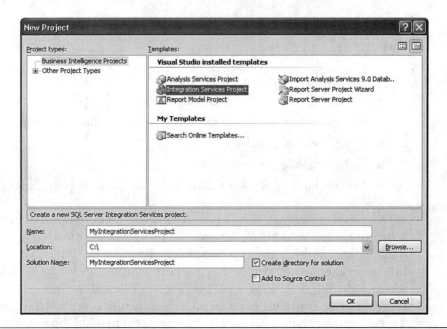

Figure 16-1 The New Project dialog box, in which you specify the project type, name the project, and optionally add the project to the source control.

You use the Integration Services project type to create packages and the data sources and data source views that packages use. If you choose the Integration Services project type, Business Intelligence Development Studio creates a project with a **Data Sources**, **Data Source Views**, **SSIS Packages**, and **Miscellaneous** folder (see Figure 16-2). An empty package is also provided.

Figure 16-2 The Integration Services project in Solution Explorer.

Many of the windows that you use when building packages are part of Business Intelligence Development studio: the **Toolbox** that provides the items for building control flow and data flow in packages, the

Properties window that lists the properties of a package or package object, and the **Solution Explorer** that manages projects and project items, including the packages, data sources, and data source views in an Integration Services project.

Figure 16-3 shows the default layout of Business Intelligence Development Studio windows. The behavior and placement of windows are configurable. If you have used Microsoft Visual Studio, this environment is familiar to you and you probably already know how to customize the development environment. If you are new to Studios, see Chapter 13, "Inside Analysis Services OLAP Tools," for more information about the features of Business Intelligence Development Studio.

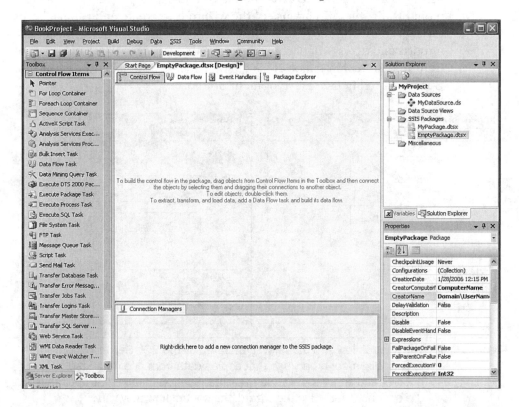

Figure 16-3   The windows that Business Intelligence Development Studio provides in their default locations, with SSIS Designer in the center window.

SQL Server Import and Export Wizard

The SQL Server Import and Export Wizard is the simplest way to create an Integration Services package. The packages that you create with this wizard can extract data from a variety of data sources such as Excel spreadsheets, flat files, and relational databases, and load the data into a similar variety of data stores. For example, the package can select data from an Excel spreadsheet with a query and write the data into a SQL Server table.

You can launch the SQL Server Import and Export Wizard from SQL Server Management Studio or an Integration Services project in Business Intelligence Development Studio. In SQL Server Management Studio, the primary use of the wizard is to create and run packages as is. Administrators typically use these packages to perform ad hoc imports and exports of data, or they save the packages to rerun as part of routine data maintenance. This chapter focuses on using the wizard in Business Intelligence Development Studio.

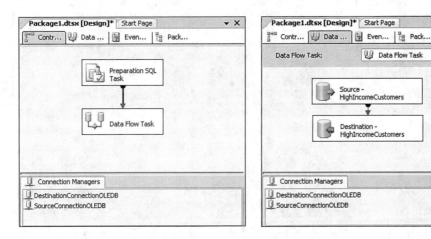

Figure 16-4 The control flow and data flow generated by the SQL Server Import and Export Wizard for a package that copies data from one database to another and creates the table in the destination database. Depending on the options selected in the wizard, the control flow may vary.

The packages that you create with the SQL Server Import and Export Wizard can perform only very limited data transformation, such as changing column metadata. However, these packages provide a great way to get a jump start on creating more complex packages. If you run the wizard from

Business Intelligence Development Studio, you cannot run the package as a step in completing the wizard. Instead, the wizard creates a package and adds it to the Integration Services project from which you launched the wizard. This package includes a basic workflow to extract and load data (see Figure 16-4). Also, depending on the options that you selected on wizard pages, the package may include tasks that prepare destination data stores, such as dropping and re-creating tables or truncating table data.

Once you have been through the wizard and the package is added to the Integration Services project, you can work with the package in SSIS Designer and enhance the package by adding other tasks, implementing advanced features such as logging and configurations and inserting transformations between the source and destination.

SSIS Designer

SSIS Designer is the graphical tool for developing packages. When you first open the designer, it consists of the four tabs: **Control Flow**, **Data Flow**, **Event Handlers**, and **Package Explorer** (see Figure 16-5). When you run the package a fifth tab, named **Progress**, is added to the designer. After you stop the package, the Progress tab is renamed to **Execution Results**.

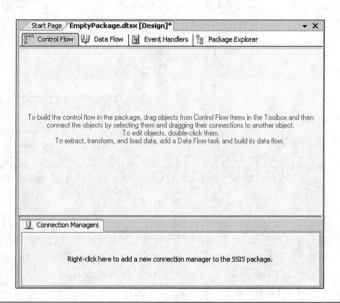

Figure 16-5   SSIS Designer shows the tabs for each designer and the tab for the package content.

SSIS Menu

When you open an Integration Services project in Business Intelligence Development Studio, the **SSIS** menu is added to the menu bar. At this time, the menu has only one option: **Work Offline (see Figure 16-6)**. This option applies to an entire project. When you select the **Work Offline** option, you are working in an offline mode. This means that Integration Services skips the aspects of package validation that make a connection to data sources and other external components.

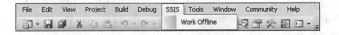

Figure 16-6 The SSIS menu option (there are multiple options) when you first open an Integration Services project.

When you open the first package in SSIS Designer, additional options become available in the SSIS menu (see Figure 16-7).

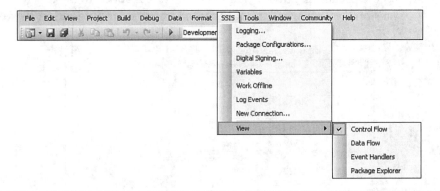

Figure 16-7 The SSIS menu options after you have opened at least one package in SSIS Designer.

From the options on the **SSIS** menu, you can access the tools for implementing more advanced features in your packages, specify whether to work in offline mode, or switch to a different tab within SSIS Designer. The **Work Offline** option applies to the current Integration Services project. This option can also be set before you open SSIS Designer. The following list describes the **SSIS** menu options:

- **Logging** opens the Configure SSIS Logs dialog box, in which you add new logs and select the events and information to log.

- **Package Configurations** opens the **Package Configuration Organizer** dialog box, from which you launch the Package Configuration Wizard to create configurations.

- **Digital Signing** opens the **Digital Signing** dialog box, from which you can select the certificate to use.

- **Variables** opens the **Variables** window, in which you add, change, and delete user-defined variables and view system variables.

- **Log Events** opens the **Log Event** window, which lists the log entries that the package generates in real time.

- **New Connection** opens the **Add SSIS Connection Manager** dialog box, in which you select the type of connection manager to create.

- **View** provides access to the Control Flow, Data Flow, and the Event Handlers design surfaces and Package Explorer.

Format Menu

The **Format** menu becomes available when you open a package in SSIS Designer. This menu includes many options for sizing the control flow and data flow items that a package contains and refining the layout of the control and data flows (see Figure 16-8). By applying these options to packages, you can make packages more legible and the control and data flows easier to understand.

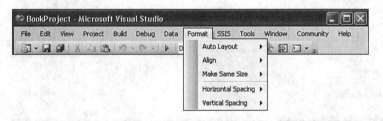

Figure 16-8   The Format menu lists the options to modify package layout.

Depending on the layout of the package and the items selected, different options are available. For all options, except for **Auto Layout**, you must select at least two items before the sub-options become available.

Control Flow Designer

The **Control Flow** tab provides the control flow designer, in which you construct the package control flow. The control flow consists of autonomous tasks and repeating sub control flows that are linked into an ordered workflow by precedence constraints. When the **Control Flow** tab is active, the **Toolbox** lists the tasks and containers that you can use to construct control flows. Figure 16-9 shows the control flow designer and the **Toolbox** when the **Control Flow** tab is active. The **Toolbox** window is in the default location. The "Common Environment Configuration Scenarios" section, later in this chapter, provides information about customizing the **Toolbox** and the behavior of control flow items.

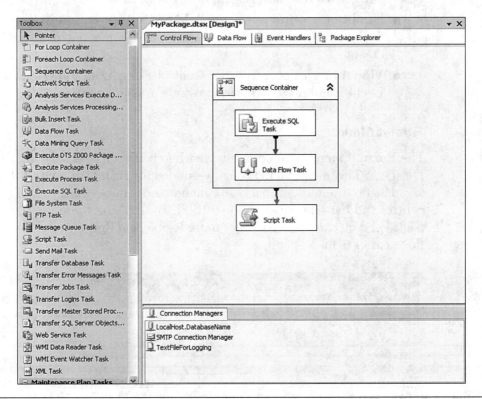

Figure 16-9   The Control Flow tab shows a control flow that consists of a Sequence container with an Execute SQL task, a Data Flow task, and a Script task.

Data Flow Design Surface

The **Data Flow** tab (see Figure 16-10) provides the data flow designer, in which you construct the data flows in the package. A package can include no, one, or multiple data flows. A data flow consists of one or more sources that extract data, transformations that modify the data, and one or more destinations that write data. The **Toolbox** lists the sources, transformations, and data control flow designer, and the default **Toolbox** when the **Data Flow** tab is active. The "Common Environment Configuration Scenarios" section, later in this chapter, provides information about customizing the **Toolbox** and the behavior of data flow items.

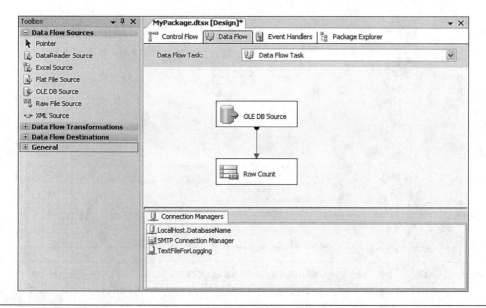

Figure 16-10   The Data Flow tab shows a data flow that consists of an OLE DB source and a Row Count transformation.

Event Handlers Designer

The **Event Handlers** tab provides the event handler designer, in which you construct an event handler for an Integration Services event. An event handler is a workflow that runs in response to an event that the runtime raises. The event handler also consists of a control flow of autonomous tasks and repeating sub control flows that are linked into an ordered workflow. If the event handler includes a data flow, then you use the data flow designer to construct the data flow.

The event handler designer is similar to the control flow designer. When the **Event Handlers** tab is active, the **Toolbox** lists the tasks and containers that you can use to construct control flows in event handlers. Figure 16-11 shows the control flow designer and the default **Toolbox** when the **Event Handlers** tab is active. The Common Environment Configuration Scenarios section, later in this chapter, provides information about customizing the **Toolbox** and the behavior of control flow items.

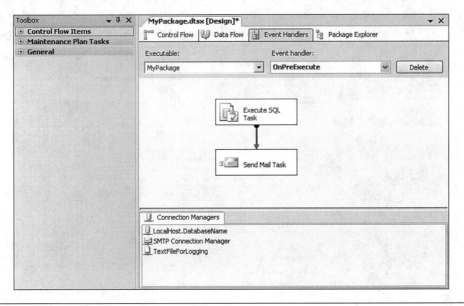

Figure 16-11   The Event Handlers tab shows a control flow that consists of an Execute SQL task and a Send Mail task. The event handler is on the OnPreExecute event.

Package Explorer

The **Package Explorer** tab provides an Explorer (why the cap?)-type view of package content. The view is built as you construct the package and provides a great way to understand the structure of the package. Figure 16-12 shows the expanded view of a fairly basic package; it has only one executable (Run SQL Statement) one connection manager (LocalHost.DatabaseName), and no user-defined variables. You can imagine how important this view is to understanding and communicating to others the structure of complex packages!

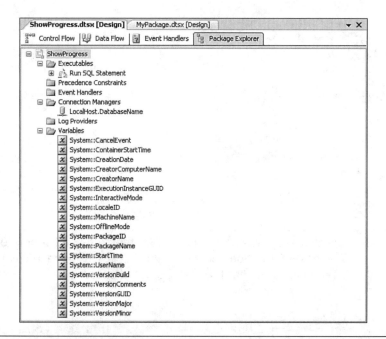

Figure 16-12   The Package Explorer view of a simple package.

Progress Explorer

The Explorer on the **Progress** tab records the progress of package execution and provides a view of package execution while the package is running. The view is built as the package makes progress in the execution of the control flow (see Figure 16-13) in the package and event handlers and in the data flow. The explorer records the beginning and completion of validation, progress percentages, and the start and end times of each executable, tasks, containers, and event handlers in the package, as well as the package itself. Depending on the tasks that the package contains, the **Progress** tab shows different types of information. For example, the Data Flow task might report the number of rows inserted into the destination data store. If errors or warnings occur, they are also listed in the Progress window.

In addition, the explorer on the **Progress** tab provides useful information about ways that you can improve the package. For example, if a data flow extracts columns from a data source and makes no subsequent use of the columns, a warning entry that identifies the unused column is written in Explorer window on the **Progress** tab.

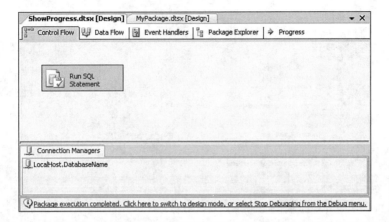

Figure 16-13 A package with a single Execute SQL task runs and generates the progress information shown in Figure 16-14. The green color on your screen indicates that the task executed successfully.

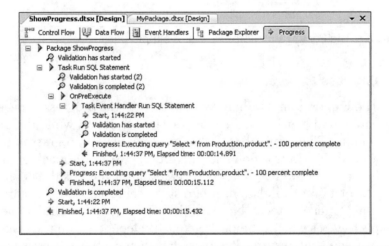

Figure 16-14 The Progress window shows the start and finish of the validation phases and the start and finish time of the package and the Execute SQL task. Progress is reported on a query that the Execute SQL task runs. In this case, the query is a simple SELECT statement.

After you stop running the package, the name of the **Progress** tab changes to **Execution Results**. The results from the previous execution of a package remain available on the tab explorer until you rerun the package, run a different package, or exit SSIS Designer.

Connection Managers Area

The **Connection Manager** area (see Figure 16-15) contains the connection managers that a package uses. Connection managers connect to data stores. They are used by sources and destinations to extract and load data, as well as many tasks, containers, and transformations that require access to a data store to do their work. You can add and configure connection managers as a separate step in the construction of a package, or you can add and configure the connection managers as you construct the control and data flows or implement logging in the package. If you choose to add and configure the connection managers as you go, Integration Services automatically makes available only the connection manager types that a particular control flow item, data flow item, or log provider can use.

Figure 16-15   The Connection Managers area lists three connection managers.

Integration Services includes a wide variety of connection managers and provides a user interface to configure each type. You configure a connection manager as a step in adding the connection manager to the package. Later, you can modify the configuration by double-clicking the connection manager in the **Connection Managers** area. Figure 16-16 shows the right-click menu where you select the connection manager type and open the dialog box to configure that type.

Figure 16-16   The Add SSIS Connection Manager dialog box lists the built-in
connection types that Integration Services support.

Variable Management Tools

Variables are used in a million different ways in Integration Services packages. Integration Services supports system and user-defined variables. System variables are the read-only variables that Integration Services provides. User-defined variables are the variables that you define to support package functionality. You will soon find that you need to add variables to packages to support package functionality.

The following are a few of the ways that packages can use variables:

- Provide values to input parameters in SQL statements and capture values from output parameters
- Serve the expressions that variables, precedence constraints, property expressions, and data flow components use.
- Provide values to use in scripts
- Capture the row count from the Row Count transformation
- Provide the SQL and XML (code) that tasks and data flow components use

The **Variables** window for working with variables is not part of SSIS Designer, but variables exist within the context of a package and you must open the package in SSIS Designer before you can add, delete, and configure variables.

To open the **Variables** window, click **Variables** on the SSIS menu. By default, the window is docked in the upper-left corner of the Business Intelligence Development Studio. Like other Business Intelligence Development Studio windows, you can move this window and configure it to be a dockable or floating window or a tabbed document and use auto-hide.

The **Variables** window can add, delete, and list variables. By default the window contains columns for the name, scope, data type, and value of variables. Figure 16-17 shows the default Variables window. You can set additional variable properties in the **Choose Variable Columns** dialog box.

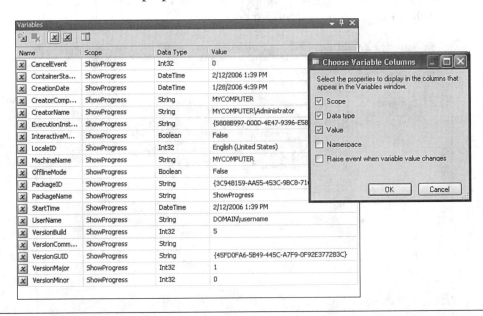

Figure 16-17   The Variables window when you click the Choose Variable Columns icon.

In the **Choose Variable Columns** dialog box, you can add the less frequently configured variable properties, the namespace, and whether an event is raised when the variable changes value to the Variables window.

TIP
Variables have properties that are not accessible from the Variables window. These properties can be set in the Properties window instead. For example, if you want to use the evaluation result from an expression as the value of a variable, then you need to configure the variable, or at least this property, in the Properties window.

Logging Configuration Tools

Integration Services include a variety of log provider types that you can use to implement logging in your packages. The log provider types include types to log to text and XML files, SQL Server Profiler, SQL Server, and Windows Events Log. You use the Configure SSIS Logs dialog box to configure logging. In this dialog box, you can specify type of log provider to implement, the logs to use, and the log entries to write to the log. The Configure SSIS Logs dialog box (see Figure 16-18) is not part of SSIS Designer, but log providers exist within the context of a package and you must open the package in SSIS Designer before you can configure logging. To open the **Configure SSIS Logs** dialog box, click **Logging** on the **SSIS** menu.

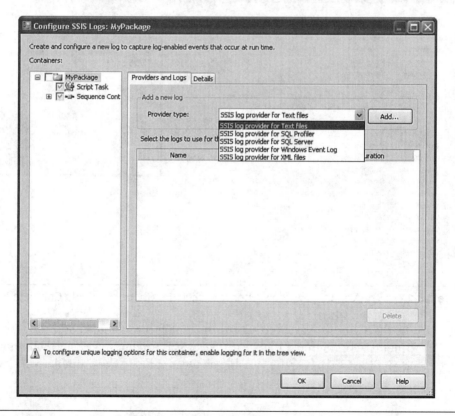

Figure 16-18 The Configure SSIS Logs dialog box shows the log provider types.

The logs are defined at the package level (see Figure 16-19). After you have defined the logs, the tasks and containers in the package can use them. A package is a hierarchical collection of objects with the package object at the top of the hierarchy. In this hierarchy, every executable (task or container), except the package itself, has a parent. If you do not want to configure logging for each executable, you can specify that an executable uses the logging specifications of its parent container.

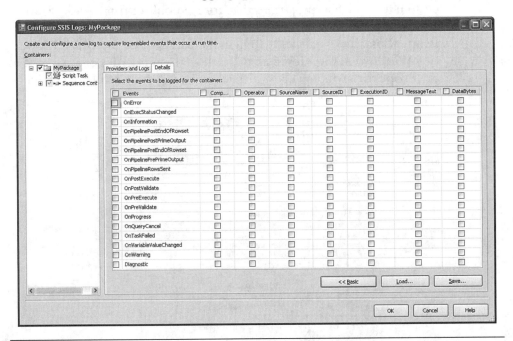

Figure 16-19   The Configure SSIS Logs dialog box shows the events and information that you can select to log for a package object.

TIP
Integration Services supports the use of logging templates. If you need to impose a consistent logging strategy across multiple packages you should consider using logging templates.

Properties Management Tools

Integration Services provides a variety of tools for setting the properties of packages and the objects that packages contain. The tools include custom tools for configuring the properties of tasks, containers, sources, transformations, and destinations, as well as the generic **Advanced Editor** dialog box that you can use to configure most data flow components.

The **Properties** window (see Figure 16-20), built into Business Intelligence Development Studio, provides an alternative way to configure package items. For packages and the Sequence container, the **Properties** window is the only tool available to set properties. In addition, the **Properties** window lists properties that are not available to configure in the custom tools such as properties that are read-only or properties for which the default values are often used. To view properties of an item in the **Properties** window, click the item in the package and then click **Properties Window** on the **View** menu. To show the properties of a package in the **Properties** window, click the background of the control flow designer.

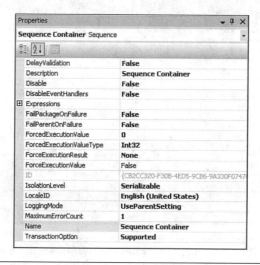

Figure 16-20 The Properties window lists the properties of the Sequence container.

You can update the value of properties with the evaluation results of expressions by implementing property expressions on properties. A property expression is an expression that you write using the Integration Services expression language and assign to a property. You can access the tools for building property expressions from the **Properties** window (see Figure 16-21).

To learn more about using property expressions, see the "Common Package Development Scenarios" section, later in this chapter.

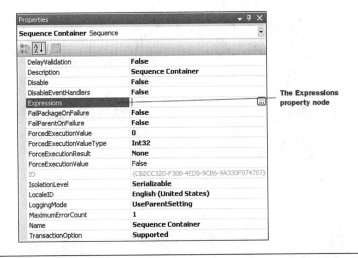

The Expressions
property node

Figure 16-21   The Expressions node, from which you open the tools you use to write
property expressions.

Package Configuration Tools

Package configurations update the values of packages and package
objects at runtime. Each configuration is a name/value pair in which the
name specifies the path of the property to update and the value specifies
the property value. By implementing configurations in a package, you
can tailor each deployment of the package to a specific environment. For
example, you can update the connection string of a connection manager
to point to a different server.

Integration Services supports a variety of configuration types. You
can store configurations in XML files, environment and parent package
variables, Registry entries, or SQL Server tables. The XML file and SQL
Server table can store multiple configurations; the other types only a single configuration. If you choose to use a SQL Server table, you can store
the configurations for multiple packages in the table and specify a filter
to identify configurations for different packages. Integration Services
provides two tools for package configurations: the **Package Configuration Organizer** dialog box and the Package Configuration Wizard.

Package Configuration Organizer

In the **Package Configurations Organizer** dialog box (see Figure
16-22), you enable the package to use configurations and specify the order

in which the configurations are loaded at runtime. The configurations are loaded in top-to-bottom order. If multiple configurations update the same property, the configuration that is loaded last wins. To launch the Package Configuration Wizard click **Add**.

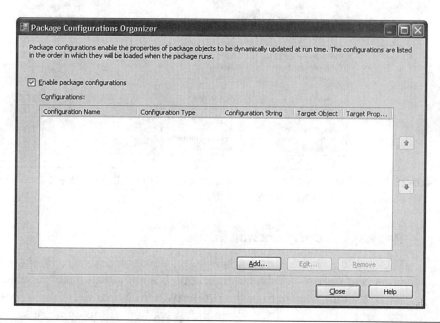

Figure 16-22   The Package Configurations dialog box, after you have enabled configurations on the package.

Package Configuration Wizard

The Package Configuration Wizard guides you though the steps to create configurations. On the Select Configuration Type page, you select the type in the Configuration type list (see Figure 16-23). You can specify the configuration location directly or choose an existing environment variable to specify the location. Table 16-1 lists and describes the various Integration Services configuration types.

Depending on whether the configuration type supports multiple configurations, you can select one or multiple package and package object properties and then complete the wizard. The configuration is added to the bottom of the list of package configurations in the **Package Configuration Organizer** dialog box. You can use the up and down arrows to position the new configuration in its correct loading position. If you want to edit the package configuration, click **Edit** and then rerun the Package Configuration Wizard.

Figure 16-23   The Package Configuration Wizard dialog box shows the configuration types.

Table 16-1   Integration Services Configuration Types

Configuration Type	Description
XML configuration file	Select an existing file or provide the name of a file to create. The file is created when you complete the wizard.
Environment variable	Select an existing environment variable from the list.
Registry entry	Type the name of an existing Registry key. The key must exist in HKEY_CURRENT_USER, and the key must include a value named Value. The value can be a string or a DWORD.
Parent package variable	Type the name of a user-defined variable with package-level scope. Variable names are case sensitive and the name you provide must be a case-sensitive match of an existing variable.
SQL Server	Select an existing OLE DB connection manager to use or create a new connection manager. The connection manager, in turn, specifies the SQL Server database that contains the table to store the configurations. You can select an existing table or create a new table. After you specify the table, you can select the filter to use for the configuration or type the name of a new filter. If a configuration already exists for a property that uses the specified filter, the configuration is overwritten.

TIP

The last page in the wizard contains lists of the paths of properties to configure. If you need to use paths when programming the Integration Services object model, you can copy them from the wizard page.

Debugging Tools

Business Intelligence Development Studio provides the same debug windows as Visual Studio. If you have debugged applications in Visual Studio, you already know how to set breakpoints and how to use the windows. If you are new to the debug environment, the Microsoft Visual Studio documentation provides information about how you access and use the debug windows.

The Integration Services breakpoints are similar to the breakpoints you may have used when writing code in Visual Studio. As in code, Integration Services breakpoints suspend execution to enable you to examine the values of variables, the call stack, and so forth to help you identify and correct errors. You can set breakpoints on packages, tasks, and other container types. To set a breakpoint you enable a break condition on the container.

In addition to enabling a break condition, you further identify break conditions by specifying how many times the break condition occurs before execution is suspended.

You use the **Set Breakpoints <container name>** dialog box to set breakpoints (see Figure 16-24).

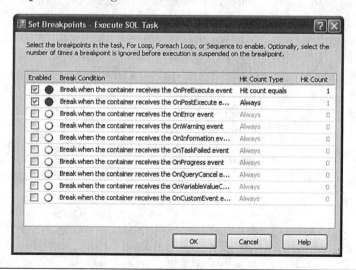

Figure 16-24 The Set Breakpoints dialog box shows that breakpoints are enabled on the OnPreExecute and OnPostExecute events of the Execute SQL task.

If a container in a package has a breakpoint, the breakpoint icon (a red dot) appears on the container shape in the control flow designer. The **Control Flow** tab represents the package, and if you enable breakpoints on the package, the breakpoint icon appears on the label of the **Control Flow** tab.

TIP

To set breakpoints on the package, place the cursor anywhere in the background of the **Control Flow** tab, right-click, and click **Edit Breakpoints**.

Package Deployment Tools

After package development is completed, you use the Build feature for Integration Services that Business Intelligence Development Studio provides to create a deployment bundle. The deployment bundle is the set of files you will copy to the target computer and then use to install the packages and their dependencies. The Build process creates a deployment manifest and includes it, the packages in the Integration Services project, package dependencies, and any files that you added to the **Miscellaneous** folder in the deployment bundle.

After you have copied the deployment bundle to the computer on which you want to install the packages, you run the Package Installation Wizard on the target computer. The wizard guides you through the steps to install packages. On the wizard pages, you must make the following decisions:

- Install packages to the file system or an instance of the SQL Server Database Engine.
- Choose whether or not the packages are validated after installation.
- Specify the folder in which packages (if deploying to the file system) and package dependencies are installed.
- If packages use configurations, whether to update the value of properties in the configurations or not.

SQL Server Management Studio

SQL Server Management Studio is the SQL Server 2005 studio for managing Integration Services packages. In SQL Server Management Studio you perform the following tasks:

- Organize packages in folders
- Import and export packages
- Assign read and write permissions to packages
- Run packages
- Monitor running packages
- View summaries of packages properties

After you connect to Integration Service, the **Object Explorer** in SQL Server Management Studio provides access to the folders for storing and running packages (see Figure 16-25). The **Stored Packages** folder and its subfolders list the packages saved to the package store; the packages can be saved to the **sysdtspackages90** table in the **msdb** database or to the file system folders that the Integration Services service monitors. The package store is a logical store that can consist of **msdb** and specified folders in the file system. To learn more about which folders are by default part of the package store and how to add other folders to the package store, read the Common Package Management Scenarios section later in this chapter.

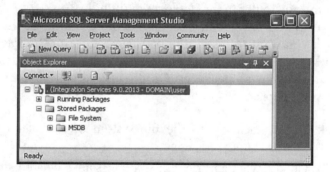

Figure 16-25   Integration Services in the Object Explorer window of SQL Server Management Studio.

From the right-click menus of folders you access the tools to perform various management tasks (see Figure 16-26). For example, expand the **Stored Packages** folder and its subfolders, right-click a package, and then click the menu option to import or export the package, run the package, assign roles to the packager, or delete the package.

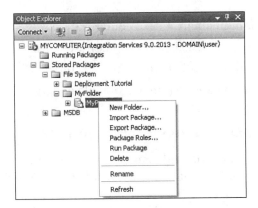

Figure 16-26   The right-click menu on a package in an Integration Services folder listed in the Object Explorer window of SQL Server Management Studio.

Command Prompt Utilities

Integration Services provides two command prompt utilities for running and managing packages. You use the **dtexec** utility to run packages, and the **dtutil utility** to manage packages. In addition, Integration Services provides the Execute Package Utility, a graphical interface on **dtexec**. The SQL Server 2005 documentation provides detailed information about the options and option arguments for both utilities. This chapter does not include this information; instead, it includes samples of command lines that you might find useful to help you write command lines that fit your business needs. For usage scenarios, see the "Common Package Management Scenarios" section later in this chapter.

Using Integration Services Tools in Business Scenarios

The life-cycle of an Integration Services solution typically has three phases: development and testing, deployment to the test or production environment, and administration in the production environment. The cycle is iterative; packages require modification and are exported to the development environment or retrieved from a storage location, updated in Business Intelligence Studio, and then again deployed to the test or production environment. This section provides answers to questions from commonly occurring scenarios in each phase of the life cycle.

- Common environment configuration scenarios
- Common package development scenarios
- Common package deployment scenarios
- Common package management scenarios

Common Environment Configuration Scenarios

This section includes information about common tasks that you do to configure Business Intelligence Development Studio.

- How to customize the Toolbox
- How to configuring Integration Services designers
- How to work offline
- How to incorporate source control in the development environment

How to Customize the Toolbox

By default the **Toolbox** lists all the control flow and data flow items that Integration Services includes. To populate the **Toolbox** with Integration Services items, you must open a package in SSIS Designer. When the **Control Flow** tab is active, the **Toolbox** lists control flow items, the tasks and containers Integration Services provides, and any custom tasks you have added. Similarly, when the **Data Flow** tab is active, the **Toolbox** lists sources, transformations, and destinations. The package must include a **Data Flow** task before you can access the **Toolbox** populated with data flow items.

    To customize Toolbox content:

1. Right-click the Toolbox and click **Choose Items**.
2. In the Choose Toolbox Items dialog box, click the **SSIS Control Flow Items**, **SSIS Data Flow Items,** or **Maintenance Tasks** tab and then clear the check box by any item you want to omit from the Toolbox.
3. Click OK.

To reset the **Toolbox**, right-click the Toolbox and click **Reset Toolbar**. To sort items, right-click the Toolbox and click **Sort Alphabetically**.

How to Configure Integration Services Designers

The **Options** option on the **Tools** menu opens the **Options** dialog box, which provides pages to configure the behavior of SSIS Designer. To access the pages for Integration Services, expand the **Business Intelligence Designers** node, and then expand **Integration Services Designers**. On the **General** page (see Figure 16-27), set options for digital signatures and accessibility. By default, the three values of precedence constraints are shown by colors: blue for completion, red for failure, and green for success. To include labels on the design surface that describe the values, select the **Show precedence constraint labels** check box.

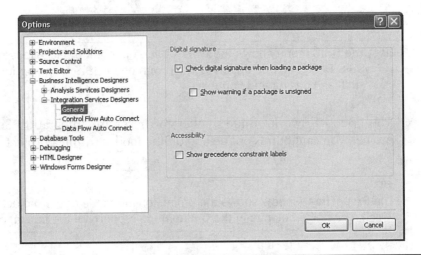

Figure 16-27   The options on the General page for digital signatures and accessibility.

Click **Control Flow Auto Connect** to open the page to configure the behavior of control flow items, tasks, and containers when you add them to the control flow designer. You can specify whether the new item is automatically connected to a selected shape, the value of the precedence constraint, and the placement of the item on the control flow design surface. Likewise, click **Data Flow Auto Connect** to configure the behavior of data flow items. You do not use precedence constraints in data flows, and the **Data Flow Auto Connect** page has only options to specify whether data flow items are automatically connected and their placement on the data flow design surface.

How to Work Offline

You can configure an Integration Services project to be offline. If you are working in an environment disconnected from the data sources and other resources that packages use, you can make your life easier by setting the project mode to offline. This way, you can avoid package validation, which inevitably generates errors. For example, connections cannot be verified because the data sources to which they connect to are not available. To work offline, click the **Work Offline** option on the **SSIS** menu (see Figure 16-28).

Figure 16-28   The SSIS menu shows the Work Offline option. If a package is open in SSIS Designer, this option is listed with other SSIS menu options such as Logging and Variable.

The option to work offline applies to the entire Integration Services project; you cannot mix online and offline modes within a project.

TIP
The **Properties** window shows the offline/online mode of the project to which a package belongs in the **OnlineMode** property of the package.

How to Incorporate Source Control in the Development Environment

Integration Services projects can be enrolled in source control. If you have source control software installed on your computer, you have the option to add the project to source control when you first create the project. To enroll the project in source control, select the **Add to Source Control** check box (see Figure 16-29).

You can also enroll existing projects in source control. From the **Source Control** option on the **File** menu, you can add a project to or from source control, exclude selected items from source control, and specify the source control software to use (see Figure 16-30).

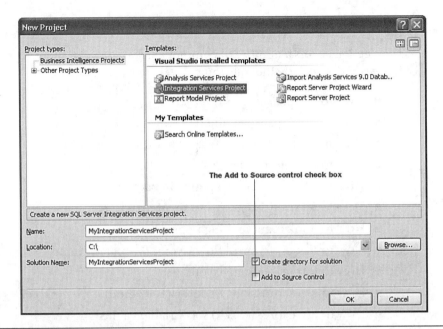

Figure 16-29 The New Project dialog box shows the option to add source control to the project.

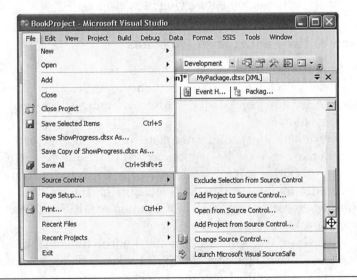

Figure 16-30 The Source Control submenu shows the options available to work with source control.

Common Package Development Scenarios

This section covers a number of common package development scenarios. The scenarios include the following:

- How to use packages as templates
- How to reuse package objects
- How to save copies of packages to different locations
- How to configure packages
- How to implement checkpoints in packages
- How to set user properties to secure packages
- How to implement looping in packages
- How to manage control flow layouts with many items
- How to format package layout
- How to use expressions to determine whether executables run
- How to use expressions to set variable values
- How to use expressions to values of properties
- How to view data during package execution
- How to implement logging in packages

How to Use Packages as Templates

Frequently groups of packages have a common set of features, or your organization may define how certain properties should be set in packages to impose consistency across packages. These scenarios call for package templates!

By default, the package template for new packages is an empty package, but you can use any package saved to the file system as a template. To use packages as templates, you copy them to the DataTransformationItems folder. The default location of this folder is C:\Program Files\Microsoft Visual Studio 8\Common7\IDE\PrivateAssemblies\ProjectItems\DataTransformationProject.

However, you cannot replace the built-in functionality of Integration Services. If you right-click the SSIS Packages node in Solution Explorer and click New SSIS Packages, Integration Services always adds a new empty package. To use the packages that you added to the DataTransformationItems folder when you add a "new" package, you need to add an existing item to the Integration Services project.

To add a new package, follow these steps:

1. Right-click the Integration Services project to which you want to add the template package, point to **Add**, and then click **New Item**. The dialog box shown in Figure 16-31 appears.
2. In the dialog box, select the package you want to use, and then click **Add**.

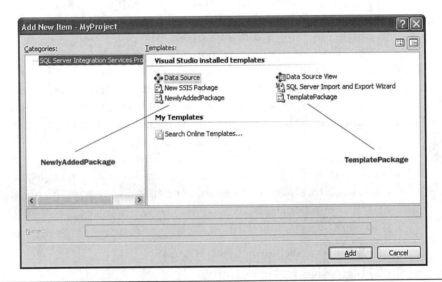

Figure 16-31   The Add New Item—MyProject dialog box lists the packages, NewlyAddedPackage and TemplatePackage, to use when adding new items that are packages. Notice the built-in templates for data sources, data source views, and the empty package New SSIS Package.

TIP
You can also add data sources and data source views to the **DataTransformationItems** folder and then use them as templates. This can be especially useful when developing a set of data source views that share core functionality.

When you add new items to an Integration Services project, the items are placed in the project folders based on their file extensions. Integration Services packages use the file extension dtsx to identify packages, and when you add a new item with this extension, it is automatically added to the **SSIS Packages** folder in **Solution Explorer**. Likewise, if you add a file that has the `ds` extension, the item is added to the **Data Sources** folder, and a file with the `dsv` extension is added to the **Data Source Views** folder.

How to Reuse Package Objects

You will probably find that you can reuse configured package objects such as tasks and connection managers in multiple packages. You might want to reuse only a single configured task or you might want to reuse an entire data flow. This is very easy to do!

SSIS Designer supports copying and pasting package objects within a package and between packages. If a solution has multiple Integration Services projects, you can copy between packages in different projects. If you copy multiple objects connected by precedence constraints or paths, then the precedence constraints and paths are copied as well. If you copy a Data Flow task, you also copy the data flows that are associated with the Data Flow task. The copy and paste functionality is built into SSIS Designer, and the packages must be opened in SSIS Designer to enable copying and pasting within a package or between packages.

To copy objects, follow these steps:

1. Select one or more objects to copy.
2. Right-click and click **Copy**.
3. If copying to different package, activate that package.
4. Click the **Control Flow**, **Data Flow**, or **Event Handlers** tab, depending on the type of objects to paste.
5. Right-click and click **Paste**.

TIP
You cannot use the standard copy and paste key combinations to copy and paste package objects.

To ensure that copied objects continue to work, you must also copy pertinent dependencies. The dependencies can be variables or connection managers that the object uses. And of course, you cannot copy data flow components to a package that has no Data Flow task.

How to Save Copies of Packages to Different Locations

From SSIS Designer you can save packages to different location types and locations. This capability is very similar to the import feature that is available to Integration Services in SQL Server Management Studio. To make the menu option to copy a package available, you must first open the package in SSIS Designer and click anywhere in the background of the control flow designer. The **File** menu includes two options that read very much alike: the **Save <package name> As** option and the **Save Copy of <package name> As** option. To save a package to a different location type (SQL Server, file system, or package store) or location, you should use the latter. During the copy and save operation, you can specify the location type and location to save the package to, and optionally, provide a new for name for the package and update the package protection level. Figure 16-32 shows an example.

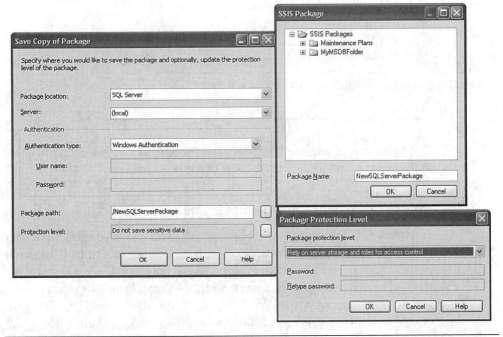

Figure 16-32 The Save Copy of Package dialog box saves a package, renamed to NewSQLServerPackage, to SQL Server and updates the package protection level from Do not save sensitive data to Rely on server storage and roles for access control.

How to Configure Packages

The package, not to be confused with the package content, is configured in the **Properties** window in Business Intelligence Development Studio. If you sort the package properties by category, you will find it easier to set related properties (see Figure 16-33).

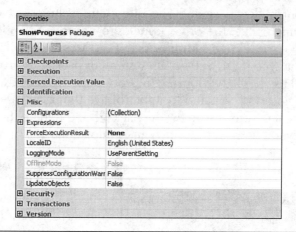

Figure 16-33   The categorized Properties window.

TIP
To display the package properties in the **Properties** window, click anywhere in the background of the control flow design surface.

How to Implement Checkpoints in Packages

Integration Services supports checkpoints. You can configure a package to use checkpoints and this way make it is possible to restart it from the point of failure, rather than rerun the whole package. If a package is configured to use checkpoints, information about package execution is written to a checkpoint file. When you rerun the failed package, the checkpoint file is used to identify where the package failed previously and restart the package from the point of failure. If the package reruns successfully, the checkpoint file is deleted.

To set the properties related to checkpoints, expand the **Checkpoints** node in the **Properties** window.

To configure checkpoints, follow these steps:

1. Set the SaveCheckpoints property to True to indicate that the package saves checkpoints.
2. Provide the name and location of the checkpoint file in **CheckpointFileName** property.
3. Set the value of the **CheckpointUsage** property (see Table 16-2).
4. To identify tasks and containers in the package as restart points, select each task or container, and in the **Properties** window set its FailPackageOnFailure property to True.

Table 16-2   The Possible Values of the CheckpointUsage Property

Value	Behavior
Never	Indicates that the checkpoint file is not used.
Always	Indicates that the checkpoint file is always used. If the checkpoint file is not found, the package fails.
IfExists	Indicates that the checkpoint file is used if it exists. If the checkpoint file is not found, the whole package is rerun.

TIP
To test the checkpoints, set the ForceExecutionResult property of tasks and containers to Failure.

How to Set User Properties to Secure Packages

Integration Services provides a variety of package protection levels to encrypt packages or to omit saving sensitive information in the package definition. When you develop a package in Business Intelligence Development Studio, you set the package protection to a level that is suitable for a single developer of a team of developers. Some package protection levels (**EncryptAllWithUserKey** and **EncryptSensitiveWithUserKey**) encrypt packages using a key based on the user profile. This means that only the same user using the same profile can load and work with the package. Obviously, these protection levels are difficult to use in a team environment because developers cannot open packages that were created by other team members. Other protection levels (**EncryptAllWithPassword** and **EncryptSensitiveWithPassword**) require that the passwords be known to all developers. Frequently the **DontSaveSensitive** protection level is used during package development. You can set the protection level to **ServerStorage** to rely only on the built-in security features of SQL Server to protect packages.

To set the properties related to package protection level expand the **Security** node in the **Properties** window.

To configure the protection level,

1. Set the **ProtectionLevel** property.
2. If applicable, provide a password in the **PackagePassword** property.

If you import or export a package in SQL Server Management Studio or save a copy of a package in Business Intelligence Development Studio, you can change the protection level that the package uses.

How to Implement Looping in Packages

In DTS, it was difficult to implement looping in packages. The solution typically included custom code. In SQL Server 2005, Integration Services introduces two new container types, the Foreach Loop and the For Loop, that make it very easy to include looping in the package control flow.

- For Loop repeats its control flow until a specified expression evaluates to False.
- The Foreach Loop repeats the control flow for each member in the collection of a specified enumerator type.

Of the two types of loops, the For Loop is probably the most straightforward to implement. To configure it, you provide the expression the evaluation results of which determine whether the loop repeats, and optionally, expressions to initialize the loop counter and increment or decrement the loop counter. The three properties to configure the For Loop are: **EvalExpression** (the evaluation expression), **InitExpression** (the initialization expression), and **AssignExpression** (the expression to increment or decrement the loop counter).

In the following very simple implementation, you use a variable, **varCounter**, to control loop execution. The variable must have a numeric data type. The loop repeats the loop repeats 5 times.

```
Set InitExpression to @varCounter = 1
Set EvalExpression to @varCounter < 6
Set AssignExpression to @varCounter = @varCounter +1
```

TIP
You must include the @ prefix to identify variables, the expression must be a valid Integration Services expression, and you must use the single equal (=) character instead of the double equal (==) characters.

To use the Foreach Loop to implement looping you first choose the type of enumerator to use. You select the enumerator type on the **Collection** page of the **Foreach Loop Editor** dialog box (see Figure 16-34).

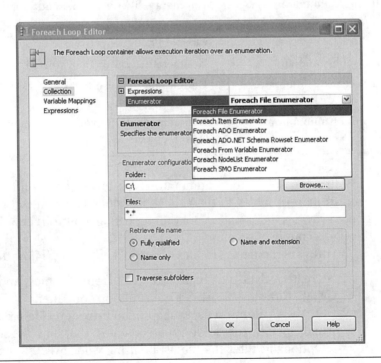

Figure 16-34   The Collection page.

The built-in enumerator types that Integration Services provides (see Table 16-3) support repeating control flows to enumerate a wide variety of objects and items. For example, you can use the Foreach File enumerator to repeat a control flow for all the files in a specified folder, regardless of the number of files present in the folder. You will learn that the Foreach File enumerator supports wildcards, which makes it possible to filter the filesand choose just those that you wish to enumerate.

Table 16-3 The Enumerator Types to Use with the Foreach Loop

Enumerator Type	Use
Foreach ADO Enumerator	Enumerate rows in an ADO recordset.
Foreach ADO.NET Schema Rowset Enumerator	Enumerate the schema information of a data source.
Foreach File Enumerator	Enumerate files in a folder and subfolders.
Foreach From Variable Enumerator	Enumerate the enumerable object in a specified variable.
Foreach Item Enumerator	Enumerate items that are collections.
Foreach Nodelist Enumerator	Enumerate the resultset of an XML Path Language (XPath) expression.
Foreach SMO Enumerator	Enumerate SQL Server Management Objects (SMO) objects.

After you select the enumerator type to use and configure it, you need to map variables to the collection value. This is how the Foreach Loop provides information to the repeating control flow. Let's walk through a couple of scenarios.

To provide the names of files to use in a data flow, follow these steps:

1. Create a data flow that reads data from flat files, and drag the Data Flow task inside a Foreach Loop container.
2. On the **Collection** page, choose the **Foreach File Enumerator** and specify the folder that contains the files to enumerate. Optionally, filter the file list by using wildcards. For example, to enumerate only text files, use *.txt.

3. On the **Variables Mapping** page, select an existing variable or create a new one. The variable must have the **String** data type. This example uses the variable **varEnumerateFiles**.
4. In the **Connection Managers** area, click the Flat File connection manager that connects to the files.
5. In the **Properties** window, add a property expression for the **ConnectionString** property of the Flat File connection manager that uses the expression **@varEnumerateFiles**.

To provide the logins on a server,

1. On the **Collection** page, choose the **Foreach SMO Enumerator** and specify the server that contains the SQL Server Management Objects (SMO) objects to enumerate, and then select the SMO objects to enumerate. The following shows the value to enumerate logins:

```
SMOEnumObj[@Name='Logins']/SMOEnumType[@Name='Objects']
```

2. On the **Variables Mapping** page, select an existing variable or create a new one. The variable must have a string data type. This example uses the variable **varLogins**. The variable must have the **Object** data type.

How to Manage Control Flow Layouts with Many Items

If the control flow in a package contains a large number of tasks and containers, the design surface can become crowded and you may not be able to view all the control flow items at one time to understand fully the functionality of the package, or you may not be able to easily locate the task or container that you want to work with. The grouping feature, available in the control flow designer, is useful in this situation.

To group tasks and containers,

1. Select the tasks and containers to group.
2. Right-click and click **Group**.
3. Optionally, rename the group.

You can then expand and collapse a group to suit your needs (see Figure 16-35). Expanding a group provides access to the properties of the task and containers in the group.

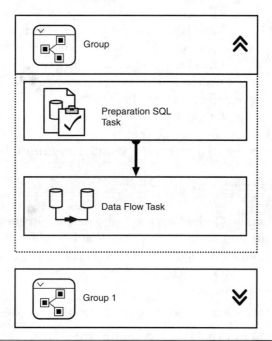

Figure 16-35   Expanded and collapsed groups.

To ungroup tasks and containers,

1. Select the group.
2. Right-click and click **Ungroup.**

The navigator is another useful feature for working with packages that have large control flows or data flows. You use the navigator to access parts of the control flow or data flow in packages when the flows are too large to view in the designer at one time.

TIP
The Sequence container also groups tasks and containers, but in contrast to the grouping feature, it is not a design-time only feature. For example, you can set properties on the Sequence container to disable it and this way disable all the tasks and containers in the Sequence container.

The navigation feature in SSIS Designer can also make it easier to work with packages in which the control flow and data flows have a large number of items. The navigation feature, also know as the navigator, is located in the lower-right corner of the control flow and data flow design surfaces (see Figure 16-36). The navigator is not available as long as all items are visible on the design surface at one time.

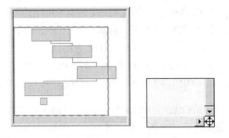

Figure 16-36　The navigator pop-up and the navigator location.

To use the navigator,

1. Click the crossed arrows in the lower-right corner of the designer.
2. Use the crossed-arrows cursor to move to the part of the design surface that you want to be visible in the designer.
3. Release.

How to Format Package Layout

As you develop a package and modify control and data flows by adding and deleting items, you might find that the package layout becomes more difficult to understand. In short, the graphical layout does not communicate package functionality in the most optimal way. You could work your way through the layout, item by item, resizing and re-placing each item on the design surface, but Business Intelligence Studio offers a much easier way to do this.

On the **Format** menu (see Figure 16-37), you will find useful options to size and align items and to set the horizontal and vertical spacing between items.

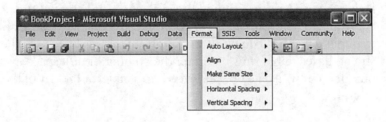

Figure 16-37　The Format menu.

To apply an option, you must select at least two items on the **Control Flow**, **Data Flow**, or **Event Handlers** tab. The item selected first is the item to which other items are sized or aligned. You can think of this item as the precedence item. You can identify the item selected first by its white handles. The items that are selected second or later have black handles. If you select items by dragging the cursor across items, the item the cursor touches first is the precedence item.

The Format menu provides the following options:

- From the **Auto Layout** option, select **Selection** or **Diagram**. The former formats the layout of selected items, the latter all items.

- From the **Align** option, you can left or right, center-align the vertical sides of items, or middle-align the horizontal sides of items.

- From the **Make Same Size** option, you can make items the same size by width, height, or both.

- From the **Horizontal Spacing** option, you can make equal, increase, decrease, or remove space.

- From the **Vertical Spacing** option, you can make equal, increase, decrease, or remove the vertical spacing between items.

How to Use Constraints and Expressions to Determine Whether Executables Run

Precedence constraints link executables (containers and tasks) in packages into a control flow and specify conditions that determine whether executables run. A precedence constraint connects two executables: the precedence executable and the constrained executable.

You can use expressions in place of or in combination with the outcome (success, failure, or completion) of the precedence executable to determine whether the constrained executable runs. The Precedence Constraint Editor is shown in Figure 16-38.

Select either **Expression and Constraint** or **Expression or Constraint** to use an expression in the evaluation operation of the precedence constraint. The expression that you use must evaluate to a **Boolean**. For example, a package could use an expression that evaluates whether the constrained executable runs based on the amount of disk space available, the number of rows a data flow inserted into a table, or the day of the month.

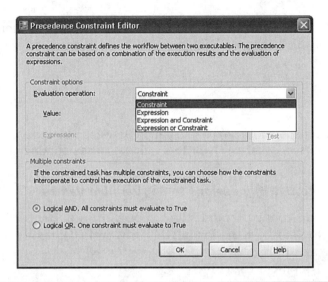

Figure 16-38   The Precedence Constraint Editor shows the available evaluation operations.

TIP
Make sure that you include the @ character as the first character in the variable name and also, because variable names are case sensitive, that the variable name you provide matches the name of the variable case-wise.

Let's look at some sample expressions. In the following expression, the variable **varRowCount**, set by a Row Count transformation in a data flow, is compared to the value 1000. You could use this expression to determine whether the package should run a task that backs up a database depending on the number of rows inserted into the destination database. The prefix @ is required when variables are used in expressions to differentiate the variables from column names. In most user interface, the @ is added for you automatically.

```
@varRowCount > 1000
```

Likewise, in the following expression, the variable @varDisk, set by a Script task, is compared to the value 20. You could use this expression to determine whether to continue package execution.

```
@varDisk >= 20
```

In the following expression, the GETDATE function determines the day. If the day is the first day in the month, the constrained executable runs.

```
DATEPART("day",GETDATE()) == 1
```

TIP
The equal operator in the Integration Services expression language is ==, that is, two equal (=) characters with no spaces between them.

How to Use Expressions to Set Variable Values

You can configure most variable properties in the **Variables** window, but you must use the **Properties** window to configure variables to evaluate as expressions.

To configure variables:

1. In the Variables window, click the user-defined variable you want to configure.
2. Set **EvaluateAsExpression** to True.
3. In the **Expression** field, type a valid expression.

You will notice that when the **Expression** field loses focus, the **Value** property is automatically updated with the evaluation result of the expression and the **ValueType** is set.

Let's look at some sample expressions. In the **Expression** field, type GetDate(). Notice, that the **Value** property now contains the current date and the **ValueType** property is set to **DateTime**.

In the **Expression** field, type "A" + "B". Notice that the **Value** property now contains AB and the **ValueType** property is set to **String**.

How to Use Expressions to Values of Properties

The value of properties can be updated with the evaluation results of expressions by implementing property expressions on properties. Property expressions are expressions that you write in the Integration Services expression language. The expressions can use variables and the operators and functions that the Integration Services expression language provides. The variables can be either system- or user-defined. The custom tools for tasks and containers include the **Expressions** page (see Figure 16-39), but you can also add property expressions in the **Properties** window.

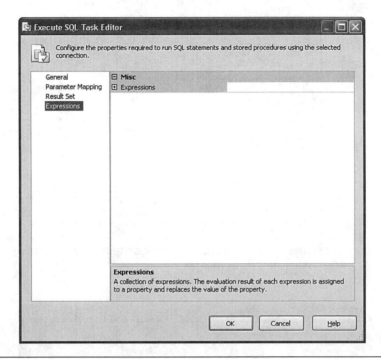

Figure 16-39 The Expressions page in the Execute SQL Task Editor on which you access the expression tools for writing property expressions for properties of the Execute SQL task.

From the **Expressions** page or the **Expressions** node in the **Properties** window, you click (...) to open the **Property Expressions Editor** dialog box (see Figure 16-40). Here you select the properties for which to create property expressions in the **Property** list, and then either type the expression directly in the **Expression** box or click (...) to use the **Expression Builder** to write expressions.

The **Expression Builder** (Figure 16-41) makes it easy to write expressions. It lists the available variables and the functions, type casts, and operators that you can use in expressions. You can type the expression in the **Expression** box or build the expression by dragging variables, functions, type casts, or operators to the **Expression** box. The advantages of using the **Expression Builder** instead of the **Property Expression Editor** are that you can verify that the syntax of the expression is valid and view the evaluation result of the expression. The value of the property with which the property expression is associated is not updated when you evaluate the expression. The values of properties are updated when you save, load, or run the package.

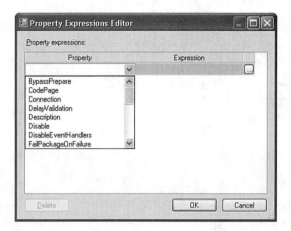

Figure 16-40 The Property Expressions Editor lists the properties of the Execute SQL task in the Property list.

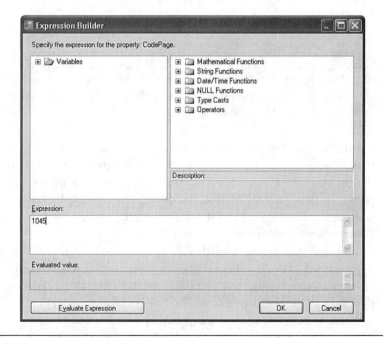

Figure 16-41 The Expression Builder shows the Variables folder, and the folders for functions, type casts, and operator. The expression sets the CodePage property of the task to 1045.

The Expression Builder lists the variables, functions, type casts, and operators for use in property expressions. Note that the name of the property, in this case **CodePage**, appears in the text at the top of the dialog box.

The Expression Builder automatically adds the @ prefix and also includes the variable namespace. If it is not necessary to include the namespace to uniquely identify a variable, you may omit the namespace.

NOTE

The Expression Builder is also available for building the expressions that data flow components use. The only difference is that the Expression Builder then includes a Columns folder, which lists the columns in the data flow that are available to use in expressions.

Let's consider some sample expressions. The following expression uses the variable, **varConnectionString**, It could be used to set the **ConnectionString** property of a file connection manager. The variable would have the **String** data type and would contain a value like "C:\MyProject\ TestLog.txt".

```
@[User:: varConnectionString]
```

The following expression uses the system variables **PackageName**, **MachineName**, and **StartTime**. Because the **StartTime** variable has a date/time datatype it must be cast to a string before the variable value can be concatenated with the other strings in the expression. This expression could be used to set the Subject property of a Send Mail task. The evaluation results would be a value like "MyPackage is running on MYLAP1started at: 2/18/2006 3:07:20 PM."

```
"The package " + @[System::PackageName] + " is running on "
➡+ @[System::MachineName] + "started at: "
➡+ (DT_WSTR, 20) (@[System::StartTime])
```

Other expressions are more simple. The following expression can set the **DisableEventHandlers** property to True and this way prevent the execution of the event handler control flow.

```
True
```

How to View Data During Package Execution

Frequently it is useful to see the data as it moves through the data flow in a package. You might want to view the data after a transformation updates values or modifies the dataset, verify that the dataset contains the columns that you need, or examine the data for unexpected values. Data viewers provide an easy way to do all these things.

TIP

In the early stages of package development, use a Row Count transformation instead of a destination as the terminating component in a data flow. This way, you can focus on getting the package to work correctly before you write any data to a data store.

Data viewers are attached to the paths that connect components in a data flow. Integration Services provides four different types of data viewers: grid, histogram, scatter plot, and column chart. The column chart and grid types are exemplified in Figure 16-42). You can only use the histogram and scatter plot types with numeric data.

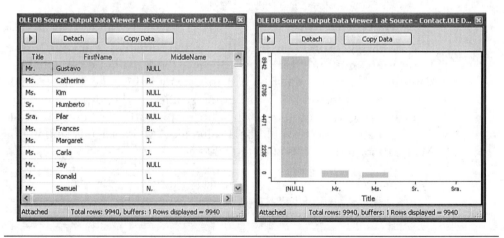

Figure 16-42   The Column Chart data viewer and the Grid data viewer.

You can copy the data in data viewers to use for further analysis. If you copy data from a Grid data viewer, the column names are copied as well.

TIP

Data viewers show data one buffer at a time. Keep that in mind when you view aggregated data, the aggregation is not necessarily applicable to the entire dataset.

How to Implement Logging in Packages

The earlier section about logging in this chapter describes the types of logging that you can implement in packages. To view the logged information, you need to exit Business Intelligence Development studio and open another tool like the Windows Event Viewer or SQL Profiler or a text or XML file, or run an SQL statement to query log entries in SQL Server tables. This is not very convenient during package development.

To view log entries in real time in Business Intelligence Development Studio, you use the **Log Events** window. There are no additional steps in the configuration of the package logging; all you do is open the **Log Events** window and the log entries are automatically written to the window. If the package is configured to log to multiple logs, the information appears only once in the **Log Events** window.

To open the **Log Events** window (see Figure 16-43), click **Log Events** on the **SSIS** menu.

Name	Source Name	Source GUID	Message	Start Time	End Time
OnPreExecute	Foreach Loop Container	{99748AD8-0658-4FA5-8B41-E8093DC5B51A}		2/19/2006 1:55:13 PM	2/19/2006 1:55:13 PM
OnPostExecute	Foreach Loop Container	{99748AD8-0658-4FA5-8B41-E8093DC5B51A}		2/19/2006 1:55:13 PM	2/19/2006 1:55:13 PM

Figure 16-43   The Log Events window lists log entries for the Foreach Loop container.

From the **Log Events** window you can copy the log entries and also view the log entry in a separate dialog box. To copy the log entries, select the entries, right-click, and then click Copy. To view a log entry in the **Log Entry** dialog box, double-click the log entry in the **Log Events** window.

Common Package Deployment Scenarios

After you complete the development or modification of packages, you need to deploy them to a test environment for further testing or to a production environment. This section includes information about common tasks that you do to prepare Integration Services projects for deployment, create the deployment bundle, and install packages on the target computer.

- How to add packages and other files to an Integration Services project
- How to configure the deployment utility and build a project
- How to prepare to install packages on the target computer
- How to install packages, package dependencies, and other files

How to Add Packages and Other Files to an Integration Services Project

The deployment bundle includes all packages in an Integration Services project. If you want to deploy only a subset of the packages, you must create a new Integration Services project and add those packages to the project. If you want to include packages from other projects, you must add the packages to the project from which you build the deployment utility. Integration Services automatically identifies and includes package dependencies in the deployment bundle, so you do not need to explicitly add those items to the project. Package dependencies include any configuration files that the package uses. On the other hand, the log files that the package uses are not automatically included. To decide whether you need to include the log files, you need to know whether the File connection manager creates a new file or uses an existing file. The easiest way to do this is to locate the pertinent File connection managers in the **Connection Managers** area of SSIS Designer, double-click it, and take a look at the **Usage type** option. If it is set to **Create file**, you do not need to include the log files, but if it is set to **Existing file**, and the file does not already exist on the target server, you do. Tasks such as the Execute SQL, XML, and WMI Data Reader tasks that execute language statements can be configured to use a direct input, a File connection, or a variable to provide the statement. If the task uses statements stored in a file, then you must add that file to the project. Again, if the file already exists on the target server, you need not do this.

If you add packages to the project, they are automatically added to the **SSIS Packages** folder; other items are added to the **Miscellaneous** folder.

TIP
Data sources and data source views are not deployed with packages. If you added connection managers that are based on data source views, the connection managers are automatically included in the package definition. The data source views are included as SELECT statements in the pertinent properties of sources, transformations, and destinations in the package definition.

How to Configure the Deployment Utility and Build a Project

Before the build process that Business Intelligence Development Studio provides for Integration Services projects will generate the deployment utility and create the deployment bundle that you use to install packages, you must update project properties. In **Solution Explorer** right-click the project and click **Properties**, or select the project and then click **Properties** on the **Project** menu. Figure 16-44 shows an example of the resulting dialog box.

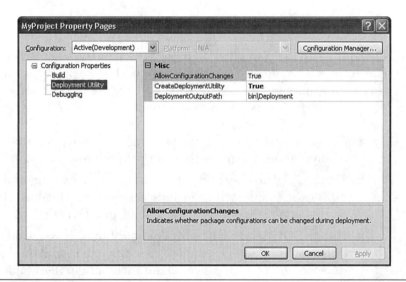

Figure 16-44   The Property Pages dialog box for the Integrations Services project, MyProject.

You need to configure only three properties for the deployment utility: **AllowConfigurationChanges, CreateDeploymentUtility**, and **DeploymentOutputPath**. To show these properties, click **Deployment Utility** in the **<project name> Property Pages** dialog box. By default, the **AllowConfigurationChanges** property is set to True. This means that you can update the values of configurations when you install the packages on the target computer. Typically, you want to allow the update of configurations the first time you deploy a set of packages. Depending on the updates to packages, you may want to disallow the update of configurations on package redeployment to ensure that package properties are not inadvertently changed and the redeployed package works the same way as the package it replaces.

To build the deployment utility when you run the build process, set the **CreateDeploymentUtility** property to True. The default value, bin\Deployment, of **DeploymentOutputPath**, specifies the folder relative to the Integration Services project for which you build the deployment utility to store the files in the deployment bundle.

Next, you right-click the Integration Services project and click **Build**. After the build process completes, the **Deployment** folder contains a deployment manifest, <project name>.SSISDeploymentManifest, the packages, and any package dependencies.

How to Prepare to Install Packages on the Target Computer

Depending on the configuration of the packages you want to deploy, you may have work to do on the target computer before packages can be run successfully in the new environment.

The following are some common tasks:

- Create environment variables. The environment variables that configurations use must exist on the target server.
- Create Registry keys. The Registry keys that configurations use must exist and they must include a value named Value. The value on the target computer can be a string or a DWORD.
- Create SQL Server tables for configurations. If you want to use a different SQL Server database than the one used during package development, you must re-create the configuration table in that database.
- Create SQL Server tables for log entries. If you want to use a different SQL Server database than the one used during package development, you must re-create the configuration table in that database.
- Create a share on the target computer to which you can copy the deployment bundle.

How to Install Packages, Package Dependencies, and Other Files

After you complete the build process to create the Deployment folder, you are ready to install the packages on the target computer.

To install packages on a different computer, follow these steps:

1. Copy the Deployment folder to the target computer.

2. Locate the deployment bundle and double-click the manifest file, <project name>.SSISDeploymentManifest. The Package Installation Wizard starts.

3. On the welcome page click **Next**.

4. On the **Deploy SSIS Packages** page, choose whether to install packages to the SQL Server Database Engine or the file system. Also, decide whether to validate packages after installation.

5. If installing on SQL Server, specify the server name and authentication type on the **Specify Target SQL Server** page.

6. On the **Select Installation Folder** page, specify the folder in the file system for the package (in a file system installation) and for package dependencies.

7. If any of the packages uses configurations, the **Configure Packages** page opens. On this page, you can edit configurations by updating values in the **Value** list.

8. Depending on whether you decided to validate packages, the packages are validated.

Common Package Management Scenarios

SQL Server Management Studio is the SQL Server 2005 studio for managing Integration Services packages.

The following sections teaches you

- How to connect to Integration Services
- How to modify the service configuration file to connect to a named instance of SQL Server
- How to add and change top-level folders in the Stored Packages folder
- How to customize the structure of subfolders within the top-level folders
- How to add folders to the package store
- How to assign read and write permissions to packages
- How to import or export packages
- How to run packages using the package execution utility
- How to run packages using the dtexec command prompt utility
- How to manage packages using the dtutil command prompt utility
- How to view summaries of package properties

Each of these tasks is covered in the following sections.

How to Connect to Integration Services

In contrast to Business Intelligence Studio, the first step to use SQL Server Management Studio is to log on to a server. In the **Connect to Server** dialog box (see Figure 16-45), you select Integration Services and specify a server. Integration Services supports only Windows Authentication and by default uses the NT AUTHORITY\NetworkService account.

Figure 16-45   The Connect to Server dialog box shows the server types with Integration Services selected.

After you have connected to Integration Services, you can work with packages from SQL Server Management Studio in the **Object Explorer** window.

TIP
If you cannot connect to Integration Services, verify that the Integration Services service is started. The **SQL Server 2005 Surface Area Configuration** tool and **Services** snap-in list the service and its state.

TIP
By default, MsDtsSrvr.ini.xml specifies a default instance of SQL Server and you must modify the file to connect to a named instance.

How to Modify the Service Configuration File to Connect to a Named Instance of SQL Server

To connect to a named instance of SQL Server, you must modify the service configuration file, MsDtsSrvr.ini.xml. By default, the file is located in C:\Program Files\Microsoft SQL Server\90\DTS\Binn. The following XML code is the content of the default configuration file.

```
<?xml version="1.0" encoding="utf-8"?>
<DtsServiceConfiguration
xmlns:xsd="http://www.w3.org/2001/XMLSchema"
➥xmlns:xsi="http://www.w3.org/2001/XMLSchema-instance">
➥<StopExecutingPackagesOnShutdown>true</
➥StopExecutingPackagesOnShutdown>
  <TopLevelFolders>
    <Folder xsi:type="SqlServerFolder">
      <Name>MSDB</Name>
      <ServerName>ServerName</ServerName>
    </Folder>
    <Folder xsi:type="FileSystemFolder">
      <Name>File System</Name>
      <StorePath>..\Packages</StorePath>
    </Folder>
  </TopLevelFolders>
</DtsServiceConfiguration>
```

Open the file in any text editor, change the `<ServerName>` element from `<ServerName>ServerName</ServerName>` to `<ServerName>ServerName\InstanceName</ServerName>`, and save the file.

You must restart the Integration Services service to use the updated service configuration file.

How to Add and Change Top-Level Folders in the Stored Packages Folder

Integration Services contains the two root-level folders: **Running Packages** and **Stored Packages**. **Running Packages** lists packages that are currently executing. **Stored Packages** contains the sub-folders that list the packages saved to the package store (the **msdb** SQL Server database or the file system). Integration Services can save packages to the file system or the **sysdtspackages90** table in the **msdb**. You can save packages to any folder in the file system, but Integration Services service monitors only packages that you save to the folders that are specified in the service configuration file, MsDtsSrvr.ini.xml. By default, the configuration file, located in C:\Program Files\Microsoft SQL Server\90\DTS\Binn, specifies the subfolders: **File System** and **MSDB** (see Figure 16-46).

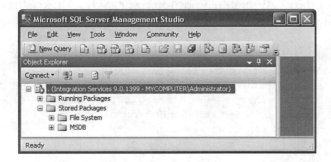

Figure 16-46   Integration Services in the Object Explorer window of SQL Server Management Studio.

You cannot modify the root-level folders, nor can you delete them; however, you can modify the sub-folders within **Stored Packages** and extend their structure to meet your needs. For example, you might want to organize your packages by the department that uses them or by the types of tasks they perform.

To add or delete top-level folders or change the names of top level folders, you must modify the service configuration file, MsDtsSrvr.ini.xml. The following XML code is the content of the default configuration file.

```
<?xml version="1.0" encoding="utf-8"?>
<DtsServiceConfiguration
xmlns:xsd="http://www.w3.org/2001/XMLSchema"
➥xmlns:xsi="http://www.w3.org/2001/XMLSchema-instance">
➥<StopExecutingPackagesOnShutdown>true</
➥StopExecutingPackagesOnShutdown>
  <TopLevelFolders>
    <Folder xsi:type="SqlServerFolder">
      <Name>MSDB</Name>
      <ServerName>ServerName</ServerName>
    </Folder>
    <Folder xsi:type="FileSystemFolder">
      <Name>File System</Name>
      <StorePath>..\Packages</StorePath>
    </Folder>
```

```
    </TopLevelFolders>
</DtsServiceConfiguration>
```

The elements `<Name>MSDB</Name>` and `<Name>File System</Name>` specify the top-level folders within the Stored Packages folder.

To add, delete, and modify the folders, open MsDtsSrvr.ini.xml in any text editor and then edit the file. Before you begin to add folders, you need to choose the type of folder you want to add. You will notice the file has two types of Folder elements: One specifies `"SqlServer-Folder"` and the other `"FileSystemFolder"`. To add a folder for packages stored in **msdb**, copy and paste the Folder element that specifies `"SqlServerFolder,"` and for packages saved to the file system use the one that specifies `"FileSystemFolder."` In the new XML Folder block, update the Name element. If you copied the Folder element that specifies `"FileSystemFolder,"` you can also update the location and folder name of the file system folder that Integration Services service monitors and add more folders to monitor. By default, the configuration file specifies the Packages folder, (..\Packages), a folder that is created when you install Integration Services. The following Folder element specifies a folder named Finance and the folder path, C:\MyPackages. A folder can monitor only one location.

```
<Folder xsi:type="FileSystemFolder">
  <Name>Finance</Name>
  <StorePath>C:\MyPackages</StorePath>
</Folder>
```

The Integration Services service must be restarted to use the updated service configuration file.

How to Customize the Structure of Subfolders within the Top-Level Folders

Unlike the top-level folders within the Stored Packages folder, you do not modify the Integration Services service configuration file to add subfolders within the top-level folders. Instead, you use the user interface that SQL Server Management Studio provides.

To add a new folder,

1. Right-click the folder to which you want to add a subfolder and click **New Folder**.

2. In the **Create New Folder** dialog box, type the name of the folder (see Figure 16-47).

3. Click **OK**.

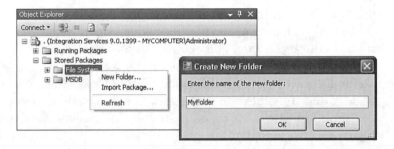

Figure 16-47 The Create New Folder dialog box, opened from the right-click menu of a folder.

How to Assign Read and Write Permissions to Packages

You can protect packages that are saved to the **msdb** SQL Server database by assigning Integration Services database-level roles that specify read and write permissions on packages. Integration Services provides the three fixed database-level roles for controlling access to packages: **db_dtsadmin, db_dtsltduser**, and **db_dtsoperator.** Table 16-4 presents the read and write permissions for each of the roles.

Table 16-4 Role Read and Write Permissions

Role	Read Permissions	Write Permissions
db_dtsadmin	Enumerate all packages	Import packages
	View all packages	Delete all packages
	Run all packages	Change all package roles
	Export all packages	
	Run all packages in SQL Server Agent jobs	
db_dtsltduser	Enumerate all packages	Import packages
	View own packages	Delete own* packages
	Run own packages	Change own* package roles
	Export own packages	

Role	Read Permissions	Write Permissions
db_dtsoperator	Enumerate all packages View all packages Run all packages Export all packages Run all packages in SQL Server Agent	None

*The package owner is identified by the value in the ownersid column in the sysdtspackages90 table in the msdb database.

To set read and write permissions follow these steps:

1. Right-click a package that is saved to **msdb** and click **Package Roles**.

2. In the **Package Roles** dialog box (see Figure 16-48), replace the default reader and write roles with the ones that you want to use.

3. Click **OK**.

Figure 16-48 The Package Roles dialog box with the db_dtsoperator role assigned to the reader role, and the db_dtsadmin role to the writer role.

TIP
Packages saved to the **msdb** database are stored in the **sysdtspackages90** table. Columns in this table contain information about the roles that are assigned to packages. The **readerrole** column specified read access, the **writerrole** column write access, and the **ownersid** column the security identifier of the package owner.

You can import packages saved to SQL Server, the package store, or the file system into SQL Server or the package store. The destination of the imported package is specified by the type of folder from which you invoke the import process. If you import packages from a folder that manages packages stored in SQL Server, the package is imported into the **sysdtspackages90** table in the **msdb** SQL Server database; likewise, if you import packages from a folder that manages packages in the file system, the packages are imported into the folder specified in the Integration Services service file; otherwise, the packages are imported into the nonmanaged file system folder.

To import a package follow these steps:

1. Right-click the folder to which you want to import a package.
2. In the **Import Package** dialog box, select the storage type of the package that you want to import in the **Package location** drop-down list.
3. Depending on the storage type selected, provide a server name and, if applicable, a username and password.
4. Click the browse button (…) for the **Package path** option and then locate the package to import.
5. Optionally, modify the name of the imported package.
6. Optionally, click the browse button (…) for the **Protection level** option, and then update the protection level of the package (see Figure 16-49).

Integration Services provides a variety of protection levels. You first set the protection level when you develop a package. However, you might want to apply a different protection level to your imported packages. For example, if you import your packages to SQL Server, you may choose to rely on the built-in security features of SQL Server to keep packages safe and update the package to use the protection level, **Rely on server storage and roles for access control**.

To learn more about package protection levels, see the section, "How to Set User Properties to Secure Packages," earlier in this chapter.

Importing packages is a quick and easy way to install packages and to change the storage format of packages. However, you should be aware that the import feature does not include package dependencies. If your packages have dependencies, or they rely on ancillary files that you have added to the Integration Services project to deploy with the packages, then you should consider building a deployment utility and importing the packages by using the Package Installation Wizard.

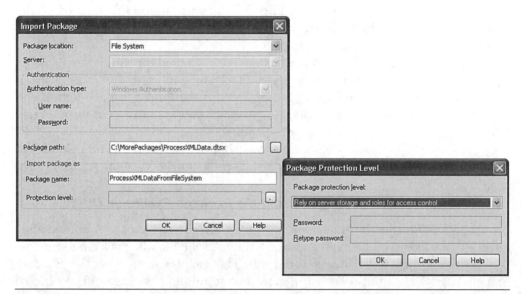

Figure 16-49   The Import Package dialog box imports a package saved to the file system, and the Package Protection dialog box updates the protection level of the package.

The export process is the reverse of the import process described previously. Import brings in packages; export sends out packages.

The steps to export a package are very similar to the steps to import a package. You can export packages to SQL Server, the package store, or the file system. If you export to SQL Server, you can export to the top-level folder for the **msdb** database or one of its subfolders.

If you export to the package store, you can specify any of the folders that Integration Services manages. The service manages two types of storage: the **msdb** SQL Server database and the folder that the configuration file for Integration Services specifies. If you export a package to the top-level folder for **msdb** or its subfolders, the package is exported to **msdb**. Likewise, if you export a package to the top-level folder that the service specifies or its subfolders, the package is exported to the file system.

If you export to the file system, you can specify any local or remote folder. The Integration Services service does not manage or monitor these packages.

To export a package follow these steps:

1. Right-click the package that you want to export.
2. In the **Export Package - <package name>** dialog box, in the **Package location** drop-down list, select the storage type to which you want to export the package.
3. Depending on the storage type selected, provide a server name and, if applicable, a user name and password.
4. Click the browse button (...) for the **Package path** option and then locate the location to which you want to export the package.
5. Optionally, modify the name of the exported package.
6. Optionally, click the browse button (...) for the **Protection level** option, and then update the protection level of the package.

How to Run Packages Using the Package Execution Utility

In SQL Server Management Studio, you can run packages immediately by using the Execute Package Utility or schedule the package to run in a step in a SQL Server Agent job. This chapter focuses on the Execute Package utility. To learn more about running packages in a job, see Chapter 8, "Inside Scheduling Tools."

The Execute Package Utility (see Figure 16-50) is a graphical interface on the **dtexec** command prompt utility; it includes the richness of the **dtexec** command line options, but it is more intuitive to use. The **dtexec** command prompt utility configures and runs packages that are saved to SQL Server, the package store, or the file system in a command prompt window. The utility provides access to package configuration and execution features. For example, you can set the values of properties, add logging capability, and specify a different package configuration file. If you are not comfortable running packages from the command prompt or you want to run packages without leaving SQL Server Management Studio, the Execute Package Utility is the tool of choice.

In the Execute Package Utility you can run the packages as they are, or you can use the pages in the user interface to modify the command line options that **dtexec** uses to run the package. The changes that you make apply only to the current execution instance; they are not saved.

To run a package using Execute Package Utility, right-click the package that you want to run and click **Run Package**.

Execute Package Utility has separate pages for different categories of options that you might want to configure. For example, the options for modifying all logging features are on the **Logging** page. You can run the package from any page. Table 16-5 presents a run-down of the pages and options you can set.

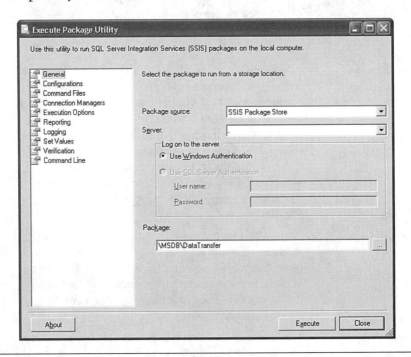

Figure 16-50   The General page of the Execute Package Utility.

TIP
The Package Configuration Wizard provides an easy and quick way to generate paths for properties. To generate multiple paths, use the XML or the SQL Server configuration type when you run the wizard.

TIP
The connection managers in the **Configuration String** drop-down list are not filtered by the selected log provider type. Make sure that the connection manager you select is compatible with the log provider type.

TIP
The Execute Package Utility provides an easy and foolproof way to generate command lines to use with the **dtexec** command prompt utility or save for reuse in command files.

Table 16-5   Execute Package Utility Pages

Page	Options to Set
General	Specify the location type, server, authentication mode, and the package to run.
Configurations	Add existing configurations files to the list of configurations to use, remove configurations, and modify the order in which configurations load. Remember, the order is important because in the case of multiple configurations updating the same property, the configuration loaded last wins, and in those cases, the configurations simply do not work if their order is not correct. For example, if an indirect configuration points to the location of the configuration file, then the indirect configuration must be loaded before the file.
Command files	Add existing command files to the list of command files to use, remove command files, and modify the order in which command files load. Remember that the order is important because in the case of multiple command files, loading the files in the wrong order may create an invalid command line.
Connection Managers	Modify the connection strings that the connection managers use. To make the connection string editable, select the check box to the left of the connection manager, and then edit the value in the Connection String column.
Execution Options	Specify how to handle package validation errors, modify the maximum number of concurrent executables within the package and choose whether to enable checkpoints. If you enable checkpoints, you can specify the file to which checkpoint information is written and the checkpoint restart option. Before you choose to enable checkpoints and select a restart option, you should read the section, How to Implement Checkpoints in Packages, in this chapter about configuring a package to use checkpoints.
	Another useful option on this page is the option to only validate the package. For example, you might want to validate the package to ensure changes in the runtime environment do not affect the package. Likewise, if you are changing a significant number of runtime options in the Package Execution Utility, you might want to make sure the package is still valid.

Page	Options to Set
Reporting	Select the events, package information, and level of information to report to the console.
Logging	Add, modify, or remove the logs to which the package writes. In the Log Provider column, select the type of log provider to use, and in the Configuration String list, select the existing connection manager that points to the location of the log.
Set Values	Add, modify, or remove the list of properties of the package or package objects to modify at runtime (in this context, "run time" is usually two words. Runtime does not refer to when, but what. For example, the runtime does this or the runtime does that). In the Package Path column, type the path of the property to set, and in the Value column type the value.
	The path notation lists the executables, delimited by backslashes, on the path to the object in the package. On the object on which you want to set a property, add ".Properties" and then in brackets, specify the name of the property.
	The following sample paths show the paths for package properties and properties on an Execute SQL task in the package, named Run SQL Statement.
	\Package.Properties[Name]
	\Package.Properties[DelayValidation]
	\Package\Run SQL Statement.Properties[SqlStatementSourceType]
	\Package\Run SQL Statement.Properties[SqlStatementSource]
	\Package\Run SQL Statement.Properties[ResultSetType]
	\Package\Run SQL Statement.Properties[MaximumErrorCount]
	\Package\Run SQL Statement.Properties[DelayValidation]
Verification	Specify the attributes to verify to allow the package to run. You can specify the package version to run, the package GUID to run, and the package version GUID to run. You can also specify whether only a signed package can be run.
Command Line	View and optionally edit the command line that dtexec will use to run the package. It is important to remember that the edited command line is not validated. If you edit the command line, it is not revalidated prior to package execution.

Table 16-5   Execute Package Utility Pages Continued

Page	Options to Set

	The following shows a simple command line that runs the package DataTransfer:
	
	`/DTS "\MSDB\DataTransfer" /SERVER "." /MAXCON-`
	`CURRENT " -1 " /CHECKPOINTING OFF  /REPORTING V`
	
	The package is stored in the msdb folder in the package store (the DTS option and the `"\MSDB\DataTransfer"` argument), on the local computer (the SERVER option and the `"."` argument), without checkpoints (the CHEKPOINT-ING option and the OFF argument), and reporting is verbose (the REPORTING option and the V argument).
	
	Notice that some arguments are enclosed in quotation marks and some are not. If an argument has no white space, it need not be enclosed in quotation marks. If a quoted string contains single quotation marks, you need to escape them by using double quotation marks. Also, in this command line all options begin with a slash (`/`), but minus sign (`-`) can be substituted.

When you click **Execute**, the **Package Execution Progress** dialog box opens (see Figure 16-51). The dialog box displays validation and progress information. While the package is running, you can click Stop to stop package execution. After the package completes, click **Close** to exit the dialog box.

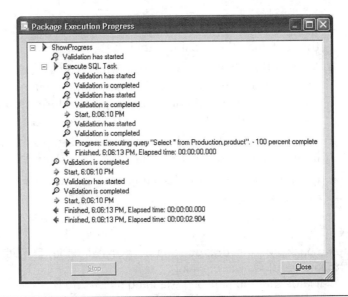

Figure 16-51   The Package Execution Progress dialog box shows validation, progress, start time, and finish times for the ShowProgress package.

How to Run Packages Using the dtexec Command Prompt Utility

You use the **dtexec** command prompt utility to execute Integration Services packages from the command prompt window. The **dtexec** command prompt utility supports access to package configuration and execution features. For example, in the command line for **dtexec** you can configure the package to use checkpoints, use a different configuration than the one specified when the package was designed, and specify the number of executable files that the package can run concurrently. The **dtexec** utility can run on packages saved to the **sysdtspackages90** table in the **msdb** SQL Server database, the package store, or the file system. Before taking a closer look at command lines for **dtexec**, let us briefly cover some basic rules for the command lines:

- Options must begin with a slash (/) or a minus sign (-). A single space delimits commands (like "/").
- The order of the options within the command line is not significant.
- Options and arguments in command lines are not case sensitive, with the exception of passwords. Variable names are case-sensitive

and the name specified by the Set command must be a case-sensitive match on the variable name.

- Most options have abbreviations, which you can use instead of the full option name. However, if you are not familiar with the **dtexec** options, you will probably find that using abbreviations makes the command line a bit more difficult to understand.

- Arguments are strings that contain no white space or are enclosed in quotation marks (like `"C:\Folder Name"`).

- Quotes within a quoted argument must be escaped by doubled quotation marks.

TIP

When a package runs, **dtexec** can return an exit code. The utility can set the following values when exiting:

0   indicates that the package executed successfully.
1   indicates that the package failed.
3   indicates that the package was canceled by the user.
4   indicates that the requested package could not be found.
5   indicates that the requested package could not be loaded.
6   indicates **dtexec** encountered an internal error or syntactic or semantic errors in the command line.

In the command line for **dtexec**, you provide the typical options and arguments; you specify the package to run, the package location type, and the package location. If the location type requires authentication, the command line also includes any applicable password and username (not usually one word).

The following command lines run a package saved to **sysdtspackages90** table in the **msdb** SQL Server database, the package store, and the file system.

To run a package saved to SQL Server using Windows Authentication:

```
dtexec /Sql MyPackage /Server MyServer
```

To run a package saved to the package store in the **MSDB** folder:

```
dtexec /DTS \MSDB\MyPackage /Server MyServer
```

To run a package saved to the file system:

```
dtexec /File c:\MyPackage.dtsx
```

A few more command line examples should prove useful. To run a package saved to the file system that uses the log file, MyLog.txt, and the XML configuration file, MyPackageConfig.dtsConfig:

```
dtexec /File c:\MyPackage.dtsx /Logger
DTS.LogProviderTextFile;c:\MyLog.txt /ConfigFile
c:\MyPackageConfig.dtsConfig
```

To run a package saved to SQL Server and set the value of the user-defined variable, MyVariable, defined in the scope of the task, MyTask:

```
dtexec /Sql MyPackage /Server MyServer /SET
➥\package\MyTask.Variables[User::MyVariable].Properties[Value];
➥newValue
```

To validate the package without running it:

```
dtexec /Sql MyPackage /Server MyServer /va
```

How to Manage Packages Using the dtutil Command Prompt Utility

You use the **dtutil** command prompt utility to manage Integration Services packages. The utility can copy, move, delete, or verify the existence of a package. You can run the utility to perform these actions on packages saved to the **sysdtspackages90** table in the **msdb** SQL Server database, the package store, or the file system. The **dtutil** command prompt utility does not support command files or redirection.

Before taking a closer look at command lines for **dutil**, let us briefly cover some basic rules for the command lines.

- Options must begin with a slash (/) or a minus sign (-). A single space delimits commands (like " /").
- The order of the options within the command line is not significant.
- Options and arguments in command lines are not case sensitive, with the exception of passwords.
- Most options have abbreviations, which you can use instead of the full option name. However, if you are not familiar with the **dtutil** options, you will probably find that using abbreviations makes the command line a bit more difficult to understand.

- Arguments are strings that contain no white space or are enclosed in quotation marks (like `"C:\Folder Name"`).
- Quotes within a quoted argument must be escaped by doubled quotation marks.

When forming the command line for **dtutil**, you provide the typical options and arguments: You specify the source and destination, package password if applicable, and depending on package source and destination, the pertinent username and password. However, when you move or copy packages you have the opportunity to reconfigure the package in significant ways; you can change the package protection level, regenerate the package GUID, or sign the package.

You use the `En[crypt]` option to encrypt the package with the specified package protection level. The syntax is: `/En[crypt] {SQL | FILE}; Path;ProtectionLevel[;password]`. The first argument indicates the package location type, the second the package path, and the third the package protection level. Depending on the protection level, you may need to include a fourth argument: the password with which the package was encrypted.

To encrypt a package saved to the file system using the password @fIH1K9, you would use the following command:

```
dtutil /Encrypt File;
C:\MyEncryptedPackages\MyEncryptedPackage.dtsx;2;
➥@fIH1K9
```

The **dtutil** command prompt utility uses numeric values to indicate the protection level. Table 16-6 describes the package protection levels.

Table 16-6   Package Protection Levels

Level	Description
0	Removes sensitive information from the package.
1	Encrypts sensitive information, using the credentials of the local user.
2	Encrypts sensitive information, using a user-defined password.
3	Encrypts the package, using the credentials of the local user.
4	Encrypts the package information, using a user-defined password.
5	Relies on SQL Server security features to protect the package.

You use the /I[DRegenerate] option create a new GUID for a package and update the package ID property. When you copy a package, the package ID remains the same and it is impossible to differentiate log entries of the original package and the package copy. If you plan on running both the original and the copy, it's a good idea to regenerate the ID in the copied package. The IDRegenerate option takes no arguments.

To copy and generate a new package ID for a package saved in the file system, you would run the following command:

```
dtutil /File c:\MyFolder\MyPackage.dtsx /Copy
➥FILE;c:\MyCopyFolder\MyCopiedPackage.dtsx /I
```

The capability to sign packages is another Integration Services security feature. You can use the /Si[gn] option to sign a package using a digital signature. The Sign option takes three arguments, which are separated by semicolon. The syntax is: /Si[gn] {SQL | File | DTS}; path; hash. The first argument indicates the package location type, the second the package path, and the third the certificate identifier, expressed as a hexadecimal string. The command line uses a sample hash.

To copy and sign a package saved in the file system you would use this command:

```
dtutil /File c:\MyFolder\MyPackage.dtsx /Copy
➥FILE;c:\MyCopyFolder\MyCopiedPackage.dtsx /Sign
➥FILE;c:\MyCopyFolder\MyCopiedPackage.dtsx;0x68DE0F55C5E86B70530
➥D484A39E12CDE13F4741
```

TIP

If the package is already signed, **dtutil** prompts for confirmation to re-sign the package. If the command line includes the Quiet option, the package is silently re-signed.

How to View Summaries of Package Properties

SQL Server Management Studio includes the **Summary** tab, which can display information about Integration Services folders and packages. If the Summary tab is not visible, press F7 or click **Summary** on the **View** menu. You can view information in a list or report format. Figure 16-52 displays the report format. Depending on whether a folder of package is selected, the list and report formats provide different types of information.

Lists and reports on folders provide information about the subfolders and packages in the folder, and on packages, lists, and reports they provide information about the selected package. The report on the Running Packages folder lists the running packages.

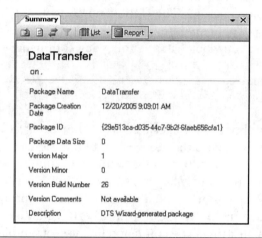

Figure 16-52   The report on the DataTransfer package.

If you run packages by using the Execute Package Utility, you can specify the package version and build version you want to permit to run. The report on the **Summary** tab lists this information.

Summary

Now you are familiar with the SQL Server 2005 Integration Services concepts and the tools that you use to create, configure, and deploy the packages that are part of an Integration Services solution.

First, this chapter covered Business Intelligence Development Studio, the IDE, in which you create Integration Services projects to manage your Integration Services solutions. You learned about the tools that Business Intelligence Studio provides for building packages, the SQL Server Import and Export Wizard that provides a great way to build simple data transfer packages and to get a head start on complex packages, and SSIS Designer to create enterprise-level packages from the ground up. We delved into SSIS Designer and discussed the design surfaces within SSIS

Designer and the package functionality that you build on each surface. Integration Services provides tools for implementing more advanced features in packages, and we covered the tools that are available from SSIS Designer to implement logging, configurations, and variables. Next you explored the tools to create a deployment bundle (a deployment utility, packages, and package dependencies) to use to deploy packages to a test or production environment. After packages are deployed, they can be run and managed in SQL Server Management Studio, and you saw the tools that this environment provides to perform tasks such as importing and exporting packages and setting the roles that control package access. To complete the tools discussion, we talked about the command prompt utilities that you can use to run or manage packages.

After the discussion of concepts and tools, this chapter provided examples of commonly occurring scenarios in each phase of the life cycle of an Integration Services solution, including detailed information about how to configure and use Business Intelligence Development Studio and how to do tasks related to the development, deployment, and management of Integration Services packages.

This chapter did not cover all the individual tools that Integration Services provides to configure connections and the control flow and data flow elements in packages. For example, we touched only on the tools for the control flow elements that implement looping, the For Loop and Foreach Loop containers that are new in Integration Services. Books Online, the documentation, provided with SQL Server 2005, contains information about the many tools that you can use to configure the tasks, sources, transformations, destinations, and connection managers that Integration Services includes.

CHAPTER 17

Inside the Reporting Services Tools

Reporting Services makes it easy for you to build data-driven reports and deploy them to a server so that everyone in your organization can access them. End users can then access these reports by using a Web browser or custom application. With SQL Server 2005, Reporting Services also enables end users to build their own reports to get the information they need for business decisions.

Compared to the other components of SQL Server, Reporting Services is a relative newcomer. The original goal of Reporting Services came from a desire to make SQL Server more immediately accessible to end users. Although SQL Server provided lots of tools and services for managing data, it didn't have much for delivering that data to end users.

The Reporting Services team began working on Reporting Services in 2001 and had originally intended it to be part of the "Yukon" release (which was eventually named SQL Server 2005). When we began showing early builds of the product to customers, the response was overwhelming and led us to release the product early. We released the first version as an add-on in early 2004. In 2005, we joined the rest of SQL Server to deliver the current version.

This chapter begins with an overview of Reporting Services tools and walks the reader through several scenarios that highlight some of key functionality of the product while also providing insights, tips, and techniques. We hope you will find many valuable how-to techniques throughout this chapter.

Reporting Services Tools Overview

This section provides an overview of the various tools used in installing and configuring Reporting Services, and designing, managing, and scheduling reports.

Setup and Configuration

The first step in deploying Reporting Services is correctly installing and configuring your server. If you are familiar with SQL Server 2000 Reporting Services, you know that configuration of the server was handled directly during setup. After setup completed, you made changes to the configuration by editing the configuration files directly or using a set of command line tools.

In contrast, setup of SQL Server 2005 Reporting Services comes in two configurations: a default server configuration that is useful for single box configurations, and a "files only," or custom, configuration. Custom configurations are useful when you want to use a remote SQL Server database to store your Reporting Services metadata or you are setting up a scale-out configuration on your server. You might also end up using a custom configuration when upgrading from SQL Server 2005 if you have made modifications to the configuration files on your server.

Reporting Services Configuration Tool

After setup is complete, you configure the report server through the Reporting Services Configuration tool, as shown in Figure 17-1. This new tool ships with SQL Server 2005 and is a vast improvement over how you configured the SQL Server 2000 version (which was basically through Notepad).

Configuring a single server is pretty easy with the tool. Like the SQL Server Configuration Manager described in Chapter 3, the Reporting Services Configuration tool works via a WMI interface. This means that you can manage a Reporting Services instance remotely and before the Web service has been initialized.

It is important to understand that Reporting Services, unlike the relational engine, is actually two services. The first is the Report Server Windows Service, which is stopped and started via the Service Control manager. The Windows Service is responsible for asynchronous or background processing tasks. The second service that makes up Reporting Services is the web service (actually hosted within Internet Information Services), which is responsible for responding to on-demand user requests.

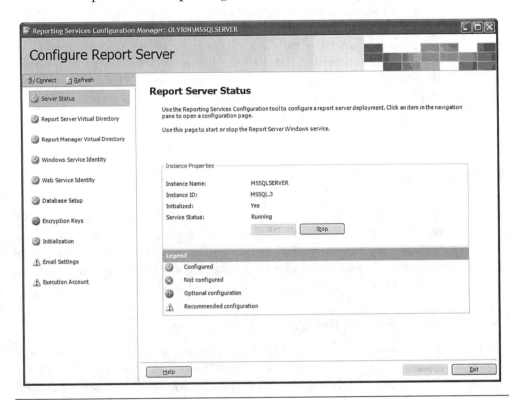

Figure 17-1   Reporting Services configuration tool.

Scale-Out Configuration

Configuration of Reporting Services in a scale-out configuration is a feature of the enterprise edition. It enables you to add new Reporting Services instances to the same catalog database, thereby accommodating additional user load. When configuring a scale-out configuration, it is important to understand the role of initialization, which occurs when a new instance is added.

All report servers in a scale-out configuration share a single key (called a symmetric key) used to encrypt certain information, generally connection strings and credentials, in the report server database. Copies of the symmetric key itself are stored in a table in the report server database, each copy encrypted using the machine key of each of the nodes in the configuration. During initialization, this key is decrypted by one machine and a row is added for the new machine. The Initialization tab in the Tool lets you control this process as well as remove machines from the configuration that are no longer necessary.

If all machines lose the capability to decrypt this key, you need to re-enter all the encrypted data. Therefore, in addition to backing up the Report Server catalog database, you should make a backup of the key, using the Configuration Tool, and keep it in a safe place in case you need to restore the database to a new set of machines.

Building Reports

After you have gotten your server up and running, you can start building reports. SQL Server 2005 Reporting Services gives you two options for building reports: Report Designer, which is the report design tool of choice for IT professionals and developers, and Report Builder, which is targeted toward end users.

Using Report Designer

The Report Designer in SQL Server 2005 is an updated version of the one that shipped in SQL Server 2000 Reporting Services. One of the nice things in SQL Server 2005 is that you don't need to have Visual Studio installed to use the Report Designer. SQL Server 2005 comes with Business Intelligence Development Studio (BIDS), which is a version of the Visual Studio 2005 shell. If you already have Visual Studio 2005 installed, the Report Designer is added alongside the existing projects. As you have seen in earlier chapters, BIDS is the same tool used to develop SQL Server 2005 Analysis Services databases and SQL Server 2005 Integration Services packages.

BIDS is the environment to use for the following type of tasks:

- Designing reports
- Editing a report built in Report designer or Report builder
- Deploying a Report project to various Reporting Servers
- Optimizing report queries
- Enhancing reports with parameters or multiple data regions

Launch BIDS from the SQL Server Program Group in the Start menu. If you select Business Intelligence Projects from the dialog, you get started with a blank report server project or use the report server project wizard to get a quick start, as shown in Figure 17-2.

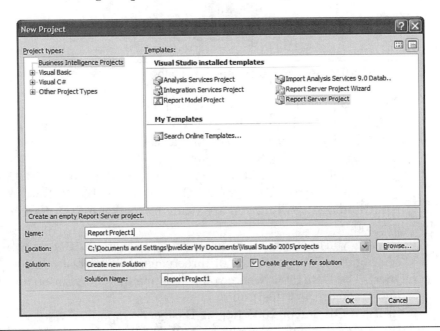

Figure 17-2   Creating a new Reporting Services project.

A report server project consists of a set of reports, resources, and data source definitions. A report server project is also the unit of deployment to a report server.

TIP

Right-clicking on the name of a report in the project window and choosing **View Code** lets you edit the report definition text as shown in Figure 17-3. Reports are defined in RDL, an XML schema that is documented in SQL Server Books Online. Some operations, such as replacing all occurrences of a string within a report, can be done more easily if you edit the RDL file directly. Just be careful when you edit the file because an invalid RDL file will not load back into the graphical editor.

Figure 17-3   Reporting Services folder security dialog.

SQL Server 2000 Reporting Services reports can be opened with the SQL Server 2005 Report Designer. When the report is saved, it changes to the 2005 Reporting Services format and cannot be used with SQL Server 2000 Reporting Services any longer.

The bottom line is this: Open the report in the SQL Server 2005 Reporting Services Report Designer available in BI Development Studio only when you are ready to stay with SQL Server 2005 for good.

After you open a report, you are presented with the Report Designer (see Figure 17-4), consisting of three panes labeled Data, Layout, and Query. The Data tab is where you will define the query (or queries for a report) and preview the results.

The SQL Server 2005 Report Designer supports a wider variety of data sources compared with the SQL 2000 version. Supported data sources include

- SQL Server Relational Database
- OLE DB
- ODBC
- Oracle
- SQL Server Analysis Services (discussed later in this chapter)
- Report Builder Models (discussed later in this chapter)
- XML
- SAP NetWeaver BI (included with Service Pack 1)

It is important to understand that Reporting Services completely separates the query from the report layout. Although each data source may have a different query designer, after the data is retrieved, it is treated the same.

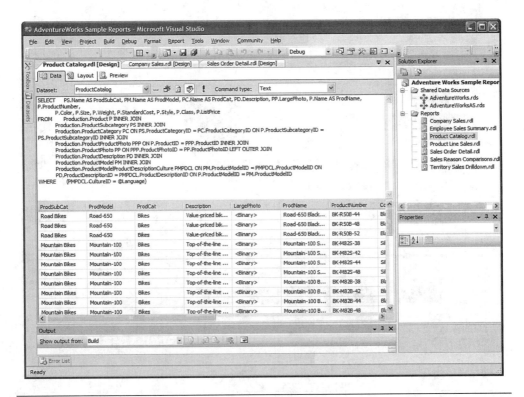

Figure 17-4 Reporting Services query designer.

After you have defined your query, you are ready to arrange the data on the report surface. This is done in the Layout tab, as shown in Figure 17-5.

TIP

If you are familiar with other report editing tools, you might wonder where the report header and page headers are. In a Reporting Services report, the report header is simply the section of the body that appears before any of the data regions. The page header and footers are available if you right-click on the Layout surface or select them in the report menu. In addition, the table and matrix data regions are capable of having elements repeat on each page. You can access this behavior through the Properties dialogs for each control.

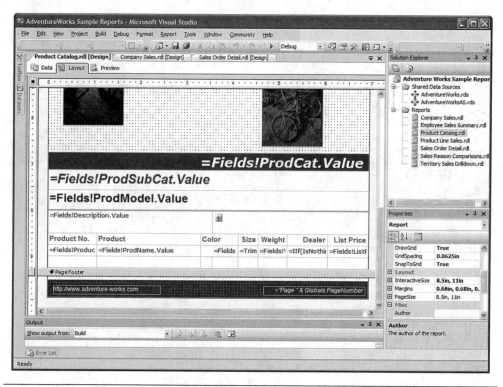

Figure 17-5 Reporting Services Layout tab.

As you start building reports, you will notice that most of the properties of the objects in your reports can be expressions (see Figure 17-6). Learning how to use expressions is critical to being able to get dynamic report behavior, such as conditional formatting or visibility. One of the nice features of the SQL Server 2005 Report Designer is a new version of the expression editor, available whenever an expression is available for a property.

Because the expression language used is Visual Basic .NET, the expression editor uses the IntelliSense features of Visual Studio to provide statement completion and syntax checking.

Deploying Reports

After you have finished editing your reports, you are ready to deploy them to your report server. If you used the Report Server Project Wizard (see Figure 17-7), you already have been prompted for a location for deployment. If not, you need to specify the URL in the project properties, as shown in Figure 17-7.

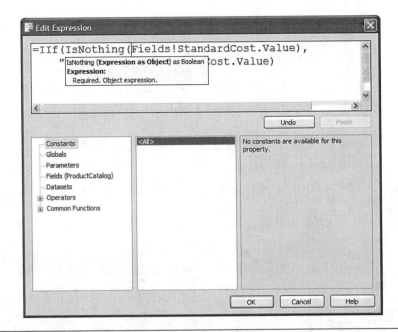

Figure 17-6   Reporting Services Expression Editor.

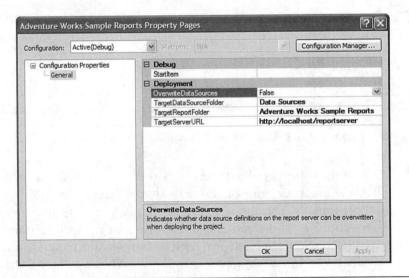

Figure 17-7   Reporting Services project properties.

After specifying the location of your Report Server, you can deploy by selecting Deploy Report Project from the Build menu.

Using Report Builder

If Report Designer is too complex for your users, you can enable them to use Report Builder, a new tool that enables end users to build their own reports. Report Builder has an Office-like interface that makes it easy to construct a report (see Figure 17-8).

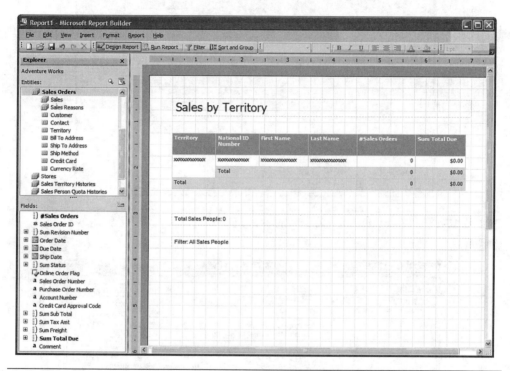

Figure 17-8 Reporting Services Report Builder.

One of the differences between Report Builder and Report Designer is that a semantic model of the data source is used to build reports in Report Builder. This model keeps the query hidden from end users, and they can focus on the contents of their queries rather than query syntax.

The semantic models for Report Builder are created in a Report Model Project in BIDS (see Figure 17-9). When you launch BIDS, you can create a new Report Model project. You can then use the Model Designer Wizard to generate a default model based on the database schema. After the wizard has generated the initial set of entities, you can customize the model based on what you would like to present end users.

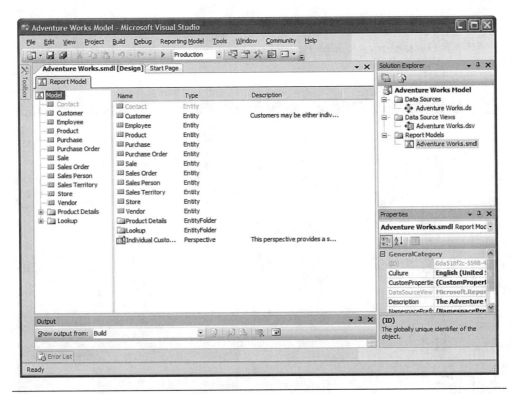

Figure 17-9   Reporting Services Report Model in BIDS.

If you are building a Report Builder model over an SQL Server Analysis Services data source, you do not need to use the Report Model Designer. You can simply use Report Manager or SQL Server Management Studio to generate the model from the SSAS schema.

Using Model Data Sources in Report Designer

Although Report Models are primarily used to power Report Builder, they can also be used within the Report Designer. Because the Report Designer has additional features and flexibility that is not present in Report Builder, you can add extra zip to a report created in Report Builder. You can also use Report Designer to craft custom click-through reports that users will see as they explore the model-based data sources (see Figure 17-10).

To use a Report Builder model as a data source in Report Designer, select Report Server Model from the connection type drop-down.

The connection string will be in the form Server=*Report Server* URL;
DataSource=*Model Path*. For example, the connection string might
look like this:

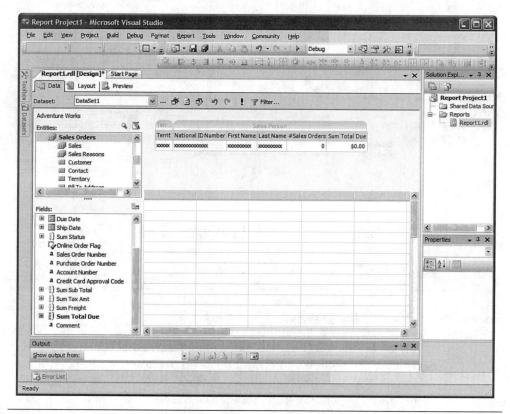

Figure 17-10 Using Report Builder in Report Designer.

```
Server=http://myserver/reportserver;DataSource=
/Models/AdventureWorks
```

The query design surface for report models in the Report Designer is
similar to what you will find in Report Builder. The main difference is
that you will build the query independently of the layout, just as with
other data sources in Report Designer.

Choosing the Correct Type of Data Source for Your Report

With all the types of data sources available to you, you might be wondering whether you should build reports directly against your source systems, build a Report Builder model on your source system or data mart, or use Analysis Services to build an OLAP database. Several questions can help you determine which is the correct approach for your environment.

- Does the report need to present aggregated or detailed information?
- What types of tools will be used to access the data?
- What is the level of expertise of the people that need to design reports?
- Does the report author have permission to modify the schema of the underlying data?

If the report simply displays detailed data that exists in the underlying relational data and can be accessed with fairly straightforward SQL statements, then building on top of the relational source might be the best option. If the reports will primarily present aggregated data, then things may be much easier if done over an OLAP source.

If calculations or extra metadata need to be added to your reports, then using a model-based approach is better than adding them to every single report. Both Report Builder Models and Analysis Services can shield report designers from the underlying relational data source design. Whereas Report Builder models are entity-based, Analysis Services uses a dimensionally based model (OLAP). Defining these calculations and extra metadata in a Report Builder model or an OLAP database may make the maintenance of the reports easier in the long run because they have to be defined only once in one place and just referred to from each report.

OLAP also enables complex calculations to be added, such as time-based calculations (e.g., Year to Date, Year over Year), cumulative sum calculations, custom aggregations (e.g., weighted average, last non empty) or hierarchically based calculations. In contrast, building a Year-to-Date (YTD) calculation in a relational system can result in over 50 lines of SQL statements because there is no notion of time hierarchy in a relational store. The calculation needs to scan the entire data set to isolate the data for the range of months, then for weeks, months, and quarters.

Which tools will users need to access the data source? If the answer is only Report Designer, then going directly against the transactional source might be the right answer. If you want to make Report Builder available to end users, you need to build a Report Builder model. If you want to make data available in analytical tools such as Microsoft Excel or ProClarity (which has been acquired by Microsoft), then an OLAP database is the way to go.

What are the levels of expertise of the report authors or of the people that will need to manage and maintain these reports? If they are familiar with writing SQL statements and understand the structure of the relational database, then writing reports over such a relational database is perfectly fine. On the other hand, if the report authors or managers are not fully comfortable with SQL and relational third normal form database design, then it may be appropriate to add a semantic layer (OLAP or Report Builder model) over the relational source.

Will report authors have permission to modify the schema of the underlying data source if need be? Some time views or additional relationships may need to be created to achieve the report's design goal. If the report author doesn't have permission to edit the underlying data source because it is a production OLTP system or it is a data warehouse owned by a different business unit, building a Report Builder Model or Analysis Services cube gives you the option to do schema modeling on the data without impacting the underlying relational data source.

Managing and Securing Reports

After you have authored reports and published them to the report server, you need to consider how to make sure that the proper people have access to them.

SQL Server 2005 comes with two tools for managing items in the Reporting Services catalog: a Web-based tool called Report Manager and the Windows-based SQL Server Management Studio (SSMS). SSMS is the same tool that you use to manage your other SQL Server components.

Using SQL Server Management Studio

SQL Server Management Studio is the environment to use for the following type of tasks:

- Defining security role and report permissions
- Defining subscriptions
- Defining shared schedules
- Defining report cache policies
- Defining linked reports
- Defining new data sources
- Scripting report server operations

You connect to your report server in Management Studio (SSMS) by selecting Reporting Services in the Server Type drop-down in the connection dialog (see Figure 17-11) and supply the name of your server, using either ServerName\InstanceName syntax or a URL (e.g., http://servername/reportserver), as shown in Figure 17.11.

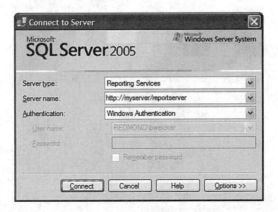

Figure 17-11 Connecting to SQL Server Reporting Services.

After you are connected to a report server, you can see the contents of the server displayed in the SSMS Object Explorer (see Figure 17-12). From here, you can bring up the Property dialog for any object in the report server catalog.

Securing Reports

Managing Reporting Services security requires an understanding of the different ways that content can be secured on the report server. The first level of security is on the objects in the report server catalog (reports, models, data sources, resources), which can be secured in a role-based security mechanism. Roles are sets of permissions that can be granted to users or groups for specific items in the report server catalog. Reporting Services comes with several built-in roles, called Browser or Content Manager, that you can assign to your users by using SSMS or Report Manager (see Figure 17-13).

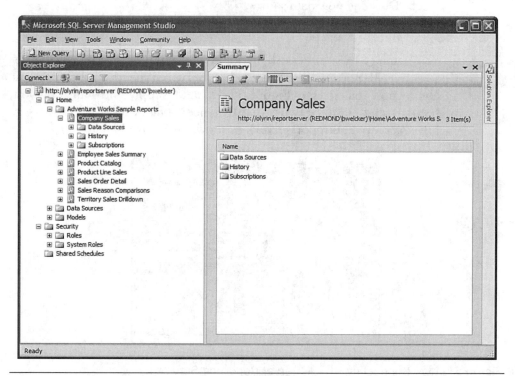

Figure 17-12 Reporting Services objects in Object Explorer.

To set security on an item, you need to break the inheritance of the security roles from the parent and then modify the roles for the item.

TIP
Like other dialogs in SQL Server Management Studio, Reporting Services property dialogs can be scripted. This makes it easy to create a set of operations that you can execute later. Although the scripts generated cannot be directly executed in SSMS, you can save them for later execution through the Reporting Services script host, `rs.exe`.

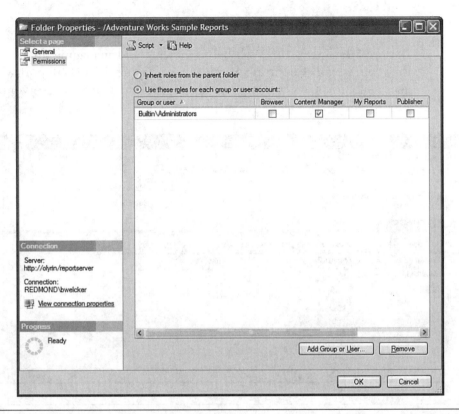

Figure 17-13   Report Designer Security Property dialog.

In addition to setting security on the reports themselves, the data source connection information can also be managed after a report is published to the server. Although reports can be built to take advantage of Windows integrated security to access the data source, this limits their usefulness. For example, if your report server is not on the same system as the data source that you are using, you cannot use integrated security unless you have implemented Kerberos delegation (for more information about delegation, see the Microsoft Knowledge Base on MSDN).

Most users use a single set of stored credentials (either SQL or Windows) to access back-end data sources. They then use the name of the user accessing the reports (available in the report through the global expression User!UserID) to potentially limit the amount of data coming back from the report queries.

Using Report Manager

Report Manager is the Web-based viewing and managing application that comes with Reporting Services (see Figure 17-14). Report Manager enables you to view and manage reports on your report server (see Figure 17-15).

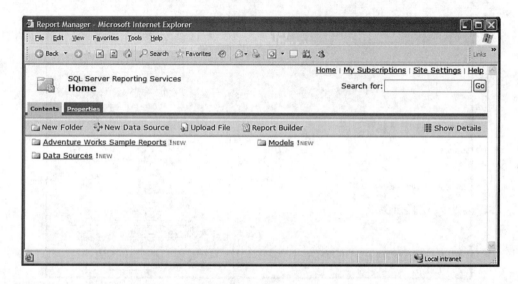

Figure 17-14 Reporting Services Report Manager.

Report Manager is the environment to use for the following types of tasks:

- Run and navigate reports
- Upload report to a server
- Define security role and report permissions
- Define subscriptions
- Define shared schedule and snapshot schedules
- Define caching policies
- Invoke Report Builder
- Define linked reports
- Define new data sources

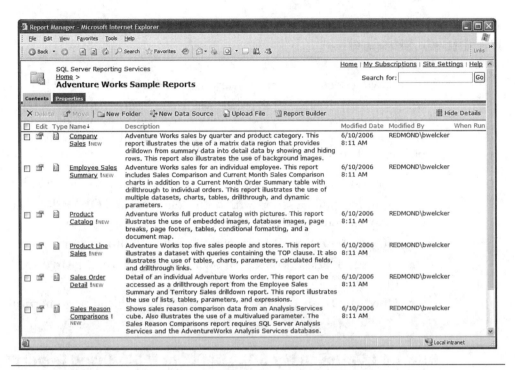

Figure 17-15   Reporting Services Report Manager (details).

Report Manager includes many of the tasks that can be accomplished through SQL Server Management Studio. So you may wonder, why the need for Report Manager? Reporting is an activity that is frequently done through a Web browser interface. As such, Report Manager allows you to perform many of the management activities remotely without the need to install SSMS. Also, many of the management tasks can be delegated to end users (e.g., scheduling snapshots, defining a new subscription). What if you don't like the look and feel of Report Manager? Report Manager was designed as a sample to demonstrate the use of the Reporting Services Web service API. As a result, every single capability of the Report Manager can be integrated in a your own custom-built application.

Now that you understand some fundamentals about the toolset, it is time to look at how it you can use it to address problems in some common business scenarios.

Using Reporting Services Tools to Solve Problems in Business Scenarios

The following section discusses various scenarios and technical situations in which you may find yourself. The goal of these scenarios is to go beyond the basic step-by-steps of how to use the designers or wizards and to provide tips about and insights into some of their less obvious capabilities. The scenarios include the following:

- How do I optimize my query report through Report Designer?
- How do I build a report with both Relational and OLAP data that share the same parameter field?
- How do I use Report Designer to bring KPI into a report?
- How can I let users pick their own languages at runtime to display the report?
- How can I use the Report Designer to build an asymmetrical report?

How Do I Optimize My SQL-, DMX-, or MDX-Based Report through Report Designer?

You can write a Reporting Services report by using SQL against a relational database, DMX against a data mining model, or MDX against an OLAP cube. Even though Report Designer provides a wizard and a graphical query builder, the database professional authoring a report can always view the generated SQL, DMX, or MDX query and tune it.

For example, if you look at a basic report sourced from the Adventure Works DW sample OLAP database, the graphical query builder embedded in Report Designer generates the query for the author shown in Figure 17-16.

The author can look at the query behind the report and edit it if necessary. In the case presented here, by clicking on the design button at the extreme right of the embedded designer toolbar, the author can now see the MDX query generated. This MDX query is actually more sophisticated than a regular MDX query because it also contains parameterization information (e.g., the @CustomerCountry parameter embedded in the query in Figure 17-17).

Now the MDX query can be copied out of the Report Designer and pasted in SQL Server Management Studio to change and optimize it.

By looking at SQL Profiler, you can assess the performance of the query, make changes, and reevaluate it. As soon as the report author is happy with the performance of the query, it can be pasted back into the Report Designer. For this exercise, the parameters have to be taken out and replaced when the MDX query is pasted back into the Report Designer.

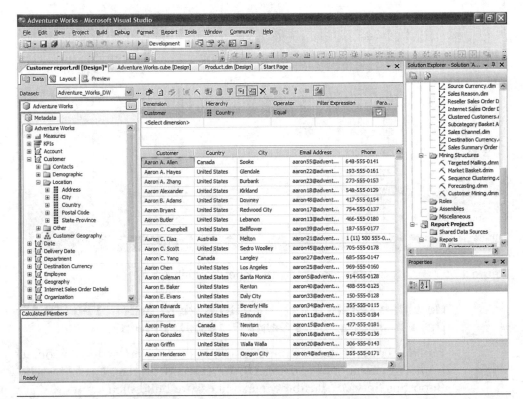

Figure 17-16   Analysis Services Query Designer (graphical).

Based on the nature of the changes, the report author may not be allowed to go back into graphical mode if the structure of the MDX query cannot be graphically displayed in simple columns format.

Similarly, this method can be used for a SQL or DMX-based report.

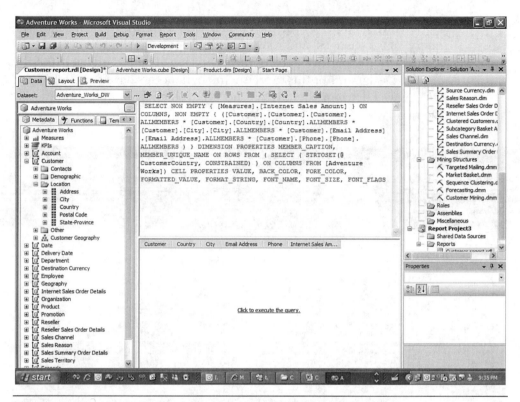

Figure 17-17   Analysis Services Query Designer (textual).

How Can I Build a Report with Both Relational and OLAP Data That Share the Same Parameter Field?

In many cases, it may be important to build a report with data coming from both relational and OLAP sources and display it side by side. Reporting Services' flexibility makes it easy to build such a report.

All you need to do is build a table or list based on data coming from the relational source and another with data coming from the OLAP data source. To do this, you need to define different queries against each source. If the report needs to show parameters, additional queries may need to be defined for each parameter, as shown in Figure 17-18.

It does not make for a very elegant report if you need to use two different sets of report parameters for each section, especially if these parameters are representing the same item.

So as long as the values for this parameter are the same between both sources, it is perfectly feasible to define only one set of parameter values, using a single parameter query, and reference it from both regions of the report.

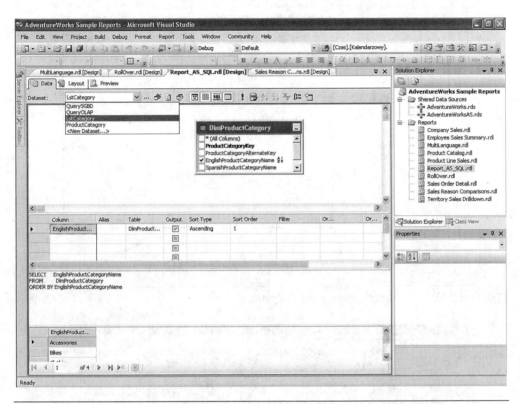

Figure 17-18   Multiple query definitions.

As shown in Figure 17-19, it is perfectly okay to have an OLAP region use a SQL-based query for parameter values.

The resulting report displays the very same information twice (see Figure 17-20). Although this is not very valuable in practice, it demonstrates the fact that the same parameter can be shared between two regions based on different data sources. The result here displays the same data, but coming from both OLAP and relational data sources.

The report presented in this scenario is provided on the book's CD, named Report_AS_SQL.rdl. The report project containing this report and others described in this chapter can be deployed on your report server as long as the AdventureWorks DW OLAP project has been deployed on this machine previously.

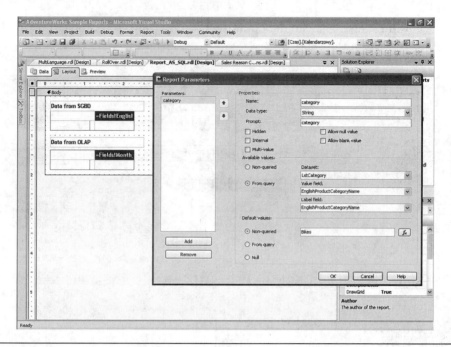

Figure 17-19   Common parameter definition.

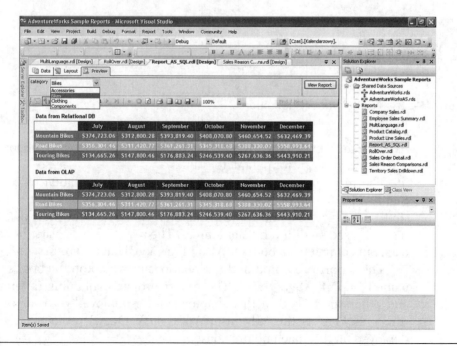

Figure 17-20   Previewing multi-source report with a common parameter.

How Do I Use Report Designer to Bring KPIs into a Report?

One of the most popular questions we get is "How do I display Analysis Services Key Performance Indicators (KPIs) in a report?" In the Analysis Services chapter, you saw how to display KPIs with Report Builder. In this case, it turns out that Report Builder is better than Report Designer in terms of exposing KPIs. The reason is that you cannot expect a business user to author formulas for displaying KPIs. Unfortunately, we did not have time to migrate the work done in Report Builder into Report Designer as it was done toward the very end of the product cycle. Although you can expect this to be addressed in a future release, for now it must be done manually. The good news is that you can achieve this in Report Designer with a little bit more work.

First, you need to add an image field in your table. When the image wizard prompt you for images, select one of the images that you have previously embedded in your report definition, as shown in Figure 17-21.

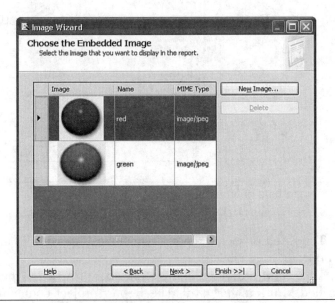

Figure 17-21   Using embedded images.

Then, define an expression that alternatively displays one image or the other, based on a conditional expression, as shown in Figure 17-22. Obviously, the expression can be more sophisticated than the example in Figure 17-22 and contain as many conditions as needed. For example, if the KPI needs to be able to show five different gauges based on five different thresholds, you can accommodate this by using the Case function or nested `if` conditions.

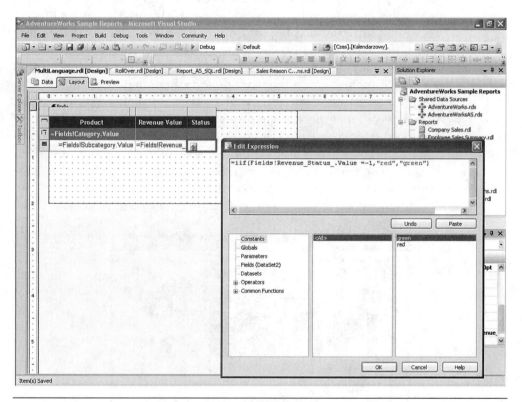

Figure 17-22   Image field conditional expression.

The result of such a report is shown in Figure 17-23 in the following section.

The report presented in this scenario is provided in the book's CD. It is called MultiLanguage.rdl. The Report project containing this report and others described in this chapter can be deployed on your server as long as the AdventureWorks DW OLAP project has been deployed on the machine previously.

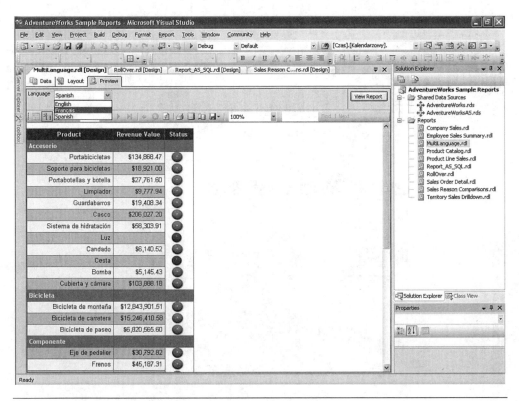

Figure 17-23   Language selection in Report Viewer.

How Can I Let Users Pick Their Own Languages at Runtime to Display the Report?

One of the advantages of building a report on top of an OLAP database is the fact that an OLAP database can be fully localized. All metadata and data can be localized in as many languages as are supported by Microsoft Windows.

The benefit is that end users can, at runtime, select the language that they want to use to display the report, as shown in Figure 17-23. The trick here is to be able to pass the selected language Locale Identifier in the connection string. As shown in Figure 17-24, you can do so by using the GetLCID() function and passing the parameter value as a parameter for it.

The report presented in this scenario is provided on the book's CD. As with the previous scenario, it uses the MultiLanguage.rdl report. The report project containing this report and others described in this chapter can be deployed on your server as long as the AdventureWorks DW OLAP project has been deployed on this machine previously.

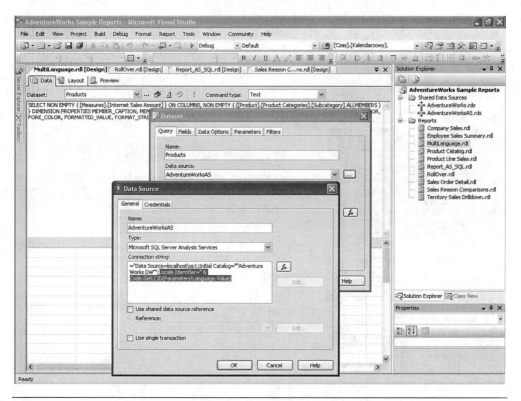

Figure 17-24   Locale Identifier dynamic definition in connection string.

How Can I Use Report Designer to Build an Asymmetrical Report?

Most reports built with Report Designer are either matrix or table-based. These are commonly used for sales and marketing analytical reports or operational reports. When it comes to financial style reports, usually an asymmetrical design is needed. A typical example is a rolling forecast report that contains two areas. The first area is made of actual data shown for every month from the first month of the year until the current month (as defined by the parameter or the computer clock, for example). The second area must display budget data for the remaining months of the year, as shown in Figure 17-25.

This is often easier said than done. Indeed, you may need to define a matrix-based report with a specific filter that will intelligently display the correct category of data for the correct month, based on the Month parameter value. As you can see from Figure 17-25, it is not just the data that needs to be filtered; in this case, the column header formatting needs to be set dynamically, based on the Month parameter.

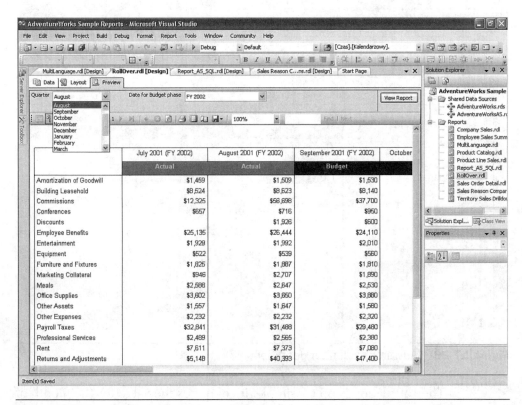

Figure 17-25 Asymmetrical report definition.

For the column header, the background color needs to be set to the following:

```
=iif(Fields!Scenario.Value="Actual","SteelBlue",
"MidnightBlue")
```

For the data, it is slightly trickier. The filter needs to be set on the matrix object, as shown in Figure 17-26.

The full expression is

```
=iif(month(Fields!Me.Value)+6 -((2002-
year(Fields!Me.Value))*12) <=
Parameters!Month.Value,"Actual","Budget")
```

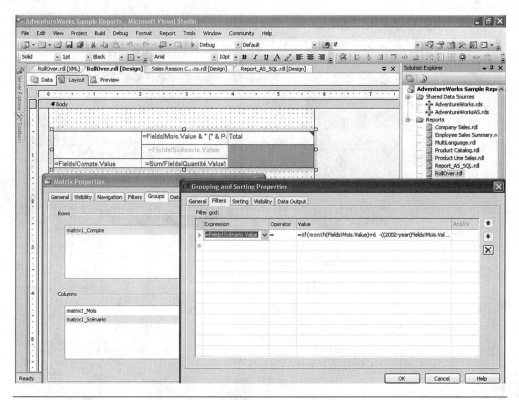

Figure 17-26   Asymmetrical filter definition.

The calculation is pretty simple; it compares the value for the month of the current matrix column with the value for the Month parameter (see Figure 17-27).

The Month parameter values are offset by 6 to comply with the fiscal year. If it was to be set on a regular calendar, it would start with January = 1 instead.

So let's review this formula above an example. Imagine that the parameter is August 2002. Then for the first column of the Matrix (July 2002), the formula becomes

```
=iif(6 + 6 -((2002-2001)*12) <= 2,"Actual","Budget")
```

which resolves as 0<2, thus "Actual."

This formula resolves similarly for the next month, August 2001, but then resolves as >2 for every other month after August 2001.

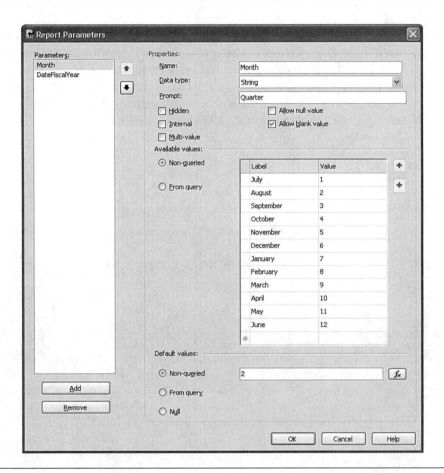

Figure 17-27   Month parameter value definition.

The report presented in this scenario is provided on the book's CD. It is called RollOver.rdl. The Report project containing this report and others described in this chapter can be deployed on your server as long as the AdventureWorks DW OLAP project has been deployed on the machine previously.

Summary

This chapter presented the breadth of tools available with SQL Server 2005 Reporting Services, from configuring your server to building reports, through deploying and managing your report server. We hope this chapter was able to convey some of the report authoring improvements in the latest release for both developers and business users and how you can manage your reporting environment through a variety of easy-to-use tools. At the same time, we have shown how you can use Reporting Services to solve various problems in typical business scenarios.

Sample KPI Client Code— Retrieving and Exposing Your First KPI

The following code needs to reference Microsoft.AnalysisServices. AdomdClient.dll:

```
string asConnectionString = "Provider=MSOLAP.3;Data
Source=localhost;Initial Catalog=Adventure Works DW";
AdomdConnection asConnection = new
AdomdConnection(asConnectionString);
try
{
asConnection.Open();
    foreach (CubeDef cubeDef in asConnection.Cubes)
        {
            if (cubeDef.Properties["CUBE_TYPE"].Value.Equals("CUBE"))
                {
                    string commandText = @"SELECT { strtomember(@Value),
                                    strtomember(@Goal),
                                    strtomember(@Status),
                                    strtomember(@Trend) }
                    ON COLUMNS FROM [" + cubeDef.Name + "]";

                    AdomdCommand command = new AdomdCommand(commandText,
                                    this.asConnection);

                    foreach (Kpi kpi in cubeDef.Kpis)
                    {
                      command.Parameters.Clear();
                      command.Parameters.Add(new
                        AdomdParameter("Value",
                        kpi.Properties["KPI_VALUE"].Value));
```

```
                    command.Parameters.Add(new
                       AdomdParameter("Goal",
                       kpi.Properties["KPI_GOAL"].Value));
                    command.Parameters.Add(new
                       AdomdParameter("Status",
                       kpi.Properties["KPI_STATUS"].Value));
                    command.Parameters.Add(new
                       AdomdParameter("Trend",
                       kpi.Properties["KPI_TREND"].Value));

                    CellSet cellset = command.ExecuteCellSet();
                    Debug.WriteLine("KPI Name:" + kpi.Name);
                    Debug.WriteLine("Value:" +
                       cellset.Cells[0].FormattedValue);
                    Debug.WriteLine("Goal:" +
                       cellset.Cells[1].FormattedValue);
                    Debug.WriteLine("Status:" +
                       cellset.Cells[2].FormattedValue);
                    Debug.WriteLine("Trend:" +
                       cellset.Cells[3].FormattedValue);
                 }
              }
          }
   }
   finally
   {
      asConnection.Close();
   }
```

KPI Utilities—Code for Parsing Display Folders and Getting Image Indexes

```
// -------------------------------------------------------
// KpiUtilities
//
// Contains re-usable KPI-related utility functions.
// -------------------------------------------------------

using System;
using System.Collections;
using System.Text;
using System.Windows.Forms;

namespace KpiDemo
{
    public static class KpiUtilities
    {
        /// <summary>
        /// Returns a collection of TreeNodes representing
        ///the display folders contained
        /// in the displayFolders parameter. These TreeNodes
        ///will be created if not found.
        /// An empty array will be returned if displayFolders
        ///does not contain any displayfolders.
        /// </summary>
        /// <param name="rootNodeCollection">nodes collection
        ///to use as the root of the KPI tree</param>
        /// <param name="displayFolders">the value of a
```

```
///DisplayFolders property</param>
/// <param name="displayFolderImageIndex">the
///ImageIndex to use for a display folder tree node
///</param> <returns>
/// An array of TreeNode objects representing the
///display folders contained in displayFolders.
/// May return an empty array but will not return
/// null.
/// </returns>
public static TreeNode[] GetDisplayFolderTreeNodes(
      TreeNodeCollection rootNodeCollection,
      string displayFolders,
      int displayFolderImageIndex )
{
  if ( string.IsNullOrEmpty( displayFolders ) )
  {
    return new TreeNode[0];
  }
  else
  {
    string[][] parsedDisplayFolders =
    ParseDisplayFolders( displayFolders );
    int pathCount =
        parsedDisplayFolders.GetLength( 0 );
    TreeNode[] displayFolderNodes =
        new TreeNode[pathCount];
    for ( int pathIndex = 0; pathIndex < pathCount;
            pathIndex++ )
    {
      string[] path =
      parsedDisplayFolders[pathIndex];
      TreeNode folderNode = null;
      TreeNodeCollection parentNodeCollection =
        rootNodeCollection;
      foreach ( string folder in path )
      {
        TreeNode[] nodesFound =
        parentNodeCollection.Find( folder, false );
        if ( nodesFound.Length > 0 )
        {
          folderNode = nodesFound[0];
        }
        else
        {
          folderNode =
          parentNodeCollection.Add( folder, folder,
          displayFolderImageIndex,
```

```
                displayFolderImageIndex );
        }
          parentNodeCollection = folderNode.Nodes;
      }
        displayFolderNodes[pathIndex] = folderNode;
    }
    return displayFolderNodes;
  }
}


/// <summary>
/// Parses the value of a DisplayFolders property
/// into an array of paths, each of which is
/// an array of folder names.
/// </summary>
/// <param name="displayFolders">string containing
/// the value of a DisplayFolders property</param>
/// <returns>
/// An array of arrays of strings. The outer array
/// may be zero-length, but will not be null.
/// The inner arrays will not be null or
/// zero-length.  Duplicate paths will be removed.
/// </returns>
public static string[][]
      ParseDisplayFolders( string displayFolders )
{
   const char pathDelimiter = ';';
   const char folderDelimiter = '\\';

   if ( displayFolders == null )
   {
      return new string[0][];
   }

   // Get paths
   int emptyPathCount = 0;
   string[] pathStrings =
      displayFolders.Split( pathDelimiter );
   string[][] allPaths =
      new string[pathStrings.Length][];
   for ( int i = 0; i < pathStrings.Length; i++ )
   {
      // Get folders
      int emptyFolderCount = 0;
      string[] allFolders =
         pathStrings[i].Split( folderDelimiter );
      for ( int j = 0; j < allFolders.Length; j++ )
```

```
    {
      allFolders[j] = allFolders[j].Trim();
      if ( allFolders[j].Length == 0 )
      {
        emptyFolderCount++;
      }
    }

    // Get currentPath without any
    // empty folders
    string[] nonEmptyFolders;
    if ( emptyFolderCount == 0 )
    {
      // This is the common case,
      // so optimize
      nonEmptyFolders = allFolders;
    }
    else if ( emptyFolderCount == allFolders.Length )
    {
      nonEmptyFolders = null;
      emptyPathCount++;
    }
    else
    {
      nonEmptyFolders =
      new string[allFolders.Length -
             emptyFolderCount];
      for ( int j = 0, k = 0; j <
      allFolders.Length; j++ )
      {
        if ( allFolders[j].Length > 0 )
        {
          nonEmptyFolders[k] = allFolders[j];
          k++;
        }
      }
    }

    // Remove duplicate paths
    if ( nonEmptyFolders != null &&
       IsPathAlreadyInPathsArray( allPaths,
       nonEmptyFolders, i ) )
    {
      nonEmptyFolders = null;
      emptyPathCount++;
    }
```

```
      allPaths[i] = nonEmptyFolders;
   }


   // Get results without any empty paths
   string[][] nonEmptyPaths;
   if ( emptyPathCount == 0 )
   {
      // This is the common case, so optimize
      nonEmptyPaths = allPaths;
   }
   else if ( emptyPathCount == allPaths.Length )
   {
      nonEmptyPaths = new string[0][];
   }
   else
   {
      nonEmptyPaths =
         new string[allPaths.Length -
         emptyPathCount][];
      for ( int i = 0, j = 0; i < allPaths.Length; i++ )
      {
         if ( allPaths[i] != null )
         {
            nonEmptyPaths[j] =
            allPaths[i];
            j++;
         }
      }
   }
   return nonEmptyPaths;
}


/// <summary>
/// Takes a normalized value such as those associated
/// with KPI Status and Trend and returns
/// a numeric index of an image based on the
/// normalized value.
/// </summary>
/// <param name="normalizedValue">normalized value
/// between -1 and 1 (values less than -1 are treated
/// as -1 and those greater than 1 are treated as
/// 1)</param>
/// <param name="firstImageIndex">value of the first
/// image index</param>
/// <param name="lastImageIndex">value of the last
/// image index</param>
/// <returns>An integer between firstImageIndex and
```

```
/// lastImageIndex, inclusive</returns>
public static int GetImageIndex( double normalizedValue,
   int firstImageIndex, int lastImageIndex )
{
   const double normalizedLowerBound = -1.0;
   const double normalizedUpperBound = 1.0;
   if ( double.IsNaN( normalizedValue ) )
   {
      return firstImageIndex;
   }
   else if ( normalizedValue <= -1 )
   {
      return firstImageIndex;
   }
   else if ( normalizedValue >= 1 )
   {
      return lastImageIndex;
   }
   else
   {
      const double inputRange =
         normalizedUpperBound -
         normalizedLowerBound;
      double outputRange =
            ( double )( Math.Abs( lastImageIndex -
            firstImageIndex ) + 1 );
      double outputSegmentsFromLowerBound =
            ( normalizedValue - normalizedLowerBound )
            * ( outputRange / inputRange );
      outputSegmentsFromLowerBound =
         Math.Round( outputSegmentsFromLowerBound,
         10 ); // round off floating point errors
         int zeroBasedIndex = ( int )(
         ( normalizedValue > 0 ) ?
         Math.Floor( outputSegmentsFromLowerBound):
         // borders between segments (whole
         //numbers) belong to the preceeding
         // segment
         Math.Ceiling(
         outputSegmentsFromLowerBound ) - 1 );
         // borders between segments (whole
         // numbers) belong to the following
         // segment

      return ( firstImageIndex < lastImageIndex )?
            firstImageIndex + zeroBasedIndex :
            firstImageIndex - zeroBasedIndex;
```

```
        }
    }

    #region ParseDisplayFolder helper methods

    /// <summary>
    /// Checks whether paths contains currentPath before
    /// currentIndex.  Used by ParseDisplayFolders.
    /// </summary>
    private static bool IsPathAlreadyInPathsArray(
        string[][] paths,
    string[] currentPath,
        int currentIndex )
    {
        if ( paths == null )
        {
            return false;
        }

        int count =
            Math.Min( currentIndex, paths.GetLength( 0 ) );
            for ( int i = 0; i < count; i++ )
            {
                if ( DoPathsMatch( paths[i], currentPath ) )
                {
                    return true;
                }
            }
            return false;
    }

    /// <summary>
    /// Checks whether path1 and path2 match.
    /// </summary>
    private static bool
            DoPathsMatch( string[] path1, string[] path2 )
    {
        if ( path1 == null && path2 == null )
        {
            return true;
        }
        else if ( path1 == null || path2 == null )
        {
            return false;
        }
        else if ( path1.Length != path2.Length )
        {
```

```
                    return false;
            }
            else
            {
                for ( int i = 0; i < path1.Length; i++ )
                {
                    if ( string.Compare( path1[i],
                        path2[i], true, System.Globalization.
                        CultureInfo.CurrentUICulture )
                        != 0 )
                    {
                        return false;
                    }
                }
                return true;
            }
        }

        #endregion ParseDisplayFolder helper methods
    }
}
```

KPI Viewer

This sample was originally written by Olivier Pieri (Microsoft Consulting Services France: opieri@microsoft.com) in his spare time. He was kind enough to share it with readers of this book.

The KPI Viewer is a small ASP.Net application that enables you to browse KPIs defined in Analysis Server 2005.

Website Installation

Create a website on your web server. Right-click on **My Computer**, choose **Manage**, and the Computer Management MMC appears. Go to **Services**, then select the Services and Applications/Internet Information Services/Web Sites/default website. Here, with a right-click, choose **New/Virtual directory**.

Give a name to your website and give the path where the web pages are located.

After your website is created, you have to remove the anonymous access to your website to not give access to your Analysis Services cube to the ASP.Net account.

Access your website using Internet Explorer. If you have an error, check the version of the .NET framework you are using (at the bottom of the error page). If it is not .NET Framework Version 2, you have to switch your website to the new framework (for this purpose, you can use the ASP.NET version switcher located at www.denisbauer.com/NETTools/ASPNETVersionSwitcher.aspx).

Website Usage

On the first page, give your server name and database name and press **Connect**. The web page shows you the list of cubes that exists on this database. Choose one and press View KPI.

On the second page, you will see your list of KPIs. Choose a dimension to drill down into and then choose your hierarchy, then click on a KPI name to drill down into your KPI.

The third page shows you the KPI that you have chosen for the hierarchy that you have selected. You can continue to drill down.

Known Issue

The link on the KPI name and on the dimension is enabled even if you haven't chosen a dimension and hierarchy.

Action will work only for the URL Action.

If you choose a hierarchy with several levels to drill down, all the levels are shown on the same page, which leads to very poor performance.

A visual representation for the display folders and parent KPI is not implemented in the sample's user interface.

Complete List of Data Mining Stored Procedures

Association Rule

```
/// <summary>
/// Generates a datatable of Edges and Nodes. The datatable
/// returned has four columns.  in_iNodes is the number of
/// nodes returned.
/// If in_iNodes = 0, then all nodes (and edges) are returned.
/// TYPE N1 N2 SCORE
/// ----------------
/// Type = 1:
/// N1: Node Unique Name
/// N2: Node Caption
/// Type = 2:
/// N1: Node Unique Name of Split Node (source)
/// N2: Node Unique Name of Target Node (target)
/// SCORE: Edge score (not same as split score)
/// </summary>
/// <returns>datatable for Nodes and Edges</returns>
[SafeToPrepareAttribute(true)]
public DataTable ARGetNodeGraph(string in_szModel, int in_iNodes)

/// <summary>
/// Generates a list of nodes.
/// </summary>
/// <returns>DataTable for Nodes.</returns>
[SafeToPrepareAttribute(true)]
public DataTable ARGetNodes(string in_szModel)

/// <summary>
/// Generates a list of edges
/// </summary>
/// <returns>Datatable for Edges.</returns>
[SafeToPrepareAttribute(true)]
```

```
public DataTable ARAddRelatedNodes(string in_szModel,
                                   string  in_newNodes,
                                   string in_existingNodes)

/// <summary>
/// Generates a list of edges
/// </summary>
/// <returns>Datatable for Edges.</returns>
[SafeToPrepareAttribute(true)]
public DataTable ARAddNodes(string in_szModel, string in_newNodes,
string in_existingNodes)

/// <summary>
/// Generates a list of edges
/// </summary>
/// <returns>Datatable for Edges.</returns>
[SafeToPrepareAttribute(true)]
public DataTable ARAddNodesConnected(string in_szModel, string
in_newNodes, string in_existingNodes)

/// <summary>
/// Generates a list of edges
/// </summary>
/// <returns>Datatable for Edges.</returns>
[SafeToPrepareAttribute(true)]
private DataTable ARAddNodesInternal(string in_szModel, string
in_newNodes, string in_existingNodes, bool in_fAddRelated)

/// <summary>
/// Return the maximum size of the result set.
/// </summary>
/// <returns>The maximum size of the result set.</returns>
[SafeToPrepareAttribute(true)]
public DataTable GetStatistics(string miningModel)

/// <summary>
/// Retrieve rules from the association rules mining model.
/// </summary>
/// <returns>DataTable containing NodeIdColumn, NodeCaptionColumn,
/// NodeSupportColumn, NodeProbabilityColumn, NodeLiftColumn,
/// NodeSizeColumn</returns>
[SafeToPrepareAttribute(true)]
public DataTable GetRules(string miningModel,
                          int   start,
                          int   end,
                          int   o,
```

```
                                double minProbability,
                                double minLift,
                                string filter,
                                bool in_fStripTableName)


        // <summary>
        /// Retrieve itemsets from the association rules mining model.
        /// </summary>
        /// <returns>DataTable containing NodeIdColumn, NodeCaptionColumn,
        /// NodeSupportColumn, NodeProbabilityColumn, NodeLiftColumn,
        /// NodeSizeColumn</returns>
        [SafeToPrepareAttribute(true)]
        public DataTable  GetItemsets(string miningModel,
                                int    start,
                                int    end,
                                int   o,
                                int    minSize,
                                double minSupport,
                                string filter,
                                bool in_fStripTableName)
```

Clustering

```
        [SafeToPrepareAttribute(true)]
        public SystemData.DataTable GetClusters(
        string strModel)


        /// <summary>
        /// An output row is a quadruple (type, N1, N2, weight)
        /// For type 1 (Node) N1, N2 are unique name and caption, weight
        /// is the frequency ? //LX:REVIEW
        /// For type 2 (Edge)    N1, N2 are unique names of the end nodes;
        /// weight is the edge weight
        /// </summary>
        /// <param name="strModel"></param>
        /// <param name="in_strClusterId"></param>
        /// <param name="in_nSize"></param>
        /// <returns></returns>
        [SafeToPrepareAttribute(true)]
        public SystemData.DataTable GetNodeGraph(
        string strModel,
        string in_strClusterId,
        int in_nSize)
```

```
/// <summary>
/// This returns a pivoted table of distribution values
/// </summary>
/// <param name="strModel"></param>
/// <param name="cAttributes"></param>
/// <param name="cSkip"></param>
/// <returns></returns>
[SafeToPrepareAttribute(true)]
public SystemData.DataTable GetClusterProfiles (string strModel,
int cAttributes,
int cSkip)


[SafeToPrepareAttribute(true)]
public SystemData.DataTable GetClusterDiscrimination(
string strModel,
string strCluster1UniqueID,
string strCluster2UniqueID,
double dThreshold
)

[SafeToPrepareAttribute(true)]
public SystemData.DataTable GetClusterDiscrimination(
string strModel,
string strCluster1UniqueID,
string strCluster2UniqueID,
double dThreshold,
bool in_beRescaled
)


[SafeToPrepareAttribute(true)]
public SystemData.DataTable GetClusterCharacteristics(string
strModel, string strClusterUniqueID, double dThreshold)
```

Decision Trees

```
/// <summary>
/// Calculate the depths of all the trees in a specified
/// mining model
/// </summary>
/// <returns>DataTable containing Tree Name, Node ID of tree root,
/// and tree depth</returns>
[SafeToPrepareAttribute(true)]
public DataTable CalculateTreeDepths(string miningModel)
```

```
        /// <summary>
        /// Get a list of trees from the model along with their
        /// scores
        /// </summary>
        /// <returns>DataTable containing Tree Name and
        /// score</returns>
        [SafeToPrepareAttribute(true)]
public DataTable GetTreeScores(string miningModel)
```

Decision Tree Dep Net

```
        /// <summary>
        /// Generates a datatable of Edges and Nodes. The datatable
        /// returned has four columns.  in_iNodes is the number of
        /// nodes returned.
        /// If in_iNodes = 0, then all nodes (and edges) are returned.
        /// TYPE N1 N2 SCORE
        /// ---------------
        /// Type = 1:
        /// N1: Node Unique Name (ID)
        /// N2: Node Caption
        /// Type = 2:
        /// N1: Node Unique Name of Split Node (source)
        /// N2: Node Unique Name of Target Node (target)
        /// SCORE: Edge score (not same as split score)
        /// </summary>
        /// <returns>DataTable for Nodes and Edges</returns>
        [SafeToPrepareAttribute(true)]
public DataTable DTGetNodeGraph(string in_szModel, int in_iNodes)

        /// <summary>
        /// Generates a list of nodes.  The whole dependency net has
        /// to be generated first.
        /// </summary>
        /// <returns>DataTable for Nodes.</returns>
        [SafeToPrepareAttribute(true)]
public DataTable DTGetNodes(string in_szModel)

        /// <summary>
        /// Generates a list of edges
        /// </summary>
        /// <returns>DataTable for Edges.</returns>
        [SafeToPrepareAttribute(true)]
public DataTable DTAddNodes(string in_szModel, string in_newNodes,
string in_existingNodes)
```

```
/// <summary>
/// Generates a list of edges
/// </summary>
/// <returns>DataTable for Edges.</returns>
[SafeToPrepareAttribute(true)]
public DataTable DTAddNodesConnected(string in_szModel, string
in_newNodes, string in_existingNodes)


/// <summary>
/// Generates a list of edges
/// </summary>
/// <returns>DataTable for Edges.</returns>
[SafeToPrepareAttribute(true)]
private DataTable DTAddNodesInternal(string in_szModel, string
in_newNodes, string in_existingNodes, bool in_fAddRelated)
```

Naïve Bayes

```
/// The actual stored procedure here
///
[SafeToPrepareAttribute(true)]
public SystemData.DataTable GetPredictableAttributes(
string strModel)


[SafeToPrepareAttribute(true)]
public SystemData.DataTable GetAttributeValues(
string strModel,
string strPredictableNodeUniqueID)


[SafeToPrepareAttribute(true)]
public SystemData.DataTable GetAttributeHistogram(
string strModel,
string strPredictableNodeUniqueID)


[SafeToPrepareAttribute(true)]
public SystemData.DataTable GetAttributeDiscrimination(
string strModel,
string strPredictableNodeUniqueID,
string strValue1,
int iVal1Type,
string strValue2,
int iVal2Type,
double dThreshold )
```

```
[SafeToPrepareAttribute(true)]
public SystemData.DataTable GetAttributeDiscrimination(
string strModel,
string strPredictableNodeUniqueID,
string strValue1,
int iVal1Type,
string strValue2,
int iVal2Type,
double dThreshold,
bool in_bRescaled)

[SafeToPrepareAttribute(true)]
public SystemData.DataTable GetAttributeCharacteristics(
string strModel,
string strPredictableNodeUniqueID,
string strValue1,
int    iValType,
double dThreshold)
```

Neural Net

```
//public SystemData.DataSet GetAttributeValues(
        //This is the new one that we will keep in the future.
        [SafeToPrepareAttribute(true)]
        public SystemData.IDataReader GetAttributeValues(
            string strModel)

//public SystemData.DataSet GetAttributeScores(
        [SafeToPrepareAttribute(true)]
        public SystemData.DataTable GetAttributeScores(
            string strModel,
            string strInputDescriptions,
            string strAttribute,
            string strValue1,
            int iVal1Type,
            string strValue2,
            int iVal2Type,
            double dThreshold)
```

Dependency Net

```
/// <summary>
/// Generates a datatable of Edges and Nodes. The datatable
/// returned has four columns.  in_iNodes is the number of
///nodes returned.
/// If in_iNodes = 0, then all nodes (and edges) are returned.
/// TYPE N1 N2 SCORE
/// ----------------
/// Type = 1:
/// N1: Node Unique Name
/// N2: Node Caption
/// Type = 2:
/// N1: Node Unique Name of Split Node (source)
/// N2: Node Unique Name of Target Node (target)
/// SCORE: Edge score (not same as split score)
/// </summary>
/// <returns>DataTable for Nodes and Edges</returns>
[ASServer.SafeToPrepareAttribute(true)]
public DataTable GetNodeGraph(string in_szModel,
                              int in_iNodes,
                              bool in_fStripTableName)




[ASServer.SafeToPrepareAttribute(true)]
public DataTable GetNodes(string in_szModel,
                          bool in_fStripTableName)




[ASServer.SafeToPrepareAttribute(true)]
public DataTable AddNodes(string in_szModel,
                          string in_newNodes,
                          string in_existingNodes)


[ASServer.SafeToPrepareAttribute(true)]
public DataTable AddNodesConnected(string in_szModel, string
in_newNodes, string in_existingNodes)
```

Others

```
ASServer.SafeToPrepareAttribute(true)]
public DataTable GetModelAttributes(string strModel)

[ASServer.SafeToPrepareAttribute(true)]
public DataTable GetModelAttributes(string strModel,
                                    int FeatureSelection)

[ASServer.SafeToPrepareAttribute(true)]
public DataTable GetAttributeValues(string strModel,
                                    int AttributeID)

[ASServer.SafeToPrepareAttribute(true)]
public DataTable GetAttributeValues(string strModel,
                                    int AttributeID,
                                    bool fQuartilesForContinuous)

[ASServer.SafeToPrepareAttribute(true)]
public DataTable
    GenerateLiftTableUsingDatasource(string encodeLiftQueries)

[ASServer.SafeToPrepareAttribute(true)]
public DataTable
    GetConfusionMatricesUsingDatasource(string encodeLiftQueries)

[ASServer.SafeToPrepareAttribute(true)]
public DataTable
    GenerateScatterTableUsingDatasource(string encodeLiftQueries)

[ASServer.SafeToPrepareAttribute(true)]
public DataTable
    GenerateLiftTableUsingXmlRowset(string encodeLiftQueries,
                                    string xmlRowset)
```

Index

Symbols

O

X–Z

Register
Your Book
at www.awprofessional.com/register

You may be eligible to receive:

- Advance notice of forthcoming editions of the book
- Related book recommendations
- Chapter excerpts and supplements of forthcoming titles
- Information about special contests and promotions throughout the year
- Notices and reminders about author appearances, tradeshows, and online chats with special guests

Contact us

If you are interested in writing a book or reviewing manuscripts prior to publication, please write to us at:

Editorial Department
Addison-Wesley Professional
75 Arlington Street, Suite 300
Boston, MA 02116 USA
Email: AWPro@aw.com

Visit us on the Web: http://www.awprofessional.com

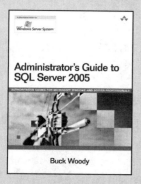

Books in the Microsoft SQL Server 2005 Series

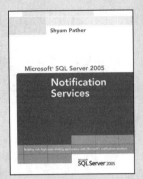

**MICROSOFT SQL SERVER 2005
NOTIFICATION SERVICES**
Shyam Pather

**MICROSOFT SQL SERVER 2005
ANALYSIS SERVICES**
Edward Melomed, Irina Gorbach, and
Alexander Berger

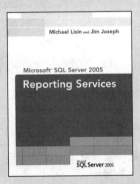

**MICROSOFT SQL SERVER 2005
REPORTING SERVICES**
Michael Lisin and Jim Joseph

**SQL SERVER 2005 PRACTICAL
TROUBLESHOOTING**
Edited by Ken Henderson

**MICROSOFT SQL SERVER 2005
INTEGRATION SERVICES**
Kirk Haselden

SAMS

For more information, including free sample chapters, visit www.samspublishing.com.

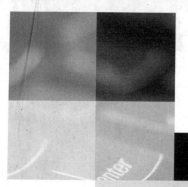